Quarto.com

© 2025 Quarto Publishing Group USA Inc.
Text © 2025 Gary Graff

First Published in 2025 by Motorbooks, an imprint of The Quarto Group,
100 Cummings Center, Suite 265-D, Beverly, MA 01915, USA.
T (978) 282-9590 F (978) 283-2742

All rights reserved. No part of this book may be reproduced in any form without written permission of the copyright owners. All images in this book have been reproduced with the knowledge and prior consent of the artists concerned, and no responsibility is accepted by producer, publisher, or printer for any infringement of copyright or otherwise, arising from the contents of this publication. Every effort has been made to ensure that credits accurately comply with information supplied. We apologize for any inaccuracies that may have occurred and will resolve inaccurate or missing information in a subsequent reprinting of the book.

This book has not been prepared, approved, or licensed by any of the artists, artists' estates, or record labels included. This is an unofficial publication.

Motorbooks titles are also available at discount for retail, wholesale, promotional, and bulk purchase. For details, contact the Special Sales Manager by email at specialsales@quarto.com or by mail at The Quarto Group, Attn: Special Sales Manager, 100 Cummings Center, Suite 265-D, Beverly, MA 01915, USA.

29 28 27 26 25   1 2 3 4 5

ISBN: 978-0-7603-9336-9

Digital edition published in 2025
eISBN: 978-0-7603-9337-6

Library of Congress Cataloging-in-Publication Data

Names: Graff, Gary, editor.
Title: 501 essential albums of the '80s : the music fan's definitive guide / Gary Graff.
Other titles: Five hundred and one essential albums of the eighties
Description: Beverly, Massachusetts : Motorbooks, 2025. | Includes index.
Summary: "501 Essential Albums of '80s is the ultimate curated list detailing dozens of the decade's most influential releases across all genres, featuring descriptions of the releases, album art, and artist imagery"– Provided by publisher.
Identifiers: LCCN 2024044859 | ISBN 9780760393369 (hardcover) | ISBN 9780760393376 (ebook)
Subjects: LCSH: Popular music–1981-1990–Discography. | LCGFT: Discographies.
Classification: LCC ML156.4.P6 A148 2025 | DDC 016.78164026/6–dc23/eng/20241002
LC record available at https://lccn.loc.gov/2024044859

Design & Page Layout: Justin Page
Cover Design: Justin Page

Printed in China

501 ESSENTIAL ALBUMS OF THE 80s

THE MUSIC FAN'S DEFINITIVE GUIDE

GARY GRAFF | EDITOR

CONTENTS

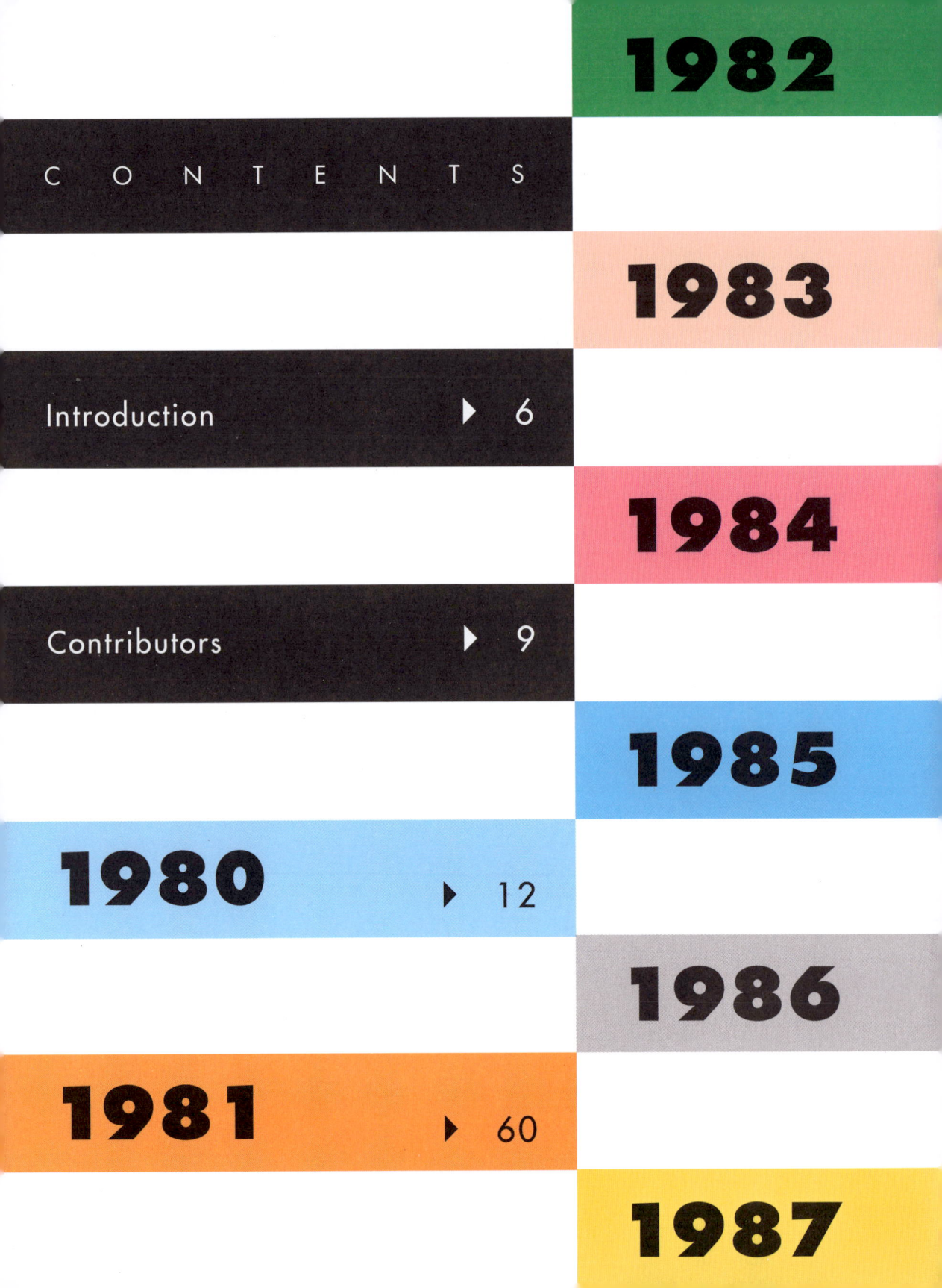

Introduction ▶ 6

Contributors ▶ 9

1980 ▶ 12

1981 ▶ 60

1982

1983

1984

1985

1986

1987

▸ 104

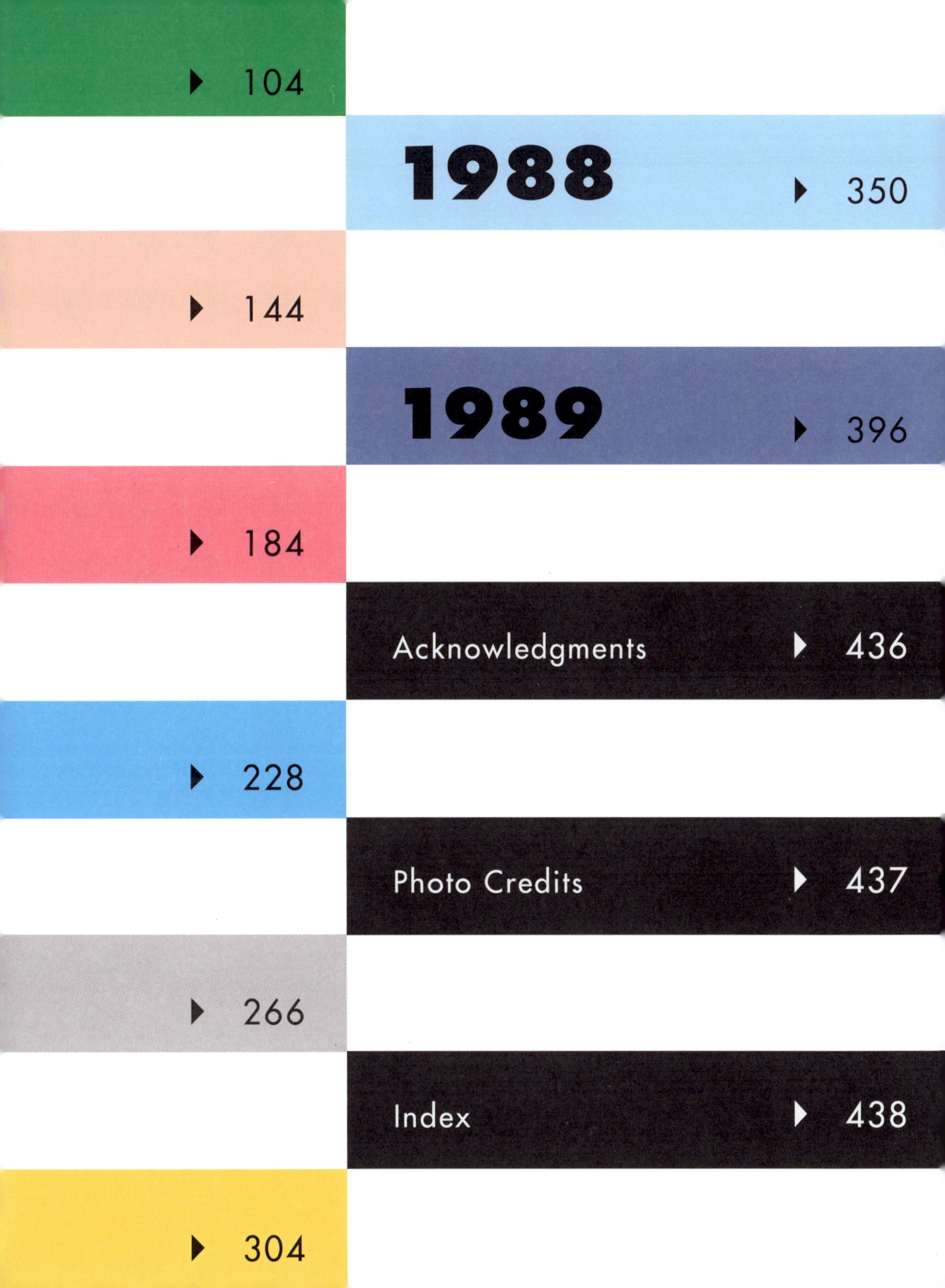

1988 ▸ 350

▸ 144

1989 ▸ 396

▸ 184

Acknowledgments ▸ 436

▸ 228

Photo Credits ▸ 437

▸ 266

Index ▸ 438

▸ 304

For older brother Harvey and sis-in-law Vicki, who inadvertently helped steer me into this music thing—and hopefully haven't figured out where all the scratches on their albums came from

Introduction

We all know the prevalent tropes of the '80s: the bright, neonlike colors; the highly poufed hair; the spandex and fishnets; the big pop music hits.

Those were all part of it, certainly. But like any given decade, the '80s encompassed more than those highly visible totems, and that was certainly reflected in the music. Rest assured, it was a lot more than we got on our MTV.

As with this volume's predecessor, *501 Essential Albums of the '90s*, we've taken a long, hard look at the '80s and worked our way through the many hundreds—even thousands—of releases that caught our collective eardrums and took music in varying directions. An argument can be made that a combination of expanding creative sensibilities and technological developments made the '80s music's most impactful decade ever. Just one example? Devices such as the Sony Walkman and boom boxes made music portable, meaning it could be in our lives 24/7—and often was. That increased not only the size of the fandom but also the intensity of the engagement. It was an unrelenting soundtrack that was with us every breath we'd take, whether we were riding in the danger zone or partying all night long, feeling hungry like a wolf or having a holiday—or experiencing a total eclipse of the heart.

And we were never gonna give it up, because we never had to. That's how ubiquitous music was to life during the '80s.

Another crucial component of that takeover was MTV. The music video channel signed on August 1, 1981, famously with the Buggles' "Video Killed the Radio Star," and became a legend as it gradually increased its reach when municipalities began to license cable television franchises into their communities. "I Want My MTV" was a rallying cry during the first half of the decade, making it arguably the most in-demand of those early cable channels (sorry, HBO . . .). While music videos were commonplace in Europe, they were a great novelty in the United States, and because they were not yet a routine part of American record companies' promotion and marketing strategies, the field was really open for acts from overseas to fill the void, the best case in point being Duran Duran, whose stylish clips and videogenic good looks (and, okay, some good tunes, too) vaulted the band into Fab Five superstar status.

Eurythmics, Culture Club, Howard Jones, Human League, Thomas Dolby . . . many others were positioned to follow the same path, and within short order the Yanks and other parts of the world caught up, allowing fans to connect to the music and the musicians on a different and even more intimate level as MTV brought the artists into our homes on a more regular basis than stodgy network programming. And while early MTV was decidedly white and pop and rock 'n' roll, the well-chronicled efforts of then–Columbia Records chief Walter Yetnikoff on behalf of Michael Jackson's "Billie Jean" video—threatening to pull all the label's clips if MTV didn't comply—opened a door that Prince, the Pointer Sisters, Cameo, and many more artists went through on their own ways to multiplatinum success.

And there were a lot of those during the '80s.

We'd gotten some taste of the mega-album during the '70s, when titles such as Boston's debut album, the Eagles' *Hotel California*, and Fleetwood Mac's *Rumours* exploded into multimillion-selling, hit-spewing phenomena. That became even more pronounced and more common during the '80s, led by Michael Jackson's *Thriller*, a sensation that's been certified more than thirty-four-times platinum in the US and has sold more than 70 million albums worldwide, basically accepted as the top-selling record of all time. A larger audience, growing industry corporatization, and a sense of a truly global market meant greater sales and new album arrivals as "events." Titles began selling in the high hundred-thousands or even a million copies during their first week of release and debuting at No. 1 on the charts. Multiplatinum certifications were more frequent than ever.

And that wasn't limited to the decade's new artists either. Old dogs such as the Rolling Stones; Aerosmith; Chicago; Yes; Journey; Fleetwood Mac; Daryl Hall & John Oates; Kiss; Alice Cooper; Earth, Wind & Fire; and even late-'70s arrivals like Van Halen and Pat Benatar learned the new tricks of the marketplace to magnify their presence and elevate their impact. For the Commodores' Lionel Richie and Fleetwood Mac's Stevie Nicks, they were tools to launch huge solo careers. For Tina Turner, music's new world order was a vehicle for a monumental comeback.

Also helping in the growth was the arrival of the compact disc. The product of a rare collaboration between major manufacturers (Phillips and Sony), the small, silver objects emerged during 1980 with pristine digital sound and a storage capacity as long as most double-vinyl albums. The standardization they presented at a time when videophiles had to choose between VHS and Beta made CDs an easy sell to consumers, and sales were boosted by those willing and even anxious to replace their vinyl, cassette, and eight-track collections with the same titles in this superior format and cast those others into the popular-culture trash heap. CDs also gave artists license to make longer albums (sometimes to a fault), while Bob Dylan's *Biograph* established what a great retrospective and archival tool they could be, launching a proliferation of carefully curated and packaged box sets.

And then there was the sheer amount of music that came at us during the '80s, thanks to a flush time for the major players and a new proliferation of independent labels, primarily from the punk revolution. Though the decade would also usher in long gaps between some albums for some acts—five years between Michael Jackson and Fleetwood Mac titles, four years between Def Leppard titles—it was still an era when significant artists were releasing genuinely significant albums nearly every year. Prince, Elvis Costello, and Joe Jackson dropped nine efforts each during the decade, Costello delivering two in the same year on two occasions. R.E.M., Billy Joel, and Linda Ronstadt put out eight each. U2, Talking Heads, the Ramones, and Eurythmics each gave us seven. The work ethic (and contractual obligations) of the '60s and '70s remained strong, nowhere more so than in the country market, where the likes of Willie Nelson, Dolly Parton, and Johnny Cash placed more than a dozen projects into the marketplace.

Burgeoning new genres, meanwhile—including rap and electronica—made their presences known, especially during the last half of the decade.

So, there was no shortage of albums from which to pick these 501 essentials, and what a challenging task *that* was. There were multiple points of consideration—merit, of course, but also impact, both artist and commercial. What we looked for and chose were albums that defined the decade, some that put a stamp on the time, others whose imprint has lasted beyond that to stand as essential works in their own right, regardless of when they were released. There was no scientific methodology at work here; these are not all the best-selling or most popular albums of the '80s, and there were plenty of personal favorites, my own and the various contributors', that are not included in these pages. Rest assured, none of those cuts were made lightly or without pain.

And we're happy to have arguments about those decisions.

What we have created is a book that can be handed to someone to fully understand and appreciate what happened musically, and to some degree culturally, during the '80s. So, get out the hairspray and the sleeveless T-shirts, pull on the fishnets, find your skinny ties and bubble shoes, plug in the Nintendo, cue up a Brat Pack movie, and read on. You may even want your MTV again—even if it doesn't look nearly like it did back then.

Gary Graff, Editor

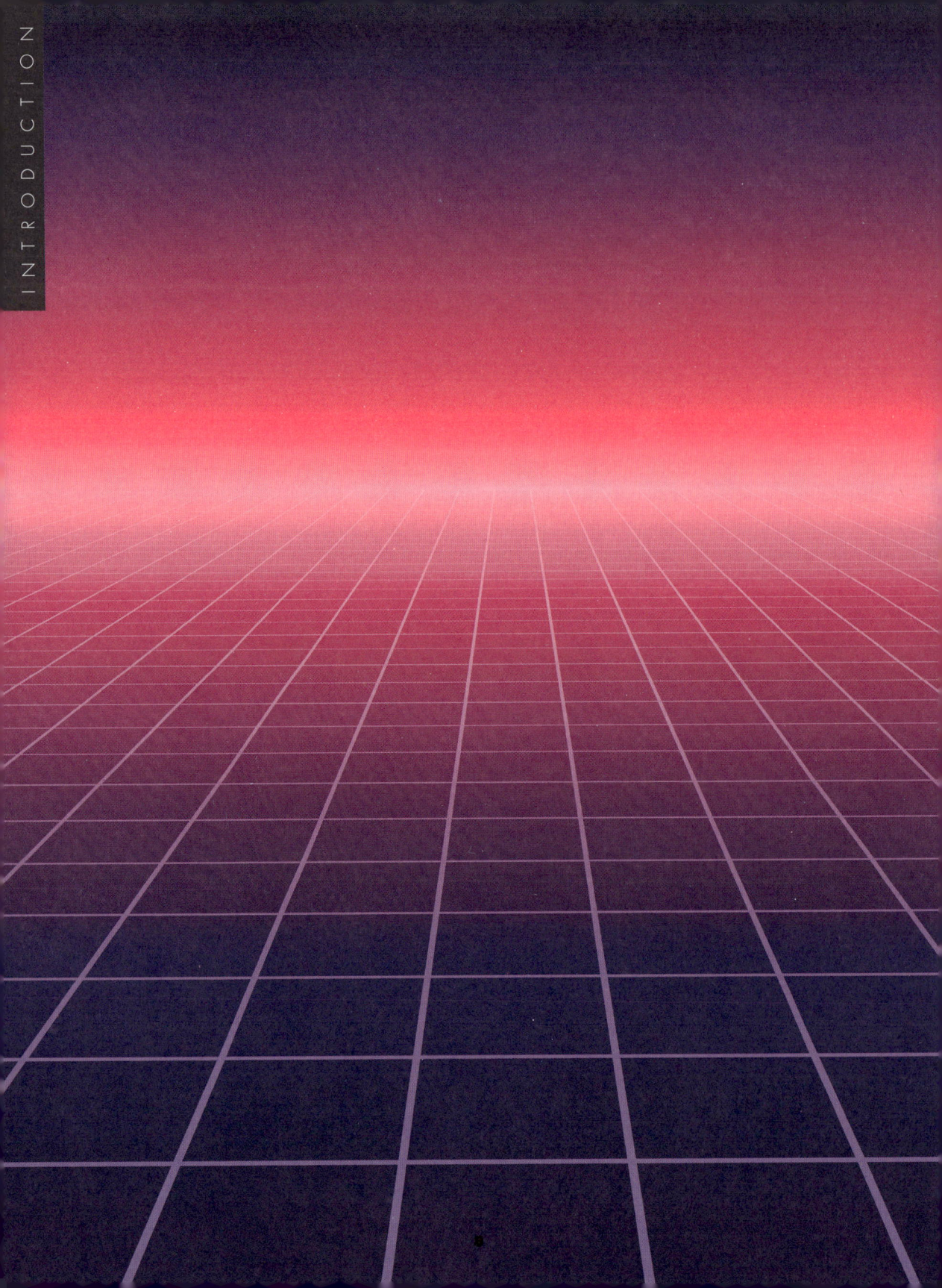

Contributors

Gary Graff (editor) (GG) is an award-winning music journalist based in Detroit. He is a regular contributor to *Guitar Player*, the Cleveland *Plain Dealer*, Media News Group, *Ultimate Classic Rock*, United Stations Radio Networks, *Music Connection*, *Classic Rock*, *VenuesNow*, and other publications and has a featured weekly music news report on WHQG-FM in Milwaukee. He is the author of *Alice Cooper @ 75* and the co-author of *Neil Young: Long May You Run* and *Rock 'n' Roll Myths: The True Stories Behind the Most Famous Legends* (both with Daniel Durchholz) and of *Travelin' Man: On the Road and Behind the Scenes with Bob Seger* (with Thomas Weschler), a Michigan Notable Book honoree. Graff also edited *The Ties That Bind: Bruce Springsteen A to E to Z* and was the series editor of the award-winning *MusicHound Essential Album Guide* series. He has contributed to other books such as *Whole Lotta Led Zeppelin*; *AC/DC: High-Voltage Rock 'n' Roll, The Ultimate Illustrated History*; *4 Way Street: The Crosby, Stills, Nash & Young Reader*; *Heaven Was Detroit: From Jazz to Hip-Hop and Beyond*; *Fleetwood Mac: The Complete Illustrated History*; and others. Graff is also co-founder and co-producer of the Emmy Award–winning Detroit Music Awards.

Cary Baker (CB) is a writer and music historian based in the California desert. The Chicago native and longtime Los Angeles resident's first book, *Down on the Corner: Adventures in Busking and Street Music*, was released in November 2024. Baker's return to writing follows a forty-two-year hiatus during which Baker headed publicity departments for six record companies (including Capitol and I.R.S.) and operated his own music PR firm, Conqueroo, from 2004 to 2022. He's also written album and box set liner notes for Universal Music, EMI, Motown, Omnivore, and Numero Group. He is presently at work on his second book, a biography.

Zach Clark (ZC) grew up in metro Detroit and graduated from the University of Arizona with a degree in journalism. He spent a decade doing sports/talk radio and then transitioned to work as a newsradio anchor. Today, Clark is an award-winning Detroit-based podcaster.

Jeff Corey (JC) was responsible for publicizing more than four thousand concerts and events during his nineteen years working for Palace Sports & Entertainment based out of The Palace of Auburn Hills in Michigan. In addition to events at The Palace, he also publicized shows at the company's other Michigan venues, including the Pine Knob Music Theatre, the Meadow Brook Music Festival, and Freedom Hill Amphitheater.

Thom Duffy (TD) is *Billboard*'s executive director of special features and power lists. He has covered all corners of the music industry for the magazine for more than three decades. Duffy was *Billboard*'s first American editor based in London and reported during the 1990s from Europe, Asia, and Australia. He has created annual *Billboard* features, including 40 Under 40, Indie Power Players, Top Business Managers, and Women in Music. He has specialized in reporting on the intersection of activism and music, covering organizations including March for Our Lives, Pete Seeger's Clearwater, and Willie Nelson's Farm Aid. Off hours, he is an Adirondack "46er," having climbed the forty-six highest four-thousand-foot peaks in New York's Adirondack Mountains.

Whether as a DJ, music journalist, marketer, or author, **Helene Dunbar** (HD) has done her best to incorporate music in every aspect of her life. As a decades-long contributor to *Irish Music* magazine, she covered traditional music in the US, later working in marketing for a Nashville-based roots music label. As a writer of fiction for young adults, particularly 2019's award-winning *We Are Lost and Found*, set in the mid-'80s, she's aimed to pay homage to the music and artists who shaped her worldview.

Daniel Durchholz (DD) is a freelance writer for many local and national publications, some of which have folded and some that probably should. He is the co-editor (with Gary Graff) of *MusicHound Rock: The Essential Album Guide* and co-author (again with Graff) of *Neil Young: Long May You Run—The Illustrated History* and *Rock 'n' Roll Myths: The True Stories Behind the Most Infamous Legends*. He lives in Wildwood, Missouri.

Michael Gallucci (MG) is the managing editor at *Ultimate Classic Rock*. His previous gigs include editor in chief at Diffuser.fm, managing editor of *Cleveland Scene*, and writing about music and movies for *All Music Guide*, *American Songwriter*, the A.V. Club, *Paste*, *Spin*, the *Village Voice*, and other publications and websites.

Adam Graham (AG) is a reporter covering music and entertainment in Detroit. A native of Rochester Hills, Michigan, he studied journalism at Central Michigan University and started his career in Palm Springs, California. He has worked at the *Detroit News* since 2002. Living Colour's *Vivid* was the first cassette tape he bought with his own money.

Mike Himes (MH) has been in the music industry since 1979, primarily in the retail sector of the industry. In 1983 he opened Record Time, an independent record store in the Detroit area that grew into a world-renowned music outlet until its closing in 2011. During the twenty-eight years it was open, Record Time became the largest independent record store in the Midwest and was known for its importance in helping to develop and promote the electronic music and rap scene in the Detroit area and beyond. Himes has contributed to many Detroit-area magazines over the years and has served on the Detroit Music Awards steering committee. Himes is still active in selling music online and still works at the local record store in his hometown.

Charlie Hunt (CH) has covered jazz and adventurous music for the *Oakland Press*, the *Detroit Free Press*, and *Billboard*. He's an inveterate musicaholic who started listening to classic British rock bands, then swerved to jazz/rock and fusion pioneers such as Santana, Mahavishnu Orchestra, Chick Corea, Herbie Hancock, Steely Dan, Frank Zappa, and Bill Bruford's Earthworks. His musical interests range from Miles Davis and Joni Mitchell to Carla Bley, Laurie Anderson, Philip Glass, Jazzrausch Big Band, and the entire ECM Records catalog. He lives in Royal Oak, Michigan.

Howard Kramer (HK) is a writer, freelance museum consultant, and the former curatorial director of the Rock & Roll Hall of Fame.

Joe Lynch (JL) serves as *Billboard*'s executive digital director, East Coast, and has nursed a lifelong obsession with music and writing. He has profiled living legends and underappreciated influencers since joining *Billboard* in 2014 and is happy to be of service to Billboard Pride since its inception. He helped *Billboard* win its first GLAAD Award and handily won the Pinewood Derby as a Cub Scout. Other outlets include *Entertainment Weekly*, *Vulture*, and *Fuse*.

Lynne Margolis (LM) published her first album review in Penn State University's *Daily Collegian* before MP3s, CDs, or even cassettes existed. She's since contributed to print, broadcast, and online media, including the *Christian Science Monitor*, *American Songwriter*, and

CONTRIBUTORS

Paste magazines; Rollingstone.com; Grammy.com; *The Bluegrass Situation*; NPR and various affiliates; newspapers nationwide; and dozens of regional and local magazines. She's collected inductee oral histories for the Rock & Roll Hall of Fame & Museum and contributed to the MusicHound Essential Album Guide series and *The Ties That Bind: Bruce Springsteen A to E to Z*. She's also toked with Willie Nelson.

David Menconi (DM) is a recovering newspaper journalist who toiled in the daily-paper trenches for thirty-four years, most of them at the *News & Observer* in Raleigh, North Carolina. He has also written for *Spin*, *Billboard*, *Rolling Stone*, *The Bluegrass Situation*, and *No Depression*. Nowadays, he edits the American Music: New Roots series for University of North Carolina Press, which published his most recent book *Oh, Didn't They Ramble: Rounder Records and the Transformation of American Roots Music* in 2023.

Dennis Pernu (DP) is an editor and writer whose words have appeared in the *Minneapolis Star Tribune*, *Vintage Guitar*, and *No Depression*. He is credited as co-author (with Jim Walsh) of *The Replacements: Waxed-Up Hair and Painted Shoes*. Dennis lives in Minneapolis, six and thirteen blocks, respectively, from Prince's and Paul Westerberg's middle schools.

Gary Plochinski (GP) spent thirty-five years as a copywriter/associate creative director at various advertising agencies, including BBDO and J. Walter Thompson. He has also taught writing at the College for Creative Studies in Detroit and was a founding member of Detroit-area polka rockers band the Polish Muslims.

Starting with Xerox fanzine journalism in high school, **Rob St. Mary** (RSM) worked as a reporter/producer in commercial and public radio and podcasts for more twenty years with stints at WWJ (Detroit), WOOD (Grand Rapids), WDET (Detroit), KAJX (Aspen), the *Detroit Free Press*, and *The Projection Booth* podcast. Rob has produced two feature films, received Michigan Notable Book Award honors for his book *The Orbit Magazine Anthology*, and is a Knight Arts challenge grant awardee for documenting Detroit's late-'70s punk rock scene.

Stacey Sherman (SS) is a veteran of the entertainment industry with more than twenty-five years of experience in radio, recording, publicity, and marketing. As a music journalist, she has contributed to numerous publications and podcasts, including *Billboard*, Media News Group, *Guitar Girl Magazine*, *The Brassy Broadcast*, MusicBizCast, and *We Spin*. She has shared her knowledge as a consultant for the CD Baby Music Convention, the Female Musicians Academy, and the Grammy Indie Collaborative and has handled press appearances on tours with Lionel Richie and the Bacon Brothers. Sherman is also part of the Emmy Award–winning production team for the 2021 Detroit Music Awards.

Ron Wade (RW) is a Detroit-area music aficionado and writer. Even though he spent much of the '90s hanging outside St. Andrew's Hall, Wade found time during the decade to write for both *Orbit* magazine and the *Detroit Metro Times*. After *Orbit* folded, Wade went back to school to earn a master's degree in sports administration from Wayne State University. He spent the next fifteen years working in professional baseball with the St. Paul Saints and Detroit Tigers but never lost his love for music, finding unique ways to combine his passion for both. Wade is currently a clinical assistant professor of sports management at the University of Michigan.

Matthew Wilkening (MW) is the founding editor in chief of UltimateClassicRock.com and UltimatePrince.com. He is based in Akron, Ohio, and his parents probably still regret giving him a copy of Kiss's *Hotter Than Hell* for Christmas in 1979.

AC/DC
BACK IN BLACK

ATLANTIC | Producer: Robert John "Mutt" Lange
RELEASED: JULY 25, 1980

● AC/DC was six albums into its four-year recording career when it finally had a breakthrough hit with *Highway to Hell*, the 1979 album that made the Australian hard rock quintet one of the biggest groups in the world. Greater things were planned for its next release—then tragedy struck. After a night of drinking, singer Bon Scott died in February 1980 at the age of thirty-three, just as AC/DC started prepping its next LP. At a crossroads, the band needed to decide how, and if, to move forward.

Two months later, at the suggestion of *Highway to Hell* producer Robert John "Mutt" Lange, AC/DC recruited Brian Johnson, formerly of the British band Geordie, to replace Scott. It wasted no time getting back to work on the record that would become *Back in Black*. Over seven weeks starting in April 1980, AC/DC, again working with Lange, recorded new songs written by Johnson and guitarist brothers Angus and Malcolm Young at Compass Point studio in Nassau. A little more than five months after Scott's death, *Back in Black* was released.

It's hard not to hear the album as a requiem to the late singer. From the tolling bells that open the record to the resolute title track to the LP's all-black cover art, death looms like a specter over *Back in Black*. There are also a few of the band's signature bawdy tunes (**You Shook Me All Night Long**, **Givin' the Dog a Bone**, **Let Me Put My Love into You**) powered by some of the Youngs' mightiest riffs. The album rose to No. 4 and eventually sold more than 25 million copies, making it one of the best-selling records of all time. More importantly, *Back in Black* helped AC/DC move on. Decades after its release, it remains a milestone in rock music. *—MG*

1980

The B-52's
WILD PLANET

WARNER BROS. | Producers: Rhett Davies, the B-52's
RELEASED: AUGUST 27, 1980

● *Wild Planet* was proof that the B-52's had more in the tank than bouffant hairdos and the quirky tunes from its self-titled 1979 debut. Oh, the Athens, Georgia, quintet's sophomore effort was just as skewed and kooky as its predecessor, but in all the best ways—and, perhaps, with better results. Returning to the Bahamas, but with a new producer (Rhett Davies), the B-52's sounded more seasoned and focused within the zany chaos that was its trademark. It also helped that many of *Wild Planet*'s nine tracks were concert staples that had been intentionally left on the table for the second album. The opening **Party Out of Bounds** certainly set a tone for what was to follow, while **Private Idaho** became deservedly part of any discussion of the best B-52's song ever. **Give Me Back My Man**, **Dirty Back Road**, **Quiche Lorraine**, the ambitious **53 Miles West of Venus**, and the manic **Strobe Light** marked a band in full, purposeful stride, while Davies's polished sonics pushed things forward and enhanced the wacky dynamics the group was exploring. Triumphant on every level, *Wild Planet* made sure that the party stayed happily and undefinably out-of-bounds. *—GG*

1980

Pat Benatar
CRIMES OF PASSION
CHRYSALIS | Producer: Keith Olsen
RELEASED: AUGUST 5, 1980

● If 1979's *In the Heat of the Night* gave Pat Benatar a foothold in the rock 'n' roll world, *Crimes of Passion* was the album that cemented her as a star. "We had some confidence and felt like we were doing more than we did the first time," Benatar said during a subsequent interview, and *Crimes* was certainly the product of a team that had gotten past its first rodeo.

Most importantly, the multi-octave singer and Neil Giraldo, the guitarist who had been brought in to help her on *Heat* (and became her husband in 1982), were more dialed in as a songwriting and arranging team; they penned three of *Crimes*' 10 tracks together, including the iconic and heartbreakingly topical **Hell Is for Children**. Some fresh faces helped push *Crimes* ahead, too—most notably, new producer Keith Olsen, a different studio (the famed Sound City in Van Nuys, California), and Myron Grombacher, the hyperactive drummer who would work with Benatar into the late '90s and joined the couple in writing *Crimes*' closing track, **Out-A-Touch**.

The defiant **Hit Me with Your Best Shot** gave Benatar not only her first Top 10 hit but also a signature character anthem that declared she would stand her ground amid the abundant sexism that surrounded her—even though it was written by a man, Eddie Schwartz. **Treat Me Right** was more command than request, and some well-chosen covers—the Young Rascals' **You Better Run** and especially Kate Bush's **Wuthering Heights**—further established a virtuosic range Benatar would explore throughout her career.

Crimes became Benatar's top-selling album at four-times platinum and scored her first Grammy Award for Best Female Rock Vocal Performance. She and Giraldo grew to be co-billed over the years and were inducted, together, into the Rock & Roll Hall of Fame in 2022. *–GG*

The Clash
SANDINISTA!

EPIC | Producers: The Clash
RELEASED: DECEMBER 12, 1980

● With its 1979 double album *London Calling*, the Clash set a new standard for punk groups. Jettisoning the three-chord guitar attack that made it the most celebrated of London's new breed of rock bands, its third LP dove into ska, pop, reggae, rockabilly, soul, and jazz for a decades-spanning history lesson of popular music. Where to go next? The three-disc, nearly two-and-a-half-hour *Sandinista!* was even more sprawling and ambitious than its predecessor. After this, nobody could refer to the Clash as merely a punk band.

If its experimental mix of post-punk, dub, and world music didn't always cohere, the scope of *Sandinista!* was astonishing. *London Calling* gave the Clash a wider forum to spread its global message; *Sandinista!* made it the biggest-thinking band on the planet. Few acts had ever attempted the breadth covered by these six sides. Producing itself for the first time, the Clash had no editor, no outside voices, and no dissenting opinions to distract from its vision. In many ways, *Sandinista!* may be the most representative of the Clash's albums.

It's among the most political, too (**The Call Up**, **Washington Bullets**)—not surprising, since the LP was named after a Nicaraguan left-wing political party. Scattered alongside blues, folk, jazz, and reggae covers were soul (**Hitsville U.K.**) and hip-hop (**The Magnificent Seven**) tributes, dub versions of tracks found elsewhere on the album, and a reworked version of the 1977 song **Career Opportunities**, sung by the two young sons of Ian Dury and the Blockheads' Mick Gallagher, who contributed keyboards to *Sandinista!* The album started as a knock at the record company (which initially resisted the double *London Calling*) but ended as a definitive statement on the band's aspirations. It's an exhausting process for both listener and the band. The Clash would never make an album this adventurous again. —MG

1980

Black Sabbath
HEAVEN AND HELL
WARNER BROS. | Producer: Martin Birch
RELEASED: APRIL 18, 1980

● Ozzy Osbourne, the Prince of Darkness, parted ways with Black Sabbath after eight albums, forcing the alchemists of metal to concoct a new mixture. Though the band still wrestled with darkness, former Rainbow vocalist Ronnie James Dio brought a brighter, less sludgy flavor to *Heaven and Hell*, though his willingness to invoke the fantastical, like dragons, could be corny. But critics be damned, as he sang in **Neon Knights**; sales proved that new Sabbath, unlike new Coke five years later, was a success, although never surpassing the original. —*RSM*

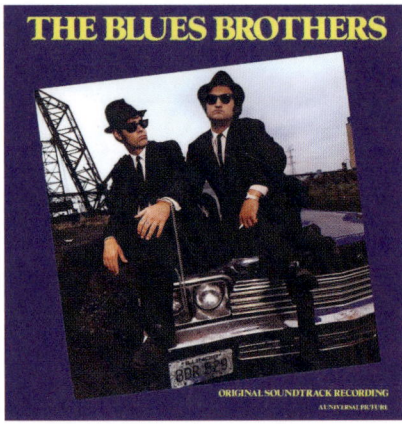

The Blues Brothers
ORIGINAL SOUNDTRACK RECORDING
ATLANTIC | Producer: Bob Tischler
RELEASED: JUNE 20, 1980

● After shocking the world by turning what began as a *Saturday Night Live* labor of love into a legitimately smoking live band with a platinum album under their belts, John Belushi and Dan Aykroyd swung for even further fences by starring in a big-budget 1980 movie. The highly entertaining if somewhat scattershot soundtrack leans more on R&B than pure blues, with the duo making plenty of room for powerful performances by the musical idols that appear in the film, including Aretha Franklin, James Brown, and Ray Charles. —*MW*

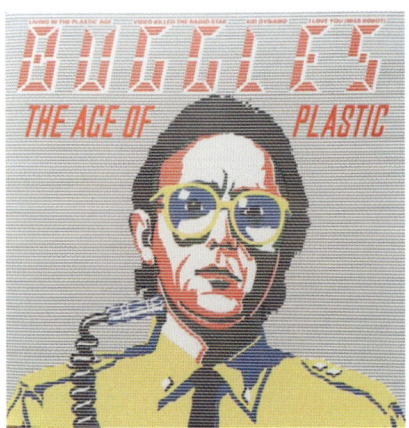

The Buggles
THE AGE OF PLASTIC
ISLAND | Producers: The Buggles
RELEASED: JANUARY 10, 1980

● Quick—name MTV's first video. It was the Buggles' (Geoff Downes and Trevor Horn) prescient electro-pop single **Video Killed the Radio Star**, which hit No. 1 in sixteen countries (not the US). By the time MTV launched in 1981, Horn and Downes had joined the prog group Yes for one album. The Buggles disbanded after one further album, freeing Horn to produce, but *Plastic* still sounds fresh and futuristic, commenting on our dependence on machines—ironic for an album dominated by synthesizers of the most glorious kind. —*HD*

Captain Beefheart and the Magic Band
DOC AT THE RADAR STATION
VIRGIN | Producer: Don Van Vilet

RELEASED: AUGUST 1980

● A lucky thirteen years after his debut album, Captain Beefheart (Don Van Vilet) was being hailed as the forefather of New Wave. His influence had sunk in, it seems, and the likes of Devo, the B-52's, and others opened ears to the wonder of the good Captain's weirdness. With song ideas Van Vilet had worked on with Frank Zappa during the late '60s, *Doc* was the strongest and most focused Beefheart outing since the legendary *Trout Mask Replica*, a triumph that was also the penultimate album released during Van Vilet's lifetime. *—GG*

Neil Diamond
THE JAZZ SINGER (ORIGINAL MOTION PICTURE SOUNDTRACK)
CAPITOL | Producer: Bob Gaudio

RELEASED: NOVEMBER 10, 1980

● The 1980 retelling of the 1925 play, starring Neil Diamond as a singer trapped between Jewish tradition and his desire to be a pop star, was gutted by critics. But the soundtrack became Diamond's biggest US hit, selling more than six million copies, with **Love on the Rocks**, **Hello Again**, and **America** hitting Billboard's Top 10. Diamond's delivery on the religious tracks were appropriately chill-inducing, but for soft rock fans, the contemporary songs allowed him to embrace the more schmaltzy style of his later albums, not unlike his film character. *—HD*

Various Artists
FAME (ORIGINAL SOUNDTRACK FROM THE MOTION PICTURE)
RSO | Producer: Michael Gore

RELEASED: MAY 16, 1980

● *Fame*, a movie about students at New York's High School of Performing Arts, spawned multiple teen musicals and launched a youthful and gritty soundtrack that catapulted the Irene Cara–sung singles **Fame** and **Out Here on My Own** high onto the Billboard chart. Both earned Grammy nominations for Best Original Song, the first time for two tracks from the same film and singer in the same category. **Fame** won, which made sure we remembered Cara's name. *—HD*

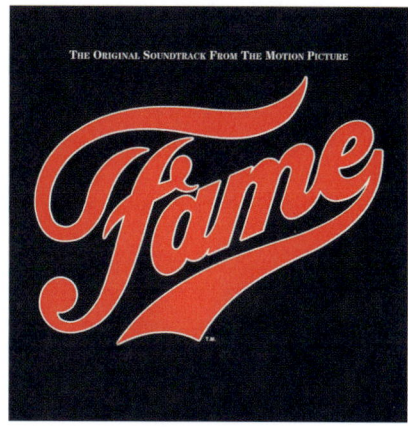

David Bowie
SCARY MONSTERS (AND SUPER CREEPS)
R C A | Producers: David Bowie, Tony Visconti
RELEASED: SEPTEMBER 12, 1980

● The dawn of the decade found David Bowie in an odd state. His 1977–79 "Berlin Trilogy" of *Low*, *Heroes*, and *Lodger* represented an adventurous peak, but sales were slipping. With his commercial stature in doubt, Bowie responded by taking another shot at the mainstream with an edgy masterpiece that still stands as his best album of the decade. Bowie brought his best set of tunes in years to *Scary Monsters (and Super Creeps)*— **Ashes to Ashes**, **Fashion**, and the title track were all about as straightforwardly catchy as the man ever got. But that's not to say this was an upbeat affair. Bowie set the tone on the very first track, **It's No Game (No. 1)**, which concluded with a raggedy scream of "SHUT UP!"

Sonically, *Scary Monsters* felt like Bowie showing the New Wave kids how it's done, with superlative off-kilter guitar flip-outs from King Crimson's Robert Fripp (among this era's most reliable quality signifiers) plus an ace cover of Television mastermind Tom Verlaine's **Kingdom Come**. Ever the visual visionary, Bowie appeared on the front cover fashionably attired in a vintage Pierrot costume, framed by a collage of his own past album covers on the back. The retrospective mood extended to lead single **Ashes to Ashes**, a sequel to Bowie's 1969 breakthrough hit "Space Oddity," accompanied by a David Mallet–directed video said to be the most expensive ever made—just in time for MTV's launch less than a year later.

By then, Bowie's next metamorphosis was already underway. After looking frail and sickly in the **Ashes to Ashes** video, he had his teeth fixed by the time **Fashion** was shot (watch for future MTV veejay Alan Hunter among the dancers). Three years later, Bowie would reemerge as a matinee-idol pop star with a new label, producer, and outlook. —DM

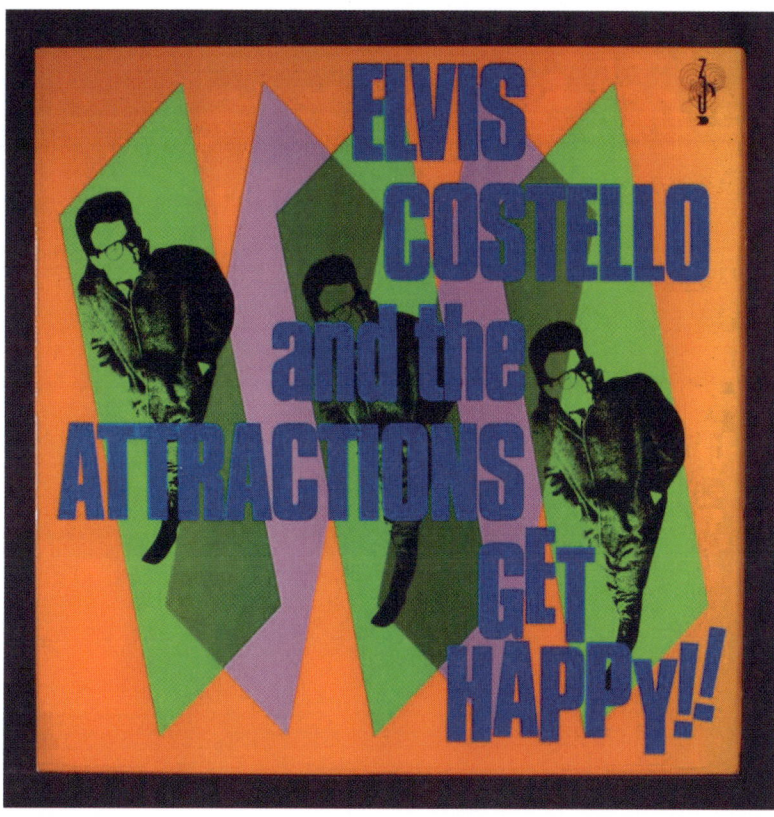

Elvis Costello and the Attractions
GET HAPPY!!

COLUMBIA | Producer: Nick Lowe
RELEASED: FEBRUARY 15, 1980

● The two and a half years following the release of Elvis Costello's debut album, *My Aim Is True*, were a whirlwind period of tours, television appearances, two additional LPs, and enough singles and leftover songs to fill another album. By late 1979, he and his backing band, the Attractions, along with producer Nick Lowe, who worked on 1978's *This Year's Model* and 1979's *Armed Forces*, were so securely locked into their relationship that they could go into the studio and lay down a couple of dozen songs within just a few weeks.

While initial sessions for Costello's fourth album, *Get Happy!!*, were scrapped for sounding too much like his earlier records, a location change and shift in direction toward '60s R&B righted the course. Even with a pair of covers—Sam & Dave's **I Can't Stand Up for Falling Down**, released as the album's first single, and the Merseybeats' **I Stand Accused**—the twenty songs on *Get Happy!!* reflected a range of songwriting styles, from **New Amsterdam**'s minimalist balladry to the fluid New Wave of **High Fidelity** and the autobiographically intense **Riot Act**.

Get Happy!! arrived at the right time for Costello, after the closing of one chapter of his career and opening another more adventurous one that found him trying out everything from country and jazz to hip-hop to classical music. Although it was originally tagged a novelty because of the number of songs and its R&B tribute aspects (complete with cover art designed to replicate a worn vintage soul LP), Costello rarely sounded this loose and muscular on record again, with more hooks and heart on *Get Happy!!* than on later, more celebrated albums. *—MG*

Peter Gabriel
PETER GABRIEL
MERCURY | Producer: Steve Lillywhite
RELEASED: MAY 30, 1980

● Ex-Genesis frontman Peter Gabriel's third self-titled solo album was known as *Melt* for its hallucinogenic, warped-Polaroid cover art, an early-1980s dorm-room staple in poster form. In a rare and stunning lapse, Atlantic Records thought so little of this album that the company declined to release it. It's hard to tell what they were thinking because it is a masterpiece and Gabriel's first important solo album. Drawing equally from Bowie-esque art rock and the newer post-punk (note the presence of both King Crimson's Robert Fripp and XTC's Dave Gregory), the album bore little resemblance to Gabriel's old band. Instead, it staked out new rhythmic territory that foreshadowed his future hits. No one does monochromatic bombast like producer Steve Lillywhite, and this album's portrait of a decaying mind was as black-and-white stark as any nightmare. The absence of drum cymbals and the use of gated reverb gave the rhythms added depth and wallop. The rolling staccato of **No Self Control** was among Phil Collins's finest moments on the drum kit, presaging his landmark "In the Air Tonight" solo a year later. **Games without Frontiers** was the hit, still heard today. And the album-closing **Biko** remains a relevant anti-apartheid anthem four-plus decades later. *—DM*

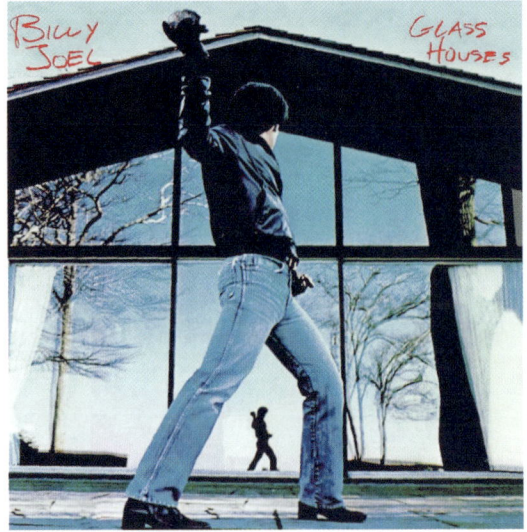

Billy Joel
GLASS HOUSES
COLUMBIA | Producer: Phil Ramone
RELEASED: MARCH 12, 1980

● Billy Joel put fans who thought they knew him and his music on notice with the cover of his seventh album. The image depicted the leather-jacketed "Piano Man" preparing to throw a rock through a literal house of glass—an indication he was about to shatter expectations when the needle hit the grooves back in those vinyl-dominated days. Having become a superstar with pop hits and ballads from *The Stranger* and *52nd Street*, Joel came out rocking hard on *Glass Houses*, crashing into the guitar riffs of **You May Be Right** and populating the set with high-octane tracks such as **Sometimes a Fantasy**, **All for Leyna**, and the New Wavey **Sleeping with the Television On**. The nostalgic **It's Still Rock and Roll to Me**, meanwhile, gave Joel his first No. 1 single on the Billboard Hot 100. He did soften up on the light samba of **Don't Ask Me Why** and the Beatlesque album-closing lullaby **Through the Long Night**, but the overall energy remained high even on deep cuts such as **Close to the Borderline**. The change was embraced, however; *Glass Houses* was certified triple platinum and received a Grammy Award for Best Male Rock Vocal Performance. *—GG*

Pat Metheny
80/81
E C M | Producer: Manfred Eicher
RELEASED: SEPTEMBER 1, 1980

● 80/81 was a defining moment for Pat Metheny, a serious effort that pulled him musically closer to his free-jazz idol, Ornette Coleman, and recalibrated his career. The Pat Metheny Group, the guitarist's well-established, fan-friendly fusion band, was commercially popular, but some critics had doubts, thinking Metheny was at best a soft-jazz artist. The two-disc 80/81 slayed the naysayers. Metheny wrote these nine tracks for handpicked musicians, all friends, and for the first time including tenor saxophonists Michael Brecker, a rising star, and jazz legend Dewey Redman, plus bassist Charlie Haden and drummer Jack DeJohnette. During May 1980, the quintet flew to Oslo, Norway, and created a masterpiece in an all-day recording session. The achingly beautiful ballad **I Thank You** and **Two Folk Songs** are among the finest songs Metheny had ever recorded. The latter was an enthralling, nearly twenty-one-minute exhibition on which Metheny unleashed a relentless rhythm-guitar strumming, opening a platform for Brecker, who gloriously unfurled the melody and pushed enticing solos to fiercer, more atonal places. DeJohnette supplied supercharged drumming. Haden's bass solo was a deep and rugged feature of the song's second half. **Turnaround**, a Coleman original, was boiled down to a guitar/bass/drum trio, supplying an aural energy shot. *—CH*

Ozzy Osbourne
BLIZZARD OF OZZ
J E T | Producers: Ozzy Osbourne, Randy Rhoads, Bob Daisley, Lee Kerslake
RELEASED: SEPTEMBER 12, 1980

● After getting fired from Black Sabbath in 1979 due to what his bandmates deemed excessive substance abuse and unreliability, Ozzy Osbourne shocked the world not only by launching a solo career that unquestionably left his former group in the dust commercially, but also by arguably outclassing it artistically with this debut. While Sabbath successfully updated its sound on the Ronnie James Dio–fronted *Heaven and Hell* that same year, Osbourne had the good taste (or luck) to recruit Randy Rhoads, the most exciting and innovative guitarist to hit the hard rock world since Eddie Van Halen. Adding a strong classical influence on the expanded vocabulary Van Halen had popularized a few years earlier, Rhoads helped Ozzy compose an album full of instantly catchy songs that still delivered the riff quotient demanded by Sabbath fans. Think of it as the difference in the fighting styles between a heavyweight boxer and a welterweight; Rhoads and Ozzy were lighter on their feet, more complex in their attack, but still suitably epic and grandiose. Sadly, after one more nearly as excellent record—1981's *Diary of a Madman*—Rhoads died in an airplane crash, robbing the rock world of a truly unique voice. *—MW*

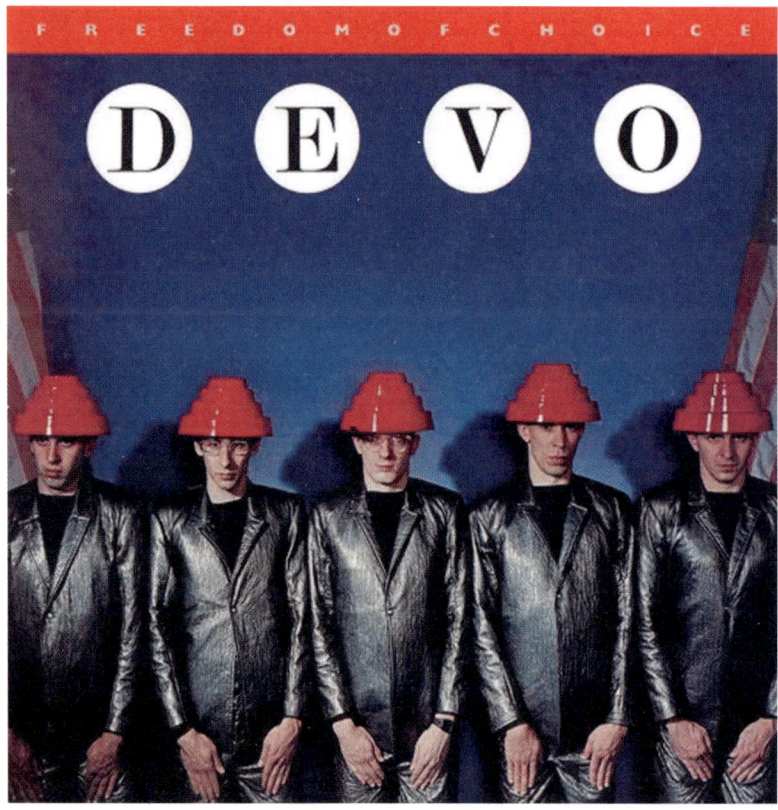

Devo
FREEDOM OF CHOICE

WARNER BROS. | Producers: Devo, Robert Margouleff
RELEASED: MAY 14, 1980

● Madonna's crucifix. Prince's purple trench coat. ZZ Top's beards. Flack of Seagulls' coifs.

Music in the '80s gave us plenty of iconic visuals, some more questionable than others. Arguably none were more iconic than the bright-red "energy dome" chapeaux adopted by Devo in time for its third LP, *Freedom of Choice*.

Devo benefited early in its career from the patronage of high-profile fans such as Neil Young, Iggy Pop, and David Bowie, the latter of whom helped the Akron, Ohio, quintet secure a Warner Bros. record deal. *Freedom of Choice* continued the art-punks-turned-New-Wavers' satirical and often surrealist music and performance, which they used to posit their theory that the human race is, in fact, *de*volving. This album, though, leaned more heavily than its predecessors on synthesizers and featured what remains the group's most famous song, **Whip It**. Written by bassist Jerry Casale and frontman Mark Mothersbaugh, the single peaked at No. 14 in the US and was explained as a satirical take on misplaced American optimism, though many thought it carried sadomasochistic tones (a misconception that the song's dude ranch–themed video did nothing to dispel).

The album's first single and lead track was the much more urgent, and in retrospect arguably superior, **Girl U Want**. Probably the band's most covered song as well, it eases fans of the band's first two albums into Devo's synth-pop era (which would really take hold with 1981's *New Traditionalists*), thanks to the repetitive and out-front guitar lines of Bob Mothersbaugh, which, granted, are often doubled by synths throughout.

The album's title track closed out the first side as more of a straight-ahead rocker and again displayed Devo's roots as a guitar-rock band, contrasting somewhat starkly with more unapologetic New Wave fare such as **Cold War**, **That's Pep!**, and **Planet Earth**. —*DP*

Dire Straits
MAKING MOVIES

WARNER BROS. | Producer: Jimmy Iovine
RELEASED: OCTOBER 17, 1980

● When Mark Knopfler chose to open **Tunnel of Love**, the first track on *Making Movies*, with a few bars of "The Carousel Waltz" from the great 1945 Broadway musical by Richard Rodgers and Oscar Hammerstein II, it was more than a thematic match. Dire Straits' songwriter, frontman, and lead guitarist signaled his ambition of creating musical stories that would endure for decades. With *Making Movies*, he succeeded beyond expectations.

Two years before the album's release, Dire Straits—Knopfler, his brother David on rhythm guitar, bassist John Illsley, and drummer Pick Withers—arrived from the UK with a self-titled debut LP and the single "Sultans of Swing." The song reached No. 4 on the Billboard Hot 100, showcasing both Mark Knopfler's storytelling skill and distinctively emotive lead guitar. Both qualities reached a new peak with *Making Movies*, the band's third album after 1979's *Communiqué*. By this point, David Knopfler had left the band, but a guest player, pianist Roy Bittan from Bruce Springsteen's E Street Band, contributed greatly to the grand, cinematic feel of these songs. So did Jimmy Iovine's production and the engineering of Shelly Yakus. In those opening moments of **Tunnel of Love**, Bittan's piano floated brightly above the organ before Knopfler's guitar comes in, accompanied by a mighty drum fill from Withers. The sonic mix is simply superb.

Knopfler was making musical movies but also telling evocative tales, with the nostalgic **Tunnel of Love**, the reimagining of **Romeo and Juliet**, the nighttime adventure of **Skateaway**, and more. The album's closer, **Les Boys**, was Knopfler's wry sketch of gay cabaret singers and this disc's musically least engaging track—a rare misstep. But return to the two-minute solo that closed **Tunnel of Love** and be reminded of how emotionally powerful rock 'n' roll guitar can be. *—TD*

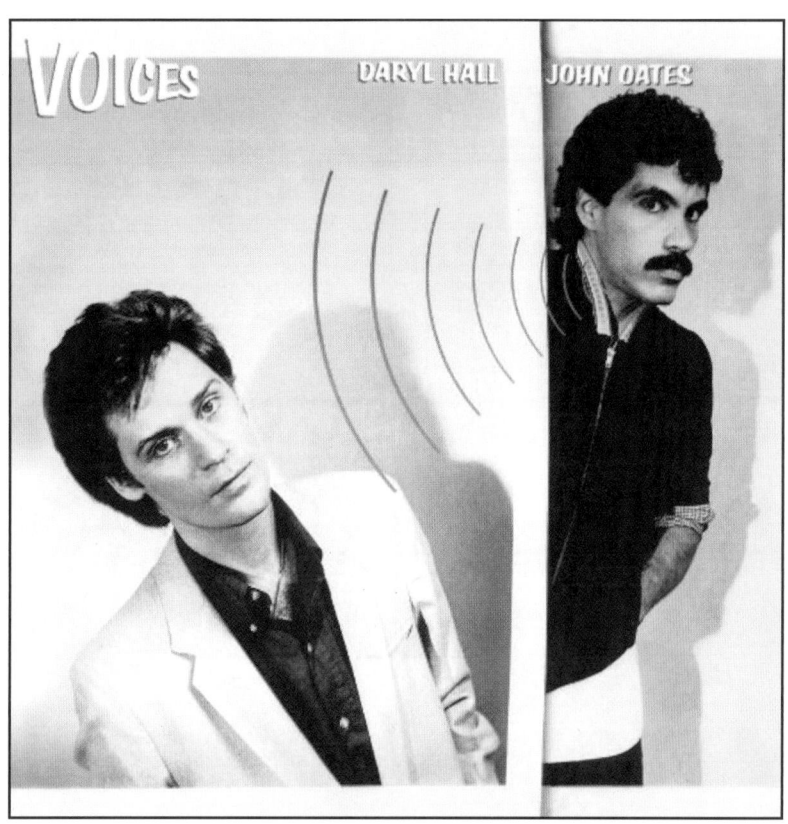

Daryl Hall & John Oates
VOICES

R C A | Producers: Daryl Hall, John Oates
RELEASED: JULY 29, 1980

● At the turn of the decade, Daryl Hall and John Oates were in need of a comeback. After a clutch of big singles and successful albums during the mid-'70s, the Philadelphia-formed duo hit a hit-less skid and was in danger of falling off a (red) ledge it was tenuously walking. *Voices*, however, was a triumphant reinvention that started Hall & Oates' reign as pop's biggest act during the first half of the '80s.

It wasn't because they were playing it safe, however. Produced solely by Hall & Oates (with engineer Neil Kernon making no small contribution), *Voices* introduced a new sound—lean, sleek, and decidedly modern. There was a perceptible space and minimalism in the mix that drew from European New Wave and synth-pop (Hall had worked with King Crimson's Robert Fripp on his first solo album, *Sacred Songs*, that came out four months earlier) and complemented the duo's blue-eyed-soul roots. Hall & Oates were still in fine form as a songwriting team, penning four of *Voices*' eleven tracks together; and Hall was also bolstered by a growing relationship, musical and personal, with Sara Allen.

The buoyant **Kiss on My List** gave Hall & Oates their first No. 1 hit since 1977, and the equally peppy **You Make My Dreams** also bopped into the Top 5. *Voices* also housed a reverent remake of the Righteous Brothers' **You've Lost That Loving Feeling** and the original version of Hall's **Everytime You Go Away**, which became a smash for Paul Young five years later.

Voices was Hall & Oates' first platinum album, too, but most importantly, it was the first strike in a four-album run that made the duo the decade's first defining act. *–GG*

Killing Joke
KILLING JOKE

E.G./POLYDOR | Producers: Killing Joke

RELEASED: OCTOBER 5, 1980

● *Killing Joke* is one of those albums that launched a thousand (maybe more) bands. The British quartet was barely together a year before it was recorded but had made a mark with singles and a previous EP. *Killing Joke* was heavier, however, veering away from the goth of its predecessors into an industrial-strength metal-funk maelstrom spotlighting Geordie Walker's guitar and accented by frontman Jaz Coleman's synthesizers. **Wardance** and **Requiem** were prototypes for a true new wave of bands, some of whom (Metallica, Helmet, Foo Fighters) would wind up covering tracks in tribute to Killing Joke's importance. —GG

Joe Henderson
MIRROR, MIRROR

MPS | Producers: Joachim-Ernst Berendt, Joe Henderson

RELEASED: 1980

● Tenor saxophonist Joe Henderson established himself by recording prolifically during the '60s and '70s with emergent jazz heavyweights. He was forty-three when he recorded *Mirror, Mirror*, which stood out for the stellar quartet enlivened by pianist Chick Corea, bassist Ron Carter, and drummer Billy Higgins. Corea's refreshing title track set off the outing with clear-voiced and tantalizing piano play. **Bolero**, Henderson's sole composition, was the album's modal centerpiece, while Carter contributed the finger-snapping **Candlelight** and **Keystone**. —CH

George Jones
I AM WHAT I AM

EPIC | Producer: Billy Sherrill

RELEASED: SEPTEMBER 8, 1980

● On **He Stopped Loving Her Today**, George Jones's unexpected first No. 1 single in six years, he sang about a man who never gave up his love for an ex-paramour. The Grammy Award–winning hit could be viewed as a parable for Jones's relationship with country music fans, who came flocking back for the track (which Jones at first hated, by the way). The Possum's label quickly capitalized with an album (Jones's first platinum set), which energized his new success, with three more Top 10 country hits launching a comeback that stretched well into the mid-'80s. —GG

Public Image Ltd
SECOND EDITION
ISLAND/WARNER BROS. | Producers: Public Image Ltd
RELEASED: FEBRUARY 1980

● With John Lydon ditching the bratty sneer of his Sex Pistols days for a mournful wail, **Albatross** opened *Second Edition* with a dour, formless descent into hell. If PiL wanted to provoke listeners on its first album, it had completely forgotten about them on its second, embracing noisy, bleak, structureless extremes. **Careering** was a disco-dub funeral, **Chant** a relentless assault, and **Poptones** a hypnotic, harrowing jam. Abandon all hope, ye who enter here hoping for a proper song. But if you want to experience one of the most potent and prophetic post-punk albums ever, step in. —*JL*

The Romantics
THE ROMANTICS
NEMPEROR | Producer: Pete Solley
RELEASED: JANUARY 4, 1980

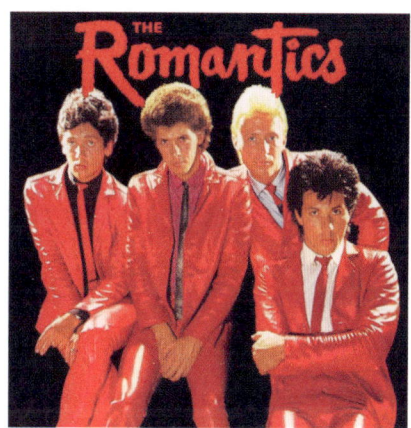

● By the end of the '70s, an entire generation of bands had modeled themselves on the Kinks, the Who, and the Beatles . . . in that order. Blazing out of Detroit came the Romantics, complete with power chords, punchy hooks, and bespoke red leather suits. Chiming Rickenbacker guitars tied the quartet to its British role models. The original songs do the heavy lifting here—pledging love in **Tell It to Carrie**, raving on **Little White Lies**, and rocking on the evergreen **What I Like About You**. An unrelenting debut. —*HK*

The Soft Boys
UNDERWATER MOONLIGHT
ARMAGEDDON | Producers: Pat Collier, Mike Kemp
RELEASED: JUNE 1980

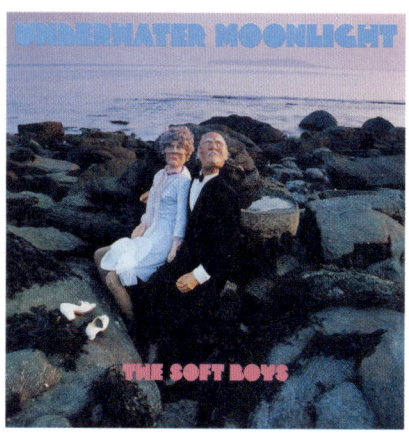

● This is one of those legendary albums that few heard at the time, but the ones who did—like R.E.M., the Replacements, and Pixies—either were forming or went on to form bands. Robyn Hitchcock and company still had a foot in '70s and even '60s power pop and psychedelia on the Soft Boys' second album, but there was something undeniably modern about its guitar-driven shimmer and a dark lyrical undertow of bracing irony and gleeful surrealism. The quartet broke up a year later, and there'd only be one more album, in 2002, but this is Soft Boys' legacy standard. —*GG*

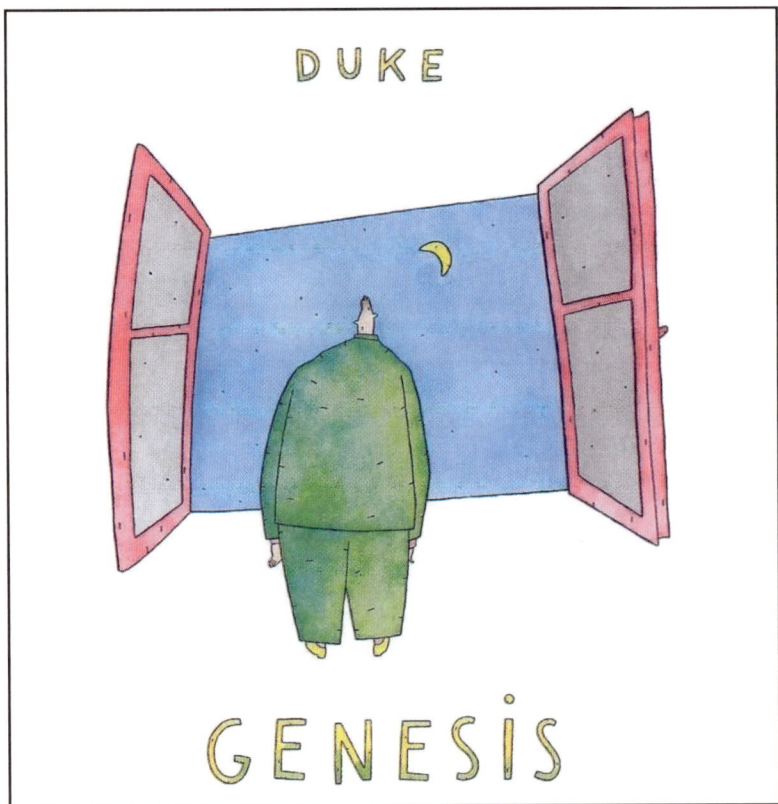

Genesis
DUKE
ATLANTIC | Producers: David Hentschel, Genesis
RELEASED: MARCH 28, 1980

● Genesis's second album as a trio struck a tone and set a course the British prog band would follow to even greater success through the rest of the '80s and into the '90s. Following its first bona fide hit single (1978's "Follow You, Follow Me"), Tony Banks, Phil Collins, and Mike Rutherford proved open to exploring more commercial—or at least accessible—possibilities while also staying true to the adventurous musicianship that was the group's stock in trade. The result was a best-of-both-worlds balance that gave Genesis its highest chart showing to date in the US (No. 11) and its first No. 1 album in its homeland, as well as additional hits in **Misunderstanding** and **Turn It On Again**.

Duke was, in fact, an album the band wasn't sure it would make at all. Collins had moved to Vancouver to attempt to patch up his failing first marriage—an estrangement documented in *Duke*'s **Misunderstanding** and **Please Don't Ask**—and had served notice that things could not continue as they were. The reconciliation didn't work out, but when Genesis began recording, it experimented with a new writing format. There were some individually penned tracks, but the opening duo of **Behind the Lines** and **Duchess**, both parts of a conceptual suite spread across the album, as well as **Turn It on Again**, were the products of trio improvisations in the studio. After that, it became the recording modus Genesis would employ for the remainder of the band's career.

The rest of *Duke*'s tracks were strong throughout, and the muscular closing of **Duke's Travels** and the instrumental **Duke's End** assured fans that a gain in commercial appeal did not cause any loss in artistry or ambition. *—GG*

Joy Division
CLOSER
FACTORY | Producer: Martin Hannett
RELEASED: JULY 18, 1980

● When Joy Division's debut album, *Unknown Pleasures*, dropped in 1979, you could still reasonably place the English rockers under the punk category. But when *Closer* came out thirteen months later, it was obvious the band was exploring far different and darker territory than any of its peers. Of course, frontman Ian Curtis's death by suicide two months before the album's release made it easy to read any number of things into the LP's sparse, searching, and lonely soundscape. The same goes for Curtis's lyrics, which were alternately inscrutable (**Atrocity Exhibition**, which takes its name from J. G. Ballard's harrowing 1970 book and later inspired the title of rapper Danny Brown's 2016 album) and gut-wrenchingly personal, such as the self-lacerating **Isolation**, which easily outpaces John Lennon's song of the same name when it comes to bleakness.

"Ian said to me that doing this album felt very strange because he felt that all his words were writing themselves," the band's Bernard Sumner, who would go on to co-found and front New Order with his surviving Joy Division bandmates, explained to the *Independent* in 2007. "He also said that he had this terrible claustrophobic feeling that he was in a whirlpool and being pulled down, drowning."

Struggling with depression and his worsening epilepsy during the recording sessions, Curtis's haunted baritone steered the band—which was already beginning to veer into dance-rock territory on songs such as **Heart and Soul**—through a gothic post-punk wasteland where tough, existential questions echoed throughout a lonely soundscape. But somehow, throughout it all, Sumner, Peter Hook, and Stephen Morris provided a tense, wiry pulse that managed to keep Curtis and the music afloat—at least for these forty-four and a half hypnotic, harrowing minutes. *—JL*

John Lennon and Yoko Ono
DOUBLE FANTASY

GEFFEN | Producers: John Lennon, Yoko Ono, Jack Douglas
RELEASED: NOVEMBER 17, 1980

● Following 1975's somewhat legally obligated *Rock 'n' Roll* album and the birth of his son Sean in October of that year, John Lennon stepped back from his career to help raise the child with his wife, Yoko Ono. For five years he was out of public view and by all accounts the happiest he had been in quite some time. In August 1980, two months before Sean turned five, Lennon returned to the studio for the first time since late 1974 with a handful of songs he had written during his hiatus.

With producer Jack Douglas in tow and Ono recording some of her new songs—which alternated Lennon's tracks on the album—*Double Fantasy* took on the aura of a dialogue between husband and wife, recounting their marital and familial bliss over the past half-decade; the album's subtitle, *A Heart Play*, said it all. Released five weeks after Lennon's fortieth birthday, *Double Fantasy* marked the former Beatle's first album of original material since 1974's No. 1 *Walls and Bridges*. Reception was initially lukewarm, both critically and commercially. Then on December 8, 1980, tragedy struck.

Returning to his New York City apartment from a recording session, Lennon was shot and killed. *Double Fantasy* soon found a mourning audience; the album shot to No. 1, as did its first single, **(Just Like) Starting Over**. And the songs about middle-aged domesticity— **Watching the Wheels**, **Beautiful Boy (Darling Boy)**, about Sean—gained even more poignancy following Lennon's death. The album's legacy is undoubtedly shaded by these events, but it's also an unfeigned reflection of the grown-up Lennon coming to terms with aging. More songs from the sessions turned up on 1984's posthumous *Milk and Honey*, the sequel to what should have been the start of a celebrated comeback. *—MG*

Judas Priest
BRITISH STEEL
COLUMBIA | Producer: Tom Allom
RELEASED: APRIL 11, 1980

● After putting an exclamation point on its decade-long rise to metal's forefront with 1979's blazing live album *Unleashed in the East*, Judas Priest kicked off the '80s with an unabashed play for more mainstream attention. *British Steel* found the band simplifying its arrangements and sharpening its hooks even further than the quintet had on 1978's *Killing Machine* (released in America early the following year as *Hell Bent for Leather*). *British Steel* was home to two of the band's most catchy and enduring anthems, **Breaking the Law** and **Living after Midnight**. Both tracks were definitive examples of how the group had learned to add a bit of breathing space into its rhythm section, a skill frontman Rob Halford later suggested Judas Priest picked up on while touring with AC/DC the previous year. **Law** and **Midnight**, both of which just missed the Top 10 in Priest's home country of England, were also notable for their more traditional anti-authority lyrics, continuing a shift away from the more fantastical subject matter of Judas Priest's '70s output.

There was plenty more to love here. The album is bookended by two blistering numbers—the opening **Rapid Fire** and the closing **Steeler**—that clearly demonstrated why Judas Priest was such a huge influence on future thrash metal pioneers such as Metallica, Slayer, and Anthrax. The slow-churning **Metal Gods** showed off the band's range, became a concert staple, and gave Halford an absolutely perfect, trademarkable nickname. Alongside 1982's more souped-up *Screaming for Vengeance*, *British Steel* is one of two all-time classic metal albums Judas Priest released during the early '80s and a major reason the band is largely considered second only to fellow Rock & Roll Hall of Famers Black Sabbath in the genre's hierarchy. —MW

1980

Motörhead
ACE OF SPADES
BRONZE | Producer: Vic Maile
RELEASED: OCTOBER 1980

● After Ian Fraser "Lemmy" Kilmister was dismissed from space-rock pioneers Hawkwind, he set up shop under the name of the last song he wrote for that band, "Motörhead," even though his first choice of band name was reportedly Bastard. Good sense prevailed, so Motörhead—Limey slang for a speed freak—it was. Hawkwind's song, which appeared on a 1975 B-side, was more leisurely than you'd expect. Lemmy's first order of business was to speed it up, which his new band did with much aplomb on Motörhead's self-titled 1977 debut.

By the time the group came to album number five three years later, the trio of singer/bassist Kilmister, guitarist "Fast" Eddie Clarke, and drummer Phil "Philthy Animal," Motörhead had gelled into an overpowering force of nature. Produced by Lemmy's Hawkwind bandmate Vic Maile, *Ace of Spades* stands as Motörhead's magnum opus. The title track remains one of the all-time great first-wavers, jittering out of the gate with a rumble-to-explosion arrangement similar to "Motörhead." With Lemmy's exhortations ("But that's the way I like it, baby / I don't wanna live for *EVAH!*"), it was the "Johnny B. Goode" of thrash-metal. **Jailbait**, **The Hammer**, and **(We Are) The Roadcrew** were just as definitive.

Despite that success, however, it would be Motörhead's lot to pave the way for others. As with the Ramones and punk rock, Motörhead's influence far outweighed its sales, serving as a bridge between punk and metal. Black Flag, Corrosion of Conformity, Metallica, and Megadeth are but a few of its descendants. Yet Motörhead was catchier than any of them—the world's loudest bubblegum band. Lemmy remained a beloved elder until his 2015 passing at age 70 from a lifetime of hard living. It's a legacy to be proud of. *—DM*

The Police
ZENYATTA MONDATTA

A & M | Producers: The Police, Nigel Gray
RELEASED: OCTOBER 3, 1980

● The Police really tried to be a punk band, but *Zenyatta Mondatta*, its third release, confirmed the trio was anything but. Sure, bassist and lead singer/songwriter Sting, guitarist Andy Summers, and drummer Stewart Copeland had plenty of cheek, but they weren't raging against the machine, and their sophisticated reggae, ska, and jazz–influenced musicianship belied punk's anybody-can-do-it ethos. The trio's allure was rooted in its ability to exude intellectualism and playfulness while laying down irresistible grooves—and look damned good while doing it.

They also craved success. On *Zenyatta Mondatta*, they merged clever literary and pop culture references (Nabokov, *The T.A.M.I. Show*) and a deepening awareness of sociopolitical issues with relentlessly catchy melodies and danceable rhythms—proclaimed "near perfect pop" by *Rolling Stone*. Though the band was unhappy with the album, which it rushed to complete, and Sting chafed at dismissals of the Top 10 hit **De Do Do Do, De Da Da Da** as nonsensical (he intended it as a commentary on the power of simplicity), the band finally broke in the US with that track and the Lolita tale **Don't Stand So Close to Me**, another Top 10. The album spent 153 weeks on the Billboard Top 200, peaking at No. 5.

Considered by some as the best of the Police's five studio albums, it scored two Grammy Awards, including one for Summers's sharp-edged, dissonant instrumental **Behind My Camel**, on which Sting refused to play. On **When the World Is Running Down, You Make the Best of What's Still Around**, meanwhile, the trio spun repeated beats, chords, and lyrics into three and a half minutes of pure funk genius. *—LM*

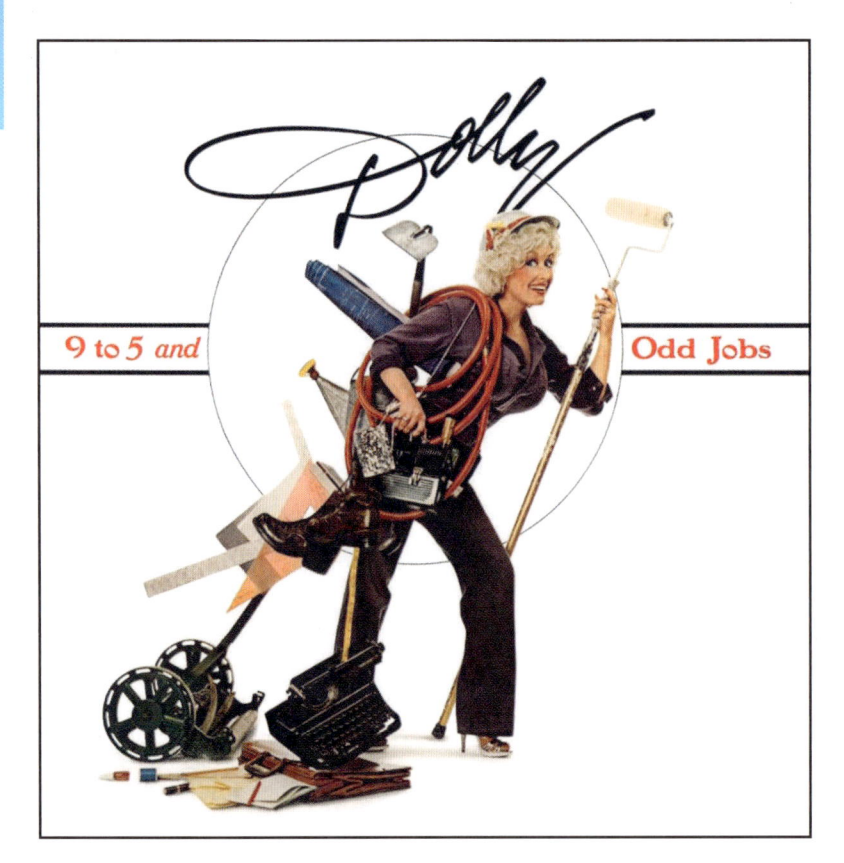

Dolly Parton
9 TO 5 AND ODD JOBS

RCA VICTOR | Producers: Mike Post, Greg Perry
RELEASED: NOVEMBER 17, 1980

● Dolly Parton could have simply enjoyed the Oscar-nominated and Grammy Award–winning success of **9 to 5**, the title theme she composed for the comedy film of the same name (in which she co-starred with Jane Fonda and Lily Tomlin), and called it a good year. Instead, the country star and future pop culture icon used it as the linchpin for one of the finest and most focused albums of her career.

9 to 5 and Odd Jobs was a rarity in the country world at the time—first of all, a bona fide *album* rather than a single or two and a bunch of filler to go with it and an actual concept album built around the idea of work and working-class struggles. Parton abetted **9 to 5** with blue-collar odes such as **Working Girl**, **Hush-a-Bye Hard Times**, and **Poor Folks' Town**, while her sister Frieda co-wrote **Sing for the Working Man**. The ten-song set's covers (Bobby Bare's **Detroit City**; the traditional **The House of the Rising Sun**, arranged with co-producer Mike Post; Woody Guthrie's **Deportee [Plane Wreck at Los Gatos]**) complemented the theme, and alongside all that, her rendition of **But You Know I Love You** gave the song a different and more poignant resonance than was felt in Kenny Rogers and the First Edition's original.

The album also benefited from some ace playing, with ringers such as Jeff "Skunk" Baxter, Larry Carlton and Reggie Young on guitar, Leland Sklar and Abraham Laboriel on bass, and Sonny Osborne on banjo.

9 to 5 spent ten straight weeks at No. 1 on the Billboard country chart, and the song took home a pair of Grammys and found itself part of US senator Elizabeth Warren's 2020 presidential campaign. Suffice to say, it all worked out just fine. *—GG*

1980

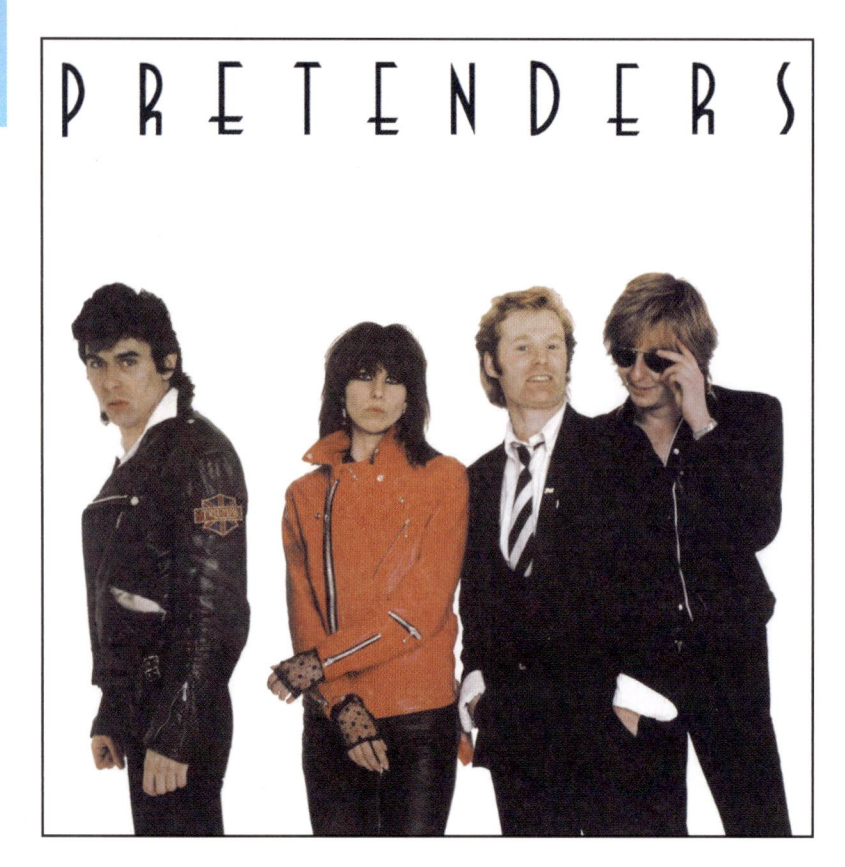

The Pretenders
PRETENDERS
S I R E | Producers: Chris Thomas, Nick Lowe
RELEASED: JANUARY 11, 1980

● The Pretenders couldn't have picked a more appropriate name. From the start, the band was never quite what it seemed. The name itself recalled a vocal group relic from the pre-Beatles era. It was based in the UK and first became famous there even though its frontwoman was born in Ohio. And though the quartet dressed like punks and was often included in discussions about that scene, it was closer at heart to a pop band. When its debut album arrived during the second week of the decade, the Pretenders had already scored three Top 40 hits in the UK, including the No. 1 **Brass in Pocket**.

Led by Akron-to-London singer and songwriter Chrissie Hynde and featuring three British musicians—drummer Martin Chambers, bassist Pete Farndon, and guitarist James Honeyman-Scott—the Pretenders made its recording debut a year prior with a cover of Ray Davies's Kinks song **Stop Your Sobbing**, produced by Nick Lowe. The next single, the Hynde-penned **Kid**, was produced by Chris Thomas, whose career dated to the Beatles' "White Album" and who helped steer the Pretenders through the recording of its first album.

Led by Hynde's vicious kiss-off **Precious**, the album found a space for both punk (the sharp-edged **Tattooed Love Boys**) and pop (the sweetly romantic **Brass in Pocket**), songs that were fully complementary within their contexts. Anyone hoping to get a handle on either Hynde or the Pretenders was turned around by their next song; as the first great album of the '80s, *Pretenders* forecasted the decade's blurring of genre lines. Subsequent releases grew up alongside Hynde, who took over the band following the deaths of Farndon and Honeyman-Scott and never allowed the Pretenders to settle into expectation. —*MG*

Prince
DIRTY MIND
WARNER BROS. | Producer: Prince
RELEASED: OCTOBER 8, 1980

● This may seem odd to say about an artist whose first single was named "Soft and Wet" and who posed nude atop a unicorn on the back of his second album cover, but Prince started off his career playing things a bit too safe. Both his 1978 debut *For You* and 1979's *Prince* showcased well-written, well-performed songs featuring an appealing mix of pop and R&B. And of course, the fact that he was a one-man songwriting/performing/producing dynamo made those albums all the more impressive. But the world didn't meet the real Prince until he unleashed the raw and risqué *Dirty Mind*.

The recordings heard on the album were originally intended only as demos, but Prince soon realized that the honesty and directness he had been seeking in his music had already been captured and, after overcoming a brief pushback from his label, released *Dirty Mind* in this primal form. The label was also understandably concerned about the subject matter of songs such as **Sister**—which toed the line between documenting and glorifying incest—and the impossibly catchy but understandably forbidden-from-radio **Head**. Luckily Prince's instincts were correct; he was at the forefront of an explosion of sexual frankness in popular music that has yet to abate—even though decades later his more conservative, religious-minded self would occasionally try to get his fellow artists to try to button up a bit.

Of course, the main ingredient in this formula was the daring new grit and genre-blending of *Dirty Mind*'s music, from the throbbing synthesizer of the opening title track to the bristling New Wave of **When You Were Mine** and the jangling rock guitar of the aforementioned **Sister**. Simply put, with *Dirty Mind*, Prince burned the cute little house he had been building down to its foundations and started building something much more unique and impressive. *—MW*

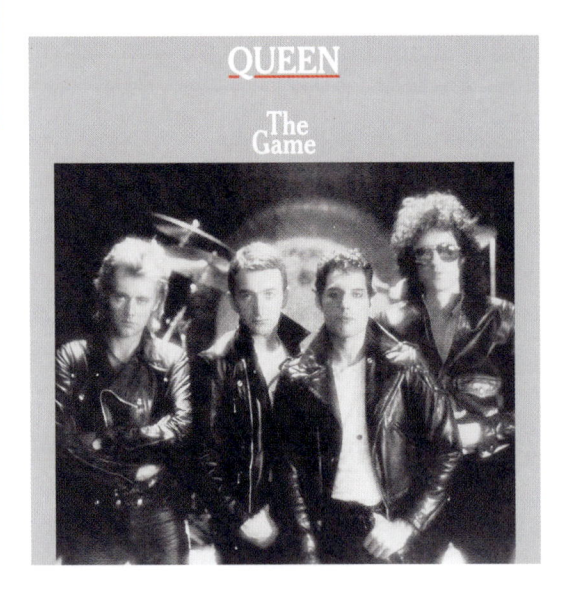

Queen
THE GAME
ELEKTRA | Producers: Queen, Reinhold Mack
RELEASED: JUNE 30, 1980

● Rules were made to be broken. And so, Queen's self-imposed "no synths" edict went out the window with *The Game*, its eighth album and the follow-up to 1978's bombastic *Jazz*. This time the group introduced an Oberheim OB-X into its sound, giving the foursome a fresh sonic approach for the new decade. It's an album that wrapped its arms around big pop sounds, from opener **Play the Game** (of love, it turns out) to the soaring power ballad closer **Save Me**. The cheeky **Don't Try Suicide** was an odd fit and far from nuanced in its acknowledgment of mental health issues; "nobody gives a damn" is one of the reasons frontman Freddie Mercury offered for not giving up. (Well, since you put it that way!) Because of its unabashed embrace of anthemic pop, *The Game* was divisive among core fans but a hit with the masses. It became the group's first US No. 1 album, and a pair of singles—the hip-swingin' rockabilly throwdown **Crazy Little Thing Called Love** and the stomping disco staredown **Another One Bites the Dust**—became the group's first Billboard Hot 100 chart-toppers. That's playing the game and winning. *–AG*

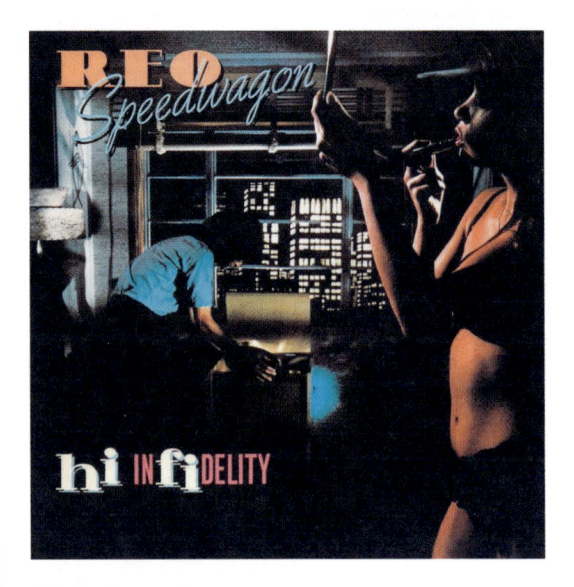

REO Speedwagon
HI INFIDELITY
EPIC | Producers: Kevin Beamish, Kevin Cronin
RELEASED: NOVEMBER 21, 1980

● REO Speedwagon didn't need to be cool to make its mark. The Champaign, Illinois, troupe weren't barechested rock gods, and the band's image wasn't ready-made for MTV, the glow from which was just around the corner. But REO spent the '70s ridin' the storm out and releasing eight albums of meat-and-potatoes rock 'n' roll, building a steady following and filling arenas coast-to-coast. All that hard work paid off on *Hi Infidelity*. The slick, catchy, and refined nine-song collection became the group's first No. 1 album and produced the radio staple **Keep on Lovin' You**. The aching-heart power ballad was an ode to sticking things out, even through infidelity, and its tender center was surrounded by wailing guitars and prom-ready theatrics. It became REO's signature song and its first No. 1 hit, and it paved the way for **Take It on the Run**, which was equally scornful but less forgiving than its predecessor. *Hi Infidelity* was a high-water mark for the group, setting REO up for a prosperous '80s and decades of touring on the summer amphitheater circuit. It was eventually certified ten-times platinum, the kind of success you can take to the bank—which is better than being cool. *–AG*

Diana Ross
DIANA
MOTOWN | Producers: Nile Rodgers, Bernard Edwards
RELEASED: MAY 22, 1980

● After taking her Supreme-ly classic Motown approach as far as she felt it could—though 1979's *The Boss* was still a gold-certified success—Diana Ross wanted to start the next decade with something new and modern. She enlisted Chic hitmakers Nile Rodgers and Bernard Edwards, which did the trick for her eleventh solo studio album. Recording in New York with much of the Chic crew, the duo brought its lean grooves and sleek, spirited songcraft to the eight tracks on *Diana*, freshening the sound, while the black-and-white Francesco Scavullo cover photo presented an equally contemporary image. Although Ross got a bit nervous and remixed it before its release (much to Rodgers's and Edwards's displeasure), the chart-topping **Upside Down** and **I'm Coming Out** blasted out of speakers at Studio 54 and radios everywhere, and there was more quality to be found in tracks such as **My Old Piano** and **Have Fun (Again)**. *Diana* was Ross's first platinum and best-selling solo outing, as well her highest charting (No. 2 on the Billboard 200). She'd team up with Edwards and Rodgers, separately and together, on 1984's *Swept Away* and 1989's *Workin' Overtime*. —*GG*

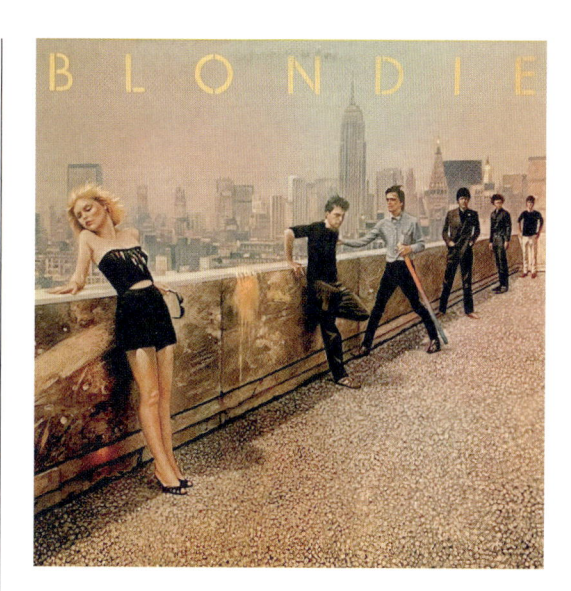

Blondie
AUTOAMERICAN
CHRYSALIS | Producer: Mike Chapman
RELEASED: NOVEMBER 26, 1980

● New Wave punk rockers Blondie's fifth studio album offered a little of this and a little of that as the band veered wildly from string-filled instrumentals (opener **Europa**) to 1920s-era pop (**Here's Looking at You**, **Faces**) to Broadway covers (closer **Follow Me**, from *Camelot*). All over the place? Sure. But the stylistic swings landed the group a pair of signature hits.

The Tide Is High, a playful cover of Jamaican group the Paragons' 1967 hit, was a sunny beachside reggae-lite kick, with frontwoman Debbie Harry letting out a couple of infectious laughs over the final chorus. And **Rapture** was a funky hybrid of disco licks and hip-hop attitude, with Harry doing her best take on "Rapper's Delight." Both songs hit No. 1 on the Billboard Hot 100, and the latter was the first chart leader to feature rap vocals.

It was also the group's last No. 1, as *Autoamerican* marked the beginning of the end of Blondie's first phase; just a few months later, Harry released her debut solo effort, *KooKoo*. Blondie put out one more album, 1982's **The Hunter**, before hanging it up, though a 1999 reunion netted a return to touring and occasional recording. —*AG*

Bob Seger
AGAINST THE WIND

CAPITOL | Producers: Punch Andrews, Bob Seger, Steve Melton, The Muscle Shoals Rhythm Section, Bill Szymczyk

RELEASED: FEBRUARY 25, 1980

● Beautifully written, arranged, and performed, the title track of *Against the Wind* is one of rock's most moving reflections on aging and loss. And with one key lyric—"Deadlines and commitments / What to leave in, what to leave out"—it is rock's greatest lament on the challenges of the creative life.

When *Against the Wind* was released, Seger was in the third decade of a career that carried him from regional bands through his first national attention with "Ramblin' Gamblin' Man" in 1969 to the massive breakthrough of *Night Moves* in 1976. He matched that peak with *Stranger in Town* in 1978 and rode that momentum into *Against the Wind*, Seger's third No. 1 album and his sole Grammy Award winner.

Seger's Silver Bullet Band was augmented once more by the superstar session players of the Muscle Shoals Rhythm Section here. He also welcomed Mac Rebennack, aka Dr. John, to play boogie-woogie piano on the roadhouse rocker **The Horizontal Bop**, which opened the album. Seger's longtime friend Glenn Frey sang on **Against the Wind** and joined fellow Eagles Don Henley and Timothy B. Schmit to harmonize on **Fire Lake**. (A year earlier, Seger co-wrote "Heartache Tonight" for the Eagles album *The Long Run*).

The medium-tempoed **Fire Lake** reached No. 6 on the Billboard Hot 100, but overall the songwriting on *Against the Wind* felt uneven. **You'll Accomp'ny Me** was a pleasant but deceptively sinister, acoustic guitar–driven song that sounded like a retread. The chugging "big train keeps on rolling" blues of **Long Twin Silver Line** was clichéd. And the sexual objectification of **Her Strut** has not aged well. On *Against the Wind*, it sounds as if this time Seger, perhaps facing deadlines and commitments, could not decide what to leave in or what to leave out. *—TD*

1980

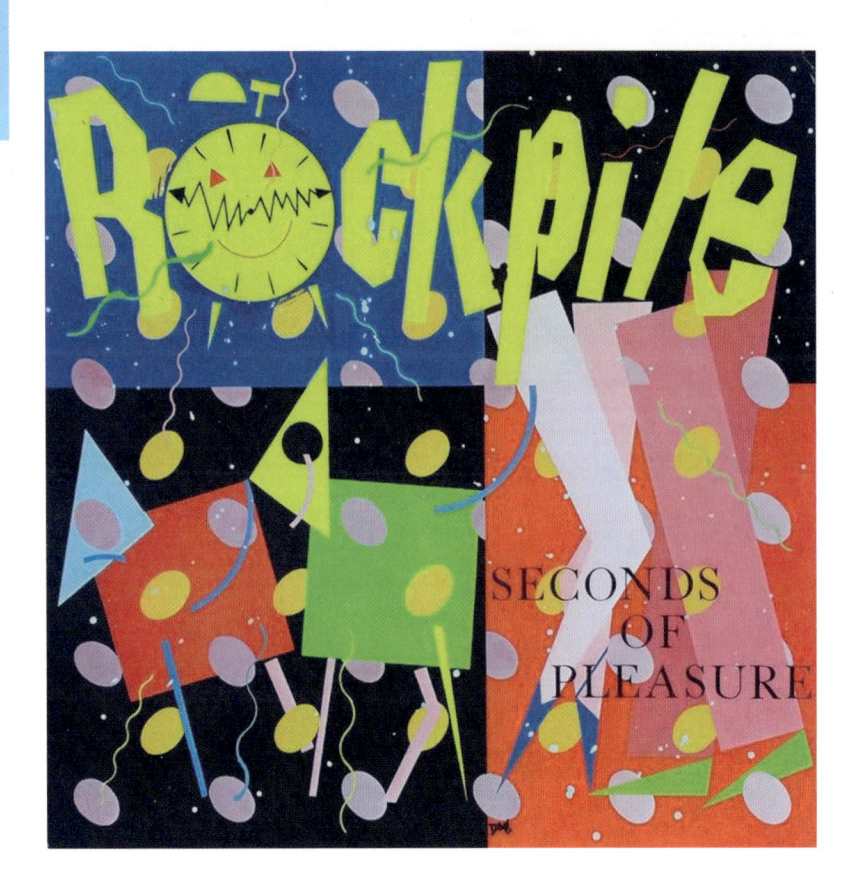

Rockpile
SECONDS OF PLEASURE

COLUMBIA | Producers: Nick Lowe and Rockpile
RELEASED: OCTOBER 1980

● Rock 'n' roll is full of coulda-shoulda-woulda stories, and Rockpile was one of them, a band with an impressive lineup with pedigrees that stretched from rockabilly and pub rock to power pop and proto–New Wave and more experience as a recording and touring unit than its sole album, *Seconds of Pleasure*, would suggest. Led by guitarist Dave Edmunds and bassist Nick Lowe, with support from guitarist Billy Bremner and drummer Terry Williams, the band played together on a number of albums—including Edmunds's *Trax on Wax 4*, *Repeat When Necessary*, and *Twangin'*, plus Lowe's *Labour of Lust*—but released only this one as Rockpile.

The twelve-track album found Edmunds and Lowe splitting lead vocals equally—five apiece—with Bremner taking two. The opening track, **Teacher, Teacher**, the only song to achieve even minor chart success, was sung by Lowe, as were the equally fine **When I Write the Book**, **Pet and Hold You**, and **Play That Fast Thing (One More Time)**. Edmunds's leads included covers of Joe Tex's **If Sugar Was as Sweet as You**, Chuck Berry's **Oh What a Thrill**, and **Wrong Again (Let's Face It)** by Squeeze's Difford/Tilbrook team. Perhaps inspired by the Everly Brothers (a four-track EP of Everlys covers was included in early pressings of the album and reissues), the two paired up nicely on **Now and Always**. Bremner's two leads, **Heart** and **You Ain't Nothin' but Fine**, were standout cuts as well.

Whether it was a clash of egos or a matter of aesthetics (Edmunds was the exacting revivalist while Lowe was purposefully nicknamed "Basher") or maybe even disappointment over the album's poor reception, the band split. Looking back on it now, though, the album ultimately delivered not just seconds but rather a lifetime of pleasure. *—DD*

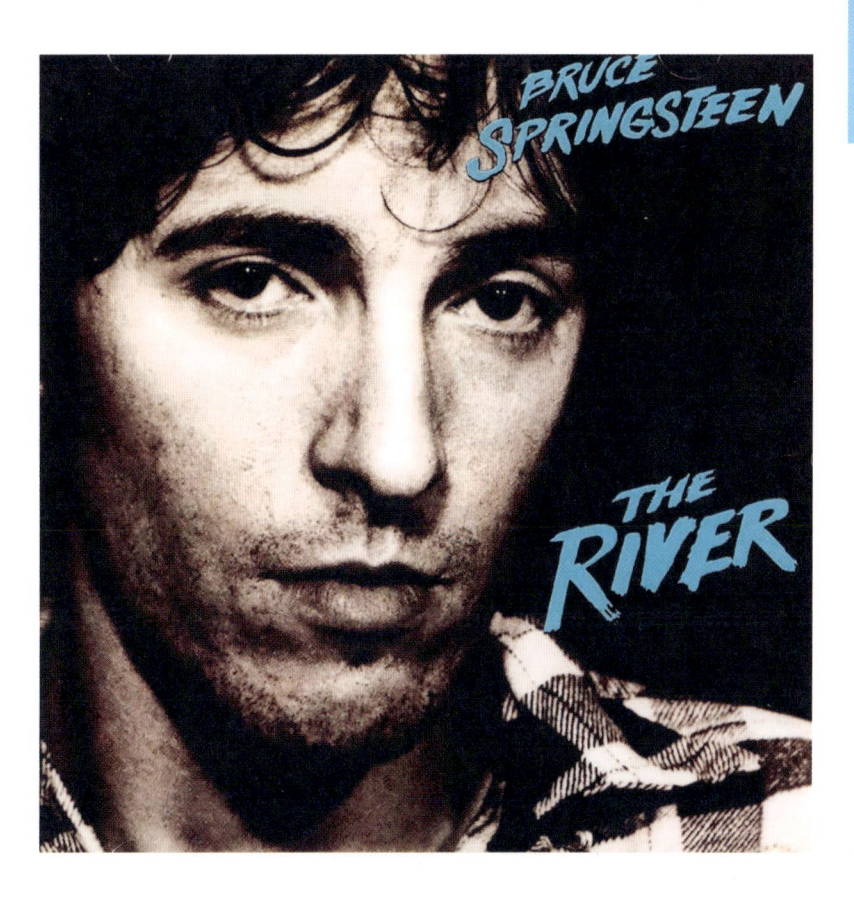

Bruce Springsteen
THE RIVER

COLUMBIA | Producers: Bruce Springsteen, Jon Landau, Steven Van Zandt

RELEASED: OCTOBER 17, 1980

● Opening his tour celebrating *The River* album back in 2016, Bruce Springsteen told a Pittsburgh crowd that "I wanted to make a record that was big enough so it felt like life . . . I wanted the record to contain fun, dancing, jokes, good comradeship, love, faith, sex, lonely nights, and, of course, tears." It was a big ambition, especially since the ultimate purpose, he added, was to "get a little closer to the home I was searching for."

At the time, of course, the New Jersey rocker's home was in rock 'n' roll, and *The River* succeeded in giving Springsteen's burgeoning nation of fans all of that—and only grew that corps thanks to *The River*'s breakthrough single, **Hungry Heart**, his first Top 5 hit. The album was a two-disc, twenty-song journey dedicated to assessing the world as Springsteen saw it and figuring out his place in it. It came from prodigious sessions that produced a wealth of legendary outtakes, which later surfaced on the *Tracks* compilation and the 2015 box set *The Ties That Bind: The River Collection*—the latter of which included an originally proposed single-disc edition of the album that felt impactful but incomplete.

The River had moments of deep, sober reflection and introspection—**Independence Day**, **Fade Away**, **Stolen Car**, **Wreck on the Highway**, and the title track among them. But Springsteen and his E Street Band also rocked up a storm in counterpoint; side one's primal opening tear of **The Ties That Bind**, **Sherry Darling**, **Jackson Cage**, and **Two Hearts** rendered a listener nearly breathless; and there was a lot more where that came from. This was Springsteen at peak productivity and fierce conceptual aspiration, striding forward into a new kind of musical promised land. *—GG*

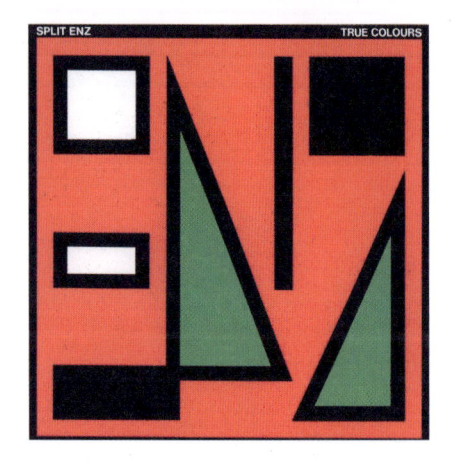

Split Enz
TRUE COLOURS
A & M | Producer: David Tickle
RELEASED: JANUARY 21, 1980

● New Zealand's Split Enz finally broke through with its fifth studio album. Brothers Tim and Neil Finn transitioned the prog-ish band to New Wave, charting internationally with **I Got You**; the taut opening riff and lyrics like "I don't know why sometimes I get frightened" hit a sweet spot between anxiety and desire for the early MTV generation. The album's sparkling vocals and manic synths brought the band out of the shadows, as did its eleven different covers and stunningly laser-etched discs. —HD

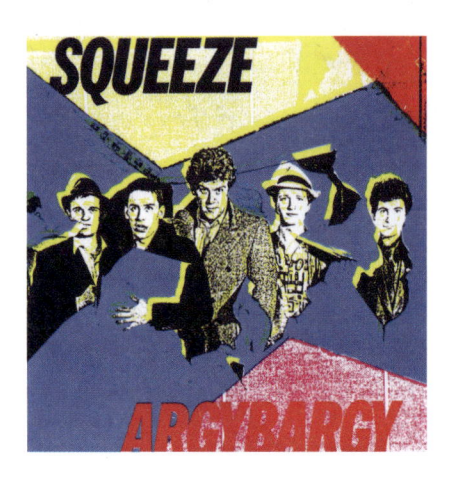

Squeeze
ARGY BARGY
A & M | Producer: John Wood
RELEASED: FEBRUARY 1980

● London-based New Wave power popsters Squeeze suffered no sophomore slump on its second album. Instead, singers/guitarists/songwriters Chris Difford and Glenn Tillbrook became tighter and more adventurous tunesmiths. **Pulling Mussels from the Shell**, which broke the band in the States, led off, transitioning effortlessly between major and minor keys and featuring an outstanding piano solo from Jools Holland. **Separate Beds** made creative use of tempo changes to craft a unique sound. Virtually every song on the disc was loaded with distinctive hooks and guitar work focused on melody rather than pyrotechnics. —GP

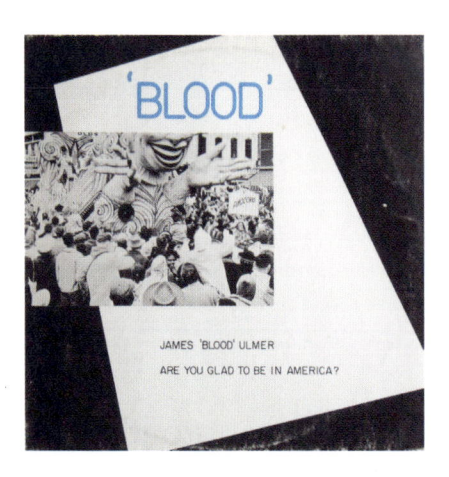

James Blood Ulmer
ARE YOU GLAD TO BE IN AMERICA?
ROUGH TRADE/ARTISTS HOUSE | Producers: John Snider, James Blood Ulmer
RELEASED: 1980

● Few artists have demonstrated as thorough an understanding of indigenous American music as the late James Blood Ulmer. *Are You Glad . . . ?*, Ulmer's second solo album, was a freer expression than 1978's *Tales of Captain Black*; it also introduced his enormously versatile Music Revelation Ensemble. Recorded in one session, *Are You Glad . . . ?* was a textbook in instinctual, interpretive communication. As the song said, **Jazz Is the Teacher (Funk Is the Preacher)**, and Ulmer's testimony was a revelation that, yes, made us glad to be a nation under his groove. —GG

UB40
SIGNING OFF

GRADUATE | Producers: Bob Lamb, UB40, Ray Falconer
RELEASED: AUGUST 29, 1980

● Birmingham, England–based UB40 hailed from the British Two-Tone movement, which featured ethnically diverse bands that combined ska and reggae with pop to produce a fresh sound. (Think Bob Marley fronting Culture Club.) The eleven songs on the band's debut were also fueled by timely statements about British colonialism (**Burden of Shame**), African famine (**Food for Thought**), and civil rights (**King**, as in Martin Luther King Jr.). Those polemics were nestled in haunting melodies featuring Ali Campbell's vocals and Brian Travers's reverb-laden saxophone, managing to make social consciousness highly entertaining. —GP

Utopia
ADVENTURES IN UTOPIA

BEARSVILLE | Producers: Todd Rundgren, Utopia
RELEASED: JANUARY 1980

● The Todd Rundgren–led Utopia's third album trimmed to a quartet was its best, a ten-track distillation of all the band did well. Intended as the soundtrack for a TV show that was never realized, the set housed punchy pop tunes (**Set Me Free**, **Shot in the Dark**) and proggy pomp (**The Road to Utopia**, **Caravan**, **Last of the New Wave Riders**), and even some kitsch in the disco-nodding album closer **Rock Love**. The troupe shared songwriting and singing duties throughout, showcasing a kind of utopian esprit de corps most bands only aspire toward. —GG

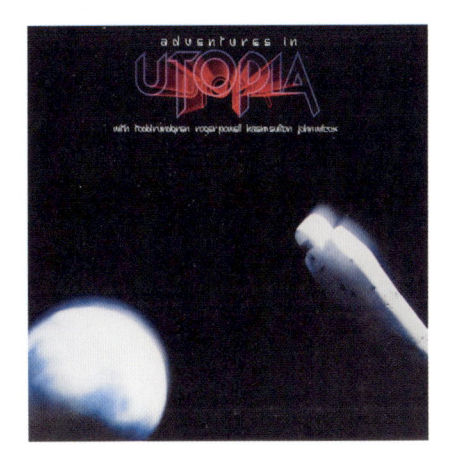

Sugarhill Gang
SUGARHILL GANG

SUGARHILL | Producer: Sylvia Robinson
RELEASED: FEBRUARY 7, 1980

● The first album by the New Jersey trio of Big Bank Hank, Master Gee, and Wonder Mike is widely considered the first full rap LP ever—even if wasn't full of rap. It housed the fourteen-minute-plus, Chic-sampling opus **Rapper's Delight**, which introduced so many to the rhythm of the boogie and the beat, but beyond that and **Rapper's Reprise**, the album was filled out by more traditional soul and disco tracks. Consequently, Sugarhill Gang doesn't have a legacy as strong as **Rapper's Delight**, but it's an important early signpost in the early days of hip-hop's ascent. —GG

Talking Heads
REMAIN IN LIGHT

SIRE | Producer: Brian Eno
RELEASED: OCTOBER 8, 1980

● When Talking Heads' *Remain in Light* dropped, fans of the nervy New Wave band were greeted with an album that owed as much to African polyrhythms as it did art school. While "I Zimbra" on the Heads' previous album was a harbinger of things to come, the real turning point was *My Life in the Bush of Ghosts*, a project frontman David Byrne and producer Brian Eno worked on between band records (released in 1981, however) that dove headfirst into looped samples, Afrobeat, and electronic mood pieces.

Fresh inspiration was exactly what the occasionally quarrelsome quartet needed. Instead of writing music to Byrne's lyrics, the band (Byrne, Chris Frantz, Jerry Harrison, and Tina Weymouth) let loose on extended Fela Kuti–inspired jams, after which they played back the recordings and decided which segments to re-create. "It was exactly what producers do these days with loops and samplers and sequencers," Byrne told *Uncut* in 2007. "We were human samplers."

It helped that the songs were among the strongest in its imposing catalog. **Born under Punches (The Heat Goes On)** was an anxious, irresistible yelp of funk. **Crosseyed and Painless** was a runaway train of polyrhythmic pleasure (boasting cowbell and an endearing robotic rap from Byrne). And **Seen and Not Seen** was a spoken-word piece about a wannabe Zelig set to percolating electronic loops.

And then there was **Once in a Lifetime**. Over a warm bubble bath of synths and a hypnotic groove, Byrne seemed to be speaking for an existentially adrift America when he asked, "Well, how did I get here?" in that inimitable alien-child voice. Despite peaking at just No. 91 on the Billboard Hot 100, **Once in a Lifetime** became a signature song, striking a chord with CEOs, socialists, and everyone in between while enjoying a popularity that's lasted, ahem, a lifetime. —JL

1980

X
LOS ANGELES
SLASH | Producer: Ray Manzarek
RELEASED: APRIL 26, 1980

● The fact that Ray Manzarek championed Los Angeles punk outfit X and produced its debut album was a bit of an eyebrow raiser. After all, his organ odysseys on several Doors classics ran longer than most songs on this twenty-eight-minute LP. But when he caught the group's sloppy, speed-of-light cover of his old band's "Soul Kitchen" at the Whisky a Go Go, he became obsessed.

No wonder Manzarek was keyed in. While X could match the burgeoning California hardcore scene when it came to breakneck brevity, volume, and social dissatisfaction, it retained some of the high(er)-brow aspirations of the so-called Hollywood punks. That was thanks to dual lead singers John Doe (also bass) and Exene Cervenka, who met at a poetry workshop a few years earlier and brought a lyrical sensibility to punk that was more Bukowski than "Blitzkrieg Bop." Ignited by guitarist Billy Zoom's Chuck Berry riffs and drummer D. J. Bonebrake's percussion, songs such as **Your Phone's Off the Hook, but You're Not** and **Johnny Hit and Run Pauline** dug into the dirt and disenfranchisement of a city of crushed dreams. This album was a document and even a cry for help from an artistic underbelly with no particular place to go in an increasingly hegemonic America—particularly on the title track, where Doe's resonant rockabilly voice and Cervenka's haunted, hoarse wail described how the pressure-cooker city brings out the worst (racism, anti-Semitism, and homophobia) in people.

There was a ragged glimmer of hope, however. Doe and Cervenka, who married the same year *Los Angeles* dropped (and divorced in 1985), closed the album with **The World's a Mess, It's in My Kiss**, a girl group–indebted romantic rager where the lovebirds seemed to find a sliver of relief in each other even as the world crumbles around them. —JL

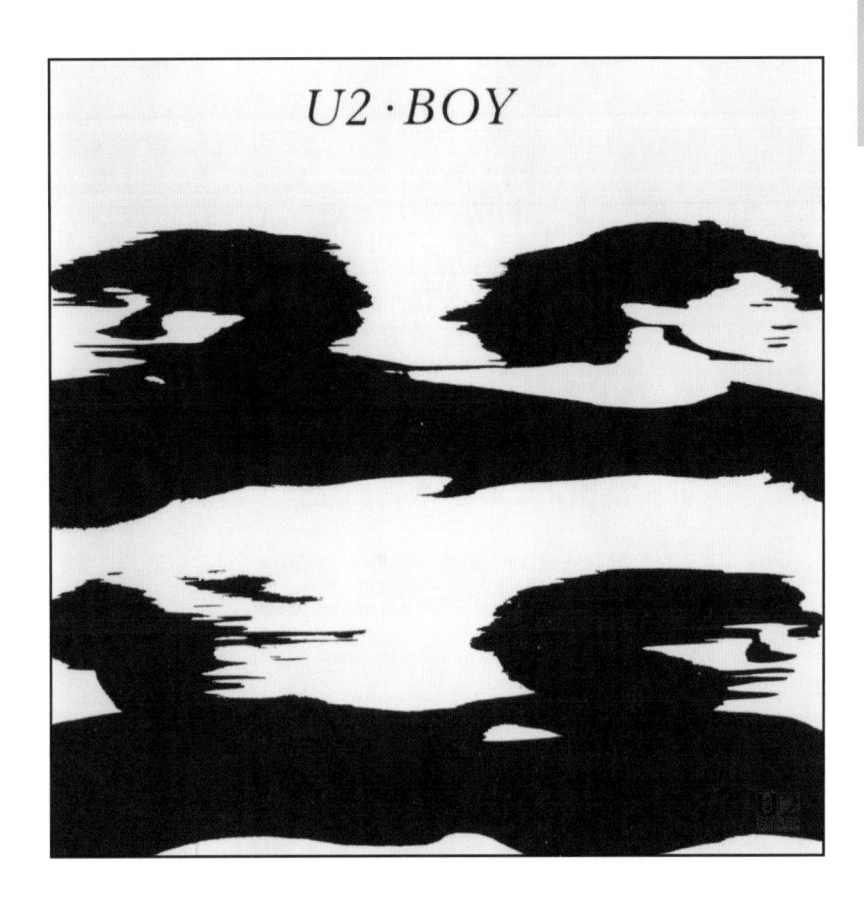

U2
BOY
ISLAND | Producer: Steve Lillywhite
RELEASED: OCTOBER 20, 1980

● U2's debut album was a lot like a puppy that hasn't grown into its huge paws yet, despite its galumphy gait, you just know that once that pup gains its footing, it'll be Best in Show.

Both thematically and musically, *Boy* conveyed that neophyte fumbling while revealing the obvious potential of an uncommonly talented young band. Deeply atmospheric and occasionally bursting with energy, it contained many moments of singular brilliance, like the way The Edge's beautifully chiming guitar chords offset Adam Clayton's thrumming bass on **I Will Follow**, while Larry Mullen Jr.'s crisp drumbeats punctuated frontman Bono's dramatically rising and falling vocals.

Bono's lyrics, however, had yet to match what a BBC reviewer described as his "vaulting ambitions and messianic zeal," though those certainly infused his passionate performances; he subsequently acknowledged their shortcomings, in fact. Exploring the progression from childhood innocence to the questioning (and questing) of adolescence and entry into manhood, *Boy*'s songs expressed the urgency of ambition, darkened by insecurity, and vulnerability. As if the possible allusion to pedophilia in **Twilight** weren't enough, the shoulders-up cover image of an apparently naked male child provoked Island Records to change the artwork for US release.

Boy seemed at times underdeveloped, simultaneously intriguing and frustrating. Several tracks started to soar, then lost focus and wandered aimlessly, like a restless teenager. **Out of Control**, for example, feels, well, out of control, uneven, possibly reflecting Bono's unsettled state after losing his mother at age fourteen.

Boy didn't herald the worldwide superstardom U2 would reach. But it instantly set the group apart from their post-punk/New Wave contemporaries and sowed the seeds for a stream of increasingly thrilling releases that led to a three-decade run of No. 1 albums. *—LM*

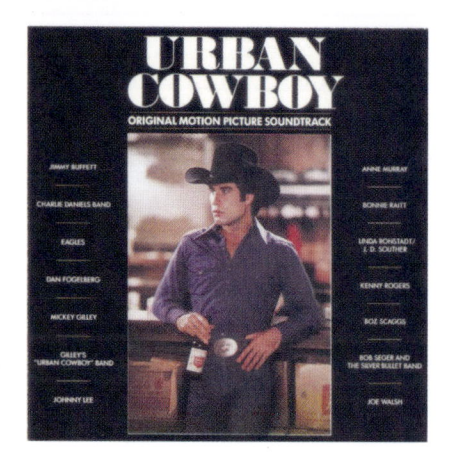

Various Artists
URBAN COWBOY (ORIGINAL MOTION PICTURE SOUNDTRACK)
FULL MOON/ASYLUM | Producer: Irving Azoff
RELEASED: JUNE 6, 1980

● There was still a fairly strong rock-country divide in 1980 when the John Travolta film *Urban Cowboy* introduced the idea that city slickers might like to line dance and ride mechanical bulls. The film's soundtrack blended the two genres with tracks by Jimmy Buffett, Eagles, Bob Seger, Bonnie Raitt, the Charlie Daniels Band, and more. Kenny Rogers's **Love the World Away** and Mickey Gilley's rendition of **Stand by Me** were more impactful as country singles, but Joe Walsh's **All Night Long** made the rock side of the equation worth noting. —*GG*

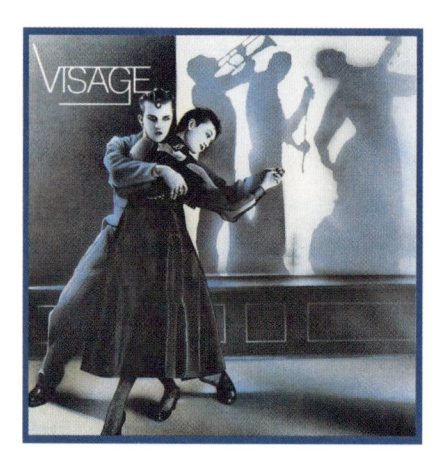

Visage
VISAGE
POLYDOR | Producers: Visage, Martin Rushent
RELEASED: NOVEMBER 10, 1980

● Steve Strange is considered the godfather of the New Romantic movement, and *Visage* was his first voyage into the artsy synth-pop genre. With help from musicians who went on to Ultravox, Magazine, and Siouxsie and the Banshees, the debut album from Visage was a groundbreaking blend of New Wave, electronica, dance, and rock with the artistically powerful Strange on vocals. Songs such as **Fade to Grey** filled dancefloors and later became a blueprint for techno pioneers. Visage delivered a masterful and highly influential record that was well ahead of its time. —*MH*

Grover Washington Jr.
WINELIGHT
ELEKTRA | Producers: Grover Washington Jr., Ralph MacDonald
RELEASED: OCTOBER 24, 1980

● Funky, groovy, sassy, and soulful saxophonist Grover Washington Jr. hit all the right R&B buttons to perfect an ultimate smooth jazz album. Its six tracks of rapturous, feel-good, and love-themed jazz became go-to dinner date background music. On *Winelight*, Washington's cozy soprano melody was buffered by Eric Gale's sweet rhythm guitar, the thumb-popping bass of Marcus Miller, and locked-in drumming by Steve Gadd. The album earned two Grammys: Best Jazz Fusion Performance and Best R&B Song for the Motown-esque megahit **Just the Two of Us**, sung by its lyricist, Bill Withers. —*CH*

Steve Winwood
ARC OF A DIVER
ISLAND | Producer: Steve Winwood
RELEASED: DECEMBER 29, 1980

● Steve Winwood had always played nice with others—the Spencer Davis Group, Traffic, Blind Faith—but on his second solo album, he took a dive as a truly one-man band, with the best results. *Arc of a Diver* was a reinvention; with help from a couple of co-writers (notably Will Jennings), Winwood found his voice in expansive, keyboard-dominated tracks such as **Night Train**, **Dust**, and **Spanish Dancer**, but retained the melodic sensibility that made **While You See a Chance** a Top 10 hit. A high spark into a new phase in Winwood's already-distinguished career. *—GG*

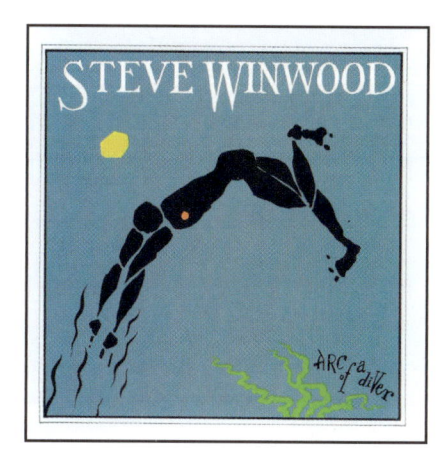

Various Artists
XANADU (ORIGINAL MOTION PICTURE SOUNDTRACK)
MCA | Producers: John Farrar, Jeff Lynne
RELEASED: JUNE 27, 1980

● There are few films kitschier than the fantastical musical *Xanadu*—and a soundtrack that paired its star, Olivia Newton-John, with Gene Kelly, the Tubes, Cliff Richards, and Electric Light Orchestra. Surprisingly, it worked. Newton-John's voice was sweet and light, while ELO displayed its usual catchy pop hooks. The two joined forces for the film's lush title track, and Newton-John's **Magic** was a No. 1 smash that helped drive the album to double-platinum sales. *—HD*

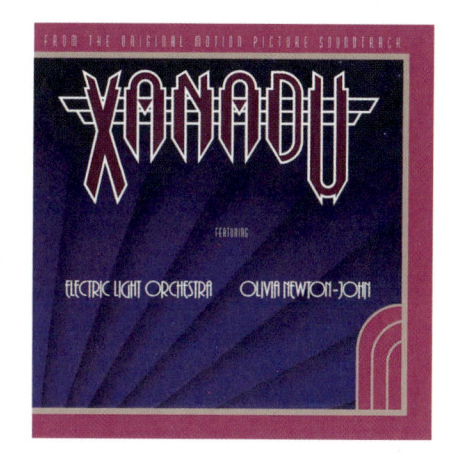

Zapp
ZAPP
WARNER BROS. | Producers: Roger Troutman, Bootsy Collins
RELEASED: JULY 30, 1980

● Zapp's influence can be measured by the hundreds of hip-hop artists who sampled their work, particularly **More Bounce to the Ounce**, the leadoff on the band's debut. Founder and frontman Roger Troutman caught the ear of funk maestro George Clinton, who signed Zapp to his label. Troutman and Bootsy Collins oversaw the recording of Zapp's debut, six tracks of elastic electro-funk jams. **More Bounce**, with its low-end bass thumps, funk guitar licks, and talkbox vocals, was signature Zapp; the sun-kissed and more laid-back **Be Alright** would form the backbone of 2Pac's 1993 hit, "Keep Ya Head Up." *—AG*

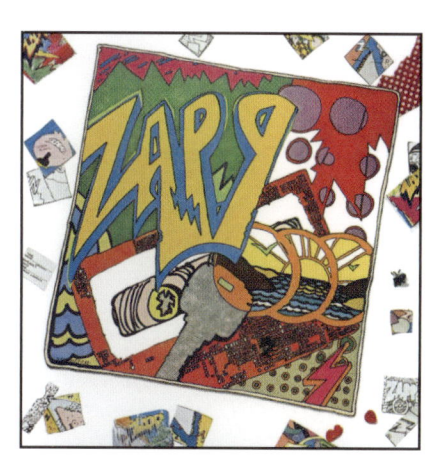

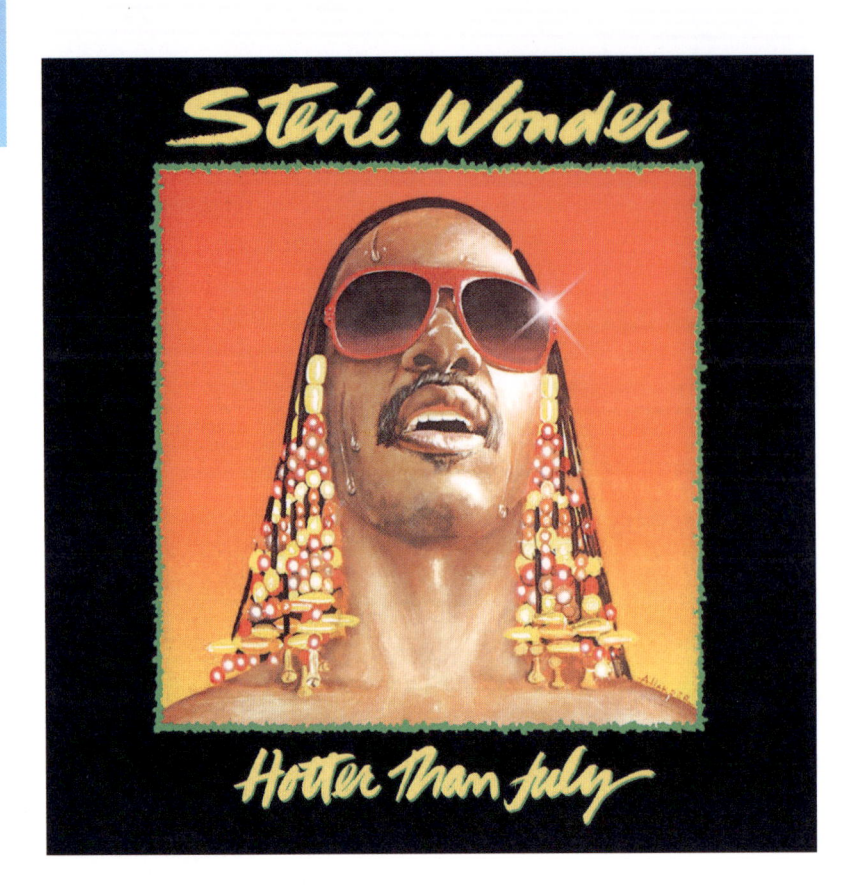

Stevie Wonder
HOTTER THAN JULY

TAMLA/MOTOWN | Producer: Stevie Wonder
RELEASED: SEPTEMBER 29, 1980

● After Stevie Wonder's remarkable '70s "classic period," becoming the only artist ever to win three consecutive Album of the Year Grammy Awards, it's no wonder he detoured into instrumental experimentation on *Journey through the Secret Life of Plants*. But he started the new decade by returning to his trademark mélange of R&B, pop, funk, and jazz. On *Hotter Than July*, his first fully digital pop production, he also retreated from grand (or grandiose) spiritual and existential statements and schmaltzy sentiments in favor of earthier commentaries about love—though ironically, *July*'s two most stylistically adventurous tracks became its biggest hits. With **Master Blaster (Jammin')**, his funkified ode to pal Bob Marley—released as the lead single days before what turned out to be Marley's final performance—Wonder made his first real foray into reggae (as opposed to his earlier "Boogie on Reggae Woman"). On **I Ain't Gonna Stand for It**, Wonder confronted a cheating lover in an almost-lampoonish country drawl. Sadly, the gorgeous lovelorn ballad **Lately** didn't earn the attention it deserved.

On *Hotter Than July*, released just as one of America's deadliest-ever heat waves subsided, Wonder pointedly called out landlords for redlining Black families. He also dedicated the album to the Rev. Dr. Martin Luther King Jr., printed disturbing photos of civil rights protests in the gatefold sleeve, and with the uplifting finale, **Happy Birthday**, launched his campaign to make King's birthday a national holiday, ultimately successful three years later.

Because Motown didn't report sales to the Recording Industry Association of America until the late '70s, *Hotter Than July* became Wonder's first official platinum album less than five months after its release. *—LM*

1980

19

81

1981

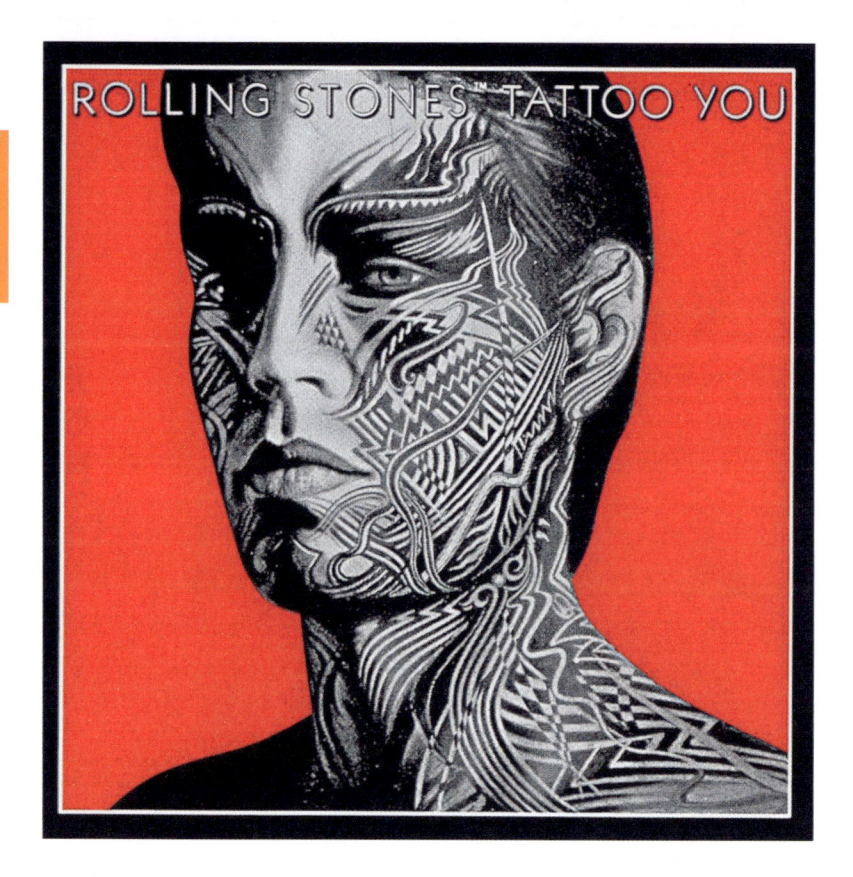

The Rolling Stones
TATTOO YOU
ROLLING STONES | Producers: The Glimmer Twins
RELEASED: AUGUST 24, 1981

● For an album that included session work that spanned almost a decade, *Tattoo You* was a surprisingly cohesive listen. It was also the band's eighth consecutive album to reach No. 1 in the States and arguably its last great album. And it all came together because the Stones' touring schedule in 1981 precluded work on a new studio record following 1980's *Emotional Rescue*. With little time to spare, the Stones' archives of unreleased performances—some completed, some in fragments—were raided, from the 1972 sessions for *Goat's Head Soup* through several *Emotional Rescue* leftovers.

Tattoo You's eleven songs ran the range of Stones recordings from the '70s: flirtations with punk (**Neighbours**), soul (**Tops**), and jazz-speckled pop (**Waiting on a Friend**) mingled with signature Stones-like rock 'n' roll songs such as **Start Me Up** and **Hang Fire**, both originated during the *Some Girls* sessions from 1978. In a way, it was the least surprising of the Rolling Stones' albums from the group's classic era; most everything is in place, from Keith Richards's familiar-sounding guitar riffs to fine-tuned Mick Jagger vocal performances. And almost every song is memorable.

Four tracks came from the pre–*Some Girls* period: **Tops** and **Waiting on a Friend** from *Goat's Head Soup* and featuring their then-guitarist Mick Taylor, and **Slave** and **Worried about You**—with Billy Preston on keyboards—from 1976's *Black and Blue*. The rest stemmed from the *Some Girls* and *Emotional Rescue* sessions, with Jagger recording additional vocals in late 1980 and the months leading up to the album's release in the summer of 1981. (Sonny Rollins's saxophone solos for two cuts were also recorded during these later touch-up sessions.) The seams barely revealed themselves in this stitched-together album, which still rates as a key record in the Rolling Stones' storied catalog. *–MG*

1981

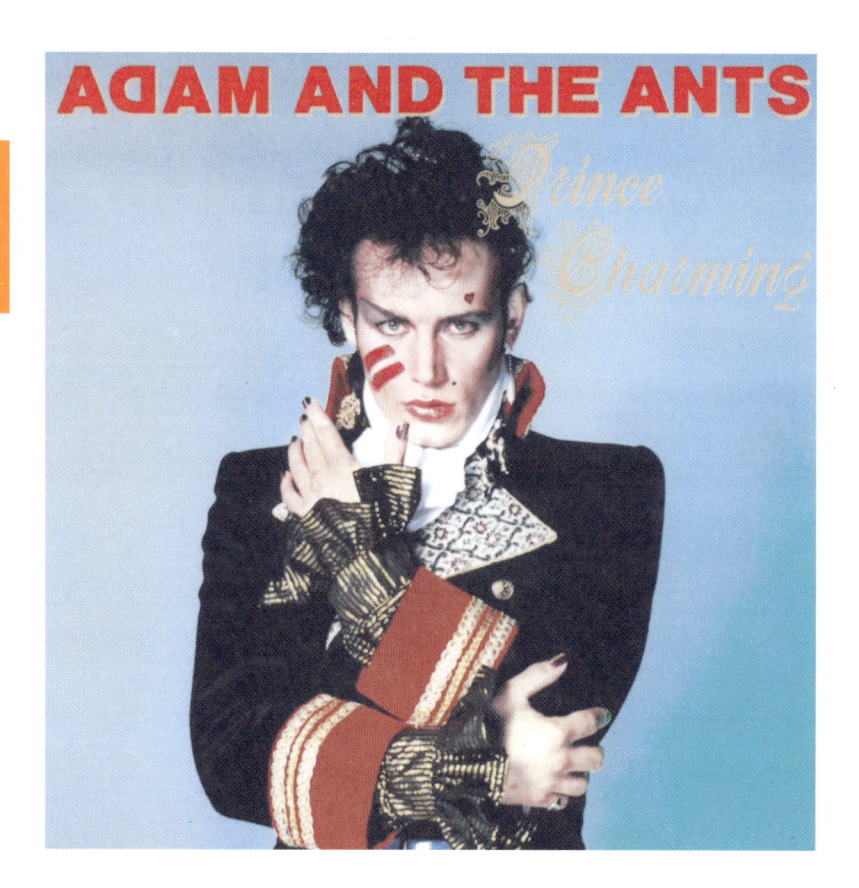

Adam and the Ants
PRINCE CHARMING

C B S | Producer: Chris Hughes
RELEASED: NOVEMBER 6, 1981

● By the time Adam and the Ants released its third album, *Prince Charming*, in 1981, the band had been through multiple lineup changes (the first iteration of the Ants marched off to back Annabella Lwin as part of Bow Wow Wow) and gone from being praised to pilloried by the press in its native England. So perhaps it was inevitable that this would be the troupe's final album before Adam Ant (Stuart Leslie Goddard) embarked upon a solo career.

But if the fashionable, flamboyant frontman was done with his bandmates, you'd be hard-pressed to detect it here. As always, Adam Ant is a king of camp on *Prince Charming*—yelping, wailing, sneering, crooning, and even rapping on this mischievous grab bag of New Wave that touches upon mariachi, Hawaiian music, country and western, and even a Māori war chant.

Prince Charming allowed the band to go out on top. The title track and lead single **Stand and Deliver** (the latter sounding a bit like the Clash's *Sandinista!* through a radio-friendly filter) both hit No. 1 in the UK, while the hip-hop-inspired **Ant Rap** reached No. 3 without any detectable chorus or hooks. You can certainly fault Adam's flow (he made Debbie Harry's "Rapture" verse sound like Rakim by comparison) but not his nerve.

Even discounting **Ant Rap**, this album's global musical palette occupied a nebulous region between admiration and opportunism; while David Byrne's world beat experiments seemed to come from a genuine love and immersion, the music here sometimes felt like the kind of cultural tourism old-school Hollywood trafficked in. But hey, cultural appropriation wasn't exactly a concern for most in 1981, and even now, you'd be cheating yourself to write off a rollicking record that's this weird, wonderful, and, yes, charming. *—JL*

Black Flag
DAMAGED
S S T | Producers: Spot, Black Flag

RELEASED: DECEMBER 1981

● For all its safety pins and sneering, punk was about returning rock to its roots—a desire to strip back the pomp and circumstance that made bands bloated with excess by the mid-'70s, and distanced from their audience, especially young men raised working class. Punk rock's bastard child known as hardcore took what it learned from its snot-nosed parents and boiled it down to a more potent fist in the face.

If readers are seeking to enter the hardcore genre, there's no better place to start than Black Flag's first full-length album. The L.A.-based band had been around about five years when *Damaged* was released. Originally co-founded by Keith Morris, who would later found and front another legendary hardcore band, the Circle Jerks, Black Flag was influenced by the Stooges and the Ramones but pared down the three-minute ditty to its essence while turning up the tempo, often writing songs that lasted about a minute or less.

With Morris's exit, a fan of the band, former D.C.-area Häagen-Dazs employee Henry Rollins, grabbed the mic to lay down vocals as fierce as the album's cover—a shaved-headed Rollins punching his own visage in the mirror, shattering it. Sonically lo-fi, the themes on *Damaged* were rich. The fifteen-track, thirty-five-minute set opened with **Rise Above**, an anthem to inner strength. Other highlights included **Six Pack**, an attack on responsibility-shirking drunks; **Police Story**, an assault on abusive cops known for beating punks and shutting down shows; and even a humorous ode to couch-potato-ism called **TV Party**.

While obviously an inspiration to future punk and hardcore bands, the sonic DNA of *Damaged* can also be heard in the thrash metal genre (especially in bands like Slayer), which arrived a few years later. *–RSM*

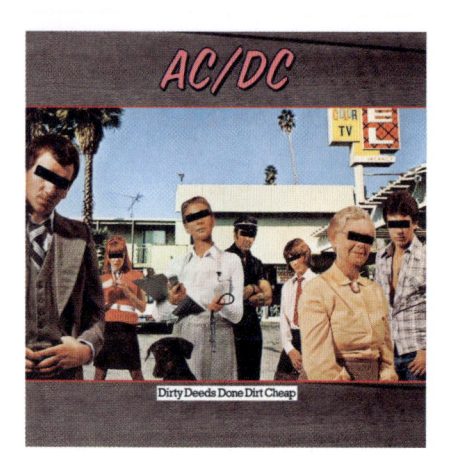

AC/DC
DIRTY DEEDS DONE DIRT CHEAP

ALBERT/ATLANTIC | Producers: Harry Vanda, George Young

RELEASED: SPRING 1981

● AC/DC's third studio album was released during 1976, only in the band's native Australia and with a different tracklist in Europe and New Zealand, but the success of 1980's *Back in Black* brought it to the rest of the world. It seemed a bit odd as new frontman Brian Johnson was still establishing himself with the group, but it did serve the purpose of introducing newbies to original frontman Bon Scott, who'd died the previous year, with particular joys in the title track, **Problem Child**, and, of course, **Big Balls**. —*GG*

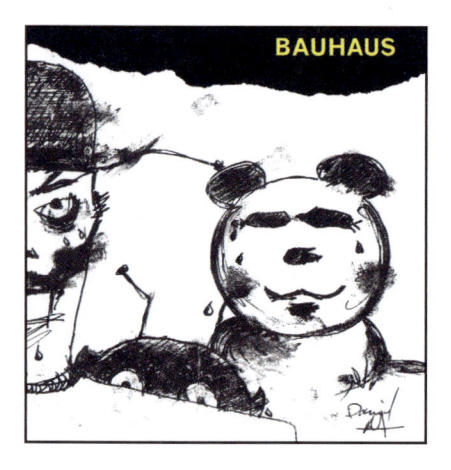

Bauhaus
MASK

BEGGARS BANQUET | Producers: Bauhaus

RELEASED: OCTOBER 9, 1981

● Having all but invented Goth rock, England's Bauhaus expanded its sound on the follow-up to its 1980 debut. Still dark, a disco ball was hung inside the quartet's cave, as **Hair of the Dog** and first single **Kick in the Eye** have defined grooves that brought Peter Murphy and his brothers in blackness out of the shadows and onto the dancefloor. The album-closing title track, meanwhile, featured a shimmering acoustic guitar outro, a ray of sunshine piercing through the dead of night. —*AG*

Lindsey Buckingham
LAW AND ORDER

ASYLUM | Producers: Lindsey Buckingham, Richard Dashut

RELEASED: OCTOBER 1981

● The quirks of Fleetwood Mac's *Tusk* in 1979 drew lines of delineation between the group's three songwriters—and, for fans of its outside the lines (i.e., weird) melodies and sonics, an appetite to hear more from Lindsey Buckingham. *Law and Order*, a mostly one-man affair, offered much of the same skewed, avant pop approach, Buckingham could pull hooks out of any orifice but also liked to deliver them with daring compositional strokes and with the sound of almost-unfinished demos, which was all part of the charm, of course. —*GG*

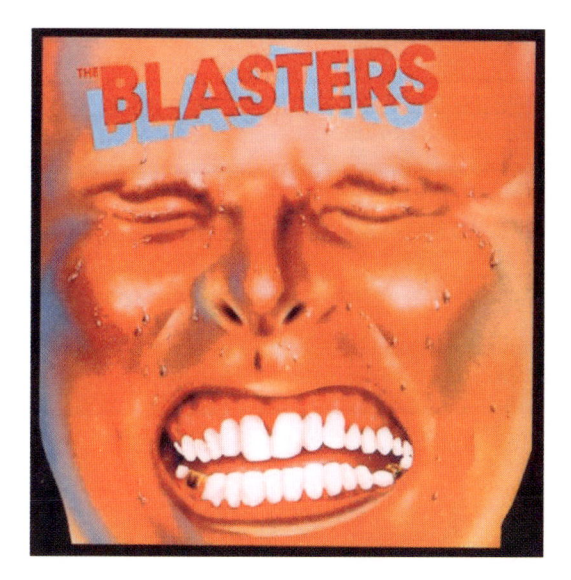

The Blasters
THE BLASTERS
S L A S H | Producers: The Blasters
RELEASED: DECEMBER 1981

● A succinct description of the Blasters' sound is right there in *American Music*, the title of the indie debut album that preceded the band's self-titled sophomore effort and a song that appeared on both. "We got the Louisiana boogie and the Delta blues," frontman Phil Alvin rhapsodized. "We got country, swing and rockabilly, too / We got jazz, country-western and Chicago blues / It's the greatest music that you ever knew." All of those vital native sounds were part of the Downey, California, roots-rock outfit's musical tutelage, and the group put that knowledge to work on L.A.'s nominally punk music scene that also nurtured such disparate outfits as X, Los Lobos, the Go-Go's, Dwight Yoakam, and Black Flag. *The Blasters* is where it all came together, from Dave Alvin's incendiary and self-defining rockers such as **Border Radio** to the come-on **Marie Marie** (another *American Music* track and a UK hit for Shakin' Stevens) and the kiss-off **So Long Baby Goodbye**, plus supercharged covers of Little Willie John's **I'm Shakin'**, Jimmie Rodgers's **Never No Mo' Blues**, and Bo Diddley's **I Love You So**. Thanks to major label distribution, the album got heard and the Alvins and company were on their way. *—DD*

Brian Eno and David Byrne
MY LIFE IN THE BUSH OF GHOSTS
S I R E | Producers: Brian Eno, David Byrne
RELEASED: FEBRUARY 1981

● *My Life in the Bush of Ghosts* displayed sonic similarities to the direction of Talking Heads, but it was entirely Brian Eno and David Byrne's project. When it arrived in 1981, it landed in like a spaceship; it was dark, dreamy, and full of rhythms from far away places. This was a time before sampling was a defined thing, and the patchwork of sounds married to non-Western rhythms was revelatory. Eno referred to it as "a vision of psychedelic Africa" and "collage music, like grafting a piece of one culture onto a piece of another," with Eno and Byrne pulling sounds that thrilled and challenged them. Accordingly, the soulful preacher in **Help Me Somebody** sounded like he's being backed by a quartet from Mali. **Mea Culpa** disassembled a radio talk show phone call and formed it into a hypnotic percussion event. These tracks, collectively and individually, represented something completely new to the world of pop music, going outside the 4/4 world of Western rock to change how many rock musicians considered their own boundaries while also exposing sounds of the Middle East and Africa to a voracious new audience. *—HK*

Rosanne Cash
SEVEN YEAR ACHE

COLUMBIA | Producer: Rodney Crowell
RELEASED: FEBRUARY 28, 1981

● All of the elements of a great country record were there on Rosanne Cash's third album and second for Columbia Records, once the label home of her father, Johnny Cash. *Seven Year Ache* had the songs, the playing, the production. But what really made *Seven Year Ache* an epochal effort was its attitude. Cash doesn't eschew her raising—by Johnny, her mother (and his first wife) Vivian, and with some influence from stepmother June Carter—but she was also a product of the era that gave us punk and New Wave. And while the album was certainly not a Clash or Elvis Costello equivalent, by Nashville standards it was something new under the sun.

That was in large part due to the title track, which Cash wrote, with its synth-heavy hook and handclaps; the insouciant, gender-switched cover of Steve Forbert's **What Kinda Girl**; as well as the rollicking, rockabilly **My Baby Thinks He's a Train**, written by Asleep at the Wheel's Leroy Preston, along with songs by rockers Tom Petty (**Hometown Blues**) and Keith Sykes (**Rainin'**). But Cash displayed an adept touch around a heartrending country ballad, too, such as the self-penned **Blue Moon with Heartache** and Merle Haggard and Red Simpson's **You Don't Have Very Far to Go**.

Coming from Nashville and not L.A. and produced by Cash's then-husband Rodney Crowell, *Seven Year Ache* scored a trio of No. 1 singles, hit No. 1 on the Billboard Country charts, and was certified gold. The title track was nominated for Grammy (as was the album) and Academy of Country Music Awards. Most importantly, it paved the way for the rule-breaking pop country and country rock to come from Cash. *—DD*

Phil Collins
FACE VALUE

ATLANTIC | Producers: Phil Collins, Hugh Padgham
RELEASED: FEBRUARY 13, 1981

● An airy synthesizer. A spectral guitar wail. A liquid drumbeat. A singer declaring he could feel something coming in the air tonight—and it wasn't good. That's how Phil Collins began his first solo album, a significant step outside of his main gig in Genesis. It turned out to be very good and much different than anything his bandmates had attempted on their own.

The thirteen-track set came out of trying times for the singer/drummer—the dissolution of his first marriage, which had caused him to take a brief hiatus from Genesis to try to make things right. In that regard, *Face Value* became one of those "gain from pain" propositions, as Collins channeled even more of the anger, loss, and sorrow that he'd put into some of Genesis's *Duke* album eleven months prior. *Face Value* also let Collins expand his breadth of styles and instruments, adding keyboards and guitar to his well-established percussion mastery.

The album's wide range surprised many who knew Collins from the worlds of Genesis's progressive rock and Brand X's jazz fusion. The freshness of the spartan **In the Air Tonight**, which built to its explosive climax, made it a worldwide smash that the other Genesis members kicked themselves for passing on. Collins fired up the Earth, Wind & Fire horns for romps such as **I Missed Again**, **Thunder and Lightning**, and a pepped-up version of Genesis's **Behind the Lines**. **If Leaving Me Is Easy** and the banjo-flecked **The Roof Is Leaking** were three-hanky heartbreakers, and **Hand in Hand** was a rich, wordless African tapestry.

The guest list was impressive, too—Eric Clapton, Alphonso Johnson, Stephen Bishop, Ronnie Scott, and Genesis adjunct Daryl Stuermer. But this Top 10, five-times-platinum outing was all about Collins and the first step in making him a dominant musical force for the next couple of decades. *–GG*

Al Di Meola, John McLaughlin, Paco De Lucia

FRIDAY NIGHT IN SAN FRANCISCO

PHILIPS | Producers: Al Di Meola, John McLaughlin, Paco De Lucia
RELEASED: AUGUST 10, 1981

● They say that speed kills, but sometimes it just melts faces—which, of course, is a preferable outcome.

Such was the case on December 5, 1980, when Al Di Meola, John McLaughlin, and Paco De Lucia—each a guitar god in his own right—joined forces for a live performance at the Warfield Theatre in San Francisco. Touring as an unadorned guitar trio, the three played not just with rocket-fueled velocity but with style, agility, and grace.

This wasn't just any trio, however.

British jazz fusion veteran McLaughlin, of course, came to the project via legendary groups including The Tony Williams's Lifetime, Miles Davis's electric band, and his own projects, Mahavishnu Orchestra and Shakti. Di Meola, an American, played with Return to Forever and the supergroup Go and had recorded several solo albums. Spaniard De Lucia was a flamenco master whose curiosity caused him to introduce elements of classical, jazz, and rock into his music—which offended purists, of course.

Put them together and you got—what, exactly? Three guitarists of astonishing ability not so much staging the ultimate cutting contest but instead working together to drive each other to new heights of creativity and technical wizardry. On the album, Di Meola, McLaughlin, and De Lucia played in various combinations and then all together, performing just five songs—including a stunning duo mash-up of Di Meola's **Mediterranean Sundance** and De Lucia's **Rio Ancho**, a raucous take of Chick Corea's **Short Tales of the Black Forest** (spotlighting McLaughlin and Di Meola), and all three firing away on Di Meola's **Fantasia Suite** and McLaughlin's **Guardian Angel**.

The excitement of the live event was palpable, too, with audience members whooping and applauding as if at a rock concert. But really, how could they not? —*DD*

Foreigner
4

ATLANTIC | Producers: Robert John "Mutt" Lange, Mick Jones
RELEASED: JULY 3, 1981

● The title of Foreigner's 4 had a double meaning. As you'd suspect, it was the popular rock band's fourth album. But the departures of keyboardist Al Greenwood and multi-instrumentalist Ian McDonald, who were unhappy with their limited role in the band's songwriting, meant Foreigner was also now down to a quartet. With help from hitmaking producer Mutt Lange—fresh off his work on AC/DC's *Back in Black*—guitarist Mick Jones and singer Lou Gramm shifted the group into more pop-friendly songwriting. **Urgent**, featuring a dramatic saxophone solo by Motown vet Junior Walker and keyboards from Thomas ("She Blinded Me with Science") Dolby, hit the Top 5 and remains a concert favorite.

Dolby's synths also played a vital role in the thumping, dramatic **Juke Box Hero**. The song tells the tale of a kid stuck outside a sold-out show who decides to become a rock star in his own right, inspired by Gramm's own experience at a Jimi Hendrix concert. It peaked at No. 26 on the charts but has gone on to become one of Foreigner's signature songs.

Of course, the big breakthrough was the lush ballad **Waiting for a Girl Like You**, which spent a remarkable two and a half months at No. 2 on the pop chart, denied the top spot for all but one of those weeks by Olivia Newton-John's exercise culture phenomenon "Physical." **Waiting . . .** turned out to be a somewhat dubious turning point for longtime Foreigner fans; the song elevated the group to new commercial heights but also drove it further away from its rock guitar–based roots and toward softer, keyboard-based fare. While the results could be impressive, such as the 1984 chart-topping smash **I Want to Know What Love Is**, Jones's increasing emphasis on ballads frustrated Gramm, who eventually departed the band to focus on a solo career. *–MW*

The Clark Sisters
YOU BROUGHT THE SUNSHINE
SOUND OF GOSPEL | Producers: Elbernita "Twinkie" Clark, Bernard Mendelson, Jeffery Hunt, Armen Boladian
RELEASED: 1981

● Detroit's Clark Sisters were well established in the gospel world, but the quintet—especially songwriter Elbernita "Twinkie" Clark—had an ear toward the pop mainstream. Stevie Wonder's reggae-flavored "Master Blaster (Jammin')" inspired the bass line for **You Brought the Sunshine (Into My Life)**, a joyous testimony that could prompt the most unrepentant sinners to throw their hands in the air. The rest of the album followed suit with plenty of sturdy grooves and polished production, a genuinely praiseworthy achievement. *—GG*

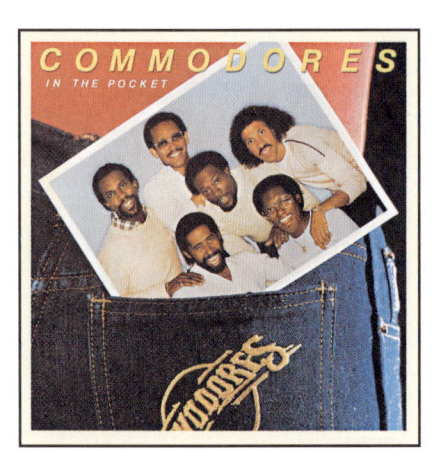

Commodores
IN THE POCKET
MOTOWN | Producers: James Anthony Carmichael, Commodores
RELEASED: JUNE 22, 1981

● Commodores was dependable R&B gold (and platinum) with certified pop crossover appeal as the Tuskegee, Alabama–formed crew slipped into its ninth studio album, its last with Lionel Richie. He left on a winning note, however, the dominant Commodore on the group's sixth consecutive platinum album, writing three of the eight tracks. *In the Pocket* showcased a slightly smoother Commodores—nothing hit as hard as "Brickhouse" or "Machine Gun," for sure—but the sextet handled the polish well, and other members' contributions showed the group would be in capable hands moving forward. *—GG*

Fela Kuti
COFFIN FOR HEAD OF STATE
BARCLAY/WRASSE/MCA UNIVERSAL | Producer: Fela Kuti
RELEASED: 1981

● There was a lot of talk about "dangerous" music—mostly referring to punk rock—around the time Nigeria's musical laureate Fela Kuti released something that was truly frightening. This nearly twenty-three-minute piece (presented with and without lyrics), was a reaction to a brutal state-sponsored attack on his Kalakuta Republic compound that led to the death of his mother. Fela responded with both heartbreaking despair and ferocious defiance plus a sprawling Afrobeat blend of jazz and funk concepts with his Africa 70 band that blended battle cry and lament, beauty with devastation. *—GG*

Loverboy
GET LUCKY

COLUMBIA | Producers: Bruce Fairbairn, Paul Dean

RELEASED: OCTOBER 7, 1981

● For New Wave fans seeking more muscle or AOR listeners curious about synth-pop, Loverboy had your back, and on its second album, the melodies, hooks, and choruses were as bright and tight as those red leather pants on the cover. **Working for the Weekend** was a note-perfect working-class anthem elevated by buoyant synths, eager vocals, industrious percussion, and an orgiastic guitar solo. **When It's Over** made perfect bedfellows of arena rock riffage and sparkling synths. Touching on glam, boozy bar band rock, and even prog, *Get Lucky* was just that for the Canadian band, going platinum four times. —JL

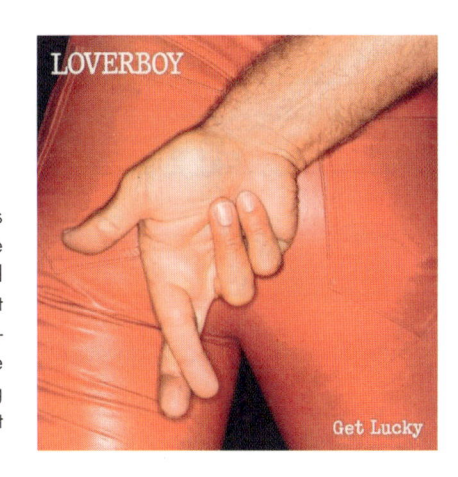

Olivia Newton-John
PHYSICAL

MCA | Producer: John Farrar

RELEASED: MARCH 13, 1981

● Oh, Sandy, indeed! The singer's eleventh studio album was a departure from the Australian-born *Grease* star's wholesome image. The title track and its accompanying video showcased Newton-John's more aggressive, mature approach to music and was highly controversial at the time for its sexual overtones. The album had a strong pop-rock feel and featured plenty of synthesizers. And with its themes of love and environmental protection, listeners definitely heard Newton-John talk on this double-platinum release. —SS

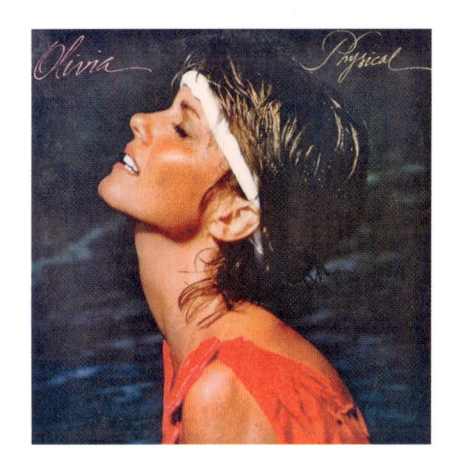

Oak Ridge Boys
FANCY FREE

MCA | Producer: Ron Chancey

RELEASED: MARCH 26, 1981

● "Who is Elvira?" and "How low can that guy sing?" were burning questions when the Oak Ridge Boys released its fifth studio album. Thanks to the platinum **Elvira** and **(I'm Settin') Fancy Free**, a fresh group of pop fans discovered what the country audience already knew. A unique blend of country, gospel, and pop sounds on the other eight tracks, combined with the quartet's signature harmonies and memorable hooks, helped establish the Oaks as one of the most recognizable bands in all of music. —SS

The Go-Go's
BEAUTY AND THE BEAT

I.R.S. | Producers: Richard Gottehrer, Rob Freeman
RELEASED: JULY 14, 1981

● The Go-Go's began life in 1978, and the all-female quintet quickly made a name for itself on the L.A. punk scene and in the UK. It then decided to inject some pop into its musical mix. Good move.

Although this directional change shed some original members, it brought the band to the attention of fledgling label I.R.S., which new bassist Kathy Valentine told *Rolling Stone* "was where you went if you couldn't get a deal with a real label." But the multiplatinum debut, *Beauty and the Beat*, put both the Go-Go's and the label on the map—largely thanks to its two hit singles. Guitarist Jane Wiedlin co-wrote **Our Lips Are Sealed** with Terry Hall about their brief affair while the Go-Go's were touring with his band the Specials in the UK. The aptly titled **We Got the Beat**, meanwhile—with its pounding drum track, driving bass line, and crunchy guitars—was released as an independent single but became a No. 2 cross-format hit after the album was released.

A deeper dig into the album reveals versatility. **Fading Fast** was a breakup song out of the '60s girl group playbook. **How Much More** was straight-ahead power pop. **You Can't Walk in Your Sleep**, **Skidmarks on My Heart**, and **Can't Stop the World** all hearkened back to the Go-Go's punk roots.

Beauty and the Beat was important not just because the Go-Go's was the first all-female band to hit No. 1 on the Billboard 200, writing its own songs and playing its own instruments, but because it was a finely crafted album that became a cornerstone of the New Wave movement. **–GP**

1981

The Gun Club
FIRE OF LOVE
R U B Y | Producers: Chris D., Tito Larriva
RELEASED: AUGUST 31, 1981

● The Gun Club was a perfect case study of what happens when the inmates get to run the asylum, as it were. Frontman and chief songwriter Jeffrey Lee Pierce was president of a Blondie fan club as a teenager, worked at Bomp Records, and was a studious fanboy whose fancies ranged from Robert Johnson to '70s prog and L.A. hardcore. Original bandmate Brian "Kid Congo Powers" Christian ran a Ramones fan club. This was music geek central, with a breadth and depth of influences that could only result in a truly classic debut album. Even *Fire of Love*'s producers, Chris D. of the Flesh Eaters and the Pugz's Tito Larriva, spoke to the Gun Club's deeply sourced music community.

What really made *Fire of Love* burn was Pierce's love of . . . well, almost everything and an effortless touch for blending sounds and sensibilities into something focused and wholly original. His brand of musical reinvention was more toward X and the Blasters than Black Flag and fully realized throughout these eleven tracks. The band's just two songs in before mining Johnson's **Preaching the Blues** into the Gun Club's own psychobilly twang, and later on Pierce stretched Tommy Johnson's **Cool Drink of Water** into more than six minutes of Hill Country lament. **Sex Beat** gave the album a ferocious opening calling card, while **Fire Spirit** channeled the Stooges. **Jack on Fire** was a West Coast "Dirty Water," and on tracks such as **Promise Me**, **Ghost on the Highway**, and **Black Train**, the Gun Club sounded like the house band in a psychedelic honky-tonk.

The rest of the Gun Club, particularly guitarist Ward Dotson, should not be discounted. *Fire of Love* certainly didn't burn up the charts, but it laid out a model from which we got the likes of the Jon Spencer Blues Explosion, the White Stripes, the Black Keys, and more. *—GG*

Merle Haggard
BIG CITY
E P I C | Producer: Merle Haggard
RELEASED: OCTOBER 1981

● As the country took a conservative turn during the early '80s, Merle Haggard read the room and released *Big City*, an album that—with its call for a return to traditional values (whether sincere or not)—struck a chord with the public, going gold and taking the title track to No. 1 on the charts. The song announced at the outset that "I'm tired of this dirty old city / And tired of too much work and never enough play." The solution, he decides, is to quit his job and start over "somewhere in the middle of Montana." Among the things he wants to leave behind is the welfare state and "your so-called Social Security."

Haggard went even further with **Are the Good Times Really Over (I Wish a Buck Was Still Silver)**, which called for a return to the time "when the country was strong," before Elvis and the Beatles and Vietnam. He wishes "coke was still cola and a joint was a bad place to be," a sure laugh line for anyone who knew Haggard personally or, years in the future would hear his duet with Willie Nelson, the pro-weed anthem "It's All Going to Pot."

Haggard had played this game before with songs such as "Okie from Muskogee" and "The Fightin' Side of Me" and it was uncertain if he meant *Big City*'s songs any more sincerely than he meant those. Reserving the right to change his mind right there in the same song, **Good Times** also took a shot at Richard Nixon, who "lied to us all on TV." Whatever the album's politics, those songs and others here—**My Favorite Memory**, **Stop the World and Let Me Off, I Always Get Lucky with You**—made *Big City* a stone Haggard classic. *—DD*

Rick James
STREET SONGS
GORDY | Producer: Rick James
RELEASED: APRIL 7, 1981

● "The name is Slick Rick." That's Rick James on **Call Me Up** from *Street Songs*, his towering fifth studio set, which found the funk-rocker—born James Ambrose Johnson Jr. in Buffalo, New York—at his slickest and most swagger-filled. Bass lines wiggled and woggled, horns blasted atop fiery punk-funk guitars, and James (thirty-three at the time) laced lived-in stories about street corners, nightlife, and very kinky girls. The result was one of the decade's funkiest albums and James's commercial peak, hitting No. 3 on the Billboard 200. It netted him a pair of monster hits with **Give It to Me Baby** and the immortal **Super Freak**, both of which kept royalty checks rolling in for decades due to their many samples and interpolations.

Street Songs was a watershed moment for James, who toiled at Motown as a writer and player before becoming a solo star in his own right. He was coming off 1980's underperforming *Garden of Love*, and he returned with both barrels loaded, stacking the decks in his favor with behind-the-scenes cameos from the Temptations (backing vocals on **Super Freak** and **Ghetto Life**) and Stevie Wonder (that's him playing harmonica on the pointed, reggae-style anti-police brutality missive **Mr. Policeman**). Meanwhile, Teena Marie nearly upstaged her mentor on the epic bedroom ballad **Fire and Desire**, which floated past the seven-minute mark.

And then there's James on the album's cover—leaning against a street pole, dressed head to toe in leather, hair in braids, bass guitar strapped to his partially exposed chest, blood-red thigh-high boots on his crossed legs. It's a look few could pull off, but Rick does it. Now *that's* slick. —AG

1981

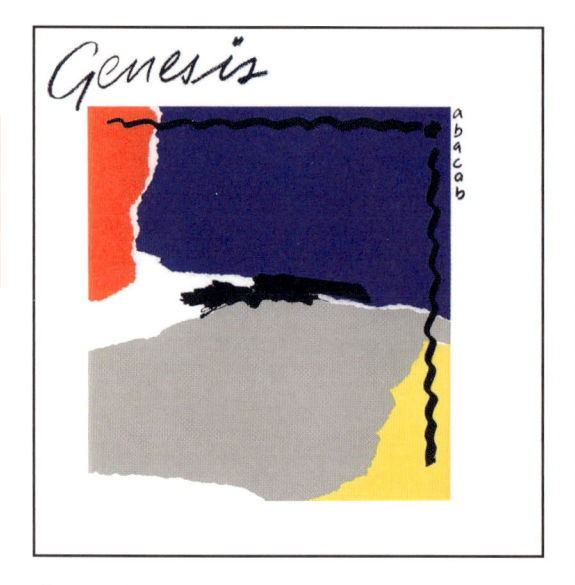

Genesis
ABACAB
ATLANTIC | Producers: Genesis
RELEASED: SEPTEMBER 24, 1981

● After being in on the ground floor of the progressive rock movement, the aptly named Genesis moved increasingly from those prog roots following the departure of founding frontman Peter Gabriel. The sleeker style adopted by the remaining trio truly came into its own with *Abacab*. Phil Collins, Tony Banks, and Mike Rutherford took on self-producing duties for the first time and used studio jams to create a slick, sophisticated recording full of pop hooks in a variety of musical styles while maintaining enough prog flavors to keep longtime fans happy. Following Collins's solo debut, *Face Value* from earlier in the year, *Abacab* achieved double-platinum status in the US, buoyed by hits such as the title track and the brassy **No Reply at All**, which featured Earth, Wind & Fire's Phoenix Horns. **Man on the Corner**, meanwhile, followed Collins's solo single "In the Air Tonight" with a simple drum machine beat under his dark, intense vocals. —*JC*

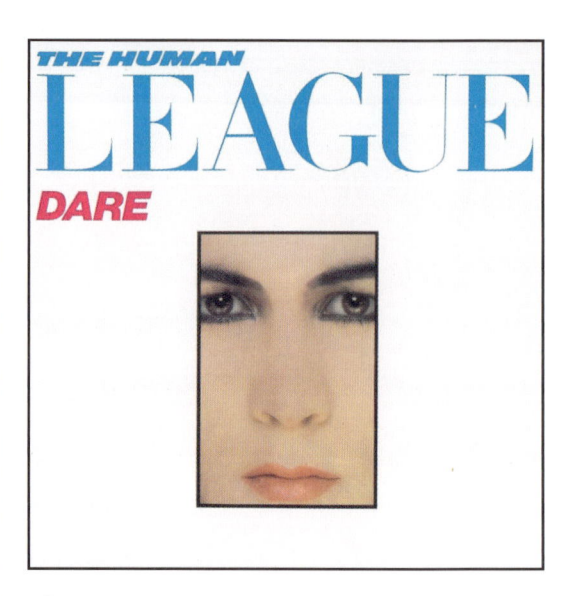

The Human League
DARE
VIRGIN | Producers: Martin Rushent, The Human League
RELEASED: OCTOBER 16, 1981

● After a lineup change left singer Philip Oakley in charge, the Human League kicked avant noodlings to the curb and embraced unabashed synth-pop on its third album. With his childlike, earnest vocal delivery, Oakley was perfectly suited to belt out the optimistic album opener **The Things That Dreams Are Made Of**, reassure wounded lovers on **Open Your Heart**, and even rap on the bouncy **Beautiful Love Action (I Believe in Love)**. So, when *Dare* took a dark turn, it hit hard, whether the band is lamenting the loss of human life to guns on the pulsating **Seconds** or giving ominous voice to Big Brother with the eerie **I Am the Law**. The crowning achievement, obviously, was **Don't You Want Me**. Over a relentless, pummeling synth beat, Oakley explored what happens when romance turns to solipsistic obsession while Susan Ann Sulley gives voice to a beleaguered woman leaving a toxic relationship. It's harrowing, but thanks to its crisp production and one of the most irresistible choruses ever, **Don't You Want Me** became one of the defining No. 1 hits of the decade—and probably the best duet you can dare to tackle at karaoke. —*LM*

J. Geils Band
FREEZE-FRAME
EMI-AMERICA | Producer: Seth Justman
RELEASED: OCTOBER 26, 1981

● *Freeze-Frame* was the chart-topping, triple-platinum-selling album that finally confirmed the J. Geils Band's stature as one of greatest rock 'n' roll acts in America—just before it broke up with its frenetic frontman Peter Wolf and nose-dived in popularity. Onstage, Wolf could rival Mick Jagger or Bruce Springsteen in their primes; in fact, the band released two live albums during the '70s seeking to capture the lightning of its shows in a vinyl bottle. But by the early '80s, Wolf and keyboardist Seth Justman blended the band's blues and R&B roots with radio-ready hooks. **Freeze-Frame** kicked off the album with a burst of Justman's carnival-house organ leading to a horn section blast over Stephen Jo Bladd's barroom drumming. Magic Dick's blues harmonica opened **Centerfold**, in which Wolf sang slyly of the heartbreak, and lust, of discovering a high school sweetheart in "a girlie magazine." The song spent six weeks atop the Billboard Hot 100. On the ballad **Angel in Blue**, Wolf sang soulfully and sympathetically of a lovely, hardened "tabletop dancer" who could "smile on cue." In **Flamethrower**, blues harmonica gave way to a rather bloodless techno-pop vibe, a style that Wolf later said led to his departure from the band just as it reached its commercial peak. *–TD*

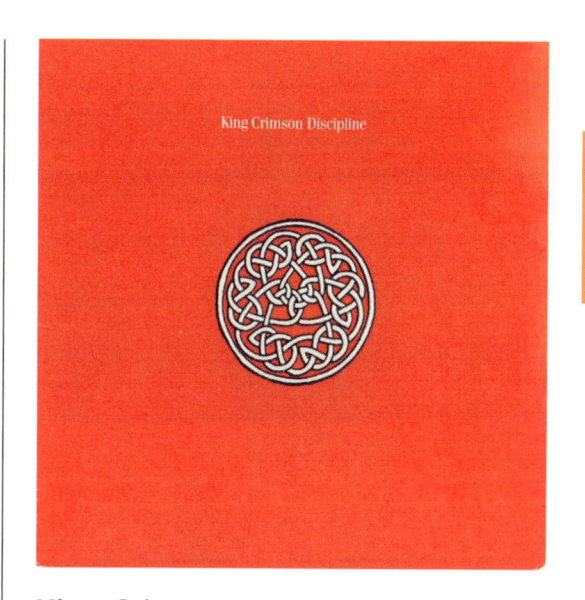

King Crimson
DISCIPLINE
E.G./WARNER BROS. | Producers: King Crimson, Rhett Davies
RELEASED: SEPTEMBER 22, 1981

● Surviving multiple lineup changes, the influential British art/prog-rock band King Crimson recorded a sequence of timeless albums from 1969 to 1974 until its founder, the enigmatic guitar mastermind Robert Fripp, pulled the plug. Ever the focused visionary, Fripp spent the ensuing years playing on and producing albums with Peter Gabriel and Brian Eno. He refined his tape-loop guitar technique (Frippertronics) and perfected his rigorous cross-picking style. In 1981, Fripp started Discipline, featuring himself and former Crimson drummer Bill Bruford and two Americans, singer/guitarist Adrian Belew (David Bowie, Talking Heads) and bassist Tony Levin (Peter Gabriel). As it built its newfangled repertoire using an arsenal of new-tech instruments, the band decided to resurrect the name King Crimson, unleashing an interlocked and unprecedented sound that broke new ground. Both guitarists sported Roland GR-300 guitar synthesizers, Bruford added a Simmons electronic drum kit, and Levin mastered the touch-sensitive Chapman Stick. Each song was intense, methodical, and tightly composed. Belew wrote crafty lyrics and sang with abandon on **Elephant Talk**, interspersing outlandish elephant, rhino, and other animal-like guitar sounds. **Frame by Frame**'s spiraling guitar parts, meanwhile, were hypnotizing. *–CH*

Joan Jett
BAD REPUTATION

BLACKHEART/BOARDWALK | Producers: Kenny Laguna, Ritchie Cordell, Mark Dodson, Steve Jones, Paul Cook

RELEASED: JANUARY 23, 1981

● Joan Jett loved rock 'n' roll well before she declared, "I Love Rock 'n Roll" (courtesy of Britain's Arrows) in the fall of 1981. Proof of that can be found in her work with the Runaways during the late '70s, of course, and most definitely on her first solo album, *Bad Reputation*, which established the former Joan Larkin's rep as a bad-ass rocker—by any gender standards, in fact.

Bad Reputation was an arrival, even more so than what came next. Jett had been laid low by the Runaways' dissolution in 1979 but found a patron saint of sorts in producer (and subsequent manager) Kenny Laguna. Using studio credits and their own money, Laguna and Jett made the album in Hollywood and in London, with a session band dubbed the Roll-ups and contributions on various tracks from members of the Sex Pistols (Steve Jones and Paul Cook on **You Don't Own Me** and **Don't Abuse Me**) and Blondie (Frank Infante and Clem Burke on three other tracks). But Jett was the real star, snarling, belting, and slashing out the album's twelve tracks like her life, or at least her life in music, depended on it—which it did.

Bad Reputation (initially released simply as *Joan Jett* in 1980 before Boardwalk Records signed her) didn't have a breakthrough single but was a cohesive rock 'n' roll party, from the title track to high-octane covers of Gary Glitter's **Do You Wanna Touch Me (Oh Yeah)**, the Isley Brothers' **Shout**, Sam the Sham and the Pharaohs' **Wooly Bully**, and Lesley Gore's **You Don't Own Me**. It straddled the line between punk and glam and sounded as good in an arena as it did in a sweaty club—a reputation Jett hasn't lost during the four-plus decades since. *—GG*

1981

GRACE JONES / NIGHTCLUBBING

1981

Grace Jones
NIGHTCLUBBING

ISLAND | Producers: Chris Blackwell, Alex Sadkin
RELEASED: MAY 11, 1981

● After releasing three disco albums to diminishing chart results, Grace Jones knew it was time for a change. In 1980, she traded Studio 54 for Compass Point Studios, a Bahamian facility Island label boss Chris Blackwell recently opened. Backed by a team of studio aces (including rhythm ringers Sly & Robbie), the Jamaica-born, New York–based Jones found her true voice (and look) as an artist. Those fruitful sessions produced 1980's *Warm Leatherette*, with enough material leftover for a follow-up album that became *Nightclubbing* the next year.

With her flat-top 'do, oversize Armani suit, and an unlit cigarette in her mouth, Jones cuts a geometric, androgynous figure on the cover. Her unflinching gaze dared you to underestimate her; after all, anyone operating under the misconception that the fashion model was a musical dilettante would have to have their ears checked after hearing *Nightclubbing*. Over muscular rhythms that felt meticulous and effortless at the same time, Jones and her band explored skanky pop, noir-ish reggae, arty New Wave, and dance-flavored R&B on nine tracks of covers and originals.

Her low voice and sing-speak delivery was perfectly suited for a post-punk revamp of Flash and the Pan's **Walking in the Rain**, a spectral take on Iggy Pop and David Bowie's **Nightclubbing**, and an ominous, seductive reworking of The Astoria Piazzolla-titled **I've Seen That Face Before (Libertango)**, which melded Argentinian tango, French chanson, and slow-grooving reggae.

The album's biggest hit, **Pull Up to the Bumper**, was also its standout. One of three tracks written or co-written by Jones, **. . . Bumper** was a sexy, spiky, and synth-y dance jam with a playfully filthy metaphor. With lyrics such as "Grease it, spray it / Let me lubricate it," this song should probably be followed by an emissions inspection. —*JL*

1981

Rickie Lee Jones
PIRATES

WARNER BROS. | Producers: Lenny Waronker, Russ Titelman
RELEASED: JULY 15, 1981

● Sometimes an artist's "difficult second album" turns out to be a masterpiece, worth the considerable time, trouble, and excessive expense it took to make it. *Pirates* is a prime example.

Rickie Lee Jones's self-titled 1979 debut caused a sensation, earning her a *Rolling Stone* cover, a *Saturday Night Live* appearance, and a Best New Artist Grammy Award—all of it too much too soon, perhaps, for an artist already enmeshed in an addiction to heroin and a messy relationship with fellow singer/songwriter Tom Waits. Taking her time, or perhaps dragging her feet during the making of *Pirates*, Jones racked up more than a quarter-million 1980 dollars in bills, which went not just to studio time but to top-notch producers and a cast of musicians that included Donald Fagen, Victor Feldman, David Sanborn, Tom Scott, Steve Gadd, Steve Lukather, Broadway arranger Ralph Burns, Randy Brecker, and others. She drove them all crazy, by the way, but again, the results spoke for themselves.

Pirates contained just eight songs, but they were exquisite. As tuneful as they may be and however much they may swing—and on both counts, that's a lot—Jones didn't write songs so much as outlines for films or Broadway plays just begging to be made. As on her debut, she brought a host of characters to life: Eddie with "one crazy eye" and C*nt-finger Louie (**Living It Up**); the titular Woody and Dutch on the **Slow Train to Peking**; Bird, who was errantly gunned down by cops in front of his pregnant girlfriend (**Skeletons**); and many others. They were all woven into a rich, complex tapestry of soul, jazz, rock, bebop stylings and revivalist Beat Generation poetry. *—DD*

Journey
ESCAPE

COLUMBIA | Producers: Mike Stone, Kevin Elson
RELEASED: JULY 17, 1981

● Four years after Journey's climb toward mainstream domination began with the hiring of powerhouse singer Steve Perry, the Bay Area–based group added the final piece of the puzzle with former Babys keyboardist Jonathan Cain—suggested by departing founding member Gregg Rolie, who had ceded the lead vocal spot to Perry with 1978's *Infinity*. This change effectively severed the last connection to Journey's early progressive rock sound. "Jonathan Cain brought in a more universal songwriting approach," drummer Steve Smith told Nick DeRiso in the book *Journey: Worlds Apart*. "There was a special kind of magic with him in the band. We were able to write some very globally accepted hit tunes that were just fantastic."

Cain immediately took on a large role in the band, earning songwriting credits on every single *Escape* song. He devised the original hook that he, Perry, and guitarist Neal Schon would develop into **Don't Stop Believin'**, the compact Top 10 epic that would become Journey's signature song. Cain and Perry proved particularly adept at writing ballads together, teaming up for the moody **Who's Crying Now** and the towering album closer **Open Arms**. Both songs reached the Top 5 on the pop charts.

Schon's inspired riffing and soloing on rockers such as **Stone in Love** and *Escape*'s title track made sure the band kept one foot firmly planted in the rock world. Journey had finally found the perfect balance, and fans rewarded it by making *Escape* the fifth best-selling album of 1981 and solidifying the group's spot as one of music's top live attractions. *Escape* went on to sell more than 10 million copies, and it's unlikely you'll spend more than a few hours on any classic rock radio station without hearing one of its songs. —*MW*

Kraftwerk
COMPUTER WORLD

WARNER BROS. | Producers: Ralf Hutter, Florian Schneider
RELEASED: MAY 1981

● A vision of the future in which an overtly computer-based society has shaped the world was the conceptual idea for *Computer World*, German electronic group Kraftwerk's eighth studio album. Three years had passed since *The Man-Machine*, and this time around Kraftwerk took on a funkier approach with most of the songs being masterfully constructed toe-tappers, layered simplistically with the group's signature futuristic rhythms.

Computer World started things off with a lush bopper in the vein of "The Model" from the preceding album. **Pocket Calculator** employed the Bee Gees Rhythm Machine, a battery-powered toy keyboard made by Mattel to give the song its signature calculator-like melody. **Numbers** was a funky electro track that made you want to break out your best robot breakdance moves. **Computer Love** was slower and mesmerizing, like a walk along the beach with your new technological friend. **Home Computer** picked up the pace with space-age interludes throughout its mid-tempo rhythms. **It's More Fun to Compute** rounded out the album and returning to the funkier feel taking listeners to the closing credits of this new computer world Kraftwerk created.

Computer World opened a new portal to music that did shape the future with Kraftwerk's pioneering use of electronics and basically gave birth to the key elements of hip-hop, electro, and techno. Countless artists in those genres have sampled and borrowed from these songs for an influence that's simply enormous. Kraftwerk was asking what the world would be like if technology was so integral. The answer is still unfolding, but *Computer World* certainly helped make the world a better place. *—MH*

1981

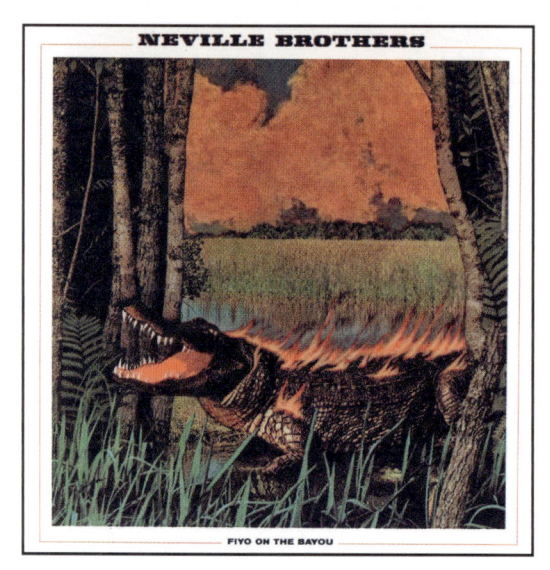

Neville Brothers
FIYO ON THE BAYOU

A & M | Producer: Joel Dorn
RELEASED: APRIL 1981

● The Neville Brothers' reputation was forged across their lengthy and lauded individual solo careers, membership in noted bands, and simply being among the best musicians New Orleans produced. The group became a must-see for attendees of JazzFest, and its performances outside of the Crescent City were rare. This record, its second as the Neville Brothers, brought the funk gospel to the world. As any New Orleans musician knows, roots must be acknowledged. In the case of this record, much of the material was already well-known; the Neville Brothers stamp was the difference. Producer Joel Dorn brought studio cleanliness to the recording, but the underlying performances remained as greasy as a chicken bone. Art, a veteran of the Funky Meters and all-around New Orleans stalwart, is a first-team soul crooner as evidenced by his take on Jimmy Cliff's **Sitting in Limbo**. Cyril made the Delta city standard **Iko-Iko** his own. At the same time, the Nevilles unashamedly played to their traditional pop strengths with Aaron's perfect takes on the Moonglows' **The Ten Commandments of Love** and Nat King Cole's **Mona Lisa**. —HK

Psychedelic Furs
TALK TALK TALK

COLUMBIA | Producer: Steve Lillywhite
RELEASED: MAY 15, 1981

● Psychedelic Furs' second album got the British group onto Billboard's Top 200 chart, but more than that, it included the original (and superior) version of **Pretty in Pink**, the song that inspired John Hughes's 1986 film of the same name. The band rose from London's '70s post-punk scene, and while this album wasn't as raw as its self-titled debut, it certainly stayed true to the band's roots, aided by Richard Butler's uniquely raspy voice and the late Duncan Kilburn's chaotic sax. The opening track, **Dumb Waiters**, and its refrain of "She has got it in for me / Yeah I mean it honestly / She's so mean" was a good intro to the jaded and often acerbic-sounding Furs, as is the frank **Into You Like a Train**. As for *that* song, Butler told *The Quietus* in 2010 that "the song was **Pretty in Pink** was a metaphor for being naked, about a girl who sleeps around a lot and thinks that she's wanted, but people are talking about her behind her back." Sorry if that bursts your bubble, but it's certainly a more Fur-ian tale than the movie. —HD

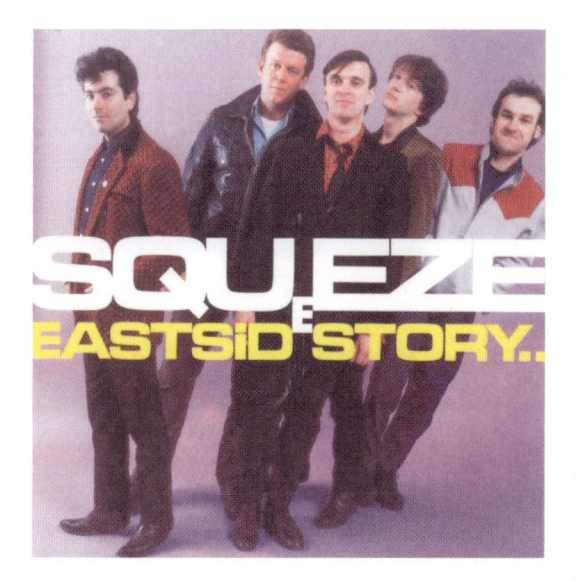

Squeeze
EAST SIDE STORY

A & M | Producers: Elvis Costello, Roger Bechrian, Dave Edmunds
RELEASED: MAY 15, 1981

● By the time UK band Squeeze released *East Side Story*, it found its true sweet spot—pure pop. Merging Chris Difford's clever lyrical vignettes with Glenn Tilbrook's irresistible melodies, the songs were crafted with tight harmonies, more hooks than a bra factory, and astonishing versatility—rockabilly, Merseybeat, country, doo-wop, and more—earning the duo comparisons to clear-cut influences John Lennon and Paul McCartney. McCartney, in fact, was slated to produce one side of the originally planned double album, with Elvis Costello, Dave Edmunds, and Nick Lowe handling the others. Costello remained, while Edmunds wound up producing on track **In Quintessence**.

Ironically, **Tempted**—Squeeze's first US-charting single and most well-known song—was sung by keyboardist Paul Carrack, who'd replaced Jools Holland and went solo himself after this album. It's one of several songs on the album alluding to infidelity, including another highlight, **Is That Love**, Difford's brilliant dissection of a faltering marriage.

Drinking and sex dominated these vivid slice-of-life tales, giving *East Side Story* an earthy relatability. The music made it agelessly cool. *–LM*

X
WILD GIFT

S L A S H | Producer: Ray Manzarek
RELEASED: MAY 1981

● When it came time for X to make its second album, the group didn't stray far from the template used on the 1980s debut, *Los Angeles*. Working with the same pedigreed producer (the Doors' Ray Manzarek) and a frantic blend of blues, country, and rockabilly whirled through a punk filter, *Wild Gift* struck with an immediacy that hammered home notions that X may have been L.A.'s best band at the turn of the decade. With married couple John Doe and Exene Cervenka writing and singing in a combined voice that spanned decades and genres for inspiration, *Wild Gift* was thirty-three minutes of Americana-reinforced punk that sounded little like the music it was often lumped with. "Our whole f*cking life is a wreck / We're desperate, get used to it," they sang on the two-minute highlight **We're Desperate**. It was both a rallying cry for a fragmented scene and a personal statement of purpose for X, which inched closer to mainstream aspirations with each subsequent release (they signed to major label Elektra for its third album, 1982's *Under the Big Black Sun*). *Wild Gift* remains the most concise and consistent record in its catalog. *–MG*

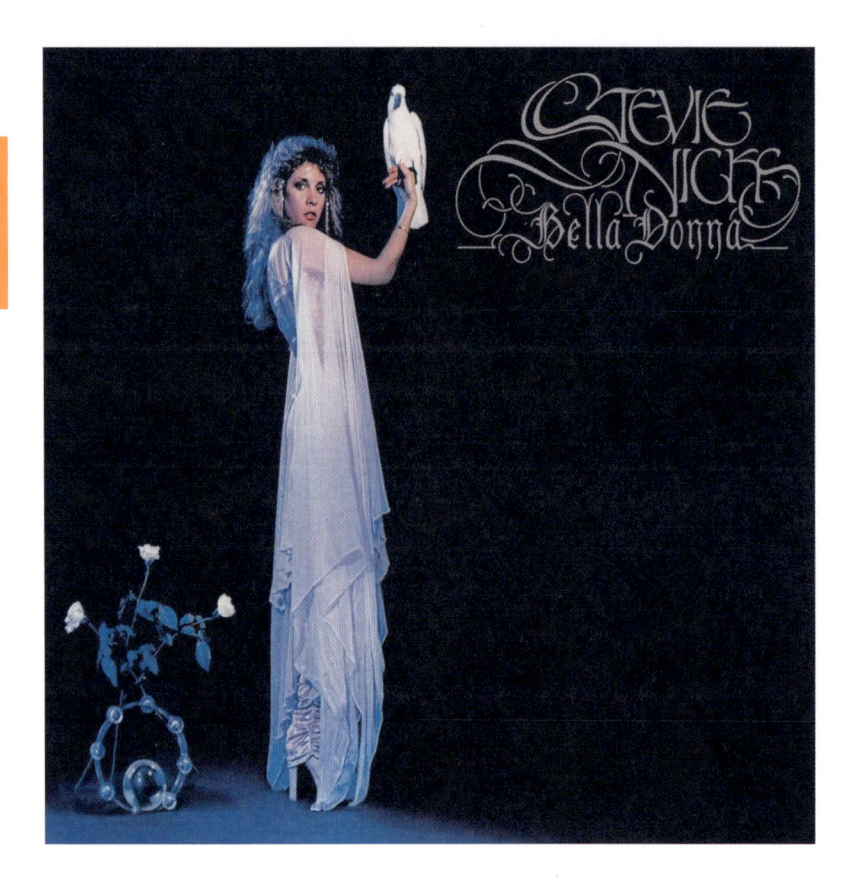

Stevie Nicks
BELLA DONNA

MODERN/ATCO | Producers: Jimmy Iovine, Tom Petty
RELEASED: JULY 27, 1981

● Of all the members of Fleetwood Mac during the group's golden era, Stevie Nicks was best teed up for a successful solo career. Without discounting the value of fellow writer/singers Lindsey Buckingham and Christine McVie, Nicks was a first among equals, loved as much by female and male fans—for different reasons, of course—and especially by the camera, which gave prominence to her flowing White Witch image at the center of the stage.

Nicks actually began working on *Bella Donna* while Fleetwood Mac was making its *Tusk* album, but her solo debut really took off after *Tusk* was finished, as she hunkered into the studio with producer Jimmy Iovine and a dream team of musicians and guests—notably Tom Petty and the Heartbreakers and onetime boyfriend Don Henley of the Eagles—for the set's first two singles. It was the Petty/Mike Campbell–penned **Stop Draggin' My Heart Around** that rocked *Bella Donna* out of the box, while the mellower Henley duet **Leather and Lace** (on which he also played drums) served the other side of Nicks's equation.

Bella Donna contained some other Nicks signature songs, including **After the Glitter Fades** and **Edge of Seventeen**, and most importantly boosted her reputation as a songwriter, since she composed seven of the tracks on her own and co-wrote two of the others, with no less than Heartbreaker Benmont Tench and Roy Bittan of Bruce Springsteen's E Street Band. It also introduced a backing vocal tandem (Lori Perry, Sharon Celani) that was also key to the sound and even wound up touring with Fleetwood Mac. *Bella Donna* hit No. 1 on the Billboard 200 and has been certified four-times platinum, with two Grammy Award nominations. If Nicks was a superstar before this, she became a super-duper star here and hasn't lost that status during the intervening years. *—GG*

1981

Tom Petty and the Heartbreakers
HARD PROMISES

BACKSTREET | Producers: Jimmy Iovine, Tom Petty
RELEASED: MAY 5, 1981

● Tom Petty and the Heartbreakers hit the jackpot with their third album, *Damn the Torpedoes*. The 1979 release saw the band become multiplatinum-selling superstars on the strength of four undeniable singles: "Don't Do Me Like That," "Refugee," "Here Comes My Girl," and "Even the Losers." To their credit, Petty and his bandmates didn't seem focused on outdoing that commercial success on the follow-up, 1981's *Hard Promises*. Instead, they followed their muse and delivered a confident, sharply written collection of songs that made perfect sense together. Only the wistful, dazzling opening track **The Waiting** earned a heavy rotation spot on classic rock radio playlists alongside its four *Torpedoes* brothers, but your favorite Petty deep track might well be from this album.

Hard Promises might be more famous for the battle that preceded its release. Petty openly campaigned against his record distributor's plans to increase the list price of the album by a dollar, to $9.98, in a naked attempt to maximize profits from their newest superstar. He even briefly floated the idea of naming the album *Eight Ninety-Eight* in protest, but fortunately MCA relented.

Although few songs here had the immediate and universal catchiness of *Torpedoes*' singles, *Hard Promises* maintained an intoxicating slow boil from start to finish. The grooves may be laid-back, but there was just the perfect amount of snarl to the guitars and venom in the lyrics and vocal delivery to keep you on the edge of your seat. Petty's growth as a Bob Dylan–style storyteller is demonstrated perfectly on **Something Big**, which told the story of a low-level criminal who falls victim to his unrealistic dreams of making one big score. —*MW*

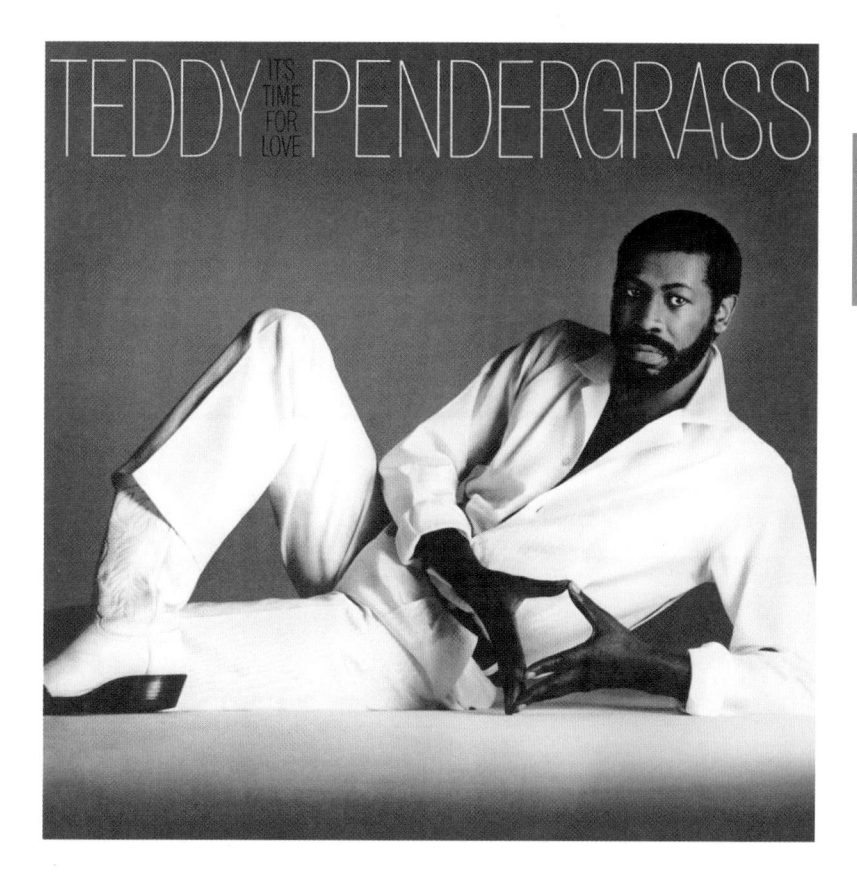

Teddy Pendergrass
IT'S TIME FOR LOVE

PHILADELPHIA INTERNATIONAL | Producers: Kenneth Gamble, Leon Huff, Dexter Wansel, Teddy Pendergrass

RELEASED: SEPTEMBER 2, 1981

● Reclining in all white—think Burt Reynolds's pose in *Cosmopolitan*, but with clothes—Teddy Pendergrass had every reason to appear relaxed on the cover of his fifth studio album. By this time, the former frontman of Harold Melvin and the Blue Notes was a solo star (some would say superstar) in the R&B world, with four platinum albums and five Top 10 R&B hits to his credit. He was king of the Philadelphia International label and a singer whose husky purr induced swooning desire whenever he performed.

All that was about to change, tragically, but *It's Time for Love* was a memorable last blast of glory.

The eight-track set was essentially more of what Pendergrass did best but was all the better for the additional experience. Label principals Kenny Gamble and Leon Huff still had the wheel here but relaxed their grip a bit, allowing Pendergrass to co-produce (with Dexter Wansel) two of the songs, the discoey **Keep on Lovin' Me** and the Barry Mann/Cynthia Weill–composed **She's Over Me**. Pendergrass's singing confidently slipped into the melodies as if he'd been living with them for years, but with formidable command, particularly on the singles **I Can't Live without Your Love** and the gospel-flavored **You're My Latest, My Greatest Inspiration**, as well as the loping title track.

Less than seven months after *It's Time for Love*'s release, Pendergrass was paralyzed from the chest down in a car crash in Philadelphia, driving his Rolls-Royce Silver Spirit even though his license had been suspended. He never walked again, and though he'd release another nine albums before his death in 2010, this was the last of his platinum successes. *—GG*

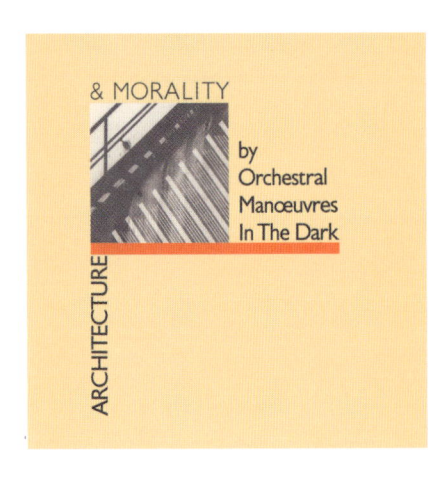

Orchestral Manoeuvres in the Dark
ARCHITECTURE & MORALITY
DINDISC | Producers: OMD, Richard Manwaring, Mike Howlett
RELEASED: NOVEMBER 6, 1981

● Initially sloughed off by critics, the third album from synth-pop pioneers OMD was later hailed as a classic of the genre as well as the high-water mark for the Liverpool lads. **Architecture & Morality** employed achingly tender melodies, heavenly choral samples, and synths that conveyed heartbreak, loss, and longing—perfect for a pair of singles named after Joan of Arc. The group's US peak wouldn't come until the *Pretty in Pink* soundtrack smash "If You Leave," but this album is where founders Andy McCluskey and Paul Humphreys built their holy temple. *—AG*

Jaco Pastorius
WORD OF MOUTH
WARNER BROS. | Producer: Jaco Pastorius
RELEASED: JULY 1981

● Star-power bassist Pastorius, a tall, athletic, and flashy showstopper, pioneered the fretless bass and elevated the jazz fusion period of Joni Mitchell (1976–1979) and Weather Report (1976–1981). This tour-de-force large ensemble album unveiled his panoramic musical vision, highlighting the bright coloration and chromatic textures of jazz harmonica and steel pans via Toots Thielemans and Othello Molineaux, respectively. **Crisis** was a risky, aggressive opener led by tenor saxophonist Michael Brecker, and on two juxtaposed tracks, Pastorious reinvigorated both Bach (**Chromatic Fantasy**) and the Beatles (**Blackbird**). *—CH*

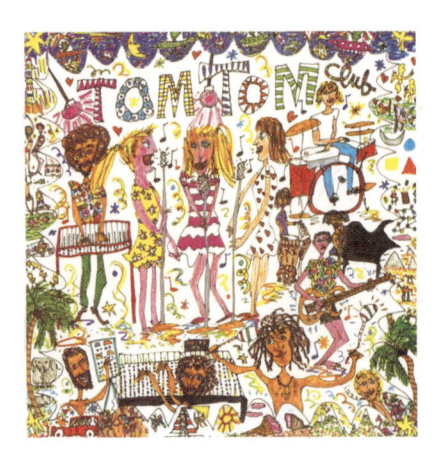

Tom Tom Club
TOM TOM CLUB
SIRE/WARNER BROS. | Producers: Chris Frantz, Tina Weymouth, Steven Stanley
RELEASED: OCTOBER 1981

● Tom Tom Club began during 1981 as a side project for Talking Heads co-founders Chris Frantz and Tina Weymouth, joined by a loose collective of musicians that on its first album included her three sisters and Heads adjunct Adrian Belew on guitar. The eight-track set, recorded in the Bahamas, was a party-ready collection of loose and playful but fully realized jams, chief among them the dizzying **Wordy Rappinghood** and **Genius of Love**, a salute to forebears that Mariah Carey sampled into her 1995 hit "Fantasy." The Club remains intermittently active, but it's never, er, beat this platinum debut. *—GG*

Luther Vandross
NEVER TOO MUCH
E P I C | Producer: Luther Vandross
RELEASED: AUGUST 12, 1981

● The first album from Luther Vandross was no mere debut. He'd been a noted working vocalist since he contributed the chorus hook to David Bowie's "Young Americans" six years earlier. Making his music on his terms for the first time, Vandross assembled a band of aces that built the stage for him to prove, from the get-go, that he was the premier male vocalist of his time. For proof, look no further than the title cut and his take on Burt Bacharach and Hal David's **A House Is Not a Home**. —HK

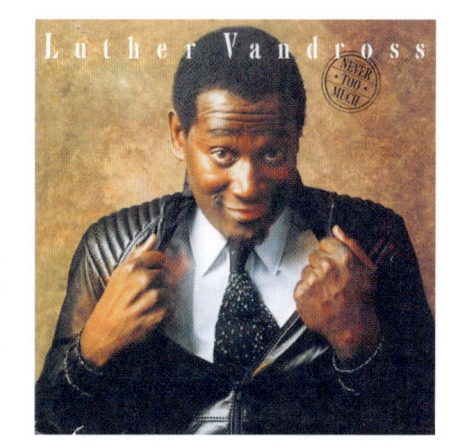

Vangelis
CHARIOTS OF FIRE (ORIGINAL MOTION PICTURE SOUNDTRACK)
P O L Y D O R | Producer: Vangelis
RELEASED: OCTOBER 1981

● Playful, triumphant, and poignant, Vengelis' music combined New Age euphoria with electronics to create one of the most memorable film themes of all time. The *Chariots of Fire* score went beyond that title track to weave a sonic tapestry that mirrored the storytelling of the Academy Award–winning film. His **Jerusalem** included a cathedral-style organ, and **Five Circles** featured keyboards simulating chiming bells and an Olympics-worthy brass fanfare. The instrumental album introduced audiences to Vangelis and has endured with every single athlete who hears the slow-motion theme in their heads. —SS

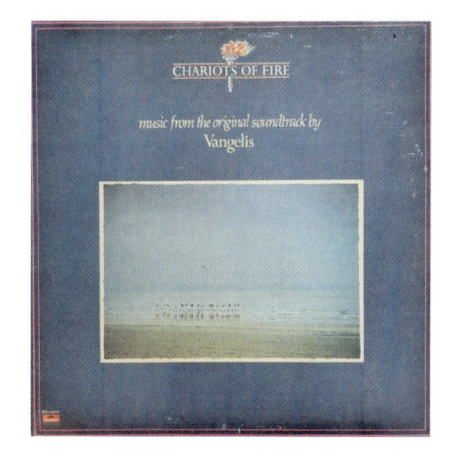

Tom Verlaine
DREAMTIME
W A R N E R B R O S. | Producer: Tom Verlaine
RELEASED: JULY 1981

● Of all the landmark works Tom Verlaine gave the world, somehow *Dreamtime* was the only one to chart in the US (at a modest No. 177). It was a customarily brilliant extension from his days leading New Wave pioneers Television, with sneaky hooks you barely notice until they've implanted themselves. Plenty of New York–scene peers back him up here, but Verlaine's guitar squalls are the stars—especially on **Penetration**, which reimagined his old collaborator Richard Hell's "Blank Generation" as beatnik pornographic fantasy. It's psychedelic rock you can drive to. —DM

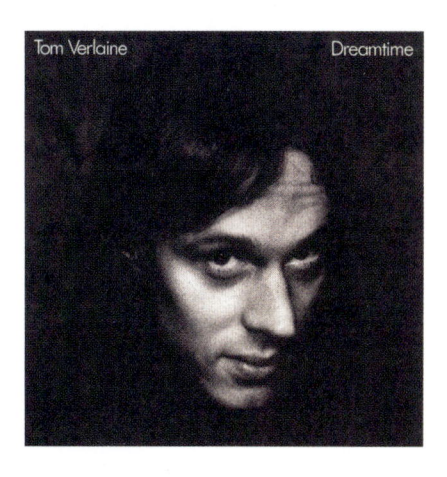

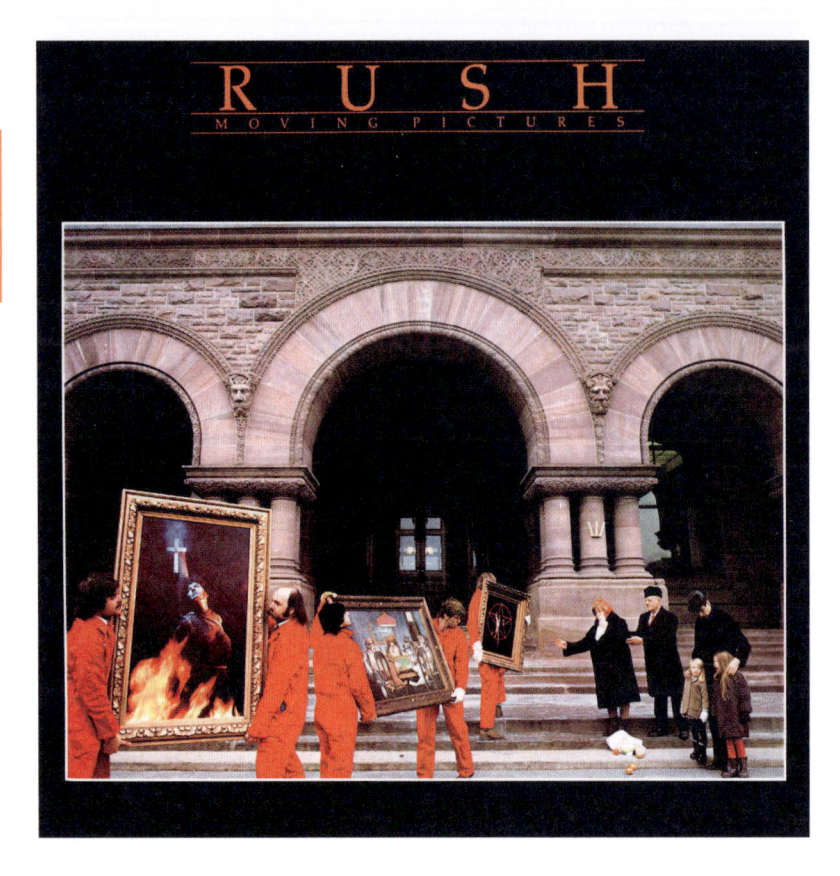

Rush
MOVING PICTURES
A N T H E M | Producers: Terry Brown, Rush
RELEASED: FEBRUARY 12, 1981

● Rush was at a new peak as it rolled into its eighth studio album. Its predecessor, *Permanent Waves*, was, according to the band, its first to ever earn a profit, and the Canadian trio and producer Terry Brown had hit on a balance of advanced sonics and (relative) song-length brevity that had made Rush a bit more radio friendly. A batch of new musical ideas, meanwhile, spurred the band to postpone its second live album in favor of returning to the studio.

There were widely chronicled difficulties in making *Moving Pictures*—mostly with the digital technology at Le Studio in Quebec—but none of that deterred Rush from crafting a masterpiece that moved the needle of its musical evolution exponentially forward. (A pressure-zone microphone taped to drummer Neal Peart's chest captured a room ambience that gave *Moving Pictures* greater immediacy.) On these seven tracks Rush found a sweet spot that made the group even more accessible without sacrificing any of its proggy, virtuosic ambitions. Best example—the Grammy Award–nominated **YYZ**, a King Crimson–like cascade that accomplished in less than four and a half minutes what Rush had taken twice as long, or longer, on previous instrumentals. Even **Tom Sawyer**, a bona fide radio classic, shifted into 7/8 sections in spots. **Limelight** and the reggae-tinged **Vital Signs** gave Rush even more entries to radio playlists, while the two-part **The Camera Eye** (subtitled **New York** and **London** and inspired by drummer/lyricist Neal Peart's walks in those cities) and **Red Barchetta** provided the requisite epics that no Rush album would be complete without.

Moving Pictures was a success by any measure and remains Rush's top-selling album in the US at five-times platinum. The delayed live album, *Exit . . . Stage Left*, came out eight and a half months later, and Rush would continue its explorations for another thirty-four accomplished years. *–GG*

1981

Rick Springfield
WORKING CLASS DOG

R C A | Producers: Rick Springfield, Bill Drescher, Keith Olsen
RELEASED: FEBRUARY 24, 1981

● Paging Dr. Noah Drake—and women from bachelorette parties everywhere—to the dancefloor. That familiar opening guitar riff of **Jessie's Girl**, the first single released from *Working Class Dog*, still serves as a, well, dog whistle that gets people up and moving. The single was also a clue to what the rest of the album held.

Working Class Dog was Australian rocker/actor Rick Springfield's fifth album but arguably the one that launched him to superstar status. The ten tracks were written mostly by Springfield and recorded at the famous Sound City Studios in Los Angeles over a period of months because he couldn't afford to pay production fees; Springfield's manager at the time, Joe Gottfried, co-owned the studio and only permitted him to work after paying customers had left for the day. Nevertheless, the result was a relentlessly catchy, power-pop collection that featured Neil Giraldo (Pat Benatar's future husband) on guitar and bass, along with other L.A. session players.

It was Giraldo who brought the hard-driving second single, **I've Done Everything for You**, written by Sammy Hagar, to the album. The song fit right in with the themes of love, lust, and betrayal, which Springfield recalled as "a very, very, very personal record. I felt free writing it." He showed his diverse style on the blues-tinged **Red Hot & Blue Love** and the ballad **Inside Silvia**.

It certainly didn't hurt that **Jessie's Girl** was released the same year MTV launched *and* while Springfield was appearing on the popular TV soap opera *General Hospital*. Critics were put off by his pretty-boy image, but Springfield's guitar-driven proclamation became a prototype for the era sound that established Springfield's status in the pop pantheon. It certainly did something for him. **—SS**

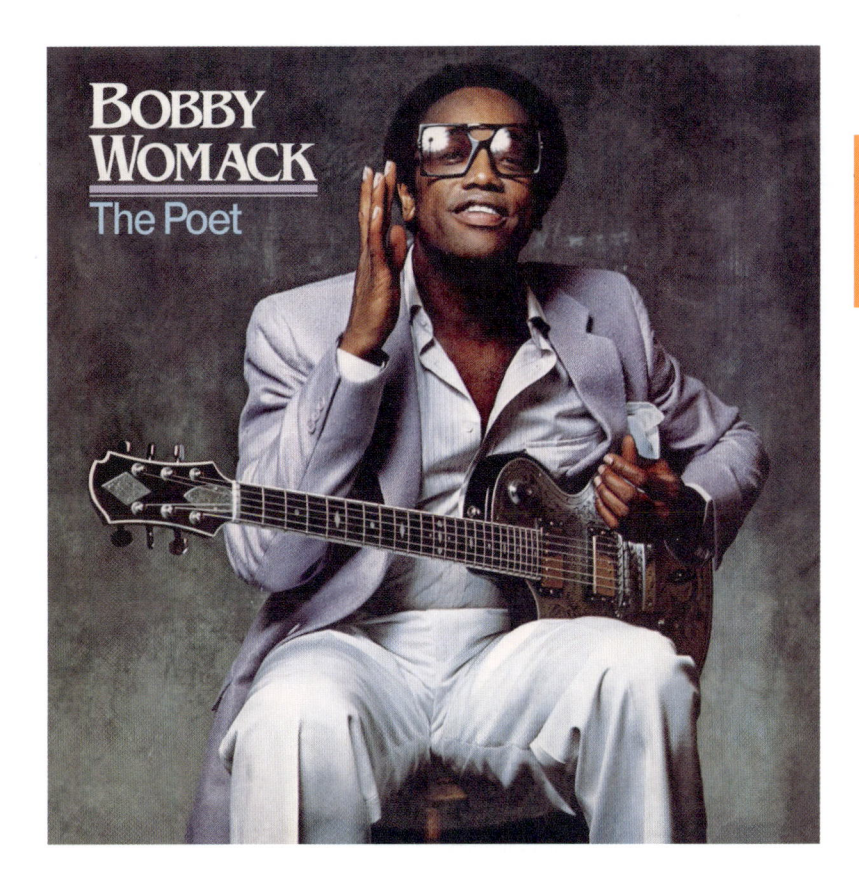

Bobby Womack
THE POET
BEVERLY GLEN MUSIC | Producer: Bobby Womack
RELEASED: NOVEMBER 1981

● As the album title indicates, Womack had become more than just a singer and songwriter by the time he reached his thirteenth studio album—and first in two years. The Cleveland native had been working since the early 1950s, backing Sam Cooke and performing in his family group the Valentinos before moving to Memphis and racking up session credits with Aretha Franklin, the Box Tops, Joe Tex, and others and writing songs for Wilson Pickett. He launched a solo career in 1969, earning props for his earthy brand of soul—especially on the soundtrack to the 1972 film *Across 110th Street*.

Like many of his old-school peers, Womack became a bit lost when disco supplanted classic R&B. He had some success collaborating with Wilton Felder of the Crusaders in 1980, and by the time he reached his first album of the 1980s, Womack sounded comfortable and contemporary in an "if you can't fight 'em, join 'em" manner—except joining on his own terms.

The Poet was a creative and commercial comeback, its eight tracks produced and mostly written by an audibly revived Womack. The reggae-flavored **So Many Sides of You** kicked things off, but it was the sultry, passionate **If You Think You're Lonely Now**—dedicated "to all the lovers tonight"—that gave Womack his first hit in five years (and was a hit for K-Ci Hailey on the *Jason's Lyric* soundtrack thirteen years later). The Temptations-referencing **Just My Imagination** and the nearly seven-minute slow jam **Games** were just as good, while tracks such as **Lay Your Lovin' on Me**, **Secrets**, and **Stand Up** put Womack credibly on the disco playlist. *The Poet* was a bona fide comeback (No. 1 on Billboard's Top Black Albums chart) and spawned a sequel in 1984, making Womack an old(ish) dog who did learn new tricks. *–GG*

Siouxsie and the Banshees
JUJU

POLYDOR | Producers: Nigel Gray, Siouxsie and the Banshees
RELEASED: JUNE 19, 1981

● Siouxsie Sioux (Susan Ballion) and Steve Severin (Steven Bailey) founded Siouxsie and the Banshees on the fly during 1976, when they had the chance to open for the Sex Pistols with a twenty-minute version of the only song they knew—"The Lord's Prayer." By their fourth album, *Juju*, they had a catalog of songs and the lineup had settled into a lasting four-piece. With Sioux's delightfully unhinged four-plus octave vocal range; Severin's unique, "upside down" bass playing; John McGeoch's inventive, effects-based guitar style; and the facile drumming of Budgie (Peter Clarke), the band came of age.

Juju produced two powerhouse singles. The first, **Spellbound**, opened with lyrics that might have described the band itself: "From the cradle bars / Comes a beckoning voice / It sends you spinning / You have no choice." There was no choice but to listen and watch. Sioux's beckoning voice was one of the most unique in pop, and her provocative outfits mixed with otherworldly makeup were attention grabbing. The second single, **Arabian Knights**, controversially addressed the treatment of women in the Middle East and remains a fan favorite today.

While the album hit No. 7 on the UK charts, where it spent seventeen weeks, it had minimal reception in the US. Still, *Juju* left a lasting mark, influencing many later bands and standing as one of the greatest post-punk albums of all time. It's also often been considered the beginning of goth, although Sioux declines that label. In the liner notes for *Juju*'s 2006 reissue, she says, in true Siouxsie fashion, "I've always thought that one of our greatest strengths was our ability to craft tension in music and subject matter. *Juju* had a strong identity, which the goth bands that came in our wake tried to mimic, but they simply ended up diluting it. —HD

1981

19

1982

82

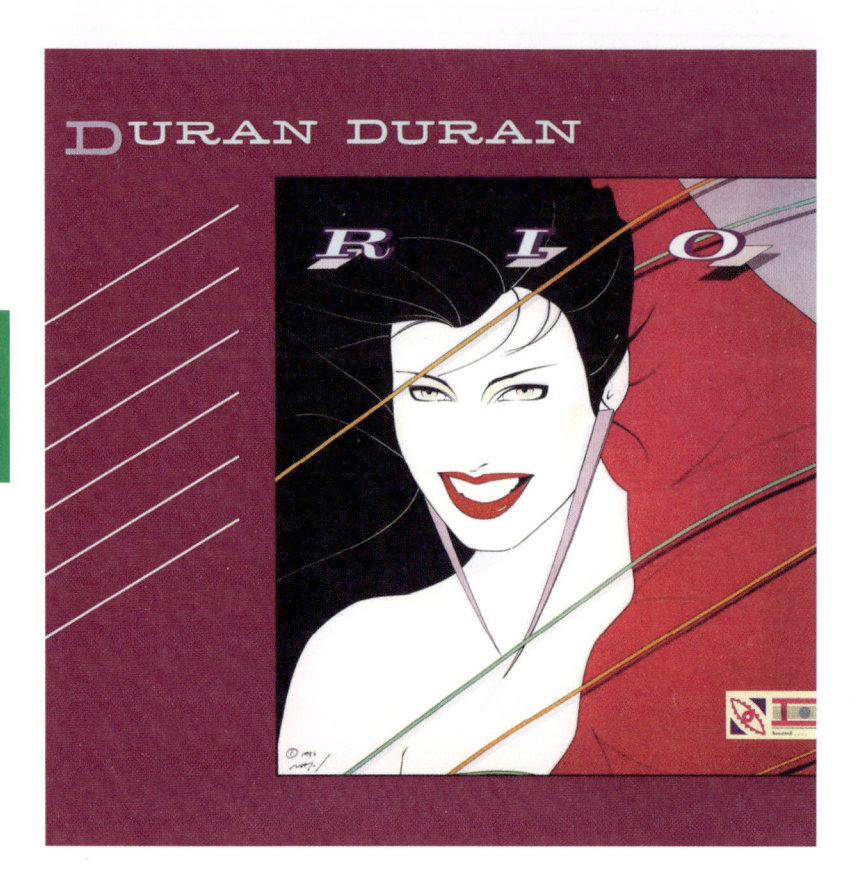

Duran Duran
RIO

E M I | Producer: Colin Thurston
RELEASED: MAY 10, 1982

● In casual early-'80s apocalyptic-fearing fashion, Duran Duran frontman Simon Le Bon said "we want to be the band to dance to when the bombs drop" months before Prince wanted to party like it was 1999. We could certainly do far worse.

Duran Duran's self-titled 1981 debut established the British quintet as a potent dancefloor force with singles such as "Girls on Film" and "Planet Earth." But it was the double-platinum *Rio* that upped the ante artistically and commercially, putting the five handsome lads on the world stage with a teen mania so potent that some media dubbed them the Fab Five.

There was substance behind the sensation, however. *Rio* was a stronger album than its predecessor, which was the stated intent. "The songs are more radio-oriented than the first album," keyboardist Nick Rhodes explained a couple of months after *Rio*'s release. "This album is much more the Duran Duran sound." Part of the ethos, he added, was that "you can make a track not specifically for dance clubs but that can cross over to dance clubs."

That was certainly how *Rio* rolled. Like a Bowie/Roxy Music summit meeting, fashion fortified the attitude in the chic, and Chic, grooves. But with more room to Andy Taylor's guitar, more dynamic arrangements, and more carefully structured melodies, songs such as **My Own Way**, **Last Chance on the Stairway**, and the saxophone-laced title track worked for the ears as well as the feet, while the breakthrough (in the US) single **Hungry Like the Wolf** and **Hold Back the Rain** offered some genuine rock crunch. **Save a Prayer**, **Lonely in Your Nightmare**, and **The Chauffeur**, meanwhile, displayed gentle moods and an ambient restraint that was a genuine addition to the group's sonic arsenal that, along with some extravagant videos, helped push the band to an iconic status. *—GG*

1982

Laurie Anderson
BIG SCIENCE
WARNER BROS./NONESUCH/ELEKTRA | Producers: Laurie Anderson, Roma Baran
RELEASED: APRIL 19, 1982

● It's not often that performance art hits the pop charts, and things might have remained that way in the early '80s if not for BBC DJ John Peel, who got behind Laurie Anderson's alternately humorous and portentous vocodered recitation **O Superman**, driving it to No. 2 on the UK Singles Chart—no mean feat, considering that the decidedly outré offering was also eight and a half minutes long.

The need to distribute the suddenly in-demand single led Anderson to sign a multi-album deal with Warner Bros., an agreement whose first fruit was *Big Science*. Anderson has said it was about "technology, size, industrialization, shifting attitudes toward authority, and individuality" and was part of a larger performance piece titled *United States I-IV*, which was recorded in 1983 and released in 1984 as the five-album set *United States Live*.

For *Big Science*, Anderson performed on keyboards and modified violins of her own design and was joined by musicians playing glass harmonica, bagpipes, bottles and sticks, woodwinds, and percussion. Her absurdist meditations were akin to short stories and were delivered in her own voice, which was often friendly and inquisitive but sometimes robotic and forbidding. The stories and characters were quirky; "I met this guy," Anderson intoned at the outset of **Let X = X**. "And he looked like he might have been a hat check clerk at an ice rink / Which, in fact, he turned out to be." Then she deadpanned the punch line: "And I said, 'Oh boy. Right again.'"

Anderson's art music may have been aimed at downtown New York City hipsters but turned out to have surprisingly wide appeal. Her work never again attained the chart heights scaled by **O Superman**, but she continued delivering her wry and often-pointed observations and unique conceptual pieces well into the twenty-first century. *—DD*

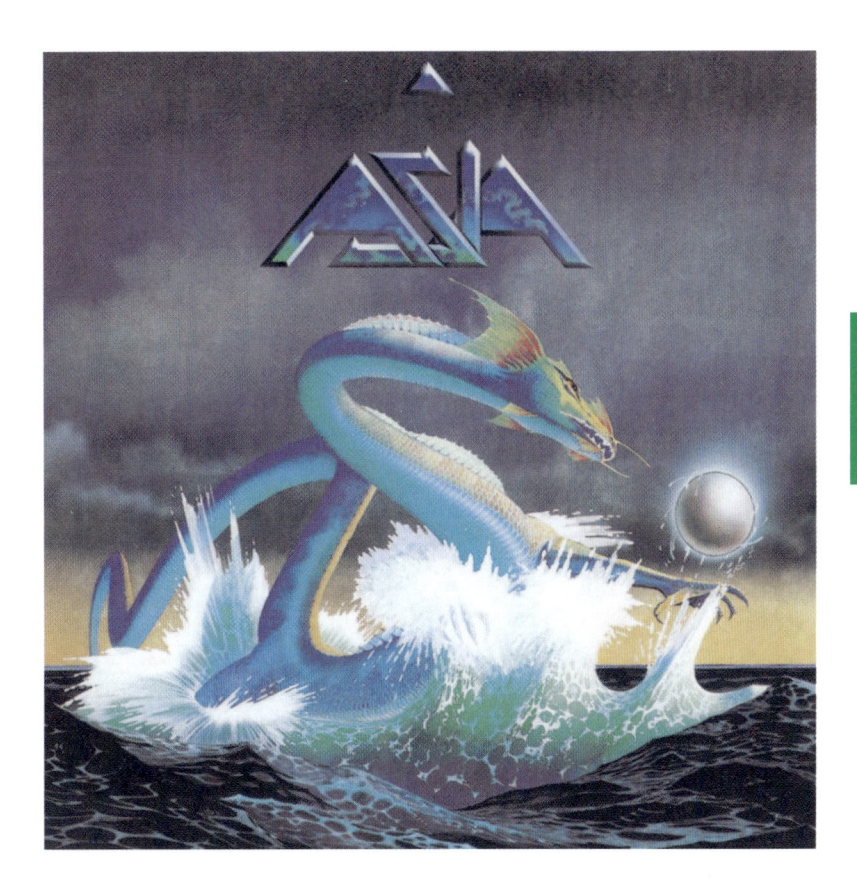

Asia
ASIA
GEFFEN | Producer: Mike Stone
RELEASED: MARCH 18, 1982

● Want to hear an extremely dubious plan for chart-topping success? Take four members of three of progressive rock's biggest '70s bands, all of whom have run their careers into the ground by losing connection with any semblance of a mainstream audience. Then put them together as a, let's face it, largely faceless supergroup, just as the visual-dependent MTV is establishing itself as the dominant force in breaking new bands.

And yet . . . somehow it worked, beyond anybody's wildest dreams. Asia—the union of Yes guitarist Steve Howe and keyboardist Geoffrey Downes; Emerson, Lake & Palmer drummer Carl Palmer; and King Crimson singer/bassist John Wetton—didn't just hit No. 1 with its self-titled 1982 debut album. It stayed in that spot for nine weeks and wound up with the year's best-selling US album.

The album featured two Top 20 pop hits—**Only Time Will Tell** and the Top 5 and career-defining future cultural landmark **Heat of the Moment**. Asia achieved that success by emphasizing the musicianship that had previously made its members kings of their genre while drastically trimming its excesses. None of the songs on Asia's first side exceeded the five-minute mark. "People said, 'No, that's not going to work. It's all keyboards now. It's all synthesizers,'" Wetton told the *Morning Call* years later. "Actually, what we did was make a sound that blew synthesizers out of the water."

Part of the credit might go to producer Mike Stone, who had just achieved massive radio success with Journey's 1981 breakthrough album *Escape*. Although the foursome never replicated the astounding success of their debut album, it's hard to imagine Howe's former (and future) Yes bandmates weren't following the Asia playbook when they released their own "prog, but concise" smash hit single "Owner of a Lonely Heart" two years later. *—MW*

ABC
THE LEXICON OF LOVE

MERCURY | Producers: Trevor Horn, Steve Brown
RELEASED: JULY 21, 1982

● Suave, jazzy, and slightly campy, ABC's debut album evoked Roxy Music but in a more romantic (i.e., less sexual) way. Singer Martin Fry's trademark was a gold lamé jacket, and his voice was as smooth as the fabric, invoking a post-punk Sinatra for the disco age. "We wanted to create a stage play, a movie," Fry said in 2004, reflecting on *Lexicon*. "We wanted to hark back to Cole Porter and his ilk, but in a very modern way." The album's singles—**Tears Are Not Enough**, **Poison Arrow**, **The Look of Love**, and **All of My Heart**—rightfully endure today, the latter possibly being the lushest track to ever hit pop radio. That was thanks to Trevor Horn's production, which leaned heavily into dense strings, keyboards (compliments of Anne Dudley, who later formed the Art of Noise with Horn), and soulful backing vocal arrangements. When ABC toured to support the album, it needed eleven backing musicians so prominent was the almost-symphonic wall of sound behind it. No time machine is needed to return to the '80s; just spin this disc. *—HD*

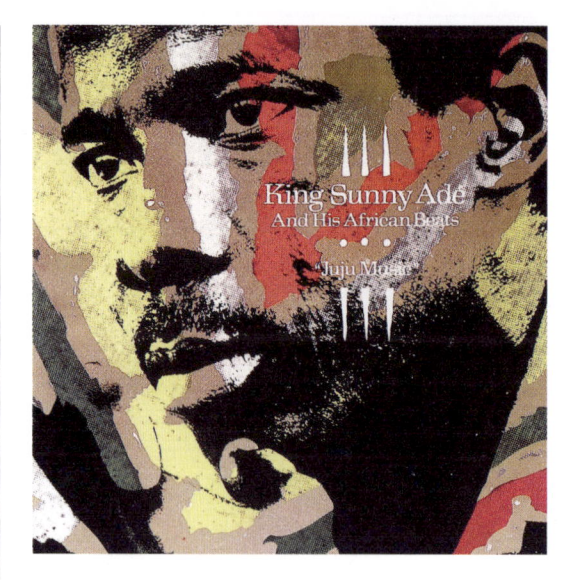

King Sunny Ade and His African Beats
JUJU MUSIC

MANGO | Producer: Martin Meissonnier
RELEASED: 1982

● Back in his native Nigeria at the dawn of the '80s, King Sunny Ade was a major cultural figure, churning out multiple albums every year. All of that was unknown in the US and much of the rest of the world until Island Records signed Ade to its Mango imprint and released *Juju Music*, an infectious distillation of the joyous, polyrhythmic delights that populate its seven tracks. The goods were there, of course, but French producer Martin Meissonnier deserves credit for turning the long, hypnotical ramble of Ade's Juju into actual songs but without losing their power or exuberance. Many of Ade's lyrics were based on Yoruban proverbs, giving the songs a spiritual gravitas amid a dance-inducing, swirling sound collage that underlined the African influence on jazz, blues, soul, folk, and reggae while never weighing down the exuberance of **Ja Funmi**, **Sunny Ti de Ariya**, **Samba/E Falaba Lewe**, and the Fillmore-caliber trippiness of **365 Is My Number/The Message**. Had this deal been made a few years earlier, Ade and company might have been the same kind of vanguard as Bob Marley and the Wailers; that said, *Juju Music* certainly opened ears and doors for the advancement of world music. *—GG*

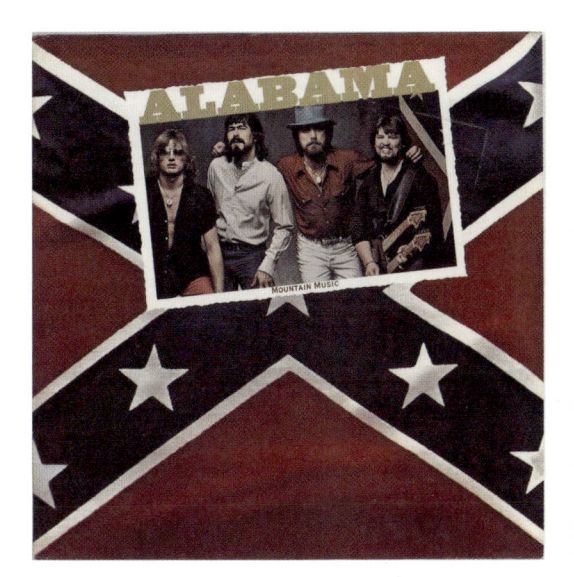

Alabama
MOUNTAIN MUSIC
RCA NASHVILLE | Producers: Harold Shedd, Alabama
RELEASED: FEBRUARY 25, 1982

● Alabama provided an aural definition of what being an urban cowboy meant during the early '80s. The Fort Payne quartet had already begun its pop crossover with 1981's *Feel So Right*, but *Mountain Music*—Alabama's sixth album overall—was even more successful both creatively and commercially, yielding five-times platinum sales, three No. 1 country chart hits, and a Top 20 on the Billboard Hot 100 with the breezy **Take Me Down**. What made Alabama work on both sides of the divide was a sound as smooth as a fresh pair of boots, more melodic than twangy, and particularly easy on the ears thanks to the earthy, soulful harmonies of vocalists Jeff Cook, Teddy Gentry, and Randy Owen. The title track gave the group a gentrified Southern signature, while **Lovin' You Is Killin' Me** felt like it could break into the Eagles' "Already Gone" at any second. Alabama's rendition of Creedence Clearwater Revival's **Green River** had a little bit of rough 'n' tumble, **You Turn Me On** came complete with Barry White murmurs, and **Never Be the One** delivered a three-hanky daddy-daughter ode. A little different than Grandma and Grandpa used to play, but they'd approve. *—GG*

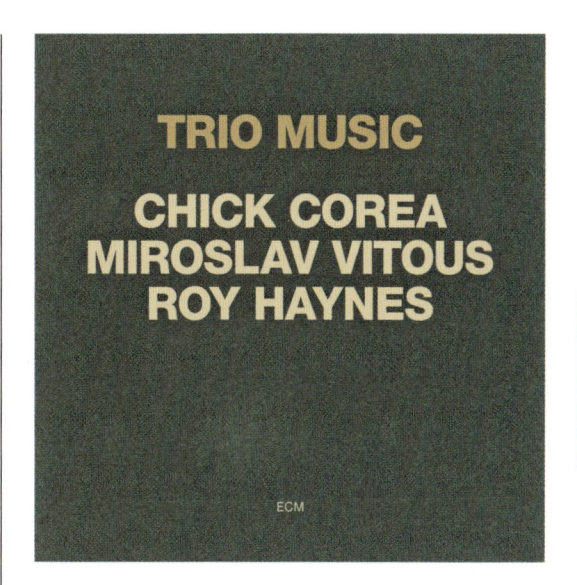

Chick Corea, Miroslav Vitous, Roy Haynes
TRIO MUSIC
ECM | Producer: Manfred Eicher
RELEASED: OCTOBER 4, 1982

● Free, abstract, and virtuosic, *Trio Music*—a double-album of impressionistic jazz piano, double bass, and drums—requires close and patient listening to fully appreciate. And the effort is rewarded, especially the second disc's showcase of the idiosyncratic music of Thelonious Monk. Pianist Corea first assembled this trio in 1968, recording his own compositions on the highly respected *Now He Sings, Now He Sobs*. Drummer Roy Haynes was already a legend, having recorded on more than 125 albums since 1947, while Corea and bassist Miroslav Vitous were rising jazz stars who played with Miles Davis. Fourteen years later, the 1982 trio was fresher, more inventive, and telepathic, playing with abandon on the first disc's five avant-garde **Trio Improvisations** and two piano/bass **Duet Improvisations**. Crafted like intricate sonic puzzles, the improvisations display the full sound palette of each instrument. Corea's **Slippery When Wet**, played as freely and off-kilter as any Monk tune, was a perfect segue; his improv around **Rhythm-a-Ning** was more elusive, more eccentric than Monk's. Haynes's brushwork on **Round Midnight** and **Eronel** was zesty and masterful. *—CH*

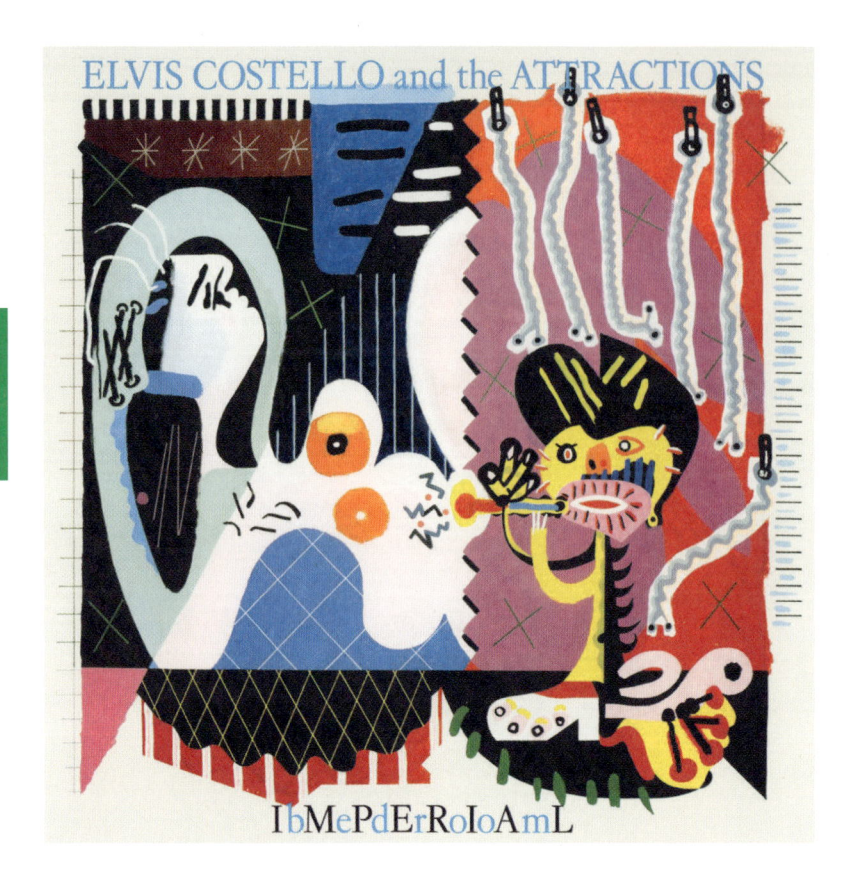

Elvis Costello and the Attractions
IMPERIAL BEDROOM

COLUMBIA | Producer: Geoff Emerick
RELEASED: JULY 2, 1982

● On Elvis Costello's first Attractions album of original music not produced by Nick Lowe, he intentionally set aside his earlier punk/New Wave punchiness and the perceived indulgence of *Almost Blue*, his country covers album, to enter a new career phase. Hiring Beatles engineer Geoff Emerick to produce gave Costello access to *Sgt. Pepper's*-level studio creativity (actual instrumental echoes appeared on **And in Every Home**), allowing for new levels of experimentation. The resulting arrangements, many incorporating elegant orchestrations by keyboardist Steve Nieve, were transformational; *Imperial Bedroom*'s sophisticated jazz and pop treatments finally matched the layered brilliance of Costello's elliptical wordplay.

His tendency toward Brechtian portrayals of humanity's wicked underbelly was still present in songs such as **Man out of Time**, a melodically gorgeous ballad inspired by a political scandal. But this album found Costello shifting toward vividly etched first-person portraits of characters plagued by self-doubt, suffering through sad circumstances or bad romances. Of course, he still peppered them with clever lines like "Spare us the theatrics and the verbal gymnastics" and sly musical and pop cultural references. Nods to the Moonglows' "10 Commandments of Love," the Beatles' "P.S. I Love You," and James Brown's "It's a Man's Man's Man's World" appeared, and amid his vocal workout on **Beyond Belief**, Costello sang, "Did you have to be so cruel to be callous," nearly mirroring Lowe's "Cruel to Be Kind."

But it's Costello's lush vocal renderings and Nieve's superb instrumental contributions that elevated *Imperial Bedroom*. Its most outstanding track, the aching torch song **Almost Blue**, remains a live-set staple. This collection set the template for Costello's Great American Songbook explorations while cementing his status as a songwriter worthy of mention alongside his inspirations. —*LM*

1982

Bad Brains
BAD BRAINS
R O I R | Producer: Jay Dublee
RELEASED: FEBRUARY 5, 1982

● Bad Brains did not like being called a hardcore band. But rest assured that its debut album was *very* hard. To its core.

The Washington, D.C.–formed quartet's very existence was revolutionary. Listen to *Bad Brains* and you'd have no idea at all this was four Black guys playing at tempos that made Ramones seem lethargic and with the intricate instrumental precision of a jazz fusion group—which is, in fact, what Bad Brains was when its members first came together as Mind Power during the mid-'70s. Then they met punk, changed the band name, and also found a way to make reggae part of its repertoire as a kind of chilled-out counterbalance to the fury.

Bad Brains, originally released on cassette only, was more of a haymaker than a slap upside the head. You practically had to put a seat belt on as **Sailin' On**, **Don't Need It**, **Attitude**, and **The Regulator** came sprinting out of the speakers—at an average of about eighty seconds per track, each a blast of pure adrenaline and ferocious energy but with chops. **Supertouch/Shitfit** in particular offered tricky dynamics and touches of metal that would make Bad Brains—and tracks such as **Fearless Vampire Killers**, **I**, and **Big Takeover**—a touchstone for a subsequent legion of speed and thrash bands.

On the flip side, the reggae tracks (**Jah Calling**, **Leaving Babylon**, the six-plus-minute **I Luv I Jah**) were all about vibe, taking their time in a pleasantly meandering fashion that allowed listeners a chance to catch their breath and steel themselves for the next fusillade of—sorry, guys—hardcore assault.

Bad Brains is not for the faint of heart, but it's an enduringly important album whose influence and inspiration have yet to ebb. *–GG*

Marvin Gaye
MIDNIGHT LOVE
COLUMBIA | Producer: Marvin Gaye
RELEASED: NOVEMBER 1, 1982

● Marvin Gaye was the premier male solo star on Motown Records. Think about that; on a label full of singers, he was the MAN. Only Diana Ross eclipsed him in fame, and she had been the voice of the biggest group on the label. Sadly, when he left the label in 1981, Gaye was a shadow of himself. His divorce from Anna Gordy had ruined him financially, and his addictions overtook him. Bouncing from California to Hawaii to England and, finally, Belgium, Gaye turned to creating new music without the constraints of his former label. A contract with Columbia Records was the lifeline he needed.

Midnight Love was a new birth. Freshly invigorated, Gaye put his instrument, that glorious voice, front and center of every track. He'd always been his own best harmonist, and his multitracked vocals give flight to everything here. The opening line of **Sexual Healing** set the direction: "Baby, I'm hot just like an oven / I need some lovin'." Gaye had always broadcast an Alpha-male-sex-god thing, and now he leaned in even harder. In lesser hands, it would have been a total mess, but Gaye was the unmatched master.

Across all tempos, he poured on the lust. On **Midnight Lady** and **Rocking after Midnight**, he was the party king. **'Til Tomorrow** was a gold-standard slow jam. In midtempo, he found his sweetest spot with **Sexual Healing**, **Third World Girl**, and **My Love is Waiting**. Unheralded across this masterwork is the use of drum machines; any concerns that this then-new technology could be legitimately funky were laid to rest on **Midnight Love**.

Gaye's reascent to the top of the charts was short lived. He couldn't outrun his demons or resolve the tumult of his family life and was murdered by his father on April 1, 1984, one day shy of his forty-fifth birthday. *—HK*

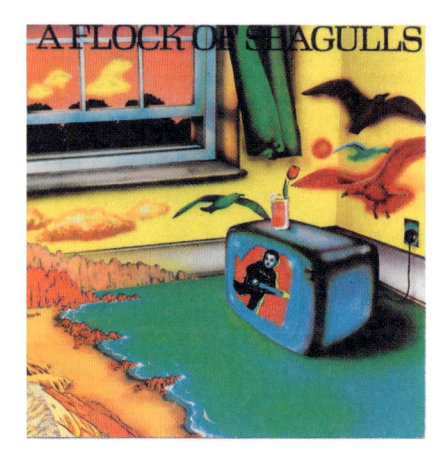

A Flock of Seagulls
A FLOCK OF SEAGULLS
JIVE/ARISTA | Producer: Mike Howlett
RELEASED: APRIL 1982

● It's not only inaccurate to call A Flock of Seagulls a one-hit wonder (the famously coiffed Liverpool band actually scored three Top 40 hits), it's a shame. Yes, **I Ran (So Far Away)**—with its sweeping, spiky guitars, propulsive percussion, and spacey synths—was its finest moment, but the self-titled debut was a stone-cold New Wave classic. From the taut, angular **Modern Love Is Automatic** to the Devo-meets-Human League **Telecommunication** and the extraterrestrial post-punk of **Standing in the Doorway**, the Flock created an immersive sound as strange as it was sweet. —JL

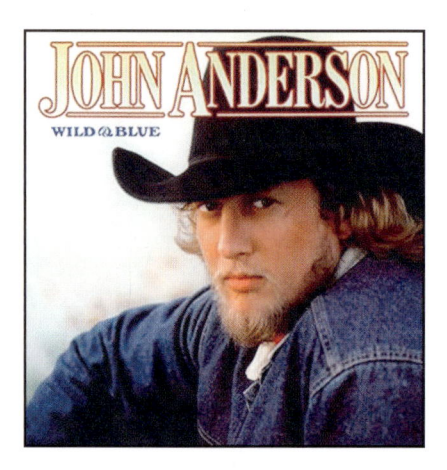

John Anderson
WILD & BLUE
WARNER BROS. NASHVILLE | Producers: John Anderson, Frank Jones
RELEASED: SEPTEMBER 18, 1982

● Four albums in, country singer John Anderson got his breakthrough. By *Wild & Blue*, Anderson had a strong sense of himself as singer, songwriter, and (co-)producer, adding string arrangements to the mix alongside collaborations with Emmylou Harris (**The Waltz You Save for Me**) and Merle Haggard (**Long Black Veil**). *Wild & Blue* was Anderson's first gold album, while **Swingin'** and the title track were Anderson's first No. 1 country chart hits—the former winning a Country Music Association Award for Single of the Year. —GG

Berlin
PLEASURE VICTIM
M.A.O./ENIGMA | Producers: Daniel R. Van Patten, The Maomen
RELEASED: OCTOBER 1982

● Short (seven songs in twenty-nine minutes), sweet, and—in the case of **Sex (I'm a . . .)**—sexy in a silly kind of way, *Pleasure Victim* was synth-pop 101, a record you'd hand somebody as prototypical of that particular musical wave. Terri Nunn's vocals have genuine character, and John Crawford knew how to write a good song and blend Euro chill with good ol' American guitar solos. The "controversy" over **Sex (I'm a. . .)** was much ado about nothing but did get attention, which the band made good on with **The Metro**, **Masquerade**, and the title track. —GG

George Clinton
COMPUTER GAMES
CAPITOL | Producer: George Clinton
RELEASED: NOVEMBER 5, 1982

● This was ostensibly funkmeister George Clinton's first "solo" album, but it was in actuality another joint from the Parliament-Funkadelic universe. The cast of characters (Bootsy Collins, Eddie Hazel, Gary Shider, Bernie Worrell, etc.) was the same and the grooves just as substantial, with some sonic tweaks to embrace the techno elements of post-disco dance music. **Atomic Dog** was its big and enduring hit, but drop the needle anywhere on the album—the title track or **Man's Best Friend/Loopzilla** especially—and you'll be able to get off your ass and jam. —*GG*

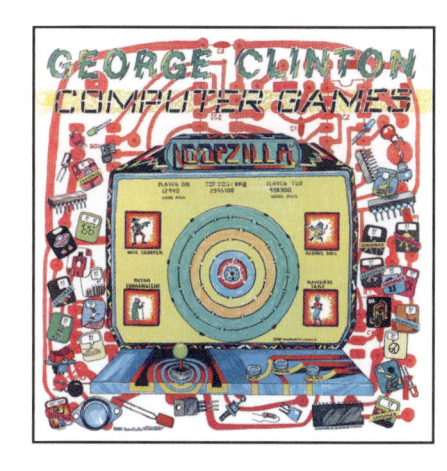

Descendents
MILO GOES TO COLLEGE
NEW ALLIANCE | Producer: Spot
RELEASED: SEPTEMBER 4, 1982

● SoCal coffee fiends Descendents brewed up melodic hardcore delivered with a nerdy sneer by future biochemist Milo Aukerman (who would indeed leave for university post-album). The pop hooks and breakneck arrangements crafted by Frank Navetta, Tony Lombardo, and Bill Stevenson (fifteen songs in twenty-two minutes) were exemplified by **Myage**, **Bikeage**, **I'm Not a Loser**, and **Suburban Home**. Though Aukerman and Stevenson have since distanced themselves from some of the youthful lyrics on *Milo*, it erected a framework for scads of pop-punk and emo acts to follow. —*DP*

The English Beat
SPECIAL BEAT SERVICE
I.R.S. | Producers: Bob Sargeant, Ranking Roger, Mike Hedges
RELEASED: OCTOBER 1, 1982

● The English Beat was one of the most popular bands to come out of Britain's 2-Tone movement of culturally diverse lineups playing Jamaican-flavored ska-rock, often with heavy political overtones. For its third album, the band took a sharp turn toward pop/rock; frontman Dave Wakeling crooned over jazzy sax and piano work on the first single, **I Confess**. The easygoing **Save It for Later** included strings. Some straight-ahead rockers and a half dozen reggae-heavy numbers completed this successful recipe. —*GP*

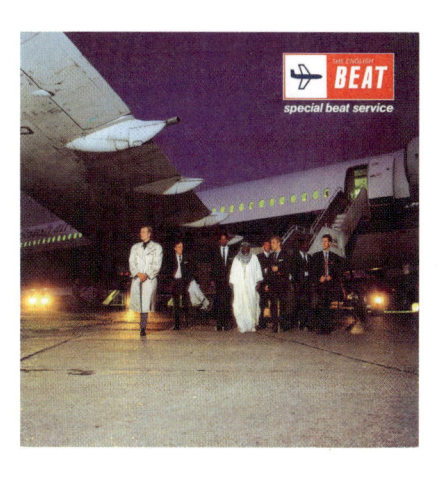

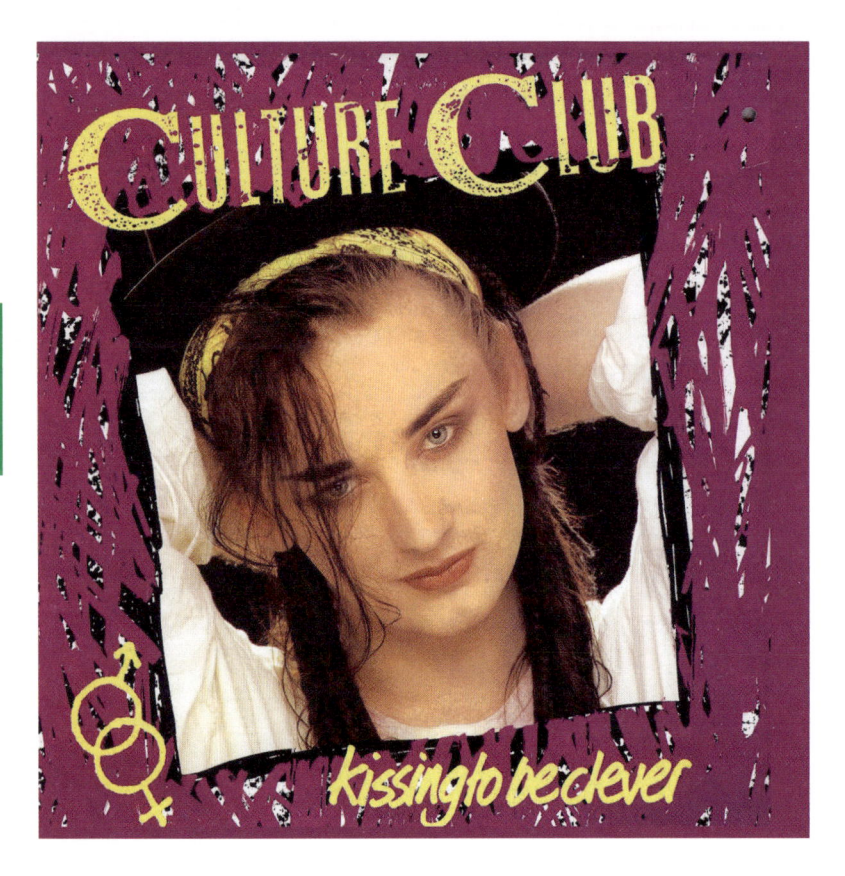

Culture Club
KISSING TO BE CLEVER

EPIC | Producer: Steve Levine
RELEASED: DECEMBER 13, 1982

● Ask people to name enduring New Wave songs and many may land on Culture Club's Grammy Award–nominated hit **Do You Really Want to Hurt Me?** While the debut album's first singles (**White Boy, I'm Afraid of Me**) tanked, the soulful and autobiographical track launched Culture Club onto the international scene so forcefully that the subsequent **Time (Clock of the Heart)** and **I'll Tumble 4 Ya** made the quartet the first debut band since the Beatles to score three Top 10 singles in the US at the same time.

It didn't hurt to have a frontman who captured public attention, and in the Reagan '80s, Boy George (nee O'Dowd) certainly did that. Androgynous and bohemian, he was unlike any other artist to be beamed into living rooms on MTV. The album broke barriers—gender, genre, and musical. Reggae beats formed the basis of many of the songs, and the band's diversity (the openly gay George, Black bassist Mikey Craig, Jewish drummer Jon Moss) was both a novelty and an important statement.

There was controversy over Julian Temple's **Do You Really Want to Hurt Me?** video, with a jury in blackface in one scene, but the overall broad-based adoration the album received never dimmed. You have to imagine that even Boy George, in his days of working as the coat check boy in the famed London Blitz Club, would have been shocked at Culture Club's level of success. Or maybe not. —HD

1982

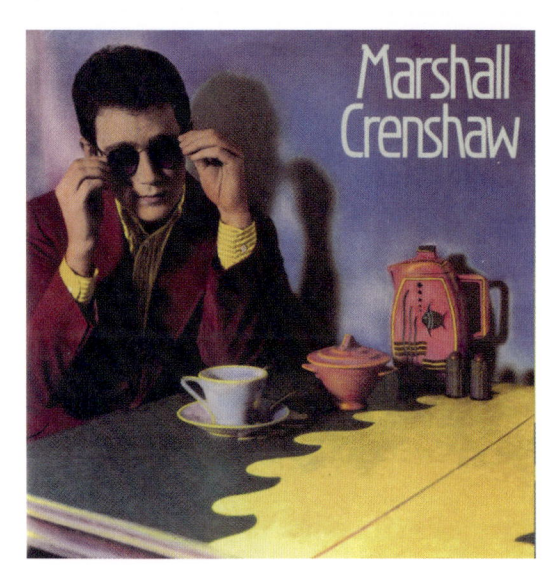

Marshall Crenshaw
MARSHALL CRENSHAW

WARNER BROS. | Producers: Richard Gottehrer, Marshall Crenshaw
RELEASED: APRIL 28, 1982

● If the title hadn't already been taken by the wonderful Nick Lowe, this album could aptly have been titled *Pure Pop for Now People*. Marshall Crenshaw's full-length major label debut was laden with hooks and harmonies. The songcraft revealed someone with an ear toward the past and one in the present. Crenshaw spent years as a working musician, playing in local bands in his native Detroit and even portraying John Lennon in a touring company of Beatlemania. He learned well from his apprenticeship, and this gem was the result. The many comparisons hung on him, mostly to guys who also wore glasses (Buddy Holly, Elvis Costello), were flattering but not accurate. Crenshaw's songs brimmed with energy and light, despite themes of isolation (**Cynical Girl**), heartbreak (**There She Goes Again**), and desire (**Brand New Lover**). Reaching into the past, he covered Arthur Alexander's **Soldier of Love**, which he took from a Beatles bootleg record. And he honored a rock 'n' roll tradition of using a girl's name as a song title (**Mary Anne**). —*HK*

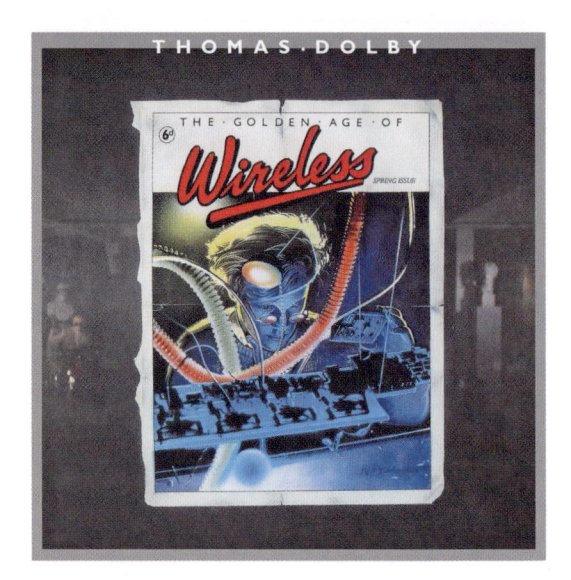

Thomas Dolby
THE GOLDEN AGE OF WIRELESS

CAPITOL | Producers: Thomas Dolby, Tim Friese-Greene
RELEASED: MAY 13, 1982

● Thomas Dolby began his music career as a songwriter/producer/session player for artists that ranged from Lene Lovich and Joan Armatrading to rapper Whodini. Using the money he made for playing synths on Foreigner's *4*, he decided to release his own work. And thus, *The Golden Age of Wireless* was born. The album opened with Dolby's signature opus, **She Blinded Me with Science**; anchored by a solid electronic bass and drum track and peppered with synth pads and samples, **Science** was a graduate-level course in how to use technology to create memorable hooks. The second-best track, **Europa and the Pirate Twins**, continued the inventive synth work but with more emphasis on vocals. The rest of the album didn't stray far from the formula, with **Airwaves**, **Radio Silence**, and **One of Our Submarines** all standout examples of New Wave synth-pop. Fun fact: The UK got five and the US got two different versions of this release with different track sequences and artwork; add later collector's editions and remixed versions and you could build a small record collection on this album alone. —*GP*

Donald Fagen
THE NIGHTFLY
WARNER BROS. | Producer: Gary Katz
RELEASED: OCTOBER 1, 1982

● After the breakup of Steely Dan the previous year, co-founder and vocalist Donald Fagen used his first foray as a solo recording artist to show the world where he came from. *The Nightfly* was an autobiographical release, focusing on the optimistic mood of his 1950s suburban upbringing and his discovery of jazz culture and an alternative world through listening to late-night radio. And the sparking lead single, **I.G.Y. (International Geophysical Year)**, articulated the era's space-age positivity. Utilizing longtime Steely Dan co-producer Gary Katz, engineer Roger Nichols, and many of the musicians employed on previous Dan albums, *The Nightfly* was crafted impeccably in smooth pop-jazz style, with precision and sophistication, and it remains a prime example of early fully digital recording in popular music. The album was a critical and commercial success, achieving platinum status in the US and the UK and earning seven Grammy Award nominations. Other top tracks included **New Frontier**, about a gawky teenager inviting a girl to visit his family's fallout shelter, and **Ruby Baby**, a slick rewrite of the Drifters' 1956 hit for additional period flavor. *–JC*

Iron Maiden
THE NUMBER OF THE BEAST
E M I | Producer: Martin Birch
RELEASED: MARCH 22, 1982

● Iron Maiden had already established itself as a rising heavy metal titan with its first two albums, but the pressures and temptations of life in a touring band quickly got the best of frontman Paul Di'Anno in the form of a massive cocaine habit, and the group replaced him with Bruce Dickinson. This was an enormous turning point for Iron Maiden and the genre as a whole. While his predecessor brought a raw, punkish, grounding element to the band's sound, Dickinson's powerful, operatic range opened the doors for Maiden to explore more epic, dynamic material. The quintet took full advantage of that on *The Number of the Beast*, delivering one of the first stone-cold classic heavy metal albums of the '80s, an all the more amazing feat considering the band only had five weeks to record and mix the album. The galloping **Run to the Hills** became Maiden's first UK Top 10 single, and the seven-minute **Hallowed Be Thy Name** is widely considered one of its most important extended compositions. There's excellence everywhere you turn here, including the soaring **The Prisoner** and the moody and atmospheric **Children of the Damned**. *–MW*

Billy Joel
THE NYLON CURTAIN

FAMILY PRODUCTIONS/COLUMBIA
PRODUCER: PHIL RAMONE
RELEASED: SEPTEMBER 23, 1982

● The '80s was a season of surprise for Billy Joel. And in between the lean rock of 1980's *Glass Houses* and the doe-eye soul of 1983's *An Innocent Man*, *The Nylon Curtain* brought us another side—sides, even—of Joel as a songwriter and record maker. "That was right in the middle of the Reagan era, and things were changing in America, and I was very aware of it," Joel reflected forty years after the album's release. "I'm very proud of that album. The songs seem to still resonate with audiences and with younger people as well."

Joel has every reason to feel that way. The piano man's eighth studio album blended social commentary with pop craftsmanship, treating each song with a kind of fully realized cinematic detail. **Allentown** put us in a bar with an unemployed steelworker lamenting his circumstances. **Goodnight Saigon** dropped us into the dark consciousness of a Vietnam veteran. The jagged, cascading **Pressure** conveyed (then) modern-age anxieties. The back-to-back **She's Right on Time** and **A Room of Our Own** offered views of relationships coming and going.

That was all on top of another set of exceptional songs—something Joel wasn't really a, er, stranger to by then. His regular band was well honed in the studio, and producer Phil Ramone helped achieve greater sonic nuances throughout, especially with the Beatlesque string arrangement for **Scandinavian Skies**. (It was also one of the very first albums to make use of digital recording, mixing, and mastering techniques.) Though it didn't sell as well as its predecessors—or *An Innocent Man*, for that matter—*The Nylon Curtain* continued Joel's Top 10 multiplatinum-album streak and is, in retrospect, a zenith achievement in a career full of high points. *–GG*

1982

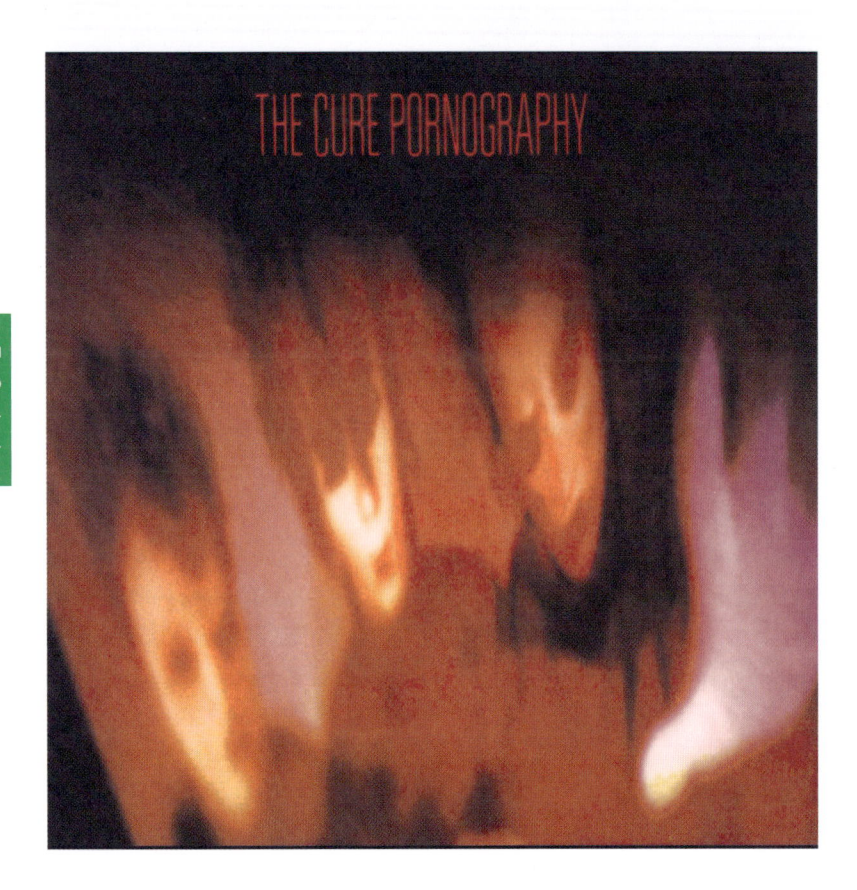

The Cure
PORNOGRAPHY

FICTION | Producers: The Cure, Phil Thornalley
RELEASED: MAY 4, 1982

● The Cure's fourth studio set was its darkest album to date, a descent into gothic gloom and doom that made the English outfit, a trio at the time, heroic to outsiders everywhere. The band would go on to masterfully balance elements of bliss with its melancholy, but *Pornography* starts out bleak and never lets up over the course of its eight-track, forty-three-minute runtime.

"It doesn't matter if we all die!" announced frontman Robert Smith less than a minute into the opening track, **One Hundred Years**, a heavy scene-setter that also contained an allusion to leaping from a tall building. (Remember, "Friday I'm In Love" was still ten years away.) Smith was in a difficult headspace at the time of recording, exhausted from touring and ready to call it quits on the band, on life, or both. *Pornography* was the sound of Smith expelling the demons from his head and attempting to move on to a better place.

To explore this morose territory, the band enlisted producer Phil Thornalley, who joined as bassist for a brief period. The mood was layered with murky keys and bass lines as dense as a thick fog, the songs a downward spiral of pain and self-loathing. The album produced just one single, **The Hanging Garden**, but it was the band's most successful album to date, hitting the Top 10 in the UK.

The Cure survived *Pornography*, and the album's thumbprint is visible on the next generation of brooding rock acts, from Deftones to System of a Down to Nine Inch Nails. It went on to become a deeply influential gateway album for generations of goth teenagers, who were drawn to its timeless themes of loneliness, isolation, and desolation, all made bearable by the beauty of Smith's emotive delivery. *–AG*

Prince
1999
WARNER BROS. | Producer: Prince
RELEASED: OCTOBER 27, 1982

● Prince's first two albums of the '80s made him a favorite with critics. Though *Dirty Mind* (1980) and *Controversy* (1981) were celebrated among tastemakers and the music elite, that support didn't push either record into the Top 20. But when *1999*, the fifth album by the 24-year-old Minneapolis-based singer, songwriter, producer, and multi-instrumentalist, arrived during the latter part of 1982, all that changed. In a couple of years, Prince would be one of the biggest artists in the world; this album is the one that helped take him there.

Acknowledging his backing band the Revolution for the first time (though it wouldn't receive a proper album co-credit until 1984's *Purple Rain*), Prince still handled most of the instrumentation by himself, including synths, guitar, piano, and drums. The double-album set featured eleven tracks in its seventy-minute running time; four singles were released, with **Little Red Corvette** becoming his first Top 10 after MTV put the song, as well as the album's title track, into heavy rotation. *1999* made it to No. 7 on the Billboard 200. The music mainstream had finally caught up with Prince.

But *1999* wouldn't have mattered if the music wasn't the best of his career so far. Beyond the singles (including the Top 10 **Delirious** and **Let's Pretend We're Married**) and the Grammy-nominated slow-jam closer **International Lover**, the album served as an introduction to the funk-based, synth-heavy Minneapolis sound that would dominate so much pop music during the mid-'80s. More so than any of Prince's other recognized masterworks, including *Purple Rain* and 1987's *Sign "O" the Times*, *1999* was the one that influenced legions of fans and followers. Its two LPs form one of the sturdiest bedrocks found in all of '80s music. —*MG*

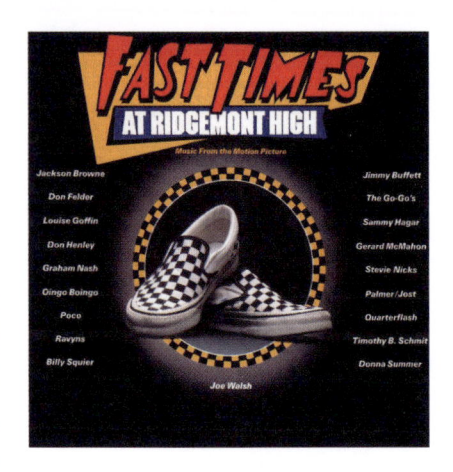

Various Artists
FAST TIMES AT RIDGEMONT HIGH (MUSIC FROM THE MOTION PICTURE)
ELEKTRA | Producers: Various
RELEASED: JULY 30, 1982

● The Cars' "Moving in Stereo," which is burned in the brains of an entire generation thanks to Amy Heckerling's quintessential early-'80s high school classic, is not on the soundtrack album. That omission aside, the companion to the Cameron Crowe–penned comedy rounds up offerings from a who's who of 1982 rock acts, including Sammy Hagar, Don Henley, Joe Walsh, the Go-Go's, Stevie Nicks, and more. It also gave Jackson Browne his highest-charting single ever, as his tender midtempo love song **Somebody's Baby** peaked at No. 7 in the US. *—AG*

Aretha Franklin
JUMP TO IT
ARISTA | Producer: Luther Vandross
RELEASED: JULY 26, 1982

● Three weeks in front of his own debut album, Luther Vandross came to Aretha Franklin's rescue after the Queen of Soul hit a nearly decade-long career skid. Pushing (and occasionally butting heads with) the esteemed singer, Vandross contemporized Franklin without diluting her power—and in some ways regaining it. The title track was Franklin's first Top 40 hit in six years and her first No. 1 R&B single in five, propelling her first gold album since 1982. And don't miss **I Wanna Make It Up to You**, a powerful summit with the Four Tops' Levi Stubbs. *—GG*

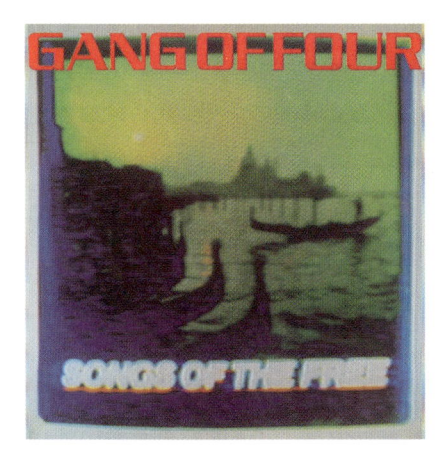

Gang of Four
SONGS OF THE FREE
EMI | Producers: Andy Gill, Mike Howlett, Jon King
RELEASED: MAY 1982

● Great change was afoot for Gang of Four on its third album. The post-punk British quartet welcomed bassist Sara Lee in place of co-founder Dave Allen, while new co-producer Mike Howlett helped steer the band in a slicker, funkier direction, with **I Love a Man in a Uniform** taking the band into the dance clubs in convincing fashion. Guitarist Andy Gill made the most of the expanded soundscape here, and Gang of Four didn't lose its strident political edge either, still railing and at times sloganeering against consumerism, militarism, bland nostalgia, and sexual politics. *—GG*

Kid Creole and the Coconuts
TROPICAL GANGSTERS
ZE / SIRE | Producer: August Darnell
RELEASED: MAY 10, 1982

● After two albums that were critically acclaimed but sales bombs, Kid Creole and the Coconuts achieved a breakthrough with what band leader August Darnell intended to be a solo album called *Wise Guy*. The eight-track *Tropical Gangsters* was more polished and focused than its predecessors but just as much fun, boasting joyous, island-invoking singles such as **I'm a Wonderful Thing, Baby**, **Stool Pigeon**, and **Annie, I'm Not Your Daddy**. It also gave the Creole gang some rare sales and chart success at home but particularly in the UK and Down Under. *—GG*

Sparks
ANGST IN MY PANTS
ATLANTIC | Producer: Reinhold Mack
RELEASED: MARCH 29, 1982

● The eleventh album by Sparks—brothers Russell (vocals) and Ron (keyboards) Mael—continued on the eclectic path of a career that ping-ponged from art rock to New Wave, avant-garde, and power pop, as well as clever, sweet, funny, profound, and nonsensical. **I Predict** was an anthemic chant and the duo's first single to chart. Subject matter ranged from a tribute to Mickey Mouse to an homage to Ron's moustache, with operetta and arena rock in the mix as well. Yet, due to the Maels' remarkable talents, it all worked. *—GP*

Little Steven and the Disciples of Soul
MEN WITHOUT WOMEN
EMI AMERICA | Producer: Steven Van Zandt
RELEASED: OCTOBER 1, 1982

● Between Bruce Springsteen, Southside Johnny & the Asbury Jukes, and Gary U.S. Bonds, Steven Van Zandt was on a roll during the early '80s. His initial Disciples of Soul, an all-star ensemble anchored by Rascals' drummer Dino Danelli and the La Bamba horn section (with E Street Band contributions as well), was an exciting and explosive soul-rock outfit with a harder rocking edge than the Jukes and a more pronounced sociopolitical outlook that preceded Van Zandt's "Sun City" initiative. Outstanding songs and ferocious ensemble playing made this an under-appreciated gem and a thrilling discovery well worth seeking out. *—GG*

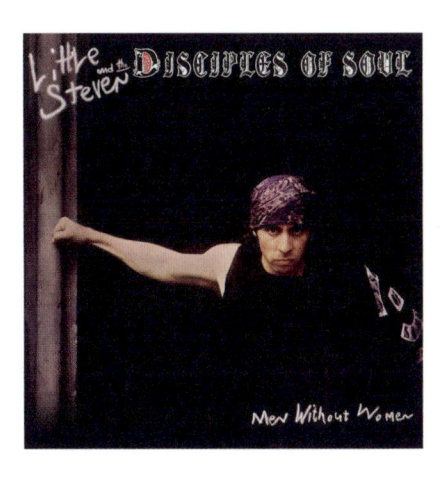

Grandmaster Flash & The Furious Five
THE MESSAGE

SUGAR HILL | Producers: Jigsaw Productions, Sylvia Robinson, Pat Thomas

RELEASED: OCTOBER 3, 1982

● **The Message**, the title rap on the debut album from Grandmaster Flash and the Furious Five, is among the most prescient tracks in the history of pop music. Ten years before the Los Angeles riots sparked by the beating of Rodney King by traffic cops and nearly four decades before the Black Lives Matter protests, ignited by the police murder of George Floyd, frontman Melle Mel chronicled four verses of urban despair and raps in slow, defiant fashion: "Don't push me 'cause I'm close to the edge."

The track was written by Melle Mel (Melvin Glover), Duke Bootee (Edward Gernel Fletcher), Clifton "Jiggs" Chase, and Sylvia Robinson. A former performer (Mickey & Sylvia's "Love Is Strange") and the founder of Sugar Hill Records, Robinson was one of the most influential women in the formative years of the male-dominated rap genre, who produced "Rapper's Delight" from the Sugarhill Gang as well as **The Message**.

Decades after its release, Melle Mel acknowledged, "We didn't actually want to do **The Message** because we [were] used to doing party raps and boasting how good we are and all that." And the Furious Five did those very well. **She's Fresh** opened the album with horn riffs that James Brown would love and a tale of a dancefloor infatuation set to a funky beat. **It's Nasty** offered great boastful wordplay. **Dreamin'** was a gentle groove dedicated to Stevie Wonder. In the context of this groundbreaking hip-hop album, the Christian pop of **You Are** was unexpected.

Beginning in 2004, reissues of *The Message* contained the 1981 single "The Adventures of Grandmaster Flash on the Wheels of Steel" as a bonus track, a seven-minute-plus DJ extravaganza whose samples included Chic's "Good Times," Blondie's "Rapture," and Queen's "Another One Bites the Dust" for an amazing sonic collage. —*TD*

1982

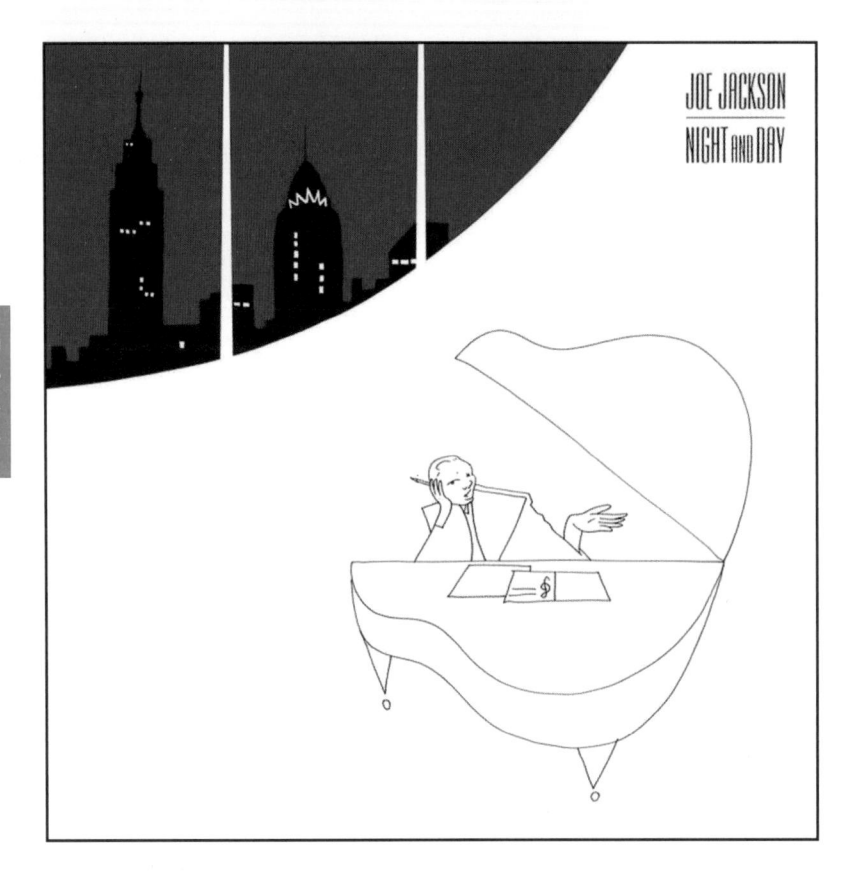

Joe Jackson
NIGHT AND DAY
A & M | Producers: Joe Jackson, David Kershenbaum
RELEASED: JUNE 25, 1982

● Along with Elvis Costello and Graham Parker, Joe Jackson was one of the "angry young men" of the British New Wave during the early '80s. By his fifth release, the sleek and stylish *Night and Day*, Jackson was full tilt into creating sophisticated popular music, and, in doing so, he utilized the album's title to pay tribute to the wit and urbane style of Cole Porter.

Although his genre-hopping began with 1980's *Beat Crazy*, it was on *Night and Day* that he really flexed his compositional chops, mixing cosmopolitan pop with jazz, salsa, Eastern sounds, and chamber music played by a tight, facile quartet of piano, percussion, vibes, and bass. Adopting New York City as his home, Jackson was inspired by its energy, rhythms, and mix of style and grittiness. As such, the album's nine tracks pulsed with dynamism of the city.

Steppin' Out, an homage to the glamour of Porter's New York with soul-lifting lyrics, twinkling piano flourishes, and stirring mechanical rhythms, was a smash on both sides of the Atlantic and Jackson's first Top 10 single (No. 6) in the US. It also scored a pair of Grammy Award nominations, including the prestigious Record of the Year. **Breaking Us in Two**, an achingly beautiful song about the battle between boredom and loneliness, was also Top 20, while **Real Men** offered a moving nod to New York's queer culture.

Thanks to those highlights, *Night and Day* was Jackson's highest-charting album (No. 4 on the Billboard 200) and a gold-certified success, a validation for an adventurous spirit that would continue to exert itself throughout his career. *—JC*

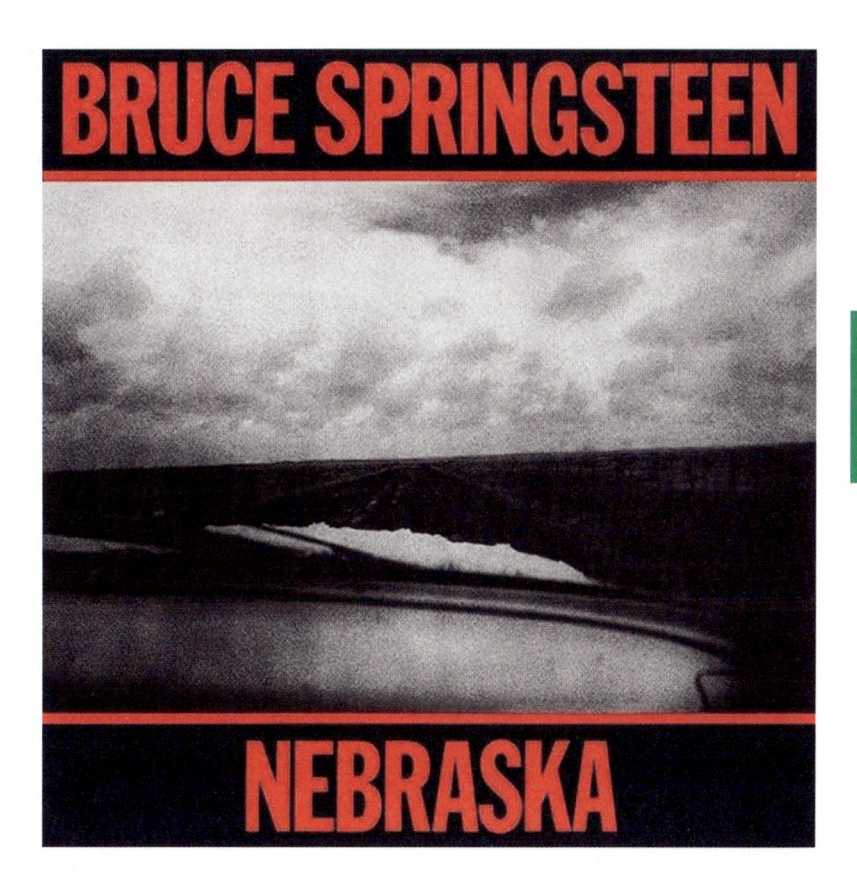

Bruce Springsteen
NEBRASKA

COLUMBIA | Producer: Bruce Springsteen
RELEASED: SEPTEMBER 30, 1982

● "I imagine America for a living, and I put it into a song," Bruce Springsteen once told a Stand Up for Heroes concert audience. But the America of Nebraska was a bleak landscape populated by non-heroes—killers, con men, and losers. In ten haunting tracks, he considered what happens when isolation, deprivation, or soul-crushing circumstance grind away hope of achieving the American Dream and replace it with desperation—or nihilism. Sung into a four-track recorder as demos, these stripped-down tunes were more intimate and personal than any he'd done before, what he called in his memoir Born to Run "an unknowing meditation on my childhood and its mysteries."

Also inspired by writers such as Flannery O'Connor and films like Badlands, Springsteen crafted taut character studies of murderer Charles Starkweather, an Atlantic City mobster, a state trooper who let his killer brother escape, and, in the final track, those who cling to irrational hope. But instead of merely depicting their struggles, for the first time, Springsteen examined what caused them, while seeking to exorcise some of his own demons.

After a trifecta of Top 5 albums, he'd earned the latitude to experiment and was rewarded when Nebraska reached No. 3 on the Billboard 200 chart. Its influence continues to reverberate across pop culture: Artists from Johnny Cash to Jason Isbell have covered Nebraska's songs, and in 2023 Springsteen himself cited it as his most definitive work. Deliver Me from Nowhere, a feature film based on Warren Zanes's book about the album, started production in 2024. —LM

Hall & Oates
H2O
RCA | Producers: Daryl Hall, John Oates, Neil Kernon
RELEASED: OCTOBER 4, 1982

● Beginning with 1980's *Voices*, Daryl Hall and John Oates unleashed a string of albums that spawned five of their six No. 1 hits and, aided by MTV, led to their sales-driven status as the most successful musical duo in history. *H2O* was the second of four consecutive Top 10 albums between 1981 and 1984, led by Hall & Oates's fifth No. 1 hit, **Maneater**. Written with Hall's longtime girlfriend, Sara Allen, the aural metaphor for New York City started with a bass riff from the Supremes' "You Can't Hurry Love," but Hall & Oates's harmony-drenched pop owed even more to Philly soul (where they formed in 1970) than to the Motown hit factory. *H2O*'s spacious **One on One** stood alongside "Sara Smile"; the duo's first chart-topper, it was a blue-eyed soul prototype with Hall's supple, seductive voice.

The rest of *H2O* further refined the sonic approach Hall & Oates began on *Voices*, using synthesizers, drum machines, and other studio technology to create a sleek modern bed that complemented the organic, soulful warmth of their melodies. While there was a sense of throwing everything against the wall to see what stuck, most of it did—in no small part due to the duo's tight corps of co-producer Neil Kernon and its regular backing band (guitarist G. E. Smith, bassist Tom "T-Bone" Wolk, drummer Mickey Curry, and saxophonist Charlie DeChant), plus programming from synthesizer whiz Larry Fast.

H2O was also highlighted by a solid rendition of Mike Oldfield's **Family Man**, which charted thirty-nine spots higher (No. 6) than his original released a few months earlier. **Art of Heartbreak** and **Open All Night** were fan-favored album tracks, and while a great deal of water went under the bridge leading up to Hall & Oates' split during the 2020s, *H2O* was an unquestioned high point. *—LM/GG*

1982

Michael Jackson
THRILLER

EPIC | Producers: Quincy Jones, Michael Jackson
RELEASED: NOVEMBER 29, 1982

● It's impossible to downplay the importance of Michael Jackson's *Thriller* on music, pop culture, and history. In many ways, there's everything before *Thriller*, and then everything after it. In a nutshell, the album changed the way we think about race, the way music is promoted, and the way a single record could dominate all walks of life. *Thriller* was a once-in-a-lifetime phenomenon that most likely could never happen again.

Is it the best album of the '80s? That's arguable. Is it the most significant record to be released during the decade? Unquestionably, yes.

Jackson had already released five solo albums since he became the eleven-year-old star of the Gary, Indiana–based Motown brother group the Jackson 5; his 1979 disco-pop record, *Off the Wall*, had taken him to another level of success. The creative team behind that album—producer Quincy Jones, songwriter Rod Temperton, and some of L.A.'s finest studio musicians—returned for *Thriller*. With contributions from Paul McCartney (the languid duet **The Girl Is Mine**) and Eddie Van Halen (whose blistering solo ignites **Beat It**), the album was a fair representation of the entire music scene in the early '80s.

Thriller was released in late November 1982; for the next two years, it dominated radio (seven singles, all Top 10), MTV (the **Billie Jean** video was credited with breaking down race barriers at the nascent music network), Billboard charts (the album was No. 1 for thirty-seven weeks), and the Grammy Awards (a record-breaking eight wins). It instantly became the best-selling album of all time, an honor it still holds. By the time the title song, *Thriller*'s final single, left the Hot 100 in the summer of 1984, Jackson was the biggest superstar on the planet. *Thriller*'s greater influence is immeasurable. —MG

1982

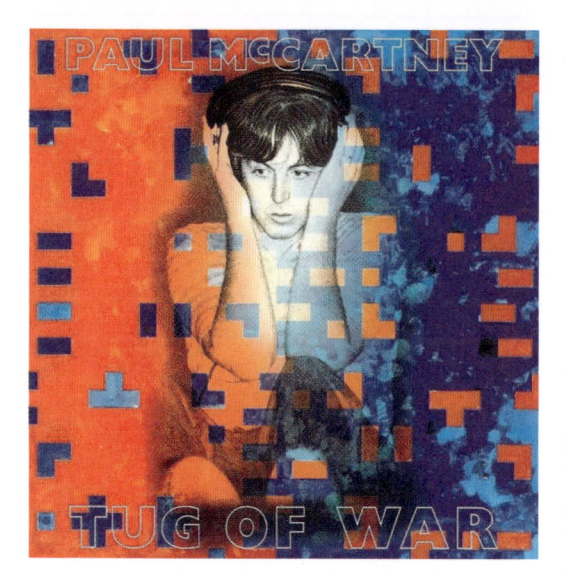

Paul McCartney
TUG OF WAR
COLUMBIA | Producer: George Martin
RELEASED: APRIL 26, 1982

● *Tug of War* was the third full-length record Paul McCartney released under just his own name, sans Wings or attribution to his wife, Linda. It was also McCartney's first release following the murder of John Lennon. Whether he felt pressure or not, the eyes of the musical world were on him. Throughout, *Tug of War* displays some of McCartney's best songcraft. It didn't hurt that Beatles cohort George Martin's gentle production hand made them outstanding records. **Wanderlust** and **Take It Away** would be standout tracks on any of his albums. Carl Perkins, a true hero to the Beatles, sat alongside McCartney to bring an authentic down-home feel that has been one of McCartney's lifelong objectives. **Ebony and Ivory**, however, did nothing to diminish criticism that Paul McCartney or Stevie Wonder were past their best days; its intention to bring people together was successful only in uniting them to slag it off. Their other collaboration, **What's That You're Doing**, was a powerful flex by two of the most important talents of their era that deserves more retrospective respect than it's been afforded. The big emotional moment is **Here Today**, McCartney's letter to Lennon. If you know the story, you'd better bring a handkerchief. *–HK*

The Jam
THE GIFT
POLYDOR | Producer(s): Peter Wilson, The Jam
RELEASED: MARCH 12, 1982

● "For those of you watching in black-and-white, this next one is in technicolor," a voice intones on the opening of *The Gift*, the Jam's sixth and final album. And technicolor it becomes when singer Paul Weller's unexpected scream leads into **Happy Together**, Bruce Foxton's funky bass lines, Rick Buckler's snappy percussion, and some Motown-style brass teaming with Weller's lyrical commentary about British life under Prime Minister Margaret Thatcher's rule. The plight of the working class was examined on **Just Who Is the 5 O'Clock Hero?** and **Town Called Malice**; the latter was the band's biggest US hit and No. 1 in its homeland, double-sided with the funkier **Precious**, a track more representative of Weller's future musical transition from the mod/punk attack of the Jam to the poppier Style Council, which Weller formed just three months after the Jam's final show. *The Gift*'s front cover depicted the band members in running stride, encased in traffic light colors (red, yellow, and green)—certainly prophetic, since the group broke up nine months later. *–HD*

Men at Work
BUSINESS AS USUAL
COLUMBIA | Producer: Peter McIan
RELEASED: APRIL 1982

● We'd heard plenty of music from Australia—the Bee Gees, Olivia Newton-John, AC/DC—but nothing nearly like Men at Work. The quintet came out of the country's gritty pub culture but retained a breezy and cheerful pop sensibility, mostly from frontman Colin Hay, as well as a wry sense of humor, especially in its videos. *Business as Usual* came out in the group's homeland six months before its US release, but Men at Work built its story with the chart-topping summer success of **Who Can It Be Now?** and a fortuitous opening spot on Fleetwood Mac's tour, which put the band in front of a decidedly mainstream audience. The Australia-advocating **Down Under** was another No. 1 hit, while other tracks (**I Can See It in Your Eyes, Underground, Be Good Johnny**) showed depth, and the seven-minute album closer **Down by the Sea** displayed a more ambitious musical stretch. All that took *Business as Usual* to No. 1 on the Billboard 200 and six-times-platinum sales, along with a Grammy Award for Best New Artist. "We are the Men, and we'll see you again," Hay said that night—and they did, albeit for only two more albums. *–GG*

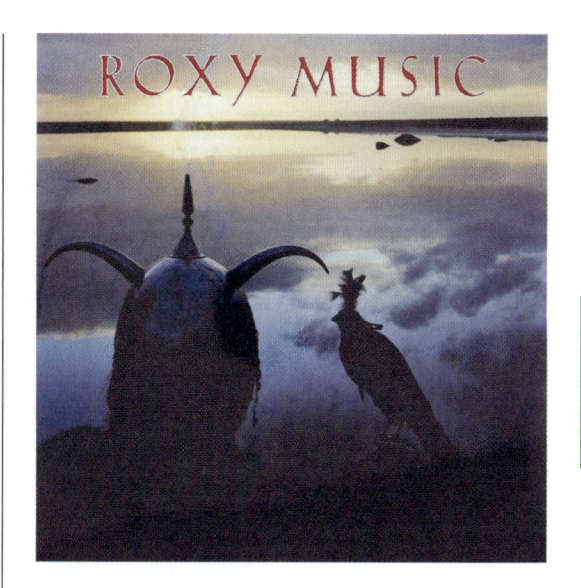

Roxy Music
AVALON
WARNER BROS. | Producers: Rhett Davies, Roxy Music
RELEASED: MAY 28, 1982

● Representing the culmination of Roxy Music's evolution from glammy art-rock to sophisticated ambient pop, *Avalon*, the band's eighth and final studio album, set the bar for much of the '80s music that followed, from ABC to Spandau Ballet and, of course, Duran Duran. Brian Ferry's elegant vocals and lush synthesizer textures, perfectly balanced by Phil Manzanera's never-overdone guitar and Andy Mackay's melodic saxophone flourishes, infused an airy sensuality into *Avalon*'s jazz- and soul-inflected dance-pop rhythms and dreamy soundscapes with an uncommon unity. Setting the tone with Ferry's wistful yet wishful **More Than This**, *Avalon* peaked with the seductive title tune, one of the most gorgeous in all of pop music—climaxed by Haitian singer Yanick Etienne's wordless aria. Ferry rightly considered *Avalon*, inspired by the enchanted isle of Arthurian legend, as his most romantic album. It took ten years for it to reach platinum status in the US, but it continues to reach new ears. Inducting Roxy into the Rock & Roll Hall of Fame, Duran Duran's John Taylor observed, "The name Brian Ferry has become a synonym for cool." Indeed. *–LM*

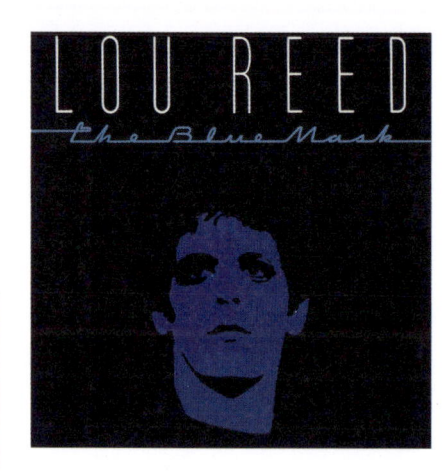

Lou Reed
THE BLUE MASK
RCA | Producers: Lou Reed, Sean Fullan
RELEASED: FEBRUARY 23, 1982

● Ambient jazz poet was an underrated aspect of Lou Reed's diverse artistic identity. That guise was most evident on *The Blue Mask*, which whipsawed between primal rage and leisurely, atmospheric songs not too far removed from Joni Mitchell during her Jaco Pastorius period (props to bassist Fernando Saunders as well as Robert Quine, one of Reed's best guitar foils). Reed tried to pass himself off as an **Average Guy** who loves **Women**, but the title track made clear he was still torn. The tension made for one of his best latter-day classics. —*DM*

Stray Cats
BUILT FOR SPEED
EMI AMERICA | Producers: Dave Edmunds, Stray Cats, Hein Hoven Producers
RELEASED: JUNE 1982

● America got rockin' big time with *Built for Speed*, a compilation from Stray Cats' two UK albums. The rockabilly trio from Long Island, led by the pompadoured Brian Setzer and his stunning guitar style and energy, captured fans with its combination of retro style and modern attitude, as well as heavy rotation on MTV. **Rock This Town** and **Stray Cat Strut** sped up the charts, while the rest of the album was solid enough to drive the twelve-song set to platinum status. —*MH*

The Time
WHAT TIME IS IT?
WARNER BROS. | Producers: Morris Day, The Starr Company (which means Prince)
RELEASED: AUGUST 25, 1982

● Prince seemed incapable of not writing infectious songs, even while working on more ambitious material for albums such as *1999* and *Purple Rain*. So, he hired Morris Day to front the Time, which, in one of music's worst-kept secrets, was just Prince writing every song and playing every instrument while Day sang and sometimes played drums. Even then, Prince couldn't help but grow creatively, as the "group's" second album featured denser grooves and a wider range of material and moods than its debut. —*MW*

Vangelis
BLADE RUNNER (ORIGINAL MOTION PICTURE SOUNDTRACK)
ATLANTIC | Producer: Vangelis
RELEASED: JUNE 25, 1982 (IN THEATERS)

● We know, we know . . . Vangelis's groundbreaking score for Ridley Scott's 1982 sci-fi hit wasn't formally released until 1994. But we include it here because it was so original and influential that it brought aspiring music makers back to theaters time and again to listen to it. Blending electronic chill, jazz and classical melodies, and Middle Eastern textures, it was a new way of considering musical alchemy in a manner that opened ears to a great many possibilities, especially in the realm that became the wide umbrella of electronica. *—GG*

Various Artists
THE SECRET POLICEMAN'S OTHER BALL—THE MUSIC
ISLAND | Producer: Martin Lewis
RELEASED: 1982

● This was the second release of music from Amnesty International's annual fundraising event and gathered performances from several different shows during the late '70s and early '80s. The focus of the event was comedy, but the UK's finest musicians lined up to participate. Former Yardbirds members Eric Clapton and Jeff Beck teamed for a rare set together, trading leads on three of each other's best-known songs, while Police frontman Sting stepped out for the first time as a solo performer and mesmerized with his versions of the Police's **Roxanne** and **Message in a Bottle**. *—HK*

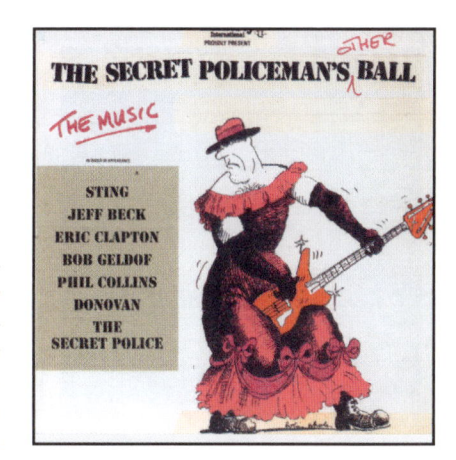

Yazoo
UPSTAIRS AT ERIC'S
MUTE | Producers: E. C. Radcliffe, Yazoo
RELEASED: AUGUST 16, 1982

● The debut album from the British duo Yazoo was a touchstone in synth-pop's ascendance. *Upstairs at Eric's* wove a sonic tapestry that juxtaposed Vince Clarke's keyboards alongside Alison Moyet's strong and soulful vocals. Fresh out of Depeche Mode, Clarke's modern beats and synthetic melodies provided a perfect contrast to Moyet's brooding delivery on **Only You** and **Situation**, while the pulsating **Don't Go** became a dance club staple. Started as an experiment, Yazoo created a seminal new blend of synthesized melodies that influenced subsequent generations of other artists. *—SS*

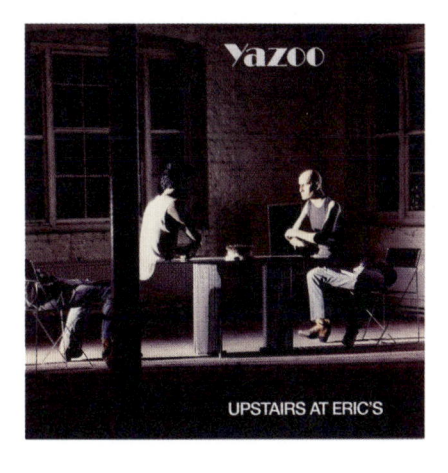

George Strait
STRAIT FROM THE HEART

MCA | Producer: Blake Mevis
RELEASED: JUNE 3, 1982

● There's no telling who actually gave him the title, but George Strait is the acknowledged King of Country. And this sophomore album was his coronation.

The hat-wearing, guitar-playing singer and occasional songwriter from Texas certainly staked a claim with his 1981 debut, *Strait Country*, which had three Top 20 genre hits and was certified platinum. But there was something decidedly more potent and forceful about *Strait from the Heart* that even the album cover attested to. On *Strait Country*, he looked young and apprehensive, but on *Strait from the Heart*, he leaned against a rail with model-caliber assurance. It was as if Strait knew exactly what was in the groove.

And it was good—no, make that great—stuff. As it still goes in Nashville, the success of *Strait Country* brought even better songs Strait's way, and he and producer Blake Mevis were adept at picking the best of them. The album clocked in at less than twenty-nine minutes but housed four Top 10 country hits, including his first chart-topper, **Fool Hearted Memory**, and Strait's second, **A Fire I Can't Put Out**. Perhaps more importantly, it had **Amarillo by Morning**, a Terry Stafford/Paul Fraser track that Strait has long identified as the best song he ever recorded and a triple-platinum single in its own right.

Also notable were **I Can't See Texas from Here**, which was Strait's first-ever released own composition, and the tasteful selection of Guy Clark's **Heartbroke**.

Strait's career skyrocketed from here and to an iconic stature that was still filling stadiums on his continuing farewell tour more than four decades later. And the septuagenarian was still wearing his wranglers as tight then as he did on the cover of *Strait from the Heart*. **—GG**

1982

Richard & Linda Thompson
SHOOT OUT THE LIGHTS

HANNIBAL | Producer: Joe Boyd
RELEASED: MARCH 15, 1982

● Richard and Linda Thompson's decade-old marriage was falling apart when they started recording their sixth album together during late 1981. The British folk-rock paragons had met in 1969 when he was a member of Fairport Convention and she was a budding singer going by the name Linda Peters. Their relationship sealed when she contributed backing vocals to his 1972 solo debut, *Henry the Human Fly*. They were married later that year and released their first album as a couple, *I Want to See the Bright Lights Tonight*, in 1974.

But as the recording of *Shoot Out the Lights* concluded, Linda was pregnant with the couple's second child, so Richard committed to a solo acoustic tour in the States, where he began a relationship that resulted in the Thompsons' separation. But the cracks were already showing by then, as heard in standout songs **Don't Renege on Our Love**, **Walking on a Wire**, and the title track. By the time the album was released in March 1982, the marriage was over.

Shoot Out the Lights was a breakup album at heart, a dialogue between the fractured couple with symbolism substituting for directness across the eight tracks. "She was broken in a hundred pieces when her body was found," Linda sang on the brooding **Did She Jump or Was She Pushed**, the only song on the album where she receives a co-writing credit with her husband. The record is neither one-sided nor places blame for the splintering; it matter-of-factly details a relationship that has run its course. On the closing **Wall of Death**, the Thompsons, singing together, likened their shared uncertainty to a carnival ride, taking chances and moving on. It's a fitting end to both the album and their union. **—MG**

Toto
TOTO IV
COLUMBIA | Producers: Toto
RELEASED: APRIL 8, 1982

● Toto was under the gun when it came time to make the band's fourth album. Its two predecessors failed to match the success of the band's self-titled 1978 debut, and Columbia Records was threatening to drop the group if it didn't come up with a hit—an ignominious situation for young but still veteran players with the enormous chops and session credentials of Toto's members. It was yellow brick road or bust this time out.

And Toto did what it had to do—hunkered down and spent many months, and a considerable amount of money, crafting what would be the band's masterwork. *IV* was a Top 5 multiplatinum outing that spawned major hits (**Rosanna**, **Africa**) and won three Grammy Awards, including Album of the Year. The songs were written and arranged with the precision of science projects, and the sonics were buffed to a lush, gleaming perfection. And Toto got by with a little help from its friends, musical luminaries from Chicago (James Pankow), Eagles (Timothy B. Schmit), countless session hands, and even the band members' own musician fathers.

Amid the polish—did pop get more middle-of-the-road than **I Won't Hold You Back** or **We Made It**, after all?—were some fine performances, particularly by guitarist Steve Lukather. Take **Rosanna** for instance, on which his fills and solos added muscle that elevated the track. The gentle polyrhythms of **Africa**, meanwhile, sounded genuinely fresh on Top 40 radio. *IV* would be Toto's true peak, but it cemented the group's validity status for decades.

Interestingly, some of the band members were concurrently playing sessions for Michael Jackson's *Thriller*, which lent a bit of extra credibility to the album that would take over the world in *IV*'s wake. *—GG*

1983

83

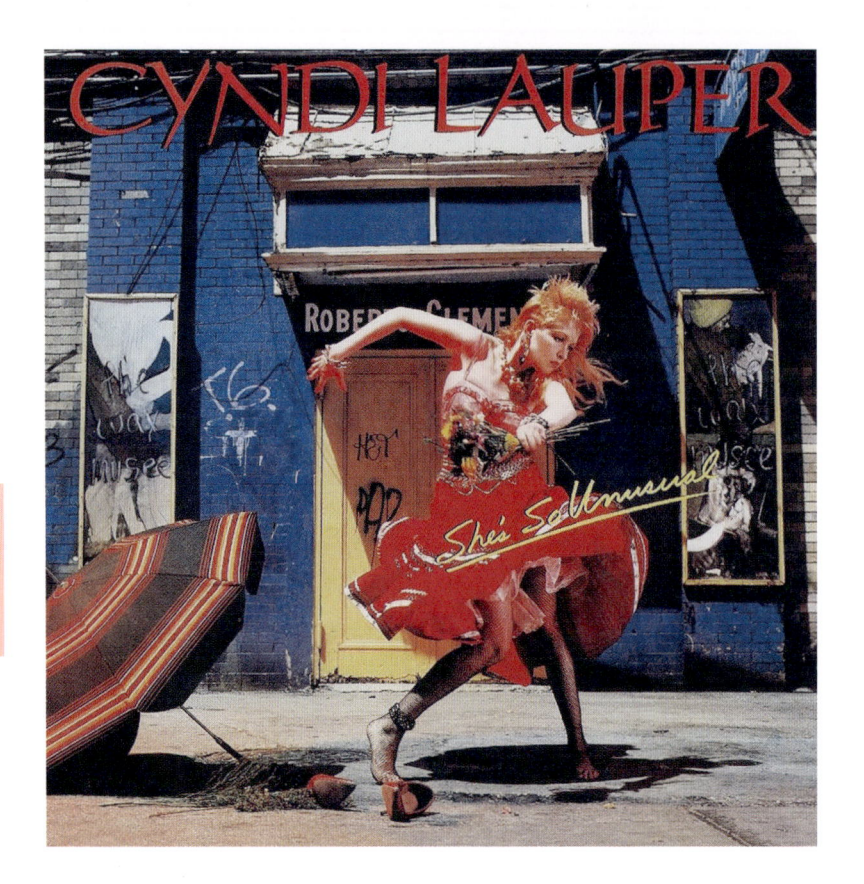

Cyndi Lauper
SHE'S SO UNUSUAL

PORTRAIT | Producer: Rick Chertoff
RELEASED: OCTOBER 14, 1983

● Cyndi Lauper's career had bottomed out before it even got a chance to go anywhere. Her band Blue Angel released a self-titled debut LP in 1980 but sold few copies, and the group soon broke up. Making matters worse, Blue Angel's manager sued Lauper, who had to declare bankruptcy. To make ends meet, the native New Yorker with a distinctive voice worked several jobs, including performing club shows around the city. It was one of these gigs that led to a solo recording deal in 1982; by mid-1983, she was recording *She's So Unusual* with members of the Philadelphia pop-rock band the Hooters.

The album wasn't an immediate hit. But its mix of bouncy New Wave and elastic synth-pop eventually caught on, thanks in no small part to MTV, which put the jovial video for the album's first single, **Girls Just Want to Have Fun**, into heavy rotation. It wasn't long before the rest of the album's quirky, catchy appeal revealed itself to a larger audience.

Leading with the glimmering **Money Changes Everything** (like most of *She's So Unusual*, a relatively obscure cover song), the record wasted no time dispensing its best tracks: **Girls**, a cover of Prince's **When You Were Mine**, and the No. 1 ballad **Time after Time**, co-written by Lauper, rounded out side 1. (Two additional hit singles were found on the album's other side.) *She's So Unusual*'s first four marked the first time a woman charted that many songs in the Top 5 from the same LP. Lauper was one of music's biggest stars by the time the album peaked at No. 4 during the first half of 1984. It's lost none of its charm after all these years. —*MG*

1983

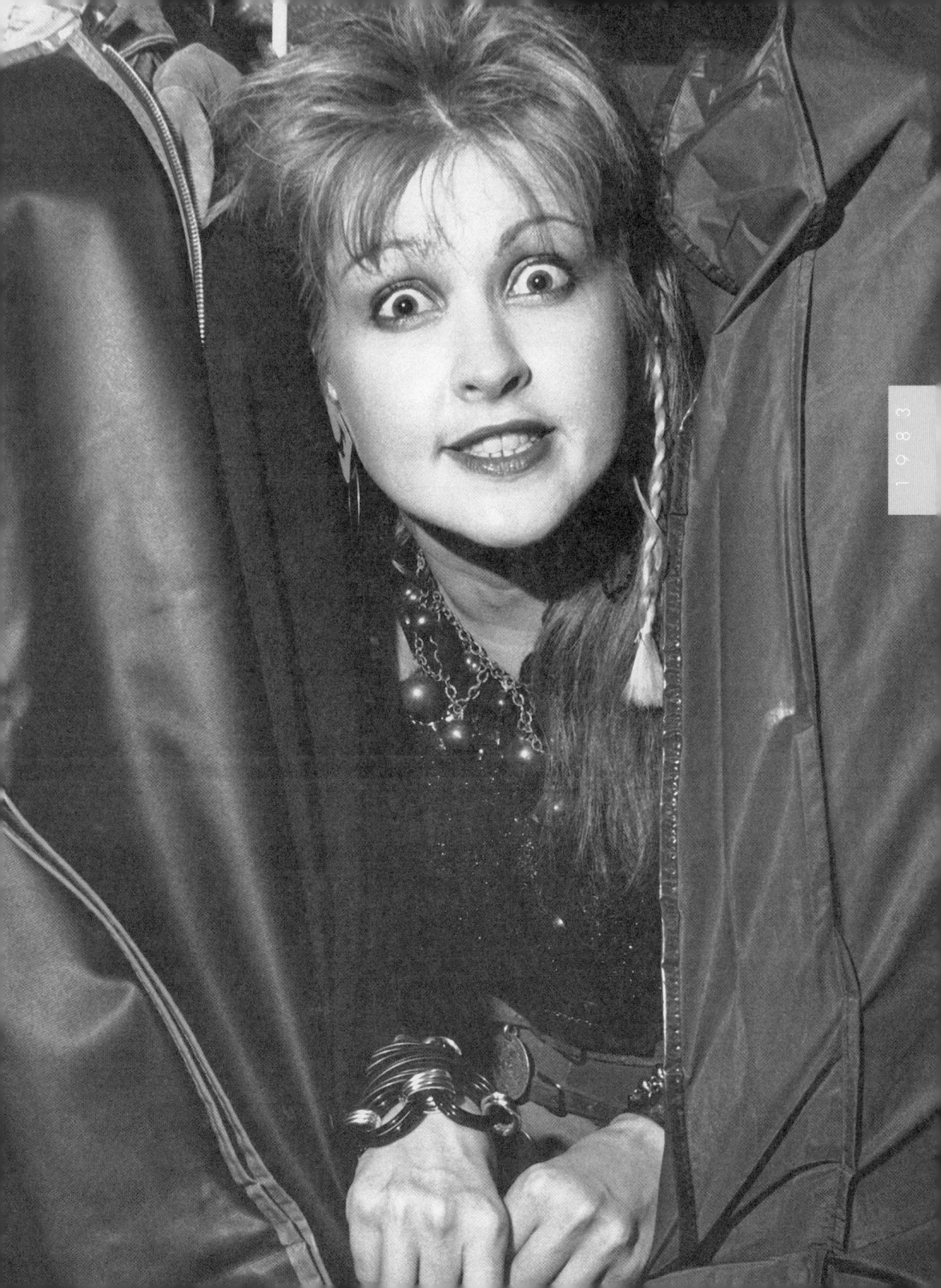

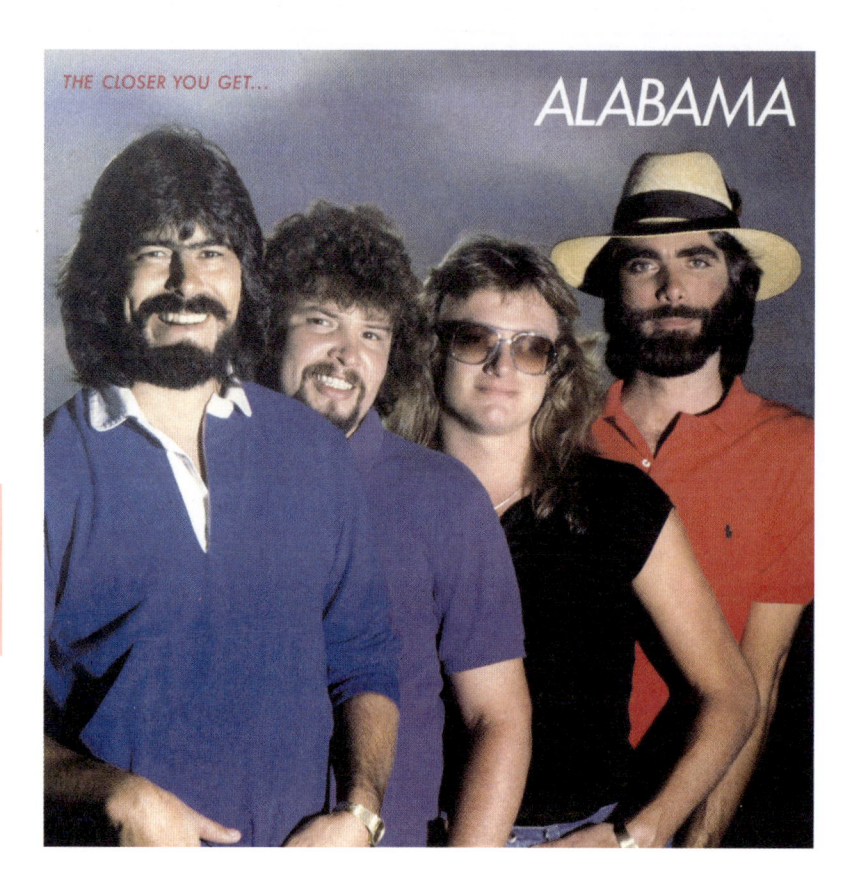

Alabama
THE CLOSER YOU GET

RCA NASHVILLE | Producers: Alabama, Harold Shedd
RELEASED: MARCH 1983

● Whether it was labeled as mountain music, Dixieland delight, or country, Alabama found its groove in the '80s. The quartet leaned further into a pop-friendly sound with the ten tracks on its seventh studio album, *The Closer You Get*. Cousins Randy Owen, Teddy Gentry, and Jeff Cook had played together for years, and the family connection shined through on their tight harmonies. Drummer Mark Herndon rounded things out with his distinctive beat—especially memorable on the title track.

The band blended traditional country with elements of Southern rock, bluegrass, and folk music and crafted a sound steeped in its Lookout Mountain roots. Even though Alabama had begun to see crossover success in the easy listening market, its music was still steeped in the Deep South. **Dixieland Delight** was a prime example, with its washboard-rhythm intro and slow, drawling lyrics. The song became a tradition at that most Southern of institutions—football—and is still played between quarters during University of Alabama games.

Owen, Gentry, and Cook were all accomplished vocalists and multi-instrumentalists (there was, in fact, a fiddle in the band) and smoothly traded playing and singing duties. The gospel-tinged **Lady Down on Love** showcased their talents and became the third track from the record to top the Billboard Hot Country Singles chart. The group had a knack for finding songs that fit its style and told relatable stories. **The Closer You Get** became one of its most recognizable hits—to the point where few people remember that the song was originally released by Exile as a pop single in 1980.

With *The Closer You Get*, Alabama solidified its role as a pioneer of country bands. There would be no Little Big Town if Alabama hadn't blazed the trail from Dixie to points well beyond the Mason-Dixon Line. —SS

Huey Lewis and the News
SPORTS
CHRYSALIS | Producers: Huey Lewis and the News
RELEASED: SEPTEMBER 15, 1983

● Huey Lewis and the News had a clear mission statement when it began working on its third studio album. "We need a frickin' hit," Lewis said on the occasion of the set's thirtieth anniversary. "It was our last record in our contract, and so far the label hadn't made any money on us. We needed hits, big hits. . . . It had to happen." And it did. *Sports* was a juggernaut that went seven-times platinum, hit No. 1 on the Billboard 200, and spawned four Top 10 hits—**Heart and Soul, I Want a New Drug, The Heart of Rock & Roll**, and **If This Is It**. Buoyed by clever, good-humored videos and the San Francisco sextet's relentless touring, it was an inescapable force that defied resistance.

It didn't come easy, of course. Even beyond the arduous writing Lewis and his News mates, particularly Johnny Colla, did for the album, the group was dealing with the purchase of its label by CBS Music, whose commitment to the News was unknown; Lewis even stashed the tapes under his bed for safekeeping while the band stayed on tour. When the business logistics worked themselves out, however, the powers that be felt the power of love for *Sports*; no less than ace promotions man Frank Dileo, Michael Jackson's future manager, pronounced, "I don't think you got to worry, kid."

Sports was sleek but not slick, filled with hooks and gentle touches of state-of-the-art technology but without losing the performance grit the News had honed in dozens of smoky venues, or the classic influences of the Beatles and Beale Street, Stax, and Motown. Sometimes **Bad Is Bad**, one song declared, but the fact was *Sports* was a winner from start to finish that's insured the News is still fresh even after Ménière's disease took Lewis out of commission in 2018. —*GG*

David Bowie
LET'S DANCE
EMI AMERICA | Producers: David Bowie, Nile Rodgers
RELEASED: APRIL 14, 1983

● Ever the master of self-reinvention, David Bowie outdid himself with *Let's Dance*, graduating from respected art-rocker to mass-appeal megastar. With Nile Rodgers of Chic fame co-producing, Bowie picked up where *Young Americans* left off, churning soul-R&B influences into pop-funk, dance club classics. The honchos at his new record label, EMI, looked like geniuses for placing a $17 million bet on him when the album reached Top 5 chart status in fourteen countries. Moving copies faster than any EMI title since *Sgt. Pepper's Lonely Hearts Club Band* and becoming the bestseller of his career, *Let's Dance* finally gave Bowie commercial success equal to his artistic influence.

The first of three MTV-aided global hits, the title track became the top-selling single of his career. Opening with a lift of the Beatles' "Twist and Shout" ending, it spun into a funky bass-and-horn tornado, punctuated by then-unknown Stevie Ray Vaughan's bluesy guitar solo and Bowie's vocals—which climaxed each time his lover trembled like a flower. The album opening **Modern Love**, meanwhile, rode a call-and-response Little Richard homage on which Bowie whipped pessimism about faith and love into a rave-up with Baptist revival fervor.

Sandwiched in between was **China Girl**, Bowie's quirky reworking of an earlier Iggy Pop collaboration that helped boost Iggy's stature, though it might not fly today. On a cover of British band Metro's **Criminal World**, Bowie altered its bisexually suggestive lyrics just as he started denying he'd ever engaged in same-sex dalliances (amid the growing AIDS pandemic) and dropped his androgynous personae for a debonair "hipster CEO" style.

Bowie would later claim this commercial success hurt him artistically, launching a creatively weak period he dismissed as his "Phil Collins years"—which seemed, then and now, disingenuous. To reenergize his music and career, he formed the more experimental and aggressive rock band Tin Machine. *—LM*

1983

Aztec Camera
HIGH LAND, HARD RAIN
ROUGH TRADE | Producers: John Brand, Bernie Clarke
RELEASED: APRIL 1, 1983

● *High Land, Hard Rain*, the highly acclaimed first album from Scotland's Aztec Camera, was primarily a vehicle for singer/songwriter/guitarist Roddy Frame to showcase his formidable skills. Frame hit the ground running with the first track and hit single **Oblivious**, featuring flamenco-inspired guitar work. Lyrics on the album were primarily poetic odes to love, both lost and found. Mostly ballads, the flavors ranged from English folk to bossa nova to country and western. This record also displayed a musical maturity, well beyond the band's teenage years. —*GP*

Various Artists
THE BIG CHILL (ORIGINAL MOTION PICTURE SOUNDTRACK)
MOTOWN | Producers: Various
RELEASED: SEPTEMBER 8, 1983

● *The Big Chill* soundtrack album contained a tasty sampler of the timeless '60s and '70s songs used in the 1983 film to create the characters' sense of nostalgia when they reunite for a weekend. The Motown label was strongly represented with half of the LP's ten tracks, from the Temptations, Smokey Robinson & the Miracles, and Marvin Gaye. The album went six-times platinum and, along with the landmark TV special *Motown 25: Yesterday, Today, Forever*, which aired a few months prior, helped to repopularize the Motown sound for a new era. —*JC*

Various Artists
CATS: COMPLETE ORIGINAL BROADWAY CAST RECORDING
GEFFEN | Producer: Andrew Lloyd Webber
RELEASED: JANUARY 26, 1983

● Joke all you want about "the dancing cats"; the Tony and Olivier Award–winning musical, based on T. S. Eliot poems, is one of Andrew Lloyd Webber's most ambitious and enduring works and home to some of his best songs, including the signature track **Memory**. The Broadway cast boasted stars such as Betty Buckley, Kenneth Ard, Donna King, and Terrence Mann, whose performances helped win this a Grammy Award for Best Cast Show album. *Cats* remains a theater favorite and, as of this writing, is nowhere close to its ninth life. —*GG*

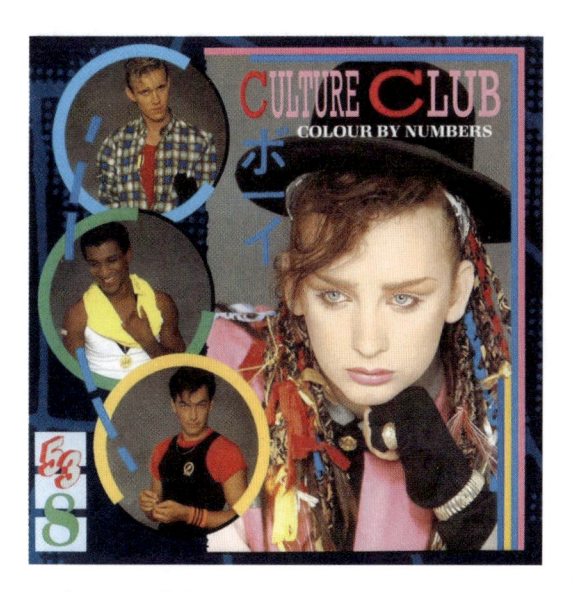

Culture Club
COLOUR BY NUMBERS
EPIC | Producer: Steve Levine
RELEASED: OCTOBER 10, 1983

● The adage of if it isn't broke, don't fix it certainly pertained to Culture Club's sophomore album. Almost a year to the day after releasing its platinum debut, *Kissing to Be Clever*, Boy George and company were still doing what they did best—blue-eyed soul-infused pop songs that had more hooks than a bait and tackle shop. The UK group's members have said they consider *Colour by Numbers* their best work, and the case can certainly be made that it's more consistent and even a touch more daring than its predecessor. **Karma Chameleon** is still a bit of an eye-roller, but there's no denying it's been an enduring signature staple for the band. **Church of the Poison Mind**, with Helen Terry's roof-raising counterpoints, was more potent lyrically and musically, however. **It's a Miracle** and **Miss Me Blind** were frothy fun, while George bolstered his diva cred on **Victims** and **Black Money**. *Colour by Numbers* gave Culture Club its only No. 1 album at home, went four-times platinum in the US, and sold more than 10 million copies worldwide—deserved success for a set that was anything but a sophomore slump. —GG

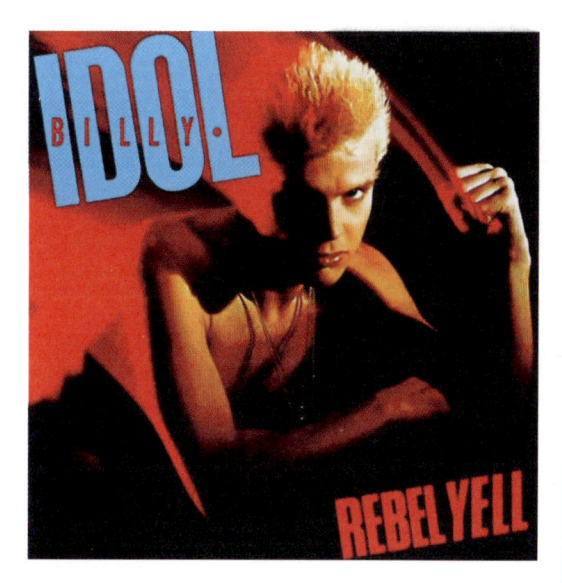

Billy Idol
REBEL YELL
CHRYSALIS | Producer: Keith Forsey
RELEASED: NOVEMBER 10, 1983

● Billy Idol fully transcended his punk rocker reputation with his career-defining second solo album, *Rebel Yell*. The former Generation X frontman had pushed forward with the hit "White Wedding" off his eponymous self-named debut release, but he pushed even further into the rock mainstream the next time out. On **Rebel Yell**, he and his primary musical partner, guitarist Steve Stevens, created an extremely listenable, slickly produced release which combined pop, rock, and New Wave, blending synthesizers, Stevens's screaming guitars, and, of course, Idol's lusty, unabashedly dramatic and versatile vocals. Four singles were released, including his first Top 10 US hit, **Eyes without a Face**, a dark, dreamy power ballad delivered with as much croon as snarl. *Rebel Yell*'s other charting singles included the grooving anthem **Flesh for Fantasy**, the sax-laden pop tune **Catch My Fall**, and the title track, which perfectly encapsulated the gusto and bluster that was Idol's stock in trade. Thanks to those hits and heavy MTV airplay, *Rebel Yell* rose to No. 6 on the Billboard 200 chart and went on to double-platinum sales status in the US while totally transitioning Idol to pop/rock stardom. —JC

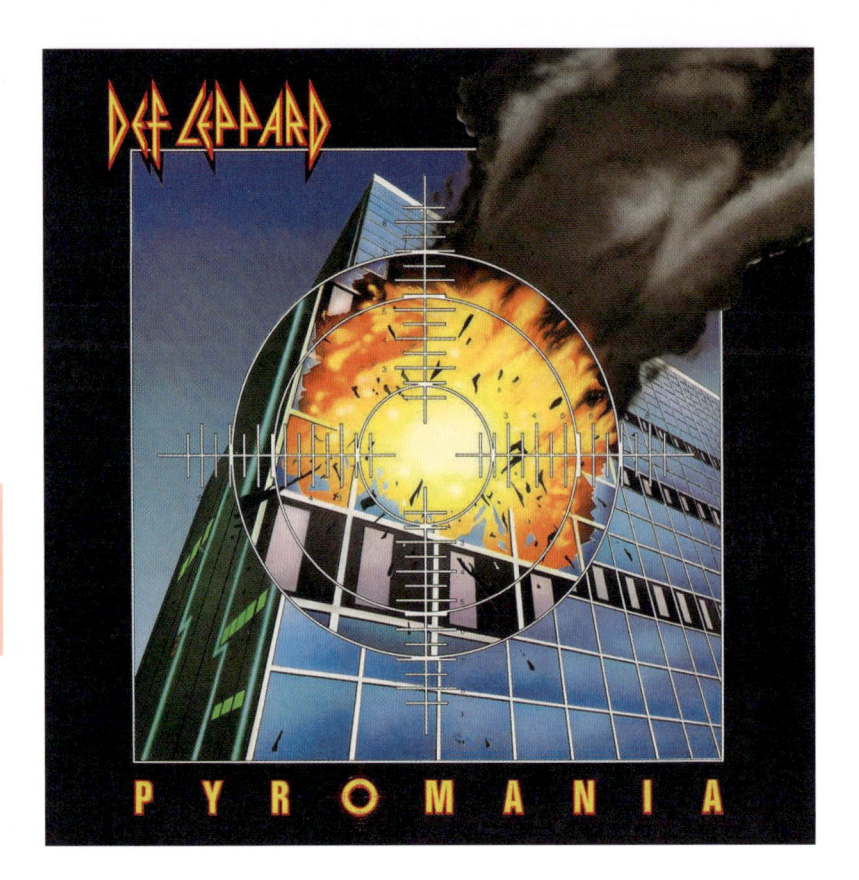

Def Leppard
PYROMANIA
VERTIGO | Producer: Robert John "Mutt" Lange
RELEASED: JANUARY 20, 1983

● Nothing on Def Leppard's first two albums pointed to its future as one of the biggest rock bands in the world in just a few short years. But the arrival of album three during the first month of 1983 changed that: *Pyromania* quickly rocketed up the charts and set a brand-new standard for heavy rock music in the '80s. While producer Robert John "Mutt" Lange worked on the group's previous album, 1981's *High 'n' Dry*, he and the band's pivot toward more pop-oriented sounds, coupled with new forms of recording, put a distinctive stamp on their respective projects over the next decade.

Pyromania marked a transitional period for the inner workings of Def Leppard, too. Original guitarist Pete Willis was fired during the making of the album because of his increasingly debilitating drinking; he was replaced by Phil Collen, who shared credit on the finished album with his predecessor. The group also approached the studio in a new way, thanks to Lange's input. All of the guitars and bass parts were recorded using drum machine click tracks, which gave the songs metronomic rhythms better suited to Top 40 radio.

In the end, *Pyromania* was a mix of the polished heavy metal heard on Def Leppard's first two albums paired with more stylized pop melodies. But it was the latter that carried the band into a whole new stratosphere and all that anyone talked about. With **Photograph**, **Rock of Ages**, and **Foolin'** netting heavy MTV airplay, the group found itself with its first US chart hits, including a monster No. 2 album. It's no surprise *Pyromania* is still talked about: The crisp, catchy music was radio-ready and at the vanguard of pop-metal's popularity during the mid-'80s. It was the spark that lit a fire. *–MG*

1983

Cybotron
ENTER
FANTASY | Producers: Juan Atkins, Richard Davis
RELEASED: 1983

● From the minds of two young men came what is considered the beginning of Detroit techno when they gathered up a few electronic devices combined with their futuristic vision. Cybotron was a euphoric electro-funk pop collaboration that changed the course of music forever. Songs such as **Clear** and **Cosmic Cars** took blended Kraftwerk and Funkadelic vibes that put the soul into the machine by using catchy synths, robotic words, and body-moving beats, a simple yet complex formula that made *Enter* a musical gem and a key part of music history. *—MH*

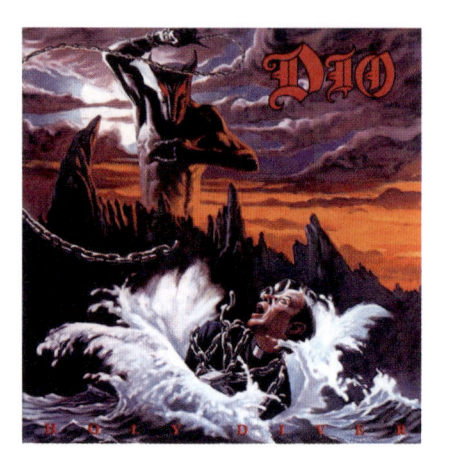

Dio
HOLY DIVER
WARNER BROS. | Producer: Ronnie James Dio
RELEASED: MAY 25, 1983

● After creative differences brought Ronnie James Dio's brief but fruitful first stint with Black Sabbath to a sudden halt, the former Rainbow singer launched his own band along with fellow Sabbath refugee Vinny Appice. Dio struck gold with the recruitment of a relatively unknown guitarist named Vivian Campbell; even at this early stage, the future Def Leppard guitarist blended technical mastery with impeccable taste on tracks such as **Rainbow in the Dark**. *Holy Diver* and 1984's *The Last in Line* cemented Dio's legacy in heavy rock's gold standard. *—MW*

Brian Eno
APOLLO: ATMOSPHERES AND SOUNDTRACKS
E.G. | Producers: Brian Eno, Daniel Lanois
RELEASED: JULY 29, 1983

● Brian Eno covered a lot of ground in the ambient sound sphere that became his domain after leaving Roxy Music in 1973. *Apollo: Atmospheres and Soundtracks*—composed for the documentary *For All Mankind*, which didn't surface until six years later—was a fully realized, tightly contextualized soundscape by Eno, his brother Roger, and Canadian colleague Daniel Lanois that cast the Apollo 11 moon landing in the quiet of space rather than the bombast of "big news" while giving it some country flavors thanks to Lanois's pedal steel. A quiet but captivating pleasure. *—GG*

ESG
COME AWAY WITH ESG
99 | Producer: Ed Bahlman
RELEASED: 1983

● ESG (aka Emerald, Sapphire & Gold) did a lot with a little on its debut album. The four Scroggins sisters from the South Bronx came into studio with bass, congas, drums, and vocalist Renee's guitar, the latter so spare it was barely detectable. Deborah's bass was the propelling force on these eleven tracks (most three minutes or under), leading a minimalist, trancey kind of funk that didn't need sonic accoutrement to make its impact. An album that made its mark more as influence, in multiple genres, than in its moment. —GG

Quiet Riot
METAL HEALTH
PASHA | Producer: Spencer Proffer
RELEASED: FEBRUARY 28, 1983

● *Metal Health* was the first heavy metal album to reach No. 1 on the Billboard 200 chart. That led to big record labels investing in similar-sounding bands, many of whom rocketed to stardom while Quiet Riot's own fortunes faltered. This left the group with the dual titles of industry pioneer and one-hit wonder. Obviously, much of the album's success was due to its excellent cover of Slade's **Cum On Feel the Noize**. But its own **Metal Health** is almost if not equally as great, and the album is packed with catchy, enjoyable hooks and riffs. —MW

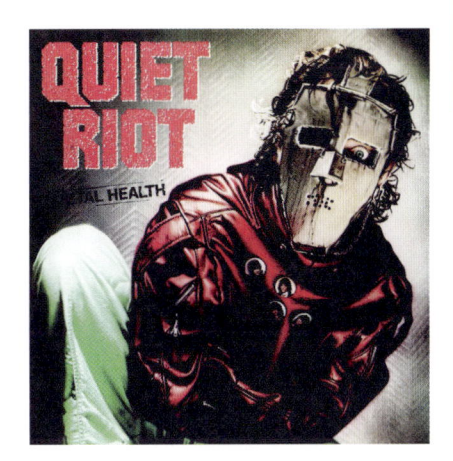

Various Artists
FLASHDANCE (ORIGINAL MOTION PICTURE SOUNDTRACK)
CASABLANCA/POLYGRAM | Producers: Giorgio Moroder, Pete Bellotte, Phil Ramone, Ronald Magness, Keith Olsen, Michael Sembello
RELEASED: APRIL 11, 1983

● The *Flashdance* soundtrack was a potpourri of songs chosen to propel the film's theme of an underdog chasing her dreams. The rock/disco concept included upbeat offerings from Laura Branigan, Kim Carnes, and others. The pulsating synthesizer beats and expansive chords captured the essence of the era and was central to the storyline. Most notable were **Maniac** by Michael Sembello, and the title track, **Flashdance . . . What a Feeling**, performed by Irene Cara, the film's central anthem that, much like ripped sweatshirts and leg warmers, became forever associated with the '80s. —SS

Eurythmics
SWEET DREAMS (ARE MADE OF THIS)

R C A | Producers: David A. Stewart, Adam Williams, Robert Crash
RELEASED: JANUARY 4, 1983

● Dave Stewart and Annie Lennox first met in 1975 and soon started a romantic and creative relationship. The first band they joined, the Tourists, achieved a moderate level of success, but Stewart and Lennox soon grew frustrated having to share creative control with other band members. They left, split up as lovers, and got together as a music duo. Thus, Eurythmics was born. The duo signed with RCA and its first album's psychedelic electropop didn't find much of an audience. For the second album, *Sweet Dreams*, Stewart shifted to more hook-laden synthesizer arrangements, and Lennox cut loose her powerful, soulful vocal cords. They hit pay dirt.

The album got off to a big start thanks to the title track, which featured Stewart's haunting, ominous synth bass track and Lennox's mournful vocals, and quickly went on to become a worldwide hit. The song was no doubt helped by a popular video, featuring an androgynous Lennox who appeared to be as comfortable in front of a camera as she was behind a microphone.

There were plenty of other gems to find here. The second single, **Love Is a Stranger**—actually a rerelease of a single that had flopped a year earlier—showcased Lennox beautifully harmonizing with herself and was aided again by heavy rotation for the video. The dark **I've Got an Angel** would have fit perfectly on the soundtrack for an episode of TV's *Miami Vice*. **Wrap It Up** was a modern electro take on a Sam & Dave song popularized by the Fabulous Thunderbirds. **This Is the House** offered a fun romp that clearly took some cues from the Talking Heads. All of that contributed to a gold-certified Top 20 success that probably exceeded the pair's sweetest dreams. *–GP*

1983

Herbie Hancock
FUTURE SHOCK

COLUMBIA | Producers: Herbie Hancock, Material (Bill Laswell and Michael Beinhorn)

RELEASED: AUGUST 15, 1983

● Keyboardist Herbie Hancock had been an innovator since his days as a Miles Davis sideman, freely ignoring conventions while fusing disparate styles into surprisingly cohesive sounds, as on his massively successful jazz-funk-rock album *Head Hunters* in 1973. But *Future Shock*, his collaboration with bassist Bill Laswell and synth player Michael Beinhorn (as the avant-funk duo Material), broke entirely new ground, mainstreaming turntable scratching and other underground hip-hop sounds and setting a template for the future shock of techno and electronica.

Jazzheads weren't enamored with the album or its genre-transcending hit, **Rockit**, which mashed staccato electronic drumbeats, twittering synth notes, and jittery needles-on-vinyl barks into an undeniable groove, but breakdancing urban kids and dance club velvet-ropers loved it. It helped that MTV played the heck out of the Godley & Crème–directed video, a brilliant collage of dancing deconstructed mannequin robots cut with TV images of Hancock. At the time, Michael Jackson was the only other Black artist in heavy rotation; at MTV's inaugural Video Music Awards in 1984, Hancock won five—two more than Jackson. The oft-sampled song also snagged his first Grammy, for Best R&B Instrumental Performance.

Future Shock's other charms included the monster jam **TFS** and Hancock's jazz interlude on **Autodrive**. The title track was a Curtis Mayfield cover, inspired by Alvin Toffler's book about societal whiplash caused by rapidly developing technology. In his liner notes for the 2013 box-set release, Bob Belden wrote, "[**Rockit**] reflected the mixing of an inclusive and collaborative urban culture but was produced with such elegance that the sound of urbanism was embraced worldwide." Hancock continued embracing musical diversity, including employing Grand Mixer DXT (then D.ST) on several tours and pursuing other directions up to the present day. *—LM*

1983

Keith Jarrett
STANDARDS VOL. 1
E C M | Producer: Manfred Eicher
RELEASED: SEPTEMBER 1983

● Always setting lofty standards, pianist Keith Jarrett joined drummer Jack DeJohnette on bassist Gary Peacock's 1977 album *Tales of Another*. Banding together again in 1983, the players focused on expansive interpretations of American Songbook standards. The players caressed the melodies, luring listeners with enough hints to recognize a familiar song, then stretching the arrangements into vigorous improvisational exercises with synergistic gusto and telepathic joy. Their **God Bless the Child** is an exquisite fifteen minutes of bluesy piano trio bliss. *—CH*

The Kinks
STATE OF CONFUSION
A R I S T A | Producer: Ray Davies
RELEASED: MAY 24, 1983

● *State of Confusion* would be these British elders' last gasp as a mainstream pop act in America, and it found Kinks mastermind Ray Davies in the mood to reminisce about dancing. That especially goes for the worldwide hit **Come Dancing**, a wistful good-old-days recollection powered by an irresistible keyboard hook. The rest of the album went back and forth between cranky and heartfelt—that title is not an exaggeration. Nevertheless, where Davies is concerned, catchiness is a given. **Don't Forget to Dance** was especially lovely, in both hook and sentiment. *—DM*

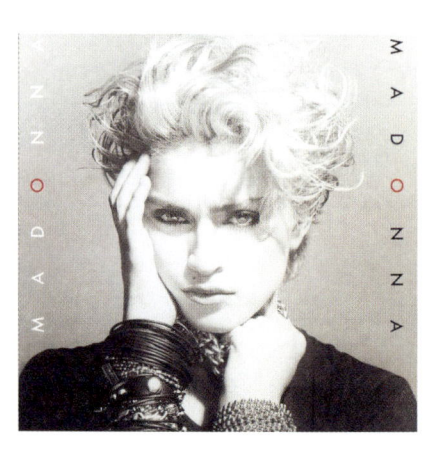

Madonna
MADONNA
S I R E | Producers: Jellybean Benitez, Reggie Lucas, Mark Kamins
RELEASED: JULY 27, 1983

● Madonna's Yellow Brick Road started here. The Michigan native was three weeks shy of twenty-five when she released her debut set, a disco dance-pop manifesto that paved the way for one of pop music's most towering careers. The mood was a sweaty New York dancefloor, as synth rhythms and programmed drums lay the foundation for Madonna's undeniable hooks. **Lucky Star** and **Borderline** were the first of many Top 10s to come; her goal was "to rule the world," she famously told Dick Clark, and she was well on her way. *—AG*

Minor Threat
OUT OF STEP
DISCHORD | Producers: Don Zientara, Minor Threat
RELEASED: APRIL 1983

● This appropriately titled album finds Washington, D.C.'s OG hardcore punks replacing many of the subgenre's rigid tropes with more complex arrangements. Ian MacKaye's throat-shearing vocals and Jeff Nelson's lockstep drumming still featured heavily, but the band's progression was also notable, especially on tracks like **Betray** and **Think Again**. Guitarists Lyle Preslar and Brian Baker offered more conventional rock 'n' roll textures, like those accompanying MacKaye's spoken-sung vocals on **Cashing In** (at 3:44, an epic in hardcore terms). Most significantly, though, *Out of Step* foreshadowed MacKaye's essential '90s post-hardcore band, Fugazi. *—DP*

Night Ranger
MIDNIGHT MADNESS
MCA | Producer: Pat Glasser
RELEASED: OCTOBER 1983

● Nobody doubted during the early '80s that you could still rock in America—or elsewhere—but Night Ranger was happy to remind us. The San Francisco quintet's second album was an undeniable leap forward, more polished and consistent, song-wise, than its *Dawn Patrol* debut. **(You Can Still) Rock in America** was a good calling card, but it was the yearning **Sister Christian** that gave the band a Top 5 breakthrough and a degree of immortality thanks to its inclusion in the film *Boogie Nights* and the musical *Rock of Ages*. *—GG*

Planet Patrol
PLANET PATROL
TOMMY BOY | Producers: Arthur Baker, John Robie
RELEASED: OCTOBER 1983

● After working with Afrika Bambaataa and Soul Sonic Force, Arthur Baker and John Robie went to work crafting a more modern style of R&B music. Using killer male singers instead of the robotic vocals from their previous work, the result was a masterful soul record with an electro feel at its core. **Play at Your Own Risk** and the funkified rockin' cover of Gary Glitter's **I Didn't Know I Loved You (Until I Saw You Rock N Roll)**, blending electronics and soul, was a fresh sound that was not your father's R&B. *—MH*

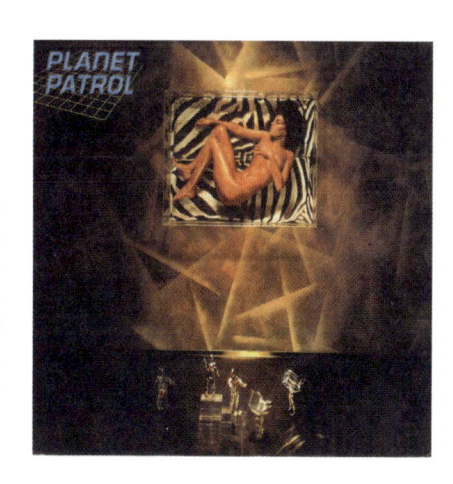

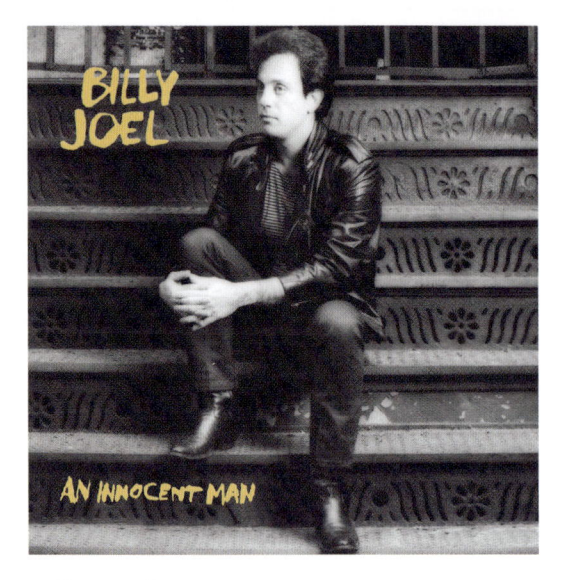

Billy Joel
AN INNOCENT MAN

COLUMBIA | Producer: Phil Ramone
RELEASED: AUGUST 8, 1983

● For his ninth studio album, Billy Joel paid tribute to the music of his adolescence. *An Innocent Man* found the Piano Man largely forgoing his keyboards to concentrate on his vocal performances; **The Longest Time** was a doo-wop tribute using only bass, hand percussion, and vocals, with all of the harmonies, claps, and finger snaps supplied by Joel himself. On **Uptown Girl**, one of his tributes to new girlfriend (later second wife) Christie Brinkley, Joel delivered a serviceable Four Seasons homage. **Tell Her About It** could have come out of Motown, **Leave a Tender Moment Alone** channeled Burt Bacharach, and **Christie Lee** saluted Jerry Lee Lewis and was one of the few songs where Joel let loose on the piano. The title track, a nod to the Drifters, makes brilliant use of dynamics, moving from just bass, finger snaps, and vocals into full-blown orchestration while Joel stretched the limits of his vocal range. Fans loved the love songs, too, as the album spawned six Top 30 singles—the most of any of his albums—and was nominated for a Grammy Award for Album of the Year. *—GP*

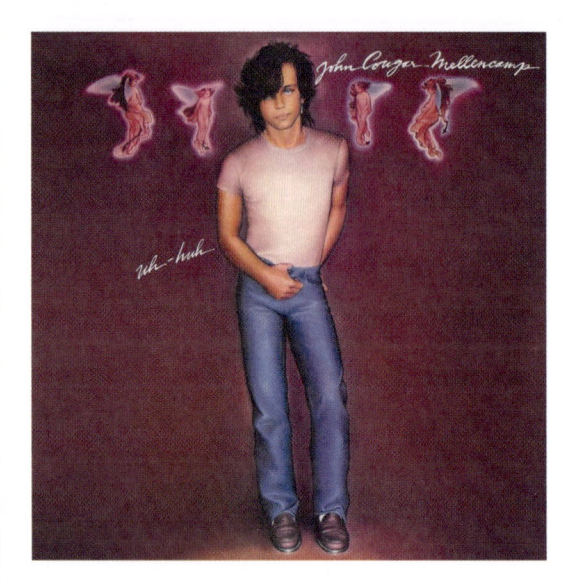

John Cougar Mellencamp
UH-HUH

RIVA/MERCURY | Producers: John Mellencamp, Don Gehman
RELEASED: OCTOBER 25, 1983

● We know what you're thinking—what about *American Fool*? Yes, that was the chart-topping breakthrough that took the (then) John Cougar from also-ran to rock star and had some memorable hits in "Hurts So Good" and "Jack & Diane." But y'know what? *Uh-Huh* was simply better. His seventh release overall and first to bear his true surname (Cougar would be gone entirely eight years later), *Uh-Huh* was more consistent and brimming with the confidence that came from its predecessor's success. His band was in white-hot form after all the *American Fool* touring, and Mellencamp's lyricism continued to advance—particularly on **Pink Houses**, a galvanizing Americana anthem that let us smell the desperation of surrender and broken dreams. And co-writer John Prine, meanwhile, helped broaden the parameters of their **Jackie O**. Mellencamp held up his own gleeful ne'er-do-well persona on **Crumblin' Down**, while **Authority Song**, **Play Guitar**, the Rolling Stones–styled **Serious Business**, and **Lovin' Mother fo Ya** (see Gary Glitter's "Rock and Roll, Part 1") were rockers that suited for both sweaty Midwestern bar and packed arenas. If *American Fool* was the breakthrough, *Uh-Huh* was the firm entrenchment, with much more where it came from ahead. *—GG*

Ministry
WITH SYMPATHY

ARISTA | Producers: Vince Ely, Ian Taylor
RELEASED: MAY 10, 1983

● Ministry's Al Jourgensen was an early player in the Chicago post-punk/industrial rock scene with his early-'80s band Special Affect, and ultimately Ministry, which began its career with an ear-turning Wax Trax 12-inch single that caught the attention of Arista's Clive Davis. While more commercial and disciplined than its predecessor, it was right in line with Depeche Mode, Yaz, and other bands receiving alt-rock airplay in the day. With **Work for Love**, **I Wanted to Tell Her**, and **Revenge** as key tracks, Jourgensen initially reveled in this direction, but that would change as Ministry embraced a more aggressive sound that would characterize its output for the ensuing forty years. While Jourgensen would later decry *With Sympathy* as a "sonic abortion," in 2020 he conceded to Metal Hammer that, "because of that record I wouldn't be who I am today . . . I wouldn't be as much of a f*cking maniac douchebag. So I'm thankful for it now." Fifteen Ministry albums later—and with side projects Revolting Cocks, Lard, and 1000 Homo DJs—Jourgensen has spent the bulk of Ministry's tenure making uncompromising albums. Yet *With Sympathy*, in its 1983 form, was one of the more listenable techno-rock albums of its day. *—CB*

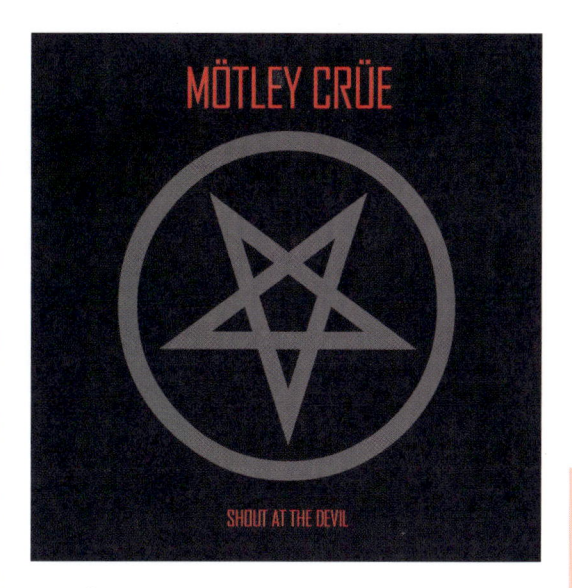

Mötley Crüe
SHOUT AT THE DEVIL

ELEKTRA | Producer: Tom Werman
RELEASED: SEPTEMBER 23, 1983

● Bad boy Los Angeles rockers Mötley Crüe followed up their bare-bones 1981 debut *Too Fast for Love* with this rollicking sophomore effort, which became their breakthrough and established them as heavy metal's lords of the Sunset Strip. The band's hard-partying off-stage antics were already becoming the stuff of legend as the album hit store shelves, a big ol' pentagram staring record buyers in the eye. The title track doubled down on the Satanic imagery—bassist and songwriter Nikki Sixx's early intention to call the album *Shout with the Devil* was eventually softened to *Shout at the Devil* —and the confrontational **Bastard** caught the ire of the Parents Music Resource Center, the Washington, D.C., censorship board, which only made the record that much more desirable to rebellious teenagers. It was free advertising for the Crüe. The album mixed the riffs of Judas Priest with the attitude of Kiss, but it was not all fun and games, and already there's a heaviness to Vince Neil's delivery that made songs like **Too Young to Fall in Love** and **Danger** sound like cautionary tales. For the Crüe, superstardom and MTV fame were just around the corner, but they'd never be this lean again. *—AG*

Metallica
KILL 'EM ALL

MEGAFORCE | Producer: Paul Curcio
RELEASED: JULY 25, 1983

● It can be hard to tell exactly when a new genre was born, as you can always retroactively point to unheralded early influencers and "almost there" building blocks. But when identifying the clearest tipping point between thrash metal and what came before it, look no further than Metallica's *Kill 'Em All*. On their 1983 debut, singer/guitarist James Hetfield, drummer Lars Ulrich, bassist Cliff Burton, and lead guitarist Kirk Hammett melded the complexities of heavy metal's fastest music with the fury and aggression of punk. This was the beginning of a powerful new underground movement that would very quickly turn the pop-friendly, overly image-conscious hard rock and metal of the era on its ear.

The precise and unbelievably fast rhythm guitar riffs on tracks such as **The Four Horsemen** and **Whiplash** set new standards for heavy metal. Burton's love of classical and jazz, demonstrated on his solo track (**Anesthesia)—Pulling Teeth**, added grandeur to the music that none of its peers could match. Metallica was irrevocably changed after his tragic 1986 death.

Metallica would go on to polish, refine, and expand its approach in astoundingly impressive ways on its next two classic albums—1984's *Ride the Lightning* and 1986's *Master of Puppets*. Those were undeniably more technically impressive, but there was a raw and unhinged edge to *Kill 'Em All* that was lost during this evolution. To make the *Kill 'Em All* era all the more impressive, another of thrash metal's biggest groups would almost immediately sprout from the Metallica bloodline. The band's previous lead guitarist, Dave Mustaine, was fired shortly before the recording of *Kill 'Em All* due to substance abuse issues. His influence on the album is clear; he's credited with co-writing four songs. Mustaine quickly formed Megadeth, universally accepted as another of thrash's "Big Four." —MW

Merle Haggard and Willie Nelson
PANCHO & LEFTY

E P I C | Producers: Merle Haggard, Chips Moman, Willie Nelson
RELEASED: JANUARY 1983

● Texas songwriter Townes Van Zandt, who wrote the title song of Merle Haggard and Willie Nelson's album *Pancho & Lefty*, was revered by his peers. "He ranks alongside Kris Kristofferson and Bob Dylan," Rodney Crowell once said. "He inspired so many songwriters to shoot for something that's timeless." But the brilliance of Van Zandt's storytelling was little known to a wider audience until Haggard and Nelson sent their version of his tale of two ill-fated outlaws to No. 1 on Billboard's Hot Country Songs chart. Never has *federales*, the Spanish word for the "Mexican police," been expressed so beautifully. The song was the highlight of this collaborative set that topped the Hot Country Albums chart.

Haggard and Nelson, part of the outlaw movement that rejected conventions of country music and both artists who found success on their own terms, brought a relaxed spirit to their performances on *Pancho & Lefty*. The title track was followed aptly by **It's My Lazy Day**, with Haggard and Nelson trading lines about going fishing, except, well, "The road to the river / Is a mighty long way." Album producer Chips Moman has a legacy as notable as his two singers, from helping craft early hits for Stax Records to co-writing "Do Right Woman, Do Right Man" for Aretha Franklin to producing Elvis Presley. On *Pancho & Lefty*, he took an understated approach, with simple piano and acoustic guitar arrangements throughout.

On one of the best duets, **Reasons to Quit**, Haggard and Nelson sang of "smoke and booze" and admitted "the low is always lower than the high." But they concluded that the reasons to quit "don't outnumber all the reasons why" not to. The song was this charming album's second hit, reaching No. 6 on the Hot Country Songs chart. *—TD*

New Order
POWER, CORRUPTION & LIES

FACTORY/QWEST | Producers: New Order
RELEASED: MAY 2, 1983

● The band started in 1980 and released its first album the following year. But *Power, Corruption & Lies* was where the New Order we know and love truly started.

Bernard Sumner, Peter Hook, and Stephen Morris brought new musical order to their lives when their tenure in Joy Division ended with frontman Ian Curtis's May 1980 suicide on the eve of a North American tour. Recruiting Gillian Gilbert, who married Morris in 1994, New Order continued on its predecessor's gloomy, gothic-flavored path for its initial singles and an album (1981's tentative *Movement*). The subsequent singles **Temptation** and **Blue Monday**, however, introduced a new direction—lighter, dancier—that led to a full-length arrival with *Power, Corruption & Lies*, the assured sound of the band finding its own true voice. And notably the group was now producing itself, having shed Martin Hannett from the Joy Division days.

There was still emotional heaviness on these ten tracks (**Blue Monday** was added to CD and cassette editions of the album), but that existed within an ambitious playfulness and inventive zeal that was missing from *Movement*. **5 8 6**, a **Blue Monday** sequel of sorts, and **Ecstasy** had dance clubs in their crosshairs, while nuanced tracks such as **Age of Consent**, **Your Silent Face**, and **Leave Me Alone** worked for the feet and for the ears. The high-stepping polyrhythmic leanings of **The Village** and **Ultraviolence**, meanwhile, would have fit on Talking Heads albums of the time.

New Order has continued to explore and expand—without Hook since 2007, and at a much slower pace—but *Power, Corruption & Lies* album was the launchpad. Suffice to say that since then, the group's brought more, or at least a different kind of, joy than Joy Division did during its all-too-short tenure. *—GG*

1983

Robert Plant
THE PRINCIPLE OF MOMENTS

ES PARANZA/ATLANTIC | Producers: Robert Plant, Benji Lefevre, Pat Moran

RELEASED: JULY 15, 1983

● The path of least resistance would have been for Robert Plant to form another guitar-based blues-rock band and replicate Led Zeppelin's sound after the legendary group broke up in 1980. This is an advantage all singers have; their voice is typically the most easily transferable and recognizable element of their former group.

But Plant chose a more difficult and far more rewarding route, trading Zeppelin's sonic palette for a cleaner, more modern, and pop-friendly sound. While there were songs such as *Worse Than Detroit* on his 1982 debut *Pictures at Eleven* that sounded like echoes or extensions of late-era Zeppelin albums such as *Presence* and *In Through the Out Door*, those traces were nearly completely eradicated on 1983's *The Principle of Moments*.

His famous Golden God wail is nowhere to be found here, replaced by a much more restrained and sophisticated vocal approach on songs like the propulsive opener **Lay Down Your Arms** and the progressive-leaning **Messin' with the Mekon**. *The Principle of Moments* was home to Plant's first two undeniably classic solo songs, the hypnotic, synth-drenched **In the Mood** and the mournful cinematic ballad **Big Log**. They hit the Top 40 and 20, respectively, on the US pop charts, sending *Moments* more than one million sales and allowing Plant to perform his first solo tour—at which he did not perform any songs from his former band.

The bravery and restlessness with which Plant started his solo career has remained intact decades later, with the singer consistently exploring and blending new genres with an impressive array of collaborators. It's hard to think of a member of a gigantic rock band who has had a more successful and creatively rewarding solo career. *The Principle of Moments* was a very important part of that journey and remains a highly enjoyable listen. **–MW**

R.E.M.
MURMUR
I.R.S. | Producers: Don Dixon, Mitch Easter
RELEASED: APRIL 12, 1983

● While well received, R.E.M.'s debut album didn't suggest the Athens, Georgia, quartet was destined to become one of the world's biggest acts. But *Murmur* did reveal something else: a band finding its intriguingly original—and captivating—sound.

Influenced by the Velvet Underground, Patti Smith, and the punk attitude of passion over proficiency, R.E.M. was labeled alternative rock but was more interested in finding its own way than in fitting any genre. Moving forward from the 1982 EP *Chronic Town*, Mike Mills's melodic bass lines sometimes functioned as leads; lead guitarist Peter Buck, meanwhile, concentrated on tone, not power chords or solos. Mills and drummer Bill Berry, bandmates since high school, had a well-honed chemistry and willingness to explore. And just as impressionist painters created the suggestion of imagery, lyricist/lead singer Michael Stipe, an art student, used words to evoke moods rather than specific statements or linear narratives.

Stipe's oblique references and abstract phrases sometimes carried meaning, though on R.E.M.'s first single, **Radio Free Europe**, he even admitted his words were babble, un-enunciated sounds strung together because he lacked actual lyrics. It didn't matter; it was the urgency in Stipe's voice, along with the compelling melody and instrumentation, that attracted attention. The achingly beautiful **Talk About the Passion**, meanwhile—with Buck's chiming chords, Mills's harmonies, and a sweeping cello—was really the sound of a band hitting its stride and moving listeners in ways that transcended language.

Critics and college radio loved it; *Murmur* ranked No. 2 on the *Village Voice*'s Pazz & Jop poll, second only to Michael Jackson's *Thriller* and ahead of the Police's *Synchronicity*, U2's *War*, and Bob Dylan's *Infidels*. And though highly influential, *Murmur* still sounds unique—the creation of a band so distinct, successful imitators simply don't exist. *–LM*

The Pointer Sisters
BREAK OUT
PLANET/RCA | Producer: Richard Perry
RELEASED: NOVEMBER 1, 1983

● After an R&B-centric '70s output, the Pointer Sisters brought their earthy, soulful pipes to the drum machines and spacey synths of the '80s for their tenth album. **Jump (For My Love)** was a bright burst of dance-pop yearning. **Automatic** was a delirious detour into funky New Wave. **I'm So Excited** brought the ecstatic release of church music to the club. And **Neutron Dance** was a runaway train of perky synth-pop and gospel harmonizing. A blockbuster smash with four Top 10 hits, *Break Out* was an unbeatable endorphin rush. —*JL*

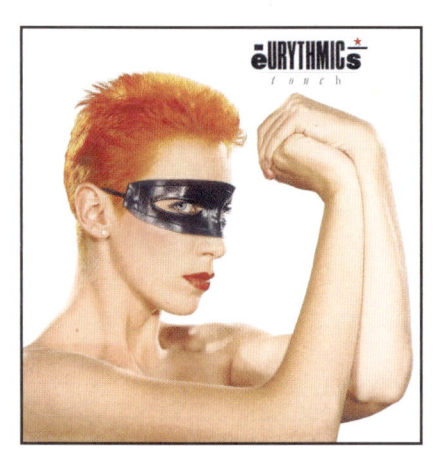

Eurythmics
TOUCH
RCA | Producer: David A. Stewart
RELEASED: NOVEMBER 14, 1983

● If Eurythmics' videogenic image(s) made the duo seem like a potential flash in the pan, this was the album that insured its longevity. The third Eurythmics album was more complete and consistent than *Sweet Dreams (Are Made of This)* just ten months earlier, with undeniable synth-pop classics such as **Here Comes the Rain Again** and **Who's That Girl?** and some stylistic broadening with the calypso swing of **Right by Your Side**. And the funky **Regrets** was, for our money, one of, if not *the* best, nonhit album track in Eurythmics' estimable catalog. —*GG*

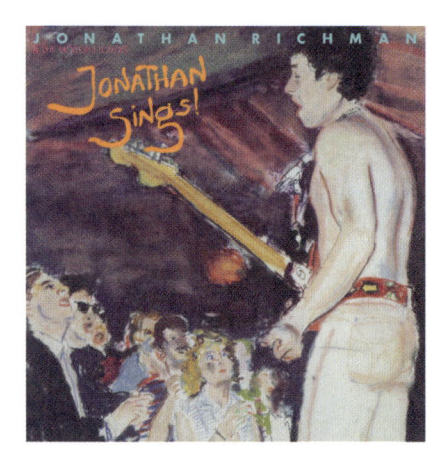

Jonathan Richman and the Modern Lovers
JONATHAN SINGS!
SIRE/WARNER BROS. | Producer: Peter Bernstein
RELEASED: SUMMER 1983

● Although billed to "and the Modern Lovers," this should be thought of as a Jonathan Richman work, with the second incarnation of the band in a decidedly support role. And with songs this strong and a frontman in fine form, it's not hard to churn out a winning set like this. It truly has **That Summer Feeling**, as Richman sings on the opening track, and the other nine fly by with tight, economic bonhomie and lots of romance via tracks such as **You're the One for Me** and **Someone to Hold Me**. —*GG*

Spandau Ballet
TRUE
CHRYSALIS | Producers: Tony Swain, Steve Jolley, Spandau Ballet
RELEASED: MARCH 4, 1983

● Spandau Ballet represented the New Romantic movement with impeccable fashion, with self-described "white European dance music" and more than a little eyeliner. Its third album, *True*, cemented the British group's legacy when songwriter/guitarist Gary Kemp led the band out of the clubs and onto the radio with singles such as **Communication**, **Lifeline**, and the lush title track and **Gold**. Saxophone, an insistence on managing its own image, and singer Tony Hadley's velvety voice made the band unique. But it's the suave songs that keep us swooning and dancing today. —HD

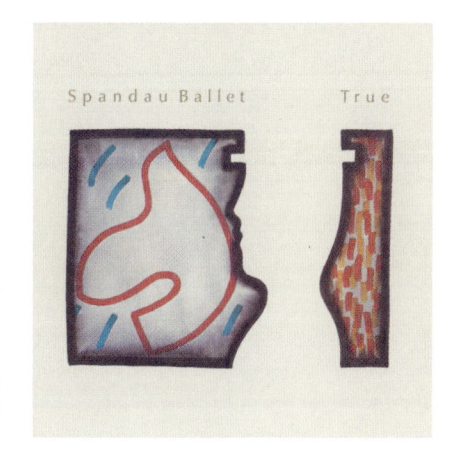

Yello
YOU GOTTA SAY YES TO ANOTHER EXCESS
ELEKTRA | Producer: Boris Blank
RELEASED: APRIL 1983

● Picture Salvador Dalí using electronics instead of paint and the result would be comparable to the masterpiece Yello created here. Simple sophistication: A fusion of funky fun mixed with addictive synth-laden beats and quirky vocals made the duo's third album a captivating, unique classic. Yello pulled out all the tools from its sonic Swiss Army knife to construct upbeat gems such as **I Love You** and **Lost Again**, proving that, while good-humored, its music was to be taken seriously. —MH

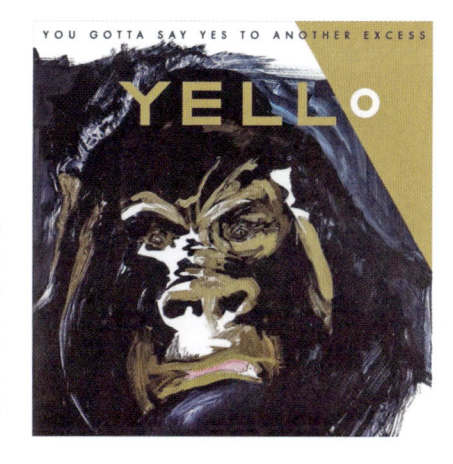

Yes
90125
ATCO | Producers: Trevor Horn, Yes
RELEASED: NOVEMBER 7, 1983

● There's that thing about teaching old dogs new tricks—we give you Yes's unexpected eleventh studio album. Some longtime fans felt pop veneer replaced prog ambition and that short-term Yes frontman Trevor Horn's production was too sleek, but it was the right sound at the right time. *90125* was the only Yes album to launch four Top 10 hits, with **Owner of a Lonely Heart** hitting No. 1, and became the veteran band's top-selling album. It was an affirmative move that gave Yes fresh life in a new decade. —GG

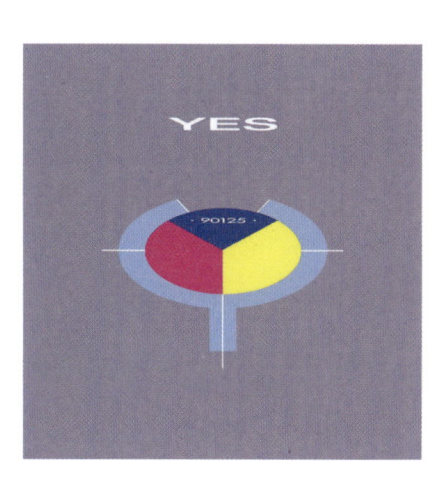

The Police
SYNCHRONICITY

A & M | Producers: The Police, Hugh Padgham
RELEASED: JUNE 1, 1983

● For a band that had earned worldwide fandom with its first four albums, the Police saved the best for last with its final studio effort, *Synchronicity*. The album cemented the trio's legacy as one of the era's biggest bands, reaching No. 1 on both US and UK charts and being added to the Grammy Hall of Fame in 2009.

Following the successful *Ghost in the Machine*, which was overstuffed with synthesizers and horns, the Police returned to a more basic instrumentation (with overdubs) but still achieved a rich, textured feel. The cohesion and success belied the combustible group's interpersonal issues as charismatic singer/bassist Sting became the band's dominant personality above drummer Stewart Copeland and guitarist Andy Summers. Compounded by nonstop years of touring and recording, the combustible trio had splintered to the point where they recorded their respective parts separately—albeit in the comfortable tropical climes of Montserrat—and often clashed while making *Synchronicity*.

This stress, compounded by the breakup of Sting's marriage, can be felt throughout the deeply personal lyrics on the songs he penned for the album (nine if you include the bonus track **Murder by Numbers**). His angst comes through on three of the album's singles— **Wrapped Around Your Finger**, **King of Pain**, and the Grammy Award–winning **Every Breath You Take**, which was the biggest hit of 1983. A fourth single, the surging rock track **Synchronicity II**, encapsulated the LP's theme of meaningful coincidences.

Perhaps sensing the impending end of the band, Sting did offer olive branches to his bandmates by letting them each write and sing a track. Summers penned and sang **Mother**, an abrasive spoken-word rant about his own mom, while Copeland's **Miss Gradenko** was inspired by the Cold War with the Soviet Union. *–JC*

1983

Linda Ronstadt
WHAT'S NEW
ASYLUM | Producer: Peter Asher
RELEASED: SEPTEMBER 12, 1983

● Linda Ronstadt has claimed that her longtime producer and manager Peter Asher barely blinked an eye when she suggested a stylistic swerve for *What's New*. "I'd thrown a lot of goofy ideas at him before," she recalled later. But it's fair to say this one—lush pop standards arranged by the legendary Nelson Riddle—was goofier than most. Ronstadt was, after all, the hitmaking queen of country-pop throughout the '70s and had successfully pivoted to more of a rock direction at the turn of the decade. But she'd also done a turn on Broadway in Gilbert & Sullivan's *Pirates of Penzance*, which seemed like an outlier indulgence at the time but became an obvious precursor to this particular musical turn.

"The Nelson Riddle stuff is timeless for me," Ronstadt explained. "That kind of music is so rich and sophisticated, and the melodies are just so wonderful to sing." She certainly made her case on these nine tracks, melting her voice into the title track and George and Ira Gershwin classics such as **I've Got a Crush on You** and **Someone to Watch Over Me**, both of which were also released as singles. Ronstadt deftly straddled the divide between technique and instinct, delivering renditions of **Crazy He Calls Me**, **What'll I Do**, **Guess I'll Hang My Tears out to Dry**—everything, really—as if she was born singing them.

Ronstadt wasn't the first pop/rock singer to pay tribute to the Great American Songbook, but she did it best (to that point), and an audience certainly recognized it. *What's New* was a surprising No. 3 on the Billboard 200 and certified triple platinum. Ronstadt recorded two more Riddle albums before continuing on to other left turns, including sets delving into her Hispanic heritage. *—GG*

Talking Heads
SPEAKING IN TONGUES

S I R E | Producers: Talking Heads

RELEASED: JUNE 1, 1983

● Talking Heads may have been labeled as art-rockers (or art punks), but *Speaking in Tongues*, its fifth album and first self-produced effort after three with Brian Eno, left no doubt that it was a funk band at heart. As guitarist Adrian Belew, who'd played on Talking Heads' previous album, *Remain in Light*, observed, it was music "for your body *and* your mind." Nowhere was that convergence more evident than on *Speaking in Tongues*, which *Rolling Stone* deemed "the album that finally obliterates the thin line separating arty white pop music and deep black funk."

Quirky didn't begin to describe the vastly varied sounds and Afrobeat-meets-trance rhythms Talking Heads juxtaposed, but frontman David Byrne's oddly disjointed lyrics and off-kilter delivery couldn't obscure one fact: The indelible grooves made you want to move. In a rare feat, every track on the album reached No. 2 on Billboard's Dance Club Songs chart, while the album opener **Burning Down the House**, bolstered by *Remain in Light* touring percussionist Steve Scales, gave the group its only US Top 10 single.

Tina Weymouth's extraordinary bass lines, Chris Franz's firecracker drumbeats, and Jerry Harrison's guitar and keyboard flights formed a tight trampoline for Byrne's vocal somersaults, but the quartet also used other touring band members to enhance the syncopated sonic gymnastics—most notably Nona Hendryx and Dolette McDonald, who delivered gospel harmonies on **Slippery People**, and Parliament-Funkadelic's Bernie Worrell, who injected trippy synths all over **Girlfriend Is Better**. The latter contained the line that titled Jonathan Demme's now-classic concert film *Stop Making Sense*.

Speaking in Tongues may not be considered Talking Heads' most "important" album, but as the impetus for that film—which directly informed Byrne's eventual *American Utopia* stage show and film—its relevance to musical and pop culture history cannot be overstated. *–LM*

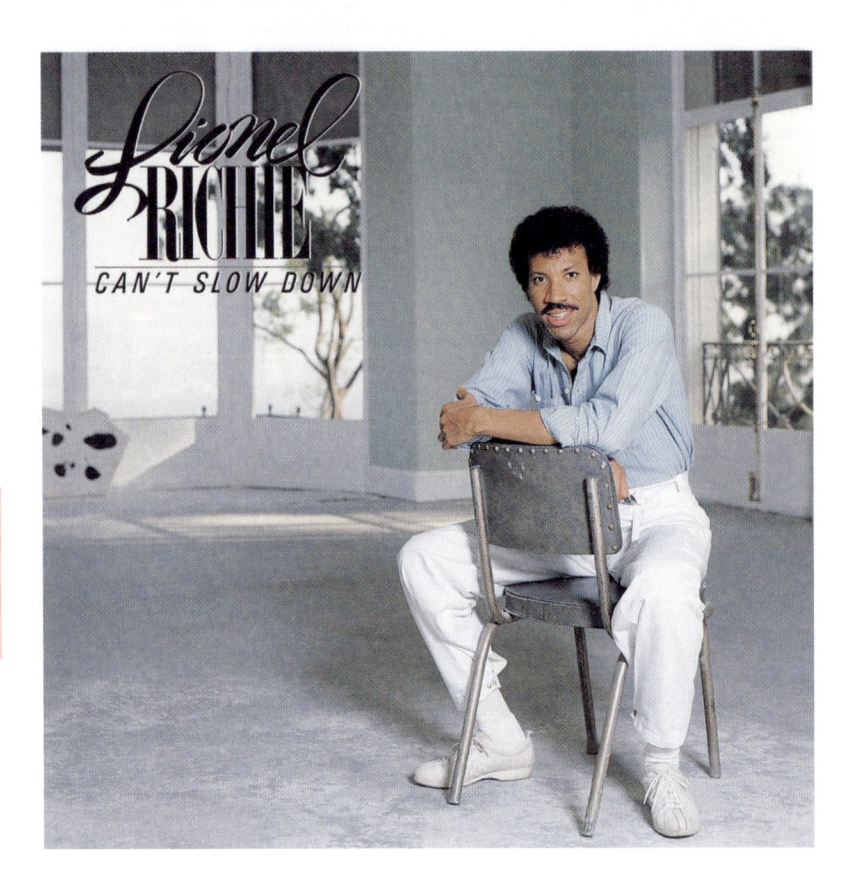

Lionel Richie
CAN'T SLOW DOWN

MOTOWN | Producers: James Anthony Carmichael, Lionel Richie, David Foster

RELEASED: OCTOBER 14, 1983

● The year after the solo debut album that bore his name became a multiplatinum, hit-spewing smash, Lionel Richie explained that "it was actually designed to be a solo album and then I'd go back to the Commodores." Fat chance. Richie not only stood as the Commodores' primary hitmaker, but his work producing and writing for Kenny Rogers and Diana Ross made his departure inevitable—if only to avoid further eclipsing his brothers-in-arms bandmates.

Can't Slow Down, then, came with high expectations and a bit of a mission statement to entrench Richie as a commercial force. If Lionel Richie was a side project, Can't Slow Down was the main event, planting a flag for brand Richie as a full-time concern. And it couldn't have gone much better. The album topped the Billboard 200, sold more than 20 million copies worldwide, and won the Grammy Award for Album of the Year. It launched five Top 10 hits, two of which—**All Night Long (All Night)** and **Hello**—reached No. 1. It's *the* album when anyone thinks of Richie and one of the tentpoles of '80s pop in general.

And a listen, even now, proves that success was anything but fluky. There's nary a wasted note on the album's eight tracks, with more hooks than a Bass Pro Shop. The three non-singles could well have been hits, too, and pro forma ballads like **Hello**, **Penny Lover**, and **Stuck On You** were elevated by Richie's skill and sincerity. **All Night Long (All Night)**, meanwhile, was a joyous breath of Caribbean fresh air, and **Running with the Night** featured a hot guitar solo from Toto's Steve Lukather —one of many top-shelf players who were part of the project. Richie pushed the pedal down on Can't Slow Down, to winning effect. *—GG*

1983

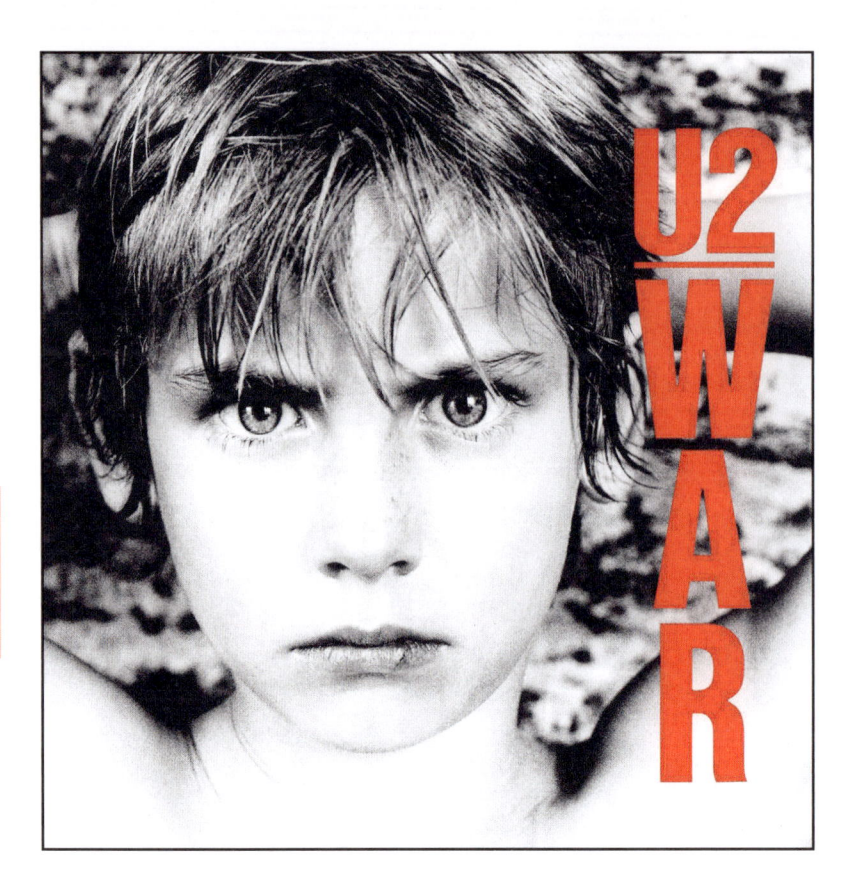

U2
WAR

ISLAND | Producer: Steve Lillywhite
RELEASED: MARCH 1, 1983

● Following its post-punk coming-of-age debut *Boy* and the conflicted religious fervor of *October*, which had the Irish quartet wondering if it should keep making music, U2 looked outward on their third album. Opening with **Sunday Bloody Sunday**—Larry Mullen Jr.'s military drumbeats, The Edge's feedback-laden guitar, and Bono's impassioned voice singing, "I can't believe the news today / Oh, I can't close my eyes and make it go away / How long . . . must we sing this song"—*War* was an unapologetic call to arms, the "arms" in this case being truth and love.

Sunday Bloody Sunday wasn't a one-off burst of social conscience. **Seconds** followed, about the threat of nuclear war, and the album's first single, **New Year's Day**, was about Polish solidarity. Thirteen minutes into the album, there was no denying where U2's heart lay. Bono and bandmates, including bassist Adam Clayton, have taken no small amount of grief over the years for their heart-on-their-sleeves humanitarian and political pontifications, but on *War*, their sincerity shined through. The Edge told *Guitar Player* magazine in 2023, "It was on *War* where we cut our teeth on activism and social justice issues." Still, the album wasn't devoid of love songs. Bono famously spent time during his honeymoon writing lyrics, which showed on *War*'s dancey second single, **Two Hearts Beat as One**, and on the shimmering, underappreciated **Drowning Man**.

Appropriately, *War*—which sold more than 4 million copies in the US and more than 11 million worldwide—ended with **40**, based on Psalm 40, which has become a moving singalong closer at U2 concerts, including its final show at The Sphere in Las Vegas. "How long to sing this song?" Bono asked again. How long, indeed? *—HD*

Stevie Ray Vaughan and Double Trouble
TEXAS FLOOD
EPIC | Producers: Stevie Ray Vaughan, Richard Mullen, Double Trouble
RELEASED: JUNE 13, 1983

● Texas guitarist Stevie Ray Vaughan was everywhere at once during the summer of 1983, starting with David Bowie's massively popular *Let's Dance* album, single, and video (which depicted Bowie playing Vaughan's stinging guitar solo). That was just a warm-up act for *Texas Flood*, Vaughan's debut album, which introduced him as one of the finest guitarists of his generation.

Yet this "overnight success" wouldn't have happened without a decade-plus of woodshedding around Texas, much of it in the shadow of big brother Jimmie Vaughan's Fabulous Thunderbirds. But that pecking order was quickly reversed. About the least kind thing you can say about *Texas Flood* is that Vaughan never really topped it. The rest of his catalog hardly pales in comparison, but *Texas Flood* was just so fully realized in presenting his strengths as a guitarist in ways to build on, not surpass.

Recorded at Jackson Browne's Los Angeles studio, *Texas Flood* might be even more of a "live" album than any of Vaughan's actual live albums. It closely mirrored a typical gig, with Vaughan and his Double Trouble rhythm section of bassist Tommy Shannon and drummer Chris "Whipper" Layton set up in a corner as if onstage, playing their live set—ten tracks, three of them instrumentals, and two of those positioned as either introductory or set-ending break songs. The third instrumental was the closing track, **Lenny**, named for Vaughan's wife Lenora, which made his debt to Jimi Hendrix clear. Vaughan would cover "Voodoo Child (Slight Return)" on the following year's *Couldn't Stand the Weather*, but **Lenny** echoed the quieter side of Hendrix's "Little Wing."

Vaughan spent the rest of the 1980s building a Hall of Fame résumé before dying in a 1990 helicopter crash on the eve of the release of his first album with brother Jimmie. He was just thirty-five years old. *—DM*

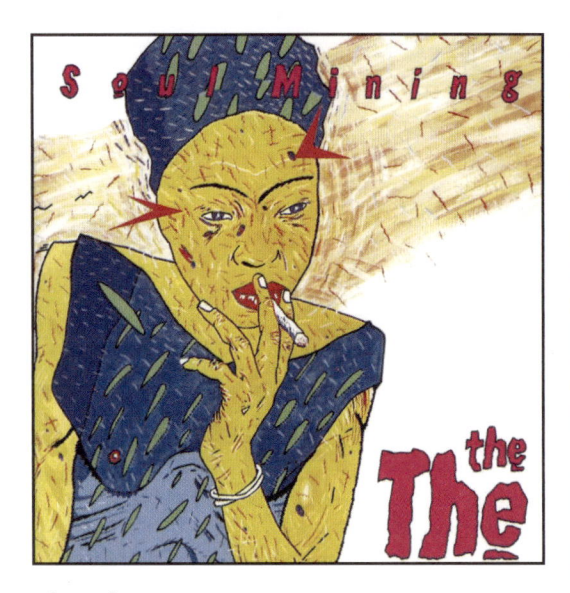

The The
SOUL MINING
EPIC | Producers: Paul Hardiman, Matt Johnson
RELEASED: OCTOBER 21, 1983

● The eight tracks on *Soul Mining* were firmly planted on the hyphen in synth-pop, straddling both genres with a sound that was both familiar and unique for the era. It took only one listen to realize that Matt Johnson was a brilliant crafter of songs, and the lyrics could only be written by a young adult riding the roller coaster of insecurity, depression, and self-discovery. Johnson was only twenty-one when he began recording *Soul Mining*, and its subject matter is what he knew best. The title, in fact, was an accurate description of the artist trapped in the nostalgia of the past but hoping to find any scrap of self-worth inside to provide optimism for the future. It's difficult to imagine that the person who wrote "My memory my fond deceiver / Is turning all my past into pain / While I'm being raped by progress / Tomorrow's world is here to stay" is observing these feelings as an impartial outsider. This raw angst may not have helped *Soul Mining* onto the US charts, but it did help two songs, **Uncertain Smile** and **This Is the Day**, work for multiple movie soundtracks afterward. —*RW*

Violent Femmes
VIOLENT FEMMES
SLASH | Producer: Mark Van Hecke
RELEASED: APRIL 13, 1983

● Punk is about stripping away the excesses that rock accrued over the years, yes? If so, you can't strip away much more than Violent Femmes, which achieved their songs of adolescent angst with minimal instrumentation—Gordon Gano's acoustic guitar, Brian Ritchie's acoustic bass, and Victor DeLorenzo's "traceaphone"—a tom-tom covered by a metal bushel basket, played with steel brushes. It was a sound and an aesthetic born of necessity. "It came from a lack of places to play. Nobody would let us play," Gano said in a 2019 interview. The Femmes busked in the streets of Milwaukee, which led to their discovery by the Pretenders' James Honeyman-Scott and eventually a deal with Slash Records. What their songs lacked in volume, they made up for in intensity. Gano's nervous, nerdy vocals, manic delivery, and disaffected, frustrated lyrics resonated sufficiently with like-minded punks and Violent Femmes eventually went platinum. The desperation of songs such as **Kiss Off**, **Add It Up**, and **Gone Daddy Gone** was palpable. And, proving that the world has a sense of humor, the opening riff of **Blister in the Sun** has become—of all things—a ballpark staple, used to rouse baseball fans out of their between-pitch torpor. —*DD*

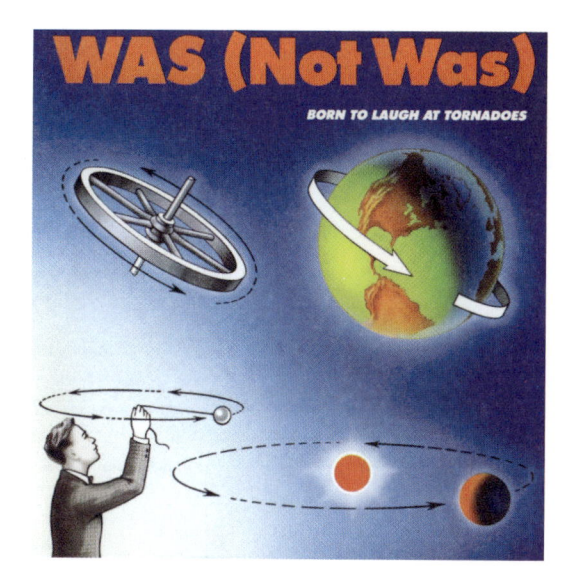

Was (Not Was)
BORN TO LAUGH AT TORNADOES
GEFFEN/ZE | Producers: Don St. Was, David St. Was, Jack Tann
RELEASED: SEPTEMBER 1983

● How can a record cover so much ground and remain cohesive? The roster of guest vocalists included Ozzy Osbourne, Mel Tormé, the Knack's Doug Fieger, and soul legend Mitch Ryder. What?!? And Was (Not Was) had two of its own singers, Sweet Pea Atkinson and Sir Harry Bowens, neither of whom is anything less world-class. That was the challenge that David St. Was and Don St. Was confronted with their second full-length release. They played into the endless contrast with joyful musical abandon and creeping lyrical darkness. David St. Was writes words that question the basic humanity of the characters, and that's not meant as a bad thing. **Knocked Down, Made Small** opened the record with a cry for respect that's never achieved. **Betrayal's Just a Game** was the refrain sung by Fieger with a sense of resolve. Perhaps the most fascinating character here is **Professor Night**; he's clearly a monster: "Pound for pound, he's a loser, a destroyer, not a cruiser"—perhaps presaging the worst of our political leadership. The songs get lifted by the ensemble of Detroit musicians who lay down the funk, notably Don St. Was on bass and Randy Jacobs on screaming guitar. *—HK*

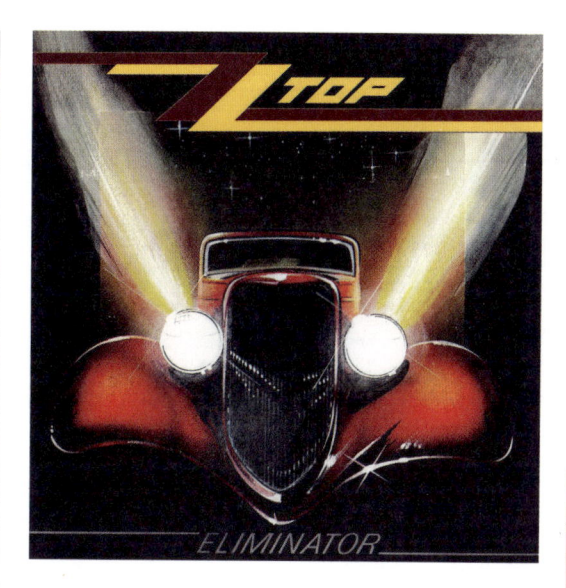

ZZ Top
ELIMINATOR
WARNER BROS. | Producer: Bill Ham
RELEASED: MARCH 23, 1983

● ZZ Top may have been the '70s band least likely to conquer the '80s. After all, the Texas trio had built its reputation on a highly organic strain of blues-rock. But singer/guitarist Billy Gibbons's fascination with New Wave, keyboards, and synthesizers began to show itself on 1981's *El Loco*, particularly on "Groovy Little Hippie Pad." Two years later, ZZ Top fully jumped into the digital world with the multiplatinum worldwide smash *Eliminator*. Using drum machines and synths to crank up the tempos and maintain an ultra-precise beat gave Gibbons's guitar more room to roam. He took full advantage throughout, not just on hit singles such as **Legs**, **Sharp Dressed Man**, and **Gimme All Your Lovin'** but on tracks like the ferocious **Got Me Under Pressure** and the extended blues of **I Need You Tonight**. The band also parlayed its unique, bearded look and a red 1933 Ford Coupe into a series of incredibly popular MTV videos, completing one of the most unlikely and wildly successful career transformations in rock history. The best part is—all these years later and purists be damned—*Eliminator* is completely worthy of all this success and adulation. *—MW*

19

84

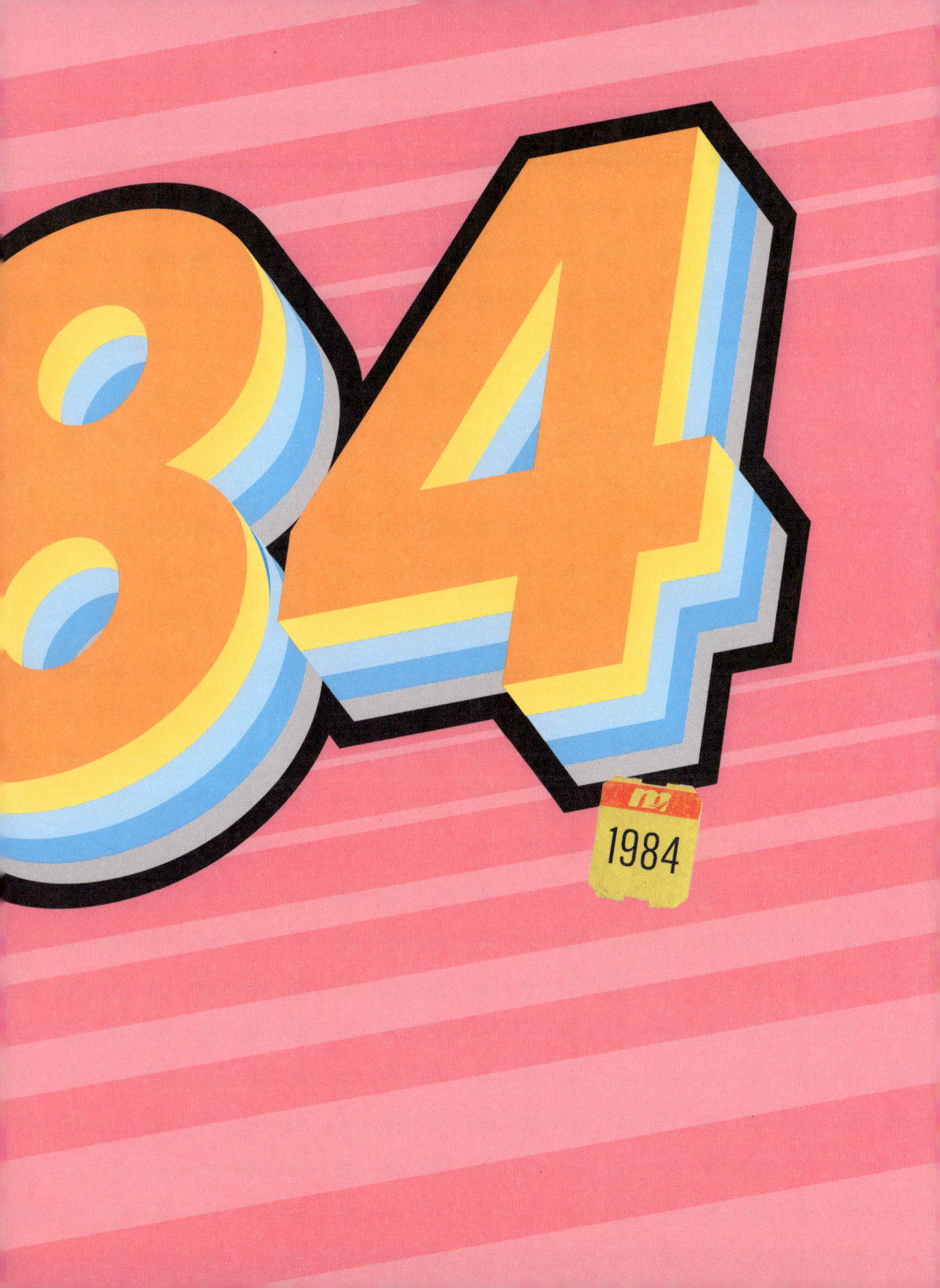

1984

Prince
PURPLE RAIN

WARNER BROS. | Producers: Prince and the Revolution
RELEASED: JUNE 25, 1984

● For all his flamboyance as a performer, the most audacious aspect of Prince's career was how he conducted it: demanding—and getting—what he wanted based simply on his vast talent, matched only by his enormous self-confidence. In the early '80s, before he'd even had a Top 10 hit, he made starring in "a major motion picture" a condition of renewing his management contract. That film was *Purple Rain*; its soundtrack album would make Prince a superstar. Though 1987's *Sign "O" the Times* is often cited as an even greater musical achievement, *Purple Rain*'s seismic impact on popular culture and Prince's career was enormous. Ignoring racial, gender, and genre boundaries, Prince catalyzed rock, pop, R&B, soul, gospel, jazz, funk, classical, and other idioms into nine boldly original tracks, several co-credited to his band, the Revolution.

Incorporating Hendrix-channeling guitar-god solos, lush string arrangements, drum-machine samples, keyboards, and advanced sonic wizardry with his high falsetto to deep baritone vocals, Little Richard/James Brown screams, and Wendy-and-Lisa harmonies, Prince turned each song into another affirmation of his genius. While sometimes referencing spirituality (**Let's Go Crazy** opened the album with a pseudo-sermon), he also stomped on sexual taboos; the masturbation and kinky sex in **Darling Nikki** helped prompt the Parents Music Resource Center and its lobby for content advisory stickers.

Spending twenty-four weeks atop the Billboard 200 and becoming one of the best-selling albums in history, *Purple Rain* also gave Prince his first No. 1 singles with the synth-pop/soul classic **When Doves Cry** and the exuberant **Let's Go Crazy**. The epic title track became an anthem as well as the highlight of Prince's stunning, rain-soaked 2007 halftime performance at Super Bowl XLI. The album's many accolades include placement on the Library of Congress's National Recording Registry. *—LM*

1984

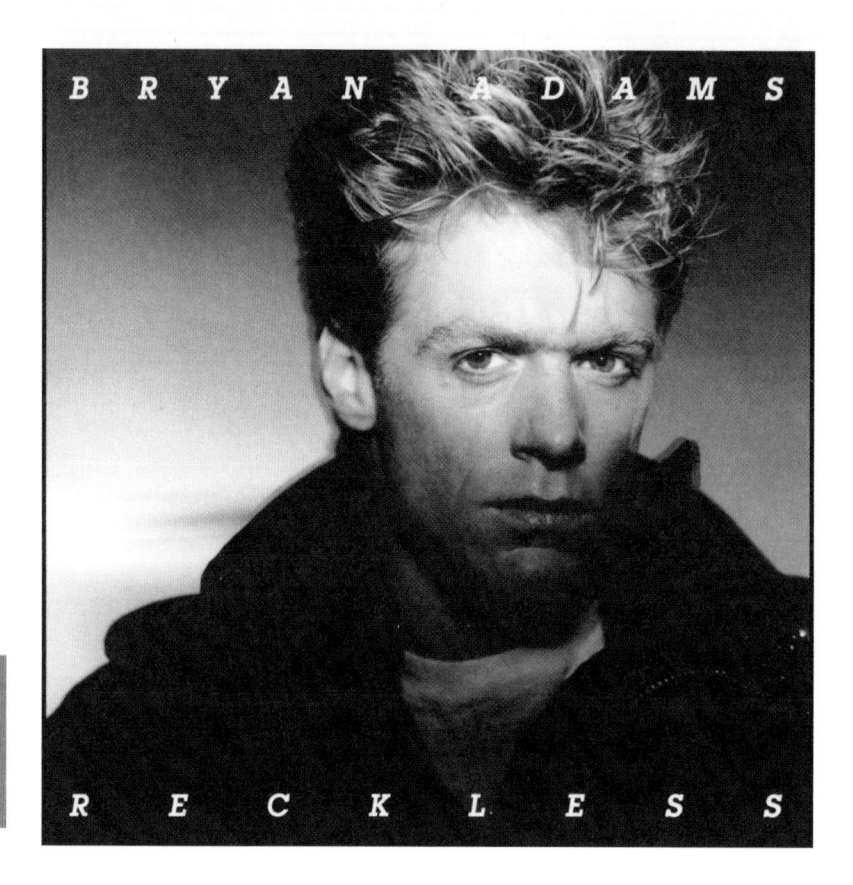

Bryan Adams
RECKLESS
A & M | Producers: Bob Clearmountain, Bryan Adams
RELEASED: NOVEMBER 5, 1984

● Bryan Adams's trajectory was sharp and upward as he rolled into his fourth studio album. The Canadian rocker and songwriting partner Jim Vallance had already had songs recorded by the likes of Loverboy, Kiss, and Bachman-Turner Overdrive, and Adams's *Cuts Like a Knife* in 1983 gave him Top 10 platinum footing with hits such as "Straight from the Heart," "This Time," and the title track. But the next step would be exponential.

"Looking back on *Reckless*, I kind of consider that album part of a trilogy of songs that started with Jim Vallance and I writing from 1981–1984," Adams said as the album turned 30. It was indeed the peak of that time period, and of Adams's career, a hit-spewing, five-times platinum onslaught that gave him his only No. 1 entry on the Billboard 200 and five Top 20 hits. The year before, Adams was giving Journey a run for its money as the group's opener; *Reckless* made him an arena headliner in his own right.

Songcraft and sound were the primary components behind *Reckless*'s triumph; Adams and Vallance were firing on all cylinders, whether it was rockers (**Run to You**, **Somebody**, **Kids Wanna Rock**, **It's Only Love** with Tina Turner) or the romantic balladry of the chart-topping **Heaven**. Adams and co-producer Bob Clearmountain made it all sound sharp and cracking, while Adams was also honed by heavy touring—and got backing vocal help from Foreigner's Lou Gramm and John Eddie. And **Summer of '69** was a nostalgic anthem that continues to resonate more than four decades later.

Reckless's five-times platinum success—including a Canadian Juno Award for Album of the Year—also gave Adams a license to push and experiment in the future, certain that these songs would ensure an audience for the rest of his career. *–GG*

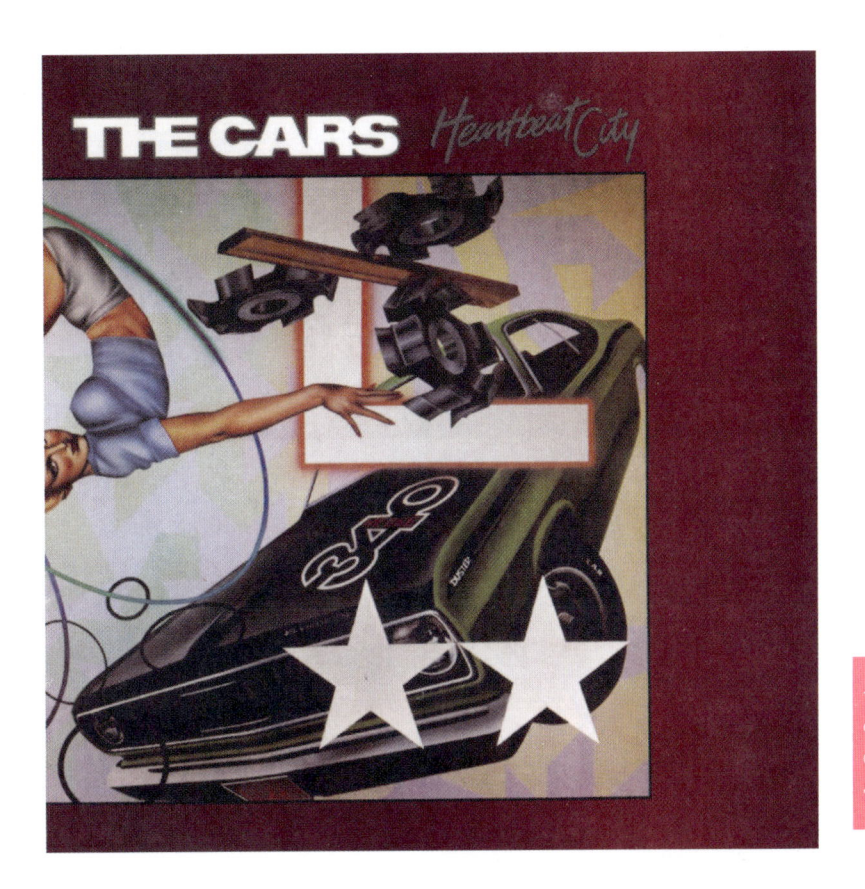

The Cars
HEARTBEAT CITY

ELEKTRA | Producers: Robert John "Mutt" Lange, The Cars
RELEASED: MARCH 13, 1984

● Though it had never really been out of the US charts or off the radio, the Cars had never been able to re-create the level of success it saw with its first two albums. So, for *Heartbeat City*, the group changed it up, splitting with longtime producer Roy Thomas Baker to work with Robert John "Mutt" Lange, recording in London rather than Boston, and sampling drummer David Robinson rather than recording him live. Sonically, the songs were diverse. The mix of beautiful ballads (**Drive**, **It's Not the Night**), powerhouse arena anthems (**Hello Again**), and pure radio hits (**You Might Think**, **Magic**), along with the plaintive title track and **Why Can't I Have You** showed how far the band had progressed.

The payoff was a No. 3 peak on the Billboard 200 and quadruple-platinum sales, with three Top 10s on the singles chart and a revival of the Cars' stature in the marketplace. And, of course, by the mid-'80s, video was king. The Cars' clips from the album were embraced by MTV, which threw its considerable weight behind **You Might Think**, **Magic**, and **Drive** in particular. The *Heartbeat City* videos even provided some fun trivia as well. **You Might Think** won Video of the Year at the first MTV Video Music Awards. The stark **Drive** featured model Paulina Porizkova, who later became Ric Ocasek's third wife (they met on the set, in fact), while the video for **Hello Again** was directed by Andy Warhol, who also appeared in it but was forced to create a second version after the original was censored for nudity and on-screen sex.

Not at all trivial, *Heartbeat City* gave the Cars a thoroughly modern upgrade while still retaining enough of the DNA from its early hits to keep longtime fans satisfied. —*HD/GG*

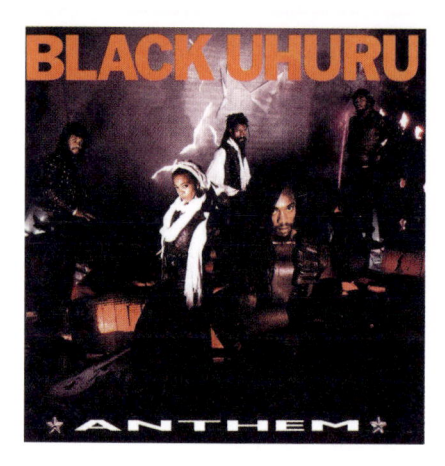

Black Uhuru
ANTHEM
MANGO/ISLAND | Producers: Sly Dunbar, Robbie Shakespeare
RELEASED: JUNE 1984

● Too often eclipsed by Bob Marley & the Wailers, fellow Jamaican troupe Black Uhuru was arguably as potent if not as productive in the same sphere. *Anthem* remains the group's zenith, the deserving winner of the first Grammy Award for Best Reggae Recording despite a confusing history of different editions and record company interference that altered Sly Dunbar and Robbie Shakespeare's production and changed the track sequence and collections. But 2004's *The Complete Anthem Sessions* box set revealed how fruitful and focused the group was at the time. —*GG*

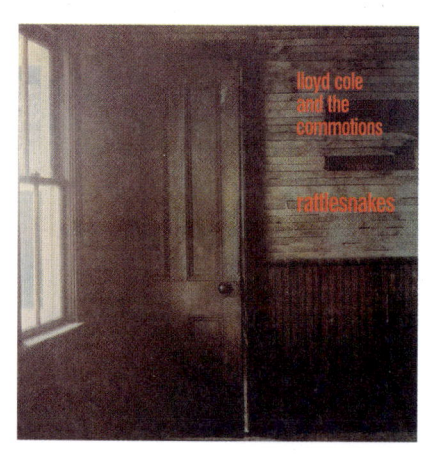

Lloyd Cole and the Commotions
RATTLESNAKES
GEFFEN | Producer: Paul Hardiman
RELEASED: OCTOBER 12, 1984

● Equal parts torrent of verbiage and sublime pop hook, **Perfect Skin** sounded an inspiring opening note to this unusually mature debut. It's to Lloyd Cole's credit that the rest of *Rattlesnakes* lived up to it, playing like pop-wise, highly literate pub rock with nary a word, syllable, or even punctuation mark out of place. Only twenty-three years old, Cole showed sly self-awareness on **Speedboat** when he sighed, "Lord you know wits / They come three to the pound." While he'd go on to make many fine records, this first-kiss debut remains Cole's signpost. —*DM*

Julian Cope
WORLD SHUT YOUR MOUTH
MERCURY | Producer: Steve Lovell
RELEASED: FEBRUARY 17, 1984

● Julian Cope's first solo album shared the same musically up-tempo but lyrically bleak formula of his previous band, the acid-fueled The Teardrop Explodes. Two singles—the catchy **Sunshine Playroom**, whose gory video was banned by the BBC, and **The Greatness and Perfection of Love**—were released, but Cope didn't have a hit until two years later when he re-used the title **World Shut Your Mouth** for a new song. Controversial for his eccentric behavior on- and offstage, Cope's music deserved more respect than he ever gave it. —*HD*

Andraé Crouch
NO TIME TO LOSE
WARNER BROS. | Producers: Andraé Crouch, Bill Maxwell, Bruce Lowe, Phyllis Saint James
RELEASED: SUMMER 1984

● Andraé Crouch was already accepted as the father of modern gospel by the time he was four albums back into his solo career, following the breakup of his band the Disciples. This was his first No. 1 on the gospel charts as Crouch infused its nine tracks with contemporary R&B, funk, and electronic flavors that took listeners to the club—righteously, of course—as well as the church with the title track, the slinky **Livin' This Kind of Life**, and **Got Me Some Angels**. *—GG*

The dB's
LIKE THIS
BEARSVILLE | Producers: Chris Butler, The dB's
RELEASED: SEPTEMBER 12, 1984

● From New York by way of Winston-Salem, North Carolina, the dB's was one of the early New Wave–era combos to put the power in power-pop, adding a modicum of soul, rhythm, and drive to the hooks. *Like This* was its first release on a US label after two stellar imports (*Stands for Decibels*, *Repercussion*), and the first after founding member Chris Stamey's departure. But Bearsville Records imploded as soon as *Like This* was released, dooming it—a shame because every track rang the bell, starting with the should've-been-a-hit **Love Is for Lovers**. *—DM*

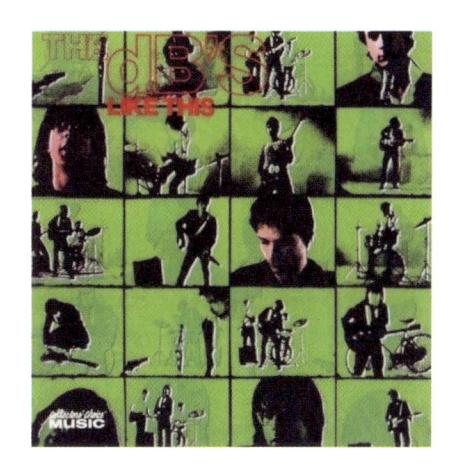

Jack DeJohnette's Special Edition
ALBUM ALBUM
ECM | Producer: Jack DeJohnette
RELEASED: SEPTEMBER 1, 1984

● On his four Special Edition recordings, culminating with *Album Album*, drummer/keyboardist DeJohnette proved he could push his bandmates to excel. The opener, **Ahmad the Terrible**, merged two melodic lines, a front line of blended saxophones and an alternate line played by bassist Rufus Reid. The Miles Davis *Bitches Brew* drummer brought rock 'n' roll hipness to add dynamic energy and funky delight on **Festival** and **New Orleans Strut**. On the melancholy **Monk's Mood**, the three saxophones serenaded in perfectly harmonized unison. On **Third World Anthem**, their delirious soloing was ferocious. *—CH*

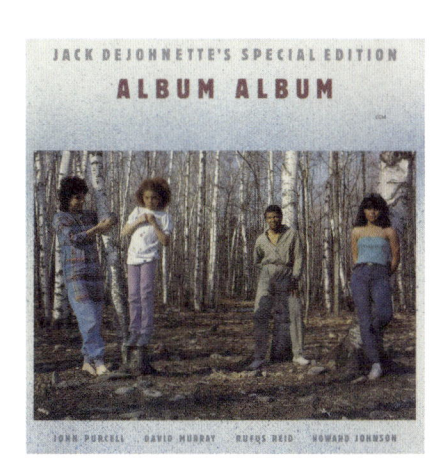

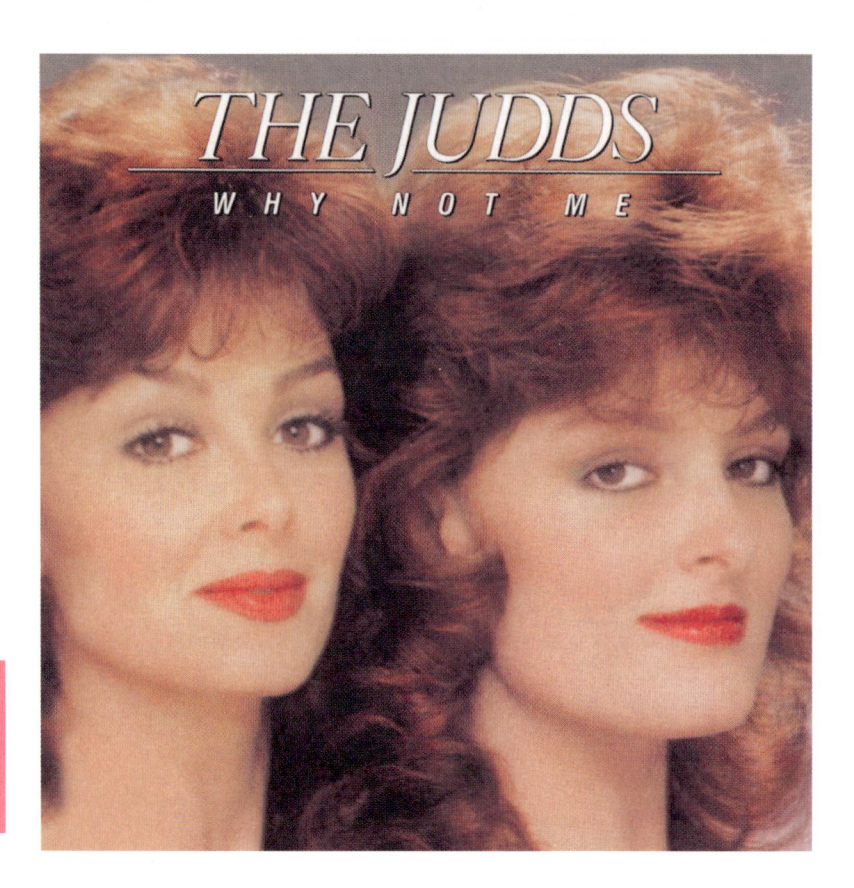

The Judds
WHY NOT ME

RCA | Producer: Brent Maher
RELEASED: OCTOBER 15, 1984

● The Judds pondered *Why Not Me* on their first proper studio release and backed up that thought with a distinct acoustic country sound that made it hard for Nashville to come up with a reasonable answer. The mother-daughter duo's back-to-basics approach was clearly influenced by bluegrass and folk but updated for the more modern, neo-traditional style of the time. The album jump-started what became one of the most successful runs in country music, then and to this day.

Naomi and Wynonna's music had an old-time sensibility countered by out-of-this-world harmonies and vibrant arrangements. The family connection was clear by the way their voices blended effortlessly—Wynonna on lead and Naomi with her lilting harmonies. They became one of country music's first true duos, eschewing the traditional formula of two well-known artists coming together for a duet, à la Loretta Lynn and Conway Twitty.

The pair had already gained notice from the success of **Mama He's Crazy**, a previously released No. 1 single subsequently included on *Why Not Me*. Old-school pedal steel and simple instrumentation enhanced the song's urgency, which was conveyed by Wy's soulful delivery. Her voice was clear and wrung every bit of emotion out of **Love Is Alive**, the final single released from the album. And while the songwriting trended toward the losing side of love (**Mr. Pain**, **Bye Bye Baby Blues**), it was saved from being dark and moody by the bouncy, almost-plucky feel of tracks such as **My Baby's Gone** and **Girl's Night Out**.

The Judds proved they had the sweet and the salty covered. The album had a timeless simplicity that made it warm and inviting like a handmade quilt, with enough edge to believe there was a jug of white lightning somewhere on the porch. —SS

1984

Don Henley
BUILDING THE PERFECT BEAST

GEFFEN | Producers: Don Henley, Danny Kortchmar, Mike Campbell, Greg Ladanyi

RELEASED: NOVEMBER 19, 1984

● Don Henley took a big step forward with his second solo record, *Building the Perfect Beast*. Never one to shy away from speaking his mind, the ten tracks covered the spectrum from human relationships to social consciousness. There was an intellectual undercurrent to the album, which helped establish Henley's solo identity outside of Eagles. Henley and Danny Kortchmar embraced the slick sounds of the decade with a full complement of synthesizers and drum machines. The pair put their Rolodexes to good use, too, and called upon numerous well-known musicians and vocalists to make appearances on the record—including Belinda Carlisle, Lindsey Buckingham, and Patty Smyth.

The haunting tap of a cymbal followed by Mike Campbell's twangy guitar riff perfectly embodied the wistful nostalgia of **Boys of Summer**. And the swelling keyboards on **Sunset Grill** may have been machine made, but the arrangement by Benmont Tench, also of Tom Petty's Heartbreakers, made them memorable. The percolating beat underneath the popular **All She Wants to Do Is Dance** turned a protest song about the US government's foreign policy into a Billboard Top 10 hit. Henley's views on the plight of working-class America took center stage in **A Month of Sundays**, and he wasn't afraid to wear his heart on his sleeve with **Land of the Living**. When broken down, in fact, the original sides of the record reflected two different aspects of Henley—side 1 focused mainly on love and emotion, while side 2 leaned into social commentary.

Henley's distinct voice and "everyman" delivery gave the album a timeless feel and universal appeal. Whether he was reminiscing about lost love or essaying on the world at large, *Building the Perfect Beast* showed what Henley was made of. *—SS*

Bob Marley
LEGEND

ISLAND | Producers: Chris Blackwell, Errol Brown, Bob Marley, Steve Smith, The Wailers

RELEASED: MAY 1984

● The comedy troupe the Kids in the Hall once joked that "greatest hits albums are for housewives and little girls," and there may be some validity to their criticism about how labels package compilations. Regardless, Legend not only launched millions of Bob Marley posters onto dorm room walls but opened American ears to reggae.

Bob Marley and the Wailers had been around since the early '60s selling well in the UK due to the influence of Jamaicans who had moved to England seeking better working opportunities, rebuilding the country after World War II. Back then, working-class British kids started digging the sounds of their Caribbean neighbors, later influencing UK punk, New Wave, and post-punk bands like the Clash, the Police, and Public Image Ltd. But by the time Marley died of cancer in 1981 at the age of thirty-six, he had barely made a dent in the US.

Understanding this, Island Records stacked Legend to highlight Marley's top-charting UK tracks with heavy emphasis on romance and rebellion. Songs such as the sunny **Three Little Birds** and **Satisfy My Soul** met anthems like **Jamming** and **Get Up, Stand Up**. Americans would have likely heard Eric Clapton's 1974 cover of **I Shot the Sheriff**, so the original is included here. While **Redemption Song** on Legend mentioned the slave trade, it's not as directly confrontational on issues of racism and oppression as "Slave Driver" and "400 Year," found on Marley's 1973 full-length Catch a Fire (Jamaican slang for "Burn in Hell").

Island's choices made Legend the perfect gateway record to reggae. In doing so, Legend became the best-selling reggae album of all time and the second-longest-running album on the Billboard 200 as of early 2024. So, apparently Bob Marley was a big hit with more than just "housewives and little girls." **—RSM**

Sheila E.
THE GLAMOROUS LIFE

WARNER BROS. | Producers: Sheila E., The Starr Company (aka Prince)
RELEASED: JUNE 4, 1984

● Although Sheila E. rose to pop fame on the strength of a hit single and album largely written and co-performed by Prince, you'd be foolish to write her off as a protégé. The percussionist's credits included Marvin Gaye, Diana Ross, Herbie Hancock, and Lionel Richie. An exuberant Latin flavor ran throughout *The Glamorous Life*, from the borderline psychedelic opener **The Belle of St. Mark** to the hit title track and the dazzling instrumental **Strawberry Shortcake**. And, in retrospect, *The Glamorous Life* also influenced Prince's next album, 1985's *Around the World in a Day*. —MW

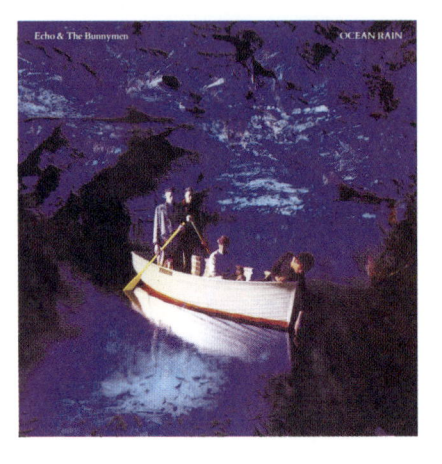

Echo & the Bunnymen
OCEAN RAIN

SIRE | Producers: Echo & the Bunnymen, Gil Norton, Henri Loustau
RELEASED: MAY 14, 1984

● Most of Echo & the Bunnymen's fourth album was recorded with a thirty-five-piece orchestra, giving the album a full, lush sound. Its first single, **The Killing Moon**, remains the band's top-seller; uniquely beautiful and almost gothic in its lyrics, its chord structure was endearingly based on David Bowie's "Space Oddity" played backwards. "It's a psalm, almost hymnal," frontman Ian McCulloch told *The Guardian* in 2015. "It's about everything, from birth to death." The entire album, including the singles **Silver** and **Seven Seas**, was dreamy, poetic pop that still impresses. —HD

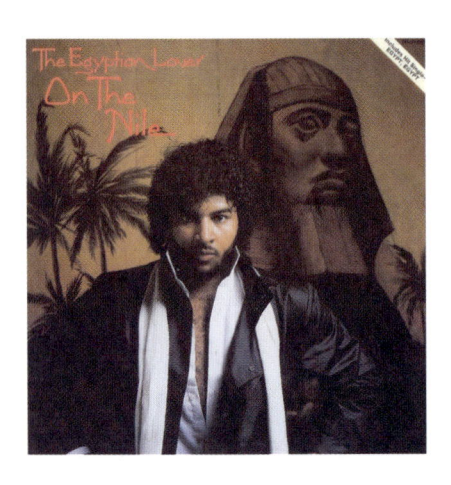

Egyptian Lover
ON THE NILE

EGYPTIAN EMPIRE | Producer: Egyptian Lover
RELEASED: NOVEMBER 1984

● Greg Broussard was a bit of a novice when he decided to produce an album under his Egyptian Lover alias. His fun-loving, uninhibited approach resulted in a record that turned the electro hip-hop world on its ears. Produced as if a DJ was cutting up beats, the album emits a fresh, almost-live feeling with the iconic **Egypt Egypt** leading the way. Just try getting these earworms out of your head while you bop around to some of the rawest and crisp electro ever produced courtesy of the Egyptian Lover. —MH

Various Artists
FOOTLOOSE (ORIGINAL MOTION PICTURE SOUNDTRACK)
COLUMBIA | Producers: Kenny Loggins, Sammy Hagar, David Foster, Keith Olsen, Jim Steinman, Bill Wolfer, George Duke, John Boylan, Lee DeCarlo
RELEASED: JANUARY 27, 1984

● The '80s were an era of teen films, and *Footloose* checked all the boxes, including a soundtrack full of mainstream pop and well-placed rock anthems. The nine tracks ran the gamut from Kenny Loggins's hit title track to Deniece Williams's foot-tapping **Let's Hear It for the Boy** and the clever use of Bonnie Tyler's **Holding Out for a Hero** during a pivotal scene. The music was an essential part of the film's success; quite simply, it would have been hard to cut loose without something to dance to. *—SS*

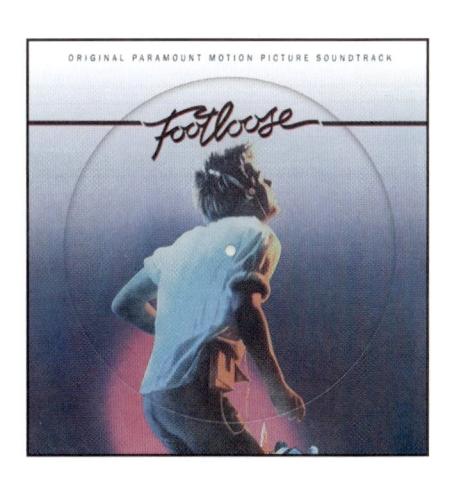

Various Artists
GHOSTBUSTERS (ORIGINAL SOUNDTRACK ALBUM)
ARISTA | Producers: Various
RELEASED: JUNE 8, 1984

● Who you gonna call? In 1984, it was Ray Parker Jr. who was tapped for a soundtrack megahit. He might not have been the obvious guess for the biggest hit from a soundtrack featuring Laura Branigan, Thompson Twins, Air Supply, and others, but the former Raydio frontman's **Ghostbusters** spent three weeks at No. 1 and was nominated for an Academy Award, though Parker also had to settle with Huey Lewis and the News due to similarities to its "I Want a New Drug." *—RW*

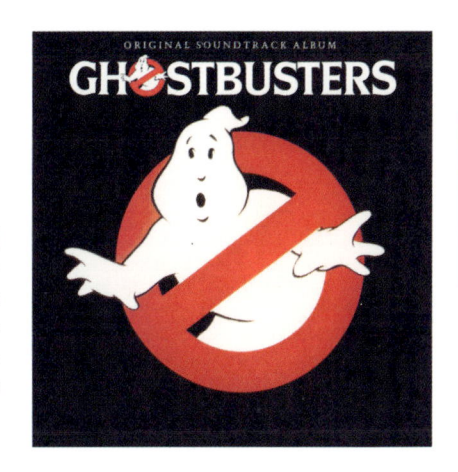

Manuel Göttsching
E2-E4
INTEAM GMBH | Producer: Manuel Göttsching
RELEASED: 1984

● It's highly unlikely that a progressive rock guitarist would compose one of the most influential albums in electronic music history, but Manuel Göttsching accomplished just that. The one-hour-long voyage of minimalistic electronica with a bit of guitar caught on in the New York underground scene, and the legend of *E2-E4* was born. The beautiful textures and floating rhythms delivered pure aural pleasure with enough underlying beat to subconsciously sway the body. Cited by numerous electronic artists as a major inspiration, *E2-E4* is considered the soul of techno. *—MH*

Los Lobos
HOW WILL THE WOLF SURVIVE?
SLASH/WARNER BROS. | Producers: T Bone Burnett, Steve Berlin

RELEASED: OCTOBER 1984

● Formed during the first half of the '70s in East Los Angeles, Los Lobos came to prominence in the local scene at the top of the '80s. The Mexican-American group initially got together to celebrate its heritage, playing traditional boleros and cumbia along with region-influenced soul and rock 'n' roll. Its 1983 EP, . . . *And a Time to Dance*, extended its reach outside of East L.A. When the band returned the following year with its second album (six years after their self-released debut), it retained co-producer T Bone Burnett from the EP, as well as its mix of English- and Spanish-language roots rock with a Tex-Mex flair.

Work began on *How Will the Wolf Survive?* not long after the Los Lobos completed touring in support of . . . *And a Time to Dance*. Burnett—along with saxophonist Steve Berlin, who co-produced the EP before becoming a member of Los Lobos—helped pull together the album's eleven songs, all but one written by group members David Hidalgo, Louie Perez, and Cesar Rosas. But its center was held firm by the quintet's expert playing.

With accordion, lap steel, and mandolin blending with traditional bajo quinto, bajo sexto, and guitarron, plus rock standbys bass, drums, and guitars, and various percussion and saxophone, the music on *How Will the Wolf Survive?* presaged much of the Americana movement that came of age later in the decade. Lyrically, the songs often explored the struggles of the working-class people whose race was an additional hurdle; on **A Matter of Time**, a migrant worker bids farewell to his family as he searches for a new life for them. The title track sums up the struggle through symbolism and self-mythology. When Hidalgo asks, "Will the wolf survive?" hope is always on the horizon. *—MG*

1984

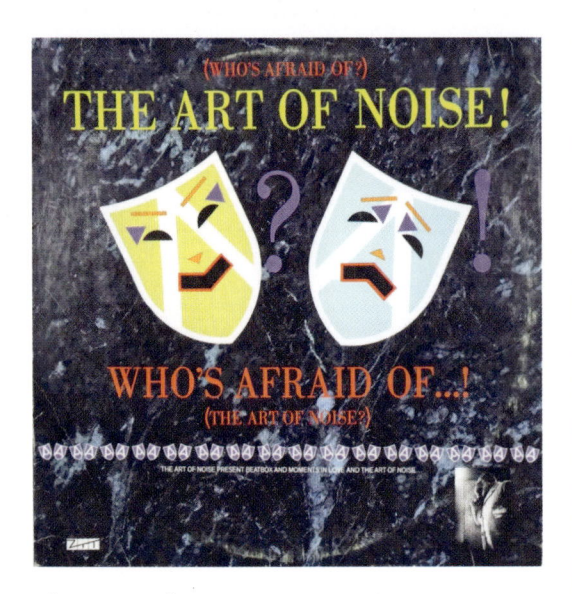

The Art of Noise
WHO'S AFRAID OF THE ART OF NOISE
ISLAND/ZTT | Producers: The Art of Noise
RELEASED: JUNE 1984

● What happens when you put basically every style of music into a creative blender, then add a genius use of electronics? The Art of Noise, with its many musical personality disorders, answered the question with this unique and groundbreaking album. The beauty and the beast are well represented here, as the band name reflects—art in a way that ears had not previously been exposed to. The album captivated and yet stirred the senses, and no matter how you try to resist, the production and cleverness kept bringing you back in. Included in this avant-garde, synth-pop-laden gem were heavy beat thumpers such as **Beat Box (Diversion One)**, **Close (To the Edit)**, and **A Time for Fear (Who's Afraid)** that got your very soul bopping to their organized chaos and rhythms. Hard and at times industrial-type beats with samples woven together created some of the most unique songs ever created. Then, out of nowhere, came **Moments in Love**, a beautiful down-tempo electronic masterpiece that delivered a hauntingly surreal feel, similar to Kool & the Gang's "Summer Madness," as it mesmerizes and floats into nirvana. Was this art? Or noise? Why not both? *—MH*

Chicago
CHICAGO 17
FULL MOON/WARNER BROS. | Producer: David Foster
RELEASED: MAY 14, 1984

● Love them or hate them, power ballads were a mainstay for *Chicago 17*, ten tracks of pure David Foster pop production that gave the band its highest-charting album (No. 4) in seven years. Despite being only his second time working with the band, Foster was instrumental in creating the swelling synthesizer sound and expansive vocals that firmly planted the group into Adult Contemporary territory. Peter Cetera's lead vocals on the two biggest singles, **Hard Habit to Break** and **You're the Inspiration**, were a perfect fit for the sweeping, lush arrangements. The horn section, which had been Chicago's signature, was relegated to the background—which made die-hard fans and purists unhappy—and likely contributed to strife within the band and Cetera's subsequent departure. This was more arena rock drama with catchy lyrics and an easy-to-follow melody. The driving drum machine of **Stay the Night** swelled into a slick chorus, and the funky keyboards on **Along Comes a Woman** had almost a New Wave dance feel. While it was a vast departure from the original Chicago Transit Authority, the new sound became the inspiration for the big songs, big hair, and even bigger voices (we're looking at you, Michael Bolton) that would define the power ballad generation. *—SS*

Hüsker Dü
ZEN ARCADE
S S T | Producers: Hüsker Dü, Spot
RELEASED: JULY 1, 1984

● Even while employing the loud-fast playbook of '80s underground rock, Minneapolis division, Hüsker Dü was always a lot catchier than the average punk band going all the way back to the head-banging hooks of its very first release, 1983's *Everything Falls Apart* EP. But what truly set this unlikely power trio apart from its punk peers was its massive, sprawling sense of ambition. That was never more obvious than on *Zen Arcade*, a landmark double album that came out just a year later.

With twenty-three tracks clocking in at a little over an hour, *Zen Arcade* was basically guitarist Bob Mould and drummer Grant Hart yelling at each other as bassist Greg Norton tries to mediate in the middle. And if that doesn't sound appealing, know that it made for a fascinating listen. For all the mood swings, the hooks were sharpened to the point of industrial strength, all the more so for the whiplash tempos and volume (kudos to producer Glenn Michael "Spot" Lockett for capturing it). There's even an actual acoustic song, **Never Talking to You Again**, pointing the way toward future directions for both Hart and Mould. By the following year, Hüsker Dü was actually making straight-up pop records. *—DM*

Branford Marsalis
SCENES IN THE CITY
C O L U M B I A | Producers: Thomas Mowrey, George Butler
RELEASED: FEBRUARY 10, 1984

● Branford Marsalis channeled years of rigorous preparation before recording his debut album as a leader, presaging his bright future with a solid and assured jazz effort in the vein of John Coltrane and Sonny Rollins. The eldest of the six New Orleans–bred Marsalis brothers, he was initially home taught by his father, Ellis, and rode the coattails of his more famous brother, trumpeter Wynton, who helped him land the alto sax chair in drummer Art Blakey's Jazz Messengers hard-bop band. Woodshedding with Blakey and later Wynton's band, Branford perfected his tone, embouchure, style, and technique and locked into soprano and tenor saxophones. For *Scenes in the City*, he hired veteran bassist Ron Carter, who ably followed Marsalis's tenacious tenor improvisation on **No Backstage Pass**; notable "Young Lion" contemporaries, pianists Kenny Kirkland and Mulgrew Miller; and drummers Jeffrey Watts and Marvin Smith. The title track, a remake of Charles Mingus's 1957 original, was a nostalgic ode to jazz life in New York with narration by Wendell Pierce. **Solstice** kicked off with feisty tenor with pungent soprano notes after the bridge. On the Miller ballad **Parable**, Marsalis's piercing, mystic soprano improv echoes Wayne Shorter. *—CH*

1984

Kool & the Gang
EMERGENCY
DE-LITE | Producers: Jim Bonnefond, Ronald Bell, Kool & the Gang
RELEASED: NOVEMBER 15, 1984

● Four years after celebrating good times, Kool & the Gang had even more reason to rejoice with *Emergency*, the best-selling album of the R&B group's then fifteen-year recording career. The band's penultimate outing with singer James "J. T." Taylor brought the funk with the singles **Fresh** and **Misled** and even tried out the rock lane on the title track. But it was the mellower **Cherish** that really opened a new avenue, hitting No. 1 on multiple charts. That pushed *Emergency* to double-platinum sales for the first and only time. —GG

Let's Active
CYPRESS
I.R.S. | Producers: Mitch Easter, Don Dixon
RELEASED: NOVEMBER 1984

● Mitch Easter oversaw R.E.M.'s landmark early work with co-producer Don Dixon. But Easter's legacy includes many other notable production clients and his own group, Let's Active, whose original trio line-up comprised singer/guitarist Easter, bassist/vocalist Faye Hunter, and drummer Sara Romweber. *Cypress* was made amid Easter's and Hunter's breakup, and Hunter practically spits her vocal on **Blue Line**. Yet the hooks are to die for, starting with the guitar jangle on opener **Easy Does**. Easter would make two more Let's Active albums with different players, shuttering the group by the end of the 1980s. —DM

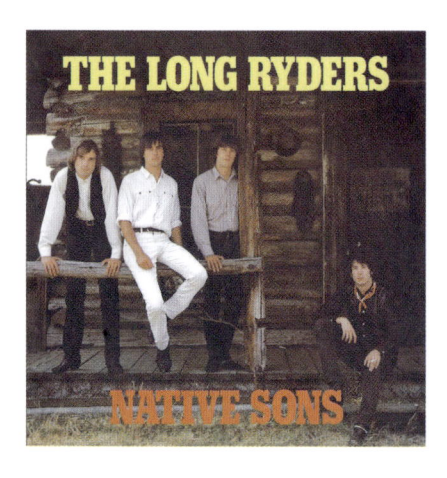

The Long Ryders
NATIVE SONS
FRONTIER | Producer: Henry Lewy
RELEASED: OCTOBER 1984

● Considered the big-bang moment for what became alt-country/Americana, the Long Ryders' debut album proudly flaunted Beatles, Byrds, and Nuggets-era psychedelic garage-rock allegiances. The Sid Griffin–led L.A. band even used the Flying Burrito Brothers' producer, put an ex-Byrd on a track, and re-created the cover of a never-released Buffalo Springfield album. *Native Sons* led to a major label deal. Unfortunately, its career soon fizzled, but its roots-music influence reverberated through Uncle Tupelo, the Jayhawks, Old 97's, and others who fused country instruments, rock attitude, and folk harmonies into a new genre. —LM

Barry Manilow
2:00 AM PARADISE CAFÉ
ARISTA | Producer: Barry Manilow
RELEASED: NOVEMBER 15, 1984

● A hipster might think it a stretch to put a Barry Manilow album in any list dubbed "Essential," but go with us on this one. Ten albums into a career of writing the songs a lot of the world was singing, Manilow veered left into smoky jazz club territory, recruiting ace players such as saxophonist Gerry Mulligan and guitarist Mundell Lowe and duet partners Mel Tormé and Sarah Vaughan to show some genuine and credible musical chops that were welcome not only for Manilow but for the market in general at the time. *—GG*

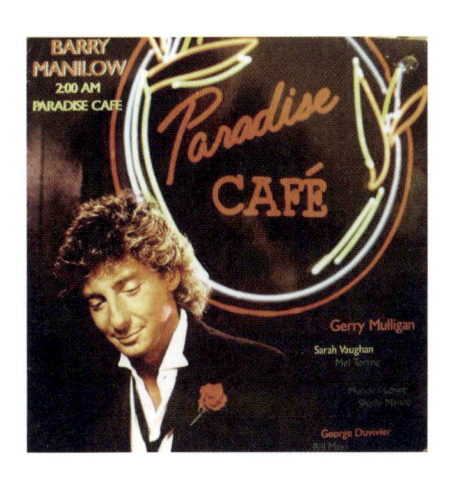

Metallica
RIDE THE LIGHTNING
MEGAFORCE | Producers: Flemming Rasmussen, Mark Whitaker, Metallica
RELEASED: JULY 27, 1984

● If *Kill 'Em All* got Metallica attention, its successor won the band respect. *Ride the Lightning* was more ambitious and sophisticated, still dark and thrashing at its heart but expanding Metallica's sound compositionally and sonically. The title track, **For Whom the Bell Tolls**, and **Creeping Death** became instant thrash classics, while **Fade to Black** introduced quieter dynamics that proved just as intense. It was truly a tremendous step forward. Lightning would strike many times for Metallica in the coming years, but this bolt's aim was fully on target. *—GG*

Pat Metheny Group
FIRST CIRCLE
ECM | Producer: Pat Metheny
RELEASED: 1984

● On the heels of two breakthrough albums and relentless touring, the Pat Metheny Group was a rare contemporary jazz band that attracted non-jazz fans. The uncanny rapport between guitarist Metheny and keyboardist Lyle Mays was crucial. The duo abounded in enthusiasm and creative artistry, co-composing soaring, highly melodic tunes and artfully blending acoustic and electric instrumentation. *First Circle* added new drummer Paul Wertico and Argentinean multi-instrumentalist/singer Pedro Aznar, whose floating wordless vocals harmonized alongside Metheny's sky-high guitar synthesizer and earned the band's third consecutive Grammy Award, for Best Fusion Jazz Performance. *—CH*

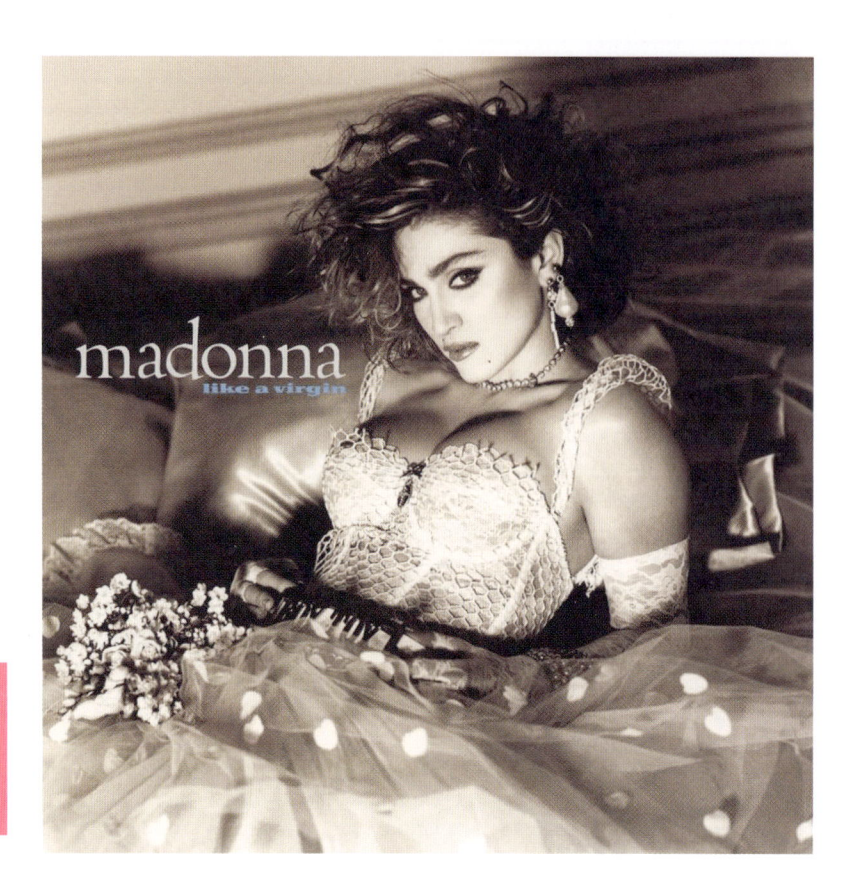

Madonna
LIKE A VIRGIN
SIRE/WARNER BROS. | Producer: Nile Rodgers
RELEASED: NOVEMBER 12, 1984

● Although Madonna made a splash with her 1983 debut, most industry prognosticators predicted the Michigan-born, New York City–based pop singer would have a limited shelf life. When she hit the stage for the inaugural MTV Video Music Awards on September 14, 1984, however, history changed. Wearing a thrift store wedding dress and Boy Toy belt, Madonna sang the suggestively titled **Like a Virgin** while writhing around, flashing her underwear and simulating masturbation (the words "like a" are key to understanding this song). Afterward, music biz naysayers doubled down, predicting the nascent star's career was done; teenage viewers, on the other hand, dropped their jaws for a different reason entirely—they wanted more, pronto.

Her sophomore album picked up where the scandal left off. *Madonna* had personality, charm, and hooks, but *Like a Virgin* had swagger, seduction, and grooves. The lattermost came courtesy of Nile Rodgers, who was in the midst of a hitmaking production hot streak after disbanding Chic. With Rodgers and Madonna working in tandem, a new breed of dance-pop that would define the '80s (and to a large extent, pop music for the next twenty years) was forged.

Listeners ate it up. **Like a Virgin** topped the Billboard Hot 100 for six weeks, and follow-up **Material Girl**—a winking send-up of consumerism that arrived with a Marilyn Monroe–inspired music video—hit No. 2. Two Top 5 hits followed—**Angel** and **Dress You Up**, both energetic encapsulations of yearning and lust that clicked with her growing army of teenage wannabes at suburban malls from sea to shining sea. And while the album topped the Billboard 200 and went ten-times platinum, its greatest impact on music was simple: This was the soundtrack to the Queen of Pop's coronation. *—JL*

1984

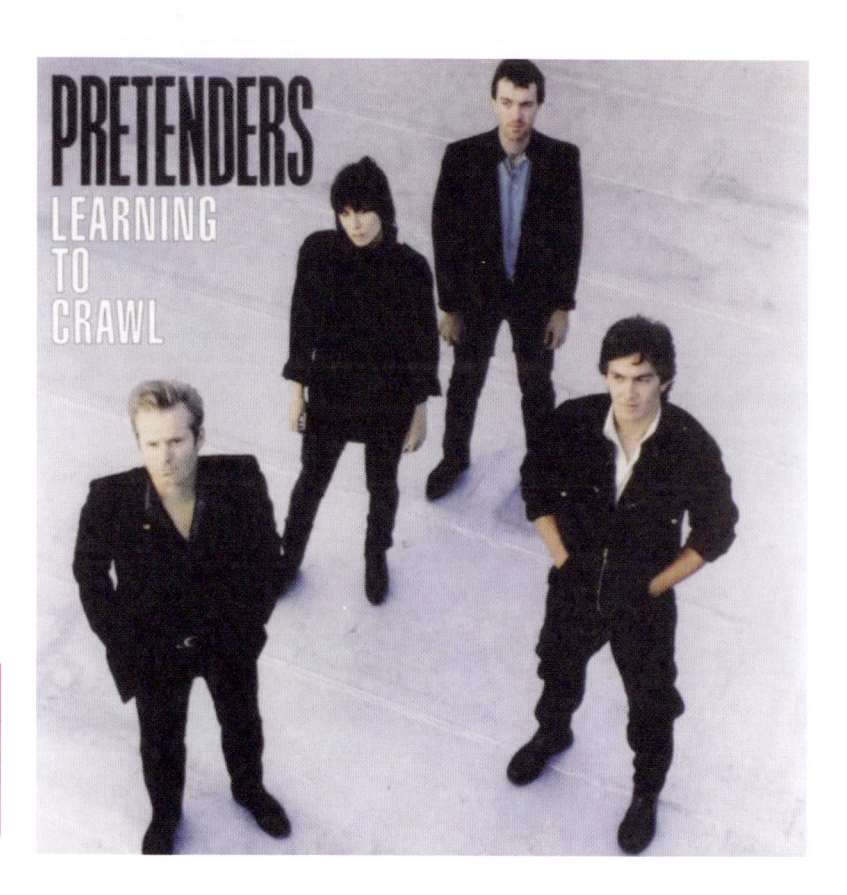

The Pretenders
LEARNING TO CRAWL

SIRE | Producer: Chris Thomas
RELEASED: JANUARY 13, 1984

● After the release of the Pretenders' second album, bandleader Chrissie Hynde was faced with a basket of life-changing personal and professional challenges. Bassist Pete Farndon was removed from the band for excessive drug use and passed away shortly after. Guitarist James Honeyman-Scott died from a drug overdose two days after Farndon's dismissal. Hynde's on-again, off-again relationship with the Kinks' Dave Davies was finally off for good; the silver lining was giving birth to a beautiful baby girl. Despite, and perhaps because of, all that, Hynde ended up producing one of the finest albums of her career, Learning to Crawl, the title a reference to her new daughter.

Like all Pretenders work, the album was powered by Hynde's distinctive songwriting and vocals, which ranged from gentle purr to an angry growl, sometimes in the same verse. Many songs here were quite personal. **Show Me** was a tender, mid-tempo message from a first-time mother to her newborn child. In **My City Was Gone**, Hynde found the gorgeous countryside of her hometown of Akron, Ohio, devoured by excessive development. **Thin Line Between Love and Hate** covered the 1971 Persuaders song about infidelity that was guessed to be aimed at a certain someone in Hynde's life.

It wouldn't be a Pretenders album if there weren't some unadulterated rockers. **Middle of the Road** cooked with new guitarist Robbie McIntosh laying down lines that proved him a spectacular replacement for Honeyman-Scott. **Back on the Chain Gang** and **Time the Avenger** added to the locomotion. There were even forays into country (**Thembelina**) and rockabilly (**Watching the Clothes**). All in all, Learning to Crawl produced five successful singles and demonstrated that great turmoil can result in great art. *–GP*

1984

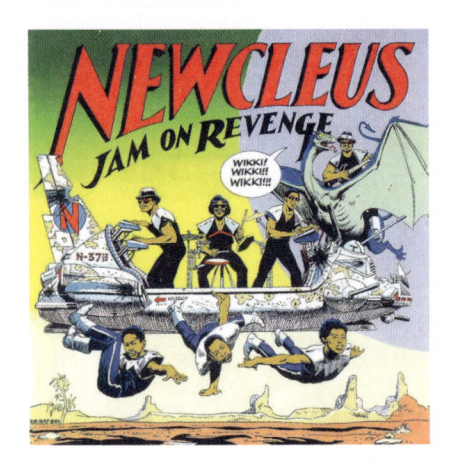

Newcleus
JAM ON REVENGE

SUNNYVIEW | Producers: Frank Fair, Joe Webb

RELEASED: 1984

● Newcleus flew its electro hip-hop mothership into a new world when it landed this funky robotic dance gem onto Earth. The duo's modern electronic, free-flowing robotic sound transformed the planet with iconic songs such as **Jam on It**, which had the masses shouting "Wikki! Wikki! Wikki!" **Computer Age (Push the Button)** delivered a futuristic blend of funk and synths that blasted listeners into a space-age dance frenzy. A fresh new sound was transmitted to the people, and the world was a better place. Mission accomplished. —MH

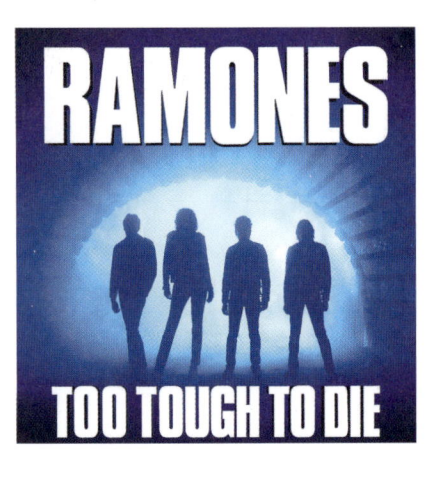

Ramones
TOO TOUGH TO DIE

SIRE | Producers: Tommy Erdelyi, Ed Stasium

RELEASED: OCTOBER 1, 1984

● Irony reigned on Ramones' eighth studio album. It was the quartet's worst-performing album to date on the charts, but it was also not so arguably its best since *Rocket to Russia* and one that delightfully straddled the group's early punk attitude and heavyweight energy that leaned into metal. The pop trimmings of more recent efforts, particularly the Phil Spector–produced *End of the Century*, were replaced by a muscular, hard-hitting attack with plenty of blast-furnace, 1-2-3-4 punk and even Ramones' first-ever instrumental, the fifty-six-second **Durango 95**. —GG

Scorpions
LOVE AT FIRST STING

MERCURY | Producer: Dieter Dierks

RELEASED: MARCH 1984

● Scorpions had been around nearly two decades when the German quintet's ninth studio album made it a worldwide sensation. The group had entered the platinum ranks with its two predecessors. *Love at First Sting* perfected the attack with producer Dieter Dierks, serving up stadium anthems (**Rock You Like a Hurricane**, **Big City Nights**), earnest power ballads (**Still Loving You**), and an epic tempo-changing track (**Coming Home**) for a triple-platinum smash that could be held up as the prototypical '80s rock album. A controversy over the sexy original cover only helped the cause. —GG

The Style Council
CAFÉ BLEU
GEFFEN | Producers: Paul Weller, Peter Wilson
RELEASED: MARCH 16, 1984

● The Style Council was born from guitarist/vocalist Paul Weller's desire to escape the rigid format of his punk band, the Jam. And escape he did. Collaborating with keyboardist Mick Talbot, *Café Bleu* was a mix of styles, from the boogie-woogie to bossa nova, jazz, torchy cabaret, and the soulful single **My Ever Changing Moods**—all on the A-side only. While off-putting to fans of the Jam, Weller's talent shined through, and the album was deservedly well received by critics and found its own fanbase. *—GP*

Thompson Twins
INTO THE GAP
ARISTA | Producers: Alex Sadkin, Tom Bailey
RELEASED: FEBRUARY 17, 1984

● Thompson Twins certainly knew its east from its west as the British trio grooved into its fourth album, building on the momentum from the polyrhythmic ecstasy of its predecessors. Songcraft was the focus this time out, and the three Twins came up with their best tunes yet, including the Top 5 love song **Hold Me Now**, **Doctor! Doctor!**, **The Gap**, the refreshingly rootsy **You Lift Me Up**, and the sublimely constructed **Sister of Mercy**. Platinum and Top 10, it was a career peak whose merits have remained obvious in the decades since. *—GG*

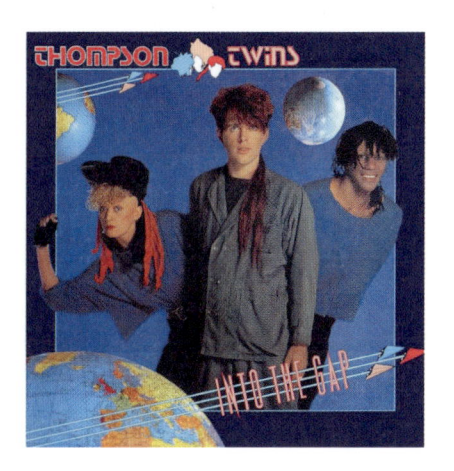

Twisted Sister
STAY HUNGRY
ATLANTIC | Producer: Tom Werman
RELEASED: MAY 10, 1984

● The world at large considers Twisted Sister a one-hit wonder, which is wrong in so many ways. *Stay Hungry*, home to the breakthrough **We're Not Gonna Take It**, was the third excellent album the group released after over a decade. The album offered more than that; the follow-up, **I Wanna Rock**, might be even better, and the rest of *Stay Hungry* was filled with smart, memorable songs such as **Burn in Hell** and **The Price**, which frontman Dee Snider wrote almost instantaneously while feeling homesick on an overseas tour. *—MW*

New Edition
NEW EDITION
MCA | Producers: Vincent Brantley, Richard Rudolph, more
RELEASED: SEPTEMBER 29, 1984

● Sure, there were boys in bands before New Edition, but the contemporary notion of boy bands more or less started with this Boston five-piece. While modeled after the Jackson 5, New Edition set the template that everyone from New Kids on the Block to Backstreet Boys, *NSYNC, and One Direction followed: Take five young male singers who individually appeal to different fans (the bad boy, the shy one, etc.), pair them with the pop sound of the day, dominate the charts, and take over the world.

It sounds easy, but there's a science to pulling it off, and New Edition—teenagers Ricky Bell, Michael Bivins, Bobby Brown, Ronnie DeVoe, and Ralph Tresvant (Johnny Gill joined later)—did it so well that generations of others duplicated their success. (Meanwhile, the predatory business practices inflicted upon them became a cautionary tale for the stars that followed in their wake.)

The group's self-titled second album (following 1983's *Candy Girl*) took New Edition to the masses; led by the hit **Cool It Now**, the album hit No. 6 on the Billboard 200 and went double platinum. It was filled with catchy pop-R&B sounds, from the modern doo-wop of **Mr. Telephone Man** to the junior high slow-dance ballad **Lost in Love** to **My Secret (Didja Gitit Yet?)**, which played like an answer to Deniece Williams's earlier 1984 hit "Let's Hear It for the Boy."

The group members went on to successful careers, as Brown became one of the biggest pop stars of the late '80s and Bell, Bivins, and DeVoe formed a trio that shaped the sound of early '90s new jack swing. After breaking up in 1990, New Edition re-formed for a 1996 reunion album and tour and became a steady stage presence following a second reunion in 2004. *—AG*

1984

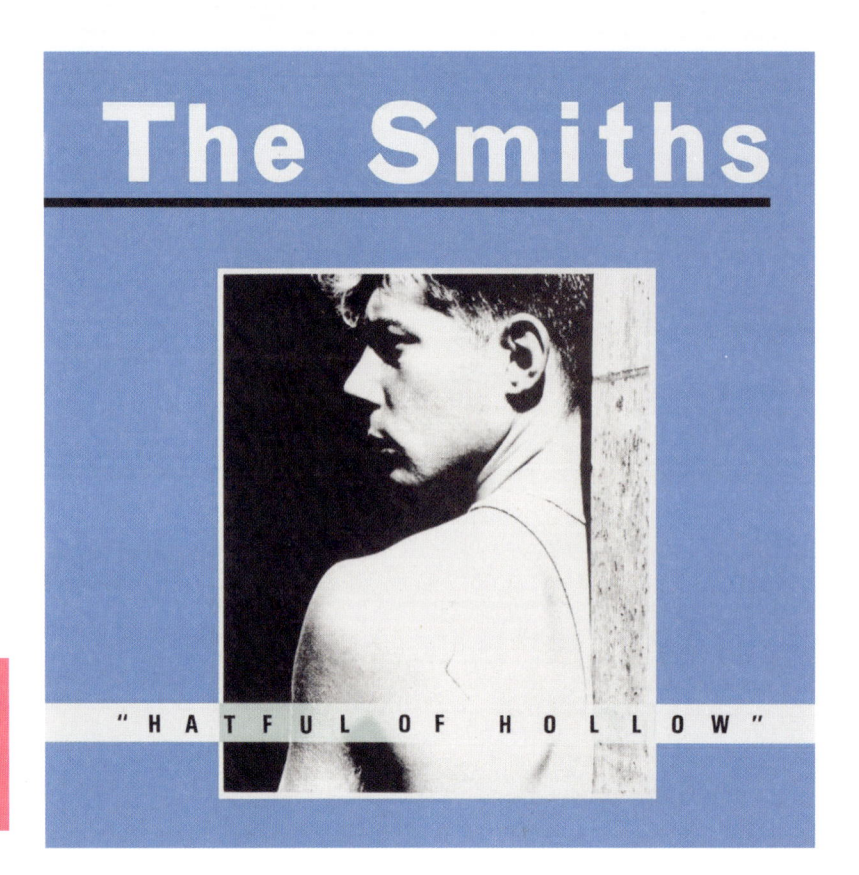

The Smiths
HATFUL OF HOLLOW

ROUGH TRADE | Producers: John Porter, The Smiths, Roger Pusey, Dale "Buffin" Griffin

RELEASED: NOVEMBER 12, 1984

● Before the political rants (by frontman Morrissey), the never-ending gig cancellations (by Morrissey), and the inflammatory statements to the press (again by Morrissey), there was the music. Bleak yet hummable. Musically complex and lyrically poetic, The Smiths (Morrissey, Johnny Marr, Andy Rourke, and Mike Joyce) formed in 1982 and quickly became the darlings of pre-emo teens everywhere.

By eschewing the synth-pop and dance music that had taken over the charts and adopting the guitar/bass/drum construct of basic rock, the Smiths projected a happy, jangly style, which was offset by Morrissey's darker-than-dark, despairing lyrics about self-loathing, celibacy, animal rights, and political injustices. In the UK, the band released a self-titled album and saw several non-album singles rise through the charts before *Hatful of Hollow*, a compilation of BBC Radio 1 tracks, which differed from the previously released versions, two new songs, B-sides, and a subtly remixed version of its first single, **Hand in Glove**. It stayed in the UK charts for almost a year. The band's US label, meanwhile, released two other different compilations instead, holding onto *Hatful of Hollow* until 1993.

While most compilations sound like unrelated songs thrown together in a blender, *Hatful*, released less than two years after the band formed, sounded cohesive and included one banger after another. From the yearning of **Please Please Please Let Me Get What I Want** to the sexual ambiguity and angst of **This Charming Man** to the bleakness of **Heaven Knows I'm Miserable Now** to the underappreciated beauty of **Back to the Old House** and the unapologetically homoerotic **Reel Around the Fountain**, this may be an album to cry to in your best black clothes—but also one to crank to eleven and appreciate. —*HD*

Run-D.M.C.
RUN-D.M.C.
PROFILE | Producers: Russell Simmons, Larry Smith
RELEASED: MARCH 27, 1984

● When Run-D.M.C.'s self-titled debut arrived, it broke a lot of ground in the still-evolving rap genre. In addition to being the first album-length work to mark itself in a singles-dominated market, the nine-track LP contained some of the first socially conscious rap songs in a genre that still hadn't grown out of its party-music stage. In essence, Run-D.M.C. was a pioneering record that launched a new era in hip-hop. Its release effectively closed all doors to the music's past.

Grandmaster Flash and the Furious Five's "The Message" got the ball rolling in 1982. A strident protest song about inner-city conditions ("It's like a jungle sometimes / It makes me wonder how I keep from going under"), the track pushed rap music out of complacency and into a more active state. The next year, Queens, New York–based Run-D.M.C.—Joseph "Run" Simmons, Darryl "D.M.C." McDaniels, and Jam Master Jay—released its debut single, **It's Like That**, a similarly themed survey of the streets: "Unemployment at a record high / People coming, people going, people born to die." Rappers Simmons and McDaniels, trading verses, barked rhymes with gravity miles above rap's usual singsong approach.

The music on *Run-D.M.C.* matched this toughness, particularly **Rock Box**, which featured a rhythm heavily inspired by Billy Squier's "The Big Beat" and a metal guitar solo from session player Eddie Martinez. (Run-D.M.C. would blend rap and rock even further in 1986 when it covered "Walk This Way" with members of Aerosmith.) The three singles leading to the album's release—**It's Like That, Hard Times** (and its B-side, the DJ/sample showcase **Jam-Master Jay**), and **Rock Box**—were matched by **Hollis Crew, Sucker M.C.'s,** and **30 Days**. Rap music was never the same after this. How could it be? —*MG*

Minutemen
DOUBLE NICKELS ON THE DIME

SST | Producer: Ethan James
RELEASED: JULY 3, 1984

● There's a snarky old tenet that states a good double album is a wasted shot at a *great* single album. Of course, many artists have produced exceptions to this rule . . . Dylan, the Stones, Miles, and the Clash come to mind. Add to that list Minutemen; upon learning that their pals Hüsker Dü were recording a double album (*Zen Arcade*), the San Pedro, California, trio are said to have quickly woodshedded a few dozen new songs to beef up their own forthcoming record, thus minting *Double Nickels on the Dime*.

But haste did not make waste. *Double Nickels* was an aural feast comprising forty-five tracks in eighty-one minutes. Central to the '80s SoCal punk scene, Minutemen was "punk" by virtue of its fiercely "econo" DIY work ethic rather than any conventional fashions, sonic or otherwise. Musical omnivores veering toward intensely personal lyrics (see the autobiographical **History Lesson—Part II** and the chugging **Political Song for Michael Jackson to Sing**), former school chums D. Boon and Mike Watt were augmented by the percussive athleticism of drummer George Hurley. Watt, who would become one of the world's preeminent bassists, often provided a melodic counter to Boon's trebly, blues- and jazz-influenced guitar stabs. And what better way to flout hardcore dogma than by offering "covers" of Van Halen (**Ain't Talkin' 'bout Love**) and Steely Dan (**Dr. Wu**)? Even the album's most straightforward original, **This Ain't No Picnic**, betrayed the band's love of classic rock.

Considering Boon's political awareness, it's ironic that the Norteño-flavored **Corona**, written about the poverty he witnessed in Mexico, became *Double Nickels'* most widely known song when MTV licensed it as the theme for its crass-a-palooza *Jackass* two decades later. Boon would die in a tragic van accident in December 1985, leaving Watt and Hurley to form fIREHOSE. **—DP**

BIG FOOT
TREAT
TOADIES
ANXIOUS MO-FO
STATIC
SEARCH
CUT
PLIGHT
WORKING MEN ARE
ACK ACK ACK
LIFE AS A REHE
BEACON SIGHTED

1984

Sade
DIAMOND LIFE
E P I C | Producer: Robin Millar
RELEASED: JULY 16, 1984

● Born in Nigeria but raised in the UK, Sade Adu traded her career as a fashion designer and part-time model for music, singing backup for the British band Pride. There, she formed a songwriting partnership with guitarist/saxophonist Stewart Matthewman, and the two soon struck out on their own, taking the rhythm section with them and forming the band eponymously named Sade.

Its first release, *Diamond Life*, crossed over from soul to pop to smooth jazz to lounge and could legitimately be found in any one of those bins in your favorite record store. It was the way the band fuses all of those elements that made this such an interesting listen. Perhaps it can best be described as cool soul. It's not Aretha Franklin demanding respect or Al Green imploring you to take him to the river but more like soul with an English stiff upper lip. The subject matter mainly concerned love in its various permutations, and the general musical style showcased Sade's jazzy vocals fixed on the foundation of a solid, prominent bass line and accentuated by Matthewman's tasteful sax and guitar flourishes.

Sade displayed cool detachment, like in the hit **Smooth Operator** and **Frankie's First Affair**, chastising cheating men in both, and when delivering good advice in **Hang On to Your Love**. But when things get more personal, as in **Your Love Is King** or **Cherry Pie**, about a man who broke her heart, Sade allowed more emotion to creep into her singing.

This formula worked extremely well. The quadruple-platinum album launched four hit singles and became the best-selling album ever by a British female vocalist, a record it held for twenty-four years. With *Diamond Life*, cool soul certainly got a warm reception. *—GP*

1984

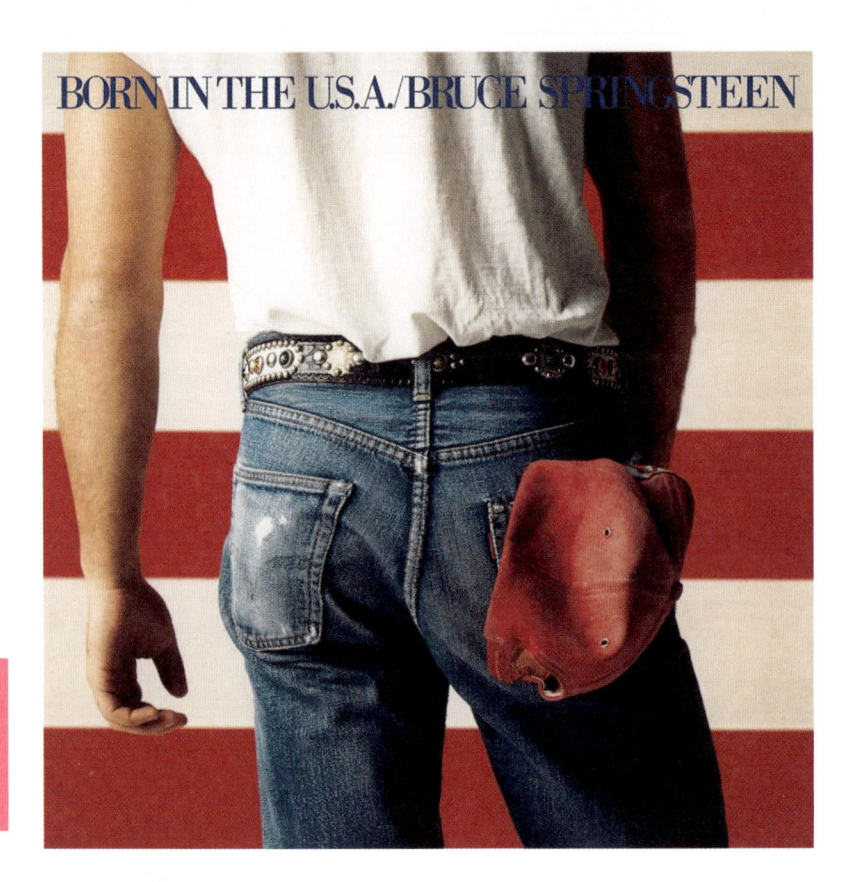

Bruce Springsteen
BORN IN THE U.S.A.

COLUMBIA | Producers: Jon Landau, Chuck Plotkin, Bruce Springsteen, Steven Van Zandt

RELEASED: JUNE 4, 1984

● Bruce Springsteen started work on the follow-up to his fifth album, the chart-topping *The River*, not long after the album's tour concluded in September 1981. Home demos recorded as blueprints for the E Street Band were eventually released in their basic forms as Springsteen's sixth album, the solo *Nebraska*, in 1982. Unused songs from this period plus an expanding set of newly written ones were tracked in New York City over the next two years, forming the basis of the album that would catapult Springsteen into one of the biggest artists on the planet.

By the time *Born in the U.S.A.* was released, Springsteen was already most popular as a live performer. Expectations weren't any higher than those for Springsteen's other albums released since *Newsweek* and *Time* put him on their covers after 1975's *Born to Run*. But *Born in the U.S.A.* immediately became his most popular LP, shooting to No. 1, as the first single, **Dancing in the Dark**, written and recorded late in the sessions to placate his manager's request for a hit, went to No. 2, his highest charter. Six more songs from the album followed into the Top 10.

Lyrically, the twelve songs touched on subjects familiar to Springsteen's catalog—working-class frustration coupled with cautious optimism and characters beaten down by personal and political circumstances. Musically, however, they were sharper and more to the point than anything he'd done before. From the emotionally and physically wounded Vietnam vet returning home to an unsympathetic country depicted in the title song to the closing **My Hometown**'s survey of a city battered by poverty and despair, *Born in the U.S.A.* disguised its desperation in crisp melodies. After this, Springsteen's music often turned inward, but his place in history was forever altered. *—MG*

1984

Tina Turner
PRIVATE DANCER

CAPITOL | Producers: Terry Britten, Carter, Leon "Ndugu" Chancler, Wilton Felder, Rupert Hine, Joe Sample, Greg Walsh, Martyn Ware

RELEASED: MAY 29, 1984

● It's fair to say Tina Turner wasn't at a peak leading up to the release of her fifth studio album, *Private Dancer*. After leaving abusive husband Ike Turner and their band, she struggled as a solo artist until finding the right team in Roger Davies (her manager) and Capitol Records executive John Carter. Turner may have been down, but *Private Dancer* proved she wasn't done—not by a long shot.

Channeling her life experience, Turner took the lyrical themes of the album and made them her own. She was unapologetically a tough, sexy woman who had been through rough times. **What's Love Got to Do with It** was a brassy, bold middle finger to stereotypes of love and romance, while **Better Be Good to Me** put her strong message across with a drum machine–laden New Wave twist.

The slick, synth-heavy production feels dated now, but Turner's self-assured attitude made the songs stand out. The record also benefited from song contributions from David Bowie (**1984**) and Mark Knopfler (**Private Dancer**). The album's British producers were able to smooth out the raw, frenzied sound of Turner's past while still maintaining her soulful R&B edge. Her distinct, raspy voice embodied the persona of the title track, while her rendition of Al Green's **Let's Stay Together** remains second only to the Reverend's himself.

The album was part personal liberation, part comeback, and part sonic reinvention. All of the power, passion, and self-empowerment came through in the music. This was a rock/pop record by a solo female artist, and it launched her into superstardom. Turner hit her stride with *Private Dancer* and proved that she was just fine, proudly rollin' on the river without any ballast to weigh her down. —SS

1984

U2
THE UNFORGETTABLE FIRE

ISLAND | Producers: Brian Eno, Daniel Lanois
RELEASED: OCTOBER 1, 1984

● As U2 set out on tour to support its fourth studio album, guitarist The Edge opined that "as a group we never doubted that what we did would be successful." And U2 had indeed hit new peaks with 1983's *War* and the live *Under the Blood Red Sky*, which had produced an MTV favorite with "Sunday Bloody Sunday." But staying the course was not in the Irish quartet's nature.

U2 changed a great deal for *The Unforgettable Fire*. Switching studios to Slane Castle in Ireland's county Meath, the band replaced Steve Lillywhite, its producer since 1980's *Boy*, with the team of Brian Eno and Daniel Lanois. It retained touches of its trademark power rock but added layers of mood and texture that gave Edge's guitar more nuanced spaces to explore and provided a wider, cushier airspace for frontman Bono and the album's overall vocal attack. "We've always felt inclined to occasionally change the base of what we did," Edge explained, and despite some initial surprise, it became clear that *The Unforgettable Fire* was the right move at the right time, pushing the band forward into fresh and adventurous sonic territory that established a template for future adventures.

Pride (In the Name of Love) checked the stirring anthem box, while the title track, **Wire**, and **A Sort of Homecoming** explored expansive new dynamics. **Bad** and **Elvis Presley and America**, both longer than six minutes, were hypnotic tone poems, and **MLK** closed the album as a rich, settling hymn. *The Unforgettable Fire* became an acknowledged classic that gave U2 its second straight Top 15 album in the US and set up the phenomenon of *The Joshua Tree* three years later. Give the last word to Edge here: "I'm amazed that having set out to do something new, we've come up with the most classic U2 [album] of all time." —GG

Wham!
MAKE IT BIG

COLUMBIA | Producer: George Michael
RELEASED: OCTOBER 15, 1984

● Never judge a book by its cover (unless it led you to buy this one). Thanks to MTV, artists' looks had oversize importance for their promotion and success. Wham!, the UK duo of George Michael and Andrew Ridgely, came along straight out of "pop superstar" central casting. Their second album, *Make It Big*, introduced most people in the US to their music through the inescapable earworm **Wake Me Up Before You Go-Go**; paired with a video of Wham! jumping around like the most excited aerobics instructors this side of Richard Simmons, the song was easy for many to dismiss as frothy pop, even though it spent three weeks at No. 1.

What fans knew, and non-fans would soon find out, was there was substance along with the style. The other songs on *Make It Big* were not merely bubblegum pop for teenage girls. **Freedom** would not have been out of place at Motown, and the Isley-Jasper-Isley composition that followed it, **If You Were There**, demonstrated some deep R&B tastes. The track list was crafted to give listeners a big pop single up front as an appetizer, but those willing to consume the album in one sitting were treated with the best song at the end.

When asked years later, Ridgely said that after hearing **Careless Whisper**, he knew that Michael needed to go solo. The power ballad, with a killer saxophone solo from Steve Gregory, was Wham!'s biggest hit, topping charts on both sides of the pond. It was impossible not to feel the regret in Michael's voice when he sings "Tonight the music seems so loud / I wish that we could lose this crowd." At that moment, you knew that Wham! was worthy for more than just its good looks. *—RW*

Van Halen
1984
WARNER BROS. | Producer: Ted Templeman
RELEASED: JANUARY 9, 1984

● Van Halen always worked hard to project a happy-go-lucky image, but the band was actually crumbling internally while recording their original lineup's final album. Guitarist Eddie Van Halen was still mad about being pressured into rush-recording 1982's covers-heavy *Diver Down* and went so far as to build a studio at his own house so he could more tightly control the recording process for *1984*. This power move rankled singer David Lee Roth, as did Van Halen's insistence on bringing keyboards to the forefront of the band's sound for the singles **Jump** and **I'll Wait**. "Hey man, you're a guitar hero. No one wants to see your dead ass playing keyboards," is how Eddie remembered Roth reacting in a 1986 *Rolling Stone* interview.

If Diamond Dave did indeed say that, he couldn't have been more wrong. **Jump** became Van Halen's only No. 1 single, elevating the band to previously unimagined levels of fame and earning its second 10 million–selling album. **I'll Wait** just missed the Top 10; so did the hard-rocking **Panama**, which had the added benefit of reassuring longtime fans that Eddie wasn't anywhere close to relinquishing his guitar hero crown.

1984's masterpiece just might be **Hot for Teacher**. In addition to being one of the best-ever displays of Eddie's fretboard magic, it showcased all of the band members' individual and collective strengths, from Roth's humor and unconventional arrangement to Michael Anthony's bass and soaring background vocals to Alex Van Halen's dazzling drum intro. The album tracks were nearly as impressive, particularly **Drop Dead Legs** (the best ZZ Top song Billy Gibbons never wrote), and the album's videos were memorable gems. It's a shame Van Halen's original lineup had to end, but it certainly went out on top. —MW

1984

David Sylvian
BRILLIANT TREES
VIRGIN | Producers: David Sylvian, Steve Nye
RELEASED: JUNE 25, 1984

● Casting off the facade he hid behind as a member of Japan, David Sylvian rose from the ashes of the band he created (and is still vilified for destroying) with *Brilliant Trees*. Sylvian's songwriting matured with the ethereal "Ghosts" just as Japan was imploding; fittingly, *Brilliant Trees* opened with the funky, Japan-esque **Pulling Punches**. But the next track, the Picasso-inspired **The Ink in the Well**, quickly revealed Sylvian's intentions to embrace unpredictable sounds and introspective lyrics. His baritone vocals less overly affected, the first single, **Red Guitar** (Sylvian's highest-charting single), was deceptively simple, while the closing title track was unapologetically layered. The evocative sounds between them were that of an artist redefining himself, thanks to adventurous collaborations with Steve Jensen and Richard Barbari (of Japan), Holger Czukay, Ryuichi Sakamoto, Danny Thompson, Mark Isham, Ronny Drayton, and Jon Hassel, among others. "I'm cutting branches from the trees / Shaped by years of memories / To exorcise their ghosts from inside of me," Sylvian sang on **Nostalgia**. But this album incinerated those branches to allow for new growth. No mere pop album, *Brilliant Trees* was a sonic meditation. Listen to it, headphones on, lights off, tipple of choice in hand. Then, breathe. *—HD*

Spinal Tap
THIS IS SPINAL TAP
POLYDOR | Producers: Christopher Guest, Michael McKean, Harry Shearer
RELEASED: MARCH 2, 1984

● In the pantheon of fake bands, one towers above the rest, symbolizing how absurd rock 'n' roll can be—Spinal Tap. The 1984 mockumentary from director Rob Reiner featured comedians Christopher Guest (aka Nigel Tufnel), Michael McKean (David St. Hubbins), and Harry Shearer (Derek Smalls) as the titular band embarking on its next world tour. The soundtrack, like the film, delightfully skewered rockers whom we might all know, and maybe even love, who lack self-awareness. The music was solidly in the hard rock/heavy metal camp of the '70s and early '80s, with comically accurate odes to rocking hard (**Heavy Duty**), absurd sexuality (**Sex Farm**, **Big Bottom**), and fantasy (**Stonehenge**). At the same time, a flashback to Spinal Tap's British Invasion era on **Gimme Some Money** is so credible, casual listeners might feel they'd happened upon a rare early-'60s track. Like any good joke, it's all about the delivery and execution. Guest, McKean, and Shearer understood their targets, and Spinal Tap satirized them by creating an album of songs so well made and humorous that even real bands, including Soundgarden, have covered them to great effect. *This Is Spinal Tap* is worth turning up to "eleven." *—RSM*

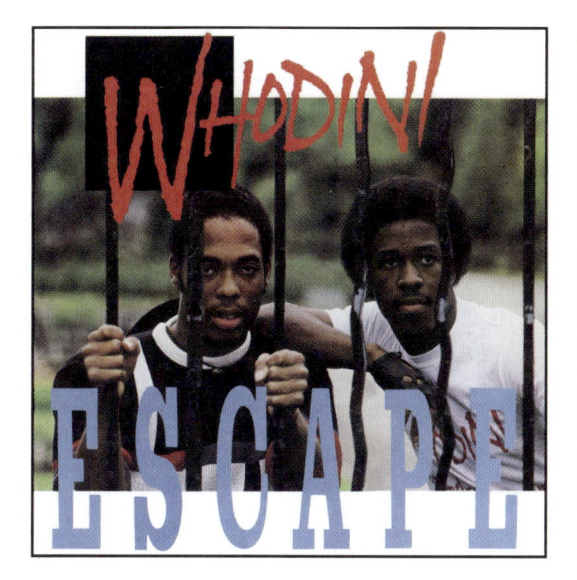

Whodini
ESCAPE
JIVE | Producer: Larry Smith
RELEASED: OCTOBER 1984

● Fate has a way of flexing its muscles, and by chance, Whodini found itself graced with the opportunity to work with producer Larry Smith on its second album, just after his stint with Run-D.M.C. It certainly wasn't planned, but the rap gods aligned, and the New York trio delivered one of the most quintessential albums in the genre's history. Smooth, crisp, funky, and lyrically topical, *Escape* was a perfect blend of R&B and hip-hop, an album with literally no filler. **Friends** was a huge single and was followed by the dancefloor-packing **Freaks Come Out at Night**, which rivaled fellow artists such as Prince and Rick James. The funky electro masterpiece **Five Minutes of Funk** had a spacey undertone that floated listeners into another dimension as the vocoder counts down until the party ends. (It was subsequently sampled by Nas and 2Pac, among others.) **Big Mouth** and **Escape** delivered a more traditional rap feel showing off their exceptional MC skills. One of rap's early million-sellers, *Escape* proved that sometimes when you let destiny take over and allow creativity to shine, some of the greatest records are made. *—MH*

The Replacements
LET IT BE
TWIN/TONE | Producers: Steve Fjelstad, Peter Jesperson, Paul Westerberg
RELEASED: OCTOBER 2, 1984

● Paul Westerberg was beginning to rethink his band the Replacements as it set to record its third album, *Let It Be*, during the latter half of 1983. The singer and songwriter of the Minneapolis punk band was growing weary of the hard-and-fast approach the group had taken in so many of its songs; on 1983's *Hootenanny*, he opened up a little, embracing the '70s pop gold he treasured. He also showed sensitivity many of his peers wouldn't dare display. While *Let It Be* still had its bratty side (**Tommy Gets His Tonsils Out**, **Gary's Got a Boner**, that Beatles-looting album title), Westerberg matured as a songwriter, penning tracks—**Unsatisfied**, **Sixteen Blue**, and **Answering Machine**—that incorporated piano, less frantic tempos, and, most importantly, lyrics about growing up with uncertainties and unshakable awkwardness. Over the next half-decade, Westerberg increasingly moved the Replacements toward a middle ground and then past that until its final LP, 1990's *All Shook Down*, was essentially a solo record with no trace of a punk past. *Let It Be* was the pivotal moment when Westerberg took a giant leap toward becoming one of the best songwriters of his generation. *—MG*

1984

1985

85

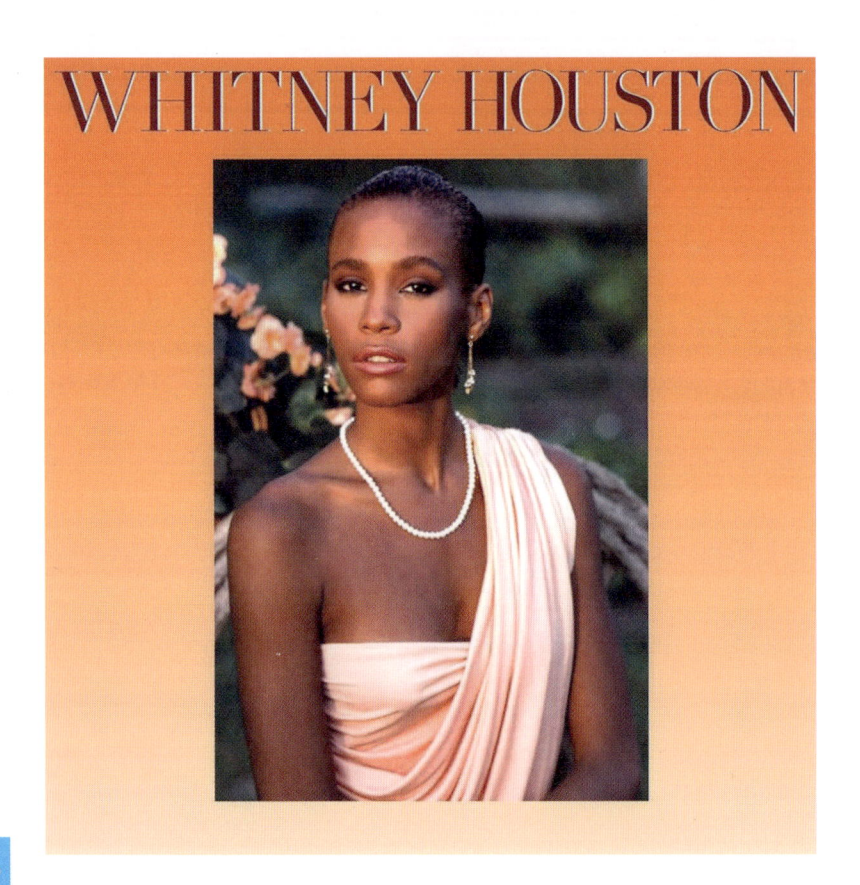

Whitney Houston
WHITNEY HOUSTON

ARISTA | Producers: Jermaine Jackson, Kashif, Michael Masser, Narada Michael Walden

RELEASED: FEBRUARY 14, 1985

● Released on Valentine's Day, the self-titled debut album from Whitney Houston heralded a bright new pop and soul talent. Except few people were listening . . . at least at first. The twenty-one-year-old singer—daughter of the Sweet Inspirations' Cissy Houston and cousin of Dionne Warwick—made her chart debut a year earlier in a duet with Teddy Pendergrass called "Hold Me" that stalled outside the Top 40. **You Give Good Love**, the first single from *Whitney Houston*, however, climbed to No. 3. By the time the album had run its course with a final single, **Greatest Love of All**, in mid-1986, she had racked up three No. 1s. Suddenly everyone was listening.

Arista Records head Clive Davis signed Houston in 1983, grooming her for pop stardom. But he had trouble connecting the big-voiced singer from New Jersey to suitable songs or producers. So *Whitney Houston* became a stitched-together debut, with contributions from songwriters and producers Jermaine Jackson, Kashif, Michael Masser, and Narada Michael Walden, who honed their respective work to radio-ready sharpness while never pulling away from the album's main sell, Houston's voice.

Once the record caught fire, three singles shot to No. 1—**Saving All My Love for You**, **How Will I Know**, and **Greatest Love of All**—claiming a pair of firsts in the process: the first debut and the first album by a female solo artist to have three No. 1s. The album also spent fourteen weeks atop the Billboard 200, setting a new standard for '80s pop that carried over to the next century. Artists from Mariah Carey to Lady Gaga have been influenced by Houston and her acrobatic vocals approach to pop-soul singing. *Whitney Houston* remains the crowning achievement of her career and a standard-bearer for '80s pop. *—MG*

1985

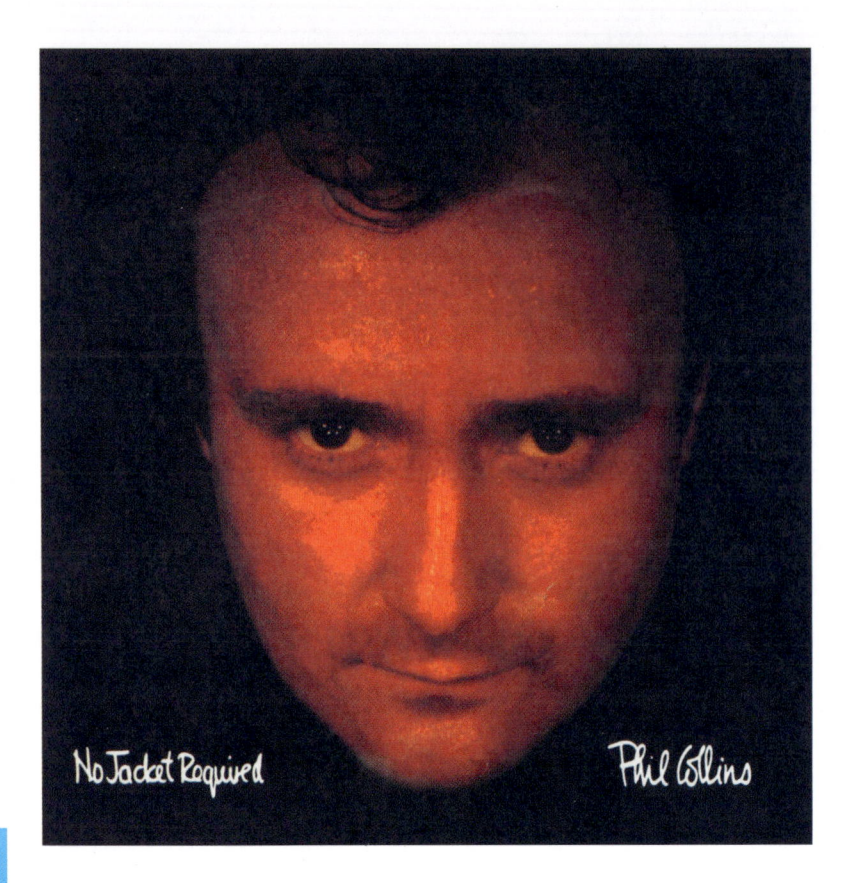

Phil Collins
NO JACKET REQUIRED

ATLANTIC | Producers: Phil Collins, Hugh Padgham
RELEASED: FEBRUARY 18, 1985

● By 1985, Phil Collins was on a roll coming off Top 10 hits with his first two solo albums—*Face Value* and *Hello, I Must Be Going!*—in addition to the same success of *Abacab* with his longtime mates in Genesis. Not one to settle for just being good, he responded with the biggest album of his career, *No Jacket Required*, titled from a personal story of Collins being denied entrance to a restaurant for not wearing proper attire. The album included softer ballads dealing with personal themes such as divorce and political angst, but he also consciously decided to write more up-tempo and danceable tunes. With ten tracks (eleven including the CD bonus **We Said Hello Goodbye**), the blend of well-written and expertly performed and recorded Adult Contemporary and pop sounds made *No Jacket Required* a veritable hitmaking machine. The album's first two released singles—**Sussudio**, a Prince-inspired rollicking song about a schoolboy crush, and **One More Night**, a soulful paean about lost love—both reached No. 1 on Billboard's Hot 100 chart. Those were followed by the Top 10 likes of **Don't Lose My Number**, with melodramatic lyrics and Collins's gated reverb drum sound (and a comically elaborate video), and **Take Me Home**, whose soaring lyrics refer to the distressed pleas of a mental patient.

No Jacket Required earned three Grammy Awards for Collins, including Album of the Year, and went on to become one of the best-selling releases of all time, with worldwide sales of more than 25 million copies. Its extraordinary success started him down the path from rock star to international music icon, with ubiquitous collaborations with other artists and a spot playing *both* Live Aid concerts, in London and Philadelphia, during the summer of 1985. —*JC*

1985

a-ha
HUNTING HIGH AND LOW
WARNER BROS. | Producers: Tony Mansfield, John Ratcliff, Alan Tarney
RELEASED: OCTOBER 28, 1985

● You have to love a band that chose the studio for its debut album (Eel Pie in London) because it had a Space Invaders machine. But Norwegian a-ha's brand of synth-pop went well beyond mere beeps and electronic noodles. There was plenty of melodic integrity that raised *Hunting . . .* beyond its genre and time period and plenty of songs that stood up in the wake of **Take on Me**, the global smash that's still a dependable multi-sports anthem. It also gave a-ha the first-ever Grammy Award nomination for a Norwegian band. *—GG*

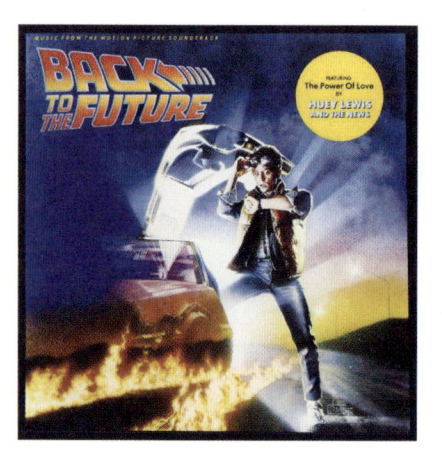

Various Artists
BACK TO THE FUTURE (MUSIC FROM THE MOTION PICTURE SOUNDTRACK)
MCA | Producers: Various
RELEASED: JULY 17, 1985

● The power of Huey Lewis fueled the soundtrack to 1985's top-grossing movie. Lewis and the News contributed a pair of songs to Robert Zemeckis's comic blockbuster: the pop-rock steamroller **The Power of Love**, which became the group's first chart-topper (for two weeks), and **Back in Time**, which, unlike **The Power of Love**, drew its inspiration from the movie itself. The soundtrack is rounded out by offerings from Lindsey Buckingham, Eric Clapton, and composer Alan Silvestri's iconic score. *—AG*

Beat Happening
BEAT HAPPENING
K | Producer: Greg Sage
RELEASED: NOVEMBER 1985

● Beat Happening is a band that makes the Violent Femmes' earliest releases sound polished—lo-fi, we mean to say. The *Beat Happening* album was a prototype of doing more with less; everything was short (most of the ten tracks were under two minutes, the album nineteen minutes total), stark, and pleasingly unsubtle. A 1990 reissue titled *1983–85—1990* offered a whopping twenty-seven tracks drawn from the sessions with Greg Sage of the Portland band the Wipers, but it missed the point of what gave the original *Beat Happening* its audacious charm. *—GG*

Big Audio Dynamite
THIS IS BIG AUDIO DYNAMITE
COLUMBIA | Producer: Mick Jones
RELEASED: NOVEMBER 1, 1985

● After getting the boot from the Clash, Mick Jones regrouped to pursue his old band's more rhythmic tangents. Comparing Big Audio Dynamite's debut LP with the Clash's swan song *Cut the Crap* (which came out the same week), Jones apparently made off with his old group's pop sense, too. Thanks to his movie director bandmate Don Letts, *This Is Big Audio Dynamite* offered a veritable film class worth of iconic soundbites from master directors such as Nicolas Roeg and Sergio Leone. But what lingers is the stately gliding hook to **E=MC2**. *—DM*

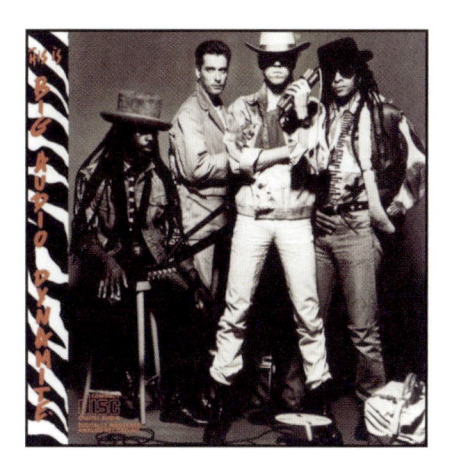

Various Artists
THE BREAKFAST CLUB (ORIGINAL MOTION PICTURE SOUNDTRACK)
A & M | Producers: Various
RELEASED: FEBRUARY 19, 1985

● "Hey, hey, hey, hey!" The opening of Simple Minds' **Don't You (Forget about Me)** immediately conjures visions of the John Hughes coming-of-age classic for many of a certain age. By far the most successful single from *The Breakfast Club* soundtrack, the song also became a signature for the band. The album featured songs by mostly rock and New Wave artists, including four instrumental tracks by producer Keith Forsey. The music reflected a point in time, much like the film distilled a Saturday detention into distinctive memories for each character. *—SS*

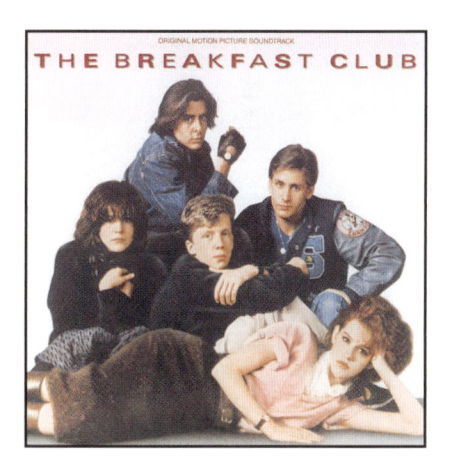

Albert Collins, Robert Cray, and Johnny Copeland
SHOWDOWN!
ALLIGATOR | Producers: Bruce Iglauer, Dick Shurman
RELEASED: 1985

● In this trio, Albert Collins was the seasoned vet who brought along two of his protégés to share the limelight and cut loose. Collins and Johnny Copeland had been friends since their youth in Houston. Robert Cray, twenty-two years young, was the up-and-comer who could hold his own and then some. Their contrasting tones and styles blended and clashed in loose perfection. The least known of these gents, Copeland, was the secret MVP with his hot, gravelly vocals and equally cool picking. *—HK*

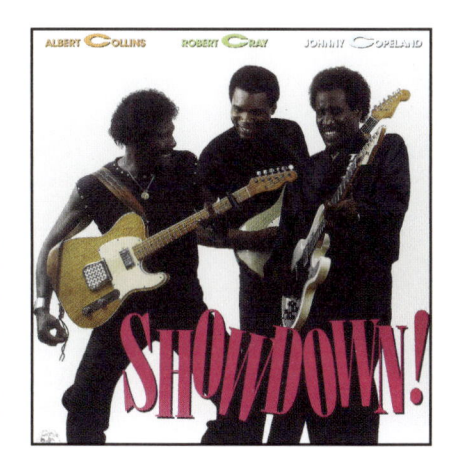

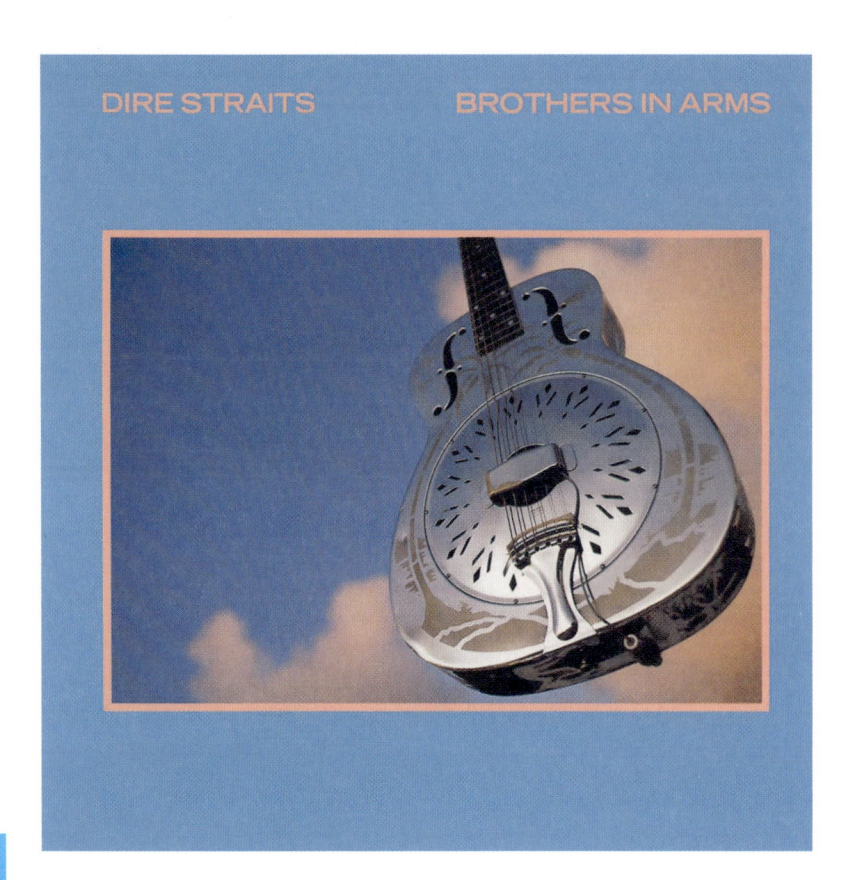

Dire Straits
BROTHERS IN ARMS

WARNER BROS. | Producers: Neil Dorfsman, Mark Knopfler
RELEASED: MAY 17, 1985

● The historical significance of Dire Straits' fifth LP stretches further than the music. As one of the first albums to be digitally recorded, the 1985 work came out around the time compact disc players were beginning to move into the mainstream. As such, *Brothers in Arms* became the first million-selling CD, a distinction served by the record's clean, clear sound and the rising format's upgrade in sonic quality. (CD buyers were also given expanded versions of the album's songs, allowing more space for the nine pristine tracks to move within.)

But the technical accolades would have meant less if the songs didn't support them. Starting with 1980's *Making Movies*, Dire Straits began recording lengthier, artier songs that willfully branched out from the group's carefully constructed 1978 debut single, "Sultans of Swing"; the five tracks on 1982's *Love Over Gold* averaged eight minutes each, with the longest clocking in at more than fourteen minutes. That album set the stage for *Brothers in Arms* and the expanse that greeted the expertly crafted and deliberately paced **Your Latest Trick**, **Why Worry**, and the title track.

But it was the album's oddest track, **Money for Nothing**, that sent it to the top of the charts and made Dire Straits one of the biggest bands in the world during the mid-'80s. With a vocal assist from Sting, a fuzzy guitar line inspired by ZZ Top, and an award-winning computer-generated video that illustrated the song's working-class takedown of pampered pop stars ("That ain't working, that's the way you do it / Money for nothing and your chicks for free"), the No. 1 hit was an inescapable part of the culture in 1985. But its success wore down frontman Mark Knopfler, who disbanded Dire Straits a decade later, after one last album. *–MG*

1985

Bob Dylan
BIOGRAPH
COLUMBIA | Producer: Jeff Rosen
RELEASED: AUTUMN 1985

● Before there was *The Bootleg Series*, there was *Biograph*. And before that, of course, there were Bob Dylan's *Greatest Hits* albums—three of them. But *Biograph* was not a best-of, per se, though it does contain a substantial number of Dylan's best-known songs.

No, instead, it's a fifty-three-track career-spanning collection that was released as a five-LP/three-cassette/three-CD box set containing previously released material, studio outtakes and demos, unreleased songs, and live performances, all of which date from 1962 to 1981. Somewhat illogically (but this is Dylan, right?), the set was not arranged chronologically, although small themes emerge here and there from the songs' groupings—love songs, political songs, etc. Ultimately, though, the Bob-Dylan-has-come-unstuck-in-time order evinced his enduring talent, never mind that his critical fortunes sometimes foundered during that span.

The real draw here, of course, was the rarities—eighteen previously unreleased songs, some of them known to the Dylan cognoscenti but not the general public. Some are revelatory, such as **Caribbean Wind**, and a smoking live take of **Groom Still Waiting at the Altar**, both of which hail from the mostly unloved *Shot of Love* era. There were also great tracks from the Rolling Thunder tour, from the *Blood on the Tracks* album sessions, and much more.

Beyond the material itself, there was much more that *Biograph* got right, most notably the booklet and accompanying materials, which offered rare photographs; a long, insightful essay by Cameron Crowe; and, perhaps best of all, direct comments about many of the songs by Dylan himself. Because it turned out to be a commercial success—going platinum, even—*Biograph* was a game changer for the way archival material was presented, paving the way for a thousand box sets to come and presaging Dylan's own vast (and still-in-progress) *Bootleg Series*. *—DD*

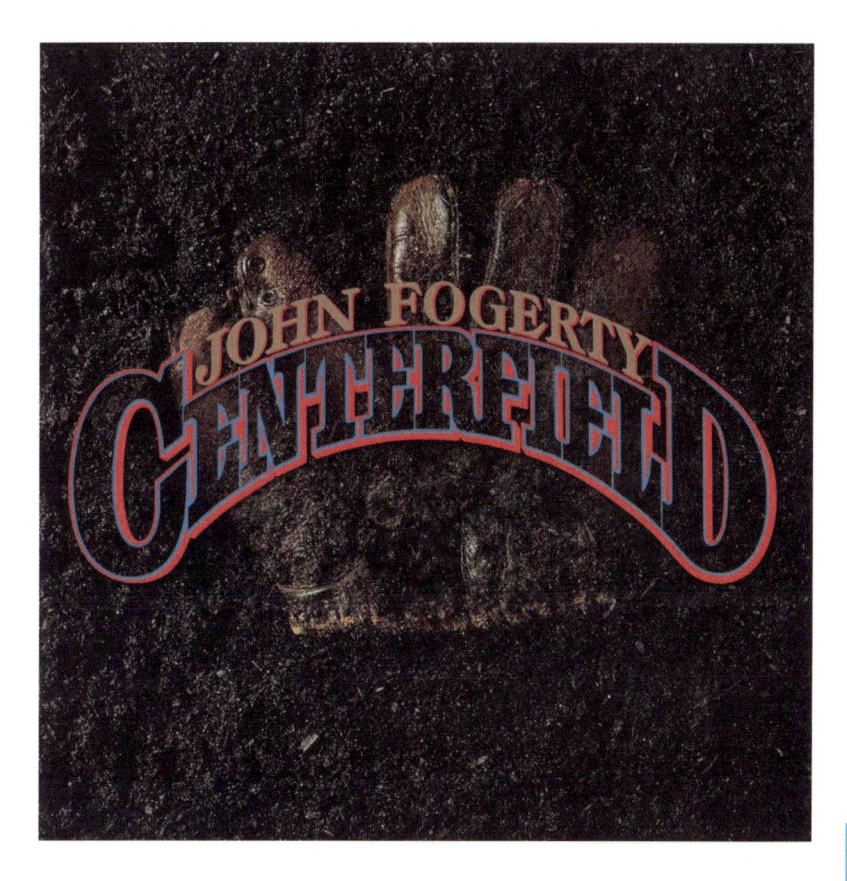

John Fogerty
CENTERFIELD

WARNER BROS. | Producer: John Fogerty
RELEASED: JANUARY 7, 1985

● With a howl like Little Richard's and guitar riffs that rival Chuck Berry's, John Fogerty is one of the great primal forces in rock 'n' roll. The hits he recorded with Creedence Clearwater Revival—more than a dozen in the Top 15 of the Billboard Hot 100 between 1968 and 1972—ranked among the genre's enduring classics. After Creedence broke up, Fogerty recorded two solo albums to little acclaim. After a decade out of the spotlight, he returned in 1985 with *Centerfield*.

"Put me in, coach, I'm ready to play!" the singer declared joyfully in the album's title track, with allusions to Berry's "Brown Eyed Handsome Man" and poet Ernest Thayer's "Casey at the Bat." The song opened with programmed drumbeats that mimic a baseball crowd's rhythmic claps—one of several moments that highlight that Fogerty apparently crafted this entire album without any other musicians in the room.

The Old Man Down the Road opens the album with a swamp rock hook that echoed CCR's "Run through the Jungle"—so much so, unfortunately, that Fogerty was sued by Saul Zaentz, then-owner of the Creedence publishing rights and the inspiration for the sharply penned **Mr. Greed** and **Zanz Kant Danz** on *Centerfield*. (Zaentz lost the "Jungle" suit in a case that went to the US Supreme Court and set a new precedent over damages in copyright cases.)

Score-settling aside, *Centerfield* was packed with exceptional songwriting, often bittersweet. **Big Train (From Memphis)** recalled the inspiration of Elvis Presley, who, like the big train, "is gone gone gone." Echoing "Fortunate Son," the aging narrator recounting baby-boomer memories in **I Saw It on T.V.**, tells of the politicians who "took my only son from me." With double-platinum sales, *Centerfield* brought Fogerty back to where he so richly deserved to be—No. 1 on the Billboard 200 chart. *—TD*

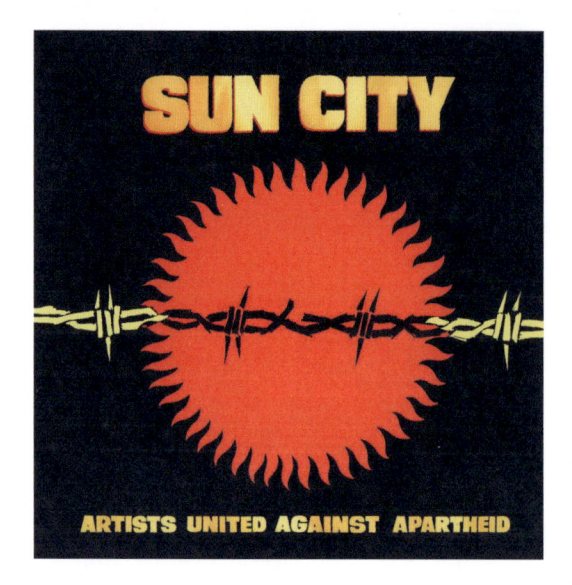

Artists United Against Apartheid
SUN CITY
MANHATTAN | Producers: Little Steven, Arthur Baker
RELEASED: DECEMBER 7, 1985

● Inspired by Peter Gabriel's musical eulogy for activist Stephen Biko and "We Are the World," USA for Africa's famine fundraiser, Little Steven Van Zandt wrote **Sun City** to spotlight South Africa's racist apartheid policies and encourage performers to boycott the exploitative white resort. Van Zandt recruited fifty-three rock, hip-hop, jazz, soul, reggae, Latin, and African music artists, including Bruce Springsteen, Bob Dylan, Lou Reed, Bonnie Raitt, Run-D.M.C., Ringo Starr, Darlene Love, George Clinton, Jimmy Cliff, and Ruben Blades, all proclaiming, "I ain't gonna play Sun City!" Originally a single, it became an album when Herbie Hancock, Tony Williams, Ron Carter, and Stanley Jordan added to Miles Davis riffs for **The Struggle Continues**. **Let Me See Your I.D.** combined raps from Gil Scott-Heron, Melle Mel, and Duke Bootee. Percussionist Keith LeBlanc looped political statements into **Revolutionary Situation**. Gabriel's chanting was hypnotic on **No More Apartheid**. **Sun City** also got a rockin' remix (**Version II**), and U2's Bono offered the bluesy **Silver & Gold** with Rolling Stones' Keith Richards and Ron Wood (later rerecorded by U2). MTV loved the title track's star-studded video, and *Sun City* raised $1 million for anti-apartheid causes and inspired a wider boycott. South African apartheid officially ended in 1992. *–LM*

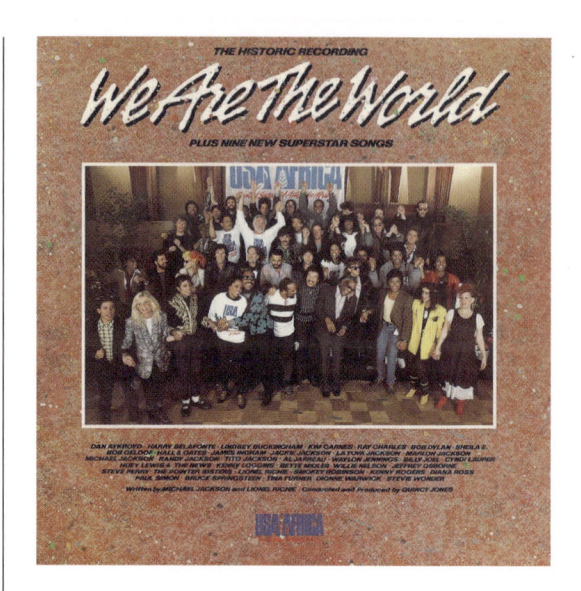

Various Artists
WE ARE THE WORLD
COLUMBIA | Producers: Various
RELEASED: MARCH 29, 1985

● Focused on making a brighter day for the less fortunate, **We Are the World** was a USA for Africa answer to Britain's Band Aid effort to raise funds for African famine relief. The album is often overshadowed by the title track, written by Lionel Richie and Michael Jackson, and famously recorded in a marathon one-night session after the 1985 American Music Awards. Forty-six celebrities were brought together for the Quincy Jones–produced extravaganza and accompanying video. The result was a snapshot of '80s music culture at the time and what became one of the most iconic songs of the decade. The rest of the album was rounded out by nine previously unreleased songs with some rare gems, including live recordings from Bruce Springsteen and Huey Lewis and the News. Prince, Tina Turner, Journey's Steve Perry, and Chicago also contributed, and the set also featured **Tears Are Not Enough**, the Canadian super-group equivalent single written by Bryan Adams, David Foster, and others. In an era that included several charity single recordings, **We Are the World** was the epitome of musical activism and sold more than 20 million copies. *–SS*

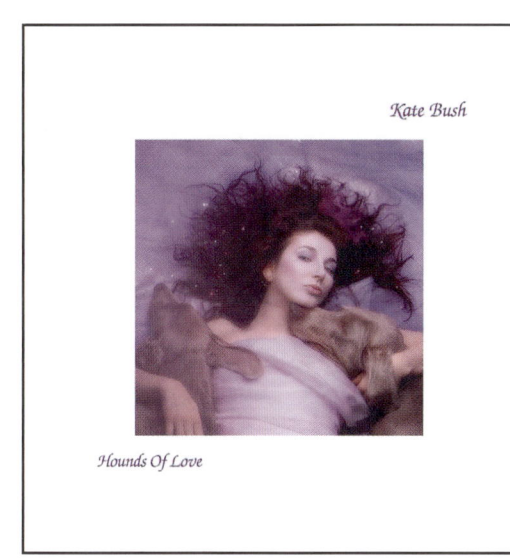

Kate Bush
HOUNDS OF LOVE
E M I | Producer: Kate Bush
RELEASED: SEPTEMBER 16, 1985

● If CDs and streaming took away the tactile aspect of turning over a record, *Hounds of Love* merits its return, as each side has its own properties. Side A was one of the greatest achievements in the history of British popular music. Bush set the table with five songs, four of which arguably became her most important. **Running Up That Hill** (the title track that would become a 2022 hit thanks to its inclusion on the streaming series *Stranger Things*), **The Big Sky**, and **Cloudbusting** perfectly illustrated Bush's singular talent. Her artistic voice—the singing, the palette of her songs, the persona she shared with the public—contained hope, desire, abandon, and passion, all communicated perfectly through those songs. The material on side B, a suite of seven songs under the banner **The Ninth Wave**, didn't get the spotlight that the singles on the other side did. When Bush made her return to live performing in 2014, an event that few people ever expected to happen, she made **The Ninth Wave** the core of her performance. Her choice said everything about what those songs mean to her. *—HK*

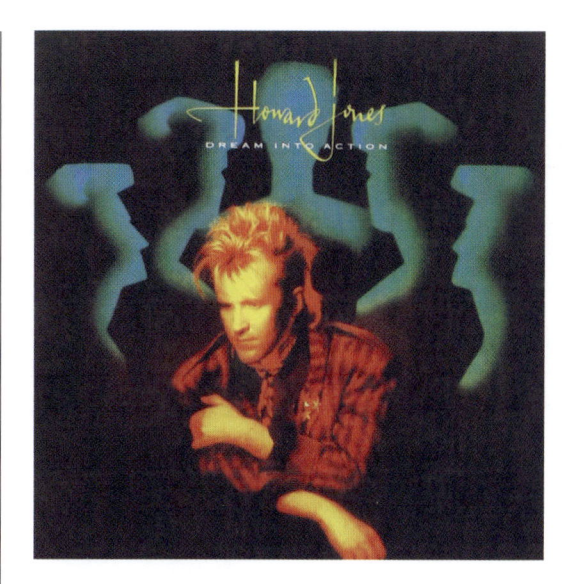

Howard Jones
DREAM INTO ACTION
E L E K T R A | Producer: Rupert Hine
RELEASED: MARCH 11, 1985

● "My songs are not about drug-taking or debauchery or rock 'n' roll," Howard Jones told the UK's *Telegraph* in 2006. "They're about positive thinking and challenging people's ideas." The singer/songwriter/keyboardist's debut album, *Human's Lib*, introduced that philosophy, and *Dream into Action* played even better with critics and proved there was a sizable international audience for his upbeat, synth-based tracks. A leading innovator of the era, Jones was backed on *Dream into Action* by Afrodiziak, a trio who appeared on far more '80s albums than you can name. The ingredients seemed disparate, but Jones displayed a knack for pulling them together. Many of the album's singles, including **Things Can Only Get Better**, **Life in One Day**, and a subsequent rerecording of **No One Is to Blame** (with Phil Collins) blazed up the charts in multiple countries. The album spent nearly a year on the Billboard 200 chart in the US. Jones indeed put his own dreams into action by writing songs you could dance to—before returning home to analyze their insightful and uplifting lyrics. *—HD*

1985

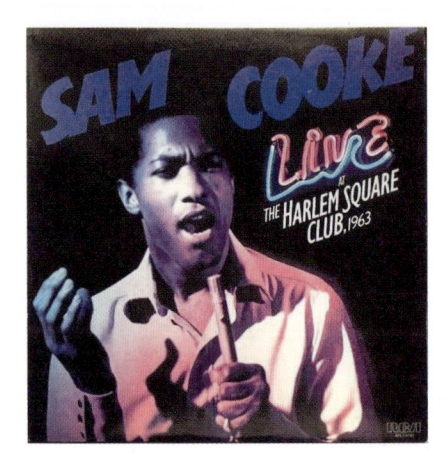

Sam Cooke
LIVE AT THE HARLEM SQUARE, 1963
RCA | Producer: Rob Santos
RELEASED: APRIL 29, 1985

● Recorded in Miami on January 12, 1963, but shelved until 1985 for fears the intensity of the performance may frighten off casual pop fans, Sam Cooke's *Live at the Harlem Square, 1963*, captured the legendary R&B singer in a sweat-soaked room surrounded by a suitably passionate audience. The hits were performed—**Cupid, Twistin' the Night Away**, and **Having a Party**—but it was Cooke's raw-to-the-point-of-hoarseness vocal execution that brought them to another level. A rare live album that transcends the medium. *—MG*

Sandra Crouch
WE'RE WAITING
LEXICON MUSIC | Producers: Sandra Crouch, Andraé Crouch
RELEASED: 1985

● Well before she launched a solo career in the '80s, Sandra Crouch had percussionist credits working with the Jackson 5, Neil Diamond, and Janis Joplin, and with twin brother Andraé's band the Disciples. Her 1983 debut *We Sing Praises* won a Grammy Award, but its follow-up, *We're Waiting*, was even more focused and exuberant, recorded in church with a full choir and guests, including Crouch's brother on the title track. Drop the needle anywhere and you'll praise the music as well as the Lord. *—GG*

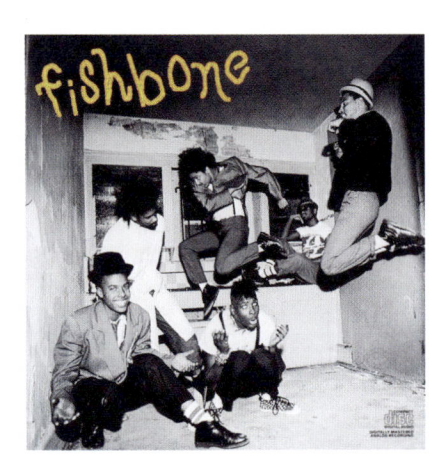

Fishbone
FISHBONE
COLUMBIA | Producer: David Kahne
RELEASED: SEPTEMBER 21, 1985

● During the mid-'80s, there was no more thankless task than to have Fishbone as your opening act. One of that era's most incendiary live bands, it put on a show that was a tall order to follow—a combustible cocktail of punk, funk, ska, and revved-up R&B that put the smart into smart-ass, shaken not stirred. All the group's virtues are present on this six-song EP, which clocked in at a breathless and action-packed twenty-six minutes. Decades later, **Party at Ground Zero** sounds like it could be coming out tomorrow. *—DM*

Paul Hardcastle
PAUL HARDCASTLE

CHRYSALIS | Producer: Paul Hardcastle

RELEASED: 1985

● With a sophisticated mesh of brilliant electronics and jazzy electro rhythms, Paul Hardcastle gave the world an innovative masterpiece that laid the foundation for what would become the chill-out sound. Delivering a fresh melodic and captivating feel, songs such as the iconic **Rainforest** took listeners on a journey that mesmerized with its smooth richness. Funky gems such as **Don't Waste My Time** and the clever anti-war statement song **19** shined and established Hardcastle as a master of his craft, light years ahead of his time. —MH

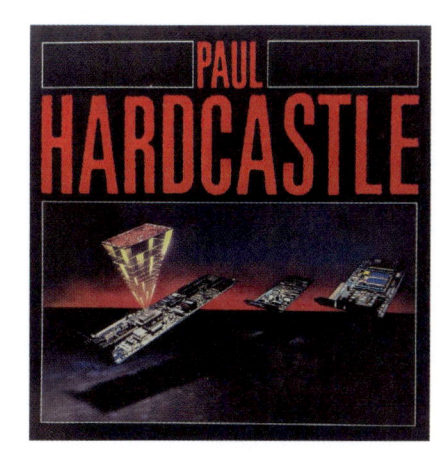

The Hooters
NERVOUS NIGHT

COLUMBIA | Producer: Rick Chertoff

RELEASED: MAY 6, 1985

● You may not know what a melodica is, but you've probably heard it. The combination harmonica/keyboard was a staple (and band namesake) on *Nervous Night*, the second studio album by the Hooters. The ten-song effort by the Philadelphia-formed group perfectly represented the carefree mindset of the '80s. Co-founders and co-songwriters Rob Hyman and Eric Bazilian created a peppy, danceable record that spawned pop hits in **And We Danced** and **Day by Day**, both filled with distinctive, hooky earworms, proving that, counter to the latter song's lyrics, some things do last forever. —SS

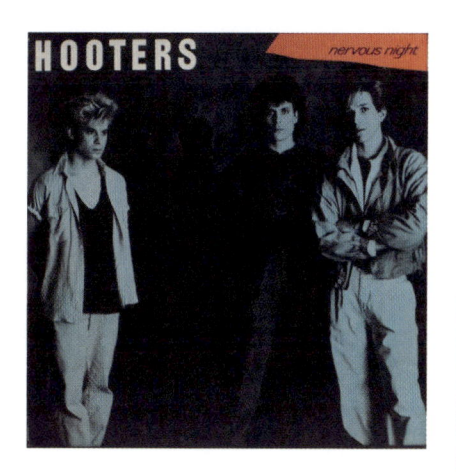

Various Artists
THE INDESTRUCTIBLE BEAT OF SOWETO

SHANACHIE | Producer: Trevor Herman

RELEASED: APRIL 16, 1985

● While ear-opening, Paul Simon's *Graceland* didn't come from a vacuum. Among its forerunners was this landmark compilation of South African township jive, which combined Western influences with Zulu and Sotho to create Mbaqanga. The hints of reggae, jazz, blues, and even bluegrass felt mind-blowing, and it doesn't get more country than the sounds of squawking poultry and a crowing rooster that turned up as rhythmic devices on the album-opening **Awungilobolele**. Ladysmith Black Mambazo's closing **Nansi Imali** felt like a dream you slip into at the end of a long day. —DM

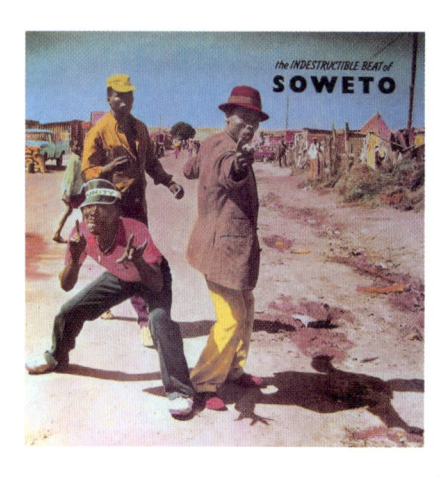

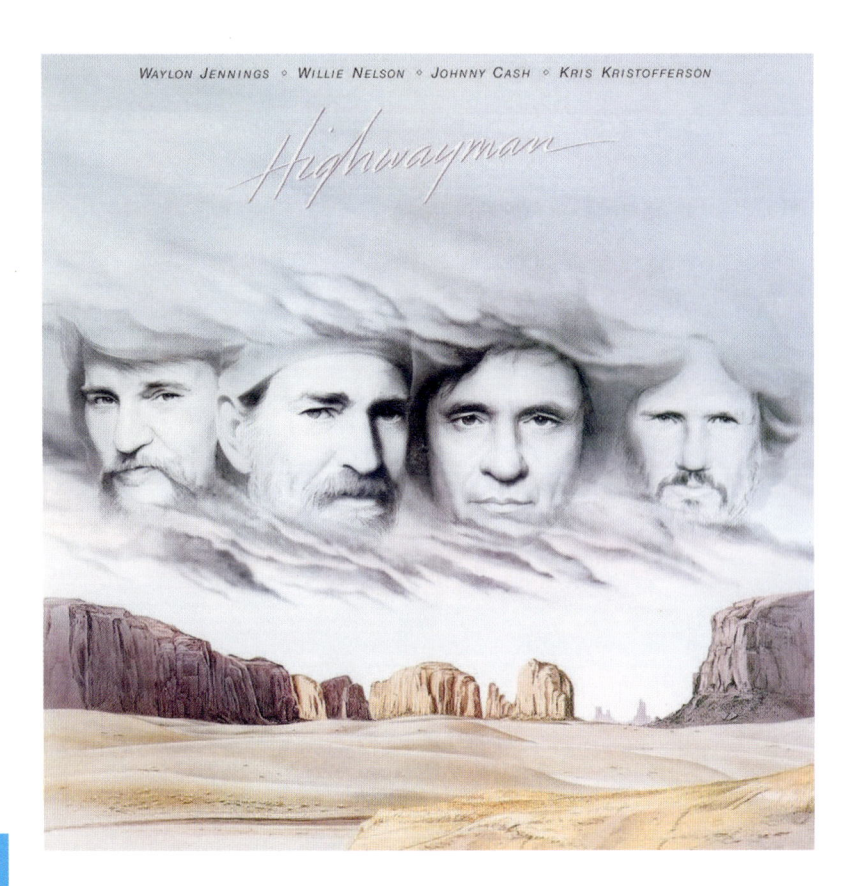

The Highwaymen
HIGHWAYMAN
COLUMBIA NASHVILLE | Producer: Chips Moman
RELEASED: MAY 6, 1985

● If you were of a mind to create a Mount Rushmore of outlaw country music—or maybe even country music in general—you could do a lot worse than to carve in stone the craggy visages of Johnny Cash, Waylon Jennings, Willie Nelson, and Kris Kristofferson. The true stories of those artists' lives and careers are extraordinary enough, but what did that reporter say in *The Man Who Shot Liberty Valance*? "When the legend becomes fact, print the legend."

Mythmaking is what this album was all about. The title track, penned by Jimmy Webb, found each of the four artists taking a verse that posited them as an adventurer or working-class hero—Nelson is the titular highwayman, Kristofferson a sailor, Jennings a dam builder, and Cash an astronaut. They all meet untimely ends, but here's the thing—they didn't die. Each was still alive, in song if not in fact.

That's a legend-cum-fact as worthy of these country music titans as they were of it.

The rest of the album strived to continue in a similar larger-than-life vein with Guy Clark's **Desperadoes Waiting for a Train**, Bob Seger's **Against the Wind**, and Ed Bruce's **The Last Cowboy Song**. Elsewhere, as befits the exalted yet humble, the quartet speaks up for the downtrodden with Cash's own **Committed to Parkview**, Woody Guthrie's **Deportee (Plane Wreck at Los Gatos)**, and Paul Kennerley's **Welfare Line**.

All of that material and the Highwaymen's performances were fine, though they paled somewhat alongside the truly memorable title track. That song rang so true that it may be time to get going on that Mount Rushmore idea. The album cover even has the design all set to go. *—DD*

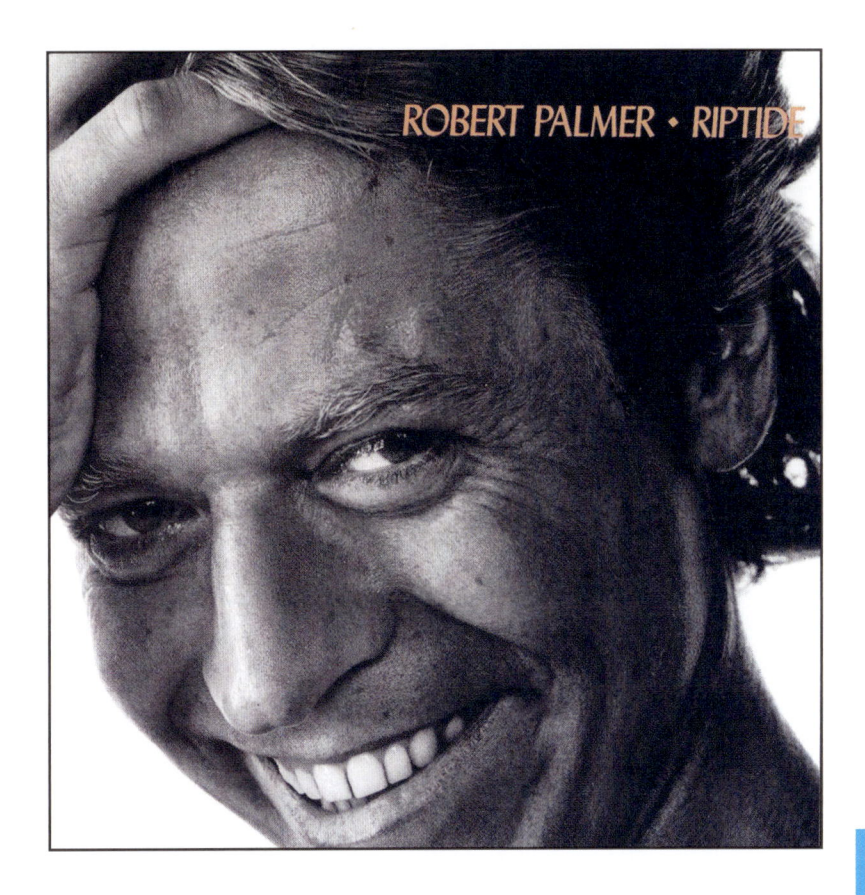

Robert Palmer
RIPTIDE
ISLAND | Producer: Bernard Edwards
RELEASED: NOVEMBER 1985

● The depth of the late Robert Palmer's genius can only truly be appreciated in retrospect, and for those who haven't done so, the rabbit hole of his music is definitely worth falling into. For most of his career, Palmer played with genres and a great wardrobe while garnering a respectful following. His short stint in the Power Station with Duran Duran's Andy and John Taylor catapulted him to something near stardom, although he left the band in the lurch to work on his own material.

That led to his eighth album, *Riptide*, and its breakthrough single, **Addicted to Love**. A rocking singalong played by musicians from the Power Station and Chaka Khan's band, it became Palmer's signature hit and was a bona fide earworm—though what people remember most is the video, in which Palmer sings while five identically styled models barely dance behind him while holding instruments they obviously aren't playing. MTV had the clip in perpetual rotation, searing its vapid imagery into the eyeballs of history while pushing the song—which won a Grammy Award—to No. 1 on the Billboard Hot 100. Palmer hit big again with his cover of Cherrelle's **I Didn't Mean to Turn You On**, whose video replicated **Addicted to Love**'s cloned models with similar success. "I hardly ever get asked about music," Palmer told the UK's *Guardian* in 2002. "I do, however, get asked about the **Addicted to Love** video and my suits on a daily basis."

Riptide had more to recommend it than those two juggernauts, however, including the first single, **Discipline of Love**, **Hyperactive**, and the title track. The double-platinum success of the album and those two videos may have minimized the brilliance of some of Palmer's previous work—notably 1980's *Clues*—but it ensured he *is* remembered. –HD

Aretha Franklin
WHO'S ZOOMIN' WHO

ARISTA | Producers: Narada Michael Walden, Aretha Franklin, David A. Stewart

RELEASED: JULY 9, 1985

● The Queen of Soul had become something of the queen of comebacks as she neared the quarter-century mark of her legendary career. By the mid-'80s, Franklin had already been through jazz, soul, and gospel eras before being ushered into early-'80s pop relevance by Luther Vandross. A voice like hers could elevate even the most mundane material, of course, but **Who's Zoomin' Who** was another new peak that few saw coming.

For her thirtieth overall studio album, Franklin connected with Narada Michael Walden, who agreed with her desire for "a younger sound" and was also willing to accommodate her dislike of travel by laying down backing tracks in California and then coming to Detroit to record her vocals. Walden co-wrote five of *Zoomin*'s nine tracks—including the hits **Freeway of Love** and the title track, with Franklin putting her pen on two. The result was one of the most solid and consistent track-for-track albums of Franklin's career, if not a, er, crowning achievement, and a sturdy collection that spotlighted her voice, still a force of nature. And like Tina Turner's *Private Dancer*, it gave Franklin a fresh berth in the MTV generation. The latter was partly thanks, too, to her collaboration with Eurythmics on **Sisters Are Doin' It for Themselves**, which the British duo had released on its own album shortly before. Other guests included Carlos Santana, Dizzy Gillespie, Peter Wolf, Martha Wash, Sylvester, and members of Tom Petty's Heartbreakers.

A sense of comeback was cemented by the album's showing. It was her highest-charting entry (No. 13) on the Billboard 200 since 1972 and her first and only studio album to be certified platinum. **Freeway of Love**, which featured a saxophone solo by Clarence Clemons of Bruce Springsteen's E Street Band, also added another Grammy Award to Franklin's overflowing trophy case. *–GG*

1985

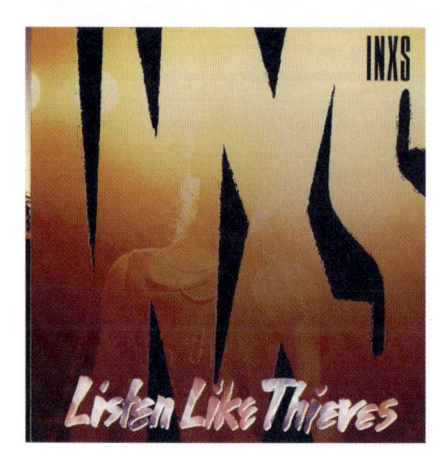

INXS
LISTEN LIKE THIEVES
ATLANTIC | Producer: Chris Thomas
RELEASED: OCTOBER 14, 1985

● Australia's INXS was hoping to break internationally with *Listen Like Thieves*, but when producer Chris Thomas said it lacked a hit, the group hustled to turn guitarist/keyboardist Andrew Farriss's "Funk Song No. 13" into **What You Need**. And boy, was it funky. With teasing guitar chords, sax attacks, slinky bass, pummeling percussion, and Michael Hutchence's punchy vocals, plus his sheer sexual charisma, the album's second single jumped to No. 5, and the album's double-platinum sales paved the way for world domination with 1987's *Kick*. —LM

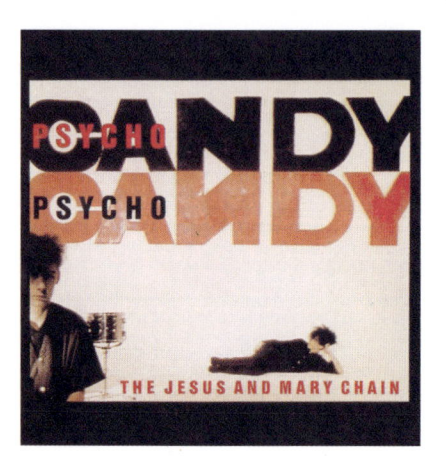

The Jesus and Mary Chain
PSYCHOCANDY
BLANCO Y NEGRO | Producers: The Jesus and Mary Chain
RELEASED: NOVEMBER 18, 1986

● Shoegaze was not a thing when the Jesus and Mary Chain released its debut album, but *Psychocandy* unquestionably set up a tentpole on which a subgenre was built. Starting with the exquisite **Just Like Honey**, Scottish brothers Jim and William Reid wrapped their songs in dense layers of fuzzy sonics, alternatingly spacious and exuberantly noisy (**The Living End**, **In a Hole**) but never losing the melodic thread couched within Jim's deadpan vocals. Unprecedented at the time, *Psychocandy* is still gloriously original, and just as enveloping, decades later. —GG

Lone Justice
LONE JUSTICE
GEFFEN | Producer: Jimmy Iovine
RELEASED: APRIL 15, 1985

● The music world was still grappling with what to call bands like Lone Justice (Country rock? Cowpunk?) when its debut album was released. It was not the first to synthesize those rock and country elements, which we now call Americana, but there was a fresh kind of energy across these ten tracks and also the arrival of Maria McKee as an exciting new singer and songwriter—even if the best track, **Ways to Be Wicked**, was written by Tom Petty and Mike Campbell. —GG

Various Artists
LOST IN THE STARS: THE MUSIC OF KURT WEILL

A & M | Producers: Hal Willner, Paul M. Young
RELEASED: OCTOBER 1985

● Hal Willner aggregated an intriguing cast ranging from Sting, Lou Reed, Todd Rundgren, and Tom Waits to Charlie Haden, Van Dyke Parks, Aaron Neville, and Carla Bley, some of whom succeeded by playing Weill's Weimar-era decadence reasonably straight (Sting's stage-worthy reading of **Mac the Knife**, Marianne Faithfull's world-weary **The Ballad of the Soldier's Wife**, and Waits's barking **What Keeps Mankind Alive?**). Others recast Weill's compositions in their own image (Parks's deftly arranged **Johnny Johnson Medley**, John Zorn's chaotic **Der Kleine Leutnant des Lieben Gottes**, and Charlie Haden's minimalist **Speak Low**). Perhaps most satisfying was Reed's surprisingly sweet **September Song**. –DD

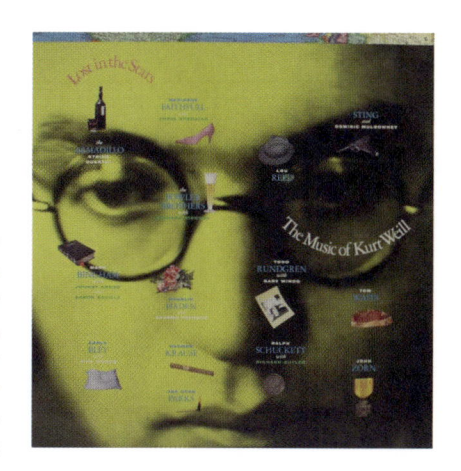

Manhattan Transfer
VOCALESE

ATLANTIC | Producers: Tim Hauser, Martin Fischer
RELEASED: SEPTEMBER 3, 1985

● All it took for Manhattan Transfer to become forever hip was teaming up with legendary scat singer/lyricist Jon Hendricks and adopt his language of vocalese, which swaps lyrics in place of jazz instrumental solos. Already known for pop hits such as "The Boy from New York City" and "Birdland," the flashy four-part harmony coterie hit its prime with *Vocalese*, earning two Grammy Awards. It sang Hendricks's magnificently crafted lyrics with panache on a collection of jazz classics, including with Dizzy Gillespie's **A Night in Tunisia**, featuring guest Bobby McFerrin. –CH

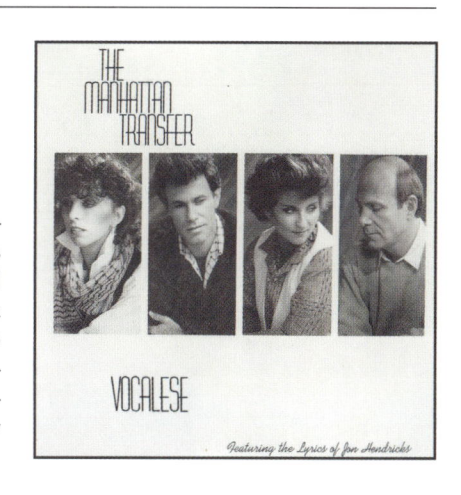

Mantronix
THE ALBUM

SLEEPING BAG | Producers: Kurtis Mantronik, MC Tee
RELEASED: 1985

● The hip-hop world was in pure awe when Mantronix exploded onto the scene with a futuristic wizardry that revolutionized the genre. Its use of the TRS 808 drum machine entered uncharted territory as the duo produced an energetic fun and enjoyable high-tech masterpiece. Danceable and infectious songs such as **Needle to the Groove** and **Fresh Is the Word**, along with the funky **Bassline**, were pure genius. With the use of raw, strong beats and hardcore melodic synth lines, *The Album* shaped the history of electronic music forever. –MH

Heart
HEART
CAPITOL | Producer: Ron Nevison
RELEASED: JUNE 21, 1985

● "Some people told us we might have hits if we did these songs," Ann Wilson said about Heart's eighth studio album. "We hadn't had hits for a while, so we listened to them." And the *Heart* album indeed began a new era for the band fronted by Ann and younger sister Nancy Wilson.

The group had, of course, started out great runs in the album rock world of the mid-'70s, drilling fans with four straight platinum or better albums and hits such as "Magic Man," "Crazy on You," "Barracuda," and more. But the hit parade waned by the turn of the decade. Heart was released by its label, ironically winding back with the company that had distribution rights for its first two albums.

The guidance from a new home and producer (Ron Nevison) helped Heart regain its beat here—mightily, though its five singles all came from outside writers, including Elton John cohort Bernie Taupin and Q-Feel leader Martin Page (**These Dreams**), hitmaker Holly Knight (**Never**), and Bryan Adams cohort Jim Vallance (**What About Love**). The band's input (five tracks) was decidedly second fiddle to these guns for hire.

The ten-song set was significantly more polished and poppy than the early contingent of Heart's fanbase was used to. But with MTV's support, a new generation was secured, sending *Heart* to No. 1 on the Billboard 200 with five-times platinum sales and four of the singles into the Top 10. The album also scored Heart its first-ever Grammy Award nomination for Best Rock Performance by a Duo or Group with Vocal.

The Wilsons later expressed some regret about the capitulation, but that seemed disingenuous; had they resisted, it's likely there would not be a Heart still around now to complain about it. *–GG*

1985

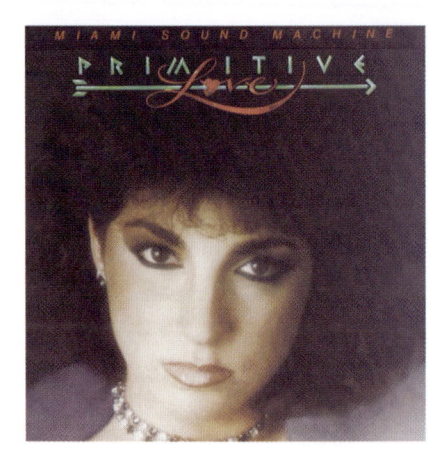

Miami Sound Machine
PRIMITIVE LOVE
E P I C | Producer: Emilio Estefan Jr.
RELEASED: AUGUST 13, 1985

● For most Anglo listeners, Miami Sound Machine came out of nowhere in 1985, when the muscular tattoo of **Conga** announced the arrival of what was the Florida group's ninth album. That was the first of three Top 10 hits and multiplatinum sales, and while more impressive statistics were ahead with 1987's *Let It Loose* and singer Gloria Estefan's subsequent solo career, *Primitive Love* was the starting point to that ascent and still had a few rough edges that made this album that much more interesting. —*GG*

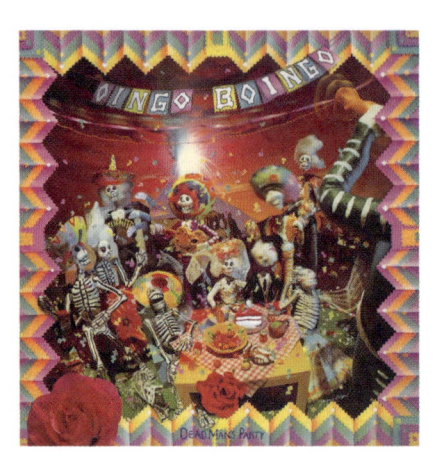

Oingo Boingo
DEAD MAN'S PARTY
M C A | Producers: Danny Elfman, Steve Bartek
RELEASED: OCTOBER 28, 1985

● In the years before Danny Elfman became an acclaimed soundtrack auteur, he led Oingo Boingo—less a conventional band than a rendering of a Halloween party as New Wave performance art. That vibe was the perfect opening act for Elfman's future work. Released just in time for Halloween, the breathlessly catchy *Dead Man's Party* came out the same year as Elfman's first big soundtrack, for the Tim Burton–directed *Pee Wee's Big Adventure*. The album only peaked at No. 98 but still earned a US gold record, thanks to the singles **Stay** and **Weird Science**. —*DM*

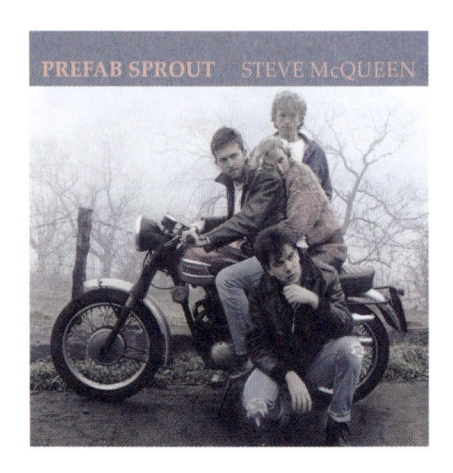

Prefab Sprout
TWO WHEELS GOOD
C B S | Producers: Thomas Dolby, Phil Thornalley
RELEASED: JUNE 22, 1985

● Prefab Sprout's Paddy McAloon earned an obsessive fanbase with the band's second album, *Two Wheels Good* (*Steve McQueen* in the UK and changed over fear of legal repercussions from the actor's estate). With its lush production, the album was a witty, moody summer song about love that cuts too deep, from the vulnerable lead single **When Love Breaks Down** to the catchy **Appetite** and the wounded **Desire As** and its acerbic lyric "I've got six things on my mind / You're no longer one of them." —*HD*

Various Artists
ROCKY IV (ORIGINAL MOTION PICTURE SOUNDTRACK)
SCOTTI BROS. | Producers: Various
RELEASED: NOVEMBER 27, 1985

● While *Rocky IV* marked a commercial peak for the film franchise, its soundtrack was a high point for '80s workout and training music. Survivor's **Burning Heart** was a worthy successor to its smash *Rocky III* contribution **Eye of the Tiger** (also included here). John Cafferty's **Hearts on Fire** was designed to squeeze those last drips of sweat from a conditioning session, Vince DiCola's instrumentals **War** and **Training Montage** could inspire anyone to get off the couch, and James Brown's **Living in America** was the celebration at the end of a hard day's work. *–AG*

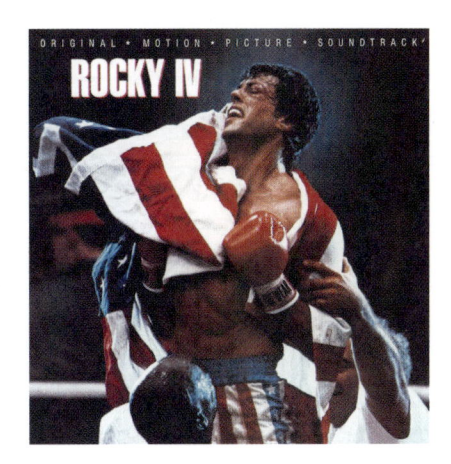

Simply Red
PICTURE BOOK
ELEKTRA | Producer: Stewart Levine
RELEASED: OCTOBER 11, 1985

● British group Simply Red's soul-filled debut album cut through the glut of mid-'80s synth-pop with **Holding Back the Years**, a gorgeous ballad sung with heartstring-pulling sincerity by sometimes-polarizing frontman Mick Hucknall. It was a stellar performance and served as a calling card for an equally gorgeous album that earned two Grammy Award nominations and offered plenty more behind it, including covers of the Valentine Brothers' **Money's Too Tight to Mention** and Talking Heads' **Heaven**. It was a platinum peak in the US, though the rest of the world would find the group simply irresistible for some years to come. *–GG/HD*

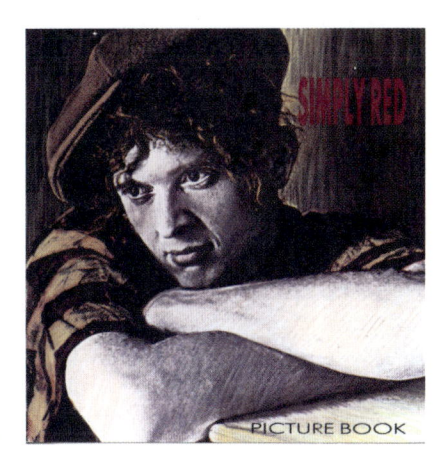

'Til Tuesday
VOICES CARRY
EPIC | Producer: Mike Thorne
RELEASED: APRIL 30, 1985

● 'Til Tuesday served as the launching pad for the solo career of lead singer Aimee Mann, and the title track from its first album was the Saturn booster that sent her into orbit. **Voices Carry**, reportedly inspired by an argument between Mann and drummer Michael Hausman, became a Top 10 hit on the strength of her lilting vocals and its unforgettable chorus. It was far and away the best of the album's eleven tracks, but *Voices Carry* was a Top 20 gold-certified arrival from which Mann went on to do even greater things. *–GP*

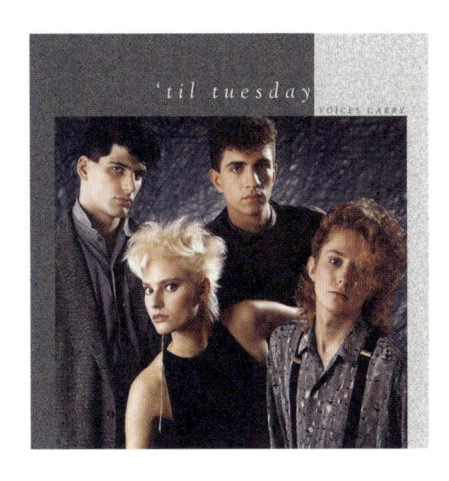

LL Cool J
RADIO
DEF JAM | Producer: Rick Rubin
RELEASED: NOVEMBER 18, 1985

● Hip-hop needed a solo star, and LL Cool J answered the call: The seventeen-year-old from Queens, New York, arrived on the scene armed with rhymes for days, attitude aplenty, and charisma to spare.

LL Cool J—born James Todd Smith, his rap name a stand-in for Ladies Love Cool James—released his debut single, **I Need a Beat**, in 1984. The hard-hitting B-boy anthem landed him a deal with Rick Rubin and Russell Simmons's upstart hip-hop label Def Jam Recordings. An appearance in 1985's *Krush Groove* greased him for success, and *Radio*, with a remix of **I Need a Beat**, became Def Jam's first album release.

Radio took everything LL did well and cranked it to eleven. With sparse production from a young Rubin, LL's rhymes are laced atop a skeletal frame of sampled rock riffs, boom bap drums, and record scratches. Rubin's production credit read "reduced by Rick Rubin," and his less-is-more approach made LL sound like he was rapping over the blown speakers of a portable jambox. As an aesthetic, it's perfect.

The first single and album opener, **I Can't Live Without My Radio**, was LL in a nutshell: He spits rhymes with the savoir faire of a young Cassius Clay, bragging how his radio is better than everyone else's, making *him* better than everyone else. "Get fresh BATTERIES if it won't rewind!" he says with the power of a war general, making even the act of replacing Duracells sound like a threat to an opponent's manhood.

Rock the Bells, **You'll Rock**, and the hilarious callout **That's a Lie** kept the energy high, and LL showed his soft(er) side on **I Want You**, a precursor to the full-on hip-hop ballad "I Need Love" on his next album. Befitting rap's first solo star, *Radio* was one of the genre's brightest moments. *–AG*

1985

Wynton Marsalis
BLACK CODES (FROM THE UNDERGROUND)

COLUMBIA | Producers: Steven Epstein, Exec Producer George Butler
RELEASED: JUNE 9, 1985

● Wynton Marsalis, the second oldest of six boys in an esteemed New Orleans jazz family, emerged as the de facto leader, a trumpet prodigy whose exceptional tone and proficiency earned him, unprecedentedly, two Grammy Awards in two genres—jazz and classical. An evangelist for no-nonsense, straight-ahead jazz, Marsalis also heralded a generation of twenty-something players dubbed Young Lions, accomplished instrumentalists steeped in tradition and determined to carry on its legacy.

When Marsalis released *Black Codes*, his sixth album, he took home two more Grammys. His compositional skills for quintet, across seven tracks, showed maturity. The album simultaneously made a bold statement: That's not a school-aged Wynton on the cover; it's his seven-year-old brother Jason, getting a lesson on the Black Codes, the oppressive post–Civil War rules that only applied to African Americans in the South in an effort to keep slavery alive. Marsalis was determined to push back against the remnants of the Black Codes, via jazz, aka "America's classical music."

Black Codes housed some of Marsalis's most elegant tunes—sweet, swinging, and locked into the hard-bop groove. The title track opened melodically with an assertive, hard-charging rhythm section of Kenny Kirkland on piano and Jeff "Tain" Watts on drums. Enter Wynton and older brother, Branford, on saxophone, who play polished and precise at high speed in tight unison, note for perfect note. When Wynton's first solo kicks in, the velocity of his compressed breath streams through his horn. He grabs the center of attention with penetrating and unsurpassed clarity.

For Wee Folks splits the melodic intro between muted trumpet and soprano sax. Equally beautiful is **Aural Oasis**, interlaced with delicate piano and cymbals accompaniment. **Blue** closes the set with Marsalis soloing expressively over Charnett Moffett's walking bass. —*CH*

1985

The Pogues
RUM, SODOMY & THE LASH
STIFF | Producer: Elvis Costello
RELEASED: AUGUST 5, 1985

● The Pogues' arrival struck a nerve, particularly in England. The younger members of the Irish diaspora in England and Scotland heard the sound and intuitively recognized the energy of the group's spirit. It reached back centuries and punched like punk rock; even the ballads had a kick. While the Chieftains were taking the metaphorical high road in spreading the gospel of Irish music, the Pogues harnessed the passion of the Clash with a tin whistle, accordion, banjo, guitar, bass, and drums. Tradition was served in a nontraditional way through contemporary songs such as Ewan MacColl's **Dirty Old Town** and Woody Guthrie's **Jesse James**. These compositions flattered the group's strengths and served to spotlight the depth of its own songwriting. Frontman Shane McGowan rapidly established himself as a composer of lyrical depth; he summoned Johnny Cash and James Joyce while illustrating the bleakness of Margaret Thatcher's England. "I took the jeers and drank the beers and crawled back home at dawn, and ended up a barman in the morning," McGowan sang in **Sally MacLennane**, a documentary of failure and despair played as a springy jig. And if anyone ever looked like their music sounded, it was McGowan and his ramshackle demeanor. *—HK*

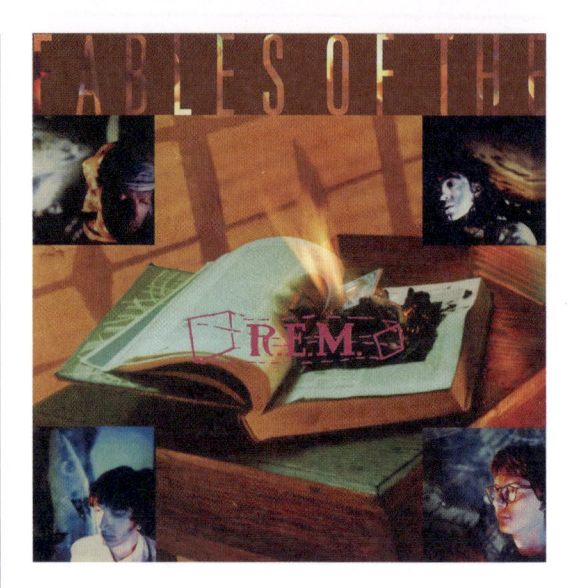

R.E.M.
FABLES OF THE RECONSTRUCTION
I.R.S. | Producer: Joe Boyd
RELEASED: JUNE 10, 1985

● Since its debut, R.E.M. shrouded itself in the mistiest Southern gothic it could conjure. Onstage there were no spotlights, the vocals were a melodic blur, and guitar solos barely existed. It could seem off-putting, but the group defined itself on its own terms. It served the quartet well, particularly by the time it got to *Fables of the Reconstruction* (or *Reconstruction of the Fables*, depending on how you read the cover). Working with Joe Boyd, the American who produced early Pink Floyd, Fairport Convention, and Nick Drake, R.E.M. found a platform to show its rapid maturation. The group appeared whimsical and bright on **Can't Get There from Here**, layered and jangly on the train song **Driver 8** and **Kohoutek**. Its sense of Southern-ness manifested itself in both darkness (**Old Man Kensey**) and warmth (**Wendell Gee**). What hasn't been said enough about this band is the deep collaborative work that is the foundation of R.E.M.—there was no one main songwriter or hotshot instrumentalist. It took until this record to get the singer to be heard above the band on occasion. That said, bassist/keyboardist Mike Mills is one Swiss Army knife of a player. *—HK*

The Replacements
TIM
SIRE | Producer: Tommy Erdelyi
RELEASED: SEPTEMBER 18, 1985

● Arriving on the heels of its much-ballyhooed third LP, *Let It Be* (1984), the hotly anticipated major label debut from Minneapolis's critical faves further highlighted songwriter/frontman Paul Westerberg's developing versatility, especially as guitarist Bob Stinson and his singular contributions from previous recordings reached the end of their line (Stinson would be ousted in 1986). *Tim* kicked off promisingly with **Hold My Life**, a lurching ode to underachievers from a band many feel superseded all others in its inability (or unwillingness) to grasp the brass ring. Drawing from the group's diverse palette were the roots-leaning **Kiss Me on the Bus** and **Waitress in the Sky** and the bordering-on-maudlin **Swingin Party** and **Here Comes a Regular**. The fillers **Dose of Thunder** and **Lay It Down Clown** were more than offset by *Tim*'s trio of essential college-rock anthems: **Bastards of Young**, **Little Mascara**, and **Left of the Dial**. The Replacements tapped Tommy Erdelyi (aka Tommy Ramone) as *Tim*'s producer; fans often cited the erstwhile drummer's work as a contributing factor to *Tim*'s somewhat-disappointing commercial returns (never mind the band's penchant for self-sabotage), a situation rectified in 2023's rerelease featuring Ed Stasium's unanimously celebrated remix. *–DP*

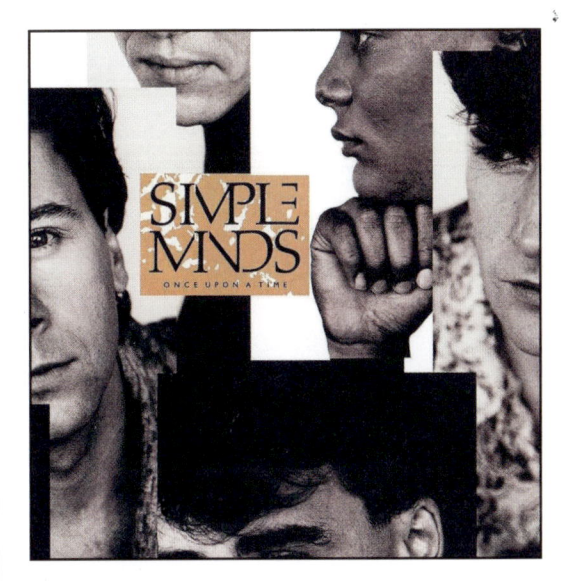

Simple Minds
ONCE UPON A TIME
A & M | Producers: Jimmy Iovine, Bob Clearwater
RELEASED: OCTOBER 21, 1985

● Scotland's Simple Minds was big in the UK and Europe with six successful albums, but it was the No. 1 hit "Don't You (Forget about Me)" from the Brat Pack film *The Breakfast Club* earlier in 1985 that broke the group in America and set the table for its biggest album. The band teamed with American producers Jimmy Iovine and Bob Clearwater to punch up its already-anthemic sound, bringing in more guitar drive and accentuating frontman Jim Kerr's yearning vocals. The result radiated a raw energy and solid structure not fully realized on its previous releases. *Once Upon a Time* reached No. 10 on the Billboard 200 and topped UK's albums chart. **Alive and Kicking** scored another abundance of radio play with its hymnlike melody and a coda featuring backup singer Robin Clark's gospel-inspired vocals. There was a spiritual vibe to the Sly & the Family Stone–influenced **Sanctify Yourself**, while **All the Things She Said** was inspired by quotes from Polish political prisoners in Russia. *–JC*

1985

John Mellencamp
SCARECROW

RIVA/MERCURY | Producers: John Mellencamp, George Green
RELEASED: JULY 31, 1985

● The maturity—and there is no other word for it—that John (then) Cougar Mellencamp began with *American Fool* in 1982 and continued on the following year's *Uh-Huh* took another step with the Indiana rocker's eighth studio album. He still liked to **R.O.C.K. in the U.S.A.**, but most of the eleven songs—including that one—mined deeper terrain, whether it was **Rain on the Scarecrow**'s paean to the plight of America's family farmer, the poignant statement of character in the biographical **Small Town**, the sociopolitical outlook in **The Face of the Nation**, or the soulful self-realization in the sweeping **Minutes to Memories**.

The penultimate track was even called **You've Got to Stand for Somethin'**, and this time Mellencamp really did—albeit with a bit of kicking and screaming to get there.

"Up until this year I was just a guy in a band in a bar. I didn't want to go beyond that," Mellencamp, acknowledging he also wanted to dodge specific comparisons to Bruce Springsteen, said as he started touring to support *Scarecrow*. "Then I started to realize, 'What's wrong with *two* people putting their best foot forward?'" Writing a "terrible" screenplay, meanwhile, put him in a different kind of mode, with characters and narrators even more fleshed out than those he drew in "Jack & Diane" and "Pink Houses."

Mellencamp, joined by guests Rickie Lee Jones and Ry Cooder in spots, also deepened the musical well here. He made his band members learn a bunch of mostly '60s garage rock tunes, opening their minds to different ways to approach music and draw from a larger palette. *Scarecrow* let us know that Mellencamp was an American fool no more but was, rather, ready to join the ranks of thoughtful, resonant heartland troubadours—and still let it R.O.C.K. when he wanted. *—GG*

1985

Sting
DREAM OF THE BLUE TURTLES

A & M | Producers: Sting, Pete Smith
RELEASED: JUNE 1, 1985

● The Police's hiatus after its *Synchronicity* album and tour was supposed to be temporary. But the massive success of Sting's solo debut, *Dream of the Blue Turtles*—released on *Synchronicity*'s two-year anniversary and containing a reworked version of *Zenyatta Mondatta*'s **Shadows in the Rain**—helped put the kibosh on reconciliation plans.

Playing guitar with a band of rising jazz stars including Branford Marsalis on sax and future Rolling Stone Darryl Jones on bass, Sting revisited his pre-Police roots, as well as his love for composer Kurt Weill (on the vampire-inspired **Moon Over Bourbon Street**). He also editorialized about sociopolitical issues such as Cold War tensions (**Russians**), British coal miners' strife (**We Work the Black Seam**), and war, child exploitation, and drugs (**Children's Crusade**). He also counterbalanced his stalkerish "Every Breath You Take," the Police's biggest hit, with the upbeat opener and first single, **If You Love Somebody Set Them Free**; reaching No. 3 on Billboard's Hot 100 chart, it remains his highest-ranking solo single. Three more singles climbed inside the Top 20; the album itself hit No. 2 on Billboard's Top 200 and launched Sting's remarkable run of seven consecutive Top 10 solo studio albums.

He actually quoted "Every Breath . . ." in the feel-good calypso track **Love Is the Seventh Wave**, then leavened its somewhat reverential lyrics with the line "Every cake you bake / Every leg you break." Marsalis's and keyboardist Kenny Kirkland's instrumental flights offset the lyrical density of songs such as **Children's Crusade** and the gorgeously arranged **Fortress Around Your Heart** and, with Omar Hakim's drumming, found a cool-jazz/funk groove on tracks such as **Consider Me Gone**. *Turtles* was all-killer/no-filler and kept any Police reunion plans cuffed for another two-plus decades. *—LM*

Tears for Fears
SONGS FROM THE BIG CHAIR

MERCURY | Producer: Chris Hughes
RELEASED: FEBRUARY 25, 1985

● Roland Orzabal and Curt Smith, aka Tears for Fears, worked out their childhood traumas on their first album *The Hurting*, freeing their psyches for the poppier *Songs from the Big Chair*. Where the debut was deeply introspective and heavily synth-based, the duo's sophomore effort had more intentionally "joyful," guitar-driven songs, though the joy was mitigated by tracks such as **Everybody Wants to Rule the World**, overtly about the Cold War (as were many other songs during the mid-'80s). It hit No. 1 on the US charts, as did the follow-up single, the more personal but equally intense **Shout**.

Based on the Jungian theory that the way to move past childhood trauma is to (literally) scream, **Shout** made the loudest noise of Tears for Fears' career. The song opened with the anthemic mantra "Shout, shout, let it all out / These are the things I can do without" and went on to profess that "If I could change your mind / I'd really like to break your heart." It was brutally candid, but overall the album offered a bold, explosive sound from an otherwise-cerebral band.

Songs from the Big Chair was relentless with hooks and beats that made listeners need to sing along—nowhere more true than on the unapologetically romantic **Head over Heels**, a third Top 5 hit from the album. Whatever sonic magic Tears for Fears unleashed on this album, the band's heart still shined through. As *Stylus* magazine noted twenty-one years after the album's release, "Even today, when all rock musicians seem to be able to do is be emotional and honest, the brutality and power of *Songs from the Big Chair*'s catharsis is still quite shocking." –HD

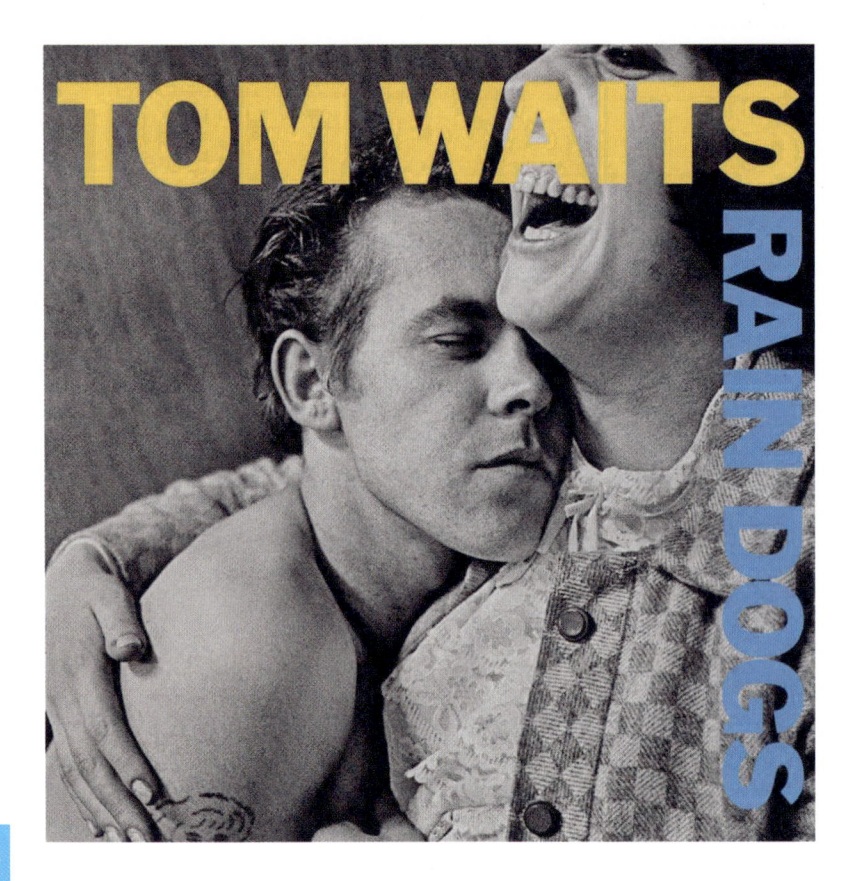

Tom Waits
RAIN DOGS

ISLAND | Producer: Tom Waits
RELEASED: SEPTEMBER 30, 1985

● When Tom Waits reached a turning point with 1983's *Swordfishtrombones*, his eighth album, there was no looking back. From his 1973 debut, *Closing Time*, through 1980's *Heartattack and Vine*, the Los Angeles singer/songwriter mined a persona of the grizzled but affable barfly, quick with a story about down-and-out characters, scat-sung or spoken over vaguely jazzy backing music. *Swordfishtrombones* transplanted Waits and his songs to a post-apocalyptic wasteland soundtracked by trash can percussion and found sounds; *Rain Dogs*, which was released two years later, went down darker, dirtier streets.

 Swordfishtrombones was a test pattern of a record for the more fully formed and confident *Rain Dogs*. More than fifty-three free-form minutes, Waits and his collaborators—including guitarists Marc Ribot and the Rolling Stones' Keith Richards and a selection of musicians on saxophone, marimba, accordion, banjo, and bowed saw—visited the outskirts of several forms of American music while never settling comfortably into any one. Waits wrote much of the album in New York, capturing the various sounds of the city streets on a cassette recorder that helped locate the downtown noises that directly and indirectly inspired the album.

From the opening boozy sea song **Singapore** to the mournful (and also boozy) closer **Anywhere I Lay My Head**, *Rain Dogs* switched course so frequently that its conceptual center—a theme LP devoted to New York City and the middle part of a trilogy concluded with 1987's *Franks Wild Years*—was nearly lost. The bluesy shuffle **Big Black Mariah** seemingly had little in common with the tortured ballad **Downtown Train** (a Top 5 hit later in the decade for Rod Stewart), but Waits positioned them as a single piece in his haunted and scarred travelogue. A template was laid out on *Rain Dogs*: avant-garde experimentalism laced with scant commercial concession. Waits finally found his groove. *—MG*

1985

19

86

1986

Janet Jackson
CONTROL

A & M | Producers: Jimmy Jam, Terry Lewis
RELEASED: FEBRUARY 4, 1986

● *Control* was Janet Jackson's third album, but for all intents and purposes, it's where her music career began. She was nineteen when it was released but had been in the public eye for years, appearing with her family on *The Jacksons* variety show as early as age ten and later acting on TV's *Diff'rent Strokes* and *Fame*. But her first two albums, 1982's self-titled debut and 1984's *Dream Street*, were commercial and artistic duds, so Jackson broke away from her domineering father-manager and took, well, you know what of her career.

The mission statement couldn't be any clearer: "This is a story about control. My control. Control of what I say, control of what I do," Jackson said on the album-opening title track. "And this time, I'm gonna do it my way. I hope you enjoy this as much as I do." Listeners did: The album launched five Top 5 singles, including Jackson's first No. 1, **When I Think of You**, and set in motion one of the most successful pop careers of all time.

Jackson was in control, but she didn't do it alone. *Control* marked the beginning of her creative partnership with producers Jimmy Jam and Terry Lewis, the Minneapolis duo who would be her musical partners for decades. They gave her a funk-driven, pop-R&B, electro-soul sound that let Jackson assert herself as a confident, modern woman who was nobody's fool. "No, my first name ain't baby / It's Janet, Miss Jackson if you're nasty," she announces on **Nasty**, a line that became her calling card.

The album eventually hit No. 1, and its videos made Jackson a fixture on MTV, where she shared airspace with fellow network staples such as Madonna and her older brother. But no longer was she Michael Jackson's kid sister; *Control* made Janet Jackson a superstar in her own right. *—AG*

1986

Bon Jovi
SLIPPERY WHEN WET

MERCURY | Producer: Bruce Fairbairn
RELEASED: AUGUST 18, 1986

● It was the smile. Bon Jovi frontman Jon Bon Jovi wasn't afraid to flash his pearly whites, and that friendly, genial attitude made Bon Jovi an approachable, and even cuddly, hard rock band. It wasn't about scaring people off; it was about inviting them in.

That smile can be heard throughout *Slippery When Wet*, the New Jersey group's mainstream breakthrough. It was one of the decade's biggest commercial juggernauts, spending eight weeks at No. 1 and selling more than 28 million albums worldwide. And it launched the monster singles **Livin' on a Prayer**, **You Give Love a Bad Name**, and **Wanted Dead or Alive**, songs that are still rock radio and karaoke staples and paved the way for the band's 2018 induction into the Rock & Roll Hall of Fame.

Slippery When Wet was Bon Jovi's third album, following 1984's self-titled debut and 1985's *7800° Fahrenheit*. The band swung for the fences, enlisting songwriter Desmond Child (Kiss, Cher) and adopting a bigger, more radio-friendly sound. Child co-wrote four songs with Jon Bon Jovi and guitarist Richie Sambora, and two of those (**Prayer** and **Bad Name**) hit No. 1 on Billboard's Hot 100. The album was produced by Bruce Fairbairn (Loverboy, Blue Öyster Cult) and mixed by Bob Rock to sound as big as their home state Meadowlands Arena.

Beyond the gigantic singles, there was the prom anthem **Never Say Goodbye**, while **Raise Your Hands** showed up in the Mel Brooks spoof *Spaceballs*. The band even caught a break with the album cover, featuring the title crudely scrawled onto a wet garbage bag; it was a last-second replacement for an image of a model in a wet T-shirt, which might not have gone over in middle America. Everything worked out on *Slippery When Wet* and gave Bon Jovi plenty to smile about. —*AG*

Steve Earle
GUITAR TOWN

MCA | Producers: Emory Gordy Jr., Tony Brown
RELEASED: MARCH 5, 1986

● Brandishing rock 'n' roll attitude, outlaw-country influences, and a drawl matching his Texas-sized self-confidence, Steve Earle swaggered into Nashville with one solid asset: killer songwriting chops. His break came when MCA's Tony Brown heard his songs, signed him, and co-produced his full-length debut. Informed as much by Springsteen as Townes Van Zandt, Earle's hero, *Guitar Town* lassoed country's twang, rock's testosterone, and folk's true confessions into an alternative-country sound that chiseled a cornerstone for what became Americana.

Starting with its title-tune pledge of allegiance to the rock 'n' roll road life, *Guitar Town* revealed the restless, brash but self-effacing spirit of a thrice-divorced father done with conforming to others' expectations. Instead, Earle turned his wandering ways into a theme threading through explorations of working-class struggles, ragged dreams of better days, and the hopes that keep us traveling.

Amid Bucky Baxter's pedal steel and the tremolo twang of Rick Bennett's down-tuned guitar or six-string bass (or, on **Hillbilly Highway**, slap bass and chicken pickin'), one could hear the occasional Rolling Stones riff (**Good Ol' Boy [Gettin' Tough]**), Rick Nelson nod (**Think It Over**), or a straight-outta-Asbury-Park line like "There ain't a lot that you can do in this town / You drive down to the lake, and then you turn back around" (**Someday**). Charmers such as **Fearless Heart** ("I admit I fall in love a lot / But I nearly always give it my best shot") and the more traditional ballad **My Old Friend the Blues** helped *Guitar Town* top Billboard's Top Country Albums chart. Its four singles all reached the country Top 40. **Goodbye** hit No. 8, and **Guitar Town** went to 7—and earned a Best Country Song Grammy nomination. The album snagged a nod for Best Country Vocal Solo Performance, Male—and is now widely acknowledged as a groundbreaking classic. —*LM*

Beastie Boys
LICENSED TO ILL

DEF JAM | Producers: Rick Rubin, Beastie Boys
RELEASED: NOVEMBER 16, 1986

● Creating the first rap record to top the Billboard Top 200 is a neat trick for a group originally conceived as a hardcore punk band. During the early 1980s, the Beastie Boys fell in love with what they heard in New York City clubs and streets and began incorporating rap into their sets. A few years later, they met Rick Rubin and Russell Simmons, co-founders in the fledgling rap label, Def Jam. Simmons, the brother of Run of Run-D.M.C., the first hip-hop group to earn a gold record, felt rap could go wider and the Beastie Boys could be the vehicle.

Licensed to Ill featured a range of samples and sounds familiar not only to hip-hop heads but also to rockers. The lead track, **Rhymin' & Stealin'**, lifted John Bonham's thudding drum opening from Led Zeppelin's "When the Levee Breaks," while **No Sleep till Brooklyn** featured a distorted guitar solo. The production was similar to the success Rubin recently had with the Run-D.M.C./Aerosmith mash-up cover of "Walk This Way."

The album is lyrically focused on what you might expect from three guys barely twenty-one—partying, braggadocio, and sex. The themes are typified by the frat anthem **(You've Got to) Fight for Your Right (To Party)**, the chest-thumping bounce of **The New Style**, and the cheeky misogyny of **Girls**. The album's success ended up being not what the Beastie Boys wanted, and they distanced themselves from it after they saw how young men took their lyrics as unintended inspiration. Ultimately, the group returned to playing live instruments, blending jazz, funk, and rock with rap on future releases.

Historically, Licensed to Ill brought white mainstream audiences to hip-hop, another Black art form that has dominated the music world ever since, and proving it needn't be limited to one race. —*RSM*

1986

Anita Baker
RAPTURE
ELEKTRA | Producers: Michael J. Powell, Marti Sharron, Gary Skardina
RELEASED: MARCH 20, 1986

● You had to have ice in your veins and around your heart not to be, yes, caught up in the *Rapture* of Anita Baker's second solo album—at once contemporary and retro. Baker was singing in Detroit clubs as a teenager and was whisked out of the group Chapter 8 for her own career. *The Songstress* did not quite connect in 1983, but for *Rapture*, Baker found a collaborator in Chapter 8 bandmate Michael Powell, who knew exactly how to present her unique blend of silk and smoke—although they recorded amid legal actions by her previous record label to block the project. **Sweet Love**, with its murmurs and swoops, established co-writer Baker as a true force with an original sensibility curated from the sum of her many influences—and there was more where that came from on the album's other seven tracks. Five Billboard chart hits followed **Sweet Love**, with **Caught Up in the Rapture**, **Same Ole Love (365 Days a Year)**, and **No One in the World** joining it in the R&B Top 10. It also gave Baker her first two Grammy Awards and the opportunity to give the best that she got on subsequent releases. —*GG*

Afrika Bambaataa & Soul Sonic Force
PLANET ROCK: THE ALBUM
TOMMY BOY | Producers: Afrika Bambaattaa, Arthur Baker, John Robie, Keith LeBlanc, Doug Wimbush, Skip McDonald, Fats Comet Productions
RELEASED: DECEMBER 1, 1986

● "From a different solar system, many galaxies away, we are the force of another creation, a new musical revelation . . ." Those lyrics from **Renegades of Funk** summarized exactly what Afrika Bambaataa and Soul Sonic Force was about. This set of previously released singles from 1982 to 1986 showcased the collective's iconic blend of raw hip-hop and electronics. In the process, it created an entirely new genre and took hip-hop into an electro-funk direction that changed the landscape of music forever. Iconic songs such as **Planet Rock** and **Looking for the Perfect Beat** as well as **Renegades of Funk** blended Kraftwerk and Parliament-Funkadelic with a touch of James Brown—putting the soul into the machine, in other words, as breakdancers sweated on hot club floors. The "perfect beat" was realized, and the Soul Sonic Force crew put the world on notice of its arrival. It's hard to find a record that changed the culture and music to the extent *Planet Rock: The Album* did; as Bambaataa and company commanded on **Planet Rock**, "Our world is but a land of a master jam / Get up and dance." —*MH*

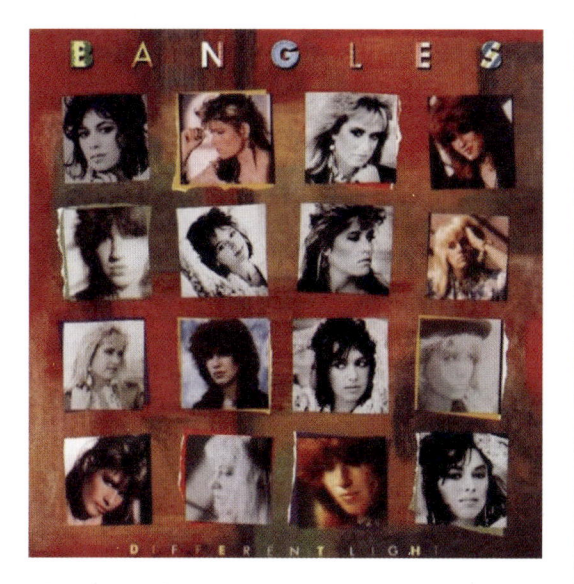

The Bangles
DIFFERENT LIGHT

COLUMBIA | Producer: David Kahne
RELEASED: JANUARY 10, 1986

● The Bangles came out of the Los Angeles Paisley Underground club scene, as the Bangs, during the early '80s but could definitely be seen in a, well, different light by the time the all-female group's second full-length studio album rolled out. While 1984's *All Over the Place*, the Bangles' major label debut, showed off the group's MTV-friendly looks and accessible mainstream pop/rock sound, it was two major hits from *Different Light* that really vaulted the quartet to triple-platinum status. The Prince-penned **Manic Monday**, originally intended for Apollonia 6 and featuring Susanna Hoff's breathy vocals, gave the Bangles its first chart hit at No. 2 on the Billboard Hot 100, while **Walk Like an Egyptian** did it one spot better—along with an equally popular video that preserved Hoff's unforgettable side-to-side glance for posterity. *Different Light* boasted more strong material, too, whether originals (**Walking Down Your Street, Following**, the title track) or covers of Jules Shear's **If She Knew What She Wants** and Big Star's **September Gurls**. It was the best the Bangles ever did, but it also guaranteed the group a spot in any discussion of the '80s—and beyond. *–JC/GG*

Cameo
WORD UP!

ATLANTA ARTISTS | Producer: Larry Blackmon
RELEASED: SEPTEMBER 9, 1986

● This breakthrough crossover set made Cameo new to a lot of its listeners, but it was already a veteran act by that time, with twelve years and twelve albums already in the books. The New York troupe had a knack for adapting to times and trends, and in Larry Blackmon it had a genuinely visionary leader with a killer instinct in recognizing what he and his bandmates needed to do in order to stay relevant—but still be funky. On *Word Up!*, then, Cameo embraced slick sonics, synthesizers, and the burgeoning rap scene to sound contemporary and even futuristic with its nods to the forthcoming electronic dance culture. The title track became a Cameo gateway drug with its hard-hitting groove, Wild West whistle (out of Ennio Morricone's *The Good, The Bad and the Ugly* theme), and Blackmon's playful robot with an adenoid vocal. It was a Top 10 hit on the Billboard 200, taking the album to No. 8 and platinum sales—by far Cameo's greatest success. And the party continued past *Word Up!*, with tracks such as **Candy**, **Back and Forth**, and **Don't Be Lonely** stretching out and compelling everybody to wave their hands up in the air. *–GG*

Miles Davis
TUTU

WARNER BROS. | Producers: Marcus Miller, Tommy LiPuma, George Duke

RELEASED: AUGUST 31, 1986

● Endless jazz debates surround the groundbreaking trumpeter Miles Davis, who once bragged, "I've changed the course of music five or six times." As he relentlessly and unapologetically followed his muse, early admirers and critics were aghast when he shifted from acoustic jazz to plug-into rock, fusion, electro-funk, and hip-hop starting with In a Silent Way and Bitches Brew in 1969. The sonically breathtaking album Tutu supercharged the debates yet again, while it stands out as an exciting high point of his comeback and final career phase during the '80s.

Davis entrusted his young bassist and multi-instrumentalist Marcus Miller to conceptualize and write music for Tutu. Miller came through with a mesmerizing soundscape using combinations of sequencers, synthesizers, pulsing drum machines, industrial sounds, and effects expressing a dark, ambient, and mystical beauty. His own electric bass, bass clarinet, and soprano sax solos added radiant coloration to the outing.

Davis was the clear star of Tutu, though his personality saturated every track via dynamic solos, riffing freely, cutting loose, and feeling the high-tech karma. His incomparable and immediately recognizable horn centered within the cosmic mix—emotional, sublime, gorgeous, rapturous. Every track was uniquely delicious, with accessible melodies, catchy hooks, and infectious grooves.

Davis favored his distinct Harmon-muted trumpet throughout the album. On the title track, he squeezed the notes in short phrases, echoing the melody and the rhythmic cadence. On the sensual ballad **Portia**, his intonations curled alongside Fairlight synth washes and gurgling bass. **Perfect Way**, his surprising and inventive cover of the Scritti Politti song, became a hit.

On the reggae-infused **Don't Lose Your Mind**, Davis cavorted with sidewinding trumpet solos, cast against twangy guitar licks. It was all such wild fun and won a Grammy Award for Best Jazz Instrumental Performance, Soloist. —*CH*

1986

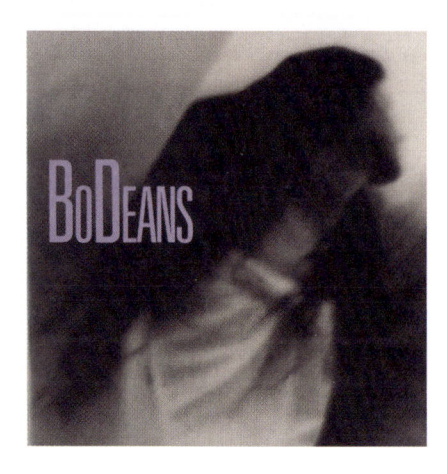

The BoDeans
LOVE & HOPE & SEX & DREAMS
SLASH/WARNER BROS. | Producer: T Bone Burnett
RELEASED: APRIL 16, 1986

● Among the first Midwest roots-rock bands offering an antidote to hair metal and synth-pop's shellacked-coif artifice, Milwaukee's BoDeans helped forge what eventually became Americana. On its debut, *Love & Hope & Sex & Dreams* (titled from the Rolling Stones' "Shattered"), Kurt Neumann and Sam Llanas caught ears and attention with earnest songs full of retro rock and pop influences, country twang, and distinctive harmonies. The chicken pickin'-meets-reggae of **Still the Night**, the Buddy Holly charm of **Angels**, and the insistent drive of **Fadeaway** remain some of their best work. *—LM*

Commissioned
GO TELL SOMEBODY
LIGHT | Producer: Alan V. Abrahams
RELEASED: FEBRUARY 25, 1986

● Commissioned's original sextet forged a path for what could be considered "accessible" gospel music, following Andraé Crouch's lead in incorporating elements of secular R&B and funk. The grooves were eternal, and the message was there if you wanted it. The Detroit troupe's sophomore effort was a bit less aggressive than its 1984 debut, *I'm Going On*, but more accomplished in terms of songcraft, its eight tracks tight and melodic enough—highlighting Commissioned's ensemble harmonies and Fred Hammond's commanding bass—to forgive the sonic vestiges of decidedly '80s production. *—GG*

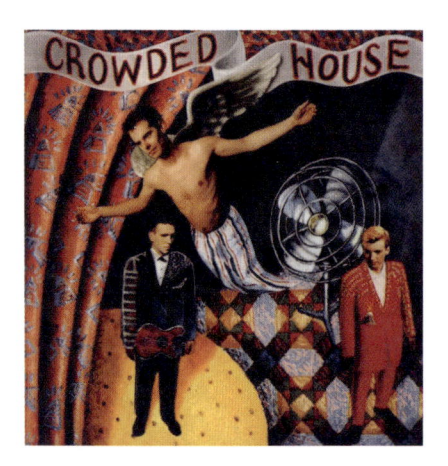

Crowded House
CROWDED HOUSE
CAPITOL | Producer: Mitchell Froom
RELEASED: JULY 1986

● Neil Finn was barely twenty-six when New Zealand's Split Enz split up. Forming Crowded House in Melbourne, Australia, with Enz drummer Paul Hester and bassist Nick Seymour, Finn had a new platform for his Beatlesque pop sensibilities and songs that shed the deliberate quirkiness of his previous band. History has centered this album around the evergreen Top 5 single **Don't Dream It's Over**, but that view marginalizes the many expertly crafted songs here such as **World Where You Live**, **Something So Strong**, and the heartbreaking **Hole in the River**. *—HK*

Bob James/David Sanborn
DOUBLE VISION
WARNER BROS. | Producer: Tommy LiPuma
RELEASED: MAY 19, 1986

● Keyboardist Bob James and alto saxophonist David Sanborn hit pay dirt by mining the smooth jazz vein. They could play anything, even avant-garde, but took the path of least commercial resistance. Their sensuous and enchanting fare went all the way, ultimately winning a Grammy Award for Best Fusion Album. Sanborn's alto was consistently invigorating and grounded, bathing listeners in polished melodies and sleek solos amid the lush and celestial ear candy deployed by James on synthesizers. Guest singer Al Jarreau turned his charisma on a potent love song, **Since I Fell for You**. *–CH*

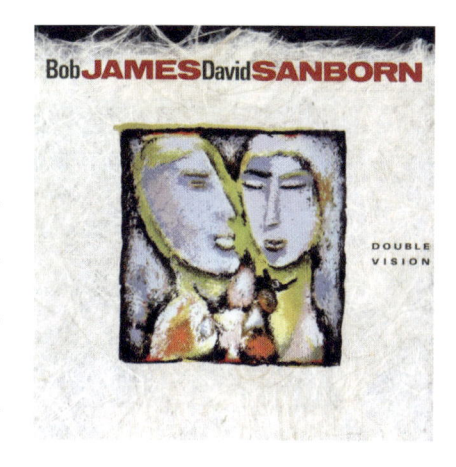

Kraftwerk
ELECTRIC CAFÉ
WARNER BROS. | Producers: Ralph Hutter, Florian Schneider
RELEASED: OCTOBER 1986

● Taking a bit of a detour, Kraftwerk went in a funkier and more accessible direction and still showed the world it was a master of electronics. From start to finish *Electric Café* was a fun and fresh excursion of catchy, head-bobbing hypnotic rhythms. **Musique Non Stop** and **Electric Café** offered a minimal electro feel with their hard, toe-tapping beats. **The Telephone Call** and **Techno Pop** lent a fresh, renovated feel to the group's trademark sound. Simply infectious electronica from pioneers of the genre. *–MH*

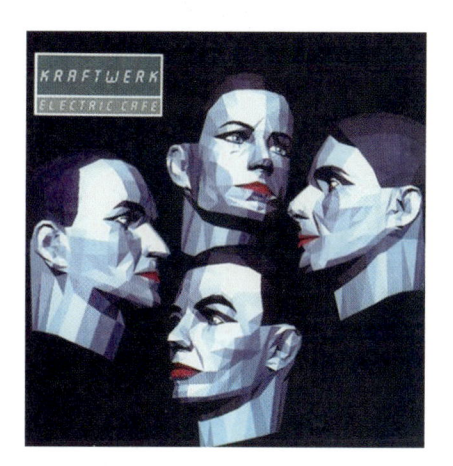

Reba McEntire
WHOEVER'S IN NEW ENGLAND
MCA NASHVILLE | Producers: Jimmy Bowen, Reba McEntire
RELEASED: FEBRUARY 10, 1986

● Reba McEntire found a theme and stuck to it with her tenth studio album. The title track was the definition of a female-oriented ballad—full of emotional turmoil and dramatic storytelling—and was McEntire's first music video. While the bulk of the album was composed of ballads, the second single, **Little Rock**, was more upbeat—and also about cheating. Delivered in McEntire's unmistakable voice, the album navigated the rocky coast of romance all the way to a No. 1 spot on the Billboard Country charts. *–SS*

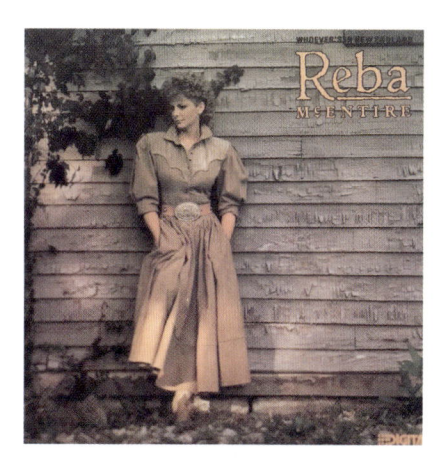

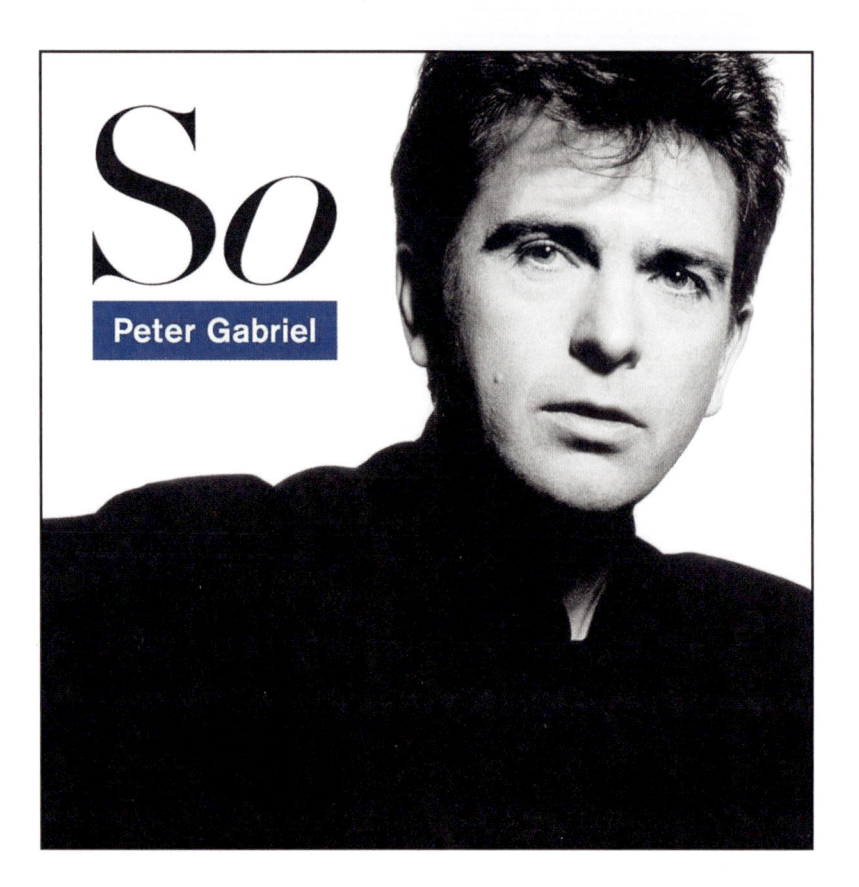

Peter Gabriel
SO

GEFFEN | Producers: Peter Gabriel, Daniel Lanois
RELEASED: MAY 19, 1986

● Going into his fifth album, Peter Gabriel was forced to confront the often-inaccessible nature of his music. Four records into his solo career since he left Genesis in 1975—each titled *Peter Gabriel* (the fourth was renamed *Security* in the US)—he submitted to a record company request that he give his fifth LP a proper title. But he took it a step further, writing songs that mostly avoided the artsy, experimental tones of his earlier albums and embraced the synth-pop sounds of his more commercially successful peers.

Working with producer Daniel Lanois, who collaborated with Gabriel on the soundtrack to the 1984 film *Birdy*, the singer and songwriter shaped tracks using his past as a springboard, including prog and world music plus some of the art-pop signposts that graced his other records. The result was one of the decade's best and most popular albums: *So*. Distinctly Gabriel in sound, but with an awareness he was in danger of being left behind, the record was a profile-boosting compromise with winners on all sides.

So's opening song, the vaguely political **Red Rain**, wasn't too far removed from what he had been doing on previous records; it's the second track where a new persona was revealed. **Sledgehammer**, a not-too-subtle metaphor about carnal desire, arrived loaded with radio-friendly pop moves, from a gigantic synth-based riff to one of Gabriel's most playful performances. An innovative and award-winning video helped push the song and the album to No. 1. Follow-up singles **Don't Give Up** (an unguarded duet with Kate Bush), **Big Time** (**Sledgehammer** without the sex), and **In Your Eyes** (featuring Senegalese singer Youssou N'Dour) rank among the greatest of Gabriel's career. Meeting the mainstream halfway on *So*, he found an ambitious eternal groove and a bold new career path. *—MG*

1986

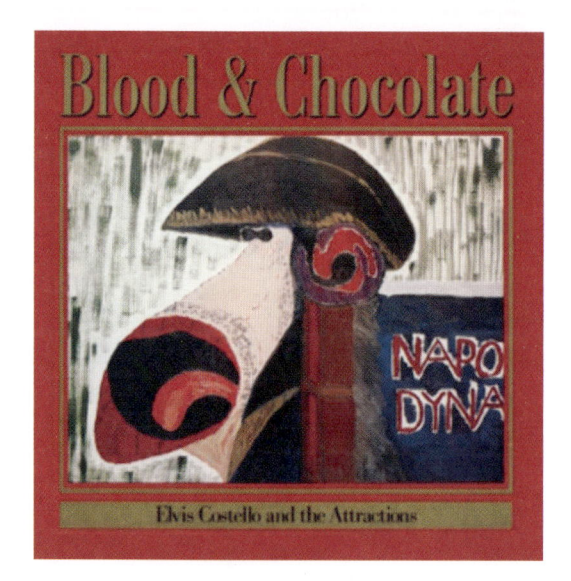

Elvis Costello and the Attractions
BLOOD & CHOCOLATE
COLUMBIA | Producers: Nick Lowe, Colin Fairley
RELEASED: SEPTEMBER 15, 1986

● No less than Radiohead's Thom Yorke declared this "the album that made me change the way I thought about recording and writing music, lyrics too. Everything about that record . . . is just awesome." After two pop-leaning records with producers who favored tracking instruments instead of capturing performances, Costello enlisted his trusted friend Nick Lowe to reprise his producing role, and Blood & Chocolate was essentially cut live in the studio. This is where its power was established. The Attractions was the best working band of the era; its ability to play at full-throttle or at the threshold of silence framed Costello's raw nerve lyrics at every turn. The hooks and riffs never obscure the acerbic and often-raging emotions. Nothing says **I Hope You're Happy Now** like "you make him sound like frozen food, his love will last forever." Reflecting on the album for Blood & Chocolate's 2002 reissue, Costello said, "The record might as well have been a blurred Polaroid: a smashed-up room, a squashed box of chocolates, some broken glass, and a little blood smeared on the wall." Considerably less than awesome for the artist, don't you think? But definitely awe-inspiring for the listener. —*HK*

Depeche Mode
BLACK CELEBRATION
MUTE | Producers: Depeche Mode, Gareth Jones, Daniel Miller
RELEASED: MARCH 17, 1986

● While Depeche Mode had flirted with darkness on its previous album, *Some Great Reward*, *Black Celebration* was its full-on pivot to goth—as in gothic literature, with all its haunted longing, wounded romance, and poisonous lust. The foreboding synth-pop pointillism of the album-opening title track could easily be mistaken for the soundtrack to a Freddy Krueger or Dario Argento film, at least until singer Dave Gahan—in his mesmerizing, eerie baritone—invited you "To celebrate the fact / That we've seen the back of another black day." Even with lead songwriter Martin Gore's comparatively sweet tenor popping up throughout the band's fifth LP, each song seemed to find the English synth-rock troupe throwing a spade of dirt on the coffin of its teen heartthrob past. While critics at the time didn't quite get it, the band's fans (including Trent Reznor) intuitively grasped that these dark, morbid themes served only to enhance the band's sensuality. When Gahan declared, "Death is everywhere" on **Fly on the Windscreen—Final**, it only heightened the urgency of the chorus, where he begged, "Come here, kiss me now." As Dracula once said, "Children of the night, what music they make." —*JL*

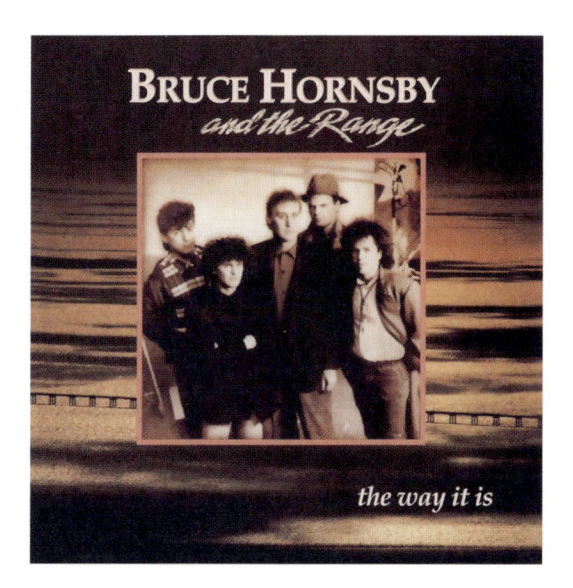

Bruce Hornsby and the Range
THE WAY IT IS
R C A | Producers: Bruce Hornsby, Huey Lewis, Elliot Scheiner
RELEASED: APRIL 1, 1986

● The spare opening notes of a piano solo set the tone for **The Way It Is**, the title track from Bruce Hornsby and the Range's debut album, and also became a signature sound, instantly tied to the lanky Virginian. The album went on to multiplatinum success and led to the group's Best New Artist Grammy Award in 1987. That sound was achieved by combining Hornsby's evocative arrangements, made up of jazz, country, and bluegrass influences, with a set of musicians so talented and tight one would think they had played together since birth. The peppy, upbeat **Every Little Kiss** featured a bright pop melody and the instruments layered on **Mandolin Rain**—including accordion and (surprise!) mandolin—showcased the group's versatility, while the lush, anthemic **On the Western Skyline** allowed the band to rock out a bit more. The album was a success, based mostly on the popularity of those three singles, and remains one of the finest debuts by an artist. The Range never reached the same sales levels with subsequent releases, but *The Way It Is* was key for Hornsby's further exploration of various musical styles, whether with a band or as a solo artist. —SS

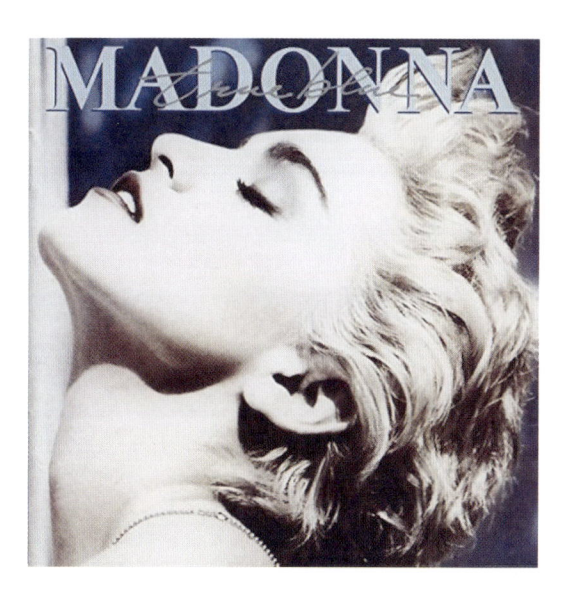

Madonna
TRUE BLUE
S I R E | Producers: Madonna, Stephen Bray, Patrick Leonard
RELEASED: JUNE 30, 1986

● You could quibble about whether it was more accurate to call Madonna a star or a superstar before the release of 1986's *True Blue*. But once her third album was done storming the charts worldwide, there was no doubt she was permanently established as a musical and cultural icon. With the singer taking on a larger role in songwriting and production, *True Blue* featured deeper, warmer grooves than her first two albums. Madonna's singing also took a leap forward, allowing her to confidently branch out into new genres and styles. The five singles released from *True Blue* represented an impressive career all by themselves. The aching ballad **Live to Tell**, the deceptively peppy teenage pregnancy tale **Papa Don't Preach**, and the blissful **Open Your Heart** all reached No. 1. The '60s-styled title track and the gorgeous Latin-flavored **La Isla Bonita** weren't far behind in the Top 5. The album's remaining four tracks aren't quite as memorable, keeping *True Blue* just shy of being labeled a start-to-finish masterpiece. But not to worry; she'd hit that mark next time out with 1989's *Like a Prayer*. —MW

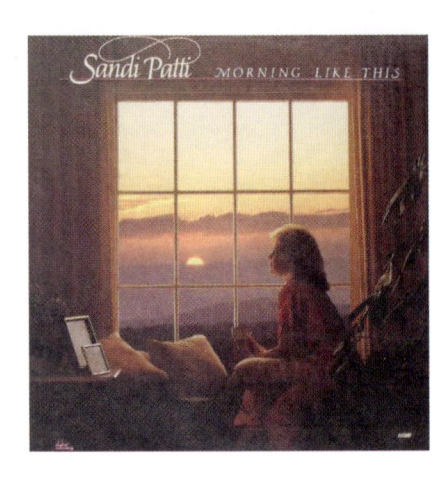

Sandi Patti
MORNING LIKE THIS
W O R D | Producers: Greg Nelson, Sandi Patti
RELEASED: MARCH 1986

● Sandi Patti was a bit like music's equivalent of *Grease*'s Sandy Olsson — clean, sweet, and kind, attributes that made her brand of Christian pop go down easy. Patti was the queen of the form at the time of her ninth album; she won a Grammy Award for it and took a second at the same ceremony for a duet with Deniece Williams. Patti was in top form here, too; she co-wrote only two of the ten tracks but performed everything beautifully, including **Hosanna** with the 2nd Chapter of Acts trio. *—GG*

Various Artists
PRETTY IN PINK (ORIGINAL MOTION PICTURE SOUNDTRACK)
A & M | Producer: David Anderle
RELEASED: FEBRUARY 28, 1986

● The soundtrack to this quirky film goes so brilliantly all-in on '80s New Wave that it landed on *Rolling Stone*'s greatest soundtracks of all time list. From the Psychedelic Furs' title track and O.M.D.'s hit **If You Leave** to Suzanne Vega's chiming **Left of Center** and New Order's underrated **Shellshock**, the album never lets up. Add in Echo & the Bunnymen and the Smiths and you get a soundtrack that perfectly captured the flavor of growing up in the '80s, when most songs on the radio were this cool. *—HD*

Lionel Richie
DANCING ON THE CEILING
M O T O W N | Producers: Lionel Richie, James Anthony Carmichael, Narada Michael Walden
RELEASED: AUGUST 5, 1986

● The third solo album by former Commodore Lionel Richie reflected his changing worldview with more thoughtful writing and deeper themes. It included the Academy Award–winning **Say You, Say Me** from the film *White Nights* and **Ballerina Girl**, dedicated to Richie's daughter. The upbeat title track, meanwhile, was a signature hit for Richie, reflecting a party attitude with its synthesizers and programmed drums. Although the album was a worldwide success, it also marked the start of a long hiatus for Richie, who didn't release any new music until 1992. *—SS*

Various Artists
ROUND MIDNIGHT (ORIGINAL MOTION PICTURE SOUNDTRACK)
COLUMBIA | Producer: Herbie Hancock
RELEASED: OCTOBER 1986

● Three years after his improbable pop-star cameo with the global hit "Rockit," Herbie Hancock got back to where he once belonged with this Academy Award–winning trad-jazz companion to Bertrand Tavernier's moody tone poem about an expatriate American jazz cat in Paris. Saxophonist Dexter Gordon starred as Dale Turner (a fictional composite of Bud Powell and Lester Young) as well as on the soundtrack, alongside key contributions from Wayne Shorter, Chet Baker, and Bobby McFerrin. With updated chestnuts from Thelonious Monk and George Gershwin, this was definitive '80s-vintage bop. —DM

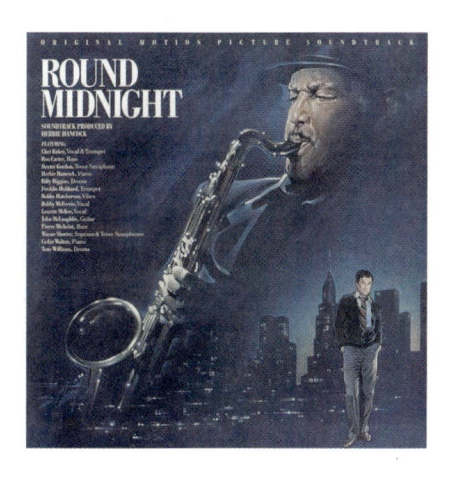

The Smithereens
ESPECIALLY FOR YOU
ENIGMA | Producer: Don Dixon
RELEASED: JULY 29, 1986

● The Smithereens' debut was an alt-rock gem. The instantly impactful **Blood and Roses**, with its stirring bass line, and the poppier **Behind a Wall of Sleep** broke through the omnipresent Britpop and hit the Billboard charts thanks to catchy melodies and the understated croon of New Jersey's Pat DiNizio. The album's other tracks were equally compelling, particularly the yearning **Alone at Midnight** and the Suzanne Vega–backed **In a Lonely Place**. These were songs to dance to, fall in love to, and mend a broken heart to. What more could anyone want? —HD

Stryper
TO HELL WITH THE DEVIL
ENIGMA | Producers: Stephan Galfas, Stryper
RELEASED: OCTOBER 24, 1986

● Mötley Crüe wanted to shout at the devil; Stryper wanted to send him to Hell—which seemed a bit redundant, no? But the band in the black-and-gold-striped spandex was adept at straddling a line between kitsch and commitment, earnest in its faith-based message and convincing enough musically to ride alongside with the more prurient Sunset Strippers and the other glam metal rockers on MTV—to the tune of Christian metal's first platinum album. The gods, or God, certainly smiled on this one. —GG

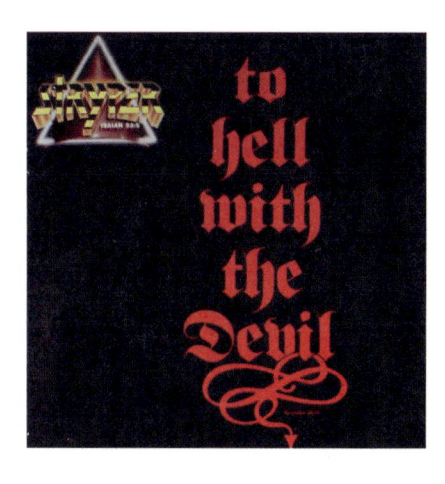

Metallica
MASTER OF PUPPETS

ELEKTRA | Producers: Flemming Rasmussen, Metallica
RELEASED: MARCH 3, 1986

● To call *Master of Puppets* just a thrash metal album is like calling the *Mona Lisa* a nice portrait. Metallica's third full-length release was a masterpiece. It deserves the moniker due to the band's solid advancement in performance and songwriting. Much of it related to a better understanding of the value of dynamics to build tension and heaviness while, at times, leaning into progressive/classical influenced elements.

The opening **Battery** announced Metallica's growth, but it was the title track—a ride through the psychological terrors of addiction—that delivered that experience to the listener in spades: Various stops illuminated an asylum revolt, the callousness of wars on those who fight them, and even a visit to the Lovecraftian underworld, all of which cut like razors thanks to improved studio production. Flemming Rasmussen, who also helmed the first two albums, captured solid performances to create a clear, crisp, tighter-sounding set instead of using chorusing effects to smooth and fatten up the guitar and vocals.

Sadly, Metallica's greatest triumph of the '80s would be tainted by the band's greatest tragedy when bassist Cliff Burton died in a bus accident in September 1986 while on tour in Sweden. Although only twenty-four years old when he died, Burton's musical ability and influences—especially classical composition—were in full flight on **Orion**, an instrumental statement the band has never surpassed.

Metallica arrived around the same time in the early '80s when mainstream metal was playing with fantastical ideas, big hair, and glam styling. As part of a cadre of bands—along with Megadeth, Slayer, and Anthrax that offered faster, hardcore punk tempos and more real-life lyrics—Metallica and *Master of Puppets* provide a key to understanding why thrash went on to dominate in the '90s and still influences today's heavy music. *–RSM*

1986

Megadeth
PEACE SELLS . . . BUT WHO'S BUYING?

CAPITOL | Producers: Dave Mustaine, Randy Burns, Paul Lani
RELEASED: SEPTEMBER 19, 1986

● Though considered one of thrash metal's Big Four, Megadeth was relegated to second-fiddle status and often carried a Rock of Gibraltar–sized chip on its shoulder, mainly due to Dave Mustaine creating his metal outfit after he was booted from Metallica. Then his former band went on to astronomical success. But Mustaine's competitive streak often led Megadeth to faster and more technical songwriting than his previous band. On this second outing, the growth was evident from the lead track. The time changes, orchestrated sections, and Arabesque solos on **Wake Up Dead** offered something unique beyond speed. Meanwhile, the album's title track—featuring a memorable galloping opening bass riff and a call and response verse structure—commented on politics, capitalism, and religion in Reagan's America. This put Megadeth more ideologically in line with the punks than the metalheads of the era. *Peace Sells . . .* was an album that not only rewarded those seeking something a little different from their metal but signposted where Megadeth would head sonically and ideologically on releases such as 1992's *Countdown to Extinction* and 1994's *Youthanasia*, where it found more commercial success. *—RSM*

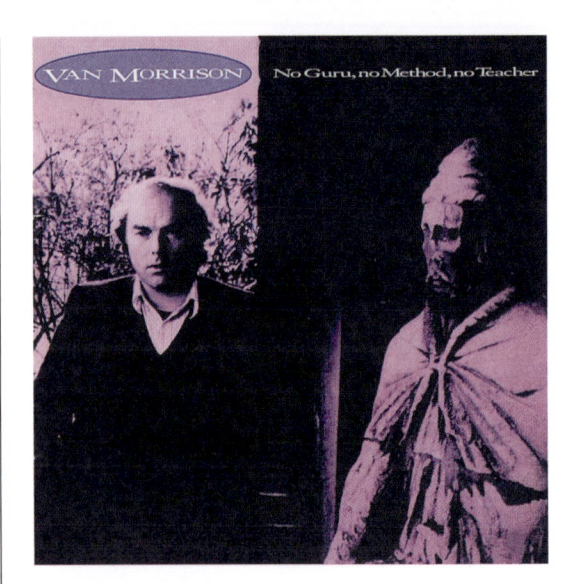

Van Morrison
NO GURU, NO METHOD, NO TEACHER

MERCURY | Producer: Van Morrison
RELEASED: JULY 1986

● Van Morrison was—and still is, as of 2025—one of music's most productive cats, maintaining a steady stream of albums since the first breakup of Them in 1966. *No Guru . . .* was Van the Man's sixteenth solo effort and was rightly hailed as a kind of comeback following a series of underwhelming titles between it and 1978's *Wavelength*. With its reflective, meditative mien and pastoral flavor, the ten-track set hearkened back to Morrison's celebrated 1968 album *Astral Weeks*. **In the Garden** most directly brought listeners into a kind of Celtic Zen state, wandering without meandering as it referenced the 1966 Jiddu Krishnamurti quote that gave the album its title. **Tir Na Nog** was steeped in Irish mythology, while in **One Irish Rover**, Morrison traipsed on more earthy terra firma and **Got to Go Back** and **Oh, the Warm Feeling** offered sentimental remembrances of his youth. And **Here Comes the Knight** found Morrison downright playful—punning, of course, on Them's "Here Comes the Night" and also quoting from the gravestone epitaph of W. B. Yeats (after the Yeats estate had denied Morrison permission to turn one of his poems into a song). Easily his best outing of the '80s. *—GG*

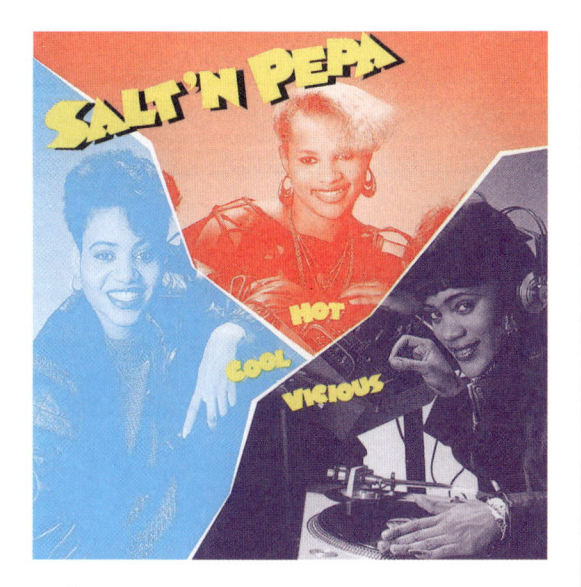

Salt-N-Pepa
HOT, COOL & VICIOUS
NEXT PLATEAU | Producers: Hurby Luv Bug, Stephen Keitt
RELEASED: DECEMBER 8, 1986

● The debut album by this New York trio was the first release by a female rap act to be certified platinum. How'd that happen? Just drop the needle on the opening track, **Push It**—itself a Top 20 hit—to get a flavor of what's to come, which was indeed hot, cool, and vicious. Unlike TLC's *Crazy Sexy Cool*, however, those monikers applied across the board to Cheryl "Salt" James, Spinderella (Deidra Roper), and Sandra "Pepper" Denton. The writing and production here came under the Svengali aegis of Hurby "Luv Bug" Azor, with occasional infusions from Parliament-Funkadelic (**I'll Take Your Man**), the Pointer Sisters (**Chick on the Side**), and Lowell Fulson (**Tramp**). But the trio's performances elevated the material with hot attitude, cool countenance, and, yes, vicious delivery that kicked open the hip-hop doors for their gender. **Push It**, by the way, was not part of the original album; it was the B-side of **Tramp**, flipped by radio and club DJs to turn it into a generational hit and a calling card that, like other Salt-N-Pepa tracks to come, still fills a floor with ecstatic dancers any time it blasts over the speakers. *—GG*

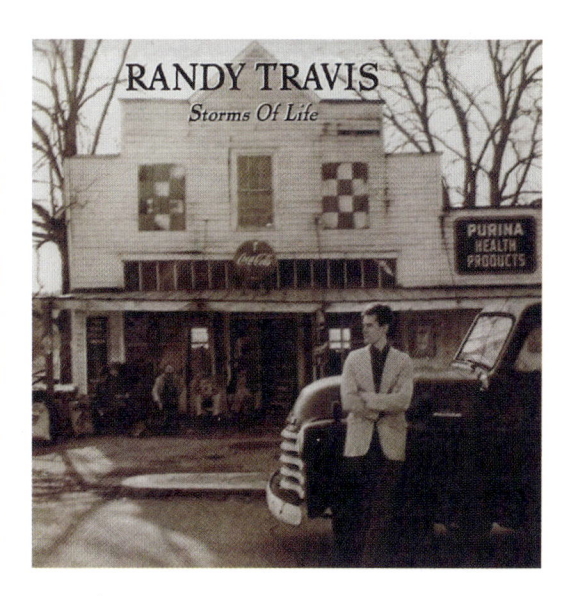

Randy Travis
STORMS OF LIFE
WARNER BROS. | Producers: Kyle Lehning, Keith Stegall
RELEASED: JUNE 2, 1986

● *Storms of Life* was one of the great debut albums of the '80s, of any genre, and a triumph of country's new traditionalism, which rejected pop production and re-embraced classic songwriting. Travis, only twenty-seven at the time, brought a heart-wrenching, world-weary ache to lyrics about cheating spouses, broken homes, and love gone wrong. The songwriters are the stars of this set, too, beginning with the great lyrical twists of the album-opening **On the Other Hand**, from Paul Overstreet and Don Schlitz (previously recorded by Keith Whitley). On the title track, Max D. Barnes and Troy Seals gave Travis lines like "I left my soul out in the rain." The country chart-topping and Grammy Award–winning **Diggin' Up Bones**, co-written by Overstreet, found Travis "resurrectin' memories of a love that's dead and gone." Travis himself wrote **Reasons I Cheat**, an all-too-believable litany of an aging man's laments and the album's vocal tour de force. Selling more than three million copies, *Storms of Life* went to No. 1 on Billboard's Top Country Albums chart. *—TD*

1986

Run-D.M.C.
RAISING HELL

PROFILE | Producers: Russell Simmons, Rick Rubin
RELEASED: MAY 15, 1986

● Run-D.M.C.'s *Raising Hell* was an album of firsts. It was the first hip-hop album to top Billboard's R&B Albums chart. It was the first hip-hop album to reach platinum status. Its big single, **Walk This Way**, was the first song by a hip-hop artist to make the Top 5 on Billboard's Hot 100. It was the first hip-hop album to include collaboration with rock artists. On top of all that, it's one of the most significant hip-hop releases of all time, a boundaries-breaking record that did more to bring the genre into the mainstream than any other LP.

Joseph "Run" Simmons, Darryl "D.M.C." McDaniels, and Jason "Jam Master Jay" Mizell, along with producers Russell Simmons and Rick Rubin, began assembling Run-D.M.C.'s third album during late 1985 following a tour in support of that year's *King of Rock* LP. The finished record sounds bigger and bolder than its predecessors; part of this can be attributed to rap's natural evolution, but there's more to it. With Rubin (who helped mix and received a song co-writing credit on *King of Rock*, and fresh from LL Cool J's pivotal *Radio*) on board full-time, *Raising Hell* was like a summit of the genre's most important figures at a crucial point in its history.

The album adds to Run-D.M.C.'s already-substantial list of foundation-building tracks: **Peter Piper**, **It's Tricky**, **My Adidas**, and **You Be Illin'** became instant hip-hop classics. And then there's **Walk This Way**; Run-D.M.C. didn't so much restructure Aerosmith's 1975 song as they decontextualized it. Enlisting the band's singer Steven Tyler and guitarist Joe Perry to reprise their parts from the original, the refreshed **Walk This Way** resurrected the Boston rockers and introduced rap music to new audiences. It's the centerpiece of *Raising Hell*, a turning point album of the '80s—and beyond. *—MG*

1986

Slayer
REIGN IN BLOOD

DEF JAM | Producers: Rick Rubin, Slayer
RELEASED: OCTOBER 7, 1986

● As early-'80s Los Angeles metal bands went glam, Slayer went gore. Finding influence in British metal such as Judas Priest and Venom, along with American hardcore like Black Flag and Minor Threat, Slayer led the charge into thrash metal along with Metallica, Megadeth, and Anthrax in bending hardcore's fast tempos with metal's dark themes.

When Rick Rubin came into the picture, Slayer had already released two full albums and an EP. But poor studio production diminished the group's strength. Rubin, known at the time for rap acts but holding hardcore roots, brought clean, clear, razor-sharp sonics to *Reign in Blood*—and it paid off. The album music was pummeling, and its lyrics were stark. Like the best slasher films of the same era, it is a fantastic horror show front to back on its ten tracks over just about twenty-nine minutes.

For the uninitiated, the lead track opened with a guttural scream on top of muscular athletic drumming supporting careening guitars and caterwauling solos as the lyrics catalogued the horrors of Nazi torturer Dr. Josef Mengele (**Angel of Death**). *Reign in Blood* announced clearly and early that this was not your father's metal through brutal and often blood-soaked first-person narratives. Dynamic highlights included the tempo swings of **Criminally Insane**, the furious gallop of **Altar of Sacrifice**, and the time change pivots in **Reborn**.

As metal continued to mutate, bands from Cannibal Corpse and System of a Down to Slipknot listed *Reign in Blood* as an inspiration. Even pianist/singer Tori Amos covered the track **Raining Blood** for her 2001 album *Strange Little Girls*. *Reign in Blood* showcased the course Slayer would ultimately take across its future releases but without ever surpassing it. —*RSM*

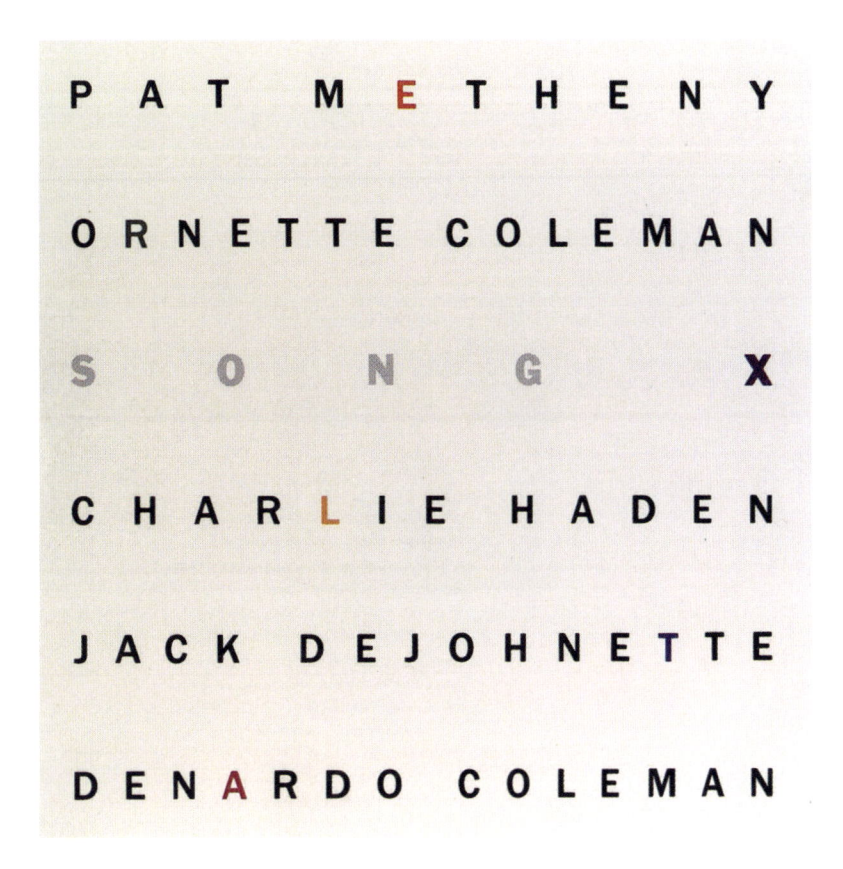

PAT METHENY

ORNETTE COLEMAN

S O N G X

CHARLIE HADEN

JACK DEJOHNETTE

DENARDO COLEMAN

Pat Metheny/Ornette Coleman
SONG X
GEFFEN | Producer: Pat Metheny
RELEASED: 1986

● The free-jazz extravaganza *Song X*, co-led by legendary alto saxophonist Ornette Coleman, was Pat Metheny's most daring and monumental career achievement. The album was the culmination of the guitarist's quest to perform with his jazz idol, whose music he first encountered while exploring records as a young teen at his hometown record store in Missouri. He was drawn to Coleman's enthusiasm and melodic spirit, irrespective of its genre. Over time, Metheny absorbed Coleman's unique Harmolodic improvising techniques, gaining more freedom and individuality as an improviser.

Metheny injected aspects of Coleman's sound textures on earlier albums, most notably on *80/81* and *Rejoicing*, a 1984 homage to Coleman performed with bassist Charlie Haden and drummer Billy Higgins, who both played in the saxophonist's band. Coleman attended the trio's New York City tour stop, met with Metheny afterward, and talked about recording together. "His spirit is so unbelievably good," Metheny said on his website podcast. "He's really one of the best human beings I've ever been lucky enough to know."

Coleman's infectious exuberance and positivity powers the music's sheer intensity. *Song X* could have come with a warning label, though; for the uninitiated, which includes casual Pat Metheny Group fans, the loud, high-octane thrashing could be a foreboding experience, a jazz cacophony. But with intent listening, there's an ebullient aspect, the joyful discovery of incredible musicians delivering spontaneous collective improvisation at its highest level.

The hard-bop tune **Mob Job** danced, with Coleman jamming on high-pitched violin. **Endangered Species** was liberating, full-throttle mayhem with aggressive alto sax squeals, distortion-tinged guitar runs, the relentless double-drumming attack of Jack DeJohnette and Denardo Coleman, and repeated tension and release of the unifying main theme. Haden's supple bass leads the enticing ballad **Kathelin Gray** over the graceful synergy of harmonized alto sax and guitar. *–CH*

Paul Simon
GRACELAND
WARNER BROS. | Producer: Paul Simon
RELEASED: AUGUST 25, 1986

● When Paul Simon's infatuation with a mixtape of township accordion jive music inspired him to record with South African musicians, he wasn't expecting to rejuvenate his sagging career, much less alter the fabric of popular culture. But by seamlessly integrating his pop sensibilities and lyrical acumen with their exuberant rhythms and transporting harmonies, Simon not only reconnected American music to its origins and drew the world's attention to South Africa's vibrant music; he composed an album consistently ranked among the most significant in recorded-music history.

Simon and his collaborators improvised their accordion- and bass-forward rhythms for **Boy in the Bubble** and other songs in Johannesburg; with Ladysmith Black Mambazo, Simon crafted the stunning Zulu a cappella composition **Homeless** in London and the stirring **Diamonds on the Soles of Her Shoes** in New York, where he also recorded the ebullient Afro-pop hit **You Can Call Me Al** and the spellbinding Linda Ronstadt duet **Under African Skies**. Simon also recorded with Louisiana Zydeco band Good Rockin' Dopsie & the Twisters and Los Angeles group Los Lobos. His conversational lyrics, while not overtly political, contained allusions to poverty, oppression, and other issues he saw in Africa and elsewhere, offset by references to "miracle and wonder," spiritual healing, or simply witty repartee.

Simon courted controversy by recording in Johannesburg despite UN-imposed cultural sanctions against apartheid and by using Ronstadt, who'd performed at the segregated Sun City resort. But *Graceland* still won the Grammy Award for Album of the Year, and a year later, the captivating title track won Song of the Year. *Graceland* sold 16 million copies, becoming Simon's most successful solo album, giving international exposure to Ladysmith and other participants (and to the abuses they endured in their homeland), and earning placement on the Library of Congress's National Recording Registry. Apartheid officially ended in 1994. *–LM*

1986

Van Halen
5150

WARNER BROS. | Producers: Mick Jones, Donn Landee, Van Halen
RELEASED: MARCH 24, 1986

● Time has obscured the fact that when Sammy Hagar joined Van Halen, he was not a star. A solid performer with a tough and soulful voice, his solo career was middling. Van Halen, on the other hand, was a superstar group. It had the hottest guitarist on earth and a frontman who could work a crowd, but he wasn't best known for his singing. When David Lee Roth split to make his own way, there was no crisis, only an opportunity. Hagar and Eddie Van Halen found in each other someone who could push them and their symbiosis is on full arena rock display on 5150.

At its core, 5150 didn't mess with the formula, but Van Halen's hook-filled, muscular rock was elevated to a new plateau. The revamped lineup allowed Eddie to expand his musical arsenal. The continuing use of keyboards, front and center, helped achieve a new depth of song composing skills. Having a guy who could flat-out sing just about anything didn't hurt either. The singles from this album—**Why Can't This Be Love**, **Dreams**, **Love Walks In**, and **Best of Both Worlds**—boast a different kind of anthemic sensibility than the Roth-era records, with more fully formed melodies.

Hagar never let up on the energy, and he didn't have to lean on a wink and a smile like his predecessor. Alex Van Halen and Michael Anthony, a rhythm section as reliable as a traffic jam on L.A.'s 405, provided a continuity that underpinned the Van Halen sound every bit as much as Eddie's guitar.

This new era of Van Halen answered the question the group posed itself: "Only time will tell if we pass the test of time." Passed, with flying colors. *–HK*

Steve Winwood
BACK IN THE HIGH LIFE

WARNER BROS. | Producers: Russ Titelman, Steve Winwood
RELEASED: JUNE 30, 1986

● Steve Winwood was just eighteen years old in 1966 when the Spencer Davis Group released "Gimme Some Lovin'" and his organ riff and spirited vocals sent the song to No. 7 on the Billboard Hot 100. Three decades later, the same joy was evident on Winwood's fourth solo album, *Back in the High Life*.

An ear-grabbing mix of percussion and keyboards introduced the album with **Higher Love**, on which Winwood declared, "I could light the night up with my soul on fire." Lyricist Will Jennings co-wrote five of the album's eight tracks. **Higher Love** hit No. 1 on the Billboard Hot 100 and won two Grammy Awards—the coveted Record of the Year and Best Pop Vocal Performance, Male.

Back in the High Life continued Winwood's embrace of technology, but after two mostly one-man-band albums (1980's *Arc of a Diver* and 1982's *Talking Back to the Night*), he was more collaborative this time out. **Higher Love**, for instance, featured Chic's Nile Rogers on guitar, Chaka Khan on backing vocals, and her Rufus bandmate John "JR" Robinson on drums. **Freedom Overkill** lined up Joe Walsh on slide guitar and drummer Steve Ferrone from Tom Petty's Heartbreakers, along with a five-piece horn section that included trumpeter Randy Brecker. Walsh, meanwhile, co-wrote and played some mean licks on **Split Decision**. James Taylor joined a mandolin-playing Winwood on the standout title track on which both sang, while James Ingram and Dan Hartman provided backing vocals on another hit, **The Finer Things**.

Back in the High Life was Winwood's most successful album, peaking at No. 3 on the Billboard 200 on its way to triple-platinum sales. It also returned him to the concert stage for the first time since his days with the band Traffic. *—TD*

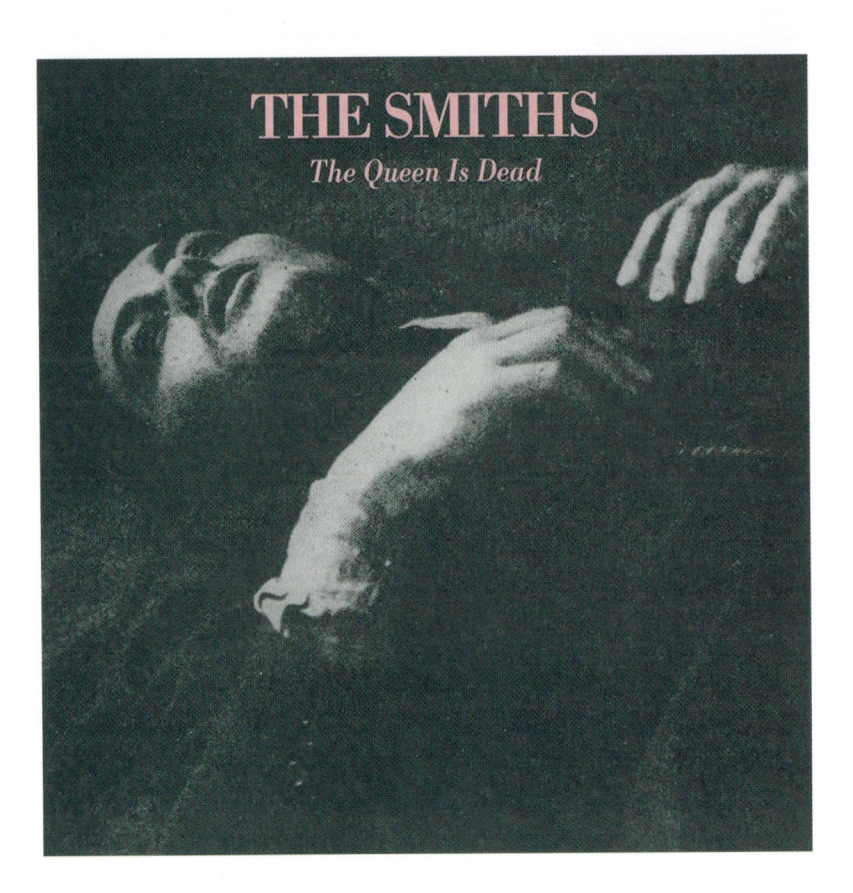

The Smiths
THE QUEEN IS DEAD

SIRE | Producers: Morrissey, Johnny Marr
RELEASED: JUNE 16, 1986

● The Smiths were on top of the world as the band recorded its third album, *The Queen Is Dead*, throughout 1985. Just as R.E.M. had revolutionized college rock in the States, the Manchester-based quartet had done the same for indie music in the UK. Over two albums and a handful of increasingly witty and catchy singles, singer Morrissey, guitarist Johnny Marr, bassist Andy Rourke, and drummer Mike Joyce had altered the landscape of popular music in the '80s. A critical as well as a commercial success, the Smiths approached *The Queen Is Dead* with all eyes on it.

They didn't disappoint. The album was an immediate hit in 1986, a funny and tuneful record that helped shape British music going into the new century. Written and produced by Morrissey (lyrics) and Marr (music), *The Queen Is Dead* wasn't so much commentary on life under Prime Minister Margaret Thatcher as it was a barbed view of the social ills that have plagued mankind since the dawn of existence. In a voice that brought shyness and awkwardness to new levels of discomfort, Morrissey theorized on his personal views of hell, often of his own making, in **Bigmouth Strikes Again** and **The Boy with the Thorn in His Side**.

It's on the album highlight **There Is a Light That Never Goes Out** where the Smiths reach an apex: "If a double-decker bus crashes into us, to die by your side is such a heavenly way to die," Morrissey sang, his fatalism clashing with a melody as resilient as any written in the decade. Nineties Britpop started here, with an album the Smiths—which broke up the next year—would never top. *The Queen Is Dead* is one of the '80s' essential British records. *—MG*

1986

Dwight Yoakam
GUITARS, CADILLACS, ETC., ETC.
REPRISE | Producer: Pete Anderson
RELEASED: MARCH 12, 1986

● Spurned by Nashville, Kentucky native Dwight Yoakam moved to Los Angeles and developed what he defiantly defined as "hillbilly music," performing on the punk-rock scene that also produced roots rockers X, Los Lobos, and the Blasters. The *Etc., Etc.* of the album title stands in for the offending descriptor, a sop to Yoakam's record label and the country music industry that, for years, had sought to cast off its yokel yoke. Not that that bowdlerization made Yoakam any less abhorrent to Nashville; he still had to make it on his own terms.

The album grew out of a six-song EP released independently in 1984. All of those tracks were included on the Warner Bros. album, which added four more. Yoakam wrote seven of the ten, establishing himself as more than just a singer and performer. An essential part of the album's success was Pete Anderson's arrangements and production, which honed Yoakam's take on the Bakersfield sound to a knife edge.

Some of those songs, though, spoke of Yoakam's roots back in Kentucky, including **South of Cincinnati** and the bluegrass-fueled **Miner's Prayer**. Yoakam also proved adept at the kind of classic country requisites such as the barroom weeper and story songs—**It Won't Hurt** and **Twenty Years**, respectively—that preceded Nashville's pop-friendly Urban Cowboy sound. **Bury Me** was a twanging, two-stepping duet with Lone Justice's Maria McKee. And the Grammy-nominated **Guitars, Cadillacs** made the hillbilly music it invokes rock like nobody's business.

Yoakam's choice of cover tunes helps defined his more-country-than-country aesthetic: Johnny Horton's **Honky Tonk Man**, Johnny Cash's **Ring of Fire**, and the Harlan Howard–penned **Heartaches by the Number**. Ultimately, *Guitars, Cadillacs, Etc., Etc.* was the album that made country acceptable for rockers, and vice versa. *–DD*

1986

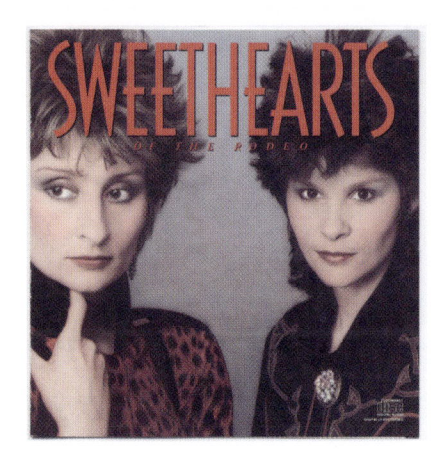

Sweethearts of the Rodeo
SWEETHEARTS OF THE RODEO
COLUMBIA | Producers: Steve Buckingham, Hank DeVito
RELEASED: JULY 26, 1986

● Naming your band after a landmark album (in this case, the Byrds' 1968 country-rock hybrid) takes guts, but Los Angeles sisters Janis Oliver and Kristine Arnold had those in abundance. The Wrangler Country Showdown contest winners had chops, too, enough to make their self-titled debut a Top 10 country hit with four Top 10 singles and a bunch of other good songs. Sweethearts never quite got the amount of love they deserved, but this was welcome proof that sisters *could* do it for themselves—and very well, indeed. *—GG*

Various Artists
TOP GUN (ORIGINAL MOTION PICTURE SOUNDTRACK)
COLUMBIA | Producers: Various
RELEASED: MAY 15, 1986

● Great soundtracks immediately evoke scenes from the film with certain songs. *Top Gun*'s had that in Berlin's Academy Award–winning **Take My Breath Away**, which decades later still brings the film's love scene to mind, and in the upbeat dance energy of Kenny Loggins's **Playing With the Boys**, a perfect match for the shirtless beach volleyball game. And **Top Gun Anthem** by '80s movie go-to Harold Faltermeyer captured the film's drama and power from its first resonating low synthesizer note and prepared listeners for the ride. *—SS*

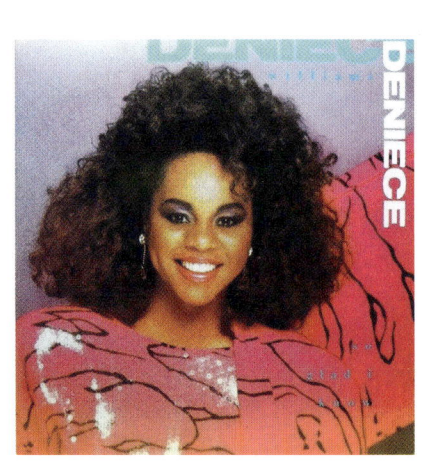

Deniece Williams
SO GLAD I KNOW
SPARROW | Producer: Brad Westering
RELEASED: MAY 1986

● Deniece Williams's career was a blessed one by the mid-'80s, with stints singing backup for Stevie Wonder, Minnie Ripperton and more, and a parade of her own hits as a solo artist—including the *Family Ties* theme song "Without Us." *So Glad I Know* was her first full-scale gospel outing and was equally successful, hitting Top 10 on the Gospel and Christian charts and winning a Grammy Award for her duet with Sandi Patti on a remake of **They Say** from Williams's 1983 album *I'm So Proud*. *—GG*

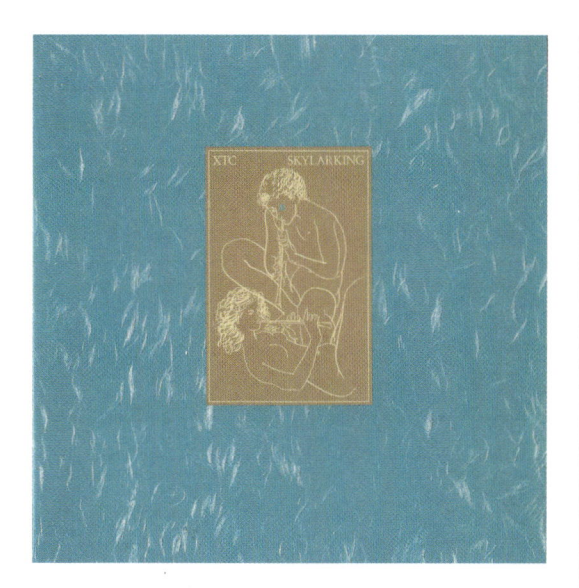

XTC
SKYLARKING
GEFFEN | Producer: Todd Rundgren
RELEASED: OCTOBER 27, 1986

● Due to steadily declining sales of their past few releases, Virgin Records insisted that XTC use an outside producer instead of letting guitarist Andy Partridge helm its next record. The band chose Todd Rundgren, who sifted through the band's demos and chose songs that he felt worked as a loosely based concept album, *Skylarking*. Rundgren and Partridge loved using a wide variety of unusual sounds and instruments along with unique chord and rhythm patterns, which created a plethora of touchpoints where the two creative leaders butted heads. In less capable hands, this could have easily resulted in an overproduced mess, but instead, it produced what is generally regarded as XTC's finest work. Virtually every song on the album treated listeners to pleasant sonic surprises—an unusual instrumental flourish here, lush strings there, interesting chords and harmonies everywhere. Influences ranged from '60s spy movie soundtrack elements in **The Man Who Sailed Around His Soul** to the Beach Boys–inspired **Season Cycle**. There's even controversy, thanks to the agnostic anthem **Dear God**, which was left off of original pressings of the album due to its provocative subject matter but was returned after it became a college radio hit. *—GP*

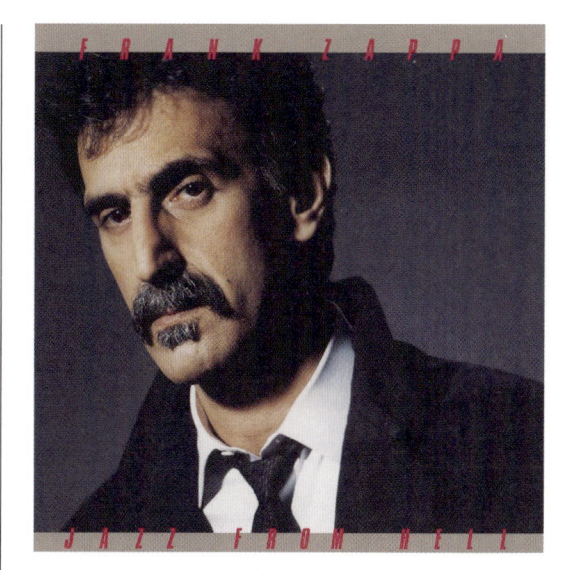

Frank Zappa
JAZZ FROM HELL
BARKING PUMPKIN | Producer: Frank Zappa
RELEASED: NOVEMBER 15, 1986

● The last studio album released during Frank Zappa's lifetime is perhaps also the strangest and most forbidding, which, for the iconoclastic and uncompromising Zappa, is saying something. Throughout his career, Zappa sought out incredible musicians to perform his complex compositions. Yet he remained frustrated that even they couldn't perfectly perform the music he heard in his head. What would it sound like if he was presented with the possibility of removing human fallibility from the equation entirely? The invention of the Synclavier—a digital sampler and synthesizer—offered him that opportunity. Inputting his work through the computer interface, Zappa was able to play and record music exactly as he intended, making *Jazz from Hell*, except for one track that features his band, a true solo album. Some critics found its "performances" cold and its '80s synths/samples dated. Yet this was the sound of Zappa's imagination completely unfettered, and the results were dazzling, most notably **Night School**, the theme song for a TV talk show Zappa was pitching; the breathtaking, hypersonic **G-Spot Tornado**; **Jazz From Hell**, which won a Grammy for Best Rock Instrumental; and yes, the band track, **St. Etienne**, a reminder that, in addition to his compositional genius, Zappa was one hell of a guitarist. *—DD*

87

1987

Guns N' Roses
APPETITE FOR DESTRUCTION

GEFFEN | Producer: Mike Clink
RELEASED: JULY 21, 1987

● Rock music wasn't in the best shape as the 1980s neared an end. Off-road detours such as college rock were thriving in all the right places, but hard rock music—like that made by heavyweight bands AC/DC and Aerosmith during the late '70s—had reached a stagnant state, replaced on radio and MTV by a spate of relatively safe, fashion-conscious hair-metal acts. Then L.A.'s Guns N' Roses arrived on the scene, and suddenly rock music was once again dark, dirty, and forbidden in certain parts.

It took some time for the band's debut, *Appetite for Destruction*, to make itself known. Released during the summer of 1987, the album faced problems from the start, including a controversial original cover design that had to be replaced and band members whose prodigious intake of sex and drugs came close to derailing the quintet more than once. Before long, though, the primal, near-punk draw of *Appetite*'s best tracks—**Welcome to the Jungle**, **Mr. Brownstone**, **Paradise City**, **Rocket Queen**—found an audience. After the song most resembling a ballad on the album, **Sweet Child O' Mine**, became a chart-topping pop single, there was no stopping the momentum.

More than a year after its release, *Appetite for Destruction* reached No. 1 on the Billboard 200. By the time the album started its slow descent on the chart, Guns N' Roses was the biggest rock band in the world. The success didn't tame it, though; if anything, it exacerbated their habits and vices until only singer Axl Rose was left to carry on the group by the mid-'90s. By then, the album's influence was strongly established. Nirvana's 1991 masterpiece *Nevermind* got much credit for shifting rock music away from its benign state in the '80s; *Appetite for Destruction* deserved a lot of that credit, too. *–MG*

1987

Eric B. & Rakim
PAID IN FULL
4TH & B'WAY | Producers: Eric B. & Rakim
RELEASED: JULY 7, 1987

● There is no overstating Rakim's importance to hip-hop. The original God MC took rap and singlehandedly elevated it, introducing complex rhyme structures and wordplay into the art form and shifting what was possible through lyricism with his use of language and metaphors. Known as The R, he owns a letter of the alphabet for a reason: Once he picked up a microphone, the game was never the same again.

Rakim was born William Griffin Jr. on Long Island, New York, and he was rhyming at an early age, inspired by New York City's burgeoning hip-hop scene. He partnered with Queens DJ Eric Barrier—in hip-hop's early days, the DJ was the star, which is why he had top billing in the duo—and the pair released their groundbreaking debut album **Paid in Full** during summer 1987.

"I ain't no joke, I used to let the mic smoke / Now I slam it when I'm done and make sure it's broke," Rakim spit at the top of **I Ain't No Joke**, one of the most famous album-opening lines in hip-hop history. For the next forty-five minutes he and Eric B. took listeners to school, with Rakim running circles over Eric. B's booming beats and furious turntable scratches, expanding and reinventing hip-hop's sound and scope at every step along the way.

The album is essential to hip-hop's DNA: **I Know You Got Soul** introduced James Brown samples into the genre, and the **Paid in Full** instrumental was so elemental to hip-hop's core it should be on rap's periodic table. "This is how it should be done / This style is identical to none," Rakim declared on **I Know You Got Soul**. Revisiting the album is a reminder that hip-hop once didn't sound like this and that a new era entirely began here. —*AG*

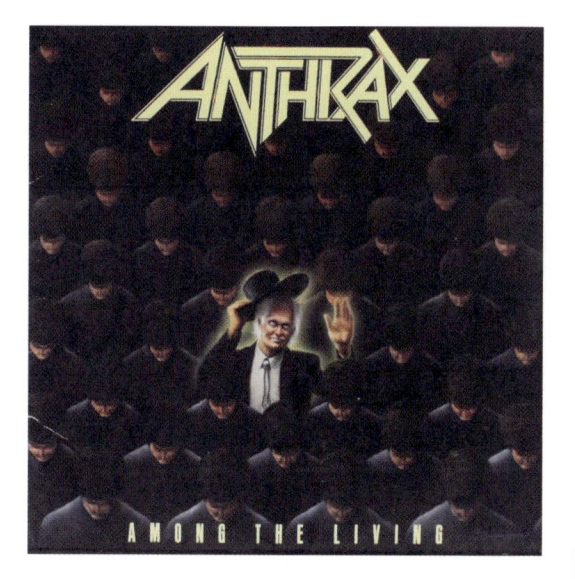

Anthrax
AMONG THE LIVING

MEGAFORCE/ISLAND | Producers: Anthrax, Eddie Kramer
RELEASED: MARCH 16, 1987

● Anthrax locked down its spot in thrash metal's Big Four by tightening up its already-winning formula on its third album, 1987's *Among the Living*. The success of its previous two records had earned the Queens, New York–born metal pioneers the time and freedom the group needed to focus on making the album everything it wanted it to be. It had the vision to hire legendary producer Eddie Kramer to help better replicate the energy of its live show and the courage to make him reverse course when Kramer tried to add too many modern studio touches to the mix. The result was a near-perfect blend of thrash riffs, hardcore gang backing vocals, and soaring performances from lead singer Joey Belladonna, a noted lover of classic rock singers such as Steve Perry and Lou Gramm. The album also featured a big leap forward in lyrical quality, whether the band was singing about serious issues such as the treatment of Native Americans in **Indians** or its love of the Judge Dredd comic books in **I Am the Law**. As if that wasn't enough, the album's sessions also yielded the stand-alone single **I'm the Man**, which kick-started the rap-metal genre. *—MW*

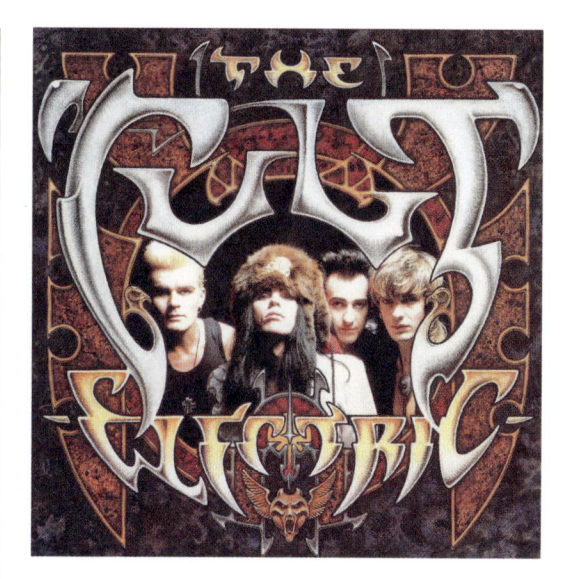

The Cult
ELECTRIC

SIRE | Producer: Rick Rubin
RELEASED: APRIL 6, 1987

● *Electric* is big, loud Rawk–and it is glorious. But as is often the case with things that seem so obvious, so guileless, this album had a backstory. The Cult broke through in 1985 with its goth-rock opus *Love* and three hit singles from it, including "She Sells Sanctuary." For the follow-up, the band found itself in the studio with Rick Rubin, best known back then for his hot hand producing the Beastie Boys and Slayer. Rubin swapped Cult guitarist Billy Duffy's chimey Roland Jazz Chorus amplifier for Marshall stacks and then comped the guitarist to AC/DC's Young brothers and vocalist Ian Astbury to Robert Plant. Tracks such as **Wild Flower**, **Lil' Devil**, and **Bad Fun** were highlights of the resulting riffalicious affair. The lone single, **Love Removal Machine**, illustrates the Zeppelin influence, especially when Astbury, a force of nature throughout, exclaims "Babybabybabybabybaby!" *Electric* was a whole lotta rock, but it had roll, too, a hip-shaking swing perhaps down to drummer Les Warner playing a bit behind Duffy. The only fly in the ointment is a cover of Steppenwolf's **Born to Be Wild**, but because this one goes to eleven, there are ten other absolute bangers to compensate. Play 'em loud. *—DP*

1987

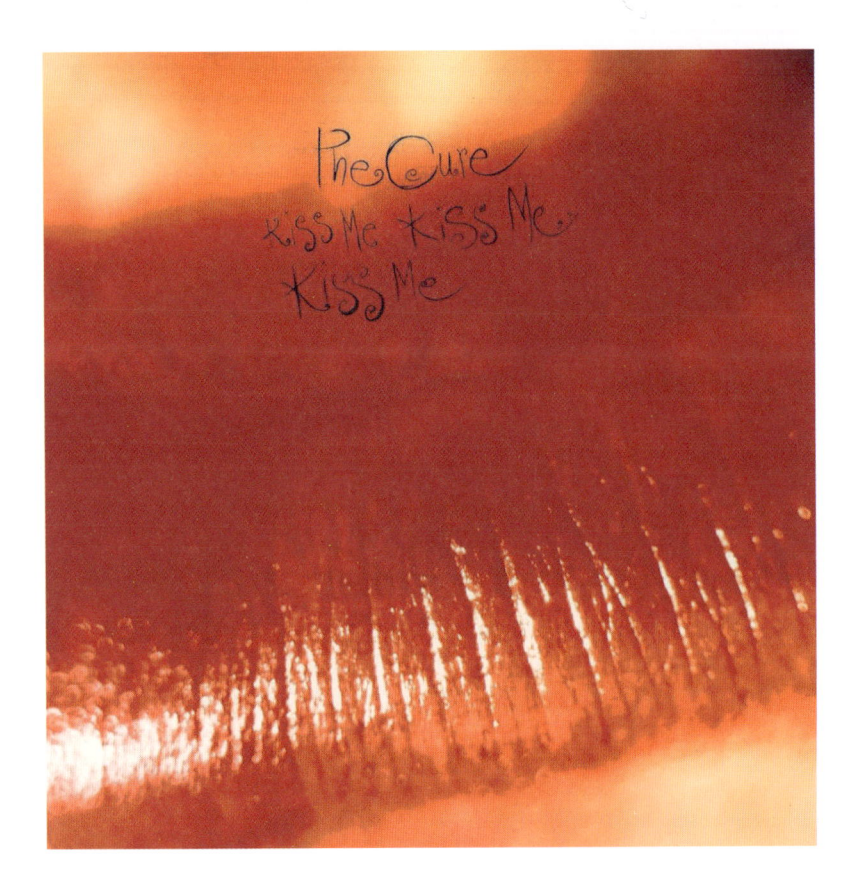

The Cure
KISS ME, KISS ME, KISS ME

FICTION/ELEKTRA | Producers: David M. Allen, Robert Smith
RELEASED: MAY 26, 1987

● Prior to its seventh studio album, the Cure was rock's goth godhead, as dark and doomy as could be over the course of its three previous albums and a long way from any of the brighter pop that was part of its early albums. For *Kiss Me . . .* , however, Robert Smith and company sought to right the equilibrium and largely succeeded, delivering what could be considered a gateway to the sensibility the world would come to know and, for those so inclined, love about the Cure moving forward.

The idea, of course, was to bring more hooks and buoyant melodies back into the mix. In doing so, Smith loosened the reins a bit and sought greater input from his bandmates, who each brought a selection of demos that were decided upon by group vote. The result was more diversity and a healthy batch of good material—enough, in fact, to make *Kiss Me . . .* a double (vinyl) album, with eighteen songs that covered a lot of stylistic ground and broadened the production punch with meatier guitars as well as strings and horns in parts.

The pop(pier) songs were back, too, led by the shimmering **Just Like Heaven** and also including **Catch**, **Perfect Girl**, **How Beautiful**, and **Hey You**. **The Kiss** started the album with a wall of barely penetrable guitar noise over its six-plus minutes, while **Like Cockatoos** and **One Thousand Days** also laid on the heavy. The Cure tried its hand at funk with **Hot Hot Hot**, while **If Only Tonight We Could Sleep** slipped an Aisan flavor into the mix.

It was messy and at times random, but *Kiss Me . . .* proved a great mass gateway into the Cure. The album was its first Top 40 entry on the Billboard 200 and the band's first platinum album in the US. Even Smith could smile about that. *—GG*

Terence Trent D'Arby

INTRODUCING THE HARDLINE ACCORDING TO TERENCE TRENT D'ARBY

COLUMBIA | Producers: Martyn Ware, Terence Trent D'Arby, Howard Gray
RELEASED: JULY 13, 1987

● Terence Trent D'Arby hit the music world like a lightning bolt with his debut, which featured a stunningly fully formed and eager-to-please blend of R&B, pop, and soul. Following in the footsteps of Stevie Wonder and Prince (who had released his own masterpiece *Sign "O" the Times* just months earlier), D'Arby was a multi-instrumentalist who wrote all his own songs—and delivered them with vocal power and range even those two legends would be hard-pressed to top.

The immodestly titled *Introducing the Hardline According to Terence Trent D'Arby* spawned a string of worldwide hit singles, including the infectious horn-charged makeup plea **If You Let Me Stay**, the strutting **Wishing Well**, and the sultry ballad **Sign Your Name**. He showed his love and respect for the history of soul music with a cover of Smokey Robinson's **Who's Loving You** and the James Brown–inspired rave-up **Dance Little Sister** while also pushing the genre forward on songs such as the dramatic, gospel-tinged **If You All Get to Heaven**.

The album sold more than eight million copies worldwide, but D'Arby's commercial demise was nearly as sudden as his ascent. After generating controversy with boastful (and possibly playful) statements—such as declaring that *Hardline* was the most important album since the Beatles' *Sgt. Pepper's Lonely Hearts Club Band*—his half-amazing but also overly ambitious and sometimes self-serious 1989 sophomore album *Neither Fish nor Flesh* was a commercial flop. Apart from some relative success in England, 1993's excellent and diverse *Symphony or Damn* also failed to connect. In 2001, D'Arby changed his name to Sananda Maitreya. He has released nine albums in relative obscurity since that time, and the titles of his '80s and '90s albums have been changed on streaming services to reflect his new name. —MW

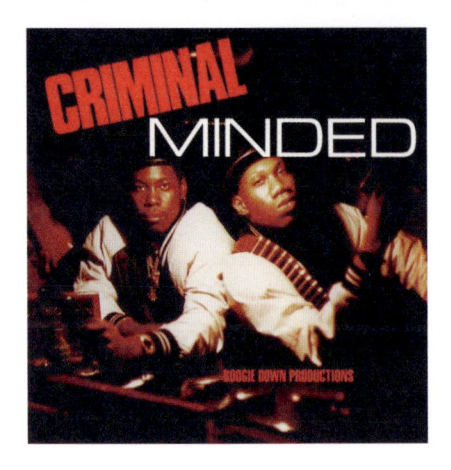

Boogie Down Productions
CRIMINAL MINDED

B-BOY | Producers: Scott La Rock, KRS-One, Ced-Gee
RELEASED: MARCH 3, 1987

● The debut album from South Bronx trio Boogie Down Productions—KRS-One, D-Nice, and Scott La Rock, who was murdered five months after the album's release—is one of hip-hop's early building blocks and a pioneering text in what would become gangsta rap. Hip-hop was still very regional. The wars were not between coasts; they were between boroughs, and KRS-One handily brought the fight to Queens (**South Bronx**, **The Bridge Is Over**). The album's stark production lent itself to samples, and everyone from Gang Starr to Rihanna eventually borrowed from it. *—AG*

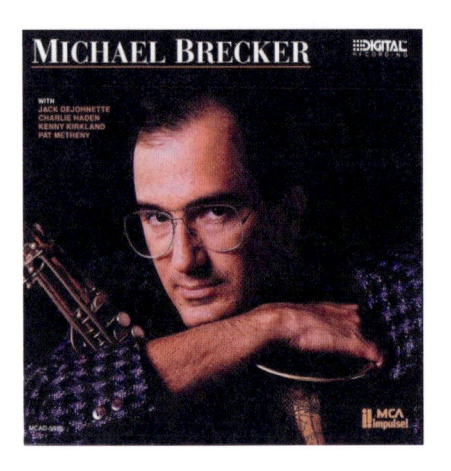

Michael Brecker
MICHAEL BRECKER

MCA IMPULSE | Producers: Don Grolnick, Michael Brecker, Ricky Schultz
RELEASED: APRIL 20, 1987

● Paybacks can be splendid. For Michael Brecker's first solo album, several jazz musicians who benefited from his saxophone brilliance on their albums reciprocated. Impressively. He landed guitarist Pat Metheny, bassist Charlie Haden, and drummer Jack DeJohnette, all from Metheny's *80/81* outing, plus keyboardist Kenny Kirkland. Brecker was an enormously in-demand studio talent and bandleader who flourished in any context. His brazen, full-bodied tenor embellished **Sea Glass**, a moody atmospheric opener, and **Choices**, a jaunty modal jazz delight. On **Original Rays**, he trailblazed the unusual EWI (Electronic Wind Instrument). *—CH*

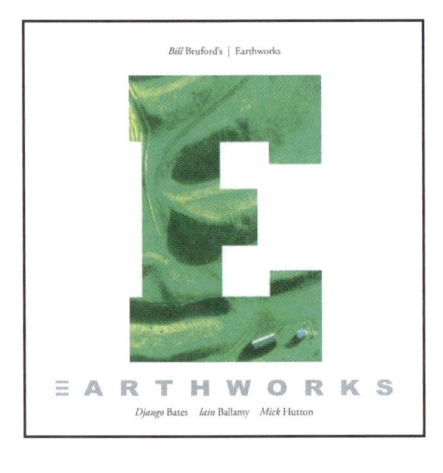

Bill Bruford
EARTHWORKS

E.G. | Producers: Dave Stewart, Bill Bruford
RELEASED: MARCH 6, 1987

● When Bill Bruford strikes his snare drum, his telltale rim shot sound is immediately recognizable. The prog-rock drummer developed the unconventional technique to be heard over louder bandmates in Yes, UK, Genesis, and King Crimson. His idiosyncratic style subsequently created a bridge from rock to jazz in acoustic/electric combos such as Earthworks. Enlivened by vigorous solos by British bandmates Django Bates (keyboards, tenor horn, trumpet), Iain Ballamy (saxophones), and Mick Hutton (double bass). Ever innovative, Bruford fluently blended acoustic and electronic drums, enabling him to create almost any sound imaginable. *—CH*

Ry Cooder
GET RHYTHM
WARNER BROS. | Producer: Ry Cooder
RELEASED: NOVEMBER 1987

● Ry Cooder's gift is his seamless ability to connect directly, musically, and spiritually to the music that ignited his soul. Unlike many of his generation, Cooder created records that didn't have the feeling of generationally being once removed. *Get Rhythm* collected many songs written by his role models, like the title cut, which echoes Johnny Cash's energetic command. Crowning this album is the ageless **Across the Borderline**; co-written by Cooder, Jim Dickinson, and John Hiatt, its meaning has only become more powerful over time. *—HK*

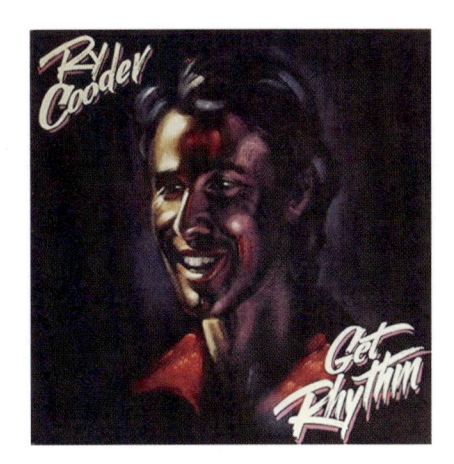

Various Artists
DIRTY DANCING (ORIGINAL SOUNDTRACK FROM THE VESTRON MOTION PICTURE)
RCA | Producers: Various
RELEASED: AUGUST 4, 1987

● Who knew Patrick Swayze could sing? It's a question still being asked about **She's Like the Wind**, one of only two original songs recorded for the *Dirty Dancing* soundtrack. The other, **(I've Had) The Time of My Life**, by Bill Medley and Jennifer Warnes, won Academy Award and Golden Globe honors. Mostly the twelve-track album's oldies piqued nostalgia, supporting the film's portrayal of Catskills vacation culture of the '60s and taking people back to when, and where, they had the time of their lives. *—SS*

Fat Boys
CRUSHIN'
TIN PAN APPLE/POLYDOR | Producers: Fat Boys, Gary Rottger, Eddison Electrik
RELEASED: AUGUST 14, 1987

● Fat Boys, the plus-size Brooklyn rap trio, got even bigger during summer 1987 thanks to their big-screen comedy *Disorderlies* and their fourth album *Crushin'*, both of which were released the same day. *Crushin'* became the Boys'—Prince Markie Dee, Kool Rock-Ski, and Buff Love—first (and only) Top 10 release, thanks in no small part to **Wipeout**, the trio's playful collaboration with the Beach Boys. That hit embodied the group's good-time, party rap ethos, which was as accessible and inclusive as an all-you-can-eat buffet. *—AG*

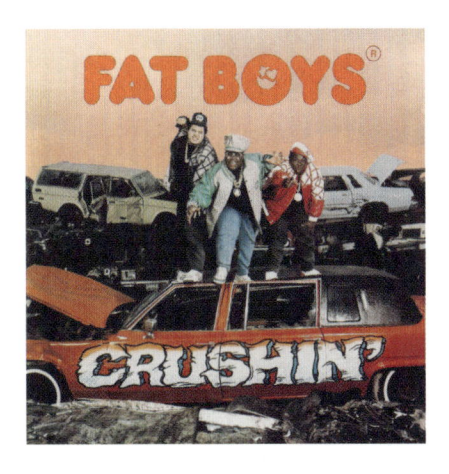

Def Leppard
HYSTERIA
MERCURY | Producer: Robert John "Mutt" Lange
RELEASED: AUGUST 3, 1987

● *Pyromania* lit a multiplatinum fire for Def Leppard in 1983. For its successor, the British hard rock troupe and its producer wanted to make something even more combustible. "With *Hysteria*," recalls guitarist Phil Collen, "Mutt (Lange) said, 'OK, what do we do for an encore?' Let's do a rock version of *Thriller*. Let's do an album where there's seven songs that can genuinely be singles.' So that was the thing—and to not make *Pyromania 2*."

Suffice to say, the Leps sussed it out—but it wasn't easy. First, Lange was initially unavailable and subsequent sessions with Meat Loaf's *Bat out of Hell* cohort Jim Steinman were, well, hellacious and ultimately scrapped. The group decided to try producing itself, but when drummer Rick Allen lost his left arm in a New Year's Eve 1984 car accident, the recovery and rehabilitation period caused a delay that enabled Lange to come back into the fold.

Recording *Hysteria* was long and piecemeal, exacting and expensive—but fruitful. The album was indeed thrilling, blasting forth with sleek, state-of-the-art force, its sixty-two-plus minutes loaded with hooks, sturdy melodies, and sophisticated arrangements. And despite a slow commercial start in the US, it achieved Lange's goal, producing seven hit singles on Billboard's Mainstream Rock chart; four also made the Top 10 on the Hot 100—the title track, **Armageddon It**, the No. 1 **Love Bites**, and the enduring stadium anthem **Pour Some Sugar on Me**. It's not only Def Leppard's best-seller but one of the best-selling and, not so subjectively, best rock albums of all time, comfortably ensconced well outside its time frame.

Hysteria was also the group's last with co-founding guitarist Steve Clark, who passed away in 1991 at the age of thirty from the effects of substance abuse as the group was working on what would become the following year's *Adrenalize*. *—GG*

Fleetwood Mac
TANGO IN THE NIGHT

WARNER BROS. | Producers: Lindsey Buckingham, Richard Dashut
RELEASED: APRIL 13, 1987

● This album could appropriately be titled *Last Tango*, period, as it became the final studio album put forth by Fleetwood Mac's most successful lineup of Mick Fleetwood, John McVie, Christine McVie, Stevie Nicks, and Lindsey Buckingham, as the latter departed acrimoniously shortly after its release.

Tango in the Night began as a Buckingham solo project two years prior but evolved into Fleetwood Mac's first studio recording since *Mirage* in 1982, as he became its main producer and guided the rest of the group through their paces. The gap between albums did little to ease the band's well-documented interpersonal tension. Several members had released solo albums, and Nicks had become a star in her own right. But, because Nicks was fighting her personal demons, she was in the studio for only two to three weeks, making it essentially a Buckingham/Christine McVie recording as they handled the bulk of songwriting and vocal duties.

Throughout the recording, the band made a conscious effort to get back to the ultra-successful pop/rock sound that made its *Rumours* a megahit a decade prior. Although *Tango . . .* did not reach the same level of mammoth success, it did sell more than 15 million copies worldwide while spawning four Billboard Top 20 hits along the way. Its biggest hit, **Little Lies**, hit No. 4; it was co-written and sung by Christine McVie with Nicks and Buckingham harmonizing and became one of the catchiest tunes of the summer of 1987. The Buckingham-penned and -sung **Big Love**, featuring rhythmic sexual panting during its outro, was the album's first single and reached No. 5. Christine also wrote and sang lead on **Everywhere**, featuring a soaring melody and bell-like synthesizers. Nicks, meanwhile, co-wrote and sang the wistful **Seven Wonders**.

It was by all measures a success, though it would be another decade before this lineup would come together again, for *The Dance*. –JC

Grateful Dead
IN THE DARK
ARISTA | Producers: Jerry Garcia, John Cutler
RELEASED: JULY 6, 1987

● By the late '80s, the prospects for a new Grateful Dead album were about as likely as the band having a Top 10 hit. The veteran group had a reticent, even hostile attitude toward the recording studio, preferring the concert stage as its palette. It had been seven years since its last non-live release, the dismal *Go to Heaven*. "Making records was never a very pleasant experience in the past," percussionist Mickey Hart noted in 1988. "That wasn't the Dead."

So, *In the Dark*'s success was a "holy crap" moment of surprise for the music world, including the Deadheads and even the Dead itself. "We thought it was OK, but I didn't think there were *hits* on it," Hart said.

Touch of Grey, with its defiant declaration that "We will survive!," was the Dead's biggest hit, its only Top 40 single ever. The video went into heavy rotation on MTV, and the platinum-certified *In the Dark* was the band's only Top 10 album. One of the Dead's most consistent sets overall, it also included ace material such as **Throwing Stones**, **Hell in a Bucket**, **West L.A. Fadeaway**, and the elegiac **Black Muddy River**.

What worked? Recorded after Dead head Jerry Garcia recovered from a near-fatal diabetic coma, the group eschewed the studio and instead set up in the Marin Veterans Memorial Auditorium in San Rafael, California, recording as if it was performing a concert. "The spirit of the record was very much, 'Keep it simple, stupid,'" Hart said. The sextet had also been playing most of the songs live for five or so years, meaning they'd gone through the Dead's intuitive process well before anyone ran tape. It, as well as the Dead (in spirit), still survives as a high point in the band's discography. *—GG*

1987

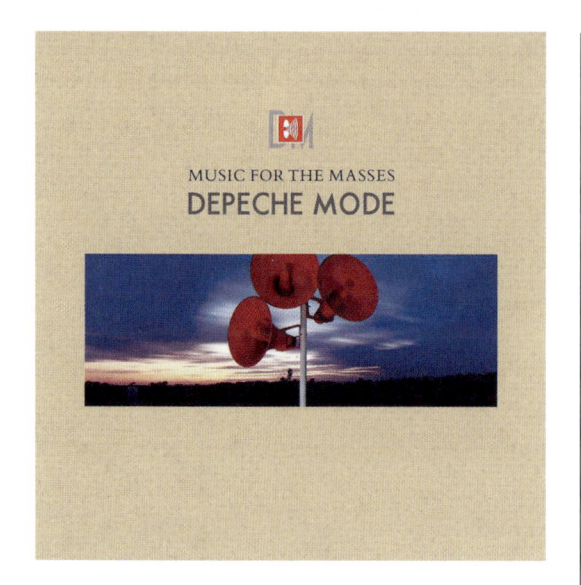

Depeche Mode
MUSIC FOR THE MASSES
MUTE | Producers: Depeche Mode, David Bascombe
RELEASED: SEPTEMBER 28, 1987

● That grandiose title was an inside joke—the English synth-rock outfit was never anyone's idea of a conventionally commercial outfit—but it proved prophetic as it bridged the band's early work with its later, stadium-worthy successes. *Music for the Masses* was the group's sixth album in seven years, and it kicked off with **Never Let Me Down**, a stadium anthem in its own right: "I'm taking a ride with my best friend," vocalist Dave Gahan announced in the opening line, over a churning electronic beat and hammering percussion meant for packed houses around the world. The song's heavy subject matter plainly deals with a soaring drug high—it's not about a road trip, at least in the conventional sense—and it sets the table for the moody journey into beautiful darkness that follows. Producer David Bascombe (Tears for Fears' *Songs from the Big Chair*) helped the band hone its massive sound, which carried through to towering instrumental closer, **Pimpf**. Sure enough, *Music for the Masses* sent Depeche Mode skyrocketing. It played California's Rose Bowl the following year, chronicled in 1989's live album and documentary *101*; and Depeche Mode never put its feet back down on the ground again. *—AG*

Debbie Gibson
OUT OF THE BLUE
ATLANTIC | Producers: Fred Zarr, Debbie Gibson
RELEASED: AUGUST 18, 1987

● The debut album from Debbie Gibson arrived in stores eight weeks after the self-titled debut from Tiffany, and together the pair set off a teen-pop craze that wouldn't be rivaled until Britney Spears and Christina Aguilera hit the scene a dozen years later. Tiffany won the immediate chart battle, but Gibson persevered in the career war. The Brooklyn-born, Long Island–raised performer grew up writing and recording her own music, and she was signed to Atlantic Records off the strength of her demo tape for the bubbly **Only In My Dreams**. That became her lead single, and she was sent on a club tour to promote it while recording her first album with Fred Zarr, who played on and helped arrange Madonna's "Holiday." Gibson wrote every song on the album (and co-produced a handful of tracks), and the set was released two weeks before her seventeenth birthday. The album, which is full of catchy melodies and highly syncopated teen-pop production, sold three million copies in the US. It sent four songs into Billboard's Top 5, including the mid-tempo ballad **Foolish Beat**, which made Gibson the youngest performer ever to write, produce, and perform a No. 1 single. *—AG*

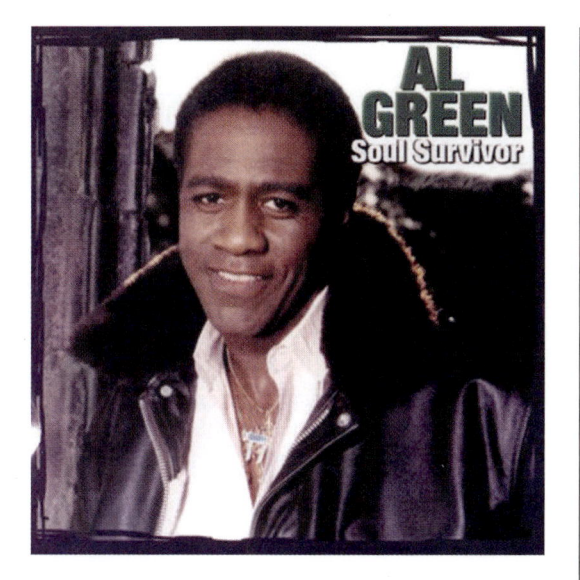

Al Green
SOUL SURVIVOR

A & M | Producers: Errol Thomas, Paul Zaleski
RELEASED: MAY 1987

● By 1987, the Rev. Al Green had lived several lifetimes. By this point in his career, the then-forty-one-year-old—who scored a string of gold and platinum albums in the early '70s and had already released two greatest hits compilations—was deep in gospel mode, and *Soul Survivor* found him praising Jesus over late-'80s production beds. Album opener **Everything's Gonna Be Alright** and the title track had the funk-R&B sound of Jimmy Jam and Terry Lewis, while **You Know and I Know** and **Yield Not to Temptation** were built like slow jam ballads in the Lord's image. Key here were a pair of cover songs: Green took Carole King to church on his version of her *Tapestry* standout **You've Got a Friend**, on which he duets with Billy Preston, and on **He Ain't Heavy . . . He's My Brother**, he laced the Hollies' hit with his signature Memphis soul. The nine-track album closed with **23rd Psalm**, a bare-bones gospel track where he knelt before God: "I will dwell in the house of the Lord forever," he sang over a simple arrangement, backed by an organ, an acoustic guitar, and a percussion track. Amen. *–AG*

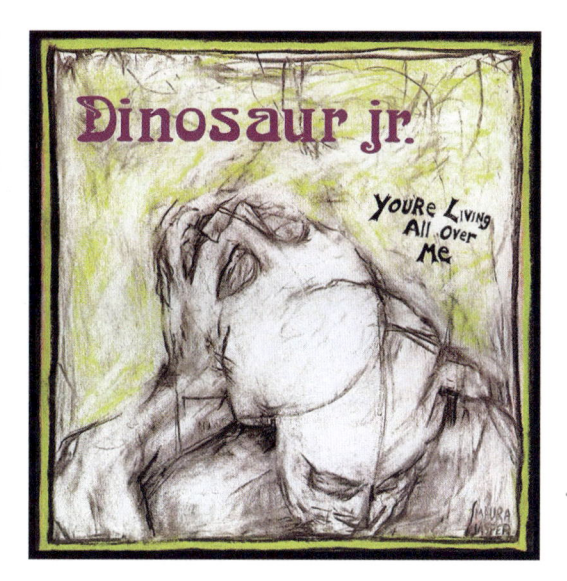

Dinosaur Jr.
YOU'RE LIVING ALL OVER ME

S S T | Producer: Wharton Tiers
RELEASED: DECEMBER 14, 1987

● *Bug* may have signaled the end of Dinosaur Jr.'s first act, but its predecessor, *You're Living All Over Me*, underlined the major plot points: punishing volume, a pummeling rhythm section, Gen X ennui, and the guitar heroics of frontman J Mascis. Cited as a major influence on the shoegaze genre, the album's opener, **Little Fury Things** (background vocals from Sonic Youth's Lee Ranaldo), is arguably still the track you'd play to the uninitiated to describe the band. Mascis's unhinged solo break highlighted **Kracked**, which segued seamlessly into **Sludgefeast**, its metal-flavored opening riff giving way to an epic song structure and Mascis's Neil Young warble. Indeed, Mascis has attracted frequent comparisons to Young over the years, for both his vocals and guitar work. And like Uncle Neil, Dinosaur Jr. has never been all about sheer volume; there are dynamics at play, as with mellower (all things being relative) offerings like **The Lung** and **In a Jar**. Also notable were the two closing tracks from bassist Lou Barlow, particularly the lo-fi THC-friendly folk suite **Poledo** that portended his future project, Sebadoh. Later reissues included Dino Jr.'s covers of the Cure's **Just Like Heaven** and Peter Frampton's **Show Me the Way**. *–DP*

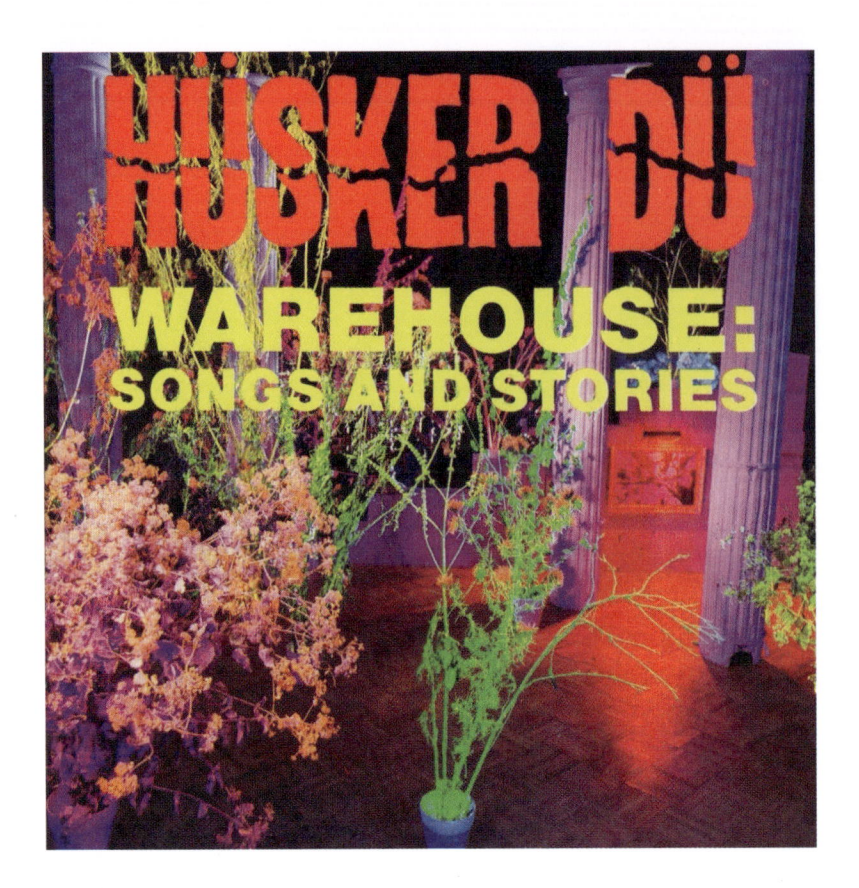

Hüsker Dü
WAREHOUSE: SONGS AND STORIES

WARNER BROS. | Producers: Bob Mould, Grant Hart
RELEASED: JANUARY 19, 1987

● Nirvana's *Nevermind* is often credited (or blamed) for turning major label attention to the alternative universe during the early '90s, but in fact, a slew of indie bands had inked big-league deals in the previous decade. Midsize Minneapolis/St. Paul alone had graduated the Suburbs, Replacements, Soul Asylum, and crosstown pals Hüsker Dü to the majors.

Like Nirvana, Hüsker Dü was a loud power trio with a knack for pop hooks. It was also on the rocks by the time *Warehouse* arrived, suffering the conflicts common to bands with two principal songwriters/vocalists, in this case Bob Mould (guitar) and Grant Hart (drums). Recorded in Minneapolis's Nicollet Studios (the room that also birthed the Trashmen's "Surfin' Bird" and the Castaways' "Liar, Liar"), *Warehouse* was the band's second double LP—twenty tracks mostly sequenced to alternate between Mould and Hart compositions.

No mere post-punk noise merchants, Hüsker Dü could evoke Byrdsian folk-rock and psyche through the ferocious squall of Mould's Ibanez V guitar, as on the guitarist's **Friend, You've Got to Fall** (the Hüsker-curious are encouraged to dial up the band's 1984 cover of the Byrds' "Eight Miles High"). *Warehouse*'s first and third singles, **Could You Be the One?** and the minor-key **Ice Cold Ice**, exemplified Mould's sheets of distorted yet somehow jangly guitar, Hart's instantly recognizable drum sound, and Greg Norton's melodic tugboat bass lines.

On the Hart side of the ledger, **She's a Woman (And Now He Is a Man)** was an interesting choice for the second single over his superior **Charity, Chastity, Prudence, and Hope**. More intriguing, though, was the shanty-like **She Floated Away**, which telegraphed some of Hart's later solo work.

Road warriors to the end, Hüsker Dü toured *Warehouse*, but Hart's drug use and the band manager's suicide proved insurmountable, and the group called it quits a year after the release. *—DP*

1987

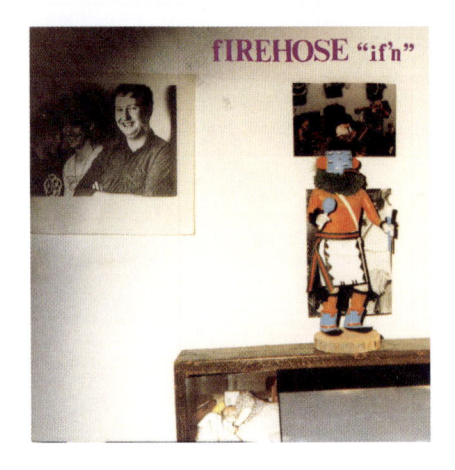

fIREHOSE
IF'N
S S T | Producers: Ethan James, Mike Watt
RELEASED: NOVEMBER 4, 1987

● If'n there were any misconceptions that fIREHOSE was a one-album distraction for bassist Mike Watt and drummer George Hurley following the death of their pal and Minutemen bandmate D. Boon, their second album served notice the trio was dug in. Featuring Minutemen superfan Ed Crawford on guitar and vocals, the trio explored more traditional alt-rock terrain than Minutemen (**Sometimes** and **Honey, Please**) while benefiting from the rhythm section's jazz influences and chief lyricist Watt's Beatnik-like patois (check the hilarious **Me & You, Remembering**). The highlight, however, might be Crawford's wistful **In Memory of Elizabeth Cotton** [sic]. —DP

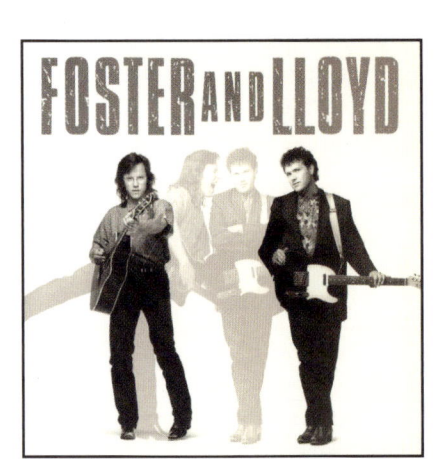

Foster and Lloyd
FOSTER & LLOYD
RCA NASHVILLE | Producers: Radney Foster, Bill Lloyd
RELEASED: SEPTEMBER 27, 1987

● A meeting at their joint song publishing company put Radney Foster and Bill Lloyd together for a short duo arrangement that deserved more credit and commercial success than it got. Their first release put them on Billboard's Country charts with the likes of **Crazy Over You**, **Sure Thing**, **What Do You Want From Me This Time?** (with Vince Gill on guitar), and **Texas in 1880**. This was good stuff but just enough ahead of the Young Country radio and Americana movements that it could not really find a proper home base. —GG

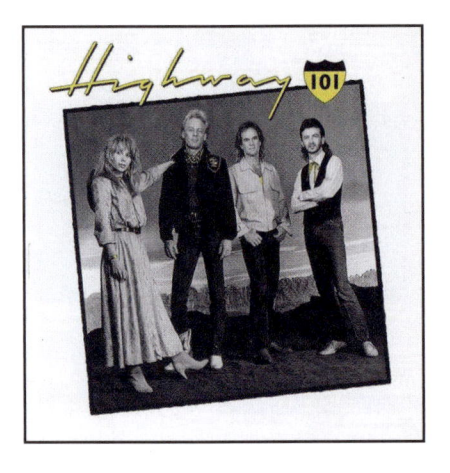

Highway 101
HIGHWAY 101
WARNER BROS. | Producer: Paul Worley
RELEASED: JULY 1987

● Highway 101's road started in Los Angeles, not exactly country music ground zero. But the quartet had promise that was realized on its ten-track debut, mostly thanks to the husky vocals of frontwoman Paulette Carson, who also made three writing contributions. The group also cut songs by Matraca Berg, Harlan Howard and Rodney Crowell, and Emmylou Harris, hitting No. 1 with two (**Somewhere Tonight** and **Cry, Cry, Cry**) and netting Academy of Country Music and Country Music Association awards as the year's top new vocal group. The shining moment of a largely forgotten career. —GG

Various Artists
LA BAMBA (ORIGINAL MOTION PICTURE SOUNDTRACK)
SLASH/WARNER BROS. | Producers: Mitchell Froom, Steve Berlin, Don Davis, Garry Tallent, Marshall Crenshaw, Don Gehman, Willie Dixon
RELEASED: JUNE 30, 1987

● The chart-topping success of this soundtrack to the Ritchie Valens biopic (starring Lou Diamond Phillips) consigned Los Lobos to singing the title track every night for eternity. Still, you could do worse, especially since the album outshines the movie. Los Lobos handled eight of twelve songs, with Marshall Crenshaw standing in for Buddy Holly and Brian Setzer for Eddie Cochran (with The Big Bopper forgotten, as usual). A year later, Los Lobos used its newfound commercial clout to make 1988's all-Spanish acoustic album *La Pistola y El Corazón*. —DM

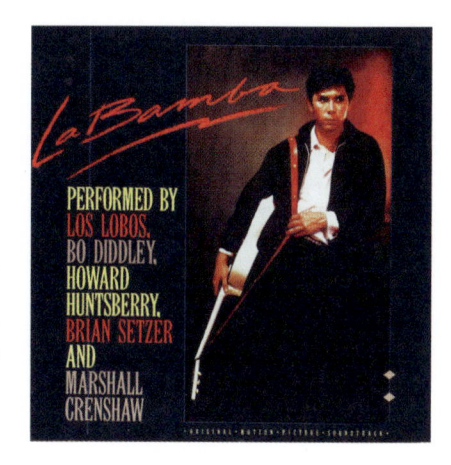

Ladysmith Black Mambazo
SHAKA ZULU
WARNER BROS. | Producer: Paul Simon
RELEASED: MARCH 1987

● The story goes that Joseph Shabalala formed Ladysmith Black Mambazo after dreaming he heard perfect-harmony singing. This South African a cappella group's layered rise-and-fall chants did feel like the stuff of dreams or waking up and trying to recall specifics of last night's nocturnal visions. *Shaka Zulu* was made in the wake of Paul Simon's *Graceland*, on which Ladysmith featured, and it might be the group's most overtly Western album with almost half its songs in English. It's some of the most beautiful grown-up lullaby music you'll ever hear. —DM

Lisa Lisa & Cult Jam
SPANISH FLY
COLUMBIA | Producers: Full Force
RELEASED: APRIL 8, 1987

● Lisa Lisa & Cult Jam's platinum second album proved she could play the pop ingenue image while the group maintained its R&B feel. Lisa Velez had a strong vocal presence that played well over Alex Moseley and Mike Hughes's heavy percussion beats; she shined particularly on the high end of the chart-topping **Head to Toe**, the album's first single. **Lost in Emotion** showcased vocals reminiscent of the Supremes and featured Motown-inspired bass lines James Jamerson would've been proud of, along with a cheeky nod to Doris Day. —SS

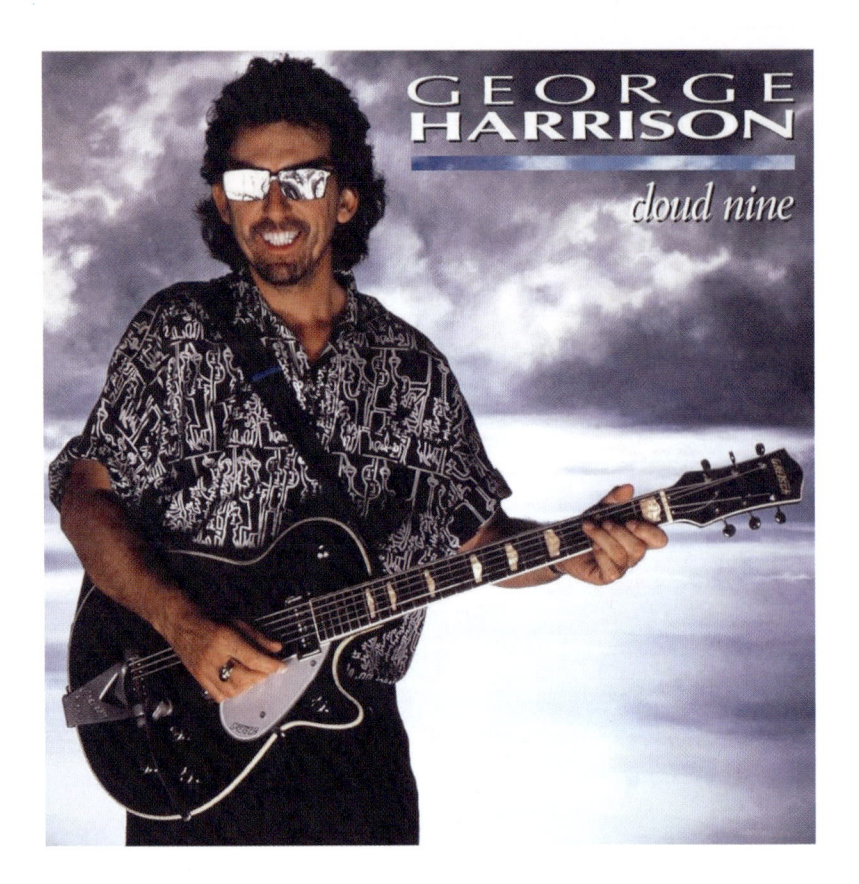

George Harrison
CLOUD NINE

DARK HORSE | Producers: George Harrison, Jeff Lynne
RELEASED: NOVEMBER 2, 1987

● Once a Beatle, always a Beatle. But George Harrison was more a legend than a man, plowed under by albums that . . . well, to say they did not live up to his legacy would be the polite way of putting it. (If you know anybody who likes 1982's *Gone Troppo*, there are treatments for that.) A comeback seemed decidedly far-fetched.

About that . . .

Harrison, who was concentrating on film production at that point (including the ill-fated Madonna/Sean Penn flick *Shanghai Surprise*, for which he wrote some songs), decided he indeed had more music to make and enlisted friend Jeff Lynne from Electric Light Orchestra to co-produce. The fruitful collaboration produced a reported seventeen songs in less than three months, eleven of which became the unexpectedly successful—artistically and commercially—*Cloud Nine*.

The album won with the charm of sounding like it was of course trying but not trying too hard. There was an audible ease and comfort to the recordings, whether it was the peppy cover of Rudy Clark's **Got My Mind Set on You** that put Harrison back at No. 1 on the Billboard Hot 100, the sentimental **When We Was Fab** (one of three tracks co-written with Lynne), or the likes of **Devil's Radio**, **That's What It Takes**, and the title track. Harrison got a little help from other friends here, too—including longtime cohort Eric Clapton, Elton John, Gary Wright, and Beatles mate Ringo Starr.

Back in the game, Harrison went on to join Lynne, Bob Dylan, Roy Orbison, and Tom Petty in the Traveling Wilburys; tour with Clapton; and record one more studio album, *Brainwashed*, released a year after his death in 2001. But it was *Cloud Nine* that made sure Harrison's last chapter was memorable. *–GG*

John Hiatt
BRING THE FAMILY

A & M | Producer: John Chelew
RELEASED: MAY 29, 1987

● You can't call it a comeback if you never really made it. And while that may be a harsh thing to say about John Hiatt's career prior to *Bring the Family*, the fact is that he had released seven—seven!—albums in twelve years without much to show for it save a few covers of his songs by high-profile artists. Then, too, those early albums were stylistically muddled, following trends rather than setting them.

Bring the Family changed all that. Part of the album's success and enduring influence is no doubt due to the incredible band Hiatt was somehow able to muster for the sessions: Ry Cooder on guitar, Nick Lowe on bass, and Jim Keltner on drums. On *Bring the Family*, the musicians' playing is every bit as astonishing as Hiatt's songs, especially Cooder's expressive slide guitar.

And those songs! Maybe it was due to maturity, sobriety, or just wisdom bought at great expense, but Hiatt began singing about adult concerns, which, back then, was still a rarity in rock circles. He took a realistic look at relationships—how much they're worth, what they cost (**Thing Called Love**, **Thank You Girl**, **Learning How to Love You**) then bottomed out (**Alone in the Dark**), sobered up (**Stood Up**), threw a lover a lifeline (**Have a Little Faith in Me**), and, in a comic interlude, realized he's turning into his father (**Your Dad Did**). But he still wanted to rock, too (**Memphis in the Meantime**).

Hiatt's voice was gravelly and lived-in, but you could sense in every song just how much he was going for it, and you can't help but root for him. The album found its audience and gave Hiatt the career he always sought—not just as an artist in his own right but as a songwriter whose work others would now clamor for. *–DD*

INXS
KICK
ATLANTIC | Producer: Chris Thomas
RELEASED: OCTOBER 19, 1987

● With a whispered "come over here," Michael Hutchence welcomed listeners into a smoldering new world of INXS. **Need You Tonight** was the first single from *Kick*, the sixth and most commercially successful studio album by the Australian sextet. It was more than just an '80s pop album; it was a combination of musical styles that was a real, well, kick for fans.

Strong and adventurous songwriting by Michael Hutchence and bandmate Andrew Farriss, combined with producer Chris Thomas's detailed production, left an impression—as did Hutchence himself. The frontman exuded sexuality with runway-ready looks and a slinky, Mick Jagger–meets–Jim Morrison presence that hovered over *Kick*'s hook-filled blend of danceable pop-funk, string-heavy ballads, and earnest soul.

Those R&B elements in particular nearly scrapped the album before it was released. Record label executives were so nervous about the new direction that INXS manager Chris Murphy said it was offered $1 million to ditch the record and re-cut something else. The band pressed on, however, and the result was an ambitious triumph that made INXS a heavy rotation staple on radio stations and MTV for nearly a year. *Kick* spawned four Top 10 singles, including **Devil Inside** and **New Sensation**. Best of all was **Never Tear Us Apart**, a ballad featuring Hutchence's yearning vocal atop angsty strings and a slow-marching beat; the enduring favorite was used as Hutchence's funeral recessional after his suicide in 1997.

Kick was the culmination of momentum that had been building for close to a decade and propelled INXS to global superstar status. Subsequent albums never achieved the same level of success, but *Kick*, more than any other release, ensured the band's immortality. **–SS**

1987

Michael Jackson
BAD
EPIC | Producers: Quincy Jones, Michael Jackson
RELEASED: AUGUST 31, 1987

● It's safe to say that, even by Taylor Swift standards, there's been no album awaited with as much universal anticipation as Michael Jackson's seventh solo effort. The global phenomenon that was *Thriller* was the reason for that, of course, its domination of the collective zeitgeist setting an impossibly high bar for its successor. Not that Jackson didn't try, of course, setting a goal of selling 100 million copies for *Thriller*'s follow-up.

Bad was not *Thriller*, of course, and couldn't be, as Jackson had used his lightning-in-a-bottle moment. But by any measure *Bad*—which sold a record 2.25 million copies during its first week on sale and was, for a time, the second-best-selling album ever—was another triumph, a slick, sleek, and dynamic collection that took some creative chances and invested Jackson even more in its process.

At producer Quincy Jones's behest, Jackson joined him behind the board and did more songwriting this time; he wound up penning all but two of the ten tracks, although, ironically, *Bad*'s most personal moment, **Man in the Mirror**, was one of those, co-written by Glen Ballard and Siedah Garrett, Jackson's duet partner on the first single, **I Just Can't Stop Loving You**. In all, according to Jones, more than sixty songs were considered and thirty recorded, although he balked at Jackson's idea of a triple album.

There was undeniable filler on *Bad*; **Dirty Diana**, with Billy Idol guitarist Steve Stevens, was no "Beat It," for instance. But its best songs—including **The Way You Make Me Feel**, **Smooth Criminal**, and the title track—were exceptional, and a record five No. 1 singles showed the fanbase was still rabid, despite all those reports of Jackson's quirky personal life. *Bad* was simply really, really good, which is all he really owed his audience, after all. *—GG*

Whitney Houston
WHITNEY

ARISTA | Producers: Narada Michael Walden, Michael Masser, Jellybean Benitz, Kashif

RELEASED: JUNE 2, 1987

● What do you do after your first album makes history—as Whitney Houston's self-titled set did in 1985, going fourteen-times platinum, spawning three No. 1 singles, and winning gobs of awards? How about not fixing what's not broken? "I believe if the formula works, that's what you stick with," Houston said while she was making her sophomore release, *Whitney*. That meant "taking my time, picking and choosing carefully, making sure it's absolutely perfect"—with a corps of top-shelf producers and writers whom she'd worked with on the debut.

With label Svengali Clive Davis presiding, the formula worked again. While it didn't have the arresting, out-of-the-blue arrival of its predecessor, *Whitney* was another sharp and immaculately put-together album that once again piled on the hits, including another four chart-toppers (the first female performer in history to achieve that). There was range, too, as Houston took listeners from the upbeat (the Grammy Award–winning **I Wanna Dance With Somebody (Who Loves Me)**, **So Emotional**) to the heartstring pullers such as **Didn't We Almost Have It All** and **Where Do Broken Hearts Go**. Kenny G played alto saxophone on **For the Love of You**, while Roy Ayers contributed vibes to **Love Will Save the Day**. But the best team-up was the album-closing **I Know Him So Well**, a gospel duet with her Grammy Award–winning mother, Cissy Houston, which showed us the apple had fallen straight down from the proverbial tree.

Whitney came with great expectations—and achieved them. It was only the fifth album in history, and first by a woman, to debut at No. 1 on the Billboard 200 after its first week of release. It was Houston's second consecutive Diamond-certified album (for more than 10 million copies in the US), with more than 20 million sold worldwide. —**GG**

Lyle Lovett
PONTIAC
MCA/CURB | Producers: Tony Brown, Lyle Lovett, Billy Williams
RELEASED: APRIL 1987

● For a bright shining moment during the mid-'80s, the subgenre not yet known as Americana looked like it might break through to the country music mainstream. Lyle Lovett was one of that nascent movement's leading lights, but for him (and most of the others), it wasn't to be. That *Eraserhead* haircut never really fit underneath a Stetson. He became a star anyway, but before that, *Pontiac* showed that Lovett had the goods. He wrote all eleven songs here, and their range was impressive. Country radio coulda-shoulda latched onto a few of them, especially those from the album's first half: the ballads **I Loved You Yesterday** and **Walk Through the Bottomland**, the high-stepping **Give Back My Heart**, and heck, even the murderous story song, **L.A. County**. But on the rest of the album, Lovett showed why no single genre could contain him. There was the surrealist opener **If I Had a Boat** and the grim, minimalist title track, which stuffed a movie script's worth of material into two and a half minutes. Meanwhile, the jazz and R&B–fueled **She's No Lady**, **M-O-N-E-Y**, **Black and Blue**, and **She's Hot to Go** offered a glimpse of Lovett's looming Large Band era. —DD

Sinéad O'Connor
THE LION AND THE COBRA
CHRYSALIS | Producers: Sinéad O'Connor, Kevin Moloney
RELEASED: OCTOBER 25, 1987

● Before Sinéad O'Connor's 1990 hit "Nothing Compares 2 U," there was her debut. *The Lion and the Cobra* was a hard album to discuss without relying on platitudes such as fierce, vulnerable, uncompromising, heartbreaking, majestic, electrifying, sexual, political, and socially aware. Even O'Connor defined it as "emotional, heartrending, exciting" to Ireland's *Hot Press* magazine. She was twenty, seven months pregnant with her first child, recording songs she wrote during her late teens on a guitar gifted by a nun—and with a voice that could pivot from tears to anger in a breath. Her first single was, fittingly, **Troy**—a complicated, transcendent anthem based on W. B. Yeats, the abuse she suffered at the hands of her mother, and her affair with a married Baptist minister. The singles—**Mandinka**, which showed off her multi-octave vocal range, and the funky, no-room-for-misunderstanding **I Want Your (Hands on Me)**—drove the album onto charts worldwide. From O'Connor's shaved head to the album's UK cover, which caught her in mid-scream (the US version was softer), *The Lion . . .*, and her entire career, dared listeners to pigeonhole her, an impossible task for an artist whose whispers were as loud as her screams. —HD

Bruce Springsteen
TUNNEL OF LOVE

COLUMBIA | Producers: Bruce Springsteen, Jon Landau, Chuck Plotkin
RELEASED: OCTOBER 5, 1987

● Imagine that you're a musician. And imagine if you have achieved everything you thought you ever wanted as a musician. Fame. Accolades. Adulation. Respect. Except, deep inside, you knew it really wasn't everything. Coming off the phenomenal success of *Born in the U.S.A.*, *Tunnel of Love* was a surprise. This was a deeply introspective solo record that posed the questions that pawed at Bruce Springsteen's soul and spirit. Identity is a central theme, addressed in several ways. **Brilliant Disguise** asked if two people ever truly reveal themselves to their partner. The title track used a boardwalk amusement ride as a relationship metaphor ("the house is haunted and the ride gets rough"). And **Two Faces** spoke to the duality that can tear you apart and drive away those you love. *Tunnel of Love* was not an entirely dour ride; Springsteen poked fun at the trappings of fame, in the context of desire, in **Ain't Got You**. The relationship between sons and fathers, so often pondered by Springsteen, is conjured in the childhood reflection of **Walk Like a Man**. And love is triumphant and vulnerable in the album closer **Valentine's Day**. Even in a catalog of superior material, this album rates among Springsteen's finest. *–HK*

Warren Zevon
SENTIMENTAL HYGIENE

VIRGIN | Producers: Warren Zevon, Niko Bolas, Andrew Slater
RELEASED: AUGUST 29, 1987

● At the end of side 1 of *Sentimental Hygiene*, Warren Zevon stated his case: "Reconsider me," he begged someone he's probably burned once too often. But he was really addressing his audience—the fans who ate up songs like "Poor Poor Pitiful Me," "Excitable Boy," and "Lawyers, Guns and Money" before Zevon went on a king-hell bender and didn't record for five years. Rehabbed and recovered, he deserved the second (or maybe twenty-second?) chance he was asking for. It didn't hurt that he came bearing a collection of songs that were tough and tender, literate, acerbic, and appropriately self-effacing. Much of the album was spent poring over his transgressions with a gimlet eye: **Trouble Waiting to Happen**, **Bad Karma**, the title track, and **Detox Mansion** didn't spare any details but managed to be hilarious, too. Perhaps feeling his old oats, Zevon also showed a touch of his trademark macho bluster (**Boom Boom Mancini**) and willingness to bite the hand that feeds (**Even a Dog Can Shake Hands**). An all-star cast—Bob Dylan, Neil Young, R.E.M., Don Henley, and others—helped Zevon get right with himself and his sound. And if those folks were willing to reconsider Zevon, shouldn't we be, too? *–DD*

1987

John Mellencamp
THE LONESOME JUBILEE

MERCURY | Producers: John Mellencamp, Don Gehman
RELEASED: AUGUST 24, 1987

● It's wholly intentional that the cover of John Cougar Mellencamp's ninth studio album bills it simply to Mellencamp. The Indiana rocker spent the '80s first coming out of his Johnny Cougar identity, reclaiming his birth surname, and digging deeper into emotions and issues with his songwriting. And having big hit records. *The Lonesome Jubilee* was the next step in that evolution.

Perhaps the album's biggest story was how Mellencamp and his band, who worked on enough material to consider a double album, expanded the instrumentation to include violin, accordion, mandolin, autoharp, penny whistle, banjo, dulcimer, and more. "I know those would definitely make an interesting sound, particularly if we didn't use them in a traditional fashion," Mellencamp explained at the time. "We never wanted to get away from making a rock 'n' roll album, but every now and then an artist has to change himself, redesign his career. That's what this record did for us."

And it still rocked, particularly on the lead single **Paper in Fire**, while Mellencamp also continued his push into serious subject matter—although he complained that critics were "taking me too seriously . . . I'm just reporting on the human condition"—on tracks such as **Down and Out in Paradise**, **We Are the People**, and **Hard Times for an Honest Man**. **Cherry Bomb** and **Hotdogs and Hamburgers** were slices of small-town heartland nostalgia, while **Check It Out** offered an everyman rumination as relevant now as it would have been one hundred years before.

Mellencamp's audience embraced the change, too. *The Lonesome Jubilee* was his fourth consecutive Top 10 album, with triple-platinum sales and a pair of No. 1 Mainstream Rock chart singles. It was critically acclaimed as well (a status Mellencamp eyed with skepticism), making the Top 10 of the *Village Voice*'s prestigious Pazz & Jop critics poll that year. *–GG*

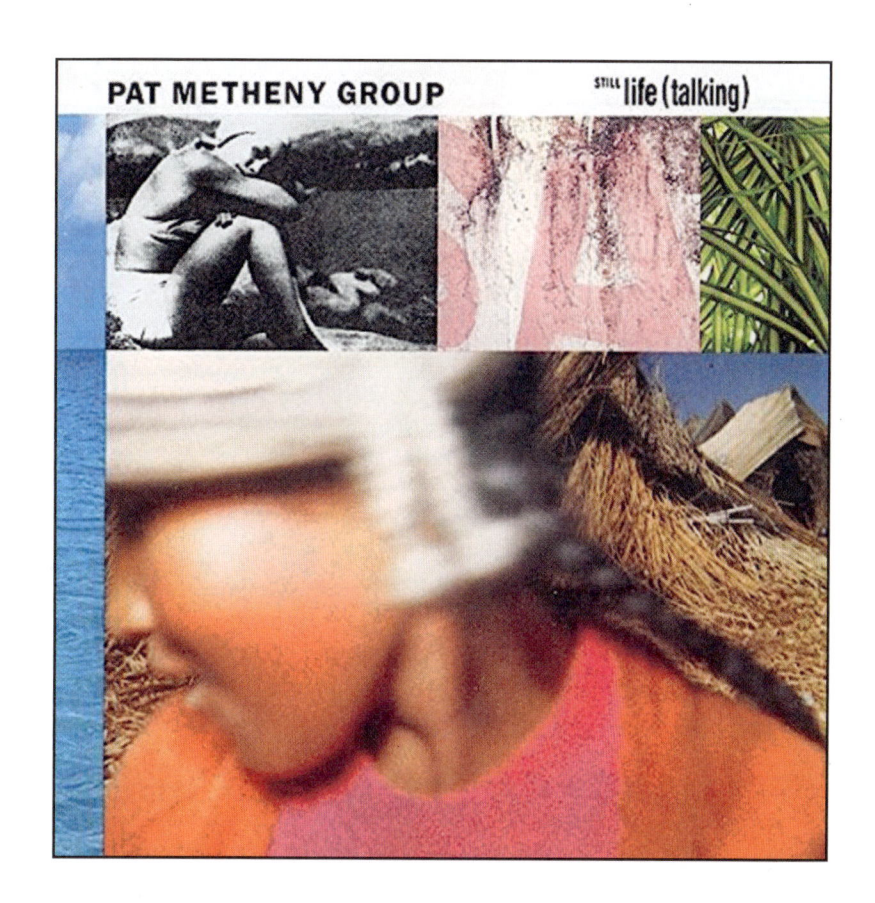

Pat Metheny Group
STILL LIFE (TALKING)
GEFFEN | Producers: Pat Metheny, Lyle Mays, Steve Rodby, Paul Wertico

RELEASED: JULY 7, 1987

● *Still Life (Talking)* marked a huge leap forward for the ten-year-old Pat Metheny Group (PMG), both sonically and for the future of the enterprising jazz band. It won the Grammy Award for Best Fusion Album and was the group's first certified gold record. It stood between *First Circle* (1984) and *Letter from Home* (1989) within a trilogy during the group's charismatic Brazilian-inflected phase.

Up to 1987, guitarist Metheny and keyboardist Lyle Mays navigated a do-it-yourself collaborative musical odyssey that started and flourished on the small, jazz-oriented European record label ECM. Not only were Metheny and Mays the prolific creative wizards who conceptualized, wrote, and performed all the music; they also recruited the band members, organized their demanding touring schedules, and handled most of the promotion. Recognizing that PMG had outgrown ECM, Metheny signed with the American juggernaut Geffen, which provided generous studio, marketing, and distribution budgets. He also formed Metheny Group Productions, which gave him complete creative control.

Initially, Metheny put PMG on hold while he produced his first Geffen release, *Song X* (1986), with alto saxophonist and avant-garde icon Ornette Coleman. When he restarted the approachable, atmospheric, and fusion-based PMG for *Still Life (Talking)*, Metheny, who lived in Brazil part-time, accentuated chic percussive textures employing newcomer Armando Marçal. Bassist Steve Rodby's recording engineer background enabled Metheny to use the studio as an instrument on lush, evolving, story-form compositions such as **Minuano (Six Eight)**, **So May It Secretly Begin**, and **Third Wind**, incorporating Mays's synthesizer array and blending in the sublime wordless vocals of David Blamires and Mark Ledford.

The mesmerizing effect of drummer Paul Wertico's fast brushwork and cymbal pacing on **Last Train Home** reimagined a dreamy, long-haul Midwestern train passing in the distance as Metheny played a twangy electric sitar-guitar. *—CH*

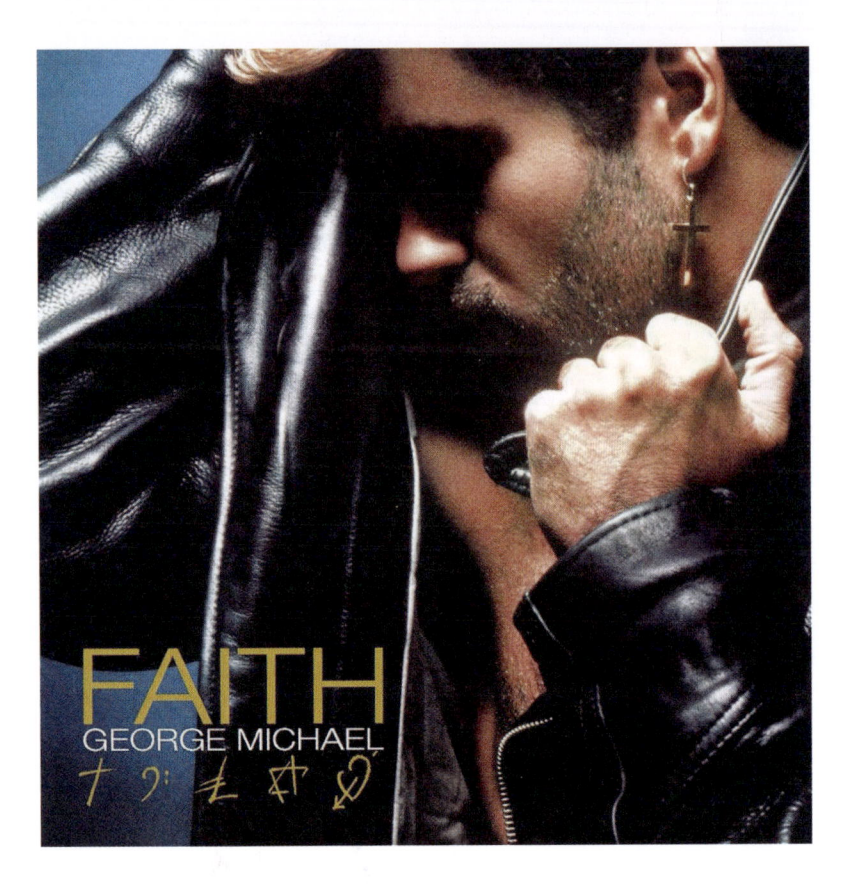

George Michael
FAITH

COLUMBIA | Producer: George Michael
RELEASED: OCTOBER 30, 1987

● George Michael's first solo album (there would only be five during his lifetime, one of covers) completed his journey from boy band to man. He just had to have . . . faith.

Michael came into *Faith* as the singer from Wham!, British pop favorites with a capital P, whose enormous success did not translate into artistic respect. "After awhile you go through a process of asking, 'Why do people believe that when I make the music I make, when I write the songs, that they're not genuine?'" Michael lamented while touring to promote *Faith*.

The album changed the tide for him, however.

The nine songs here, written and produced by Michael, were undeniably from the heart and from the pen of an enormously talented craftsman who would earn comparisons to forebears such as Paul McCartney and Elton John upon *Faith*'s release. The language and melodic choices were more sophisticated and carefully executed than anything he'd done with Wham! And even when he was having fun on **I Want Your Sex**, Michael was trying to make a serious point about monogamy that was lost in the ensuing, and perhaps deliberate, controversy that followed its release in front of the album.

The rest of *Faith* had the goods to support the attention that generated, however. Still riding a wave from his duet with Aretha Franklin (her "I Knew You Were Waiting (For Me)"), Michael had listeners jitterbugging to the title track, hitting dance club floors for **Hard Day** and **Monkey**, holding up lighters for **Father Figure**, and going through tissue boxes during **One More Try**. It all put him at a twelve-week run atop the Billboard 200 with four No. 1 singles as well as a Grammy Award for Album of the Year. His faith, in himself, was richly and deservedly rewarded. *–GG*

1987

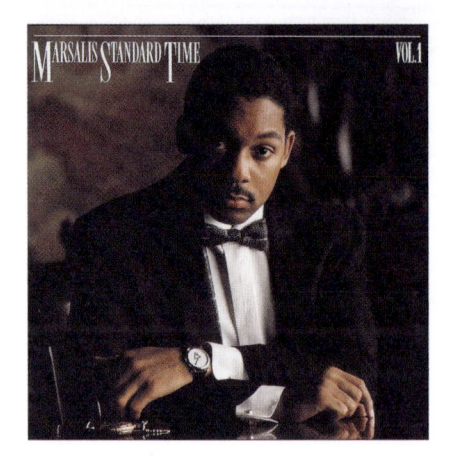

Wynton Marsalis
MARSALIS STANDARD TIME, VOL. 1
COLUMBIA | Producer: Steven Epstein
RELEASED: SEPTEMBER 8, 1987

● Trumpeter extraordinaire Wynton Marsalis stocked his late-'80s working quartet with like-minded jazz traditionalists—pianist Marcus Roberts, bassist Robert Hurst Jr., and drummer Jeff "Tain" Watts. The jazz purist forged his indelible stamp on ten standards and two originals, creating polished, elegant, and perpetually swinging arrangements of **Caravan**, **April in Paris**, **Autumn Leaves**, and **Cherokee**. The attention to detail—subtly reframing a melody, injecting bluesy grooves, adding expressive textures and supple shapes to the arrangements—earned a Grammy Award for Best Jazz Instrumental Performance, Group. *—CH*

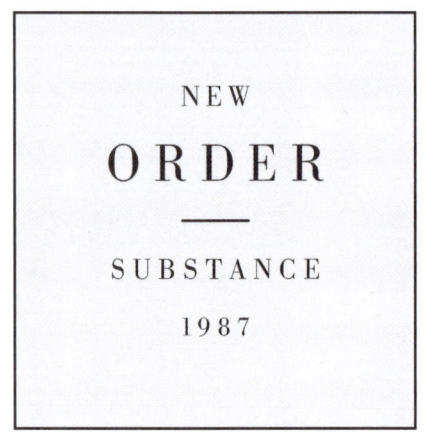

New Order
SUBSTANCE 1987
FACTORY | Producers: Various
RELEASED: AUGUST 17, 1987

● New Order's first compilation set rounded up singles from its first four albums and became a catchall for the post-punk outfit, or an entry point for newbies who weren't in on the ground floor. It's a sparkling showcase for the band's sublime, sadness-spiked synth-pop; the band rose from the ashes of Joy Division after the suicide of lead singer Ian Curtis. Several rerecords are featured, including what became the essential version of 1982's **Temptation**, while a second disc of B-sides houses the underheralded **1963**, which later became a UK hit. *—AG*

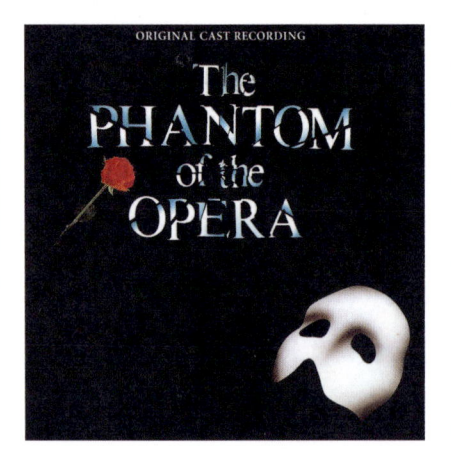

Andrew Lloyd Webber
THE PHANTOM OF THE OPERA (ORIGINAL CAST RECORDING)
POLYDOR | Producer: Andrew Lloyd Webber
RELEASED: 1987

● Andrew Lloyd Webber, he of the dancing *Cats* and *Jesus Christ Superstar*, struck gold again with this adaptation of a Gaston Leroux novel. Known as a horror movie before, Webber's *Phantom* gave us more romance and historical intrigue—along with a solid batch of memorable songs captured on this recording of the original London cast, including **The Music of the Night**, **All I Ask of You**, and the title song. There's a truncated *Highlights from* . . . set, too, but one should really listen to this *Opera* even after the fat lady sings. *—GG*

Red Hot Chili Peppers
THE UPLIFT MOJO PARTY PLAN
EMI MANHATTAN | Producer: Michael Beinhorn
RELEASED: SEPTEMBER 29, 1987

● After two attention-getting but uneven releases, the third time was a charm for the Red Hot Chili Peppers. This was the only album to feature the original lineup on every track, a tragic distinction as guitarist Hillel Slovak died from a drug overdose nine months later. The group's punk-funk–metal-rap rubric really gelled on tracks such as **Fight Like a Brave**, **Me and My Friends**, **Backwoods**, and **Behind the Sun**, albeit still in an agreeably spicy, raw form that preceded the polish of the Chili Peppers' future outings. *–GG*

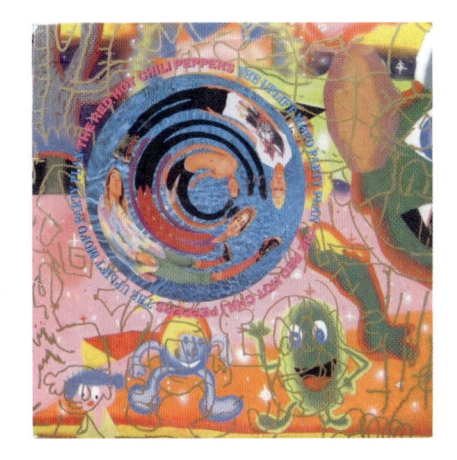

Robbie Robertson
ROBBIE ROBERTSON
GEFFEN | Producers: Daniel Lanois, Robbie Robertson
RELEASED: OCTOBER 27, 1987

● Best known as part of the Band, Robbie Robertson had established himself as a film score composer (primarily for Martin Scorsese) since going on his own in 1978. The wait for a solo album was worth it, however. *Robbie Robertson* was front-to-back solid thanks to Robertson's killer songs and co-producer Daniel Lanois's sympathetic ambience. **Broken Arrow** went on to be a hit for Rod Stewart, while the BoDeans brought extra magic to **Showdown at Big Sky** and **Somewhere Down the Crazy River**. A welcome "return" for a true creative force. *–GG*

Joe Satriani
SURFING WITH THE ALIEN
RELATIVITY | Producers: Joe Satriani, John Cuniberti
RELEASED: OCTOBER 15, 1987

● Joe Satriani's claim to fame before his second album was as teacher to fellow guitar heroes such as Steve Vai, Metallica's Kirk Hammett, Primus's Larry LaLonde, and others. *Surfing With the Alien* was its own master class in both technique and composition; as flashy and intricate as his playing was, these ten instrumental tracks were bona fide songs, rich in melodic credibility and texture. The album, made for just $13,000, went platinum and scored a pair of Grammy Award nominations—creating a wave Satriani's been able to ride ever since. *–GG*

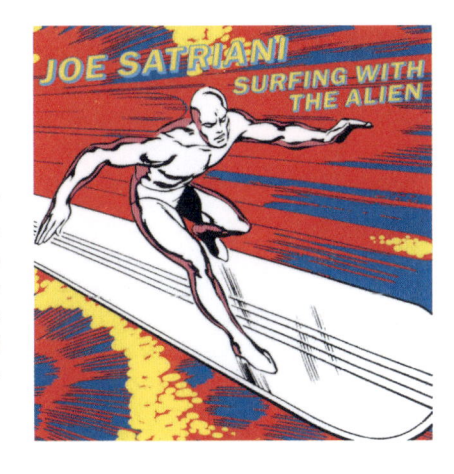

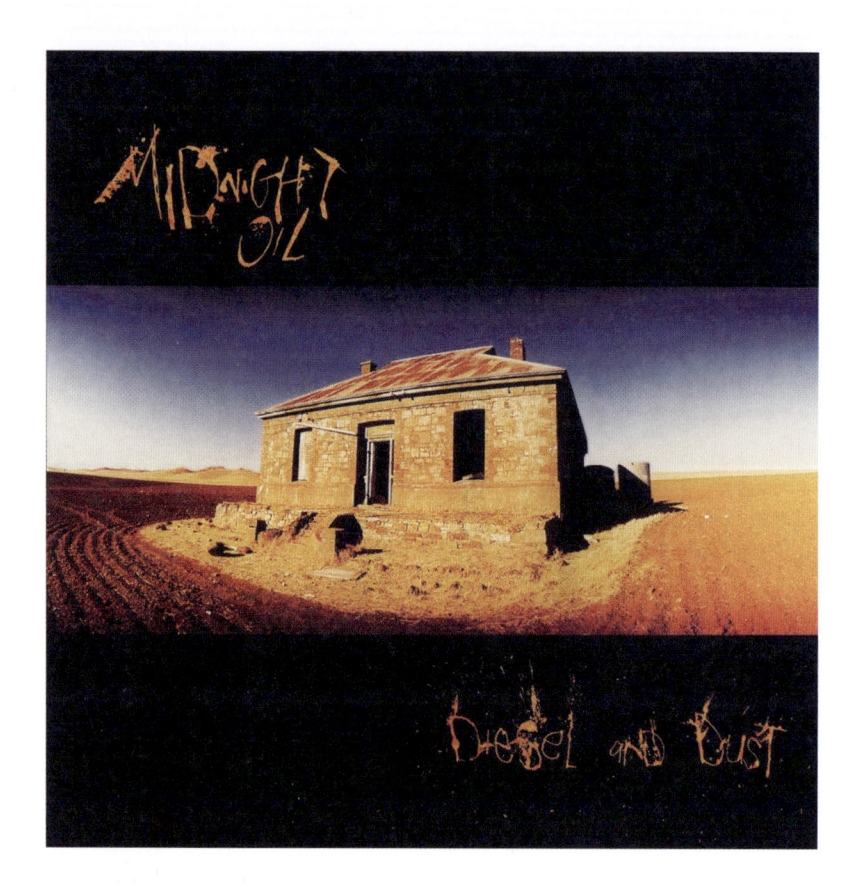

Midnight Oil
DIESEL AND DUST

SPRINT/COLUMBIA | Producers: Warne Livesey, Midnight Oil
RELEASED: AUGUST 2, 1987

● Midnight Oil was already popular in its native Australia by the time its sixth studio album was released. Formed in 1972, frontman Peter Garrett, bassist Peter Gifford, drummer Robert Hirst, guitarist Martin Rotsey, and guitarist/keyboardist Jim Moginie had gained national acclaim and a solid local following with their in-your-face messaging of Aussie political and social issues through their edgy rock music.

The band was inspired to create the concept album *Diesel and Dust* after its 1986 Blackfella/Whitefella Tour of outback Australia, in which it played to remote Aboriginal communities and witnessed firsthand the gravity of the many issues faced by the natives. While addressing those concerns, a conscious effort was made during its recording to polish the group's harsher edges and emphasize the more melodic side of its songwriting in order to spread its message to a wider international audience.

The Dead Heart, commissioned for a documentary about one of the tribes, was the first single and snagged listeners with its guitar/vocal call and response and its catchy "doo doo" backing vocals. **Beds Are Burning**, the album's opening track, became a worldwide hit and the band's biggest single with its jarring subject matter, intense rhythm, horns, a chugging bass line, and the sense of urgency in Garrett's growling, warbling vocals as he begs, "It belongs to them / Let's give it back." The song's dramatic video, which showcased Garrett's striking stature and spasmodic dancing, enjoyed heavy play on MTV in the US, which helped push it and the album even higher on the charts.

Diesel and Dust hit No. 1 on the Australian charts and went platinum in the US. It was named Album of the Year in 1988 by *Rolling Stone* magazine. *–JC*

Dolly Parton, Emmylou Harris, Linda Ronstadt
TRIO
WARNER BROS. | Producer: George Massenburg
RELEASED: MARCH 2, 1987

● Though they'd guested on one another's albums for years, pals Dolly Parton, Emmylou Harris, and Linda Ronstadt waited a long, long time—till Parton's RCA contract ended—to record together. When Parton's Appalachian-born flutter, Harris's ethereal vibrato, and Ronstadt's controlled power finally merged, they sounded like actual angels.

Backed by Laurel Canyon players Harris and Ronstadt had known since their respective days with Gram Parsons and the Stone Poneys, the three traded leads and harmonized on an inspired range of mostly nostalgic songs. Choices included the Parton/Porter Wagoner composition **The Pain of Loving You** and the pair's hit **Making Plans**, on which the trio wrapped silver-filigreed notes around Parton's sweetly nuanced lead; Jimmie Rodgers's **Hobo's Meditation**; and the traditional **Rosewood Casket** (arranged by Parton's mother) and **Farther Along** (arranged by Harris and bluegrass guitarist John Starling, a longtime pal). Ronstadt sang lead on two breakup songs penned by women—Kate McGarrigle's **I've Had Enough** and Linda Thompson and Betsy Cook's **Telling Me Lies**—on which Ronstadt took her only full-throttle vocal turn.

According to Ronstadt, the label saw little commercial potential in their "old-timey music." Then their cover of Phil Spector's 1958 Teddy Bears classic, **To Know Him Is to Love Him**, hit No. 1 on Billboard's Hot Country Singles chart, followed in the Top 10 by **Telling Me Lies**, **Those Memories of You**, and Parton's sweet mountain-girl ode, **Wildflowers (No. 6)**. Trio spent five weeks as the No. 1 country album chart and hit No. 6 on the Billboard 200. It won a Grammy Award and was the Academy of Country Music's Album of the Year and the Country Music Association's Vocal Event of the Year, which certainly made chastened label honchos more eager for *Trio II*, released twelve years later. —*LM*

Pet Shop Boys
ACTUALLY

PARLOPHONE | Producers: Julian Mendelsohn, Pet Shop Boys
RELEASED: SEPTEMBER 7, 1987

● English synth-pop duo Pet Shop Boys—wry vocalist Neil Tennant and keyboardist Chris Lowe—made a splash with their 1986 debut album, *Please*, and its worldwide smash "West End Girls." The group's follow-up, *Actually*, doubled down on its sense of melody and song structure and its framing of pop music as a vessel for art and commentary on modern culture.

"Hit music, on the radio," Tennant sang in his signature deadpan delivery on **Hit Music**, a song about the function of pop escapism (and, yes, hit music on the radio). It's slyly ironic and matter of fact, touching on both the banality and brilliance of pop. (It was never released as a single, so it didn't get to have its moment on the radio.) **Rent** had a similarly on-the-nose chorus—"I love you, you pay my rent"—but tells a story of a relationship kept hidden in the shadows and propped up by commercial transactions. Pet Shop Boys could make their music simple, but it's never simple music.

What Have I Done to Deserve This?, which featured a vocal assist from '60s icon Dusty Springfield, and the pulsating Catholic guilt anthem **It's a Sin** were the set's big singles, both reaching the Top 10 in the US. The lush, slow-building **It Couldn't Happen Here**—co-written with legendary film composer Ennio Morricone and with an orchestral arrangement by *Blue Velvet*'s Angelo Badalamenti—swelled to an emotional climax as Tennant sang about the AIDS crisis of the 1980s and the lost innocence of youth.

Tennant was depicted letting out a huge yawn on the album's cover, just another example of the ways the group gleefully plays with expectations and imagery. But *Actually* was a triumph of synth-pop and '80s dance music, and it's anything but boring. *—AG*

1987

Prince
SIGN "O" THE TIMES

PAISLEY PARK | Producer: Prince
RELEASED: MARCH 30, 1987

● The genesis of one of Prince's greatest albums, and one of the best records of the '80s, started with three other projects by the prolific singer, songwriter, producer, and multi-instrumentalist. Not yet thirty, Prince was coming off two follow-up hit records to his life-altering 1984 album *Purple Rain* when he started work on music that eventually became his ninth LP, *Sign "O" the Times*. First conceived with his band the Revolution as a double album called *Dream Factory*, the work pivoted to a single LP titled *Camille*, based on Prince's voice-modified alter ego of the same name.

Eventually, music from both abandoned projects was compiled, along with newer tracks, for a proposed three-album set titled *Crystal Ball*. After his record company blocked the release of such an expansive record, Prince adjusted the track listing again by deleting some songs and adding others to the re-titled double album, now *Sign "O" the Times*. By the time the record came out, Prince had disbanded the Revolution—which had shared co-billing on his last three albums—for his first solo LP since *1999* five years earlier, though members of the band performed on several tracks.

Still, most of *Sign "O" the Times* was Prince alone, as he was on his earliest records. From the stuttering synths on the stripped-down opening title song to **If I Was Your Girlfriend**'s smoldering soul to the New Wave funk of **I Could Never Take the Place of Your Man**, the album was Prince's most ambitious and dynamic. Whether sprinkling psychedelic pop over **The Ballad of Dorothy Parker** or glancing back at the electro-funk of his past in **U Got the Look**, he exhibited personas both familiar and unknown across *Sign "O" the Times*. *Purple Rain* made Prince a star, but this was his masterpiece. *—MG*

Suzanne Vega
SOLITUDE STANDING

A & M | Producers: Steve Addabbo, Lenny Kaye
RELEASED: APRIL 1, 1987

● Suzanne Vega came to prominence in New York's folk scene, and her self-titled debut album stayed true to those roots. But for her second effort, she was determined to chisel away at the boundaries of traditional folk tropes—and the results were quite gratifying.

Solitude Standing had plenty of the genre's conventional acoustic guitar work, but it's heavily supplemented by the good ol' rock standbys of electric guitar, bass, and drums and often peppered with a healthy dash of synthesizer. Vega's vocals were soft and whispery, creating a sense of intimacy that made you feel like she was singing only to you.

Vega pushed those folk boundaries in a number of different directions. **Wooden Horse** sits on the foundation of a big drum line à la Phil Collins's "In the Air Tonight." **Gypsy** just needed some slide guitar to show up on country charts. **In the Eye** added some New Wave seasoning to the mix. **Tom's Diner**, an a cappella ditty that opened the album, ended up becoming a huge dance club hit courtesy of a remixed version from electronic troupe DNA. Fun fact: **Tom's Diner** was the track used by the creator of the MP3 to develop his compression algorithm.

And then we come to **Luka**, the album's Grammy Award–nominated hit single. Its bright, poppy melody contrasted to its deeply disturbing subject matter, as the song details the story of a child suffering from extensive abuse. It turned out that the song was autobiographical; years after its release Vega confessed that she was victimized as a child by her stepfather. As a result of *Solitude Standing*'s Top 15 success, Vega got a ticket to work beyond the confines of the coffeehouse circuit. —*GP*

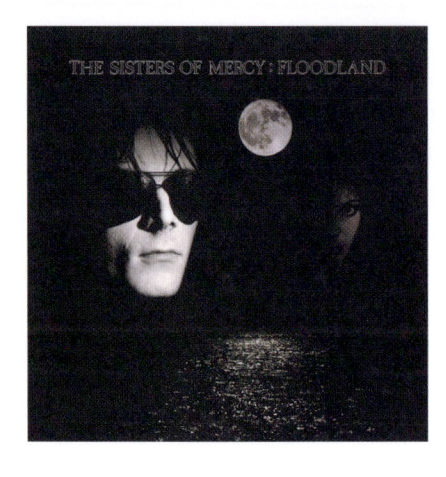

The Sisters of Mercy
FLOODLAND
MERCIFUL RELEASE | Producers: Larry Alexander, Andrew Eldritch, Jim Steinman
RELEASED: NOVEMBER 13, 1987

● The second album from English Goth rock outfit the Sisters of Mercy broadened the group's dark wave sound and buffed it to a glorious sheen. Frontman and songwriter Andrew Eldritch, who scrapped his bandmates after 1985's *First and Last and Always*, teamed with Meat Loaf sidekick Jim Steinman on a pair of tracks, and in an act of sheer indulgence, the theatrically over-the-top producer added a forty-piece choir to the eleven-minute-plus **This Corrosion**. Too much? No such thing. *Floodland* shouldered the excess and made it the sound of immortality. *—AG*

Sly & Robbie
RHYTHM KILLERS
ISLAND | Producers: Bill Laswell & Material
RELEASED: MAY 1987

● Something magical happened when Bill Laswell and a cast of brilliant musicians teamed up with the legendary reggae rhythm masters Sly Dunbar and Robbie Shakespeare. Laswell's production—with the help of Bootsy Collins, Bernie Worrell, and Gary "Mudbone" Cooper—resulted in a modern funk/dance masterpiece. The nonstop thumping beats with heavy bass infused with a touch of hip-hop and modern electronics made it irresistible. The album could well have been called *Killer Rhythms*, too, serving as a kind of aural serotonin. It's simply . . . killer. *—MH*

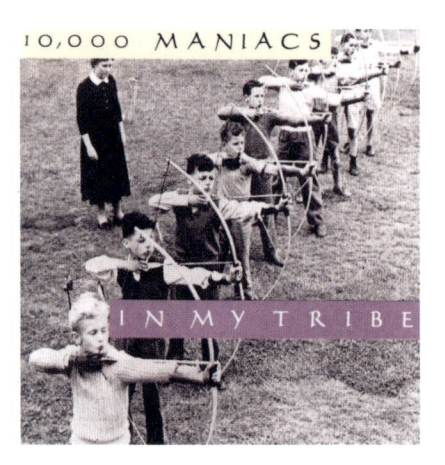

10,000 Maniacs
IN MY TRIBE
ELEKTRA | Producer: Peter Asher
RELEASED: JULY 27, 1987

● With *In My Tribe*, 10,000 Maniacs' lilting folk-pop melodies and earnest, issue-oriented lyrics reached maturity—and helped create what became AAA radio. Natalie Merchant's supple, distinctive voice and disinterest in pop-tart posing made her an intriguing focal point, but Robert Buck's superb guitar playing, Jerome Augustyniak's percussion, and Dennis Drew's keyboards helped send the upbeat but serious child-abuse alarm **What's the Matter Here** and the winsome rainy-day lament **Like the Weather** onto the charts. Merchant's R.E.M. pal Michael Stipe's cameo added further coolness. *—LM*

Whitesnake
WHITESNAKE

GEFFEN | Producers: Mike Stone, Keith Olsen
RELEASED: MARCH 23, 1987

● Big hair, sultry stare? Whitesnake tweaked its previous sound and became a pop-metal sensation with its self-titled seventh studio album. Featuring David Coverdale's soaring vocals and the expansive, somewhat-dirty guitar of John Sykes (the pair's first and only collaboration), the nine-track effort included two hit singles, **Is This Love** and what became the band's signature song, **Here I Go Again**. Coverdale and company embraced the MTV power-ballad era with a video that remains memorable to this day for Tawny Kitaen's flexibility and the durability of that Jaguar automobile. —SS

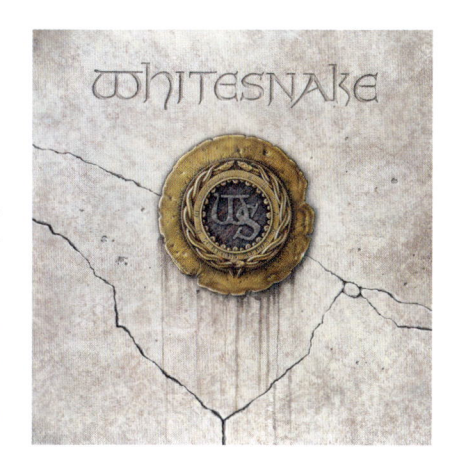

Tony Williams
CIVILIZATION

BLUE NOTE | Producers: Tony Williams, David Cole
RELEASED: MAY 15, 1987

● At seventeen, Tony Williams proved himself as a formidable jazz drummer within Miles Davis's iconic second quintet (1964–1968). Grounded in hard bop, he also veered toward fusion and rock-tinged jazz, with both Davis and his own power organ trio, Tony Williams Lifetime. On *Civilization*, **Geo-Rose** and **Warrior** best displayed his astounding polyrhythmic drumming and brisk cymbal work. Filling out the quintet were the hottest upstart players: Davis protégé Wallace Roney deftly explored melodic passages, joined by Billy Pierce on saxophones, Mulgrew Muller on piano, and bassist Charnett Moffatt. —CH

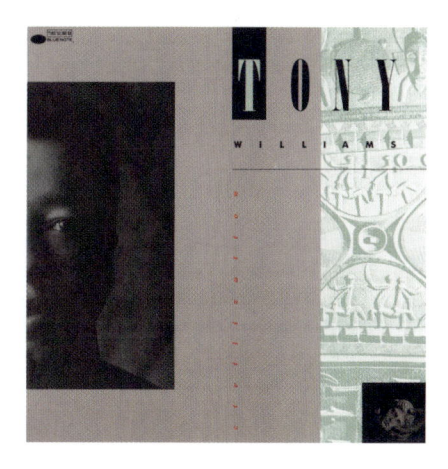

The Winans
DECISIONS

QWEST/WARNER BROS. | Producers: Marvin Winans, Quincy Jones, Barry Hankerson
RELEASED: AUGUST 1987

● There have been plenty of claims to the First Family of Gospel moniker over the decades, and certainly the Winans are as credible as any of them. The four Detroit-based brothers came with church bona fides and were discovered by Andraé Crouch, boasting a Temptations-level vocal blend that was welcoming to the faithful and nonbelievers alike. The group's fifth studio album delivered a crossover step via a Grammy Award–winning duet with homegirl Anita Baker on **Ain't No Need to Worry** and another collaboration, **Love Has No Color**, with Michael McDonald. —GG

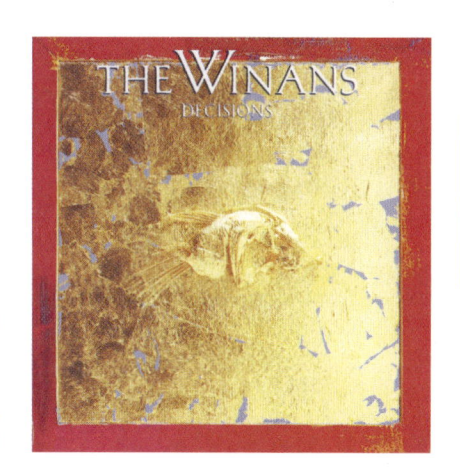

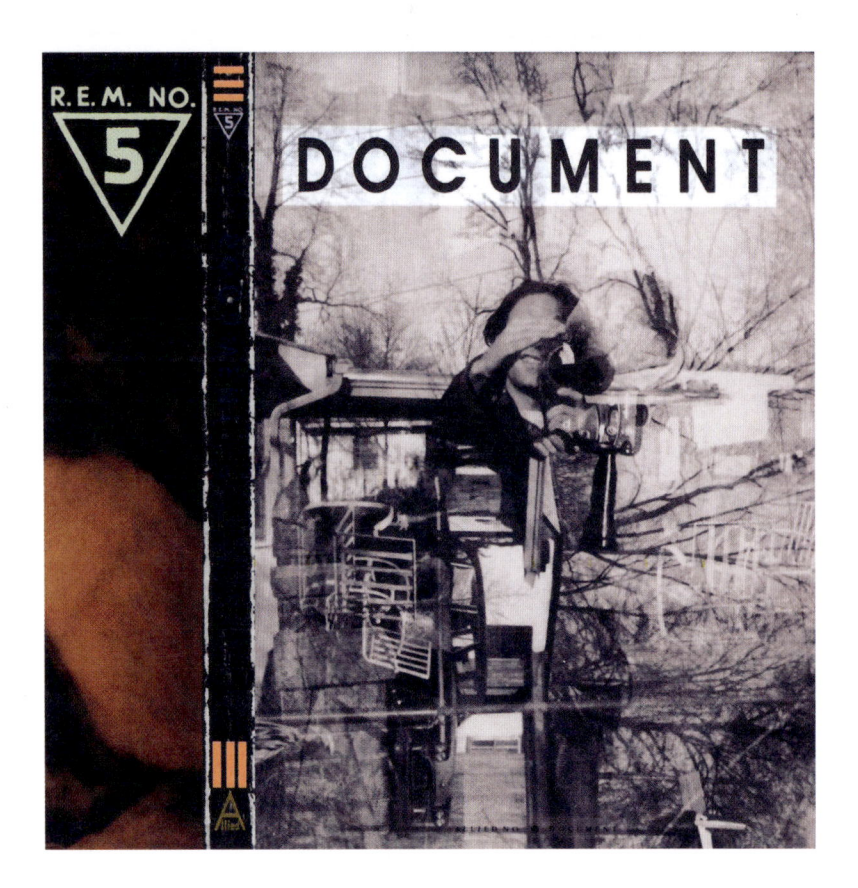

R.E.M.
DOCUMENT

I.R.S. | Producer: Scott Litt
RELEASED: AUGUST 31, 1987

● R.E.M.'s *Document*, the Athens, Georgia, quartet's fifth studio release, was also its breakthrough. It was the group's first Top 10 entry on the Billboard 200, while its flagship single, the deceptively sinister **The One I Love**, was the band's first Top 10 hit, beneficiary of I.R.S.'s long game of artist development.

Document continued to capture R.E.M.'s live energy on record, in the tradition of its two predecessors, *Lifes Rich Pageant* (1986) and *Fables of the Reconstruction* (1985). As Michael Stipe's vocals grew more assertive, lyrics became easier to make out (compared with the murmured phraseology of the band's earliest releases), if not necessarily to decipher. A listen in the present day also reveals an at-the-time-unintended relevance to the state of the nation and world today.

Consider, for instance, **Welcome to the Occupation**, ostensibly about occupation in Central America but perhaps just as applicable to the events of January 6, 2021, in Washington, D.C. **Exhuming McCarthy**'s source was obvious. And **It's the End of the World as We Know It (And I Feel Fine)** was inspired metrically by Bob Dylan's "Subterranean Homesick Blues" but with its own apocalyptic take. In the course of its mile-a-minute lyrics, the band referenced several historical notables with the initials L. B.: Leonard Bernstein, Leonid Brezhnev, Lenny Bruce, and Lester Bangs. The album was not entirely gloomy, though: **Lightnin' Hopkins** was an ode to the blues king of Houston's 3rd Ward, and there's a strong cover of UK post-punk band Wire's **Strange**.

Document did bring R.E.M.'s relationship with I.R.S. to a close; it may have seemed like the end of the world as fans knew it. But the band reemerged a year later with the rockin' *Green* on Warner Bros. Records and nine subsequent long-players prior to R.E.M.'s 2011 dissolution. *—CB*

1987

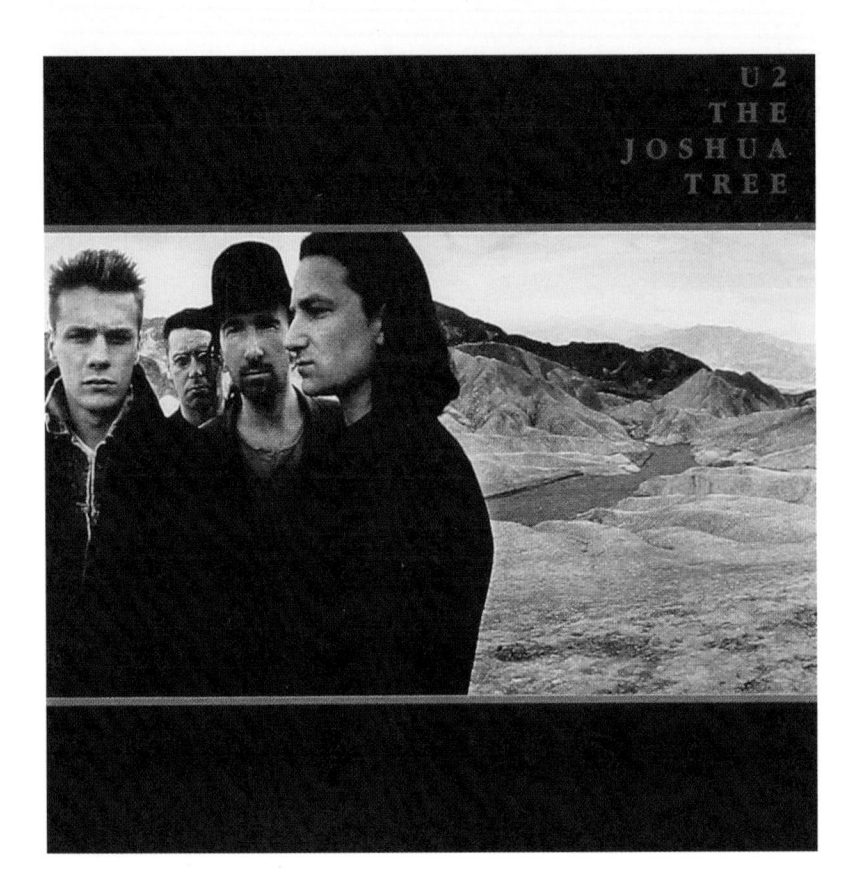

U2
THE JOSHUA TREE

ISLAND | Producers: Daniel Lanois, Brian Eno
RELEASED: MARCH 9, 1987

● U2's stock had been rising since its third album, 1983's *War*, found them at the center of buzzing media attention. Thanks to MTV and some adventurous radio stations, the Irish group's mix of traditional rock moves and post-punk edge picked up more listeners with each release. When the quartet arrived at its fifth album in 1987, thematic ambition, public anticipation, and a once-in-a-lifetime set of songs converged for one of the best and most defining albums of the '80s.

With 1984's *The Unforgettable Fire*, the four members of U2 used their experiences of touring in the US as a launching point for an album that explored American myth versus reality. The self-aware evangelizing paired hauntingly with Brain Eno and Daniel Lanois's often-ambient production. For *The Joshua Tree*, the returning team ventured further into similar musical and lyrical themes, but instead of the atmospheric soundscapes that characterized its predecessor, the album aimed for the bigger and grander gestures of arena rock. The new strategy made U2 one of the biggest bands in the world.

From the slow-building explosion of the opener **Where the Streets Have No Name** to the final benediction of the closing **Mothers of the Disappeared**, *The Joshua Tree* declared a widescreen importance. Connecting *The Unforgettable Fire*'s ambient haze with *War*'s stirring vibrancy, U2 forged a path with spiritual, hopeful, political, and personal songs. The album was about America, but it was about so much more, too—and it quickly became a No. 1 hit. The first two excellent singles—**With or Without You** and **I Still Haven't Found What I'm Looking For**—also went to No. 1. A massive stadium tour and a Grammy Award for Album of the Year followed. *The Joshua Tree* made U2 superstars; more importantly, it forever secured the band's legend. **–MG**

1987

1988

88

Paula Abdul
FOREVER YOUR GIRL

VIRGIN | Producers: Oliver Leiber, Elliot Wolff
RELEASED: JUNE 21, 1988

● Paula Abdul was a dancer and choreographer to the stars—that's her in Janet Jackson's "Nasty" video, back in 1986—who decided to give pop stardom a shot herself. She crushed it: Her debut album, *Forever Your Girl*, sold 7 million copies in the US and 12 million copies worldwide, launching four No. 1 singles—a record for an artist's debut album.

Abdul was born and raised in L.A.'s San Fernando Valley and was a cheerleader for the Lakers by the time she was eighteen. Dancing was her way into the entertainment industry, and her dance skills and sheer star power superseded her relatively limited vocal range. She signed to Virgin Records and was paired with a team of producers, including Oliver Leiber of Minneapolis collective Ta Mara and the Seen and former Peaches & Herb musical director Elliot Wolff, who helped lend her a funk-inflected pop-R&B sound.

First single **Knocked Out** nearly cracked the Top 40, but it was **Straight Up** (and its eye-catching-black-and-white video, directed by a young David Fincher) that opened the floodgates for her. **Straight Up** had hooks, mini-hooks, and hooks within hooks, and Abdul's tinny voice mattered less than her personality, which was bold and demanding. It was a defining song of the era, and it shot to No. 1 in February 1989, remaining there for three weeks.

The cutesy pop valentine **Forever Your Girl** and the slinky **Cold Hearted** followed at No. 1, and **Opposites Attract**, with its *Who Framed Roger Rabbit?*–style music video (featuring MC Skat Kat, who did not appear on the original recording), joined them, sending the album to No. 1 for nine consecutive weeks in early 1990. Abdul was undoubtedly a superstar, and she mentored the next generation of stars as an *American Idol* judge for its first eight seasons. —AG

1988

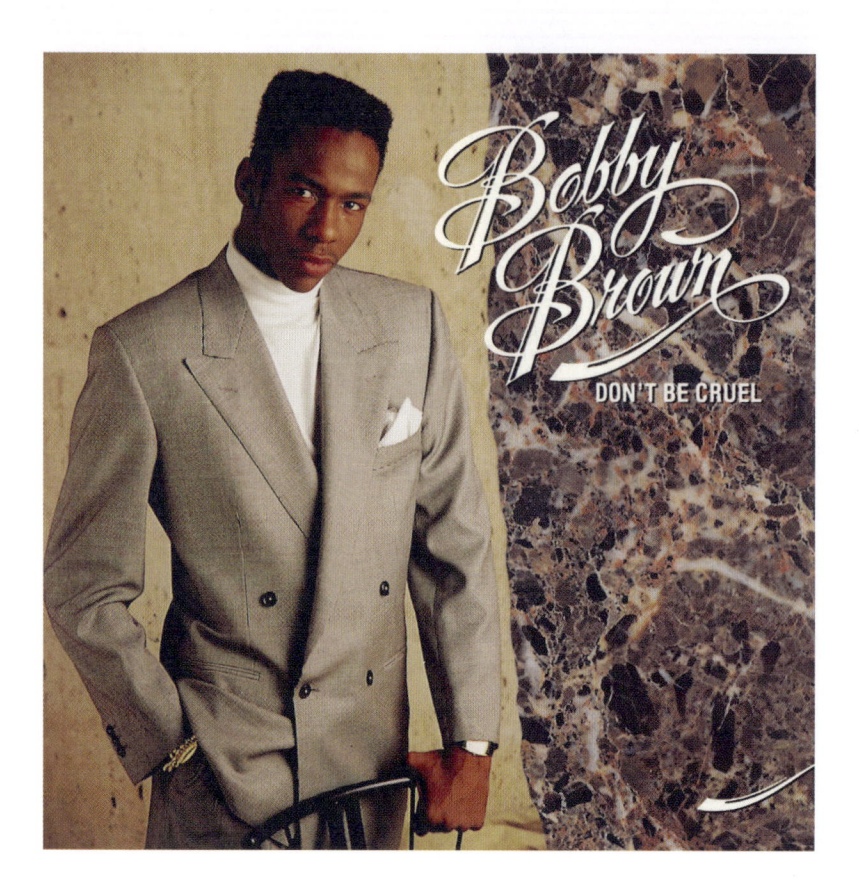

Bobby Brown
DON'T BE CRUEL

M C A | Producers: Babyface, L. A. Reid, Teddy Riley, Larry White, Bobby Brown, Gordon Jones

RELEASED: JUNE 20, 1988

● The music world already had that thing of new jack swing by 1988, coming from Junior Giscombe in the UK and Jimmy Jam and Terry Lewis in Minneapolis. But the beginning of its golden era came during June 1988, when the band Guy and Bobby Brown released key albums just one week apart—with the former's Teddy Riley and Aaron Hall also contributing to Brown's *Don't Be Cruel*, including the breakthrough, chart-topping single **My Prerogative**.

Brown's second solo album after leaving New Edition followed Guy but was even more commercially impactful. More fully developed and carefully crafted than its predecessor, 1986's lightweight *King of Stage*, the eleven-track *Don't Be Cruel* found the then-nineteen-year-old Brown in greater command of his voice and, as we'd see in music videos and onstage, his body. He may have co-written and co-produced just one song (**I Really Love You Girl**), but the album burst forth with attitude and swagger. Confident? Hell, Brown was downright cocky, and with every reason to be so.

While the Guy guys helmed two of *Don't Be Cruel*'s songs, Brown's primary overseers were Kenneth "Babyface" Edmonds and L. A. Reid. They sculpted a defined personality for the singer as well as a bit of conceptual grandeur—the title track preceded by **Cruel Prelude** and the album ending with **Cruel Reprise**. In between they kept him grooving (**Roni**), rocking (the Grammy Award–winning **Every Little Step**), and crooning (**Rock Wit'cha**).

In all, *Don't Be Cruel* topped the Billboard 200 and launched five Top 10 Hot 100 hits. It was the best-selling album in the US for 1989 and sold more than 12 million copies during its first decade of release. *Cruel* has indeed been kind, still a shining moment in what subsequently became a rocky career and life afterward. **—GG**

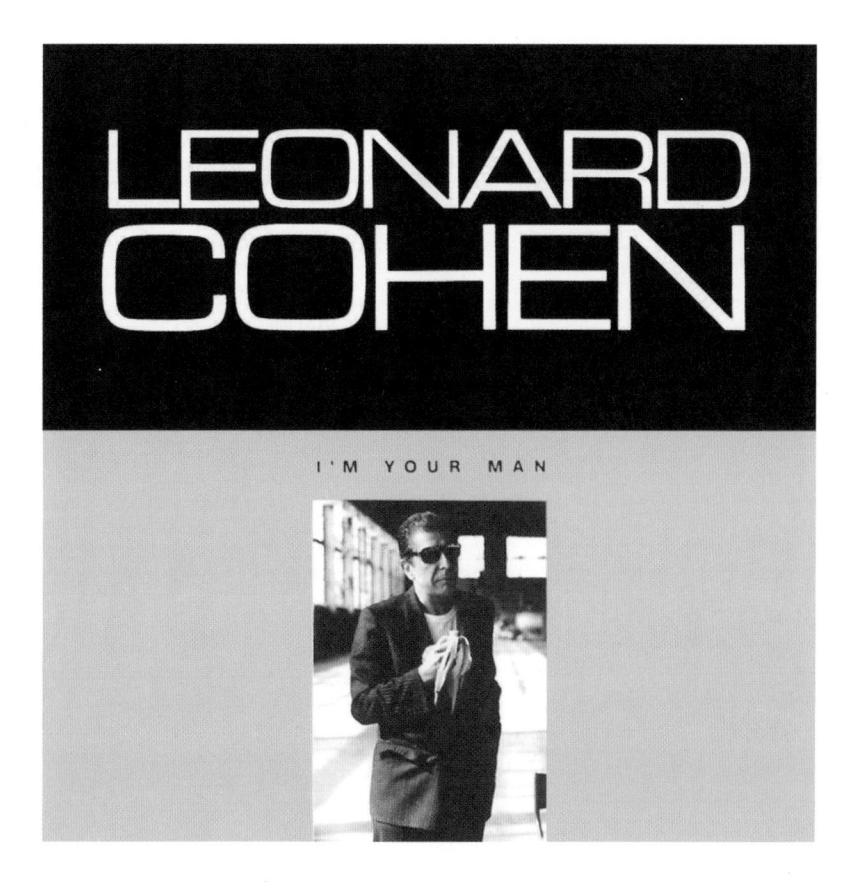

Leonard Cohen
I'M YOUR MAN
COLUMBIA | Producers: Leonard Cohen, Jean-Michel Reusser, Michel Robidoux
RELEASED: FEBRUARY 2, 1988

● Even though he "was born with the gift of a golden voice," the early 1980s had not been kind to Leonard Cohen. Columbia reluctantly released his previous album, 1984's *Various Positions*—featuring the soon-to-be-ubiquitous "Hallelujah"—because it didn't believe in Cohen's new synth-driven sound, and it didn't sell well. By the time *I'm Your Man* hit shelves, it's likely Cohen's older fans used to a more guitar-based gloomy folkie wouldn't find the contemporary dance sensibilities of the lead track compelling. But this time it worked for listeners.

What is clear to anyone willing to listen was that Cohen was not seeking to become the next Depeche Mode. Rather, he was experimenting with new sounds to propel his poetry forward, as evident on his dark catalog of the Reagan and AIDS-era, **Everybody Knows**, featuring a Middle Eastern oud playing against synthesized strings. But where the album truly connected lyrically—as is often the case for Cohen's body of work—is in the dynamics of the interpersonal and romantic in relationships. Always a keen observer of himself and similar male characters, **I Can't Forget**, **Tower of Song**, and the album's title track were all statements by Cohen as an artist and, ultimately, a middle-aged man wrestling with what the weary decades of living can do to the mind, the body, the heart, and the libido.

Although Cohen used sounds the kids of the era might have recognized, this was an album for the parents of the MTV generation, or anyone today seeking wise counsel on the eternal questions of life, love, war, and death. *I'm Your Man* was also a wayfaring sign pointing where Cohen would go, sonically and lyrically, on the rest of his albums during the next three decades. *–RSM*

Shirley Caesar
LIVE IN CHICAGO
A & M / REJOICE | Producers: Bubba Smith, Shirley Caesar
RELEASED: MARCH 1988

● North Carolina gospel legend Shirley Caesar has won eleven Grammys over the years, and one of her songs was an unlikely 2017 viral hit—the "Grandma's Thanksgiving Rap" spiel that countless DJs remixed. Still, her style of old-school gospel call and response, preacher to choir, is as aged and earthy as the hills. It was brilliantly rendered on this stellar live album, which caught Caesar on a night when she had The Spirit, and it was as much sermon as show. Lots of exhortations, some thoughts on AIDS, and a voice for the ages. *—DM*

Camper Van Beethoven
OUR BELOVED REVOLUTIONARY SWEETHEART
VIRGIN | Producer: Dennis Herring
RELEASED: MAY 24, 1988

● Would success spoil Camper Van Beethoven? That was the question when, after three delightfully eccentric indie albums, the band signed with major label Virgin. Not to worry; money may have been spent on upgraded sonics, but otherwise the band, led by frontman David Lowery, remained true to its eclectic nature on tracks such as **Eye of Fatima Pt. 1** and **Pt. 2**, **Tania**, the instrumentals **Waka** and **The Fool**, and a cover of the traditional **O Death**. Throughout, Lowery cracks wise and explores the surreal while the band visits exotic locales all over the musical map. *—DD*

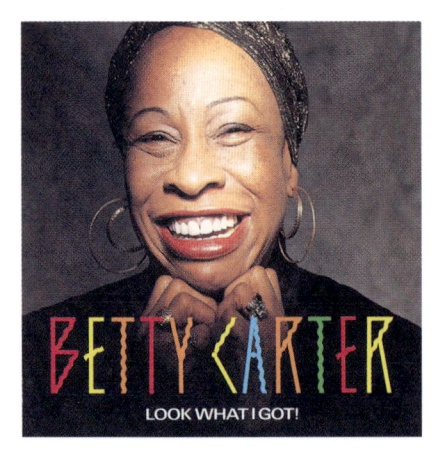

Betty Carter
LOOK WHAT I GOT
VERVE | Producer: Betty Carter
RELEASED: JUNE 13, 1988

● The late Betty Carter had it all. A deep, graceful voice. A superhuman ability to improvise and scat. Expansive and seamless range. And, with this, a Grammy Award for Best Jazz Vocal Performance, Female. After tenures with Lionel Hampton and pianist Ray Charles, Carter founded her own recording company, Bet-Car Productions, in 1969. She nurtured young talent such as pianists Benny Green and Stephen Scott and drummer Winard Harper. Here, her rendition of George and Ira Gershwin's treasure **The Man I Love** received eloquent treatment alongside Don Braden's smoky tenor saxophone. *—CH*

The Church
STARFISH

ARISTA | Producers: Greg Ladanyi, Waddy Wachtel, The Church
RELEASED: FEBRUARY 16, 1988

● From Australia, the Church emerged during the early '80s with a more polite, polished answer to L.A.'s neo-psychedelic "Paisley Underground." After a series of fine records, the Church struck commercial pay dirt with its fifth album, *Starfish*, which co-producer Waddy Wachtel helped slick up just enough for **Under the Milky Way** to register as a worldwide hit. The bagpipes at the end were the kind of go-for-broke genius touch that could have been ridiculous but instead turned out to be perfect. So is the descending guitar riff of **Reptile**. *—DM*

Cocteau Twins
BLUE BELL KNOLL

4AD/CAPITOL | Producers: Cocteau Twins
RELEASED: SEPTEMBER 19, 1998

● Ever seen the "Stop honking! I'm trying to figure out what Cocteau Twins are saying" bumper sticker? Elizabeth Fraser, lead singer of the ethereal Scottish dream-pop outfit, sings in a made-up mixture of sounds based more on feeling than words. On *Blue Bell Knoll*, the band's majestic fifth album (and first to be released in the US), Fraser conveyed beauty, heartbreak, sadness, longing, and elation—even rolling her Rs on standout single **Carolyn's Fingers**—without saying a single thing you could include on a lyric sheet. The album's luxe swooning is post-language. *—AG*

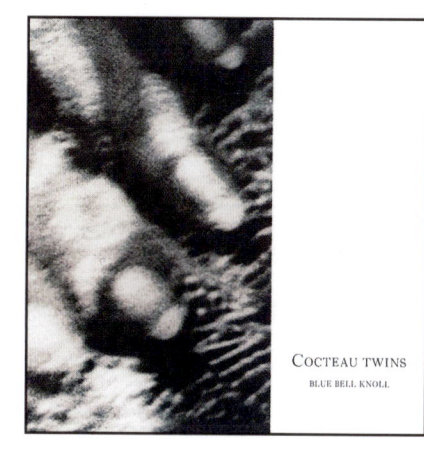

Fugazi
FUGAZI

DISCHORD | Producers: Ted Nicely, Fugazi
RELEASED: NOVEMBER 1988

● Dave Edmunds once sang that "from small things . . . big things sometimes come," which was certainly true of Fugazi's all-killer debut EP. With just seven songs, the Washington, D.C., quartet formed by a post–Minor Threat Ian MacKaye built a new template for hardcore post-punk—furious but articulate, with a bit of ska in the seminal opening track **Waiting Room** and a primal rhythm section (bassist Joe Lally, drummer Brendan Canty) driving under MacKaye's guitars and vocals (shared with Guy Picciotto). It's an ear-opening revelation, cited as an influence by scores of musicians. *—GG*

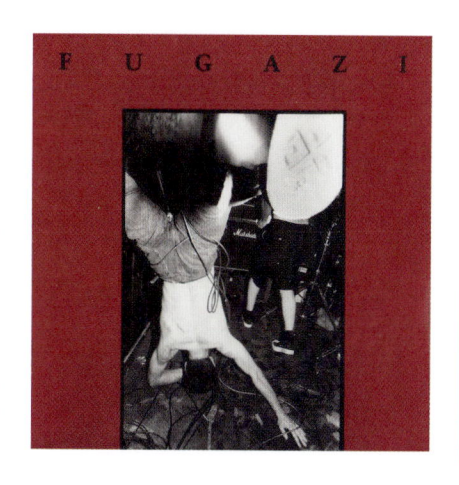

Tracy Chapman
TRACY CHAPMAN
ELEKTRA | Producer: David Kershenbaum
RELEASED: APRIL 5, 1988

● It seemed like Tracy Chapman came out of nowhere after her self-titled debut album blossomed into one of the biggest records of 1988. And in a way, she did. Before the release of the record, she was an unknown singer/songwriter working the coffeehouses and clubs around Boston. A fellow college student passed along her songs to his father, a music publisher who eventually connected the twenty-three-year-old Chapman with Elektra Records. Within a year, she had a No. 1 album and a half-dozen Grammy Award nominations, including a win for Best New Artist.

But it wasn't an easy path for Chapman. Several producers turned down the offer to work on her album because they didn't think a Black female folk singer had much commercial draw during the era of big hair and bigger guitars. But David Kershenbaum, who had collaborated with Joan Baez, Joe Jackson, Duran Duran, and others since the mid-'70s, was eager to take on an acoustic project, and over two months, he helped shape *Tracy Chapman*'s eleven original songs.

Tasteful instrumentation and sensitive production added shades and textures to the album, but it was Chapman's honeyed voice and timeless compositions that pulled the record forward from the opening notes of **Talkin' Bout a Revolution**. Politically upfront, but often tied to matters of the heart, the album's best songs blurred the lines between social and personal, none more so than the Top 10 single **Fast Car**; "I know things will get better, you'll find work and I'll get promoted / And we'll move out of the shelter, buy a bigger house, and live in the suburbs," Chapman sang, barely disguising her hopelessness.

By the dawn of the '90s, scores of women singer/songwriters were signing major label record deals thanks to Tracy Chapman's popularity and influence, still felt more than a quarter century later. —MG

407B

1988

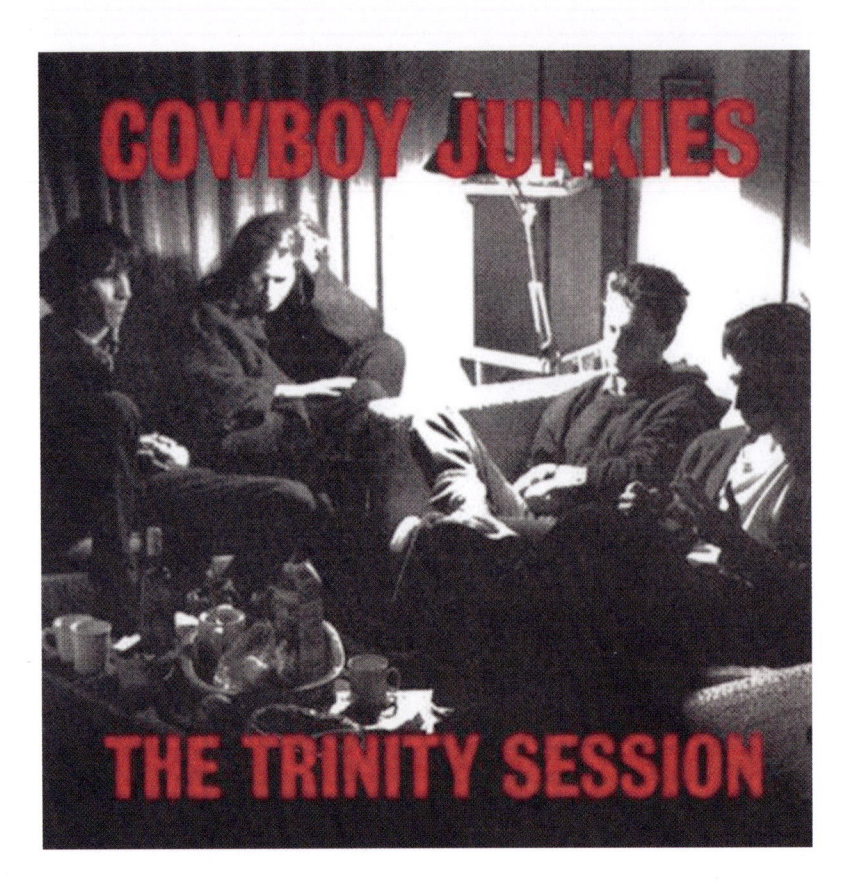

Cowboy Junkies
THE TRINITY SESSION

LATENT/RCA | Producer: Peter Moore
RELEASED: NOVEMBER 15, 1988

● It's not just what you say but how you say it. That's something Cowboy Junkies discovered early on by recording its music using an old-school technique, with the band—siblings Margo Timmins (vocals), Michael Timmins (guitar), Peter Timmins (drums), and bassist Alan Anton—performing in an intimate space, gathered around a single microphone, the better to capture the spontaneity and genuineness of the performances.

In the case of the band's second album, *The Trinity Session*, that space was inside the Church of the Holy Trinity in its native Toronto. A fortuitous meeting with self-taught producer/engineer Peter Moore, who happened to own an ambisonic microphone, led to the band's debut album, *Whites Off Earth Now!*, and the continued development of the technique—a radical reaction to the overproduced and synth-heavy sounds of the 1980s—on *The Trinity Session*. It was so radical that it drew no industry interest, prompting Cowboy Junkies to release its early efforts on their own indie label, Latent Recordings. When the band was signed by major label RCA, *The Trinity Session* was rereleased to wide acclaim and commercial success.

The rightness of the band's attempting that technique was apparent from the languid and dreamlike album's opening track, Margo Timmins's a cappella performance of the traditional tune **Mining for Gold**. From there the album mixed originals such as **Misguided Angel** and **I Don't Get It** with classic country, rock, and blues songs, including Hank Williams's **I'm So Lonesome I Could Cry**, Patsy Cline's **Walkin' After Midnight**, and, best of all, the Velvet Underground's **Sweet Jane**.

The eclectic song selection and spare performances matched the recording technique, making the album sound like the band was playing in your living room and Margo Timmins is whispering a series of special secrets in your ear. *—DD*

DJ Jazzy Jeff & The Fresh Prince
HE'S THE DJ, I'M THE RAPPER

JIVE | Producers: DJ Jazzy Jeff, The Fresh Prince
RELEASED: MARCH 29, 1988

● DJ Jazzy Jeff & The Fresh Prince took rap from the streets to the suburbs. The West Philadelphia duo's second album was a mainstream commercial breakthrough at a time when the genre was ready for it, and the pair put on a friendly face that made the medium palatable to middle America. **Parents Just Don't Understand**, the song said, but Jazzy Jeff and the Fresh Prince's spin on rap was one parents could fully get behind.

The DJ was Jeffrey Townes, who was entranced watching turntablists spin at neighborhood block parties when he was growing up, and the rapper was Will Smith, the extremely charismatic lyricist who would go on to become a sitcom star and one of the world's biggest movie stars. The pair's 1987 debut album, *Rock the House*, didn't make a splash, but it set the table for what was to come.

He's the DJ . . . was a double album that took off thanks to **Parents Just Don't Understand**, a full-on comedy tale about everyday conflicts between parents and children. Smith's storytelling and lyrical inflections were so vivid that the song didn't need a music video; he painted the picture entirely through his words. (It got a video anyway, which became a giant hit on MTV.) The song became the first rap song to win a Grammy Award, in the newly christened Best Rap Performance category, and helped the set reach triple-platinum sales.

Elsewhere, Jeff flexed his dexterity on the turntables, especially on the album's back half, and the duo created party rap tales (**Pump Up the Bass**, **Brand New Funk**) to rock the block. But they're often overshadowed by novelty tracks like **A Nightmare on My Street** and **Human Video Game**, goofy parodies that did not stand the test of time, even though Smith's superstardom certainly did. *—AG*

Billy Bragg
TALKING WITH THE TAXMAN ABOUT POETRY

ELEKTRA | Producers: Kenny Jones, John Porter
RELEASED: SEPTEMBER 22, 1986

● Billy Bragg has frequently been called a political singer. No question that he staked out his positions in the clearest terms. He's insightful and sometimes withering. It is those qualities, along with an ample well of human empathy, that made *Talking with the Taxman about Poetry* one of his finest moments. Early in his career, Bragg busked the streets of London. He learned chops that underpin his performance and songwriting. The sharpness of his guitar playing is enthralling; using little stabbing accents and chopping chords, his electric guitar rang clear and true across this album. When stacked with bass and acoustic guitar and the aforementioned humanity, you got the working-class beauty of **Greetings to the New Brunette**. A special place in heaven awaits Bragg for making **Levi Stubbs**, the Four Tops' legendary lead singer, the iconographic emotional center of a song that contained an otherwise despairing story—not an easy task and one that only highlighted Bragg's superior songwriting. And it would be shallow to not mention the aim Bragg took in **Help Save the Youth of America** or the Woody Guthrie-esque punch of **There Is Power in a Union**, two songs that have, sadly, remained relevant. *—HK*

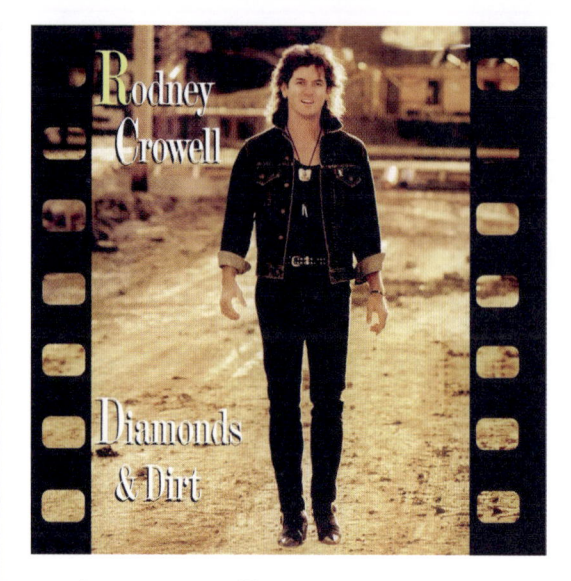

Rodney Crowell
DIAMONDS & DIRT

COLUMBIA | Producers: Rodney Crowell, Tony Brown
RELEASED: MARCH 30, 1988

● Prior to recording his classic album *Diamonds & Dirt*, Rodney Crowell made his bones as a songwriter whose tunes were recorded by Emmylou Harris, Johnny Cash, Waylon Jennings, the Oak Ridge Boys, Crystal Gayle, Bob Seger, and Crowell's wife, Rosanne Cash. He also played guitar and sang backup for Harris and produced several albums for Rosanne. His own early efforts were critically acclaimed but didn't fare nearly as well commercially. *Diamonds & Dirt* changed all that. It was a straight-up country album that lit up the charts with five No. 1 singles—something no previous country record had done. Crowell sounded completely on his game as he leaned into high-stepping fast numbers **I Couldn't Leave You if I Tried** and **She's Crazy for Leavin'**, played it tender on **After All This Time**, and turned in a fine mid-tempo duet with Rosanne on **It's Such a Small World**. The musicianship was every bit as terrific as the vocals: The stellar cast includes keyboardist Barry Beckett, drummer Russ Kunkel, fiddler/mandolinist Mark O'Connor, guitarist Steuart Smith, steel guitarist Paul Franklin, and Vince Gill singing background vocals. Crowell has always operated at a high level, but *Diamonds & Dirt* was the first time he hit the stratosphere. *—DD*

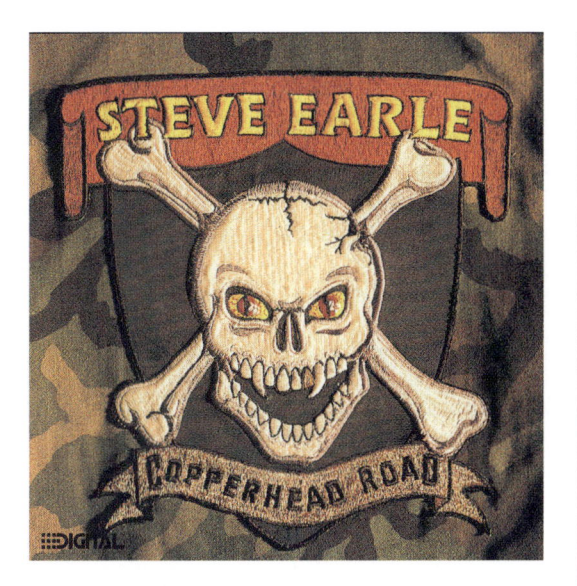

Steve Earle
COPPERHEAD ROAD

UNI/MCA | Producers: Steve Earle, Tony Brown
RELEASED: OCTOBER 17, 1988

● Neil Young isn't the only artist that "headed for the ditch" musically when the middle of the road started to look too boring. Steve Earle went there, too, and it wasn't just a casual visit. After a stint as a Nashville songwriter and two successful albums that were rowdy but didn't necessarily challenge the status quo, Earle let his freak flag fly on *Copperhead Road*. Earle was a poor fit for Nashville's music-industry machinery, so his label packed him off to its Los Angeles imprint, Uni. He also made the music outside the confines of Music City, recording in Memphis instead. The difference was obvious from the jump: cranked-up guitars, thunderous drums, and a decidedly rock 'n' roll attitude dominated. Starting with the title track, a moonshiner opus that positively roared, Earle kept the throttle wide open throughout the album's first half, including **The Devil's Right Hand**, which posited a handgun as a murder waiting to happen, and the Vietnam vet reel **Johnny Come Lately**, which featured the Pogues as his backing band. The love songs that dominated the second half showed Earle still possessed a softer side, but by then, he was well entrenched in the musical ditch. *—DD*

Enya
WATERMARK

GEFFEN/REPRISE | Producers: Nicky Ryan, Ross Cullum, Enya
RELEASED: SEPTEMBER 19, 1988

● Long before there were apps and streaming music channels to chill you out or send you into an international coffee-sipping reverie, there was Enya. Born into the Brennan family that would form Celtic band Clannad, Eithne Pádraigín Ní Bhraonáin—easy for you to say, maybe—Enya simplified her name and went solo, composing ethereal soundtrack music before becoming a multiplatinum sensation with her second album, *Watermark*. Its recording was initially done in Ireland, but then Enya rerecorded the songs digitally in a London studio, adding a few musicians to the mix. The songs were primarily synth driven, with Enya's multilayered vocals delivered in English, Gaelic, and Latin—the latter two perhaps giving seemingly heightened import to co-writer Roma Ryan's impressionistic musings about journeys, dreams, and sailing away. Sailing away, of course, is the central theme of international smash **Orinoco Flow**, which name-checked a number of exotic locations but descended into seeming gibberish: "We can steer, we can near with Rob Dickins at the wheel." What? Oh—Dickins was a label executive. That didn't damage the album's commercial fortunes, however, and it became a high-(ahem)water mark of New Age music. Taken stereophonically, it's a yummy aural gummy if there ever was one. *—DD*

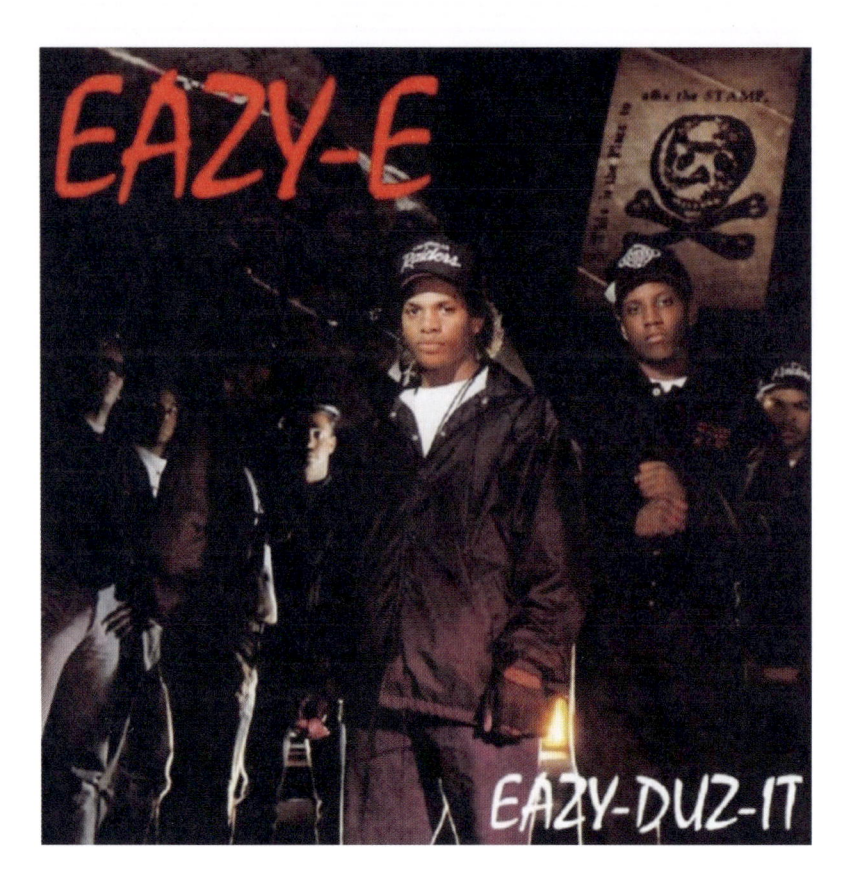

Eazy-E
EAZY-DUZ-IT

RUTHLESS/PRIORITY | Producers: Dr. Dre, DJ Yella
RELEASED: SEPTEMBER 13, 1988

● Gangsta rap was still in its infancy when *Eazy-Duz-It* was released, and Eazy-E was just the character to deliver it to the masses. The charismatic N.W.A star was the group's most magnetic personality, packing his hardcore tales with wit, fun, and humor, like a wisecracking antihero the audience loves to root for. He basically became every middle schooler's hero and every parent's worst nightmare.

Eazy-E was born Eric Wright in Compton, California, a high school dropout turned drug dealer who aspired to be on the business end of rap music. But once he got behind a microphone, his delivery had so much presence that his path was clear. He was a born star.

Released just a month after N.W.A's *Straight Outta Compton*, *Eazy-Duz-It* presented the twenty-four-year-old front and center. (He hits his age throughout the album, which becomes its own running joke.) His N.W.A cohorts—chiefly MC Ren and Ice Cube—wrote rhymes, while Dr. Dre and DJ Yella provided backing tracks. But Eazy sold the profane tales with style and loose cannon charm, like a rap version of Joe Pesci's character in *Goodfellas*. Whether spinning stories of bank robberies (**Nobody Move**) or his own mythmaking (**Still Talkin'**), Eazy-E came across larger than life, or at least bigger than his five-foot, three-inch frame would have you believe.

The centerpiece was a remix of **Boyz-n-the-Hood**, which originally appeared on the 1987 compilation album *N.W.A and the Posse* and was presented here with a new introductory verse ("I gotta get drunk before the day begins, before my mother starts bitchin' about my friends"). But Eazy retained his cool, laid-back delivery, and its casual, lived-in observations made it an iconic West Coast anthem. Ice Cube wrote it, but Eazy made it his own, and he made it all look, well, you know . . . —AG

Erasure
THE INNOCENTS
SIRE/REPRISE | Producers: Stephen Hague, Dave Jacob, Erasure
RELEASED: APRIL 10, 1988

● British synth-pop duo Erasure (Vince Clarke and Andy Bell) had already established itself in the UK, but it was this eleven-track third studio album that earned it more than a little respect in America. *The Innocents* became Erasure's signature recording and helped the group cross over from dance clubs to the pop charts on the strength of three singles. The first was surprisingly a ballad; **Ship of Fools** showcased the duo's expanded songwriting talents in dramatic fashion. The buoyant **Chains of Love** followed with its electronic, Motown-esque beats and storytelling lyrics. But it was **A Little Respect** that brought Erasure firmly into airplay's embrace with a simple, rhythmic guitar beat overlapping Clarke's swirling synthesizers to provide a backdrop for Bell's full vocal range. The escalating chorus of "to-ooo-ooo-ooo MEEEEE" was mangled by fans everywhere attempting to hit the high notes. Erasure had staked its claim on dance/synth/pop music. Whether romping to a blaze of electronic beats on a glitter-strewn dancefloor or leading a singalong plea for respect, the sound was unmistakable, and *The Innocents* came together as the perfect pop explosion. *—SS*

Everything but the Girl
IDLEWILD
BLANCO Y NEGRO/SIRE | Producer: Ben Watt
RELEASED: FEBRUARY 29, 1988

● The strain of elevated, synth-driven pop that emerged during the '80s from a mating of smooth jazz and New Wave wasn't dubbed sophisti-pop until after the fact, but that perfectly described the sound England's Everything but the Girl (the couple Ben Watt and Tracey Thorn) produced on *Idlewild*. EBTG's fourth album solidified its '80s direction with finely textured songs exuding a soothing warmth, despite the melancholy undercurrent in its lyrics and Thorn's elegant voice. Like her contemporary, Sade, Thorn's silky alto seemed tailor-made for pensive material such as **Apron Strings**, about longing for a family—a subject addressed from a different perspective on the moving, Watt-led duet **The Night I Heard Caruso Sing**. Arrangements featuring jazz piano, synths, bass, occasional horns, and programmed percussion, accented by Watt's excellent guitar work, made a comfortable bed for Thorn's vocal shadings—including an uplifting turn on **Blue Moon Rose**. But sadness was obviously her wheelhouse. Her mournful cover of late Crazy Horse guitarist Danny Whitten's **I Don't Want to Talk about It**, released as a stand-alone single, was added to the album after it became the band's first UK Top 10 hit. (EBTG finally earned US attention with *Idlewild*'s follow-up, *The Language of Life*.) *—LM*

Guy
GUY
UPTOWN | Producers: Teddy Riley, Gene Griffin
RELEASED: JUNE 14, 1988

● The year 1988 was the launch pad for new jack swing. The collaboration and collision of classic R&B and hip-hop sensibilities was around for three years or so before Guy released its debut album, with British producer Junior Giscome's "Oh Louise" and Full Force's "Alice, I Want You Just for Me" as the first swings at the sound. But Guy and Bobby Brown's *Don't Be Cruel* a week later made June 1988 its real launch pad.

Riley already had production credits (Kids at Work, Doug E. Fresh) when he, Aaron Hall, and Timmy Gatling formed a trio, with Gatling leaving over management contract conditions (he co-wrote nine of ten songs on *Guy*). Hall's brother Damion was enlisted, and the album came together as a tight set filled with exciting, groove-laced tracks that sounded hot over speakers in the disco or a boombox on the street corner. Singles such as **Groove Me**, **'Round and 'Round (Merry Go 'Round of Love)**, and **Teddy's Jams** were street but polished, a bit less sonically bright than the Minneapolis version of the sound concocted by Jimmy Jam and Terry Lewis but every bit as potent and infectious.

Guy ran deep, too. It launched four Top 5 R&B chart singles, but other songs such as **Don't Clap . . . Just Dance** and **You Can Call Me Crazy** were hardly filler. *Guy* hit No. 1 on the R&B Albums survey, was platinum less than six months after its release (eventually double platinum), and won three Soul Train Music Awards. It was somewhat eclipsed by Brown, but the group gestalt of Guy made it arguably more interesting. The trio would release only two more albums, though it has been back together, intermittently, since 2005, making this new jack legend still sound fresh even coming from old(er) jacks. —GG

Ministry
THE LAND OF RAPE AND HONEY

S I R E | Producers: Al Jourgensen (aka Hypo Luxa), Paul Barker (aka Hermes Pan), Eddie Echo

RELEASED: OCTOBER 11, 1988

● Ministry's third album was a proverbial slap upside the head, eardrums included, when it was released. Prior to *The Land of Rape and Honey*, Al Jourgensen and his Chicago collective was a synth-pop outfit, heavier perhaps than others of the ilk but definitely music of the frothy variety. But when Paul Barker came on board as a creative partner in 1986, the shift was seismic.

The turn began on *Big Sexy Land*, the 1986 debut by Jourgensen and one of his other bands, Revolting Cocks. It was still plenty of Electronic Body Music (EBM) but had a significantly harder and more industrial flavor informed by Luc van Acker's guitar; after that, Jourgensen picked up his own axe, which he'd put aside for Ministry's first two albums, to crank up both volume and texture, and, with Barker, also began working more with samples and cut-up studio production techniques and vocal distortion to craft an aggressive aural soundscape that was infectious enough to make the bodies hit the (dance) floor.

The first three tracks—**Stigmata**, **The Missing**, and **Deity**—established the new sound in one pulverizing triumvirate. But wait, there was indeed more: from the trancey, big-beat opus of **Golden Dawn** to the dark house-of-horrors maelstrom of **You Know What You Are** and the free-form(ish) techno shuffle of **Abortive**, written by British dub specialist Adrian Sherwood.

Jourgensen, Barker, and their cohorts—notably drummer Bill Rieflin—kept the noise coming throughout, and the nine tracks (eleven on CD) established a new standard for what was considered industrial and, to be sure, a fresh form of music, period. A legion of acts that came in its wake testified to its influence, and Jourgensen has often said it's his favorite Ministry album—as well it should be. *—GG*

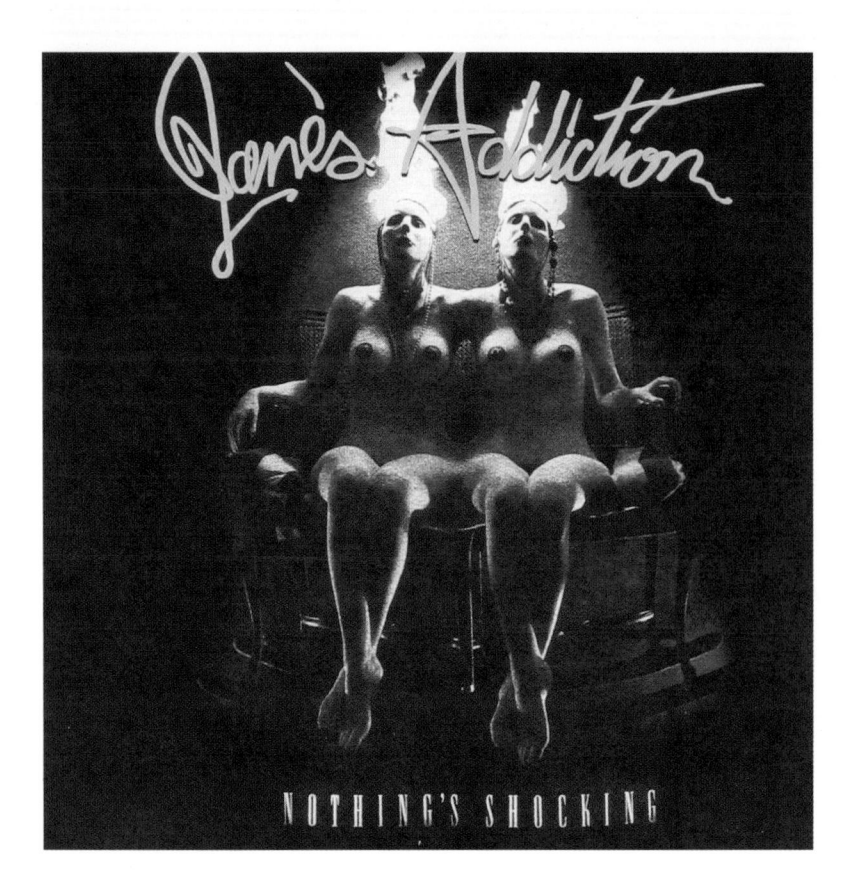

Jane's Addiction
NOTHING'S SHOCKING

WARNER BROS. | Producers: Dave Jerden, Perry Farrell
RELEASED: AUGUST 23, 1988

● When it arrived, nothing sounded quite like *Nothing's Shocking*, the debut studio album from Los Angeles rock outfit Jane's Addiction. Released the same summer Guns N' Roses and Def Leppard were trading top spots on the charts, Jane's presented a true alternative to the mainstream—a freaky, spiritual, artful, soulful collective that drew from nature, '70s rock titans, and the L.A. neighborhoods that birthed them. The band's essence had been captured on 1987's self-titled live album, but *Nothing's Shocking* put some heft behind their sound, which was big enough to move mountains.

Singer/songwriter Perry Farrell, guitarist Dave Navarro, bassist Eric Avery, and drummer Stephen Perkins had a live-wire chemistry that was always ready to explode. Dave Jerden, who had worked with Talking Heads, Frank Zappa, and fellow L.A. scenesters the Red Hot Chili Peppers, was brought in to produce the album alongside Farrell. Songs such as the opening **Up the Beach** and **Summertime Rolls** acted as picturesque scene-setters for monsters like **Ocean Size** and **Mountain Song**, towering feats of strength that showed the band's raw power. **Jane Says**, a holdover from the group's debut, was a lovely mid-tempo ballad that became the band's signature song, while **Ted, Just Admit It . . .** was an experimental odyssey that climaxed with Ferrell shouting, "Sex is violent!" and was built around a repeated refrain of the album's title. At seven-plus minutes, it packed a wallop and left you reeling.

Jane's Addiction proved to be so ahead of its time that by 1991, when the alt-rock movement it helped usher in began to fully take hold, it was already in the process of breaking up, the first Lollapalooza tour acting as its swan song. Numerous reunions and new studio albums followed, but none matched the seismic, combustible energy of *Nothing's Shocking*, the band's indisputable masterpiece and a touchstone of alternative rock. *—AG*

1988

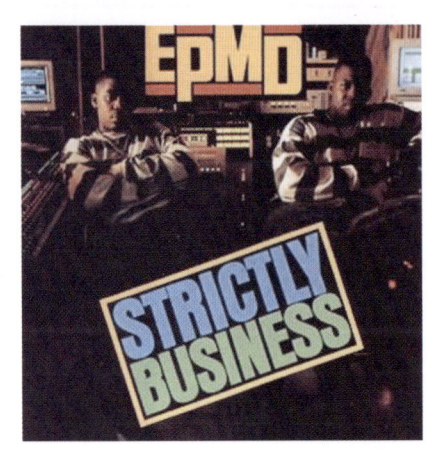

EPMD
STRICTLY BUSINESS
FRESH/SLEEPING BAG | Producers: EPMD
RELEASED: JUNE 7, 1988

● EPMD boldly flipped the script on many of hip-hop's rules with its invigorating 1988 debut album, *Strictly Business*. The duo's laid-back, largely spoken vocal style was a big and highly influential departure from the more animated deliveries of most of its peers. EPMD also made very creative use of samples from the rock world. It rearranged Eric Clapton's version of "I Shot the Sheriff" on the title track and combined ZZ Top and the Steve Miller Band on **You're a Customer**, always keeping its witty rhymes at the forefront. —MW

Jungle Brothers
STRAIGHT OUT THE JUNGLE
WARLOCK | Producers: Jungle Brothers (two songs have uncredited production from Todd Terry and Q-Tip)
RELEASED: NOVEMBER 8, 1988

● The pioneering Native Tongues collective essentially created alternative hip-hop, and Jungle Brothers' debut is where it all begins. Drawing on brittle funk, vintage soul, jazz, and club music while sampling everyone from Marvin Gaye to Prince to Gil Scott-Heron, Mike Gee, Sammy B, and Afrika Baby Bam planted a firm, thoughtful flag for Afrocentrism on classics such as **Black Is Black** and the title track. The trio's relaxed, self-assured style also lent itself well to the record's freewheeling moments, such as the Todd Terry–produced rap-house music mash-up **I'll House You**. —JL

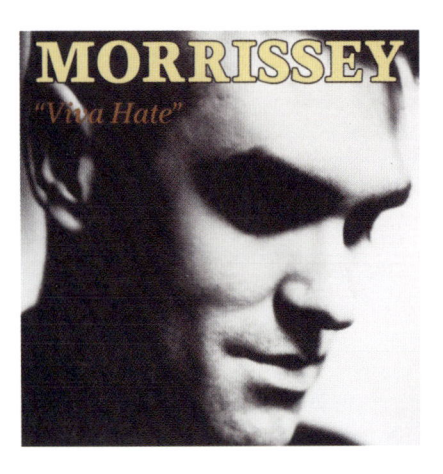

Morrissey
VIVA HATE
SIRE/REPRISE | Producer: Stephen Street
RELEASED: MARCH 14, 1988

● The Smiths' breakup in 1987 did not suddenly make Morrissey a happy camper. If anything, as a title like *Viva Hate* indicated, he was just as morose as he began his solo career but equally tuneful and more adventurous across these twelve tracks. Smiths producer Stephen Street stepped in to replace Johnny Marr as Morrissey's musical accomplice, extending the pomp of the band's last album (*Strangeways, Here We Come*) with more varied textures. The Smiths-style shimmer of the single **Suedehead**, though, made this intriguing set a solid bridge into his future. —GG

My Bloody Valentine
ISN'T ANYTHING
CREATION | Producers: My Bloody Valentine
RELEASED: NOVEMBER 21, 1988

● This monolithic Irish-English shoegaze outfit reached its apex with 1991's *Loveless*, but My Bloody Valentine's journey toward noise rock nirvana began here on the band's debut album. Underneath the dizzying layers of guitar feedback, stacked on top of each other like infinite Tetris blocks, there was quiet interplay between Kevin Shields and Bilinda Butcher, who traded vocal duties. And while the swirl of guitars was intoxicating, there were sobering indie-pop songs hidden inside the guitarmageddon, and they stood out the further you dug inside this precursor to a masterpiece. —AG

New Kids on the Block
HANGIN' TOUGH
COLUMBIA | Producer: Maurice Starr
RELEASED: AUGUST 12, 1988

● Producer Maurice Starr used his New Edition formula on a different group of Boston teens, five photogenic fellas who perfected the boy band template. Though NKOTB's self-titled 1986 debut album stiffed, its follow-up was a certified Block-buster: *Hangin' Tough* gave the boys a rougher-edged sound but still had plenty of puppy-dog ballads just for you, girl. The result: a No. 1 album, two No. 1 singles (**I'll Be Loving You (Forever)**, the title track), 14 million worldwide sales, and the future careers of every boy band to follow. —AG

Pere Ubu
THE TENEMENT YEAR
ENIGMA | Producers: Paul Hamann, Pere Ubu
RELEASED: MARCH 28, 1988

● Pere Ubu was supposedly done by 1982, but when a couple of its members backed David Thomas on his 1987 solo album *Blame the Messenger*, a connection was re-forged. Good thing, too; *The Tenement Year* was a triumphant return, a charged farewell to the group's hometown of Cleveland that incorporated more melody and a more accessible songwriting approach than the arty punk inclinations of the group's previous work. These eleven band-composed songs struck a happy medium, a direction the group delved into even more on subsequent releases. —GG

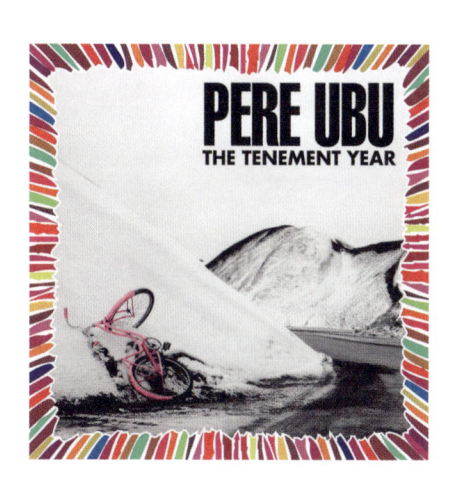

Living Colour
VIVID

EPIC | Producers: Ed Stasium, Mick Jagger
RELEASED: MAY 2, 1988

● It shouldn't be rare or even noteworthy that a band consisting of four Black men made one of the most exciting and popular hard rock albums of the '80s, but that was the case with Living Colour's debut *Vivid*—and sadly, it would probably still be the case today.

After spending four years solidifying its lineup, refining its sound, and building a following around its New York City home, Living Colour got a big break when Mick Jagger became a fan. The Rolling Stones frontman produced two demos that wound up on *Vivid*, and his interest finally helped the band land a record deal. "The fact that he had to come see us, and dig us, for us to get at the back of the line is crazy," guitarist Vernon Reid later told The Ringer. The group made the most of the opportunity, crafting a highly intelligent album that was equally accessible and uncompromising. *Vivid* melded exciting elements from a wide range of diverse genres into a unique mix with both immediate and lasting impact.

The album is best known for the smash hit **Cult of Personality**, which blended a stunning Led Zeppelin–meets–Mahavishnu Orchestra riff with insightful lyrics examining the machinery behind the deification of politicians. The song opened with a dramatic Malcolm X quote: "During the few moments that we have left, we want to talk right down to earth, in a language that everybody can easily understand." And that's exactly what *Vivid* accomplished throughout. **Open Letter (To a Landlord)** painted a disturbing portrait of lower-income housing, while the frantic **Which Way to America** put the racial division in our country into stark relief. It's up to the listener to decide what it means that most of these songs are as relevant today as they were in 1988. —MW

1988

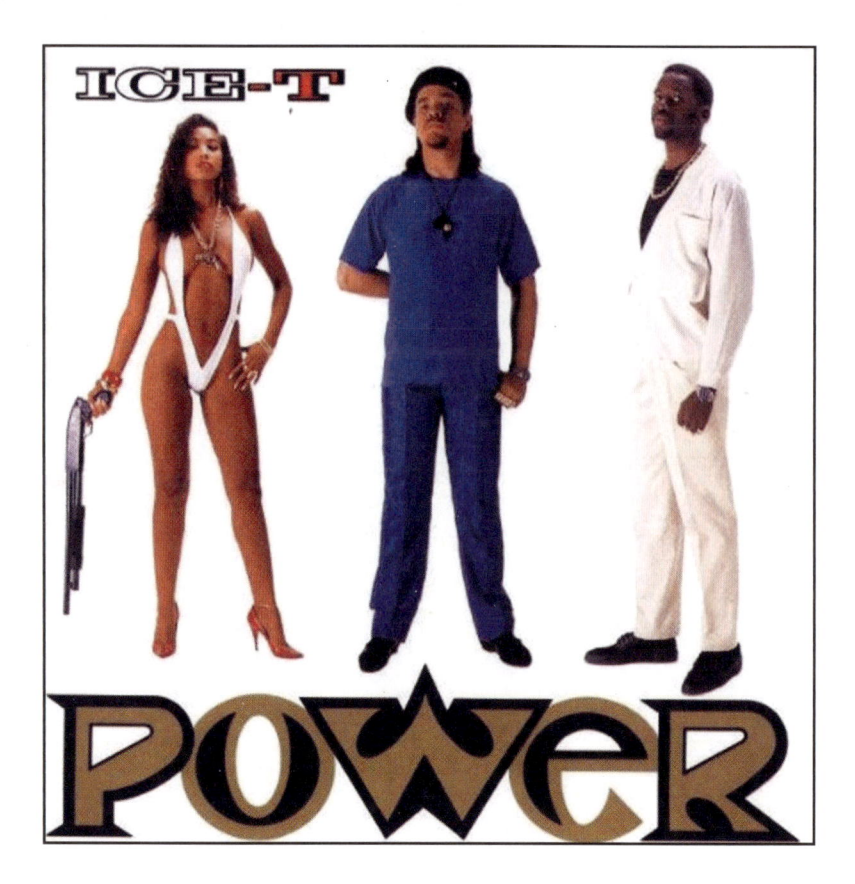

Ice-T
POWER
S I R E | Producers: Ice-T, Afrika Islam
RELEASED: SEPTEMBER 13, 1988

● After helping pioneer the gangsta rap genre with 1987's *Rhyme Pays*, Ice-T doubled down on *Power*, his second album, pushing powerful, gritty tales of Los Angeles street life to listeners across the land. The album cover, featuring Ice-T's girlfriend Darlene Ortiz wearing a provocative one-piece swimsuit and holding a sawed-off shotgun, ruffled plenty of feathers, as did randy sex songs such as **Girls L.G.B.N.A.F.** But beneath the bluster, Ice-T's rhymes frequently criticized the fast-paced hustler lifestyle; **High Rollers** didn't celebrate flashy criminal life as much as it exposed its shortcomings, calling it "a one-way ticket to death row." **I'm Your Pusher**, meanwhile, used Curtis Mayfield's 1972 "Pusherman" (from the *Super Fly* soundtrack) to weave a five-and-a-half-minute metaphor for music as drugs, with Ice as the dealer: "You wanna get high? Let the record play," he urged. (It's one of several songs that takes digs at LL Cool J, an early West Coast/East Coast beef that simmered for several years but cooled off as both rappers went on to successful Hollywood careers.) *Power* presented a complex take on gangsta rap that both entertained and educated, with Ice-T not only as pusher but professor, consistently taking listeners to school. *—AG*

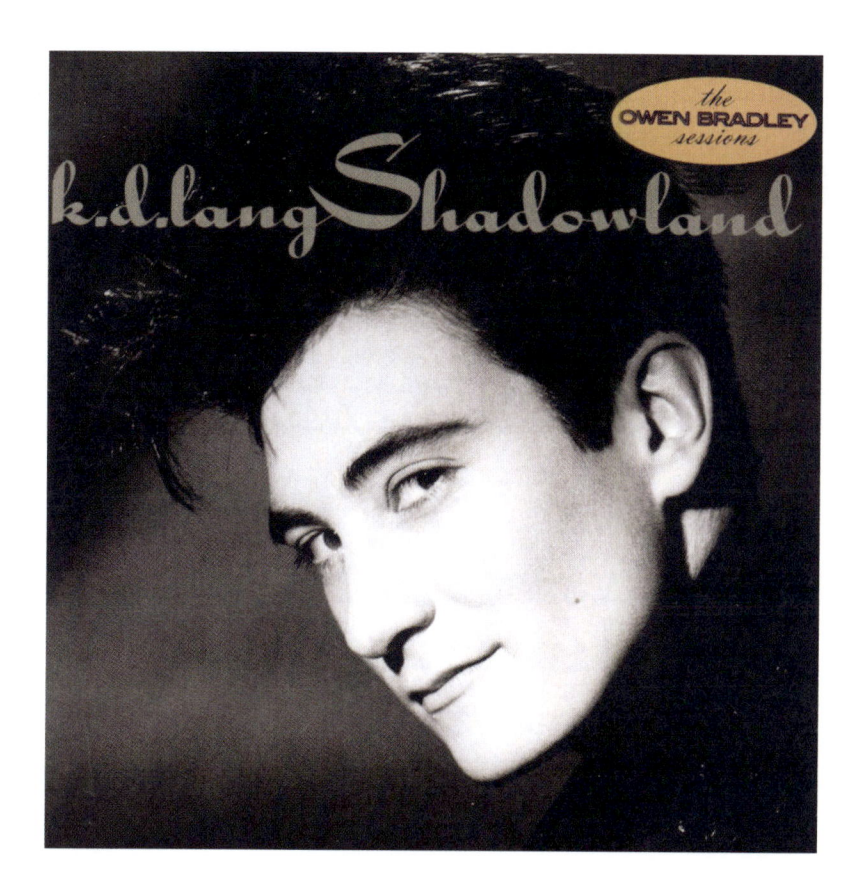

k. d. lang
SHADOWLAND

SIRE | Producer: Owen Bradley
RELEASED: APRIL 26, 1988

● It took an incredible amount of nerve to make this album. k.d. lang was a bit of a novelty at the time; she was retro but modern, country but punk, and without much beyond a buzz fronting the Reclines. She was, however, a generational singing talent with no fear. So, on this, her first album under her own name, lang walked into the hallowed Nashville ground of Owen Bradley's studio and proved she was no fluke. Shadowland was stocked with what made Nashville legendary—songs by Harlan Howard, Cindy Walker, and Roger Miller. Tracks cut with Buddy Emmons, Harold Bradley, Hargus "Pig" Robbins, and the Jordanaires. And in the middle of it all, the kid from Consort, Alberta, delivered the goods. On the ballads **Shadowland** and **Lock, Stock & Teardrops**, she fully revealed her perfect interpretive skills. Phrasing, control, timbre, and tone—it's all there. The most modern track on this set, the Chris Isaak–penned **Western Skies**, was made timeless by lang's performance. This album was not met with open arms on release; some saw it as a nostalgia trip or, worse, a sellout. No, this was an artist taking tradition in her hands and making it her own. Fearless. *—HK*

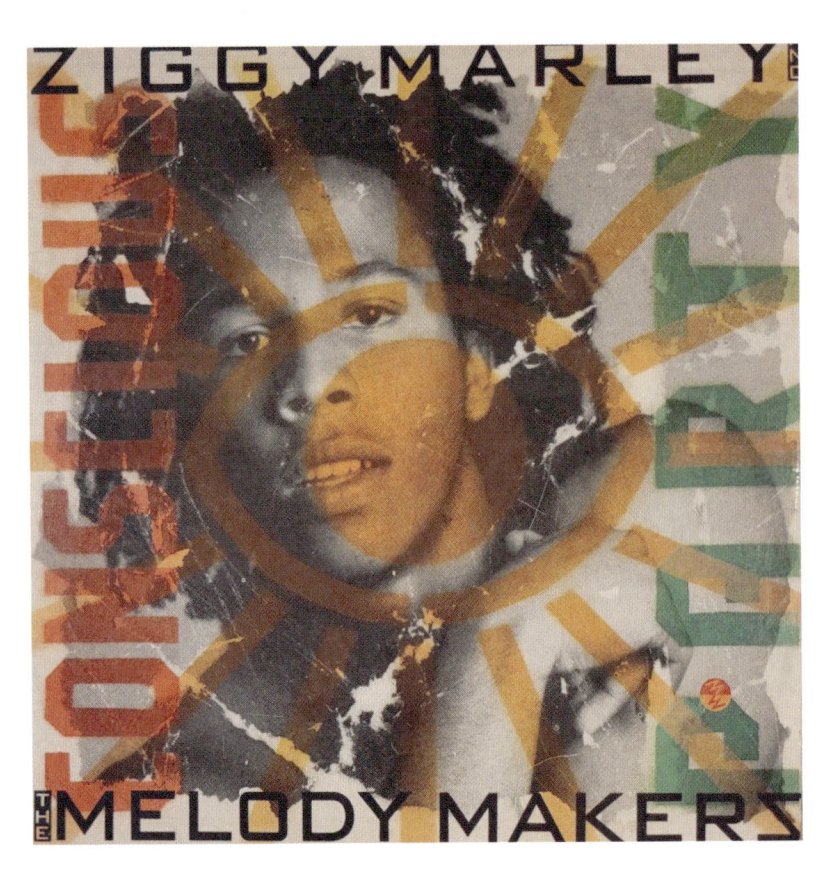

Ziggy Marley and the Melody Makers
CONSCIOUS PARTY

VIRGIN | Producers: Chris Frantz, Tina Weymouth
RELEASED: APRIL 5, 1988

● Being the progeny of an icon is not easy, and it took Bob Marley's oldest son, David (aka Ziggy), and his three siblings (Cedelia, Sharon, and Stephen) in the Melody Makers four albums to find their groove. "I want to be fulfilled myself rather than try to follow exactly in my father's footsteps," Ziggy said when *Conscious Party* was released. With a new label and new producers (Chris Frantz and Tina Weymouth of Talking Heads), the eleven-track set was as much arrival as evolution, thematically more serious and more, well, conscious (song topics included politics, race, social inequities, and the Marleys' African heritage). Sonically, meanwhile, *Conscious Party* took reggae in some new directions, with Frantz explaining, "We tried to get different sounds out of him, modern sounds you didn't hear on reggae records before." It worked—and connected. *Conscious Party* put the Melody Makers in the Top 30 of the Billboard 200 chart and won a Grammy Award for Best Reggae Album. It's a record that upheld and even advanced the family's rich musical legacy, and it's still an inspiring listen now, decades after the Melody Makers spun off into everyone's own careers. *—GG*

Van Morrison & the Chieftains
IRISH HEARTBEAT

MERCURY | Producers: Van Morrison, Paddy Maloney
RELEASED: JUNE 1988

● Much of Van Morrison's career is marked by collaborations—with Mose Allison, Georgie Fame, Lonnie Donegan, Junior Wells, and John Lee Hooker, to name a few. It all started with this unlikely pairing, a group of musical archaeologists and traditionalists from the Republic of Ireland and an R&B-mad singer from Northern Ireland. It made little sense and all the sense in the world at the same time; together, Van Morrison and the Chieftains created an album that was a high point in both of their long and storied careers. The collision of roots music on *Irish Heartbeat* is revelatory. Most of the songs were traditional Irish compositions. The Chieftains brought to that music what they always have: vitality and passion. Morrison was the unknown factor but summoned his soul influences seamlessly. If you thought "Cypress Avenue" was a spiritual adventure, listen to **My Lagan Love** here; Morrison creates a bridge between the Celtic soul and the Delta howl of Son House. **Carrickfergus** was straight-up Ray Charles by way of the Liffey. Two Morrison compositions, the title track and **Celtic Ray**, received the Chieftains treatment and came out fuller. It's too bad additional collaborations never appeared. *—HK*

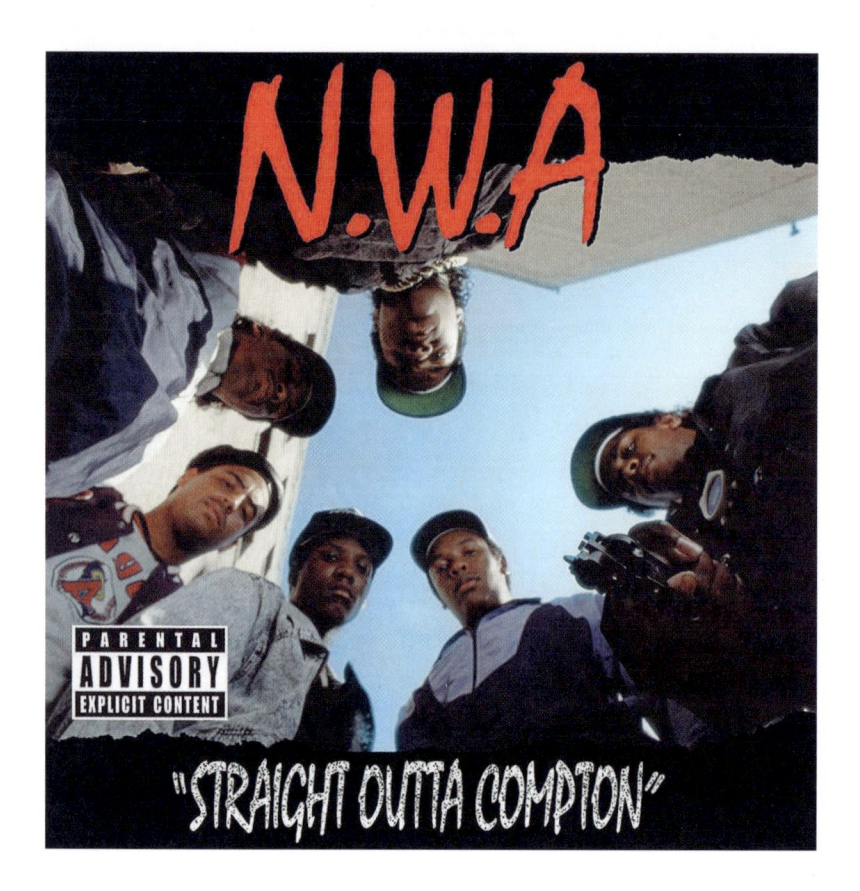

N.W.A
STRAIGHT OUTTA COMPTON

RUTHLESS | Producers: Dr. Dre, DJ Yella
RELEASED: AUGUST 8, 1988

● Rap music was still evolving, commercially and creatively, when the Compton, California–based sextet N.W.A set it off in another direction at the end of the '80s. Its debut became gangsta rap's first platinum-selling LP despite receiving little airplay because of its controversial lyrics. By the early '90s, thanks to N.W.A, the genre was among the most popular in the States, often outselling rock and pop records weekly.

N.W.A—short for "Niggaz Wit Attitudes"—first got together during early 1987 as a vehicle for rapper Eazy-E, who released the multi-artist compilation album *N.W.A and the Posse* later that year on his Ruthless Records label. While members Ice Cube, Dr. Dre, and Arabian Prince appeared on that LP, *Straight Outta Compton* introduced MC Ren and DJ Yella. The group soon changed hip-hop's landscape with an exhilarating and contentious work as significant as Elvis Presley's debut and *Meet the Beatles!* in its history-making gravity.

As soon as the opening title track storms forward, N.W.A unleashed an assault unlike any heard in popular music before. Like Public Enemy and other socially conscious rappers of the era, Eazy-E, Ice Cube, and MC Ren identified domestic injustices without offering solutions to the problems, instead firing their anger like arbitrary shotgun blasts at anyone who gets in their way. "Police think they have the authority to kill a minority," Ice Cube raged in **F*ck tha Police**, the album's most confrontational track (later the focus of an FBI investigation). It's an us-against-them moment that exemplified *Straight Outta Compton*. The members' differences would pull the group apart before long, but for one pivotal album, N.W.A repositioned rap's still-developing geography. *–MG*

1988

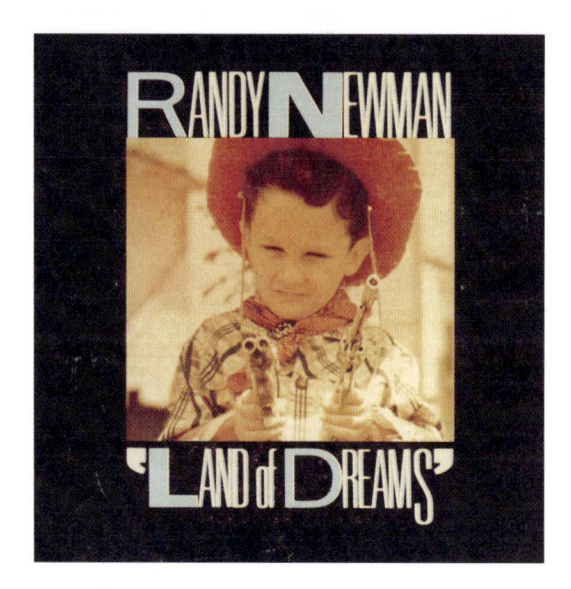

Randy Newman
LAND OF DREAMS

REPRISE | Producers: James Newton Howard, Jeff Lynne, Mark Knopfler, Tommy LiPuma

RELEASED: SEPTEMBER 20, 1988

● Which Randy Newman album contained the singer/songwriter/soundtrack maestro's sole No. 1 Billboard Mainstream Rock chart hit? It had to be *Trouble in Paradise*, with "I Love L.A.," right? Nope. It was *Land of Dreams*, whose **It's Money That Matters** hit that mark for two weeks. Did the hoi polloi finally get hip to Newman's sardonic style—the way his songs' characters tend to say the quiet part out loud, as they do here? Maybe, but it's more likely that rockers heard Mark Knopfler's serrated-edged guitar on the track and connected it with the Dire Straits frontman's own "Money for Nothing." No matter. The '80s was a transitional time for Newman. He turned more toward soundtrack work, got divorced, and on the album's opening salvos—**Dixie Flyer**, **New Orleans Wins the War**, and **Four Eyes**—he uncharacteristically, yet movingly, wrote about his own early life. He was still up to his familiar hijinks on the rap rip **Masterman and Baby J** and at his most trenchant on **I Want You to Hurt Like I Do**, **Roll with the Punches**, and **Follow the Flag**. It's enough to prove that not all of Newman's best '80s work was on the silver screen. *—DD*

Queensrÿche
OPERATION: MINDCRIME

EMI MANHATTAN | Producer: Peter Collins

RELEASED: MAY 3, 1988

● Already a kind of thinking man's metal band, the Seattle quintet Queensrÿche chose its third album to go full-blown conceptual. The Reagan era–inspired tale about a disaffected, drug-addicted youth who becomes an assassin with a revolutionary organization, *Operation: Mindcrime* was inspired by frontman Geoff Tate's own observations of Quebec's violent separatist activists while he was living in Montreal. It took a minute for Tate to convince the rest of the band, but the others eventually bought in and *Mindcrime* became a collaborative, hour-long piece that worked not only because it had a narrative but also because it rocked with a sophisticated ambition, flaunting heady musicianship—particularly by guitarists Michael Wilton and Chris DeGarmo—and epic arrangement sensibilities on tracks such as **Suite Sister Mary** and **Eyes of a Stranger**. The latter gave Queensrÿche its first Mainstream Rock chart hit, followed by **I Don't Believe in Love**. *Mindcrime* was Queensrÿche's first platinum album, too, and the attention it received set up even greater success for its 1990 follow-up, *Empire*. There was an *Operation Mindcrime II* sequel in 2006 that actually charted better than its predecessor, but the original reigned superior. *—GG*

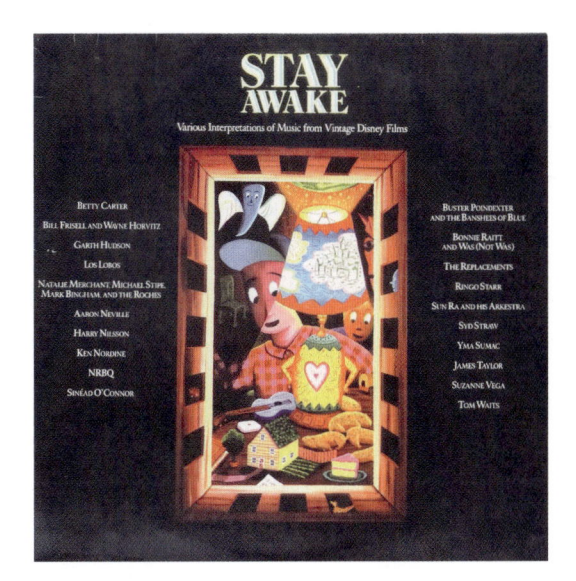

Various Artists
STAY AWAKE: VARIOUS INTERPRETATIONS OF MUSIC FROM VINTAGE DISNEY FILMS

A & M | Producer: Hal Willner
RELEASED: OCTOBER 11, 1988

● It takes a real talent to convince artists to get in the studio and reinvent songs that have anchored themselves in the minds of millions of moviegoers. But here, producer Hal Willner did just that. Tom Waits made **Heigh Ho** from *Snow White* to a futuristic, ambient blues, as one might expect from him. Bonnie Raitt and Was (Not Was) freed **Baby Mine** from the constraints of late-'30s pop music and created a soul lullaby that could have been born in Muscle Shoals. It also takes real insight to build something new out of something old; this is where Willner's vision soared. He created medleys with performances by artists with no apparent connection and made them work beyond expectation. Of the five medleys, none was as unlikely as the blended performance from the Band's Garth Hudson, NRBQ, Betty Carter, the Replacements, and Bill Frisell and Wayne Horvitz, which simply soared. —*HK*

Various Artists
TECHNO! THE NEW DANCE SOUND OF DETROIT

10/VIRGIN | Producers: Various
RELEASED: MAY 1988

● Move over, Motown, Detroit had a new sound, and it was called techno. The Detroit electronic scene was in its infancy when British DJ and journalist Neil Rushton stumbled across a record released on the Transmat label from the Motor City. He fell in love with the fresh new dance sound and, after some investigation, discovered there was a plethora of amazing and vibrant talent from the area. Soon after, he released this compilation, which became one of the most important releases in the history of electronic music, exposing the world to the artistry of Juan Atkins, Derrick May, Kevin Saunderson, Eddie Fowlkes, and Blake Baxter—all architects of this fresh new sound. Futuristic beats and plush, layered synth lines with a soulful, hypnotic backbone became the new zenith of electronic music. The Inner City song **Big Fun** was released as a single in the U.K. and became a worldwide dance smash, often cited as one of the greatest dance songs ever. One cannot understate the beauty and innovation that is represented throughout this album, nor its influence on generations of electronic music artists. —*MH*

K. T. Oslin
THIS WOMAN
R C A | Producers: Harold Shedd, Jim Cotton, Joe Scaife
RELEASED: AUGUST 1988

● Getting a recording deal at the age of forty-five is a rare feat—at any time, by anybody. But Kay Toinette "K. T." Oslin had the moxie to make that happen, and the talent to make it work at a chart-topping, platinum level. It helped that she was not only a songwriter herself (which the Arkansas native, who started in a folk trio with Guy Clark in Texas, began as a hobby) but also understood the craft inside and out, partly the result of extensive work on the musical stage, including Broadway appearances in *Promises, Promises* and *West Side Story* and in television commercials (one for a hemorrhoid cream). By the time RCA Records signed her, Oslin was what the industry would come to call a complete "package."

She was a hit from the get-go with 1987's *80s Ladies* and then further refined her singing and songcraft with its follow-up. *This Woman* was platinum like its predecessor, with four Top 20 country hits; Oslin wrote or co-wrote all ten tracks and displayed just as much unapologetic defiance and lyrical depth as she had on *80s Ladies*. The title track here made it clear that Oslin was a strong-willed woman to be reckoned with, and her performances of **Money**, **Where Is a Woman to Go**, **Hold Me**, the sultry **Hey Bobby**, and **Didn't Expect It to Go Down This Way** were stellar—and soulful.

With only six studio albums to her credit, Oslin and her forward-thinking songs have been unintentionally consigned to the deeper regions of country music history (and pop, for that matter). But from Trisha Yearwood to Shania Twain to Lainey Wilson, and maybe even Beyoncé, Oslin (who passed away in 2020 at age 78) was an underappreciated flag-bearer for women's place in the genre. *—GG*

Pixies
SURFER ROSA
4 A D | Producer: Steve Albini
RELEASED: MARCH 21, 1988

● When Pixies released its debut album *Surfer Rosa*, few would have tagged it then as one of the most important records in alternative rock history. But years of praise and influence have slung it to the top of the pile, a key album in developing the music as a genre and an innovative work that has inspired artists of subsequent generations. Taken within the context of the era, *Surfer Rosa* still sounds like a visionary moment in 1980s rock—that it's lost none of its primal appeal over the years adds to the legacy.

As the Boston-based quartet of singer and guitarist Black Francis, bassist and singer Kim Deal, guitarist Joey Santiago, and drummer David Lovering began recording *Surfer Rosa* in late 1987 with producer Steve Albini, it had one EP, that year's *Come On Pilgrim*, to its name. Made in ten days in fly-on-the-wall style—studio conversations can be heard in the finished record—the album undercut Francis's serrated vocals, occasionally sung in Spanish, with Deal's less ragged backing. Pop melodies collided with college-rock bite, while songs unexpectedly accelerated or slowed to a crawl, depending on the mood.

Yet it's the band's celebrated soft-loud dynamism that's kept interest in *Surfer Rosa* thriving for so many years. Centerpiece songs **Gigantic**, **Where Is My Mind?**, and **Cactus** signaled a turning point in indie rock, a balance that grew in popularity as the alt-rock revolution took shape during the early part of the '90s. Nirvana noted the influence of Pixies on its landmark *Nevermind*, ensuring most '90s modern-rock giants were touched, directly or indirectly, by *Surfer Rosa*. The group made three more albums—the last, 1991's *Trompe le Monde*, was released the same day as *Nevermind*—before breaking up. A reunion during the mid-2000s, continuing now without Deal, brought more records. *—MG*

Don Pullen
NEW BEGINNINGS
BLUE NOTE | Producer: Michael Cuscuna
RELEASED: DECEMBER 16, 1988

● Don Pullen's peerless and astonishing jazz piano technique, filled with waves of block chords, clusters of notes, and glissandos, was fully revealed on this trio recording with drummer Tony Williams and bassist Gary Peacock. Known as an avant-garde pianist and organist, Pullen gained notoriety in bassist Charles Mingus's band during the '70s. On **New Beginnings**, he wove cunning and thoroughly accessible melodies amid staggering amounts of swirling notes and tricky chord passages. Best was the masterwork **Silence = Death**, a gorgeous, twelve-minute piano solo. *—CH*

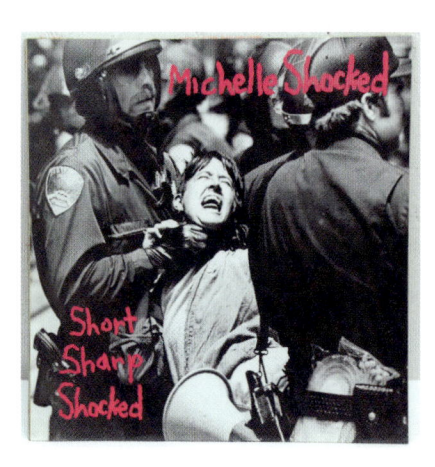

Michelle Shocked
SHORT SHARP SHOCKED
MERCURY | Producer: Pete Anderson
RELEASED: AUGUST 15, 1988

● Michelle Shocked's sophomore effort—really her first proper release following the Walkman-recorded *Texas Campfire Tapes*—revealed a still-raw talent of seemingly limitless potential. **Anchorage** is the song everyone remembers, but Shocked delivered other sharp (though not necessarily short) originals as well as a pensive cover of Jean Ritchie's **The L&M Don't Stop Here Anymore** with equal aplomb. Shocked's miscreant reputation would later sink her career, but here it's only hinted at by a tacked-on, untitled punk fusillade and an album cover showing Shocked being choked by an otherwise-bored cop. *—DD*

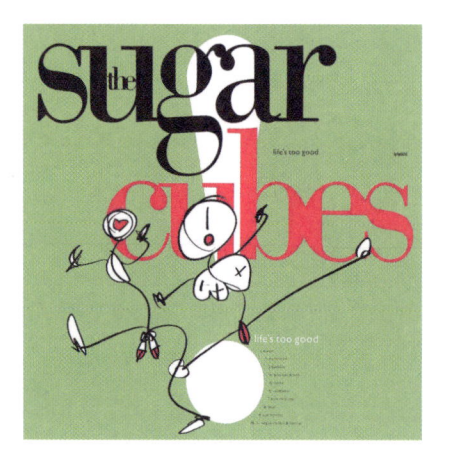

The Sugarcubes
LIFE'S TOO GOOD
ELEKTRA | Producers: Ray Shulman, Derek Birkett
RELEASED: APRIL 25, 1988

● From Reykjavik, Iceland, the Sugarcubes were literally cool, playing abundantly quirky pop that could be mesmerizing thanks in part to the sonic-boom voice of pre-solo-fame Björk Guðmundsdóttir. The troupe's 1988 debut album was the most accessible of its three studio albums and also the shortest (a brisk thirty-three minutes). It was unexpectedly successful all over the world, with the overdrive **Motorcrash** registering as a hit. That was Björk at her most accessible—immediately followed by the weird, warped, and bent **Birthday**, with the vocalist's yowl at her Björkiest. Beguilingly strange. *—DM*

Keith Whitley
DON'T CLOSE YOUR EYES

R C A | Producers: Garth Fundis, Keith Whitley, Blake Mevis
RELEASED: MAY 31, 1988

● On his second full-length album, bluegrass-turned-country singer Keith Whitley spun his buttery-rich baritone into several weepers and honky-tonkers, including three No. 1 hits; the title track, a George Jones–worthy tissue-grabber; the gentle **When You Say Nothing at All**; and **I'm No Stranger to the Rain**, a finely wrought mid-tempo depression diary. Sadly, Whitley died of alcohol poisoning at thirty-four, a year after its release. But he inspired many, from Dierks Bentley to Morgan Wallen. Alison Krauss's tribute-album version of **When You Say Nothing at All** in 1995 was a fine homage. —LM

Lucinda Williams
LUCINDA WILLIAMS

ROUGH TRADE | Producers: Gurf Morlix, Dusty Wakeman, Lucinda Williams
RELEASED: JUNE 1988

● Lucinda Williams's ascent from the coffeehouse to A-list singer/songwriter was quick. Signed to Rough Trade Records, she navigated an eight-year gap between records to emerge as a new, pure voice anchored in the music and literature of the American South. Williams owned an expressive alto with a charming lilt and a lyrical gift that quickly resulted in recognition from many major artists. Mary Chapin Carpenter and Tom Petty each had hits with songs from this record. On her own merits, this was the arrival of a truly great American artist. —HK

BeBe & CeCe Winans
HEAVEN

SPARROW/CAPITOL | Producer: Keith Thomas
RELEASED: SEPTEMBER 1988

● This brother-sister pair had already made good on the pedigree of one of gospel's great families and truly came into their own with their third album. With help from Whitney Houston on two tracks, *Heaven* was BeBe & CeCe's first No. 1 on Billboard's Gospel charts and housed their first No. 1 Christian hit, **Lost Without You**, a crossover success in the R&B Top 10, too. The actual singing was the best part of *Heaven*, however—two voices that, when together, truly became more than the sum of their parts. —GG

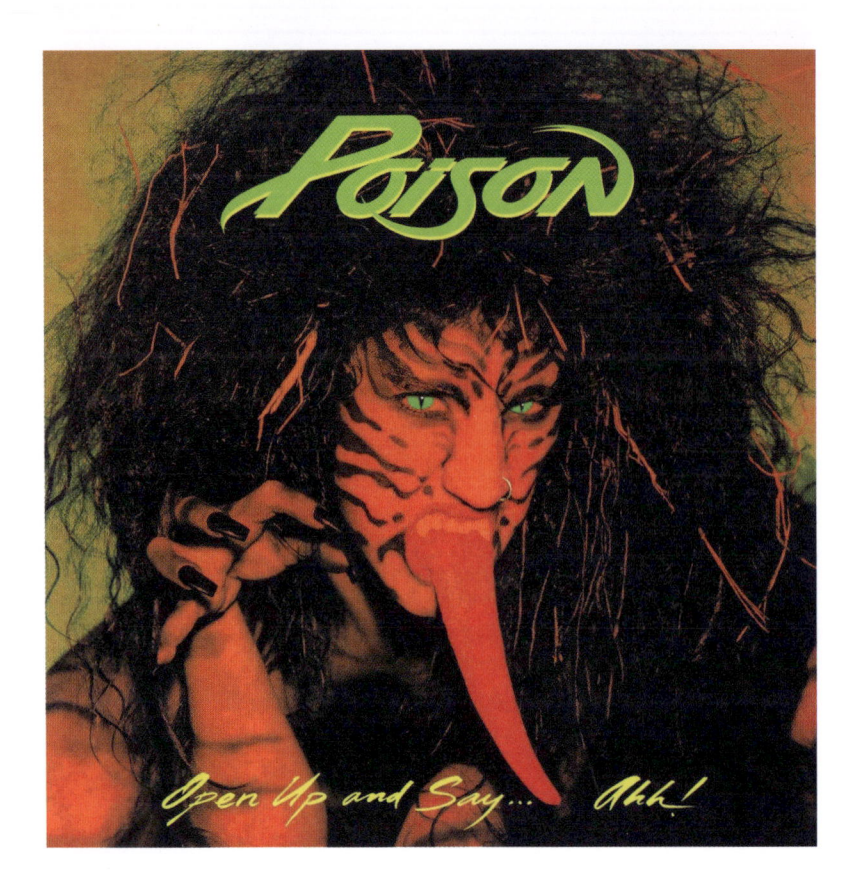

Poison
OPEN UP AND SAY . . . AHH!

ENIGMA | Producer: Tom Werman
RELEASED: APRIL 27, 1988

● Poison clearly stated the purpose for its second album with its first single—**Nothin' but a Good Time**.

That's exactly what the Pennsylvania-formed Los Angeles band was after following 1986's *Look What the Cat Dragged In*, a stake-claiming Top 5 debut that gave Poison a foothold in the Sunset Strip glam-metal scene (and was, until *Open Up and Say . . . Ahh!*, the best-selling album in independent Enigma Records' history). Poison followed that up with a cover of Kiss's "Rock and Roll All Nite" for the *Less Than Zero* soundtrack—ironic since the quartet was hoping to have Kiss's Paul Stanley produce *Open Up . . . .* That did not pan out, but the well-credentialed Tom Werman was a fine fill-in. He understood both sounds and songs, helping Poison put even more Teflon sheen on this batch of ten and make sure there were few wasted notes across its thirty-six-minute run time.

Nothin' but a Good Time, with its Kiss-derived riff, gave Poison the "big, kick-ass arena anthem" frontman Bret Michaels most wanted and the band its highest-charting single to date. There was more where that came from, too, in pop-flavored rockers such as the propulsive **Fallen Angel**, **Love on the Rocks**, **Back to the Rocking Horse**, and **Tearin' Down the Walls**. A high-octane cover of Loggins and Messina's **Your Mama Don't Dance**, meanwhile, was an effective gimmick.

But it was the power ballad **Every Rose Has Its Thorn**, which Michaels wrote in a Dallas laundromat after hearing another man's voice over the phone at his girlfriend's apartment, that was the real mainstream breakthrough—No. 1 on the Billboard Hot 100, gold certified, and capable of draining an arena's worth of Bic lighters during its four minutes and twenty seconds. Thanks to all that, *Ahh!* was definitely an exclamation of pleasure. *—GG*

1988

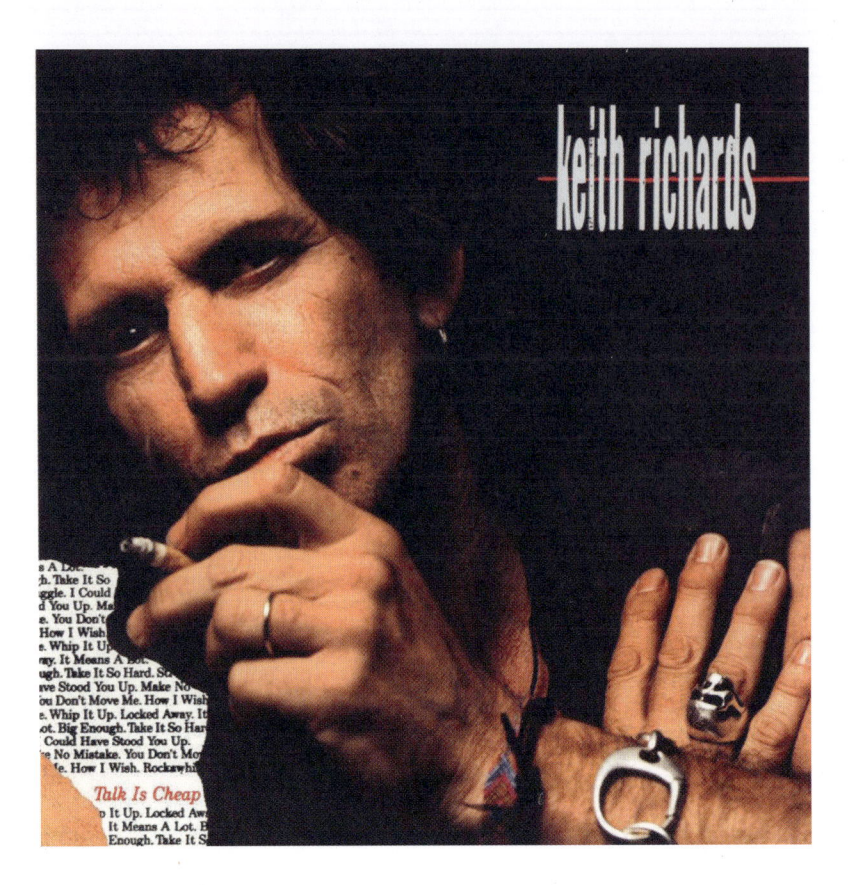

Keith Richards
TALK IS CHEAP
V I R G I N | Producers: Keith Richards, Steve Jordan
RELEASED: OCTOBER 3, 1988

● It's been said a lot and not without cause. Yes, this would have been an extraordinary Rolling Stones album. But it wasn't. And it wasn't made to be one. *Talk Is Cheap* was Keith Richards's musical statement, no different from any solo record made by a member of the Stones. Because Richards was, and is, a talismanic figure, more weight was ascribed to it than, say, *Gimme Some Neck* by Ronnie Wood. Then again, there was a lot more riding on it.

The Rolling Stones was in disarray at the time, and the arrival of Richards's first solo album was a statement. No surprise, *Talk Is Cheap* is built around grooves and riffs. It's downright filthy and stocked with the key elements Richards consistently embraced since picking up a guitar. From the funky bubbling bass of Bootsy Collins on the album opener **Big Enough**, it was practically an R&B/rock 'n' roll travelogue. That track was pure King Records funk. **I Could Have Stood You Up** sounded like the lost outtake from Chuck Berry's "Back in the U.S.A."/"Almost Grown" session, complete with Johnnie Johnson on piano. **Make No Mistake** was a map of Memphis, right down to the inclusion of Ben Cauley and Andrew Love on horns.

Attention must be pointed to the X-Pensive Winos, the band Richards and co-producer Steve Jordan assembled for this record and subsequent tour. No band Richards played in could avoid Stones comparisons, but this was a legit group that provided the "loosely tight" vibe necessary to carve out its own identity. The cuts that feature just this core band—**Whip It Up**, **Take It So Hard**, and **It Means a Lot**—were simply excellent, unadorned, swinging rock 'n' roll. Seriously, what else would you expect from Keith Richards? *–HK*

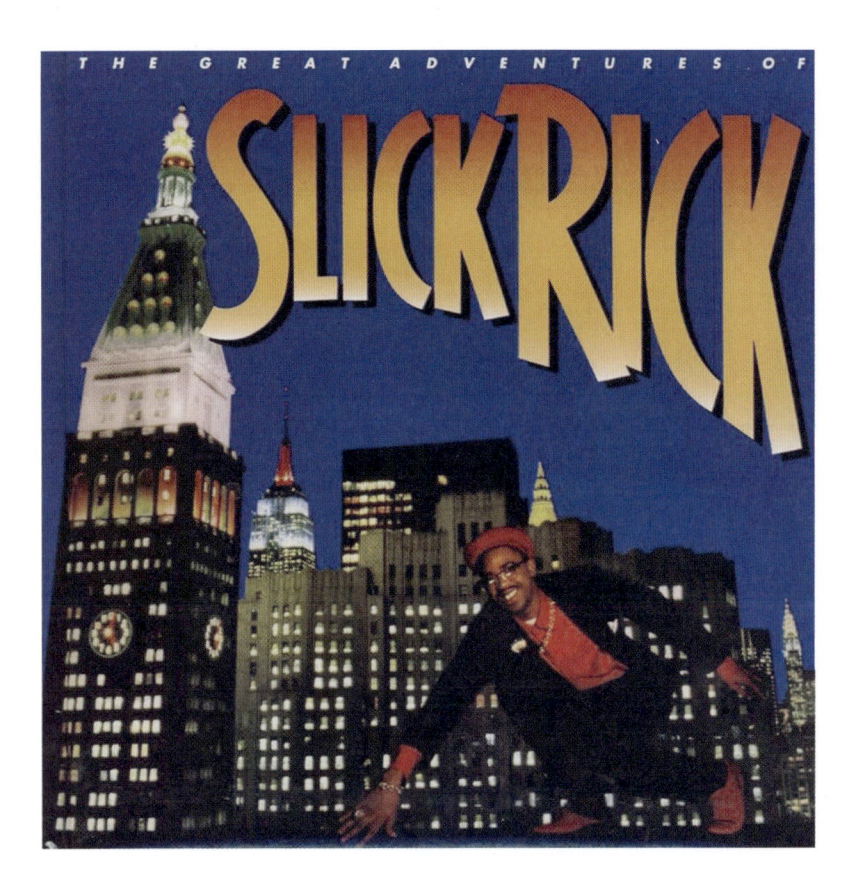

Slick Rick

THE GREAT ADVENTURES OF SLICK RICK

DEF JAM/COLUMBIA | Producers: Jam Master Jay, Jerry Martin, Slick Rick, The Bomb Squad

RELEASED: NOVEMBER 1, 1988

● On Doug E. Fresh's smash 1985 single "The Show"/"La Di Da Di," Slick Rick (then going by MC Ricky D) brought an easygoing charm to a seminal release from the Original Human Beat Box. But with the release of his debut album *The Great Adventures of Slick Rick*, the London-born, New York City–based emcee did more than deliver a classic—he created the most lyrically influential rap record of the decade.

While listeners to the nascent genre had heard brittle 808s, clever soul samples, and deft record scratches from other artists, no one had heard hip-hop storytelling on this level before. In a soothing, sly drawl, Slick Rick spun concise stories full of vivid, unobtrusive details, NSFW one-liners, and unexpected moments of humanity. His wise-ass, cartoonishly crass jokes—oft imitated but rarely bested—attracted as many critics as fans, and while it was hard not to be bothered by the rampant misogyny on the album, it was equally difficult not to be impressed by Rick's pithy punchlines. (That being said, the racist, violent **Indian Girl (An Adult Story)** was indefensible even as a prank.)

For each **Treat Her Like a Prostitute** and **Lick the Balls** there were bittersweet message songs such as **Hey Young World** and **Teenage Love**, with the latter finding the emcee dispensing wisdom and empathy to those reeling from their first heartbreak. The finest moment on the album (and, for some folks, '80s rap in general) came with **Children's Story**. A brutal, brisk account of a seventeen-year-old caught in a street violence spiral in the form of a bedtime story (complete with Rick doing high-pitched voices for the confounded kids), the haunting, hard-to-shake hit paved the way for rap raconteurs from Nas to Jay-Z to Busta Rhymes. —JL

Public Enemy
IT TAKES A NATION OF MILLIONS TO HOLD US BACK

DEF JAM | Producers: Hank Shocklee, Carl Ryder
RELEASED: JUNE 28, 1988

● There were hip-hop albums before Public Enemy's *It Takes a Nation of Millions to Hold Us Back*, but there weren't any hip-hop albums like this one: a revolutionary work that transformed an evolving genre into a respected art form. Earlier records from Run-D.M.C., Eric B. & Rakim, and Beastie Boys helped set the template for long-form rap releases, but like the initial LPs released during rock 'n' roll's beginning years, most hip-hop albums were a mix of time-filling tracks assembled around one or two great singles.

Public Enemy, whose debut album *Yo! Bum Rush the Show* was released in 1987, was determined to deliver something more ambitious for its follow-up. Using Marvin Gaye's 1971 social-change classic *What's Going On* as inspiration, rappers Chuck D and Flavor Flav, DJ Terminator X, and the Hank Shocklee–led production team the Bomb Squad opened a new chapter in hip-hop history here. A pair of previous singles—**Rebel Without a Pause** and **Bring the Noise**—were featured, but the fifty-seven-minute album was conceived and constructed as a single piece to be absorbed from start to finish.

Like *What's Going On*, *It Takes a Nation . . .* spotlighted key songs that made even more sense when fit into the bigger picture. From the appropriately distorted intro **Countdown to Armageddon** to the closing group chant **Party for Your Right to Fight**, the album surveyed societal and cultural concerns at the end of the '80s, from the Black experience to trash TV, with a combination of aggression and consciousness that helped spur a new movement in hip-hop. Not even gangsta rap, arriving with a shotgun blast the next year, would soften the impact of Public Enemy's eternal masterpiece. *—MG*

1988

Sonic Youth
DAYDREAM NATION
E N I G M A | Producers: Sonic Youth, Nicholas Sansano
RELEASED: OCTOBER 18, 1988

● **Teen Age Riot**, the Trojan horse lead-in track to Sonic Youth's fifth album, was the most accessible song the New York noisemakers had made in a career noted for its inaccessibility. *Daydream Nation*, which was also the band's most ambitious album, wound itself around art-punk, post-punk, noise rock, alt-rock, and avant-garde side trips over seventy escalating minutes. The double LP arrived with a new co-producer in Nicholas Sansano, best known for his work with hip-hop artists Ice Cube and Public Enemy; the band's fourth label since 1983's debut, *Confusion Is Sex*; and its decision to construct songs from in-studio jam sessions for the first time.

Even at nearly seven minutes, and a lengthy intro in which bassist Kim Gordon recited, over a repeated burring guitar line, what's either a stream-of-consciousness poem or random words that popped into her head, **Teen Age Riot** stood out in Sonic Youth's catalog for its use of a traditional verse-chorus-verse structure and Thurston Moore's verging-on-pop guitar and vocal melodies. The next song, the noisier but still relatively straightforward **Silver Rocket**, continued along that line. And then Sonic Youth dropped the facade.

Starting with Gordon's appropriately named, seven-and-a-half-minute **The Sprawl**, *Daydream Nation* returned to familiar territory with oddly tuned guitars, experimental no-wave noise excursions, and some musique concrete. By the closing **Trilogy**, three disparate tracks stitched together into a fourteen-minute suite, Sonic Youth had made its masterpiece. When its next album, *Goo*, came out in 1990, the quartet was on another label (and first for a major), providing enough radio support for a minor hit. A little more than a year after that, Nirvana's *Nevermind* launched a music revolution. As Kurt Cobain told anyone who'd listen, Sonic Youth's *Daydream Nation* helped pave the way. *–MG*

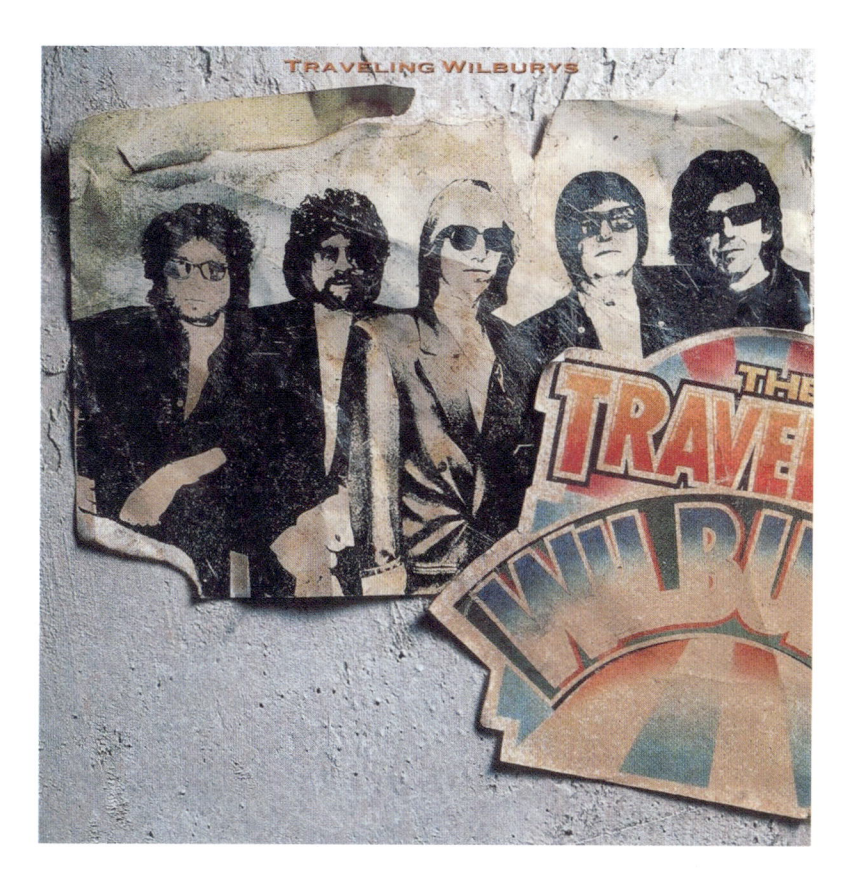

Traveling Wilburys
VOLUME 1

WILBURY/WARNER BROS. | Producers: Nelson Wilbury (George Harrison), Otis Wilbury (Jeff Lynne)
RELEASED: OCTOBER 1988

● The Traveling Wilburys was the antithesis of a rock star supergroup—except you couldn't get much more super than George Harrison, Bob Dylan, Tom Petty, Jeff Lynne, and Roy Orbison, which is why they chose pseudonyms. Dropping their identities (and egos) liberated them to create rootsy, harmony-rich rock simply as friends and respected colleagues.

The relaxed charm of Harrison's **Handle with Care**, a mini-autobiography deemed too good to "waste" as a B-side single, inspired and set the tone for *Traveling Wilburys Volume 1*, aided by the nudge-nudge, wink-wink of Monty Pythoner Michael Palin's hilariously mythologized history. More subversive humor appeared in **Dirty World**, Dylan's double entendre–filled attempt to "do one like Prince," which dropped musical references to Prince's *Dirty Mind* album, the Standells' "Dirty Water," and Dylan's own "Stuck Inside of Mobile with the Memphis Blues Again." It was some of his best work in ages—except for **Tweeter and the Monkey Man**, written in Bruce Springsteen's style and filled with his song titles, and **Congratulations**, which ends with a sweet Abbey Road choral flourish.

The Lynne-led rockabilly gave up **Rattled**, Petty's reggae-ish **Last Night**, and Orbison's operatic **Not Alone Any More**, dressed with sha-la-la-la's and twangy guitar, provided further delights; **Handle with Care**, **Heading for the Light** (another upbeat Harrison song about spiritual enlightenment), and **End of the Line** (which summarized their collaborative joy with the line, "I'm just glad to be here, happy to be alive") became hits. Petty, Orbison, and Dylan all got career boosts from the album, which grabbed a Grammy nomination for Album of the Year and won for Best Rock Performance by a Duo or Group. Sadly, the Wilbury brotherhood lost Orbison six weeks after its release but dedicated its follow-up, 1990's *Traveling Wilburys Volume 3*, to Lefty. **–LM**

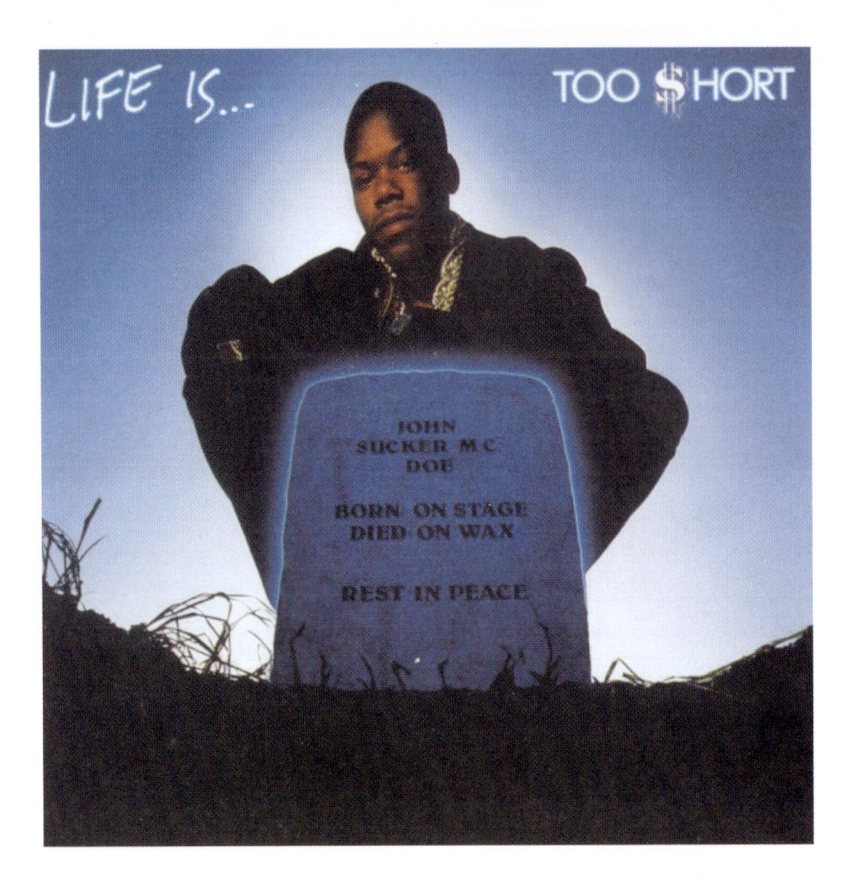

Too $hort
LIFE IS . . . TOO $HORT

DANGEROUS MUSIC | Producers: Ted Bohanon, Too $hort
RELEASED: JANUARY 31, 1988

● By 1988, Oakland, California, rapper Too $hort had established and even perfected his laid-back style, which was on full display on *Life Is . . . Too $hort*, his fifth album, and the one that brought his freaky tales to the masses.

Todd Shaw was born in South Central Los Angeles but moved to Oakland in his teen years, and he released his self-produced debut album *Don't Stop Rappin'* in 1985, when he was nineteen years old. He hustled his way through several more sets of sordid sex stories, selling tapes out of the trunk of his car, becoming a regional sensation, and eventually attracting the attention of Jive Records, which gave him a national platform for his pimp rhymes beginning with 1987's *Born to Mack*. He was never going to win any lyrical competitions with his simplistic rhyme schemes and elementary flow, but Too $hort sold them with flair, his distinctive nasally voice turning his delivery of the word "biiiitch!" into its own catchphrase—so much so that it would still be his signature even decades later.

He said it plenty on *Life Is . . .* , which mines '70s funk grooves for inspiration, filling out the bottom-heavy, trunk-rattling bass sound that became his sonic trademark. Too $hort took his time on the album, stretching four songs past the six-minute mark and recounting his own origin story on the languid **I Ain't Trippin'**. Meanwhile, **CussWords** featured nearly eight minutes of bedroom-based brags and boasts, including a story of receiving oral sex from First Lady Nancy Reagan. That specific imagery didn't so much spark outrage as it earned *Life Is . . .* a level of infamy that made it a must-hear on the nation's playgrounds and school buses, and eventually led to the album's double-platinum sales and the breakthrough moment for the rap icon in the making. *—AG*

Ultramagnetic MCs
CRITICAL BEATDOWN
NEXT PLATEAU | Producers: Ced-Gee, Ultramagnetic MCs
RELEASED: OCTOBER 4, 1988

● No one else in rap sounds quite like Ultramagnetic MCs, and rap doesn't quite sound the same without Ultramagnetic MCs. The Bronx collective's debut album marked a critical moment in hip-hop's evolution, with its dense layers of sampling helping to influence the sonic techniques favored by Public Enemy's Bomb Squad production team. Producer Ced-Gee's affinity for James Brown samples popularized the Godfather of Soul's breaks across hip-hop's spectrum, and a piano loop from Joe Cocker's "Woman to Woman" on **Funky** formed the musical bed over which 2Pac later serenaded the Golden State on "California Love."

But Ultramagnetic MCs' innovations were hardly limited to production. Critical Beatdown acted as the introduction of Kool Keith, hip-hop's most oddball presence, who even in a relatively grounded state—he didn't fully depart Earth until he adopted his Dr. Octagon guise in the mid-'90s—still made for delightfully strange company. "I pull your skull out, move it with a tractor," he rapped on **Funky**, just a few lines after bragging that his voice causes earthquakes in Michigan. His free associative non sequiturs spilled out fast and loose on Critical Beatdown and were perfectly melded to Ced-Gee's beats, even when his cadences and references made sense mainly to himself.

Critical Beatdown's influence and critical appeal outweighed its commerciality, and it was retroactively exposed to new audiences following a high-profile Prodigy sample in 1997 ("Smack My Bitch Up" is built around a line from **Give the Drummer Some**) and a deluxe repackaging in 2004. After a brief split in 1990, the group reunited and made several more albums, but none had the long tail of Critical Beatdown, a golden effort from hip-hop's new-school era that wasn't just ahead of its time—it was out of time, sounding like nothing else that came before or after. –AG

19

89

1989

Aerosmith
PUMP
GEFFEN | Producer: Bruce Fairbairn
RELEASED: SEPTEMBER 12, 1989

● With 1987's *Permanent Vacation*, Aerosmith pulled off what might be the most amazing comeback in rock history, completely revitalizing its career with a hit-filled, multiplatinum album that fully connected with the modern music world while staying true to the band's roots. Then even more incredibly, two years later, the Boston quintet topped it with *Pump*. Sticking with *Permanent Vacation* producer Bruce Fairbairn but dialing back on the outside co-writers, Aerosmith delivered a sharper, harder-hitting album, forcing the mainstream to meet the band a bit further over to their side of the fence on smash hits such as **Love in an Elevator**.

At this point it must be stated that Aerosmith's first post-reunion album, 1985's down-and-dirty, Ted Templeman–produced *Done with Mirrors*, was a tragically underrated and wrongfully ignored album that any fan of the band's '70s glory days would love.

Beyond reaffirming past strengths, as the group did by adding the yearning **What It Takes** to its repertoire of beautiful ballads, *Pump* found Aerosmith breaking exciting new ground. Nowhere was this more clear than on **Janie's Got a Gun**, a haunting tale of child abuse and revenge whose lyrics reportedly took lead singer Steven Tyler nine months to complete. Recorded in Vancouver at the same time and in the same studio where Mötley Crüe was recording its own commercial high point, *Dr. Feelgood*—Tyler sang backing vocals on three tracks on that album—*Pump* also featured plenty of bracing rock, most notably the opening one-two punch of **Young Lust** and **F.I.N.E.**

Although 1993's *Get a Grip* would match *Pump* in terms of commercial success, the band's formula also started to get a bit stale, leaving *Pump* as the undisputed peak of Aerosmith's second golden era. —MW

1989

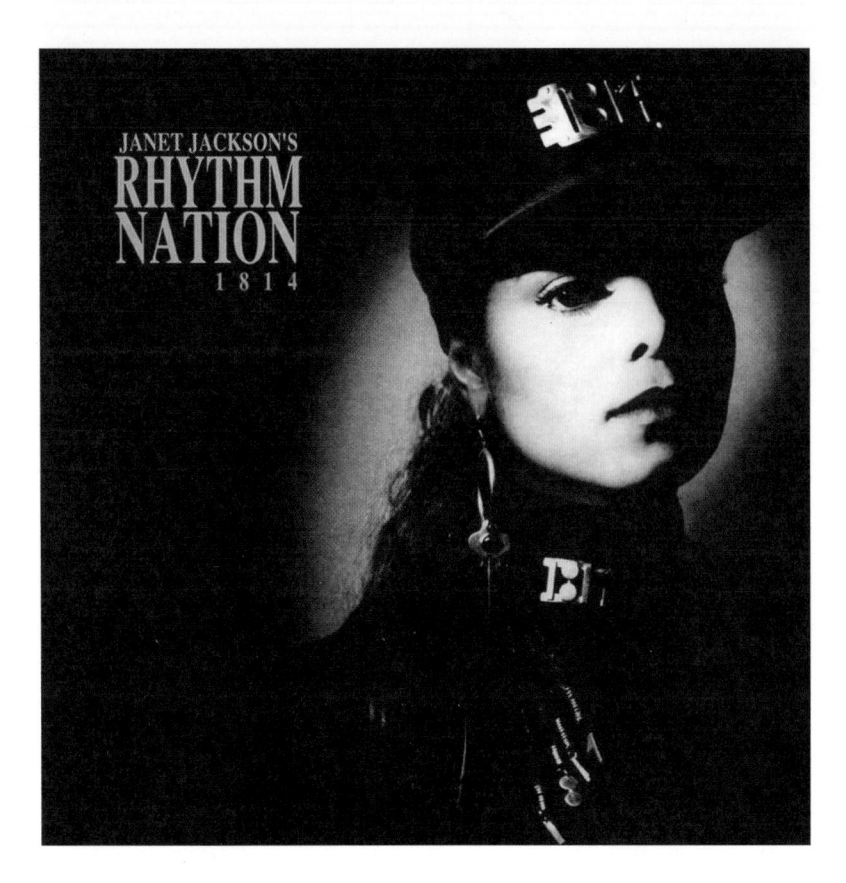

Janet Jackson
JANET JACKSON'S RHYTHM NATION 1814

A & M | Producers: Jimmy Jam, Terry Lewis, Janet Jackson, Jellybean Johnson

RELEASED: SEPTEMBER 19, 1989

● Janet Jackson was coming off a No. 1 album with five Top 5 singles when her label started pushing for a repeat. But the twenty-two-year-old singer and youngest sibling of the superstar Jackson dynasty had something else in mind, something bigger and more ambitious. Something like a concept album about sociopolitical issues of the day encompassing women's rights, Black equality, and urban decay. She'd still have songs about love and other Top 40–safe subjects, and *Control* producers Jimmy Jam and Terry Lewis would return. But, as its scholastic title implied, *Janet Jackson's Rhythm Nation 1814* was more aspiring in its scope.

The hour-plus length and eight spoken-word interludes scattered throughout the album (with titles such as **Pledge**, **Race**, and **Livin' . . . In Complete Darkness** and running from five seconds to just more than a minute) made sure of that. Yet most of the twelve songs covered the same themes found on *Control*. From matters of the heart (**Miss You Much**, **Love Will Never Do (Without You)**) to putting aside worries for some occasional fun (**Escapade**), *Rhythm Nation 1814* shrouded its politics under the guise of catchy pop songs.

Taken as a piece, the album's social consciousness was fairly obvious. But *Rhythm Nation 1814* worked just as well, if not better, as a great dance and pop record—a fact made clear by the seven singles that reached the Top 5. Not even her brother Michael achieved that feat. The 1989 album, boosted on the strength of its excellent singles, entered the new decade as the best-selling LP of 1990. In mid-1991, the last of its four No. 1s exited the charts, and Jackson, having taken control of her career, flourished as one of the most popular artists in the world. *—MG*

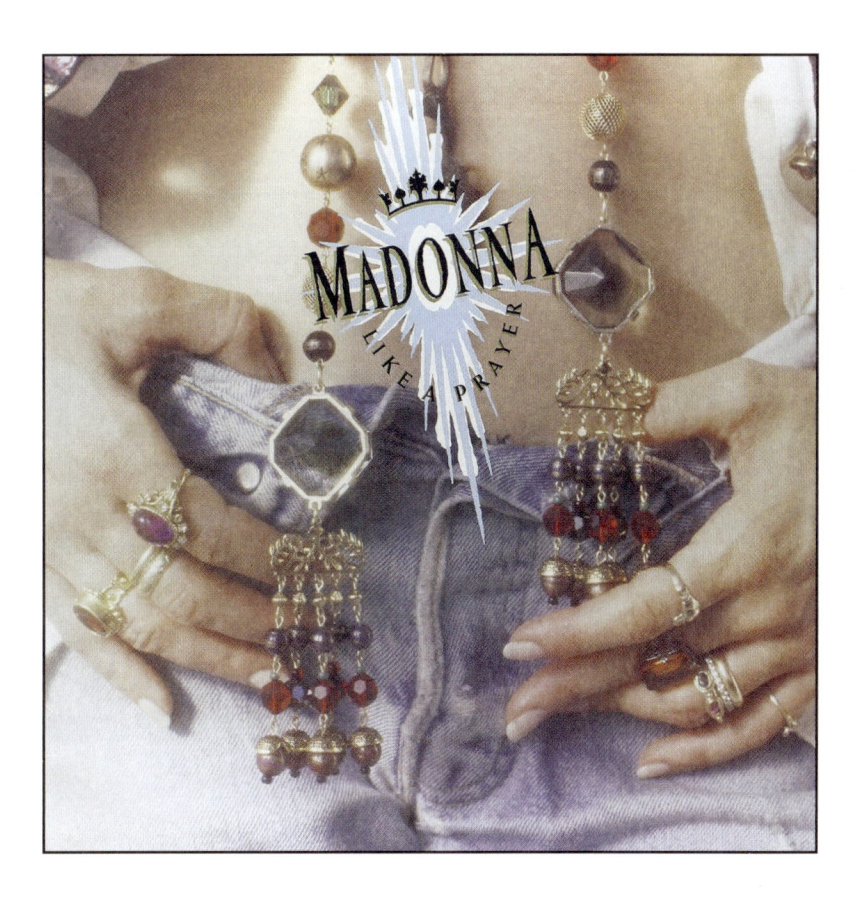

Madonna
LIKE A PRAYER

S I R E | Producers: Madonna, Patrick Leonard, Stephen Bray, Prince
RELEASED: MARCH 21, 1989

● By her fourth album, Madonna's growing confidence as an artist and her proven hitmaking status over the preceding few years sent her on a new career path. Once hesitant to disclose any semblance of her personal life in her music, the thirty-year-old singer and songwriter began writing songs that reflected her Catholic upbringing, the loss of her mother at a young age, and her fractured relationship with her dad. The result of her work, *Like a Prayer*, was a revealing look at the pieces that formed Madonna Louise Ciccone and a thrilling statement of purpose announcing her next era.

Like her earlier incarnations, the new Madonna was a provocative instigator, combining themes of sexual liberation and religious reservation, often within the same song. "I'm down on my knees / I want to take you there," she declared in *Like a Prayer*'s title track, while **Oh Father** connected lines between her dad and God: "Seems like yesterday I lay next to your boots and I prayed for your anger to end." It was an album about faith, but more than that, *Like a Prayer* was a tribute to Madonna's early years.

Take away the deeper meanings of the songs, though, and *Like a Prayer* was also a great pop and dance record. **Express Yourself** and **Cherish** touched on empowerment and devotion, respectively, through deep-club and girl-group exuberance. **Keep It Together**, about her family, was lined with late-'80s funk, including guitar by an uncredited Prince, who wrote, produced, and played on another of the album's songs. In the end, Madonna had it both ways, achieving the artistic credibility she desired and notching her third straight No. 1 album. She also set the stage for an even more remarkable decade to come. *–MG*

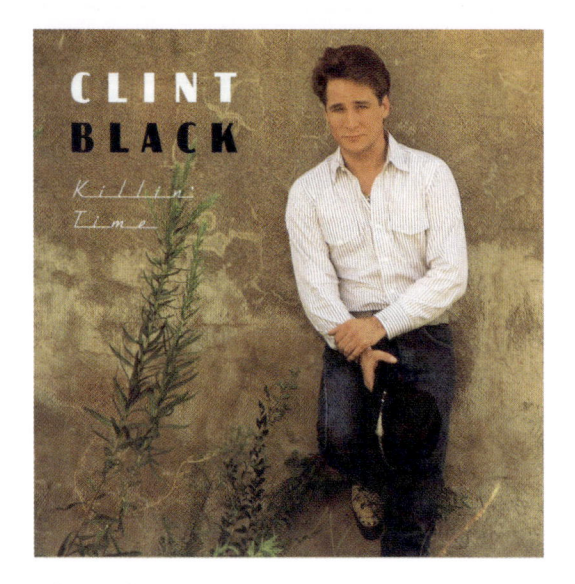

Clint Black
KILLIN' TIME

RCA NASHVILLE | Producers: James Stroud, Mark White
RELEASED: MAY 2, 1989

● There is debut success and then there is Clint Black's debut success. Black, then twenty-seven, burst onto the scene with *Killin' Time*, an album that produced four consecutive No. 1 Billboard Country hits—**A Better Man**, **Nobody's Home**, **Walkin' Away**, and the title track. Over a year after the album was released, **Nothing's News** topped out at No. 3 on the charts. *Killin' Time* certainly reflected a different time in Nashville; it's filled with slide guitars, banjos, fiddles, and harmonicas, perfect for two-stepping across the honky tonk. The album slowed down from time to time with heartbreakers such as **You're Going to Leave Me Again**. Black's first album not only showed off his Merle Haggard–like crooning ability but also showcased him as a songwriter, with credits on all ten songs. That investiture gave *Killin' Time* an even richer feel. The songs were more than just lyrics and a melody; they told the story of who Clint Black is. There is no question about the impact of Black, a member of the famed Class of '89 (along with Garth Brooks, Alan Jackson, and Travis Tritt). And that all started with the success of *Killin' Time*, a shining example of Texas Country. —ZC

Cher
HEART OF STONE

GEFFEN | Producers: Peter Asher, Michael Bolton, Desmond Child, Jon Lind, Diane Warren, Guy Roche
RELEASED: JULY 10, 1989

● Chances are you've seen some iteration of Cher's **If I Could Turn Back Time** video. It's hard to forget the icon fully, er, embracing her '80s rock persona while she straddled a giant gun turret on the battleship USS *Missouri*. It was the second single released from Cher's nineteenth studio album, *Heart of Stone*, and sales soared thanks to that provocative clip. *Heart of Stone* explored Cher's updated rock/pop sound in collaboration with some heavy hitters; Dianne Warren, Desmond Child, Jon Bon Jovi, Richie Sambora, and Michael Bolton all contributed one or more of the twelve tracks. Fresh off her Academy Award win for *Moonstruck* and seemingly happy in her personal relationships (yes, these were the Bagel Guy years), Cher delivered some of her best vocal performances on songs that felt authentic, with a slightly gritty edge. **Emotional Fire** featured plenty of power guitar chords, and the ballad **Just Like Jesse James** had a softer feel that hearkened back to her story-song days ("Half-Breed," "Dark Lady"). *Heart of Stone* triggered yet another comeback for the musical chameleon, and Cher rode the wave of success—comfortably clad in only a see-through body stocking and some strategically placed fabric. —SS

De La Soul
3 FEET HIGH AND RISING
TOMMY BOY | Producer: Prince Paul
RELEASED: FEBRUARY 6, 1989

● Gangsta rap's mainstream domination was right around the corner, and socially conscious hip-hop had already reshaped the genre's landscape. But in early 1989, a hip-hop trio from Long Island released a debut album that was both out of step with the times and an in-the-moment reflection of another side of the still-evolving music. De La Soul's *3 Feet High and Rising* was also one of the best records, rap or otherwise, ever made. The group—Posdnuos, Maseo, and Trugoy the Dove—along with producer Prince Paul, assembled the album as a reaction to hip-hop's growing obsession with materialism and the rise of confrontational rap music at the end of the '80s. Sparked by an array of samples (listen for Johnny Cash, Hall & Oates, and Steely Dan, among others) and playful lyrics that trained on the trio's nerdy interests (a game-show skit runs throughout the LP), *3 Feet High and Rising* was an outlier, a record made for the sheer joy of it. All these years later, nothing else sounds like it—a concept album stitched together with legally dubious samples and the sense that anything is possible through music. *—MG*

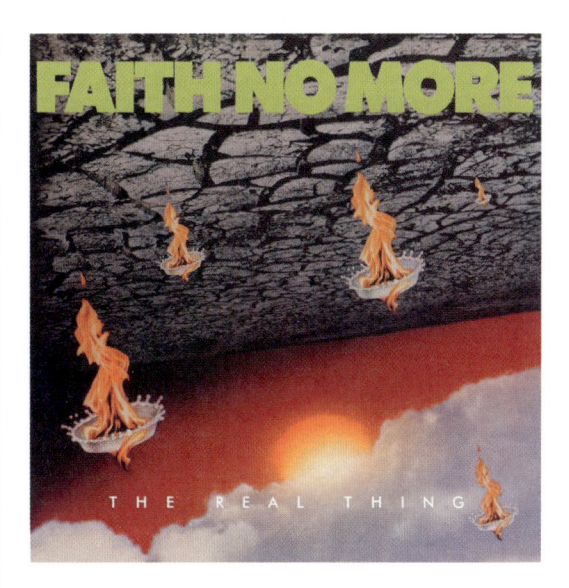

Faith No More
THE REAL THING
SLASH/REPRISE | Producers: Matt Wallace, Faith No More
RELEASED: JUNE 20, 1989

● Faith No More was already a band on the rise based on its first two albums, but a change in singers helped launch them into the stratosphere on 1989's *The Real Thing*. Replacing the punk-inspired, sometimes intentionally out-of-tune vocals of Chuck Mosley with the virtuosic and highly idiosyncratic approach of Mike Patton took the band to the next level. You could think of it as a weirder version of the evolution Iron Maiden underwent when switching from Paul Di'Anno to Bruce Dickinson. Drummer Mike Bordin, keyboardist Roddy Bottum, bassist Billy Gould, and guitarist James Martin had already perfected an innovative blend of metal, rap, funk, and alternative rock on 1987's album *Introduce Yourself*. They took everything up a notch on the follow-up, which was almost completely recorded before Patton joined the band. Unable to request even the simplest arrangement changes, the singer remarkably came up with all his lyrics and melodies in less than two weeks. *The Real Thing* was best known for the surprise Top 10 hit single **Epic**, but the band's genre-smashing genius was just as evident on the careening **From Out of Nowhere**, the thrashy **Surprise! You're Dead**, and the loungey **Edge of the World**. *—MW*

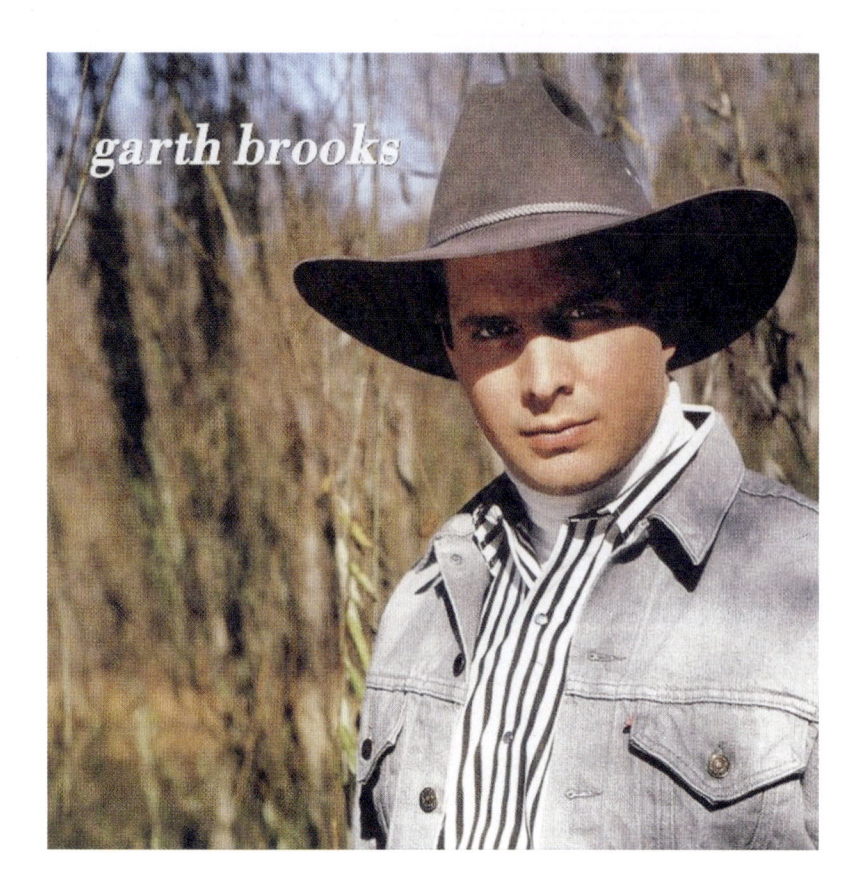

Garth Brooks
GARTH BROOKS
CAPITOL NASHVILLE | Producer: Allen Reynolds
RELEASED: APRIL 12, 1989

● Garth Brooks's debut album wasn't necessarily an obvious harbinger of the megastar he'd become in short order. But it made clear that the Oklahoma native had, as the second track announced, "a good thing going on."

Brooks came to Nashville after studying advertising at Oklahoma State University (where, legend had it, he met his first wife while breaking up a bar fight she was in—a country song if there ever was one). He was also a student of music, introduced partly by his mother, a recording artist herself during the '50s. "I love writers, great performers and great singers," Brooks said in 1992. "That's why I love Billy Joel—he does all three phenomenally." He was a studio singer for hire before getting his own deal, giving him a front-row seat to absorb other writers, performers, and producers.

So Brooks was well-formed by the time he made his first album, for which he wrote or co-wrote four of the ten tracks. Starting with the Texas swing of **Not Counting You**, this was the most traditionally country of his albums, stylistically and lyrically. But even here the upbeat tunes carried the sonic wallop of the best rock 'n' roll, while the slower fare—country chart-toppers **If Tomorrow Never Comes**, the epochal album closer **The Dance**—and mid-tempos (**Much Too Young (To Feel This Damn Old)**) displayed a warm, whisper-in-your-ear intimacy.

All of that connected to make *Garth Brooks* an out-of-the-box success with fellow Class of '89'ers such as Clint Black, Alan Jackson, and Travis Tritt. It reached No. 2 on the country charts, and, in the wake of Brooks's subsequent success, was certified Diamond. And now it's a charming start of what became a juggernaut career. *—GG*

1989

Beastie Boys
PAUL'S BOUTIQUE

CAPITOL | Producers: Beastie Boys, the Dust Brothers, Mario Caldato Jr.

RELEASED: JULY 25, 1989

● The success of *Licensed to Ill*, Beastie Boys' groundbreaking 1986 debut, came with much baggage; and by 1988, the New York City trio had parted ways with its producer, Rick Rubin, and his Def Jam record label and relocated to Los Angeles. The Beasties needed a reboot, seeking more creative control amid a growing desire to free themselves of the limitations placed on them by fans who took their frat-house rhymes at face value.

Over several months in 1988 going into 1989, Adam "Ad-Rock" Horovitz, Adam "MCA" Yauch, and Michael "Mike D" Diamond, along with engineer Mario Caldato Jr. and production duo the Dust Brothers, assembled one of hip-hop's most breathtaking albums, employing more than one hundred samples and a widescreen approach to free-form record-making. The samples heard on *Paul's Boutique* covered many types of music: rock (Led Zeppelin), soul (James Brown), reggae (Bob Marley), country (Johnny Cash), jazz (the Crusaders), and early rap (the Sugarhill Gang). These multilayered sound collages effectively pioneered a new musical art form based on samples and studio manipulation that would influence artists for decades to come.

The group also exhibited a growing maturity in its rhymes, mostly staying clear of the misogynist lyrics that hampered its debut. Still, it was the colorful assortment of samples and sounds that drove *Paul's Boutique*. Highlights **Shake Your Rump**, **Hey Ladies**, and **Shadrach** were bolstered by their playful references; **B-Boy Bouillabaisse**, the album's closing twelve-and-a-half-minute suite, included two dozen samples from the likes of Jimi Hendrix, the Isley Brothers, Led Zeppelin, the Meters, and Sweet. While the album was a commercial disappointment following the No. 1 and eventual Diamond-selling *Licensed to Ill*, its legacy has been greater. Few albums in the history of hip-hop have had as much impact as *Paul's Boutique*. —MG

The Cure
DISINTEGRATION

ELEKTRA | Producers: Robert Smith, David M. Allen
RELEASED: MAY 2, 1989

● *Disintegration*, the Cure's eighth album, was the culmination of a decade-long recording career that found the group recasting from goth heroes to pop stars and back again. The album was released following two records that were its highest charting in both its native UK and in the US. *Disintegration*, while shifting back to the Cure's original post-punk origins, brought it even more success as the band linked with its earliest days. Everything a Cure fan could want—goth, pop, post-punk, art-rock, New Wave, and alternative—was contained within its twelve tracks and seventy-one minutes.

Much of that was bandleader Robert Smith's intention, or at least what his muddled mind had initially perceived. The overwhelming mainstream reaction to 1985's *The Head on the Door* and 1987's *Kiss Me, Kiss Me, Kiss Me* left the twenty-nine-year-old singer, songwriter, guitarist, keyboardist, and producer uncertain of his path forward. Mass commercial acceptance was never in his plans, so he turned to LSD to combat depression that stemmed from his group's pop success.

Wanting to return to the Cure's darkest period from the early '80s, Smith began writing epic-length songs such as **The Same Deep Water as You** and *Disintegration*'s title track, which were at odds with the breezy pop arrangement that made it a Top 10 sensation. But Smith couldn't completely abandon his melodic instincts. Despite its seven-and-a-half-minute length, **Pictures of You** was a prime Cure ballad; the eerie **Lullaby** became its biggest hit in the UK; and the pop valentine **Lovesong** shot to No. 2 in the States. Woven within the fabric of the dark-space draw of **Plainsong**, **Fascination Street**, and **Disintegration**, the songs tell the story of the band's move away from the center and how, in the process, it became bigger and better. *—MG*

Neneh Cherry
RAW LIKE SUSHI

V I R G I N | Producers: Jonny Dollar, Cameron McVey, Mark Saunders, Time Simenon

RELEASED: JUNE 5, 1989

● Nobody who lived an ordinary life could have made an album as unique and daring as *Raw Like Sushi*. Luckily, Neneh Cherry's first twenty-five years prepared her for the job just perfectly.

Born in Sweden as the child of an acclaimed painter/artist and the musician son of an African tribal chief, Cherry was raised from a very early age by her stepfather, jazz musician Don Cherry. The family moved to New York City during the late '70s, befriending cotenants Chris Franz and Tina Weymouth of Talking Heads. She moved to England at the age of fifteen, joining a series of punk rock bands and playing rap music as a pirate radio DJ.

When it came time to record her debut album, Cherry had the confidence and outsider's perspective to rewrite or completely ignore the accepted rules of hip-hop, pop, and R&B. While she used the same building blocks as many of her contemporaries, *Raw Like Sushi* assembled them in bracingly inventive new ways. Nowhere was this more clear than on the first single, **Buffalo Stance**, which, decades later, remains magical and not completely definable. The song began in the world of minimalist '80s hip-hop, then continually added layers and complexity, including an intoxicating ascending keyboard line, while Cherry effortlessly toggled between rapping and singing.

The rest of the album was full of such delights, such as the wise-beyond-her-years **Manchild** and the effervescent **Kisses on the Wind**. Racking up more than two million sales worldwide and influencing countless future artists, *Raw Like Sushi* was both a perfect snapshot of its time and an ageless pop delight—though Cherry's own productivity has been scant ever since. *—MW*

1989

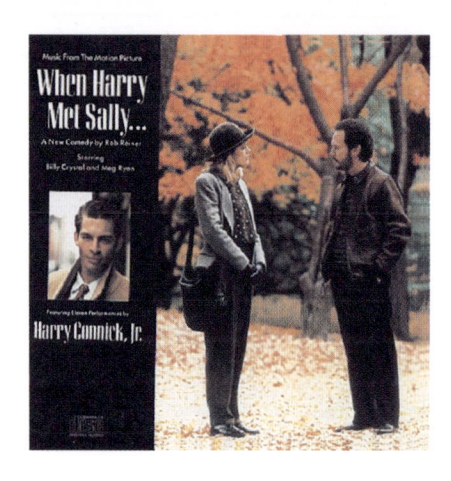

Harry Connick Jr.
WHEN HARRY MET SALLY . . . (ORIGINAL MOTION PICTURE SOUNDTRACK)
COLUMBIA | Producers: Marc Shaiman, Harry Connick Jr.
RELEASED: JULY 25, 1989

● Director Rob Reiner's romantic comedy starring Billy Crystal, Meg Ryan, and the city of New York popularized the concept of the "high-maintenance woman," as well as the career of New Orleans singer/pianist Harry Connick Jr. Connick's pitch-perfect renditions of Ellington, Goodman, and Gershwin classics perfectly evoked the Big Apple as another character in the story—where you go not just to make it but to fall in love. Best of all was the piano-trio instrumental version of **It Had to Be You**. Connick's first platinum album and also his best. —DM

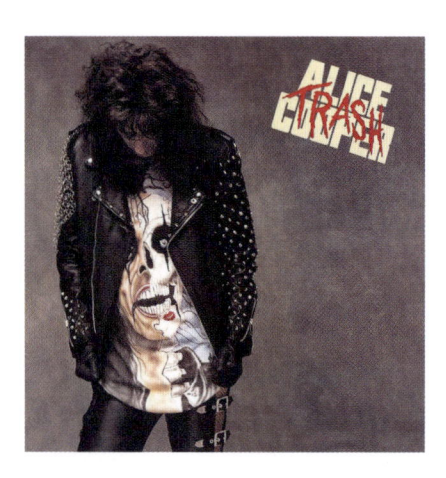

Alice Cooper
TRASH
EPIC | Producer: Desmond Child
RELEASED: JULY 25, 1989

● Two albums into his '80s comeback from rehab, Alice Cooper still needed a big hit. Enter songwriter/producer Desmond Child and **Poison**, which put the shock-rocker back on the singles chart—and in fact equaled the No. 7 showing of "School's Out" twelve years prior. The rest of *Trash*, meanwhile, was solid, melodic hard rock in keeping with Cooper's '70s heyday with guest appearances by members of Aerosmith, Bon Jovi, and Toto, while Joan Jett joined the writing team for **House of Fire** and Diane Warren chipped in for **Bed of Nails**. —GG

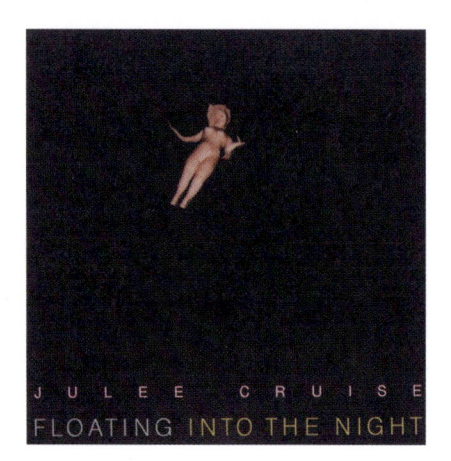

Julee Cruise
FLOATING INTO THE NIGHT
WARNER BROS. | Producers: David Lynch, Angelo Badalamenti
RELEASED: SEPTEMBER 12, 1989

● The debut album from Julee Cruise belonged to the David Lynch extended universe. The filmmaker and his musical partner, composer Angelo Badalamenti, first teamed with the Iowa-born singer for a song on the *Blue Velvet* soundtrack, Cruise's ethereal vocals perfectly embodying Lynch's surreal, dreamlike sensibilities. Lynch and Badalamenti wrote *Floating into the Night* for Cruise and used its songs throughout *Twin Peaks*—including *Falling*, the instrumental that was used as the show's theme song—as Cruise's serene sense of slow-motion beauty became forever linked to the cult TV series. —AG

Galaxie 500
ON FIRE
ROUGH TRADE | Producer: Mark Kramer
RELEASED: OCTOBER 20, 1989

● In the years before Luna, Dean Wareham led Cambridge's Galaxie 500, a group you could call quietly influential—except it wasn't really quiet. But, name aside, the band was never in a hurry to get anywhere, grooving along at an amiable saunter toward an expected explosion that never quite happened. *On Fire* was a great ride, especially **Snowstorm**, which sounded like Neil Young sitting in with Yo La Tengo, and the closing cover of George Harrison's **Isn't It a Pity**. For a bonus, producer Stephen Michael "Kramer" Bonner's liner notes are meditations about fire. —*DM*

Ghetto Boys
GRIP IT! ON THAT OTHER LEVEL
RAP-A-LOT | Producers: DJ Ready Red, John Bido
RELEASED: MARCH 12, 1989

● The second album from Houston's Ghetto Boys helped expand hip-hop's Southern reach. Replacing Sire Jukebox and Prince Johnny C, DJ Akshen (later known as Scarface) and Willie D joined Bushwick Bill and DJ Ready Red, and the group laid down shockingly frank rhymes about sex (the Steve Miller–sampling **Gangster of Love**) and violence (**Mind of a Lunatic** is gorier than a horror movie). Most of the album's tracks would be remixed and reworked on 1990's Rick Rubin–produced *The Geto Boys*, but the foundation of one of hip-hop's seminal outfits was set. —*AG*

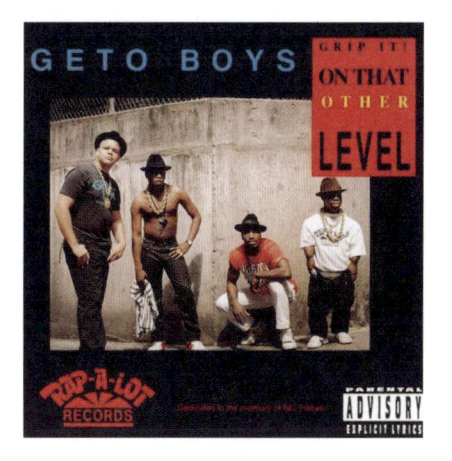

Indigo Girls
INDIGO GIRLS
EPIC | Producer: Scott Litt
RELEASED: FEBRUARY 28, 1989

● "The less I seek my source for some definitive / Closer I am to fine," the Indigo Girls (Amy Ray and Emily Saliers) sang on the single from their addictively listenable sophomore album. Recorded with Ireland's Hothouse Flowers, **Closer to Fine** led the childhood friends to a Grammy Award for Best Contemporary Folk Album. Drawing the members of R.E.M., including Michael Stipe on **Kid Fears**, the album ultimately sat nicely between coffeehouse folk and pop with tight harmonies and internally-turned lyrics about coming of age and female empowerment. —*HD*

B-52's
COSMIC THING

REPRISE | Producers: Nile Rodgers, Don Was

RELEASED: JUNE 27, 1989

● The tragic death of guitarist Ricky Wilson in 1985 from AIDS-related complications at just thirty-two years old could have spelled the end of the B-52's. But even though the group stopped recording and performing for a few years, the band members stayed in touch, helping to heal each other's emotional wounds. Spurred on by drummer-turned-guitarist Keith Strickland, the band started writing and recording again and, four years after Wilson's passing, released what may be its finest effort, *Cosmic Thing*.

The album was a return to their college frat-party roots, both musically and thematically. Strickland did an admirable job mimicking Wilson's minimalist surf-punk guitar sound while injecting it with his own funky style. Kate Pierson and Cindy Wilson (Ricky's sister) supplied the sweet singalong harmonies with Fred Schneider supplying geek-rap vocals. It was the same danceable, weird, goofy, and fun formula that brought the group success a decade prior, only this time a bit more polished, thanks to the album being helmed by two of the hottest producers in the business: Nile Rodgers and Don Was.

The band seemed to be experiencing a catharsis by revisiting its beginnings. **Dry County** conjured up '70s Athens, Georgia. **Deadbeat Club** was what the members self-deprecatingly called themselves back in the day. And the **Love Shack** of the huge hit single was an actual place where the B-52's used to hang out.

Pierson at the time said, "It wasn't until we wrote the first couple of songs that we started seeing this theme. Every song we were writing was evocative of the rural South." It worked. Along with it being the band's best-selling album, **Love Shack** and **Roam** were its first singles to crack Billboard's Top 10. *Cosmic Thing* turned out to be a triumph musically, psychically, and commercially. —GP

1989

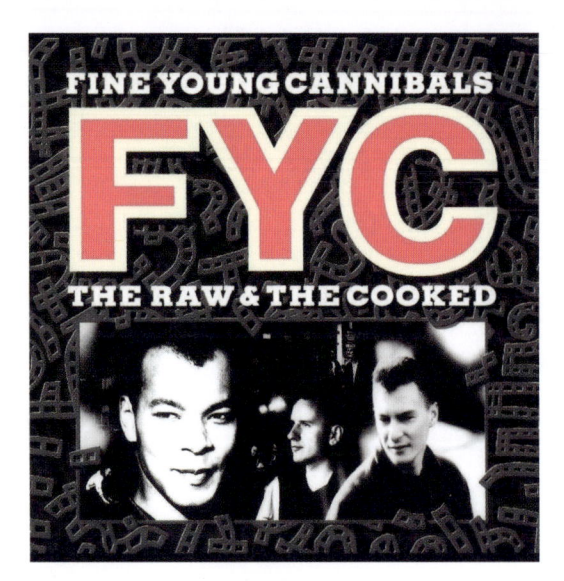

Fine Young Cannibals
THE RAW AND THE COOKED

I.R.S. | Producers: Fine Young Cannibals, David Z, Jerry Harrison
RELEASED: JANUARY 13, 1989

● After the breakup of the English Beat, bassist David Steele and guitarist Andy Cox spent eight months listening to hundreds of audition tapes before finally finding vocalist Roland Gift and forming Fine Young Cannibals. The new band walked away from the English Beat's reggae roots and went in a more soulful direction. Though the first album was well received, the boys took four years to release their second (and final) effort, but *The Raw and the Cooked* turned out to be worth the wait. The music is a trip through the history of soul, from Motown to then-contemporaries such as Prince. In a *Rolling Stone* interview, Cox described the album as "30 years of pop music in 30 minutes." The album produced two No. 1 singles—**Good Thing**, with a danceable Motown vibe, and **She Drives Me Crazy**, with a more modern-funk feel. Other gems included **I'm Not the Man I Used to Be**, with Gift channeling Otis Redding; **As Hard As It Is**, an emotional ballad; and **I'm Not Satisfied**, which threw some New Wave flavors into the mix. *The Raw and the Cooked* left you wanting another thirty-minute music history lesson. —*GP*

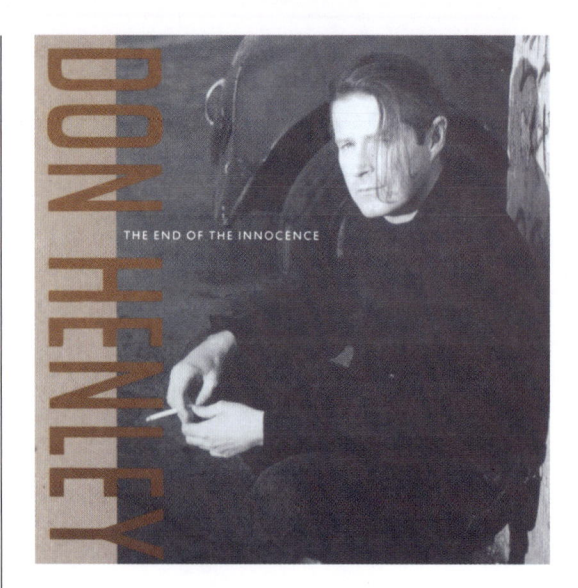

Don Henley
THE END OF THE INNOCENCE

GEFFEN | Producers: Mike Campbell, John Corey, Don Henley, Bruce Hornsby, Greg Ladanyi, Stan Lynch
RELEASED: JUNE 27, 1989

● The elegiac title song of the third solo album from Eagles member Don Henley, which reached No. 1 on Billboard's Mainstream Rock chart, featured Bruce Hornsby's distinctive grand piano alongside lyrics that evoke America's beautiful spacious skies at a time when "those skies are threatening." Henley's metaphor comparing a nation's growing somber awareness with a young woman's sexual awakening has not entirely aged well. ("Offer up your best defense," he sings in the pre-#MeToo era.) But largely, throughout this album, Henley is at the peak of his game in writing or selecting songs that combined pop craftsmanship with insightful lyrics. **New York Minute** is a chilling noir tale. **The Last Worthless Evening** is a story of redeeming love. And **The Heart of the Matter**, co-written by Mike Campbell of Tom Petty's Heartbreakers and frequent Eagles collaborator J. D. Souther, contains a great truth about emotional acceptance; "it's about forgiveness, forgiveness." *The End of the Innocence* was a commercial and critical triumph, reaching No. 8 on the Billboard 200 and earning Grammy Award nominations for Henley for Album, Song, and Record of the year, while the title track won for Best Rock Vocal Performance, Male. —*TD*

Lenny Kravitz
LET LOVE RULE
VIRGIN | Producer: Lenny Kravitz
RELEASED: SEPTEMBER 6, 1989

● It's fair to say Lenny Kravitz had solid grounding for a career in the arts. Entertainment was in his DNA thanks to a TV producer father and actress mother, and their mixed-race marriage—as well as being raised on both coasts—gave Kravitz a wide worldview at an early age. So did his exposure to a wide range of music, singing in the California Boys Choir and going to high school with future recording stars Slash and Maria McKee. It's no surprise, then, that Kravitz had a fully-formed vision when he recorded his debut album as a one-man-band affair—even producing it himself. As a first effort, *Let Love Rule* wore its rock, R&B, and funk influences on its sleeve, but Kravitz knew how to write a solid tune, evidenced by the likes of the hit title track, **I Build This Garden for Us**, the topical **Mr. Cab Driver**, and **Sittin' on Top of the World**. Then-wife Lisa Bonet wrote lyrics for two of the ten tracks, and saxophonist Karl Denson played on seven, helping to make *Let Love Rule* a gold-certified introduction that Kravitz would use as a formidable career springboard. –GG

Bob Mould
WORKBOOK
VIRGIN | Producer: Bob Mould
RELEASED: MAY 2, 1989

● Bob Mould became the first former member of the influential punk/alt-rock trio Hüsker Dü to issue a solo release. While he mostly stuck with the three-piece format he knew best (as he would throughout his career), *Workbook* found Mould freed from the tethers of band politics, the result being a much more highly produced effort than anything in Hüsker Dü's vaunted catalog. **Sunspots**, for example, a delicate fingerpicked acoustic instrumental that wouldn't seem out of place on a Leo Kottke album, was a palate cleanser for anyone expecting Hüskers Mk.II. Backing Mould on the rest of the album was Pere Ubu's rhythm section, Anton Fier (drums), and Tony Maimone (bass). Beginning with the urgent **Wishing Well**, Mould often layered his acoustic and electric guitars beneath vocals that were much more out front than in his Hüskers days and, as on **Heartbreak a Stranger**, sometimes double-tracked to great effect. Cellist Jane Scarpantoni added to the production vibe, including on **See a Little Light**, a Top 5 single on Billboard's Modern Rock Tracks chart. Mould also exercised a greater degree of dynamics within his songs, perhaps best showcased on the buildup in **Poison Years**, addressed to Mould's former bandmate Grant Hart. –DP

415

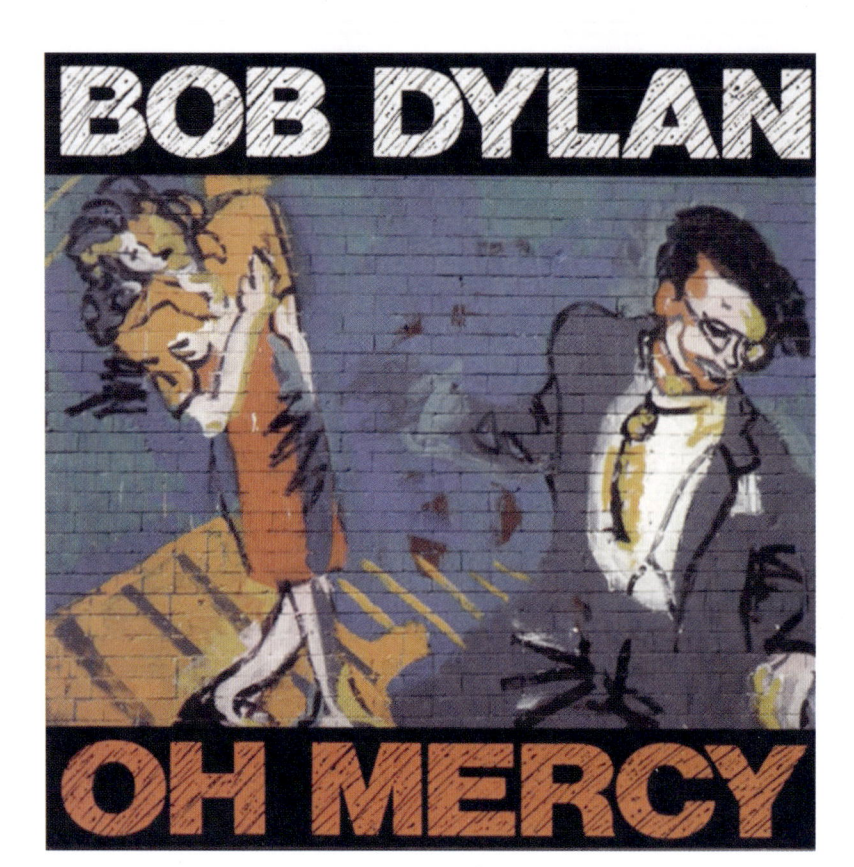

Bob Dylan
OH MERCY

COLUMBIA | Producer: Daniel Lanois
RELEASED: SEPTEMBER 12, 1989

● In his 2004 memoir *Chronicles Volume One*, Bob Dylan offered a riveting, richly detailed seventy-five-page account on the creation of the Daniel Lanois–produced *Oh Mercy*: how he'd previously injured his hand and felt creatively spent, but slowly healed, both in body and in mind; how U2's Bono introduced him to Lanois; how he traveled to New Orleans to make the record; and how creative clashes ensued but resulted in a record that ultimately had "something magical" about it.

That it did. Though Dylan had doubts about the material and continually struggled to make it feel true, *Oh Mercy* contained his best batch of songs of the decade. The opening **Political World** was relevant and razor sharp, as was **Everything Is Broken**, the two songs delivering a one-two state-of-the-world haymaker of the sort that people used to expect from Dylan. **Man in the Long Black Coat** was dark and portentous, while elsewhere, Dylan admitted self-doubt and strived for self-improvement (**Most of the Time**, **What Good Am I?**, **Disease of Conceit**). And he wrapped things up with one of his loveliest ballads, **Shooting Star**. Were these autobiographical songs? In *Chronicles*, Dylan wrote that even if they're not explicitly about him, "the stuff I write does come from an autobiographical place."

Of course, the element that truly takes *Oh Mercy* into another realm is Lanois's trademark atmospheric production work. But he doesn't overdo it; some of the songs are left simple and stark, giving Dylan's fine lyrics a wide berth. The album was recorded at night and has a terrific late-night vibe. It sounded great anytime but especially when the moon was out and the lights were low.

Though the process of *Oh Mercy* was contentious, Dylan and Lanois would work together again, though it took them almost a decade to reunite for 1997's *Time Out of Mind*. *—DD*

1989

Inner City
PARADISE/BIG FUN
VIRGIN | Producer: Kevin Saunderson
RELEASED: MAY 1989

● Detroit techno blended with Chicago house became a magical combination when Kevin Saunderson and Paris Grey got together to form Inner City. Infectious electronic beats and strings courtesy of Saunderson with killer soulful vocals from Grey turned the dance-music world upside down with the massive club hits **Good Life** and **Big Fun**. The songs were the backbone of the record, but the rest is no mere filler. The entire project was a work of modern soul bliss and, as the album title exclaims, musical *Paradise*. —MH

Joe Jackson
BLAZE OF GLORY
A & M | Producer: Joe Jackson
RELEASED: APRIL 17, 1989

● Joe Jackson's given us a lot of substantial music and surprising left turns during his career. This is one of the best. The British singer/songwriter/muso's tenth studio album was a partly autobiographical concept piece that mused on society, aging, unrealized ideologies, and sociopolitical terrain. It was delivered with expansive instrumentation (Joy Askew's an MVP here) and some of Jackson's finest songs, including **Nineteen Forever**, **Down to London**, **Tomorrow's World**, and the title track. He continues to delight and confound us, but this one's still something to rant and rave about. —GG

Kool G Rap & DJ Polo
ROAD TO THE RICHES
COLD CHILLIN'/WARNER BROS. | Producer: Marley Marl
RELEASED: MARCH 14, 1989

● *Road to the Riches* introduced Kool G Rap as one of rap's greatest MCs. Assisted by DJ Polo and Marley Marl, Kool G was a skilled battle rapper who was one of the first to infuse Mafioso rap into his lyrics; on tracks such as **Poison**, he's an assassin. The duo's debut album not only advanced the place of rap in mainstream music; it also inspired the future legends of the genre—including Nas, MF Doom, and Bell Biv Devoe, who all sampled some of its songs. —ZC

Various Artists
THE LITTLE MERMAID (ORIGINAL MOTION PICTURE SOUNDTRACK)
WALT DISNEY | Producers: Alan Menken, Howard Ashman, Robert Kraft
RELEASED: OCTOBER 19, 1989

● Disney's adaptation of Hans Christian Andersen's *The Little Mermaid* gave the studio a comeback after some relatively fallow years at the box office, and the songs, by Howard Ashman and Alan Menken, should be given some credit. The multiplatinum soundtrack had some actual hits—the lively calypso party **Under the Sea**, the heartrending **Part of Your World**, the easygoing **Kiss the Girl**—that led to Grammy, Academy, and Golden Globe awards and launched a new era of music-centric Disney princess epics that's still going on today. *—GG*

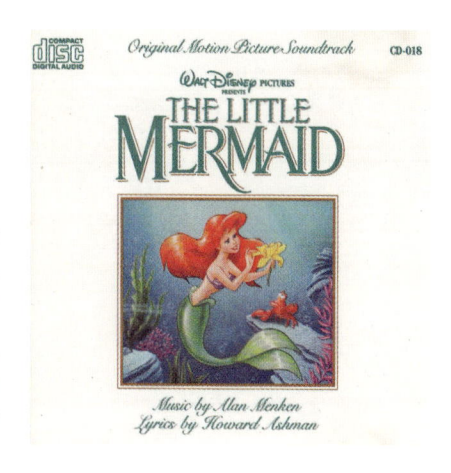

Love and Rockets
LOVE AND ROCKETS
BEGGARS BANQUET | Producers: John Fryer, Love and Rockets
RELEASED: MAY 1989

● When the bats of Bauhaus were chased from the belfry, Daniel Ash, David J, and Kevin Haskins re-formed as Love and Rockets. The trio's joyfully poppy first two albums gave way to an acoustic feel on its third, but it was this self-titled fourth album that gave the band a Top 5 glam hit, **So Alive**, which finally put this deserving band on the radio. *Love and Rockets* also generated **No Big Deal**, **Motorcycle**, and **Rock & Roll Babylon** for Love and Rockets' only gold album. *—HD*

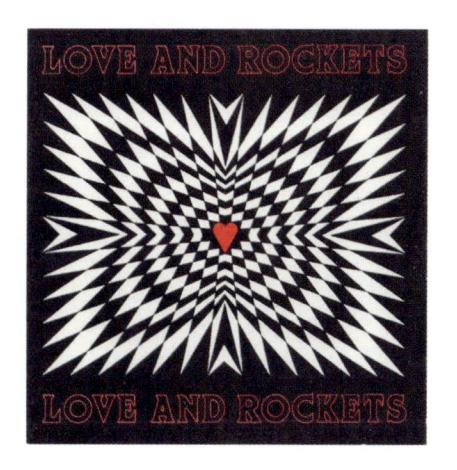

The Mekons
THE MEKONS ROCK 'N' ROLL
TWIN/TONE-A&M | Producers: The Mekons, Ian Caple
RELEASED: SEPTEMBER 1989

● One of agitprop singer/guitarist/author/artist Jon Langford's many musical outlets, the Mekons are a venerable UK punk collective that demands an exceptional level of commitment—from audience and band alike. To be a Mekon is to take a vow, and the first words on this album were a roaring call to arms: "Destroy your safe and happy lives / Before it is too late!" Revolutionary sentiments aside, *Rock 'n' Roll* is just about the most accessible the Mekons ever sounded, before or since—even as those hoedown fiddles go hard. *—DM*

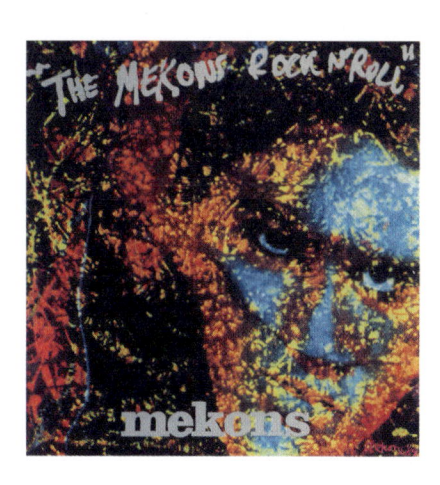

Quincy Jones
BACK ON THE BLOCK

QWEST/WARNER BROS. | Producer: Quincy Jones

RELEASED: NOVEMBER 21, 1989

● Nobody (at least nobody in their right mind) said no to Quincy Jones ever, but especially back in the '80s. His music-making legend extended back to his jazz work during the '50s, and by 1989 he'd produced the two best-selling albums (to date) of all time—Michael Jackson's *Thriller* and *Bad*—as well as the all-star charity record "We Are the World." So, when Jones flipped through his Rolodex for *Back on the Block*, his first artist outing since *The Dude* eight years before, he didn't get many turndowns.

Jones had in mind a common grounding of R&B, hip-hop, and jazz, albeit more alongside each other than together. He brought in old running buddies (Miles Davis, Ray Charles, Ella Fitzgerald, Dizzy Gillespie, Sarah Vaughan, Herbie Hancock) with new jacks such as James Ingram, El DeBarge, Al B Sure!, Kool Moe Dee, Melle Mel, Ice-T, Bobby McFerrin, Take 6 and the introduction of a twelve-year-old Tevin Campbell, members of Toto—and, of course, many more. All of them brought their A games, too, as you'd expect when summoned by a guy like Jones.

The title track was a summit meeting presided over by Jones and gospel great Andraé Crouch, while Weather Report's **Birdland** got an all-star treatment with Davis, Fitzgerald, Gillespie, writer Joe Zawinul, James Moody, and more. Barry White, Dionne Warwick, and Luther Vandross were among the singers sampled for **The Places You Find Love**.

The album put Jones back on the Grammy Award block as well. It won seven trophies, including Album of the Year, and brought Jones an honor for Producer of the Year, Non-Classical. It also reached No. 9 on the Billboard 200 and was certified platinum, and *Back on the Block* certainly ensured that those who didn't already knew Jones's name, as well as his enormous musical résumé, would soon learn. *—GG*

1989

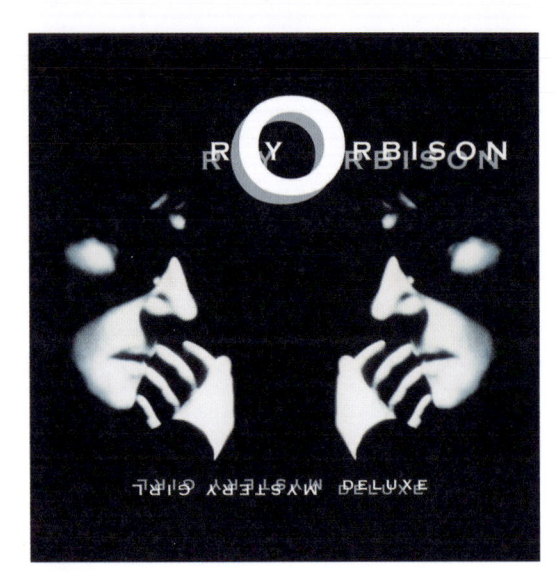

Roy Orbison
MYSTERY GIRL
VIRGIN | Producers: Bono, T Bone Burnett, Mike Campbell, Jeff Lynne, Barbara Orbison, Roy Orbison
RELEASED: JANUARY 31, 1989

● Three decades after his neo-operatic voice graced classics such as "Crying" and "Oh, Pretty Woman," Roy Orbison's popularity enjoyed a resurgence that included joining Bob Dylan, George Harrison, Tom Petty, and Jeff Lynne in the Traveling Wilburys in 1987 and the release of this solo album—two months after his untimely death at age fifty-two. For fans, the joy of his comeback was lost with the realization of how much more great music Orbison could have made. Opening the album, **You Got It** featured the Wilburys (sans Dylan) in a delightful mix of layered acoustic guitars, electric guitar leads, and lush strings driving Orbison's declaration of devotion. It became his first Top 10 hit in twenty-five years. Orbison's voice soared in a falsetto for **In the Real World**, which featured Mike Campbell of Petty's Heartbreakers; slid into a darker tenor on **She's a Mystery to Me**, written by U2's Bono and The Edge; and built dramatically on his cover of Elvis Costello's **The Comedians**. When Bruce Springsteen inducted Orbison into the Rock & Roll Hall of Fame in 1987, he acknowledged that on *Born to Run*, "I wanted to sing like Roy Orbison. Now, everyone knows that no one sings like Roy Orbison." —TD

Milli Vanilli
GIRL YOU KNOW IT'S TRUE
ARISTA | Producer: Frank Farian
RELEASED: MARCH 7, 1989

● German models and dancers Rob Pilatus and Fab Morvan were chosen to be the faces of producer Frank Farian's pop R&B act Milli Vanilli, which pumped out energetic Eurodance songs with ultra-catchy hooks over rubbery grooves and hip-hop backbeats. The duo became international superstars, landing a No. 2 hit with its debut single, **Girl You Know It's True**, and three No. 1 hits: **Baby Don't Forget My Number**, **Blame It on the Rain**, and **Girl I'm Gonna Miss You**. Their debut album sold seven million copies. There was only one problem: Rob and Fab didn't sing a single lick on the album, a fact unearthed only after Milli Vanilli won 1990's Best New Artist Grammy.

As for the music itself, it holds up as a shiny example of prefabricated late-'80s pop, highly danceable and perfectly glossy, with the Diane Warren–penned **Blame It on the Rain** showing off admirable songcraft. But ensuing scandal became much more than a cautionary tale. The press pounced, Arista dropped the pair, and "Milli Vanilli" became shorthand for inauthenticity. Attempts by the pair to prove they could indeed sing fell flat, and Pilatus died of an accidental overdose in 1998. —AG

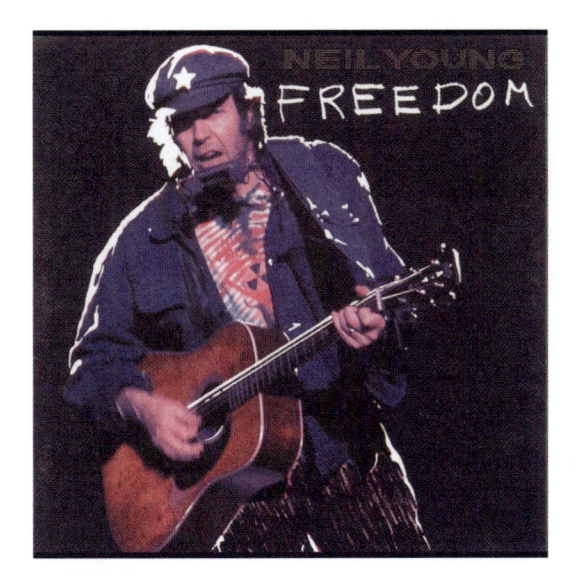

Neil Young
FREEDOM
REPRISE | Producers: Neil Young, Niko Bolas
RELEASED: OCTOBER 2, 1989

● Musically, Neil Young went walkabout during the '80s and, famously, was sued by Geffen Records for making albums that were "musically uncharacteristic" of his previous output. That can't be said about *Freedom*, an album rightly regarded as a comeback. It contained a familiar-sounding mix of acoustic and electric tracks, including two versions of **Rockin' in the Free World**—a live acoustic album opener and a hurricane-force electric closer. It was yet another signature song from a guy who's got a lot of them. Much of the material was pulled from various phases and stages of Young's career, but they held together here: hard-rocking songs that previously appeared on the *Eldorado* EP (**Don't Cry**, **Eldorado**, a bonkers cover of the Drifters' **On Broadway**); an expansive, bluesy opus (**Crime in the City**); gentle country rockers (**Hangin' on a Limb**, **The Ways of Love**); and a pair of besotted love songs, one with romance (**Wrecking Ball**), the other with booze (**Too Far Gone**). It's not like Young forgot how to be Young on those previous '80s albums, but *Freedom* was the Neil that most of his fans knew and loved—and the record they were waiting for. *—DD*

Soul II Soul
CLUB CLASSICS VOL. ONE/KEEP ON MOVIN'
VIRGIN | Producers: Jazzie B, Nellee Hooper
RELEASED: APRIL 10, 1989

● From the moment the first track's heartbeat rhythm kicked in and Caron Wheeler's seductive voice began imploring "Keep on movin', don't stop" amid orchestral strings and piano notes, London collective Soul II Soul was charting unique territory. *Club Classics Vol. One* (titled *Keep on Movin'* in the US) fused soul, funk, dub, reggae, hip-hop, and jazz into a new, multicultural groove, draping electronic and acoustic textures over rhythms designed to incite movement. Producers Jazzie B and Nellee Hooper drafted manifestos about the unifying, positive power of dance—and their tight underground club scene. Jazzie delivered them in conversational, stream-of-consciousness toasts on **Holdin' On (Bambelala)**, **Jazzie's Groove**, and his swaggering **Dance**, along with the scratch-happy **Feeling Free (Live Rap)**. Rose Windross elaborated on **Fairplay**, and Do'Reen picked up the thread on **Feel Free** and **Happiness (Dub)**. But it was Wheeler's vocal prowess on **Back to Life (However Do You Want Me)**, written about a near-death experience, that pushed the single and album atop Billboard's R&B/Hip-Hop charts. That track and an instrumental, **African Dance**, won Grammy Awards, and Soul II Soul helped launch what became known as EDM (electronic dance music). *—LM*

Nine Inch Nails
PRETTY HATE MACHINE

T V T | Producers: Trent Reznor, Flood, John Fryer, Keith LeBlanc, Adrian Sherwood

RELEASED: OCTOBER 20, 1989

● When Trent Reznor started on the first full-length Nine Inch Nails release, it might have seemed success was unlikely. First, it was released by a record label best known for cheap compilation albums of TV theme songs. But Reznor's synthesizing of darker, industrial electronic sounds with pop sensibilities created something that would influence popular music over the next few decades.

By the late '80s, drum machines and synthesizers had driven pop songs to the top of the charts. That was not new. The same could be said for groups with driving, heavy industrial sounds like Throbbing Gristle and Einstürzende Neubauten. When ideas for *Pretty Hate Machine* started, Reznor had been playing keyboards in middling Cleveland-area synth-pop bands such as Slam Bamboo. But his demos attracted producers who had worked with U2, Depeche Mode, and the pioneering hip-hop label Sugar Hill Records. What arrived was an album that didn't shy away from its influences but never felt like a retreading of familiar ground.

Tracks such as **Head Like a Hole**, **Terrible Lie**, and **Sin** made philosophical statements platformed in metallic stamping-plant rhythms and sinister synth lines—perfect for darker dancefloors of the era. Reznor's work also shined in the dynamics of electronic and acoustic interplay, best displayed with the atmospheric **Something I Can Never Have**, a track that likely lit a million candles in the bedrooms of Gen X high school goths tasting the bitterness of a lost relationship.

While Reznor has gone on to create more integrated releases for Nine Inch Nails, including 1994's *The Downward Spiral,* and Academy Award–winning film scores with collaborator Atticus Ross, revisiting *Pretty Hate Machine* is still rewarding for the quality of the tracks and a marker for where it all began. *–RSM*

1989

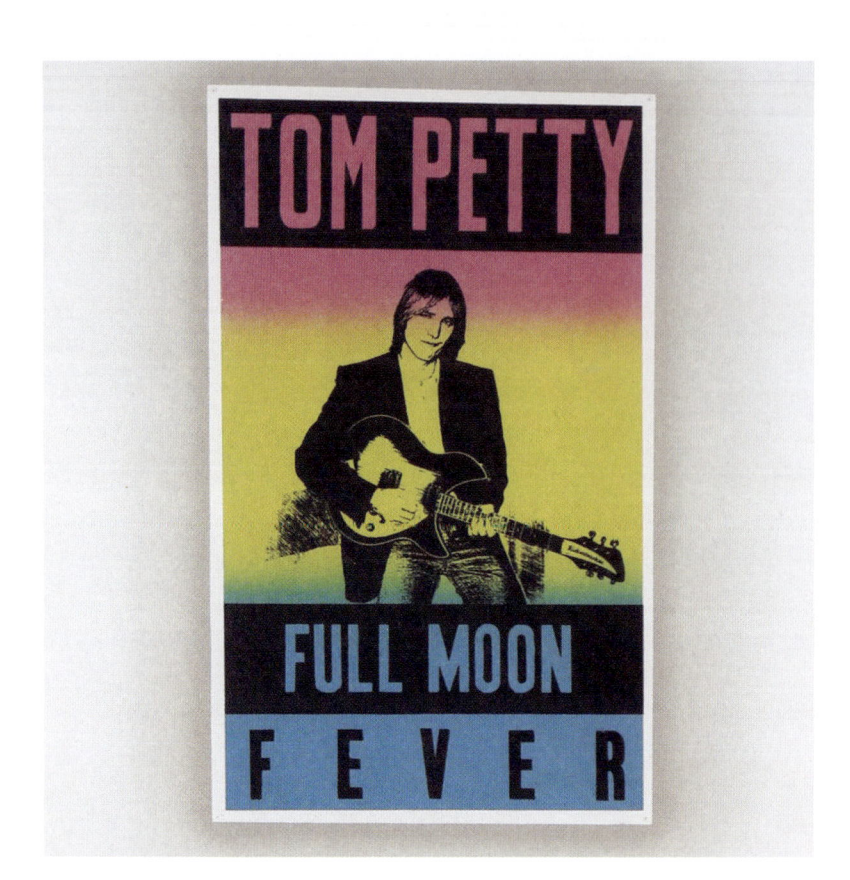

Tom Petty
FULL MOON FEVER

MCA | Producers: Jeff Lynne, Tom Petty, Mike Campbell
RELEASED: APRIL 24, 1989

● By 1988, Tom Petty's career was in a weird spot. With the Heartbreakers, he achieved full stardom with *Damn the Torpedoes* in 1979 and became an MTV favorite with "Don't Come Around Here No More" from *Southern Accents* in 1985. Petty wrote songs with Bob Dylan and, together with Heartbreakers, combined forces for a stunning tour in 1986-1987. Then Petty decided it was time to hit the reset button and cut his first solo album.

When an artist who is closely associated with a particular band (think Bruce Springsteen, Phil Collins, Elvis Costello) chooses to make a solo record, it's often because they have ideas they want to try outside of the established creative format. Petty enlisted his Heartbreakers co-pilot Mike Campbell and Electric Light Orchestra founder Jeff Lynne to help achieve that. Lynne's approach to recording provided Petty with a new freedom without obscuring his identity. Together, they took the inherent simplicity of each song and embellished them with a symphony of guitars and perfect percussion. In **Runnin' Down a Dream**, acoustic guitars mirrored the hi-hat of drummer Phil Jones, giving the song extra fuel. **Free Fallin'** was a California mash note complete with a big nod to the vocals of the Beach Boys.

Rarely does an artist hit the spot so directly and perfectly as Petty did with *Full Moon Fever*. Like AC/DC's *Back in Black* or *Revolver* by the Beatles, every track on this record was a classic full stop. **Free Fallin'** on its own could carry an entire album. The rest of side A is a pummeling sequence of **I Won't Back Down**, **Love Is a Long Road**, **A Face in the Crowd**, and **Runnin' Down a Dream**. And to think Petty's label initially didn't want to release this. WTAF? —*HK*

1989

Bonnie Raitt
NICK OF TIME
CAPITOL | Producer: Don Was
RELEASED: MARCH 21, 1989

● Few albums, ever, have been as aptly titled as Bonnie Raitt's *Nick of Time*.

Nine albums in as she entered the late '80s, Raitt was, by her own admission, "at rock bottom"—kicked off her label, drinking too much, depressed about too many ruinous relationships, angry about her curdled career. "I had to look in the mirror," Raitt said after *Nick of Time*'s release, which meant psychotherapy and Alcoholics Anonymous. And finding her way back to quality music making.

That path led her to producer Don Was, via an introduction by Hal Willner. Knowing it was a genuine make-or-break moment, they spent six months poring over songs in great detail, finding a thread of an album about growing up and coming to grips with being an adult. "We really knew what we were doing for—a personal record for her," Was explained. The idea was also to strip down the arrangements to let Raitt's voice and slide guitar be the stars of the album; in fact, Was was surprised to learn that Raitt "had never played much guitar on her albums" and insisted that she be the main guitarist on *Nick of Time*'s ten tracks—bookended by her two autobiographical compositions, the title track and **The Road's My Middle Name**.

The result was the Bonnie Raitt album the world had been waiting for, one on which even songs by other writers such as John Hiatt (**Thing Called Love**), Bonnie Hayes (**Love Letter, Have a Heart**), and David and Julie Lasley (**I Ain't Gonna Let You Break My Heart Again**) fit Raitt's own story. It hit No. 1 on the Billboard 200, won three Grammy Awards, including Album of the Year, and sold more than five million copies. It was a career (and life) saver, arriving right in the . . . well, you know. *—GG*

1989

Pixies
DOOLITTLE
4AD/ELEKTRA | Producer: Gil Norton
RELEASED: APRIL 17, 1989

● *Surfer Rosa* (from 1988) introduced the quiet-loud dynamic tied to the Pixies' sound, but it was the follow-up album, *Doolittle*, that helped shape the terrain of alternative rock during the '90s. Sharpened by Gil Norton's production and songs that lived on the outskirts of pop (**Here Comes Your Man**, **Monkey Gone to Heaven**), the Boston quartet's second LP was tighter and more tuneful than its justly praised predecessor. *Surfer Rosa* was the album to pull out for cool friends; *Doolittle* is the one with the great songs. *—MG*

Queen Latifah
ALL HAIL THE QUEEN
TOMMY BOY | Producers: DJ Mark the 45 King, Prince Paul, Queen Latifah, Louis "Louie Louie" Vega, Daddy-O, KRS-One
RELEASED: NOVEMBER 7, 1989

● There were women rappers before Queen Latifah, but most were trying to copy their male counterparts, boasting about their style and mic supremacy. But nineteen-year-old New Jersey MC Dana Owens targeted her rhymes toward gender-specific topics, flipping a page on hip-hop's developing history. Her debut album, *All Hail the Queen*, blended soul, reggae, jazz, and dance music on the female-empowerment cuts **Mama Gave Birth to the Soul Children** and the epochal **Ladies First**. De La Soul, KRS-One, Monie Love, and Daddy-O were in the Queen's court for this one, too. *—MG*

Red Hot Chili Peppers
MOTHER'S MILK
EMI | Producer: Michael Beinhorn
RELEASED: AUGUST 16, 1989

● After the 1988 death of guitarist Hillel Slovak and the departure of drummer Jack Irons, the funky L.A. freaks regrouped for their fourth album, adding guitarist John Frusciante and drummer Chad Smith and setting their trajectory toward the sun. *Mother's Milk* was loose and wild, a bouncing-off-the-walls amalgam of funk, punk, and metal; if it tended to lack focus, a revved-up cover of Stevie Wonder's **Higher Ground** landed and scored the band an MTV hit, setting the table for the Chilis' big-time breakthrough just around the corner. *—AG*

Skid Row
SKID ROW
ATLANTIC | Producer: Michael Wagener
RELEASED: JANUARY 24, 1989

● It's well known that a fledgling Skid Row got its record deal with help from guitarist Dave Sabo's childhood friend Jon Bon Jovi. But once the door of opportunity was cracked open, the band blew it off the hinges with its own power on this highly impressive self-titled debut album. Although *Skid Row* featured three huge radio and MTV hits in **Youth Gone Wild**, **18 and Life**, and **I Remember You**, the album had a more organic, timeless hard rock sound than many of its poppy, keyboard-using contemporaries. *—MW*

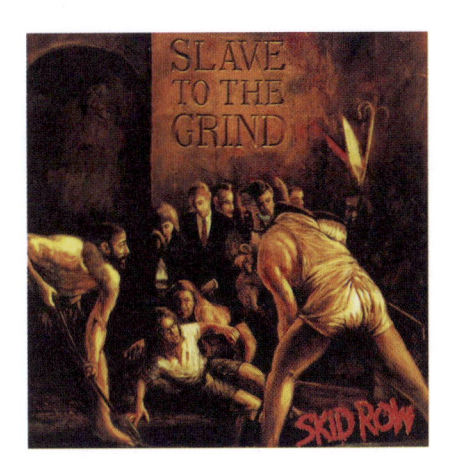

Soundgarden
LOUDER THAN LOVE
A & M | Producers: Terry Date, Soundgarden
RELEASED: SEPTEMBER 5, 1989

● The second album from Seattle's Soundgarden churned out molasses-thick grooves and was superpowered by frontman Chris Cornell's stone-cutting vocals, which even from inside a studio sounded like they were being shouted from a mountaintop. *Louder Than Love* was the band's major label debut but made no concessions to mainstream sounds of the time, favoring odd time signatures and a proudly sludgy sound, while sending up typical metal misogyny (**Big Dumb Sex**). Alt-rock superstardom was still a few years off, but *Louder Than Love* showed a band ready for the next step. *—AG*

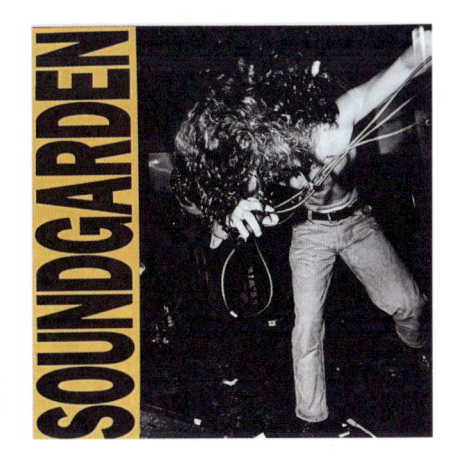

World Saxophone Quartet
RHYTHM AND BLUES
ELEKTRA/MUSICIAN | Producers: Marty Khan, the World Saxophone Quartet
RELEASED: MAY 16, 1989

● Surely, an all-saxophone jazz quartet must be the ultimate novelty act, but in the fast-fingered hands of these electrifying players, their sweet flutters and strident bleats were a bona fide blast. The WSQ originated in 1976 with Hamiett Bluiett (baritone), Julius Hemphill (alto), Oliver Lake (alto), and David Murray (tenor). Ingenious and captivating, the players divvied up the melodies of familiar pop and funk songs, reharmonizing the O'Jays' **For the Love of Money** and freewheeling on love songs such as Ray Noble's **Try a Little Tenderness** and Marvin Gaye's **Let's Get It On**. *—CH*

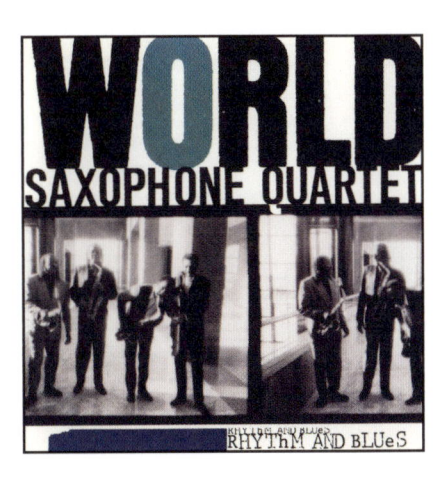

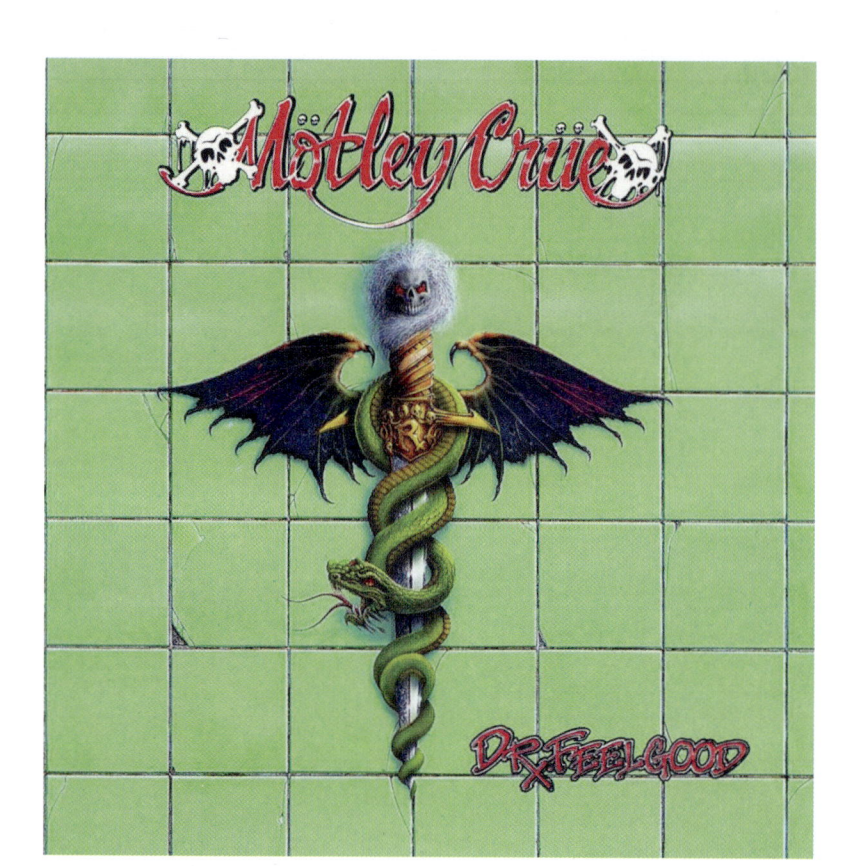

Mötley Crüe
DR. FEELGOOD
ELEKTRA | Producer: Bob Rock
RELEASED: AUGUST 28, 1989

● Although both albums sold millions of copies, Mötley Crüe and its fans knew that 1985's *Theatre of Pain* and 1987's *Girls, Girls, Girls* contained more than their fair shares of filler. After a series of scary incidents—including the time bassist and primary songwriter Nikki Sixx had to be brought back to life after a heroin overdose—the group collectively entered rehab, emerging sober and determined to improve on its recent work.

The quartet hunkered down with producer Bob Rock in Vancouver and painstakingly crafted 1989's *Dr. Feelgood*, its sleekest and most polished album to date. It was also the band's most consistent collection of songs since *Shout at the Devil*. Although it lacked some of the grit and appealing wildness of that 1983 masterpiece, *Dr. Feelgood* added just the perfect extra dash of pop smarts and arena-ready choruses to the band's hard rock formula, allowing songs such as the title track, **Same Ol' Situation (S.O.S.)** and **Don't Go Away Mad (Just Go Away)** to rule radio and MTV for a solid year.

The ballads **Without You** and **Time for Change** were not as excitingly fresh as *Theatre of Pain*'s "Home Sweet Home," but the overall strength of deep tracks such as **Sticky Sweet**, **Slice of Your Pie**, and **Rattlesnake Shake** more than made up for that.

The adrenaline-charged **Kickstart My Heart** was the unquestioned highlight. Inspired by Sixx's near-death experience, the song finds drummer Tommy Lee and guitarist Mick Mars flirting with something resembling danceable thrash metal while singer Vince Neil marveled at all the band had survived during the previous decade. Apart from the sublime 1991 single "Primal Scream," lineup changes, legalities, label struggles, and changing musical tastes would keep Mötley Crüe from ever reaching its '80s creative and commercial peaks again. *—MW*

1989

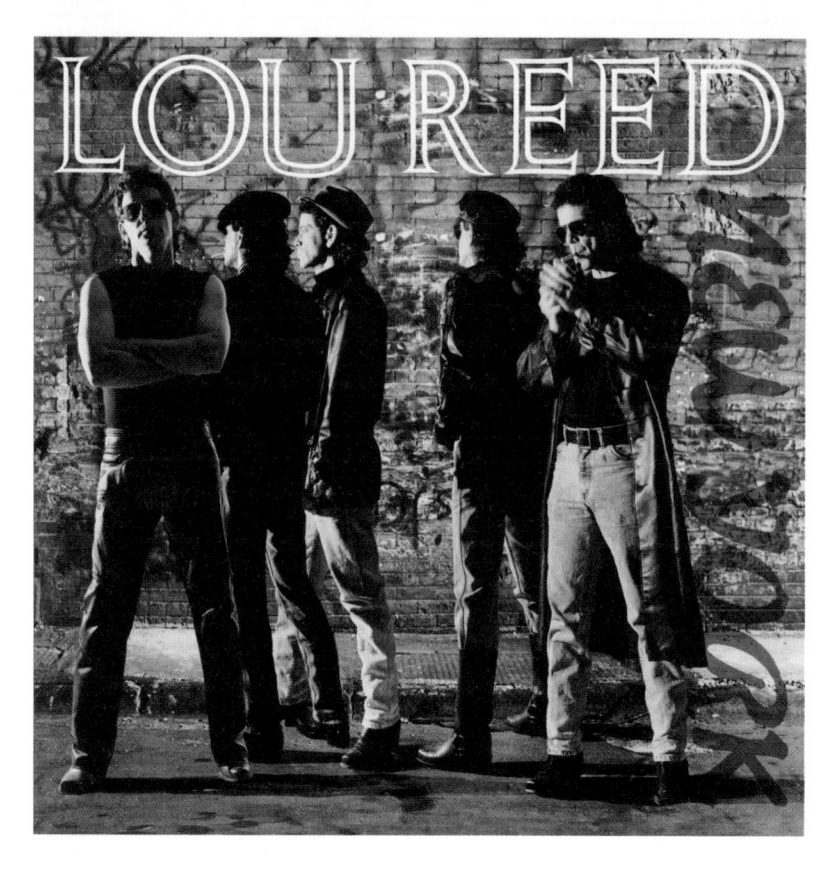

Lou Reed
NEW YORK
SIRE | Producers: Lou Reed, Fred Maher
RELEASED: JANUARY 10, 1989

● The '80s was a consistently interesting decade for Lou Reed.

Well established as iconoclastically unpredictable, the five studio albums leading up to *New York* all had merit, even if at times he seemed to be trying a bit too hard to score a hit ("I Love You, Suzanne" or "The Original Wrapper," anyone?). On studio album number fifteen, however, Reed connected tunefulness with his naturally ambitious muse and a desire "not to be disposable . . . [and be] more like a novel or a piece of literature."

New York examined, in blunt and angry detail, the deterioration of the city Reed called home. The fourteen songs were poetic and journalistic at the same time. There was no question what he was singing about, but it wasn't merely fifty-seven minutes of ranting. Rather, it was as if the passion of his despair pushed Reed to keep the language tight and direct, making points and observations that required little in the way of interpretation.

The music followed suit—deliberately, Reed acknowledged, to make sure the songs weren't eclipsed by any sort of metal machine music. He and co-producer/fellow guitarist Mike Rathke, along with bassist Rob Wasserman and drummer/bassist Fred Maher, played with muscle and economy, especially in arranging the forceful six-string attack. Fellow New Yawker Dion DiMucci provided backing vocals for the single **Dirty Boulevard**—a rare Reed hit at No. 1 on Billboard's new Modern Rock Tracks chart—while Reed's former Velvet Underground bandmate Moe Tucker added percussion on two other tracks.

New York also set a template for conceptual works that would follow, including 1990's Andy Warhol–celebrating *Songs for Drella* with John Cale and 1992's *Magic and Loss*. Reed had produced plenty of compelling work before, but on *New York*, the man found a milieu that best served his inherent artistry. *—GG*

The Stone Roses
THE STONE ROSES

SILVERTONE/RCA | Producer: John Leckie
RELEASED: MAY 2, 1989

● A number of threads came together to make the first album—and one of only two ever released—by the Stone Roses a curiosity. And a classic.

The raving Madchester and "baggy" scenes out of the quartet's native Manchester, England, were already well established by the end of the decade. The idea of dance-rock was nothing new, even in the modern context explored by Joy Division and its spawn, New Order, and the jangly guitars of the '60s were suitably embraced by L.A.'s Paisley Underground. Stone Roses was stepping into well-trod territory, in other words, but brought those elements together in a manner that was both present and future-gazing (yes, the beginning of '90s Britpop) and unquestionably arty in its intent.

The Stone Roses was also front-loaded with frontman Ian Brown and guitarist John Squire's best songs—a formidable opening of **I Wanna Be Adored**, **She Bangs the Drums**, and the chiming flow of **Waterfall**. The US edition of the album, meanwhile, added **Elephant Stone**, a stand-alone single in the UK eight months before the album's release (and produced by New Order's Peter Hook). The US album also included the epic **Fools Gold**, a subsequent single in the UK that nevertheless made the Yanks' version of *The Stone Roses* that much stronger.

The Stone Roses played with a lot of conventions here, nodding to *Revolver* and *A Saucerful of Secrets* (and *The Madcap Laughs*) in spots and even mining a bit of psychedelic country in **Bye Bye Badman**. **(Song for My) Sugar Spun Sister** and **Made of Stone** stood up to those opening tracks, and **I Am the Resurrection** offered a weighty counterbalance to the album's poppier moments. It never felt like we got our full measure out of the Stone Roses, but this album made more impact than some bands make during multi-decade careers. —*GG*

Acknowledgments

The best part of this particular enterprise was the opportunity to work with so many valued friends and respected colleagues—even if some of them may be cursing the editing changes made to their entries. (There's a reason I don't let any of them have my home address.) Everybody's skills, hard work, dedication, and enthusiasm were deeply appreciated throughout the project. Special nods go to Adam Graham, Stacey Sherman, Michael Gallucci, Daniel Durchholz, Matthew Wilkening, and Howard Kramer, who did extra heavy lifting both at the beginning of and throughout the process, providing expertise, encouragement, and opinions that helped shape this book and those that will follow.

My thanks also to Dennis Pernu at the Quarto Group; this is our fifth book together, and it's always a pleasure. The Quarto crew—Brooke Pelletier, David Martinell, and Regina Grenier—did their usual job of making it look amazing, and Steve Roth once again banged the drum tirelessly to get the word out. Also, thanks to Joseph Bellanca for his valued continuing legal counsel.

I am genuinely blessed to work day-to-day with colleagues who make the hard work worthwhile and even more rewarding, including in no particular order Michael Norman, Joe Lynch, Thom Duffy, Matthew Wilkening, Michael Gallucci, Jason Alley, Steve Frye, Brian Johnston, Eric Jensen, Bob Madden, Brian Nelson, Borna Velic, Zach Clark, Howard Handler, Kim Klein, Bryant Fillmore, Carly Somers, Kelly Franz, Clare Baker, Jackie Headapohl, Ryan Anderson, Drew Lane, Marc Fellhauer, Fraser Lewry, Sian Llewellyn, and Joseph Maltese.

Regards, too, to our growing Detroit Music Awards family.

And to my real family—Stacey, Hannah, Josh, Ben, Sean, Ari, Harvey, Vicki, and the Gallaghers in Cincy—much love and appreciation for the support and encouragement that help keep, as Queen would say, my rockin' world go 'round. *—Gary Graff*

Photo Credits

Alamy Stock Photos: 19 (Sheri Lynn Behr), 41 (Moviestore Collection), 47 (Media Punch), 53 (© Marcello Mencarini/Lebrecht Music & Arts), 119 (Pictorial Press), 123 (© Gary Gershoff/Media Punch), 133 (ilpo musto), 141 (Ron Wolfson/Media Punch), 147 (© mpi09/Media Punch), 151 (Pictorial Press), 155 (dpa picture alliance), 159 (dpa picture alliance), 187 (Ross Marino/Media Punch), 205 (dpa picture alliance), 207 (Arthur D'Amario), 217 (Trinity Mirror/Mirrorpix), 219 (Jeffrey Mayer/Pictorial Press), 221 (Ross Marino/Media Punch), 231 (Jeffrey Mayer/Media Punch), 233 (Ross Marino/Media Punch), 237 (ilpo musto), 265 (Palace Pictures/Album), 269 (dpa picture alliance), 273 (Ron Wolfson/Media Punch), 277 (Brigitte Friedrich/Süddeutsche Zeitung Photo), 287 (Ross Marino/Media Punch), 291 (Karen Petersen/Everett Collection), 307 (© Kevin Estrada/Media Punch), 327 (Pictorial Press), 335 (Trinity Mirror/Mirrorpix), 341 (Pictorial Press), 349 (© Joey Mcleister/*Minneapolis Star Tribune* via ZUMA Wire), 353 (dpa picture alliance), 369 (© Kevin Estrada/Media Punch), 399 (Jeffrey Mayer/Pictorial Press), 409 (Orjan Bjorkdahl/TT News Agency), 413 (dpa picture alliance), 417 (ilpo musto), 421 (CelebrityArchaeology.com).

AP Photos: 85 (Horst Ossinger/picture-alliance/dpa), 161 (Michael Maloney/*San Francsico Chronicle*), 281 (Fred Jewell), 295 (Gillian Allen), 301 (Mark Humphrey), 359 (John Redman).

Bridgeman Images: 33 (© Mondadori Portfolio/Archivio Tv Sorrisi e Canzoni), 83 (© Philip Grey. All rights reserved 2024), 175 (Picture Alliance/DPA/Hanne Jordan).

Getty Images: 15 (Michael Putland/Hulton Archive), 27 (Ed Perlstein/Redferns), 37 (Fin Costello/Redferns), 59 (David Redfern/Redferns), 63 (Michael Putland/Hulton Archive), 75 (Aaron Rapoport/Corbis Historical), 79 (RB/Redferns), 89 (Koh Hasebe/Shinko Music), 93 (Michael Putland/Hulton Archive), 99 (Fin Costello/Redferns), 103 (David Corio/Redferns), 107 (Koh Hasebe/Shinko Music/Hulton Archive), 113 (Michael Putland/Hulton Archive), 129 (David Corio/Redferns), 135 (Ron Galella/Ron Galella Collection), 169 (Kerstin Rodgers/Redferns), 179 (Paul Natkin), 193 (Michael Ochs Archives), 199 (Paul Natkin), 211 (Raymond Boyd/Michael Ochs Archives), 225 (Kevin Winter), 247 (Paul Natkin), 251 (Steve Rapport/Hulton Archive), 255 (John R. Nordell), 257 (Paul Natkin), 261 (Ebet Roberts/Redferns), 299 (Pete Still/Redferns), 317 (Clayton Call/Redferns), 321 (Lisa Haun/Michael Ochs Archives), 347 (Chris Carroll/Corbis Historical), 373 (Ebet Roberts/Redferns), 379 (Raymond Boyd/Michael Ochs Archives), 387 (George Rose/Hulton Archive), 391 (Michael Ochs Archives), 405 (Michael Ochs Archives), 425 (Ian Dickson/Redferns), 427 (Jeffrey Mayer/WireImage), 429 (Gie Knaeps/Hulton Archive), 433 (Paul Natkin/WireImage).

Jim Saah (jimsaah.com): 215.

Shutterstock: 8 (Rodin Anton).

Index

A

Abacab (Genesis), 80
ABC, 110
Abdul, Paula, 352
Abrahams, Alan V., 278
AC/DC, 14, 66
Ace of Spades (Motörhead), 38
Actually (Pet Shop Boys), 340
Adam and the Ants, 64
Adams, Bryan, 188
Addabbo, Steve, 343
Adventures in Utopia (Utopia), 51
Aerosmith, 398
Afrika Bambaataa, 274
Afrika Islam, 374
Against the Wind (Seger), 46
Age of Plastic, The (The Buggles), 20
a-ha, 234
Alabama, 111, 148
Albini, Steve, 383
Album, The (Mantronix), 249
Album Album (Jack DeJohnette's Special Edition), 191
Alexander, Larry, 344
All Hail the Queen (Queen Latifah), 430
Allen, David M., 310, 407
Allom, Tom, 36
Among the Living (Anthrax), 309
Anderle, David, 284
Anderson, John, 116
Anderson, Laurie, 108
Anderson, Pete, 300, 384
Andrews, Punch, 46
Angst in My Pants (Sparks), 127
Anthem (Black Uhuru), 190
Anthrax, 309
Apollo: Atmospheres and Soundtracks (Eno), 156
Appetite for Destruction (Guns N' Roses), 306
Arc of a Driver (Winwood), 57
Architecture & Morality (Orchestral Manoeuvres in the Dark), 96
Are You Glad to Be in America? (Ulmer), 50
Argy Bargy (Squeeze), 50
Art of Noise, The, 200
Artists United Against Apartheid, 240
Asher, Peter, 176, 344, 402
Ashman, Howard, 419
Asia, 109
Asia (Asia), 109
Atkins, Juan, 156
Autoamerican (Blondie), 45
Avalon (Roxy Music), 137
Azoff, Irving, 56
Aztec Camera, 152

B

B., Eric, 308
B-52's, The, 16, 412
Babyface, 354
Back in Black (AC/DC), 14
Back in the High Life (Winwood), 297
Back on the Block (Jones), 420
Back to the Future (various artists), 234
Bad (Jackson), 328
Bad Brains, 114
Bad Brains (Bad Brains), 114
Bad Reputation (Jett), 82
Badalementi, Angelo, 410
Bahlman, Ed, 157
Bailey, Tom, 209
Baker, Anita, 274
Baker, Arthur, 163, 240, 274
Bangles, The, 275
Baran, Roma, 108
Barker, Paul (aka Hermes Pan), 367
Bartek, Steve, 252
Bascombe, David, 318
Bauhaus, 66
Beamish, Kevin, 44
Beastie Boys, 272, 406
Beat Happening, 234
Beat Happening (Beat Happening), 234
Beauty and the Beat (The Go-Go's), 74
Bechrian, Roger, 91
Beinhorn, Michael, 160, 337, 430
Bell, Ronald, 202
Bella Donna (Nicks), 92
Bellotte, Pete, 157
Benatar, Pat, 17
Benitez, Jellybean, 162, 329
Berendt, Joachim-Ernst, 30
Berlin, 116
Berlin, Steve, 198, 323
Bernstein, Peter, 172
Bido, John, 410
Big Audio Dynamite, 235
Big Chill, The (various artists), 152
Big City (Haggard), 77
Big Science (Anderson), 108
Biograph (Dylan), 238
Birch, Martin, 20, 121
Birkett, Derek, 384
Black, Clint, 402
Black Celebration (Depeche Mode), 282
Black Codes (From the Underground) (Marsalis), 256
Black Flag, 65
Black Sabbath, 20
Black Uhuru, 190
Blackmon, Larry, 275
Blackwell, Chris, 84, 195
Blade Runner (Vangelis), 139
Blank, Boris, 173
Blasters, The, 67
Blasters, The (The Blasters), 67
Blaze of Glory (Jackson), 418
Blizzard of Ozz (Osbourne), 25
Blondie, 45
Blood & Chocolate (Costello), 282
Blue Bell Knoll (Cocteau Twins), 357
Blue Mask, The (Reed), 138
Blues Brothers, The, 20
Blues Brothers, The (The Blues Brothers), 20
Bock, Bob, 432
BoDeans, The, 278
Bohanon, Ted, 394
Boladian, Armen, 72
Bolas, Niko, 331, 423
Bolton, Michael, 402
Bomb Squad, The, 389
Bon Jovi, 270
Bonnefond, Jim, 202
Bono, 422
Boogie Down Productions, 312
Born in the U.S.A. (Springsteen), 218
Born to Laugh at Tornadoes (Was (Not Was)), 183
Bowen, Jimmy, 279
Bowie, David, 22, 150
Boy (U2), 55
Boyd, Joe, 142, 258
Boylan, John, 197

Bradley, Owen, 375
Bragg, Billy, 362
Brand, John, 152
Brantley, Vincent, 210
Bray, Stephen, 283, 401
Break Out (The Pointer Sisters), 172
Breakfast Club, The (various artists), 235
Brecker, Michael, 312
Brilliant Trees (Sylvian), 226
Bring the Family (Hiatt), 325
British Steel (Judas Priest), 36
Britten, Terry, 220
Brooks, Garth, 404
Brothers in Arms (Dire Straits), 236
Brown, Bobby, 354
Brown, Errol, 195
Brown, Steve, 110
Brown, Terry, 98
Brown, Tony, 271, 330, 362, 363
Bruce Hornsby and the Range, 283
Bruford, Bill, 312
Buckingham, Lindsey, 66, 315
Buckingham, Steve, 302
Buggles, The, 20
Building the Perfect Beast (Henley), 194
Built for Speed (Stray Cats), 138
Burnett, T Bone, 198, 278, 422
Burns, Randy, 288
Bush, Kate, 241
Business as Usual (Men at Work), 137
Butler, Chris, 191
Butler, George, 201, 256
Byrne, David, 67

C

Caesar, Shirley, 356
Café Bleu (The Style Council), 209
Caldato, Mario, Jr., 406
Cameo, 275
Campbell, Mike, 194, 414, 422, 426
Camper Van Beethoven, 356
Can't Slow Down (Richie), 178
Caple, Ian, 419
Captain Beefheart and the Magic Band, 21
Carmichael, James Anthony, 72, 178, 284

Cars, The, 189
Carter, 220
Carter, Betty, 356
Cash, Rosanne, 68
Cats: Complete Original Broadway Cast Recording (various artists), 152
Ced-Gee, 312, 395
Centerfield (Fogerty), 239
Chancey, Ron, 73
Chancler, Leon "Ndugu," 220
Chapman, Mike, 45
Chapman, Tracy, 358
Chariots of Fire (Vangelis), 97
Chelew, John, 325
Cher, 402
Cherry, Neneh, 408
Chertoff, Rick, 146, 243
Chicago, 200
Chicago 17 (Chicago), 200
Chieftains, The, 377
Child, Desmond, 402, 410
Church, The, 357
Civilization (Williams), 345
Clark, Elbernita "Twinkie," 72
Clark Sisters, The, 72
Clarke, Bernie, 152
Clash, The, 18
Clearmountain, Bob, 188
Clearwater, Bob, 259
Clink, Mike, 306
Clinton, George, 117
Closer (Joy Division), 34
Closer You Get, The (Alabama), 148
Cloud Nine (Harrison), 324
Club Classics Vol One/Keep on Movin' (Soul II Soul), 423
Cocteau Twins, 357
Coffin for the Head of State (Kuti), 72
Cohen, Leonard, 355
Cole, David, 345
Coleman, Ornette, 293
Collier, Pat, 31
Collins, Albert, 235
Collins, Bootsy, 57
Collins, Peter, 380
Collins, Phil, 69, 232
Colour by Numbers (Culture Club), 153
Come Away with ESG (ESG), 157
Commissioned, 278
Commodores, 72

Computer Games (Clinton), 117
Computer World (Kraftwerk), 88
Connick, Harry, Jr., 410
Conscious Party (Ziggy Marley and the Melody Makers), 375
Control (Jackson), 268
Cooder, Ry, 313
Cook, Paul, 82
Cooke, Sam, 242
Cooper, Alice, 410
Cope, Julian, 190
Copeland, Johnny, 235
Copperhead Road (Earle), 363
Cordell, Ritchie, 82
Corea, Chick, 111
Corey, John, 414
Cosmic Thing (B-52s), 412
Costello, Elvis, 23, 91, 112, 258, 282
Cotton, Jim, 382
Cowboy Junkies, 360
Crash, Robert, 158
Cray, Robert, 235
Crenshaw, Marshall, 120, 323
Crimes of Passion (Benatar), 17
Criminal Minded (Boogie Down Productions), 312
Critical Beatdown (Ultramagnetic MCs), 395
Cronin, Kevin, 44
Crouch, Andraé, 191, 242
Crouch, Sandra, 242
Crowded House, 278
Crowded House (Crowded House), 278
Crowell, Rodney, 68, 362
Cruise, Julee, 410
Crushin' (Fat Boys), 313
Cullum, Ross, 363
Cult, The, 309
Culture Club, 118, 153
Cuniberti, John, 337
Curcio, Paul, 166
Cure, The, 124, 310, 407
Cuscuna, Michael, 384
Cutler, John, 316
Cybotron, 156
Cypress (Let's Active), 202

D

D., Chris, 76
Daddy-O, 430
Daisley, Bob, 25
Damaged (Black Flag), 65
Dancing on the Ceiling (Richie), 284
D'Arby, Terence Trent, 311
Dare (Human League), 80
Darnell, August, 127
Dashut, Richard, 66, 315
Date, Terry, 431
Davies, Ray, 162
Davies, Rhett, 16, 81, 137
Davis, Don, 323
Davis, Miles, 276
Davis, Richard, 156
Day, Morris, 138
Daydream Nation (Sonic Youth), 392
dB's, The, 191
De La Soul, 403
De Lucia, Paco, 70
Dead Man's Party (Oingo Boingo), 252
Dean, Paul, 73
DeCarlo, Lee, 197
Decisions (The Winans), 345
Def Leppard, 154, 314
DeJohnette, Jack, 191
Depeche Mode, 282, 318
Descendents, 117
DeVito, Hank, 302
Devo, 26
Di Meola, Al, 70
Diamond, Neil, 21
Diamond Life (Sade), 216
Diamonds & Dirt (Crowell), 362
Diana (Ross), 45
Dierks, Dieter, 208
Diesel and Dust (Midnight Oil), 338
Different Light (The Bangles), 275
Dinosaur Jr., 319
Dio, 156
Dio, Ronnie James, 156
Dire Straits, 28, 236
Dirty Dancing (various artists), 313
Dirty Deeds Done Dirt Cheap (AC/DC), 66
Dirty Mind (Prince), 43
Discipline (King Crimson), 81
Disintegration (The Cure), 407
Dixon, Don, 171, 202, 285
Dixon, Willie, 323
DJ Jazzy Jeff, 361
DJ Mark the 45 King, 430
DJ Polo, 418
DJ Ready Red, 410
DJ Yella, 364, 378
Doc at the Radar Station (Captain Beefheart and the Magic Band), 21
Document (R.E.M.), 346
Dodson, Mark, 82
Dolby, Thomas, 120, 252
Dollar, Jonny, 408
Don't Be Cruel (Brown), 354
Don't Close Your Eyes (Whitley), 385
Doolittle (Pixies), 430
Dorfsman, Neil, 236
Dorn, Joel, 90
Double Fantasy (Lennon and Ono), 35
Double Nickels on the Dime (Minutemen), 214
Double Trouble, 181
Double Vision (James and Sanborn), 279
Douglas, Jack, 35
Dr. Dre, 364, 378
Dr. Feelgood (Mötley Crüe), 432
Dream into Action (Jones), 241
Dream of the Blue Turtles (Sting), 262
Dreamtime (Verlaine), 97
Drescher, Bill, 100
Dublee, Jay, 114
Duke (Genesis), 32
Duke, George, 197, 276
Dunbar, Sly, 190
Duran Duran, 106
Dust Brothers, 406
Dylan, Bob, 238, 416

E

E., Sheila, 196
E2-E4 (Göttsching), 197
Earle, Steve, 271, 363
Earthworks (Bruford), 312
East Side Story (Squeeze), 91
Easter, Mitch, 171, 202
Eazy-Duz-It (Eazy-E), 364
Eazy-E, 364
Echo, Eddie, 367
Echo & the Bunnymen, 196
Edmunds, Dave, 91, 138
Edwards, Bernard, 45, 245
Egyptian Lover, 196
Eicher, Manfred, 25, 111, 162
80/81 (Metheny), 25
Eldritch, Andrew, 344
Electric (The Cult), 309
Electric Café (Kraftwerk), 279
Electrik, Eddison, 313
Elfman, Danny, 252
Eliminator (ZZ Top), 183
Elson, Kevin, 87
Elvis Costello and the Attractions, 23, 112
Ely, Vince, 165
Emergency (Kool & the Gang), 202
Emerick, Geoff, 112
End of the Innocence, The (Henley), 414
English Beat, The, 117
Eno, Brian, 52, 67, 156, 222, 348
Enter (Cybotron), 156
Enya, 363
EPMD, 370
Epstein, Steven, 256, 336
Erasure, 365
Erdelyi, Tommy, 208, 259
Eric B. & Rakim, 308
Escape (Journey), 87
Escape (Whodini), 227
ESG, 157
Especially for You (The Smithereens), 285
Estefan, Emilio, Jr., 252
Eurythmics, 158, 172
Everything But the Girl, 365

F

Fables of the Reconstruction (R.E.M.), 258
Face Value (Collins), 69
Fagen, Donald, 121
Fair, Frank, 208
Fairbairn, Bruce, 73, 270, 398
Fairley, Colin, 282
Faith (Michael), 334
Faith No More, 403
Falconer, Ray, 51
Fame (various artists), 21
Fancy Free (Oak Ridge Boys), 73
Farian, Frank, 422
Farrar, John, 57, 73
Farrell, Perry, 368
Fast Times at Ridgemont High (various artists), 126
Fat Boys, 313
Fats Comet Productions, 274

Felder, Wilton, 220
5150 (Van Halen), 296
Fine Young Cannibals, 414
Fire of Love (The Gun Club), 76
fIREHOSE, 322
First Circle (Pat Metheny Group), 203
Fischer, Martin, 249
Fishbone, 242
Fishbone (Fishbone), 242
Fiyo on the Bayou (Neville Brothers), 90
Fjelstad, Steve, 227
Flashdance (various artists), 157
Fleetwood Mac, 315
Floating into the Night (Cruise), 410
Flock of Seagulls, A, 116
Flock of Seagulls, A (A Flock of Seagulls), 116
Flood, 424
Floodland (The Sisters of Mercy), 344
Fogerty, John, 239
Footloose (various artists), 197
Foreigner, 71
Forever Your Girl (Abdul), 352
Forsey, Keith, 153
Foster, David, 178, 197, 200
Foster, Radney, 322
Foster & Lloyd (Foster and Lloyd), 322
Foster and Lloyd, 322
4 (Foreigner), 71
Franklin, Aretha, 126, 246
Frantz, Chris, 96, 375
Freedom (Young), 423
Freedom of Choice (Devo), 26
Freeman, Rob, 74
Freeze-Frame (J. Geils Band), 81
Fresh Prince, The, 361
Friday Night in San Francisco (Di Meola, McLaughlin, and De Lucia), 70
Friese-Greene, Tim, 120
Froom, Mitchell, 278, 323
Fryer, John, 419, 424
Fugazi, 357
Fugazi (Fugazi), 357
Full Force, 323
Full Moon Fever (Petty), 426
Fullan, Sean, 138
Fundis, Garth, 385
Future Shock (Hancock), 160

G

Gabriel, Peter, 24, 280
Galaxie 500, 410
Galfas, Stephan, 285
Gamble, Kenneth, 95
Game, The (Queen), 44
Gang of Four, 126
Garcia, Jerry, 316
Garth Brooks (Brooks), 404
Gaudio, Bob, 21
Gaye, Marvin, 115
Gehman, Don, 164, 323, 332
Genesis, 32, 80
Get Happy!! (Elvis Costello and the Attractions), 23
Get Lucky (Loverboy), 73
Get Rhythm (Cooder), 313
Ghetto Boys, 410
Ghostbusters (various artists), 197
Gibson, Debbie, 318
Gift, The (The Jam), 136
Gill, Andy, 126
Girl You Know It's True (Milli Vanilli), 422
Glamorous Life, The (Sheila E.), 196
Glass Houses (Joel), 24
Glasser, Pat, 163
Glimmer Twins, The, 62
Go Tell Somebody (Commissioned), 278
Go-Go's, The, 74
Golden Age of Wireless, The (Dolby), 120
Gordy, Emory, Jr., 271
Gore, Michael, 21
Gottehrer, Richard, 74, 120
Göttsching, Manuel, 197
Graceland (Simon), 294
Grandmaster Flash & the Furious Five, 128
Grateful Dead, 316
Gray, Howard, 311
Gray, Nigel, 39, 102
Great Adventures of Slick Rick, The (Slick Rick), 389
Green, Al, 319
Green, George, 260
Griffin, Dale "Buffin," 212
Griffin, Gene, 366
Grip It! On That Other Level (Ghetto Boys), 410
Grolnick, Don, 312
Guest, Christopher, 226
Guitar Town (Earle), 271
Guitars, Cadillacs, Etc., Etc. (Yoakam), 300
Gun Club, The, 76
Guns N' Roses, 306
Guy, 366
Guy (Guy), 366

H

H2O (Hall & Oates), 132
Hagar, Sammy, 197
Haggard, Merle, 77, 167
Hall, Daryl, 29, 132
Hall & Oates, 132
Ham, Bill, 183
Hamann, Paul, 371
Hancock, Herbie, 160, 285
Hangin' Tough (New Kids on the Block), 371
Hankerson, Barry, 345
Hannett, Martin, 34
Hard Promises (Tom Petty and the Heartbreakers), 94
Hardcastle, Paul, 243
Hardiman, Paul, 182, 190
Harris, Emmylou, 339
Harrison, George, 324, 393
Harrison, Jerry, 414
Hart, Grant, 320
Hatful of Hollow (The Smiths), 212
Hauser, Tim, 249
Haynes, Roy, 111
Heart, 250
Heart (Heart), 250
Heart of Stone (Cher), 402
Heartbeat City (The Cars), 189
Heaven (BeBe & CeCe Winans), 385
Heaven and Hell (Black Sabbath), 20
Hedges, Mike, 117
Hein Hoven Producers, 138
Henderson, Joe, 30
Henley, Don, 194, 414
Hentschel, David, 32
Herman, Trevor, 243
Herring, Dennis, 356
He's the DJ, I'm the Rapper (DJ Jazzy Jeff & The Fresh Prince), 361
Hi Infidelity (REO Speedwagon), 44
Hiatt, John, 325
High Land, Hard Rain (Aztec Camera), 152
Highway 101, 322
Highway 101 (Highway 101), 322

Highwayman (The Highwaymen), 244
Highwaymen, The, 244
Hine, Rupert, 220, 241
Holy Diver (Dio), 156
Hooper, Nellee, 423
Hooters, The, 243
Horn, Trevor, 110, 173
Hornsby, Bruce, 283, 414
Hot, Cool & Vicious (Salt-N-Pepa), 289
Hotter Than July (Wonder), 58
Hounds of Love (Bush), 241
Houston, Whitney, 230, 329
How Will the Wolf Survive? (Los Lobos), 198
Howard, James Newton, 380
Howlett, Mike, 96, 116, 126
Huey Lewis and the News, 149
Huff, Leon, 95
Hughes, Chris, 64, 263
Human League, 80
Hunt, Jeffrey, 72
Hunting High and Low (a-ha), 234
Hurby Luv Bug, 289
Hüsker Dü, 201, 320
Hutter, Ralf, 88
Hysteria (Def Leppard), 314

I

I Am What I Am (Jones), 30
Ice-T, 374
Idlewild (Everything But the Girl), 365
Idol, Billy, 153
If'n (fIREHOSE), 322
Iglauer, Bruce, 235
I'm Your Man (Cohen), 355
Imperial Bedroom (Elvis Costello and the Attractions), 112
In My Tribe (10,000 Maniacs), 344
In the Dark (Grateful Dead), 316
In the Pocket (Commodores), 72
Indestructible Beat of Soweto, The (various artists), 243
Indigo Girls, 410
Indigo Girls (Indigo Girls), 410
Inner City, 418
Innocent Man, An (Joel), 164
Innocents, The (Erasure), 365
Into the Gap (Thompson Twins), 209
Introducing the Hardline According to Terence Trent D'Arby (D'Arby), 311

INXS, 248, 326
Iovine, Jimmy, 28, 92, 94, 248, 259
Irish Heartbeat (Van Morrison and the Chieftains), 377
Iron Maiden, 121
Isn't Anything (My Bloody Valentine), 371
It Takes a Nation of Millions to Hold Us Back (Public Enemy), 390
It's Time for Love (Pendergrass), 95

J

J. Geils Band, 81
Jack DeJohnette's Special Edition, 191
Jackson, Janet, 268, 400
Jackson, Jermaine, 230
Jackson, Joe, 130, 418
Jackson, Michael, 134, 328
Jagger, Mick, 372
Jam, The, 136
Jam Master Jay, 389
Jam on Revenge (Newcleus), 208
James, Bob, 279
James, Ethan, 214, 322
James, Rick, 78
Jane's Addiction, 368
Janet Jackson's Rhythm Nation 1814 (Jackson), 400
Jarrett, Keith, 162
Jazz from Hell (Zappa), 303
Jazz Singer, The (Diamond), 21
Jazzie B, 423
Jerden, Dave, 368
Jesperson, Peter, 227
Jesus and Mary Chain, The, 248
Jett, Joan, 82
Jigsaw Productions, 128
Jimmy Jam, 268, 400
Joel, Billy, 24, 122, 164
Johnson, Jellybean, 400
Johnson, Matt, 182
Jolley, Steve, 173
Jonathan Richman and the Modern Lovers, 172
Jonathan Sings! (Jonathan Richman and the Modern Lovers), 172
Jones, Frank, 116
Jones, Gareth, 282
Jones, George, 30
Jones, Gordon, 354
Jones, Grace, 84
Jones, Howard, 241
Jones, Kenny, 362

Jones, Mick, 71, 235, 296
Jones, Quincy, 134, 328, 345, 420
Jones, Rickie Lee, 86
Jones, Steve, 82
Jordan, Steve, 388
Joshua Tree, The (U2), 348
Jourgensen, Al (aka Hypo Luxa), 367
Journey, 87
Joy Division, 34
Judas Priest, 36
Judds, The, 192
Juju (Siouxsie and the Banshees), 102
Juju Music (King Sunny Ade and His African Beats), 110
Jump to It (Franklin), 126
Jungle Brothers, 370
Justman, Seth, 81

K

Kahne, David, 242, 275
Kamins, Mark, 162
Kashif, 230, 329
Katz, Gary, 121
Kaye, Lenny, 343
Keitt, Stephen, 289
Kemp, Mike, 31
Kernon, Neil, 132
Kershenbaum, David, 130, 358
Kerslake, Lee, 25
Khan, Marty, 431
Kick (INXS), 326
Kid Creole and the Coconuts, 127
Kill 'Em All (Metallica), 166
Killin' Time (Black), 402
Killing Joke, 30
Killing Joke (Killing Joke), 30
King, Jon, 126
King Crimson, 81
King Sunny Ade and His African Beats, 110
Kinks, The, 162
Kiss Me, Kiss Me, Kiss Me (The Cure), 310
Kissing to Be Clever (Culture Club), 118
Knopfler, Mark, 236, 380
Kool & the Gang, 202
Kool G Rap, 418
Kortchmar, Danny, 194
Kraft, Robert, 419
Kraftwerk, 88, 279
Kramer, Eddie, 309

Kramer, Mark, 410
Kravitz, Lenny, 415
KRS-One, 312, 430
Kuti, Fela, 72

L

La Bamba (various artists), 323
La Rock, Scott, 312
Ladanyi, Greg, 194, 357, 414
Ladysmith Black Mambazo, 323
Laguna, Kenny, 82
Lamb, Bob, 51
Land of Dreams (Newman), 380
Land of Rape and Honey, The (Ministry), 367
Landau, Jon, 49, 218, 331
Landee, Donn, 296
lang, k. d., 375
Lange, Robert John "Mutt," 14, 71, 154, 189, 314
Lani, Paul, 288
Lanois, Daniel, 156, 222, 280, 337, 348, 416
Larriva, Tito, 76
Laswell, Bill, 160, 344
Lauper, Cyndi, 146
Law and Order (Buckingham), 66
Learning to Crawl (The Pretenders), 206
LeBlanc, Keith, 274, 424
Leckie, John, 435
Lefevre, Benji, 170
Legend (Marley), 195
Lehning, Kyle, 289
Leiber, Oliver, 352
Lennon, John, 35
Leonard, Patrick, 283, 401
Let It Be (The Replacements), 227
Let Love Rule (Kravitz), 415
Let's Active, 202
Let's Dance (Bowie), 150
Levine, Steve, 118, 153
Levine, Stewart, 253
Lewis, Huey, 149, 283
Lewis, Martin, 139
Lewis, Terry, 268, 400
Lewy, Henry, 202
Lexicon of Love, The (ABC), 110
Licensed to Ill (Beastie Boys), 272
Life Is . . . Too $hort (Too $hort), 394
Life's Too Good (The Sugarcubes), 384
Like a Prayer (Madonna), 401

Like a Virgin (Madonna), 204
Like This (The dB's), 191
Lillywhite, Steve, 24, 55, 90, 180
Lind, Jon, 402
Lion and the Cobra, The (O'Connor), 330
LiPuma, Tommy, 276, 279, 380
Lisa Lisa & Cult Jam, 323
Listen Like Thieves (INXS), 248
Litt, Scott, 346, 410
Little Mermaid, The (various artists), 419
Little Steven, 240
Little Steven and the Disciples of Soul, 127
Live at the Harlem Square, 1963 (Cooke), 242
Live in Chicago (Caesar), 356
Livesey, Warne, 338
Living Colour, 372
LL Cool J, 254
Lloyd, Bill, 322
Lloyd Cole and the Commotions, 190
Loggins, Kenny, 197
Lone Justice, 248
Lone Justice (Lone Justice), 248
Lonesome Jubilee, The (Mellencamp), 332
Long Ryders, The, 202
Look What I Got (Carter), 356
Los Angeles (X), 54
Los Lobos, 198
Lost in the Stars: The Music of Kurt Weill (various artists), 249
Louder Than Love (Soundgarden), 431
Loustau, Henri, 196
Love & Hope & Sex & Dreams (The BoDeans), 278
Love and Rockets, 419
Love and Rockets (Love and Rockets), 419
Love at First Sting (Scorpions), 208
Lovell, Steve, 190
Loverboy, 73
Lovett, Lyle, 330
Lowe, Bruce, 191
Lowe, Nick, 23, 42, 48, 282
Lucas, Reggie, 162
Lucinda Williams (Williams), 385
Lynch, David, 410
Lynch, Stan, 414
Lynne, Jeff, 57, 324, 380, 393, 422, 426

M

MacDonald, Ralph, 56
Mack, Reinhold, 44, 127
Madonna, 162, 204, 283, 401
Madonna (Madonna), 162
Magness, Ronald, 157
Maher, Brent, 192
Maher, Fred, 434
Maile, Vic, 38
Make It Big (Wham!), 223
Making Moves (Dire Straits), 28
Maloney, Pat, 377
Manhattan Transfer, 249
Manilow, Barry, 203
Mansfield, Tony, 234
Mantronik, Kurtis, 249
Mantronix, 249
Manwaring, Richard, 96
Manzarek, Ray, 54, 91
Maomen, The, 116
Margouleff, Robert, 26
Marl, Marley, 418
Marley, Bob, 195
Marley, Ziggy, 375
Marr, Johnny, 298
Marsalis, Branford, 201
Marsalis, Wynton, 256, 336
Marsalis Standard Time, Vol. 1 (Marsalis), 336
Marshall Crenshaw (Crenshaw), 120
Martin, George, 136
Martin, Jerry, 389
Mask (Bauhaus), 66
Massenburg, George, 339
Masser, Michael, 230, 329
Master of Puppets (Metallica), 286
Material, 160, 344
Maxwell, Bill, 191
Mays, Lyle, 333
MC Tee, 249
McCartney, Paul, 136
McDonald, Skip, 274
McEntire, Reba, 279
Mclan, Peter, 137
McKean, Michael, 226
McLaughlin, John, 70
McVey, Cameron, 408
Megadeth, 288
Meissonnier, Martin, 110
Mekons, The, 419
Mekons Rock 'N' Roll, The (The Mekons), 419
Mellencamp, John (Cougar), 164, 260, 332
Melton, Steve, 46
Men at Work, 137

INDEX

Men Without Women (Little Steven and the Disciples of Soul), 127
Mendelsohn, Julian, 340
Mendelson, Bernard, 72
Menken, Alan, 419
Message, The (Grandmaster Flash & the Furious Five), 128
Metal Health (Quiet Riot), 157
Metallica, 166, 203, 286
Metheny, Pat, 25, 203, 293, 333
Mevis, Blake, 140, 385
Miami Sound Machine, 252
Michael, George, 223, 334
Michael Brecker (Brecker), 312
Michelle Shocked, 384
Midnight Love (Gaye), 115
Midnight Madness (Night Ranger), 163
Midnight Oil, 338
Millar, Robin, 216
Miller, Daniel, 282
Miller, Marcus, 276
Milli Vanilli, 422
Milo Goes to College (Descendents), 117
Ministry, 165, 367
Minor Threat, 163
Minutemen, 214
Mirror, Mirror (Henderson), 30
Moloney, Kevin, 330
Moman, Chips, 167, 244
Moore, Peter, 360
Moran, Pat, 170
Morlix, Gurf, 385
Morning Like This (Patti), 284
Moroder, Giorgio, 157
Morrison, Van, 288, 377
Morrissey, 298, 370
Mother's Milk (Red Hot Chili Peppers), 430
Mötley Crüe, 165, 432
Motörhead, 38
Mould, Bob, 320, 415
Mountain Music (Alabama), 111
Moving Pictures (Rush), 98
Mowrey, Thomas, 201
Mullen, Richard, 181
Murmur (R.E.M.), 171
Muscle Shoals Rhythm Section, The, 46
Music for the Masses (Depeche Mode), 318
Mustaine, Dave, 288
My Bloody Valentine, 371
My Life in the Bush of Ghosts (Eno and Byrne), 67
Mystery Girl (Orbison), 422

N

Native Sons (The Long Ryders), 202
Nebraska (Springsteen), 131
Nelson, Greg, 284
Nelson, Willie, 167
Nervous Night (The Hooters), 243
Never Too Much (Vandross), 97
Neville Brothers, 90
Nevison, Ron, 250
New Beginnings (Pullen), 384
New Edition, 210
New Edition (New Edition), 210
New Kids on the Block, 371
New Order, 168, 336
New York (Reed), 434
Newcleus, 208
Newman, Randy, 380
Newton-John, Olivia, 73
Nicely, Ted, 357
Nick of Time (Raitt), 428
Nicks, Stevie, 92
Night and Day (Jackson), 130
Night Ranger, 163
Nightclubbing (Jones), 84
Nightfly, The (Fagen), 121
Nine Inch Nails, 424
9 to 5 and Odd Jobs (Parton), 40
90125 (Yes), 173
1984 (Van Halen), 224
1999 (Prince), 125
No Guru, No Method, No Teacher (Morrison), 288
No Jacket Required (Collins), 232
No Time to Lose (Crouch), 191
Norton, Gil, 196, 430
Nothing's Shocking (Jane's Addiction), 368
Number of the Beast, The (Iron Maiden), 121
N.W.A., 378
Nye, Steve, 226
Nylon Curtain, The (Joel), 122

O

Oak Ridge Boys, 73
Oates, John, 29, 132
Ocean Rain (Echo & the Bunnymen), 196
O'Connor, Sinéad, 330
Oh Mercy (Dylan), 416
Oingo Boingo, 252
Olsen, Keith, 17, 100, 157, 197, 345
On Fire (Galaxie 500), 410
On the Nile (Egyptian Lover), 196
Once Upon a Time (Simple Minds), 259
Ono, Yoko, 35
Open Up and Say . . . Ahh! (Poison), 386
Operation: Mindcrime (Queensrÿche), 380
Orbison, Barbara, 422
Orbison, Roy, 422
Orchestral Manoeuvres in the Dark, 96
Osbourne, Ozzy, 25
Oslin, K. T., 382
Our Beloved Revolutionary Sweetheart (Camper Van Beethoven), 356
Out of Step (Minor Threat), 163
Out of the Blue (Gibson), 318

P

Padgham, Hugh, 69, 174, 232
Paid in Full (Eric B. & Rakim), 308
Palmer, Robert, 245
Pancho & Lefty (Haggard and Nelson), 167
Paradise/Big Fun (Inner City), 418
Parton, Dolly, 40, 339
Pastorius, Jaco, 96
Pat Metheny Group, 203, 333
Patti, Sandi, 284
Paul Hardcastle (Hardcastle), 243
Paul's Boutique (Beastie Boys), 406
Peace Sells . . . But Who's Buying? (Megadeth), 288
Pendergrass, Teddy, 95
Pere Ubu, 371
Perry, Greg, 40
Perry, Richard, 172
Pet Shop Boys, 340
Peter Gabriel (Gabriel), 24
Petty, Tom, 92, 94, 426
Phantom of the Opera (Original Cast Recording), The (Webber), 336
Physical (Newton-John), 73
Picture Book (Simply Red), 253
Pirates (Jones), 86
Pixies, 383, 430
Planet Patrol, 163
Planet Patrol (Planet Patrol), 163
Planet Rock: The Album (Afrika Bambaataa & Soul Sonic Force), 274
Plant, Robert, 170

Pleasure Victim (Berlin), 116
Plotkin, Chuck, 218, 331
Poet, The (Womack), 101
Pogues, The, 258
Pointer Sisters, The, 172
Poison, 386
Police, The, 39, 174
Pontiac (Lovett), 330
Pornography (The Cure), 124
Porter, John, 212, 362
Post, Mike, 40
Powell, Michael J., 274
Power (Ice-T), 374
Power, Corruption & Lies (New Order), 168
Prefab Sprout, 252
Pretenders (The Pretenders), 42
Pretenders, The, 42, 206
Pretty Hate Machine (Nine Inch Nails), 424
Pretty in Pink (various artists), 284
Primitive Love (Miami Sound Machine), 252
Prince, 43, 125, 138, 186, 196, 342, 401
Prince and the Revolution, 186
Prince Charming (Adam and the Ants), 64
Prince Paul, 403, 430
Principle of Moments, The (Plant), 170
Private Dancer (Turner), 220
Proffer, Spencer, 157
Psychedelic Furs, 90
Psychocandy (The Jesus and Mary Chain), 248
Public Enemy, 390
Public Image Ltd, 31
Pullen, Don, 384
Pump (Aerosmith), 398
Purple Rain (Prince), 186
Pusey, Roger, 212
Pyromania (Def Leppard), 154

Q

Queen, 44
Queen Is Dead, The (The Smiths), 298
Queen Latifah, 430
Queensrÿche, 380
Quiet Riot, 157

R

Radcliffe, E. C., 139
Radio (LL Cool J), 254
Rain Dogs (Waits), 264
Raising Hell (Run-D.M.C.), 290
Raitt, Bonnie, 428
Rakim, 308
Ramone, Phil, 24, 122, 157, 164
Ramones, 208
Rapture (Baker), 274
Rasmussen, Fleming, 203, 286
Ratcliff, John, 234
Rattlesnakes (Lloyd Cole and the Commotions), 190
Raw and the Cooked, The (Fine Young Cannibals), 414
Raw Like Sushi (Cherry), 408
Real Thing, The (Faith No More), 403
Rebel Yell (Idol), 153
Reckless (Adams), 188
Red Hot Chili Peppers, 337, 430
Reed, Lou, 138, 434
Reid, L. A., 354
Reign in Blood (Slayer), 292
R.E.M., 171, 258, 346
Remain in Light (Talking Heads), 52
REO Speedwagon, 44
Replacements, The, 227, 259
Reusser, Jean-Michel, 355
Reynolds, Allen, 404
Reznor, Trent, 424
Rhoads, Randy, 25
Rhythm and Blues (World Saxophone Quartet), 431
Rhythm Killers (Sly & Robbie), 344
Richards, Keith, 388
Richie, Lionel, 178, 284
Ride the Lightning (Metallica), 203
Riley, Teddy, 354, 366
Rio (Duran Duran), 106
Riptide (Palmer), 245
River, The (Springsteen), 49
Road to the Riches (Kool G Rap and DJ Polo), 418
Robbie Robertson (Robertson), 337
Robertson, Robbie, 337
Robidoux, Michel, 355
Robie, John, 163, 274
Robinson, Sylvia, 51, 128
Roche, Guy, 402
Rockpile, 48
Rocky IV (various artists), 253
Rodby, Steve, 333
Rodgers, Nile, 45, 150, 204, 412
Roger, Ranking, 117

Rolling Stones, The, 62
Romantics, The, 31
Romantics, The (The Romantics), 31
Ronstadt, Linda, 176, 339
Rosen, Jeff, 238
Ross, Diana, 45
Rottger, Gary, 313
Round Midnight (various artists), 285
Roxy Music, 137
Rubin, Rick, 254, 272, 290, 292, 309
Rudolph, Richard, 210
Rum, Sodomy & the Lash (The Pogues), 258
Rundgren, Todd, 51, 303
Run-D.M.C., 213, 290
Run-D.M.C. (Run-D.M.C.), 213
Rush, 98
Rushent, Martin, 56, 80
Ryan, Nicky, 363
Ryder, Carl, 390

S

Sade, 216
Sadkin, Alex, 84, 209
Sage, Greg, 234
Saint James, Phyllis, 191
Salt-N-Pepa, 289
Sample, Joe, 220
Sanborn, David, 279
Sandinista! (The Clash), 18
Sansano, Nicholas, 392
Santos, Rob, 242
Sargeant, Bob, 117
Satriani, Joe, 337
Saunders, Mark, 408
Saunderson, Kevin, 418
Scaife, Joe, 382
Scarecrow (Mellencamp), 260
Scary Monsters (and Super Creeps) (Bowie), 22
Scenes in the City (Marsalis), 201
Scheiner, Elliot, 283
Schneider, Florian, 88
Schultz, Ricky, 312
Scorpions, 208
Second Edition (Public Image Ltd), 31
Seconds of Pleasure (Rockpile), 48
Secret Policeman's Other Ball—The Music, The (various artists), 139
Seger, Bob, 46
Sembello, Michael, 157

Sentimental Hygiene (Zevon), 331
Seven Year Ache (Cash), 68
Shadowland (lang), 375
Shaiman, Marc, 410
Shaka Zulu (Ladysmith Black Mambazo), 323
Shakespeare, Robbie, 190
Sharron, Marti, 274
Shearer, Harry, 226
Shedd, Harold, 111, 148, 382
Sherrill, Billy, 30
Sherwood, Adrian, 424
She's So Unusual (Lauper), 146
Shocklee, Hank, 390
Shoot Out the Lights (Thompson and Thompson), 142
Short Sharp Shocked (Michelle Shocked), 384
Shout at the Devil (Mötley Crüe), 165
Showdown! (Collins, Cray, and Copeland), 235
Shulman, Ray, 384
Shurman, Dick, 235
Sign "O" the Times (Prince), 342
Signing Off (UB40), 51
Simenon, Time, 408
Simmons, Russell, 213, 290
Simon, Paul, 294, 323
Simple Minds, 259
Simply Red, 253
Siouxsie and the Banshees, 102
Sisters of Mercy, The, 344
Skardina, Gary, 274
Skid Row, 431
Skid Row (Skid Row), 431
Skylarking (XTC), 303
Slater, Andrew, 331
Slayer, 292
Slick Rick, 389
Slippery When Wet (Bon Jovi), 270
Sly & Robbie, 344
Smith, Bubba, 356
Smith, Larry, 213, 227
Smith, Pete, 262
Smith, Robert, 310, 407
Smith, Steve, 195
Smithereens, The, 285
Smiths, The, 212, 298
So (Gabriel), 280
So Glad I Know (Williams), 302
Soft Boys, The, 31
Solitude Standing (Vega), 343
Solley, Pete, 31
Song X (Metheny and Coleman), 293

Songs from the Big Chair (Tears for Fears), 263
Songs of the Free (Gang of Four), 126
Sonic Youth, 392
Soul II Soul, 423
Soul Mining (The The), 182
Soul Sonic Force, 274
Soul Survivor (Green), 319
Soundgarden, 431
Spandau Ballet, 173
Spanish Fly (Lisa Lisa & Cult Jam), 323
Sparks, 127
Speaking in Tongues (Talking Heads), 177
Special Beat Service (The English Beat), 117
Spinal Tap, 226
Split Enz, 50
Sports (Huey Lewis and the News), 149
Spot, 65, 117, 201
Springfield, Rick, 100
Springsteen, Bruce, 49, 131, 218, 331
Squeeze, 50, 91
Standards Vol. 1 (Jarrett), 162
Stanley, Steven, 96
Starfish (The Church), 357
Starr, Maurice, 371
Starr Company, The, 138, 196
Stasium, Ed, 208, 372
State of Confusion (The Kinks), 162
Stay Awake: Various Interpretations of Music from Vintage Disney Films (various artists), 381
Stay Hungry (Twisted Sister), 209
Stegall, Keith, 289
Steinman, Jim, 197, 344
Stevie Ray Vaughan and Double Trouble, 181
Stewart, Dave, 312
Stewart, David A., 158, 172, 246
Still Life (Talking) (Pat Metheny Group), 333
Sting, 262
Stone, Mike, 87, 109, 345
Stone Roses, The, 435
Stone Roses, The (The Stone Roses), 435
Storms of Life (Travis), 289
Straight Out the Jungle (Jungle Brothers), 370
Straight Outta Compton (N.W.A.), 378

Strait, George, 140
Strait from the Heart (Strait), 140
Stray Cats, 138
Street, Stephen, 370
Street Songs (James), 78
Strictly Business (EPMD), 370
Stroud, James, 402
Stryper, 285
St. Was, David, 183
St. Was, Don, 183, 412, 428
Style Council, The, 209
Substance 1987 (New Order), 336
Sugarcubes, The, 384
Sugarhill Gang, 51
Sugarhill Gang (Sugarhill Gang), 51
Sun City (Artists United Against Apartheid), 240
Surfer Rosa (Pixies), 383
Surfing with the Alien (Satriani), 337
Swain, Tony, 173
Sweet Dreams (Are Made of This) (Eurythmics), 158
Sweethearts of the Rodeo, 302
Sweethearts of the Rodeo (Sweethearts of the Rodeo), 302
Sylvian, David, 226
Synchronicity (The Police), 174
Szymczyk, Bill, 46

T

Talk Is Cheap (Richards), 388
Talk Talk Talk (Psychedelic Furs), 90
Talking Heads, 52, 177
Talking with the Taxman about Poetry (Bragg), 362
Tallent, Garry, 323
Tango in the Night (Fleetwood Mac), 315
Tann, Jack, 183
Tarney, Alan, 234
Tattoo You (The Rolling Stones), 62
Taylor, Ian, 165
Tears for Fears, 263
Techno! The New Dance Sound of Detroit (various artists), 381
Templeman, Ted, 224
Tenement Year, The (Pere Ubu), 371
10,000 Maniacs, 344
Texas Flood (Stevie Ray Vaughan and Double Trouble), 181
The The, 182
This Is Big Audio Dynamite (Big Audio Dynamite), 235

This Is Spinal Tap (Spinal Tap), 226
This Woman (Oslin), 382
Thomas, Chris, 42, 206, 248, 326
Thomas, Errol, 319
Thomas, Keith, 385
Thomas, Pat, 128
Thompson, Richard and Linda, 142
Thompson Twins, 209
Thornalley, Phil, 124, 252
Thorne, Mike, 253
3 Feet High and Rising (De La Soul), 403
Thriller (Jackson), 134
Thurston, Colin, 106
Tickle, David, 50
Tiers, Wharton, 319
'Til Tuesday, 253
Tim (The Replacements), 259
Time, The, 138
Tischler, Bob, 20
Titelman, Russ, 86, 297
To Hell with the Devil (Stryper), 285
Tom Petty and the Heartbreakers, 94
Tom Tom Club, 96
Tom Tom Club (Tom Tom Club), 96
Too $hort, 394
Too Tough to Die (Ramones), 208
Top Gun (various artists), 302
Toto, 143
Toto IV (Toto), 143
Touch (Eurythmics), 172
Tracy Chapman (Chapman), 358
Trash (Cooper), 410
Traveling Wilburys, 393
Travis, Randy, 289
Trinity Session, The (Cowboy Junkies), 360
Trio (Parton, Harris, and Ronstadt), 339
Trio Music (Corea, Vitous, and Haynes), 111
Tropical Gangsters (Kid Creole and the Coconuts), 127
Troutman, Roger, 57
True (Spandau Ballet), 173
True Blue (Madonna), 283
True Colours (Split Enz), 50
Tug of War (McCartney), 136
Tunnel of Love (Springsteen), 331
Turner, Tina, 220
Tutu (Davis), 276
Twisted Sister, 209
Two Wheels Good (Prefab Sprout), 252
2:00 AM Paradise Café (Manilow), 203

U

U2, 55, 180, 222, 348
UB40, 51
Uh-Huh (Mellencamp), 164
Ulmer, James Blood, 50
Ultramagnetic MCs, 395
Underwater Moonlight (The Soft Boys), 31
Unforgettable Fire, The (U2), 222
Uplift Mojo Party Plan, The (Red Hot Chili Peppers), 337
Upstairs at Eric's (Yazoo), 139
Urban Cowboy (various artists), 56
Utopia, 51

V

Van Halen, 224, 296
Van Hecke, Mark, 182
Van Morrison and the Chieftains, 377
Van Patten, Daniel R., 116
Van Vilet, Don, 21
Van Zandt, Steven, 49, 127, 218
Vanda, Harry, 66
Vandross, Luther, 97, 126
Vangelis, 97, 139
Vaughan, Stevie Ray, 181
Vega, Louis "Louie Louie," 430
Vega, Suzanne, 343
Verlaine, Tom, 97
Violent Femmes, 182
Violent Femmes (Violent Femmes), 182
Visage, 56
Visage (Visage), 56
Visconti, Tony, 22
Vitous, Miroslav, 111
Viva Hate (Morrissey), 370
Vivid (Living Colour), 372
Vocalese (Manhattan Transfer), 249
Voices (Hall & Oates), 29
Voices Carry ('Til Tuesday), 253
Volume 1 (Traveling Wilburys), 393

W

Wachtel, Waddy, 357
Wagener, Michael, 431
Wailers, The, 195
Waits, Tom, 264
Wakeman, Dusty, 385
Walden, Narada Michael, 230, 246, 284, 329
Wallace, Matt, 403
Walsh, Greg, 220
Wansel, Dexter, 95
War (U2), 180
Ware, Martyn, 220, 311
Warehouse: Songs and Stories (Hüsker Dü), 320
Waronker, Lenny, 86
Warren, Diane, 402
Was (Not Was), 183
Washington, Grover, Jr., 56
Watermark (Enya), 363
Watt, Ben, 365
Watt, Mike, 322
Way It Is, The (Bruce Hornsby and the Range), 283
We Are the World (various artists), 240
Webb, Joe, 208
Webber, Andrew Lloyd, 152, 336
Weller, Paul, 209
We're Waiting (Crouch), 242
Werman, Tom, 165, 209, 386
Westerberg, Paul, 227
Westering, Brad, 302
Weymouth, Tina, 96, 375
Wham! 223
What Time Is It? (The Time), 138
What's New (Ronstadt), 176
When Harry Met Sally . . . (Connick), 410
Whitaker, Mark, 203
White, Larry, 354
White, Mark, 402
Whitesnake, 345
Whitesnake (Whitesnake), 345
Whitley, Keith, 385
Whitney (Houston), 329
Whitney Houston (Houston), 230
Whodini, 227
Whoever's in New England (McEntire), 279
Who's Afraid of the Art of Noise (The Art of Noise), 200
Who's Zoomin' Who (Franklin), 246
Why Not Me (The Judds), 192
Wilbury, Nelson (George Harrison), 393
Wilbury, Otis (Jeff Lynne), 393
Wild & Blue (Anderson), 116
Wild Gift (X), 91
Wild Planet (The B-52's), 16
Williams, Adam, 158

Williams, Billy, 330
Williams, Deniece, 302
Williams, Lucinda, 385
Williams, Tony, 345
Willner, Hal, 249, 381
Wilson, Peter, 136, 209
Wimbush, Doug, 274
Winans, BeBe, 385
Winans, CeCe, 385
Winans, Martin, 345
Winans, The, 345
Winelight (Washington), 56
Winwood, Steve, 57, 297
With Sympathy (Ministry), 165
Wolfer, Bill, 197
Wolff, Elliot, 352
Womack, Bobby, 101
Wonder, Stevie, 58
Wood, John, 50
Word of Mouth (Pastorius), 96
Word Up! (Cameo), 275
Workbook (Mould), 415
Working Class Dog (Springfield), 100
World Saxophone Quartet, 431
World Shut Your Mouth (Cope), 190
Worley, Paul, 322

X

X, 54, 91
Xanadu (various artists), 57
XTC, 303

Y

Yazoo, 139
Yello, 173
Yes, 173
Yoakam, Dwight, 300
You Brought the Sunshine (The Clark Sisters), 72
You Gotta Say Yes to Another Excess (Yello), 173
Young, George, 66
Young, Neil, 423
Young, Paul M., 249
You're Living All Over Me (Dinosaur Jr.), 319

Z

Z, David, 414
Zaleski, Paul, 319
Zapp, 57
Zapp (Zapp), 57
Zappa, Frank, 303
Zarr, Fred, 318
Zen Arcade (Hüsker Dü), 201
Zenyatta Mondatta (The Police), 39
Zevon, Warren, 331
Zientara, Don, 163
Ziggy Marley and the Melody Makers, 375
ZZ Top, 183